Seventh Edition

QUANTITATIVE ANALYSIS
for Decision Makers

Mik Wisniewski
Freelance Consultant and Business Analyst

Farhad Shafti
Adam Smith Business School,
University of Glasgow

 Pearson

Harlow, England • London • New York • Boston • San Francisco • Toronto • Sydney • Dubai • Singapore • Hong Kong
Tokyo • Seoul • Taipei • New Delhi • Cape Town • São Paulo • Mexico City • Madrid • Amsterdam • Munich • Paris • Milan

PEARSON EDUCATION LIMITED
KAO Two
KAO Park
Harlow CM17 9SR
United Kingdom
Tel: +44 (0)1279 623623
Web: www.pearson.com/uk

First published 1994 (print)
Second edition published under the Financial Times/Pitman Publishing imprint 1997 (print)
Third edition 2002 (print)
Fourth edition 2006 (print)
Fifth edition 2009 (print)
Sixth edition published 2016 (print and electronic)
Seventh edition published 2020 (print and electronic)

The Financial Times. With a worldwide network of highly respected journalists, *The Financial Times* provides global business news, insightful opinion and expert analysis of business, finance and politics. With over 500 journalists reporting from 50 countries worldwide, our in-depth coverage of international news is objectively reported and analysed from an independent, global perspective. To find out more, visit www.ft.com/pearsonoffer.

ISBN: 978-1-292-27661-8 (print)
       978-1-292-27663-2 (PDF)
       978-1-292-27664-9 (ePub)

British Library Cataloguing-in-Publication Data
A catalogue record for this book is available from the British Library

Library of Congress Cataloging-in-Publication Data
Names: Wisniewski, Mik, author. | Shafti, F. (Farhad), author.
Title: Quantitative analysis for decision makers / Mik Wisniewski,
    Freelance Consultant and Business Analyst, Farhad Shafti, Adam Smith
    Business School, University of Glasgow.
Description: Seventh edition. | Harlow, England : Pearson, [2020] |
    Previous edition title: Quantitative methods for decision makers. c2016.
    | Includes bibliographical references and index.
Identifiers: LCCN 2019030641 (print) | LCCN 2019030642 (ebook) | ISBN
    9781292276618 (paperback) | ISBN 9781292276632 (pdf) | ISBN
    9781292276649 (epub)
Subjects: LCSH: Decision making--Mathematical models. | Management science.
Classification: LCC HD30.23 .W566 2020 (print) | LCC HD30.23 (ebook) |
    DDC 658.4/033--dc23
LC record available at https://lccn.loc.gov/2019030641
LC ebook record available at https://lccn.loc.gov/2019030642

10 9 8 7 6 5 4 3 2 1
23 22 21 20

Front cover image: © sarathsasidharan/iStock/Getty Images Plus

Print edition typeset in 9.5/12.5 pt Stone Serif ITC Pro by SPi Global

Printed in Slovakia by Neografia

NOTE THAT ANY PAGE CROSS REFERENCES REFER TO THE PRINT EDITION

Contents

3　Presenting Management Information　55

4　Management Statistics　101

5　Probability and Probability Distributions　141

6 Decision Making Under Uncertainty   181

7 Market Research and Statistical Inference   205

Appendices   559

Lecturer Resources

For password-protected online resources tailored to
support the use of this textbook in teaching, including:

• a downloadable Instructor's Manual, with full teaching
  notes and solutions to the exercises in the book
• data sets in Excel to accompany the exercises in the book
• a list of Useful Online Resources

please visit **www.pearsoned.co.uk/wisniewski**

List of 'QADM in action' case studies

Preface

Welcome to the 7th edition of *Quantitative Analysis for Decision Makers* (previously titled *Quantitative Methods for Decision Makers*).

It's 30 years since this book was first published and much has changed in the world of business and management since then. The internet was only just becoming available to businesses, with the world wide web starting to develop at the same time. Smartphones didn't exist. Apple and IBM were about to introduce their first business laptops. Microsoft was still working on its first version of Windows.

One thing that hasn't changed – and if anything it's got worse – is the pressure that managers are under at every level to make fast, effective decisions that turn out to be the *right* decisions.

The contribution that quantitative analytical techniques can make to such decision making is well researched. There is extensive empirical evidence that the relevant application of such techniques has resulted in significant improvements in efficiency – particularly at the microeconomic level – and has led to improvements in decision making in both profit and not-for-profit organisations. Numerous professional journals regularly provide details of successful applications of such techniques to specific business problems.

This is, arguably, one of the major reasons why in recent years there has been a considerable expansion of the coverage of such topics throughout business studies programmes in the higher education sector, in the UK and across much of the world. Not only postgraduate courses (such as MBAs) and professional courses (in finance, banking and related fields) but most, if not all, business undergraduate courses nowadays expose the student to basic quantitative analytical techniques. It is no longer simply the statistical or mathematical specialist who is introduced to these topics but, in numerical terms far more importantly, a large number of students who go on to a career in general management.

Coupled with this development has been the revolution that has occurred in making available powerful and cost-effective computing power on the manager's desktop, laptop or smartphone. Not only has this meant that the manager now has instant direct access to available business information but also that techniques which used to be the prerogative of the specialist can be applied directly by the manager through the use of appropriate – and relatively cheap and user-friendly – computer software such as Excel.

Because of these developments it is increasingly important for managers to develop a general awareness and understanding of the more commonly used techniques and it is because of this that this textbook was originally written and has continued to be updated.

The text aims to provide the reader with a detailed understanding of both the role and purpose of quantitative techniques in effective management and in the process of managerial decision making. This text focuses not only on the development of appropriate skills but also on the development of an understanding as to how such techniques fit into the wider management process. Above all, such techniques are meant to be of direct, practical benefit to the managers and decision makers of all organisations. By the end of the text the reader should be able to use the techniques introduced, should have an awareness of common areas of business application and should have developed sufficient confidence and understanding to commission appropriate applications of more complex techniques and contribute to the evaluation of the results of such analysis.

To assist in this each chapter includes:

- a fully worked example, usually with real data, applying each technique in a business context and evaluating the implications of the analysis for management decision making;
- short articles from the *Financial Times* illustrating the use of techniques in a variety of business settings;
- Quantitative analysis in action (QADM in action) case studies illustrating how the techniques are used in practice.

There is also a comprehensive, fully worked Instructor's Manual available for lecturers who adopt the text as the main teaching text for their class. The Manual is around 300 pages long, all end-of-chapter exercises have a full, worked solution together with supporting, explanatory text and there are suggestions for other related exercises that can be given to students. Diagrams and tables forming part of the solution are available in A4 size so they can be incorporated into PowerPoint presentations, or photocopied for students.

A number of features have been incorporated into this new edition:

- Dr Farhad Shafti joins as co-author. Farhad has considerable expertise in the areas of operations management, quality management and performance measurement.
- In line with the expanding use of business analytics, the text has been retitled and has an increased focus on the analytical aspect of quantitative methods and models.
- Additional use has been made of Excel.
- The linkages between the various quality management techniques in Chapter 8 has been strengthened.
- Chapter 12 on stock control now includes mention of the periodic review system.
- Chapter 13 on project management now focuses on the 'activity on node' method in line with industry practice.
- Chapter 14 on simulation illustrates the use of simulation software.
- *Financial Times* cases and 'QADM in action' case studies have been updated.
- A Postscript section highlighting recent developments in the quantitative analysis field

Publisher's acknowledgements

Text

2 The Financial Times Ltd: Tieman, Ross (2016) Remodelling MBAs for the digital era, 25 January © The Financial Times Limited. All Rights Reserved **3 ING Bank N.V.:** Adapted from www.ing.com/Newsroom/All-news/Data-driven-from-bytes-to-business.htm **4 The Financial Times Ltd:** Buckley, N. (2004) Numbers man bridges the Gap, 24 August © The Financial Times Limited. All Rights Reserved **6 The Financial Times Ltd:** Hale, T. (2015) Amadeus set to soar on airline data sales, 26 February © The Financial Times Limited. All Rights Reserved **8 The Financial Times Ltd:** Cookson, C. (2006) Mathematics offers business a formula for success, 13 February © The Financial Times Limited. All Rights Reserved **12 The Financial Times Ltd:** Simon, B. (2008) Cautious of creating too much complexity, 16 June © The Financial Times Limited. All Rights Reserved **13 John Wiley and Sons:** Mohamed, O. (2004) You've got direct mail, *Significance*, vol 1 (2), pp 78–80. Copyright © 2004 John Wiley and Sons **17 Springer Nature:** Based on Richardson, C. (1991) Staffing the front office, *Operational Research Insight*, 4 (2), pp. 19–22. © 1991 Macmillan Publishers Limited **23 Random House:** Blastland, M. and Dilnot, D. (2007) *The Tiger That Isn't: Seeing Through a World of Numbers*. London: Profile Books. **26 The Financial Times Ltd:** Brunsden, Jim (2016) ING to cut more than 5,000 jobs in branch cull, 3 October © The Financial Times Limited. All Rights Reserved **30 The Financial Times Ltd:** Munchau, W. (2007) Multiple answers to Europe's maths problem, Financial Times, 18 June. © The Financial Times Limited. All Rights Reserved **38 The Financial Times Ltd:** O'Connor, M. (2014) Mobiles aid Africa's women farmers, FT.com, 7 March. © The Financial Times Limited. All Rights Reserved. Pearson Education is responsible for providing this adaptation of the original article. **43 Capgemini:** Based on a Capgemini case study, with thanks to Capgemini for permission to use their material. **45 The Financial Times Ltd:** Jack, A. (2019) Almost one in three English secondary school budgets in the red, Financial Times, 11 January. © The Financial Times Limited. All Rights Reserved. **47 Crown Copyright:** The UK Cards Association UK Office of National Statistics **53 UK Finance Limited:** UK Finance **54 Newquest Media Group:** *The Herald on Sunday*, September. 2018 **57 The Economist** America's trade spats are rattling markets, The Economist, 20th June 2018. Copyright © *The Economist* Newspaper Limited 2019. All rights reserved **58 Crown copyright:** Office for National Statistics **62T Eurostat:** European Union **62B The Financial Times Ltd:** Asgari, Nikou (2019) Global spending on cards set to reach $45tn by 2023, 15 February © The Financial Times Limited. All Rights Reserved **63T The Financial Times Ltd:** Rennison, Joe (2019) US secured bond sales jump as red-hot loans cool, 18 February © The Financial Times Limited. All Rights Reserved **63B The Financial Times Ltd:** Alphabet: the algorithm section, 5 February © The Financial Times Limited. All Rights Reserved **64 The Financial Times Ltd:** Pooler, Michael

The Institute for Operations Research and the Management Sciences: Based on 'Development and Use of a Modeling System to Aid a Major Oil Company in Allocating Bidding Capital', DL Keeper, F Beckley Smith Jr and HB Back, *Operations Research*, vol. 39 (1), 1991, pp. 28–41. We are grateful to the Operations Research Society of America for permission to reproduce the figures shown in this section. **206 The Financial Times Ltd:** Bond, S. (2019) 'SAP acquires Qualtrics for $8bn' Financial Times, November 12, 2018 © The Financial Times Limited. All Rights Reserved. **208 Thomson Reuters:** Adapted from Kemp, J. (2012) Don't shoot the statisticians, Reuters. com, 26 April, © 2012 reuters.com. All rights reserved, www.reuters.com. Used by permission and protected by the Copyright Laws of the United States. The printing, copying, redistribution, or retransmission of this Content without express written permission is prohibited. **209 Capgemini:** Based on a Capgemini case study, with thanks to Capgemini for permission to use their material. **215 The Financial Times Ltd:** Warrell, H., Smith, A. and Fray, K. (2016) Doubt grows over official migration data as cabinet splits over direction of policy, 30 November © The Financial Times Limited. All Rights Reserved **217 Capgemini:** Based on a Capgemini case study, with thanks to Capgemini for permission to use their material. **218 The Financial Times Ltd:** Mundy, S(2014) Hyundai hit with lawsuit over fuel efficiency © The Financial Times Limited. All Rights Reserved **221 The Financial Times Ltd:** Jackson, F. (2014) Scottish polls: margin call, 13 September © The Financial Times Limited. All Rights Reserved. **239 The Financial Times Ltd:** Sarah O'Connor(2017) Employment Correspondent 'Britain's gig economy 'is a man's world, 27 April © The Financial Times Limited. All Rights Reserved **241 The Financial Times Ltd:** Martin Sandbu (2016) 'Free Lunch: Year-round fool's day' 1 April © The Financial Times Limited. All Rights Reserved **249 Crown copyright:** Office for National Statistics **257 The Financial Times Ltd:** (2019) IHI Corporation: cratering credentials, 6 March © The Financial Times Limited. All Rights Reserved **259 The Financial Times Ltd:** Palmer, M. (2014) Social media and big data come into play, 24 June © The Financial Times Limited. All Rights Reserved **265 Capgemini:** Based on a Capgemini case study, with thanks to Capgemini for permission to use their material. **275 The Financial Times Ltd:** (2005) Adventures in six sigma: how the problem-solving technique helped Xerox, 23 September. © The Financial Times Limited. All Rights Reserved **276 Emerald Publishing Limited:** Adapted from Yazan Al-Zain, Lawrence Alfandi, Mazen Arafeh, Samar Salim, Shouq Al-Quraini, Aisha Al-Yaseen, Demah Abu Taleb, (2019). "Implementing lean six sigma in a Kuwaiti private hospital", *International Journal of Health Care Quality Assurance*, 32:7. © Emerald Group Publishing Limited. All rights reserved. https://doi.org/10.1108/IJHCQA-04-2018-0099 **283 The Financial Times Ltd:** Chris Giles (2018), Forecasters get their 2018 UK economy predictions right, 28 December © The Financial Times Limited. All Rights Reserved **287 The Financial Times Ltd:** Gillian Tett(2019),Davos climate obsessions contain clues for policymaking, 17 January © The Financial Times Limited. All Rights Reserved **291 The Financial Times Ltd:** Myles McCormick and David Sheppard (2018), Oil tumbles after fears of tighter supply recede © The Financial Times Limited. All Rights Reserved **292 The Financial Times Ltd:** Cadman, E. (2013) UK sees steep increase in winter deaths, 26 November. © The Financial Times Limited. All Rights Reserved **296 Capgemini:** Based on a Capgemini case study, with thanks to Capgemini for permission to use their material. **301 The Financial Times Ltd:** Heaney, V. (2003), Technical analysis: How to identify your friend the trend, 24 January. © The Financial Times Limited. All Rights Reserved. **303 Crown copyright:** Office for National Statistics **305 The Financial Times Ltd:** Jackson, G. (2018) Some like it hot—but UK heatwave proves a mixed blessing, 28 July © The Financial Times Limited. All Rights Reserved **306 Capgemini:** Based on a Capgemini case study, with thanks to Capgemini

Neville, S. (2014) UK Whitehall projects worth £500bn at risk of failure, 23 May, © The Financial Times Limited. All Rights Reserved. **487 The Financial Times Ltd:** Balls, Ed (2015), Lesson I learnt tackling financial crisis that never was, 4 August © The Financial Times Limited. All Rights Reserved **500 Capgemini:** Based on a Capgemini case study, with thanks to Capgemini for permission to use their material. **506 The Financial Times Ltd:** Garrahan, M. (2006) Hedge funds eye glamour of movie land, FT.com, 9 October. © The Financial Times Limited. All Rights Reserved **508 Mike Allen:** Planning theatre time to achieve 18 week elective targets, http://clahrc-peninsu-la.nihr.ac.uk/uploads/attachments/PenCHORD/Case%20Studies/PenCHORD%20CS%20-%20 18%20week%20R2T.pdf **518 The Financial Times Ltd:** Vermaelen, T. (2008) Shareholders need better boards, not more regulation, Financial Times, 11 January © Professor Theo Vermaelen. **521 The Financial Times Ltd:** Ross, S. (2004) Is money in my account mine?, 7 April © The Financial Times Limited. All Rights Reserved. **525 Capgemini:** Based on a Capgemini case study, with thanks to Capgemini for permission to use their material. **528 The Financial Times Ltd:** Murphy, M. (2008), Terra Firma sued over 'modelling flaw, 5 February © The Financial Times Limited. All Rights Reserved. **529 The Financial Times Ltd:** Pfeifer, S., Rigby, E. and Pickard, J. (2013) Deal offers distant benefits for consumers and security for EDF, 21 October. © The Financial Times Limited. All Rights Reserved **536 The Institute for Operations Research and the Management Sciences:** Based on 'Decision Analysis and its Application in the Choice Between Two Wildcat Adventures', J Hosseini, *Interfaces*, 16 (2), 1986, pp 75–85. Copyright is held by the Operations Research Society of America and the Institute of Management Sciences, 290 Westminster Street, Providence, Rhode Island 02903, USA. **544 The Financial Times Ltd:** Burn-Murdoch, John (2018), How data analysis helps football clubs make better signings, 1 November © The Financial Times Limited. All Rights Reserved. **545 The Financial Times Ltd:** Robin Wigglesworth (2019), Opinion On Wall Street Illuminating Big Data will leave governments in the dark, 19 April © The Financial Times Limited. All Rights Reserved **548 The Financial Times Ltd:** Gray. Alistair (2019), McDonald's to buy AI company Dynamic Yield, 26 March © The Financial Times Limited. All Rights Reserved. **551 The Financial Times Ltd:** Murphy. Hannah (2019), How Facebook could target ads in age of encryption, 27 March © The Financial Times Limited. All Rights Reserved. **554 Emerald Publishing Limited:** Nelson Alfonso Gómez-Cruz, Isabella Loaiza Saa, Francisco Fernando Ortega Hurtado, (2017) "Agent-based simulation in management and organizational studies: a survey", *European Journal of Management and Business Economics*, Vol. 26 Issue: 3, pp. 313–328 **574 The Financial Times Ltd:** Smith, A. (2019), Sonification: turning the yield curve into music, 15 March © The Financial Times Limited. All Rights Reserved.

Photographs

6 Shutterstock: Andrew Barker/Shutterstock **38 Getty Images:** ullstein bild/Getty Images **45 Getty Images:** Jeff J Mitchell/Staff/Getty Images News/Getty Images **158 Getty Images:** Anwar Hussein/Contributor/WireImage/Getty Images **183 Anna Gordon:** Anna Gordon **194 Alamy Stock Photo:** Janine Wiedel Photolibrary/Alamy Stock Photo **219 Getty Images:** Bloomberg/Contributor/Getty Images **291 123RF:** Robert Gerhardt/123RF **292 Shutterstock:** Marian Weyo/Shutterstock **305 Press Association:** Danny Lawson/PA **314 Shutterstock:** Pete Pahham/Shutterstock **337 Getty Images:** Michael Bowles/Stringer/Getty Images Entertainment/Getty Images **420 Shutterstock:** huyangshu/Shutterstock **432 Shutterstock:** Mubus7/Shutterstock **545 Shutterstock:** Rawpixel.com/Shutterstock **548 Getty Images:** Bloomberg/Contributor/Getty Images **551 Alamy Stock Photo:** Reuters /Alamy Stock Photo

1 Introduction

There's no getting away from it. Quantitative data and information is everywhere in business. In the private sector the focus is on share prices, costs, income and revenue levels, profit levels, cash flow figures, productivity figures, customer satisfaction ratings, market share figures, cost and revenue information. The list goes on and on. If you're in a public sector or not-for-profit organisation comparable information is also being generated, such as service response times, patient waiting times, cost benchmarks and productivity figures. The trend seems to be: let's measure and quantify everything we can.

The problem this causes for managers is how to make sense of this mass of quantitative information. How do we use it to help make decisions and to help the organisation deal with the issues and pressures that it increasingly faces? Such decisions may be routine, day-to-day operational issues: deciding how much laser printer paper to order for the office or how many checkouts to open at lunchtime in the store today. They may be longer-term strategic decisions which will have a critical impact on the success of the organisation: which goods/services do we expand? How do we increase market share? How do we balance the pressures on our income with the demand for services?

And – no great surprise here – this is why this textbook has been written: to help managers make sense of quantitative business information and understand how to analyse and use that quantitative information constructively to help make business decisions. However, we're not looking to turn you into mathematical and statistical experts. We want to give you a reasonable understanding of how a variety of quantitative analytical techniques can be used to help decision making in any organisation. We also want to convince you that these techniques are of real, practical benefit. That's why throughout the text we focus on the business application of the techniques rather than the theory behind them. We also illustrate how real organisations have used these techniques to improve their business performance.

We hope you find this textbook useful.

The use of quantitative techniques by business

Okay, let's start with a reality check.

You're *really* looking forward to the quantitative analysis module on your course. Right?

You *really* wish there could be more quantitative analysis on your course. Right?

You *really* see quantitative analysis as the key to a successful management career. Right?

We don't think so!

Like just about every other business degree student around the world you're probably approaching this course and this textbook with a mixture of concern, worry and misunderstanding.

Concern about your ability in statistics and mathematics, especially as these probably weren't your favourite subjects in school either.

Worry about whether you'll be able to pass the exam and assessments in this subject.

Misunderstanding about why you have to do a quantitative analysis course on a business degree. After all, business is about strategy, about marketing, about finance, about human resource management, about IT and e-commerce. We know these are important to every business because company boards have directors in these areas. But whoever heard of a company with a director of quantitative analysis? Well, the world is changing.

Remodelling MBAs for the digital era

MBA programmes are being recast to keep up with developments in data

By Ross Tieman

Data will surge through business like the earlier tsunamis of personal computers, the internet and smartphones, predicts Alwin Magimay. The partner and head of digital and analytics at KPMG says: "We are entering the fourth wave of digital value creation. I think data scientists are going to be to the present time what computer programmers were in the 1990s."

If Magimay is right, then a generation of school-leavers and university graduates must think very hard about how they learn the skills for an era when digital platforms and data are at the heart of every economic and administrative activity. . . .

As data-gathering snowballs worldwide, understanding fully the story behind the numbers is vital in every field.

 Source: Tieman, R. (2016) MBA programmes are being recast to keep up with developments in data, FT.com, 24 January.

The ability to collect, analyse and act upon data is critical for every manager at every level.

ING: A data-driven business

Chief Analytics Officer Görkem Köseoğlu wants ING to be driven by data – a 'smart bank' that uses artificial intelligence (AI) to predict customers' wants and needs. The ING Group is a Dutch multinational banking and financial services organisation headquartered in Amsterdam with around 40 million customers in more than 40 countries.

As Görkem comments, 'we have over have three billion customer interactions a year . . . ' and his team focus on customer intelligence, pricing, risk management, intelligent operations and innovation. But in addition to employing a team of analytical specialists the company is also launching global ING Analytics Academy which is available to all ING employees. Görkem comments, 'Data is the language of the future. If you don't speak it yet, we'll help you master it.'

Source: adapted from www.ing.com/Newsroom/All-news/Data-driven-from-bytes-to-business.htm

ING is not alone at seeing data and analysis as key driver of business success.

One of the major reasons for writing this book was to provide business studies students at both undergraduate and postgraduate levels with a text that is relevant to their own studies, is easy to read and to understand and that demonstrates the practical application – and benefits – of quantitative analysis in the real business world. The book is *not* aimed at students whose main interest is in statistics, mathematics or computing. We assume that, like ourselves, students in the fields of management, accountancy, finance and business have no interest in these in their own right but rather are interested in the practical applications of such topics and techniques to business and to management decision making. The reason why all students in the business area nowadays need a working knowledge of these quantitative analysis techniques is clear. In order to work effectively in a modern business organisation – whether the organisation is a private commercial company, a government agency, a state industry or whatever – managers must be able routinely to use quantitative analysis in a confident and reliable manner. Today's students are striving to become tomorrow's managers. Accountants will make decisions based on the information relating to the financial state of the organisation. Economists will make decisions based on the information relating to the economic framework in which the organisation operates. Marketing staff will make decisions based on customer response to products and design. Personnel managers will make decisions based on the information relating to the levels of employment in the organisation and so on. Such information is increasingly quantitative and it is apparent that managers (both practising and intending) need a working knowledge of the procedures and techniques appropriate for analysing and evaluating such information. Such analysis and certainly the business evaluation cannot be delegated to the specialist statistician or mathematician, who, adept though they might be at sophisticated numerical analysis, will frequently have little overall understanding of the business relevance of such analysis.

Two relatively recent developments in the business world have accelerated the need for managers to make better use of quantitative information in their decision making. The first is the move towards *big data* in many organisations. The second is the development of the area known as *business analytics*. Big data refers to increasingly large, varied and complex data sets that are collected by organisations in both private and public sectors. Thanks largely to modern technology, such as laptops, smartphones, GPS systems and sensors, it has become possible for organisations to collect vast quantities of information routinely and cheaply. For example, the US-based retailer Walmart routinely collects data on over a million customer transactions *every hour* and it's been estimated that the volume of business data collected worldwide *doubles* every 12 months. The field of business analytics has developed partly to exploit big data. Business analytics focuses on developing insights and understanding of business performance based on data and statistical methods and makes extensive use of statistical analysis, including explanatory and predictive modelling and evidence-based management to drive decision making. Increasingly, organisations will be looking for people who can exploit big data using business analytics and will want managers to be able to make use of the quantitative information generated. The good news is that those managers with the necessary quantitative understanding and skills will be in a prime position.

The US clothing group's chief ignores fashion intuition, using scientific analysis to woo alienated customers.

Numbers man bridges the Gap

By Neil Buckley

The first few times Paul Pressler, chief executive of Gap, the US clothing group, reviewed the new season's products, the designers were baffled.

He would ask only a few basic questions – had they thought of this or that, why had they chosen a particular style – and he would not pass judgment. When he left the room, the designers "were, like, 'OK. Did he *like* it?'", he says, recounting the story in Gap's design office in Chelsea, New York. But for Mr Pressler, a former Disney theme park executive, "it didn't matter whether I liked it or not – what mattered was whether the consumer liked it". His refusal to air stylistic opinions was his way of showing his staff how he planned to manage the company. "I had to demonstrate to everyone that the general manager is here to lead people – not pick the buttons," he says.

Mr Pressler's anecdote illustrates how he runs Gap very differently from his predecessor, Millard "Mickey" Drexler, whom he succeeded two years ago. Whether Mickey Drexler liked things or not was very important indeed.

Popularly known as Gap's "Merchant Prince", Mr Drexler set the tone, designed products and even dictated what quantities of products buyers should order from the company's suppliers. The business was largely run on his instinct. Designers, jokes Mr Pressler, "relied on getting their blessing from the pope".

The approach was successful for 15 years, as Mr Drexler worked with Don Fisher, Gap's founder, to transform into an international fashion retailing giant what had started as a single store in counter-culture 1960s San Francisco. Yet by 2002, when Mr Pressler arrived, Gap Inc – which now includes the lower priced Old Navy and upmarket Banana Republic chains in North America as well as international Gap stores – was in trouble. Comparable sales, or sales from stores open at least a year – an important indicator of a retailer's

health – had fallen, year-on-year, for 29 straight months. It was clear Gap had lost touch with its customers.

Mr Drexler's genius had been to be absolutely in tune with the post-war baby boomers – those born between 1946 and 1964 – who were Gap's first customers. Gap grew and adapted with them; when they had children, it clothed them too, launching Gap Kids in 1986 and Baby Gap in 1990. It kept up their interest with quirky and distinctive advertising. By the late 1990s, as the boomers took over America's boardrooms, the internet took off and 'business casual' replaced suits and ties, Gap seemed unstoppable.

It increased the number of stores – and the amount of debt – tossing out Mr Fisher's previously cautious approach of opening just enough stores to ensure 15 per cent compound annual earnings growth.

But, like many of its customers, Gap was about to experience what Mr Pressler calls a mid-life crisis. Gap's massive investment in expansion was not yielding a return. Sassy, youth-orientated retailers such as Abercrombie & Fitch and American Eagle were coming on the scene, offering Gap stiff competition. "Everyone was looking at them and saying 'look how cool and hip they are' and 'Gap is now my father's brand,'" says Mr Pressler.

To address the problem, Mr Drexler decided Gap needed to go after a younger consumer. Out went the khakis and simple white shirts; in came turquoise low-rise jeans and tangerine cropped T-shirts. But the customers deserted the stores in droves. "Mickey took the fashion in a direction that was, to his credit, trying to be more hip and relevant," says Mr Pressler, "but it was too singular, too hip and youthful." At this point, Mr Drexler left Gap, having served 19 years. Mr Pressler, then running Walt Disney's theme park division and considered a possible successor to Michael Eisner as Disney's CEO, says he did not have to think too long about accepting the Gap job. Like many businessmen of his generation – he is now 48 – he felt a personal connection.

"I thought about it first as a consumer and said: 'Damn! This brand is too good and too awesome'. Many of us went to [business] school on Gap: how it reinvented itself, how it did its marketing. And as consumers we were all a little pissed off that it had alienated us."

Once inside, he spent 90 days reviewing the business, interviewing the 50 most senior people in the company. He was shocked.

"A company that I had thought was this unbelievably consumer-centric company was not a consumer-centric company at all," he says. "The truth is that we made decisions in our head, not in the real world. The tool we used was yesterday's sales – which didn't give you consumer insights, or tell you why people didn't shop at our stores."

There were other problems. The technology system was, as Mr Pressler puts it: "massively, woefully, behind anything I had ever seen in my life for a company of our size." A $15bn-a-year business was run largely on Excel spreadsheets and inventory discipline was non-existent, with little account taken of how much working capital was being tied up.

Mr Pressler set about replacing intuition with science. He carried out a detailed "segmentation" study for each brand and introduced consumer research, interviews with customers and store managers, and focus groups.

The message that came back was clear. Prices aside, consumers could see little difference between Gap and its Old Navy sister chain. In response, Old Navy was repositioned as more of a value chain and Banana Republic was taken upmarket and given a "designer" feel. That left the middle ground for Gap. Mr Pressler stuck with Mr Drexler's strategy of waving goodbye to the boomers, though. "We have brought a more youthful style aesthetic," he says, "but it's a safe one, not a scary one."

"Instead of going to the 15- to 20-year-olds, we pushed the brand back to what it has always been, which is really a 20- to 30-year-olds' brand," says Mr Pressler.

The research also helped identify new product niches that could be added to stores – petite sizes in Banana Republic, so-called "plus" sizes in Old Navy and maternity wear in Gap.

It helped each chain segment its customers into types – mums, mums shopping for families, fashionable teens and more conservative "girl-next-door" teens – so designers had a clearer idea of their likely buyers. In pursuit of what Mr Pressler calls fashion retailing's "Holy Grail" – women's trousers that fit right – Gap stopped using in-house "fit models" who were a perfect size 8. Instead, it organised "fit clinics" across the country, and designers got real people to try on their clothes.

Sizing initiatives did not stop there. Gap's chains used to ship identical proportions of different sizes of products to all stores. But in, say, fitness-obsessed San Francisco, it would be left with lots of surplus extra large sizes. In the Midwest, the surplus would be in extra small sizes.

Mr Pressler got mathematical experts to analyse Gap's electronic sales information. They divided its stores into seven different "clusters" according to the likely sizes of the customers in the local area. Each cluster now gets a different mixture of sizes. As a result, fewer products are out of stock, more customers are satisfied and fewer goods get left over to be marked down.

Meanwhile, systems were updated and sophisticated inventory management software introduced.

Mr Pressler admits that the company's designers were initially sceptical about his analytical approach. But once they saw what was happening to sales they became converts.

Comparable sales began growing again in late 2002 and continued until last month when sales fell 5 per cent year-on-year. This drop was largely attributable to poor weather and higher petrol prices. Operating margins are also getting back towards the mid-teens they reached in the 1990s.

However, at around $20, Gap's shares still remain well below their $50-plus peak in 1999 and the market is clamouring to hear where future growth will come from.

Mr Pressler says Gap is studying how to expand its core brand in its existing overseas markets – Japan, the UK and France – as well as in some other countries. It is also considering whether Old Navy and Banana Republic could work outside the US and Canada. He does not rule out departing from the existing model of company-run stores and using franchising, licensing arrangements or partnerships in these overseas markets.

In the US, Mr Pressler admits that he is contemplating a fourth brand. But he refuses to comment on speculation that Gap is considering a chain catering to boomer women – those aged 35–50 – for whom the core brand is too youthful.

If Gap is targeting the post-boomer generation now, Mr Pressler insists the brand will never lose sight of its 1960s counter-culture origins.

Its autumn advertising campaign, featuring *Sex and the City* star Sarah Jessica Parker, will, he says, affirm its cultural relevance.

"We were always right on the spot, on the cultural phenomenon happening at the moment. And we brought it to you, through our commercials, and through our product, in ways that were compelling," he says. "That piece of the DNA we still feel very strongly."

As Gap shows, an analytical approach and the use of quantitative methods can make all the difference to business success or failure.

A report by McKinsey Global Institute in 2011 concluded that the shortage of analytical and managerial talent presented a significant challenge with the United States alone facing a shortage of 1.5 million managers and analysts to analyse big data and make decisions based on their findings. There's no reason to think that this skills gap is any different round the globe.

Amadeus set to soar on airline bookings

By Thomas Hale in Madrid

Amadeus, the Spanish company that provides the technology behind airline flight bookings, is set to report results in stark contrast to the airlines it serves, as it benefits from a 40 per cent share of a growing air travel market.

On Friday, the group's full-year results are expected to show the effect of its expansion from flights into hotel reservations and the growth of its IT solutions business. Its share price has been charting a sustained upward trajectory for much of the past five years, hitting an all-time high on Monday this week, for a market capitalisation of €16bn.

Amadeus makes most of its money through its global flight distribution system, which manages transactions between customers and about 400 of the world's airlines, many of which take place on online price comparison websites. Its growth is therefore linked directly to an increase in global air traffic.

Analysts suggest that much of Amadeus's value lies in what it can glean from the billions of transactions it processes: a perspective on the purchasing habits of consumers.

Improved personalisation – from the interrogation of "big data" – enables airlines to tailor their products and services to the personal whims of individual consumers.

Amadeus has already begun to sell aggregated user information to airlines, revealing customers' search habits. It provides a growing revenue stream for the company.

Source: Andrew Barker/Shutterstock.com

 Source: Hale, T. (2015) Amadeus set to soar on airline data sales, FT.com, 26 February.

Big data and business analytics are increasingly becoming big business.

This text introduces the major mathematical and statistical techniques used to help decision making by managers of all types of business organisation: large and small, private sector, public sector, profit-oriented, not-for-profit, manufacturing or service sector. As the article on Gap illustrates, managers are expected to be able to justify the decisions they reach on the basis of logic and hard analysis not just on judgement and experience. In such an environment the quantitative techniques we shall be examining have an important part to play. We do not pretend that these techniques offer the manager an instant solution to the problems faced. However, they do offer a method of analysing a problem using proven techniques, of providing information about that problem and of assessing the potential outcomes from different decisions. Such techniques can provide valuable information about a business problem that may not be available from any other source. But such information is only part of the problem. The manager must assess the information generated by techniques alongside that available from Finance, from Engineering, from Sales, from Marketing, from Personnel and so on. Like any piece of information, the manager must be in a position to assess its reliability and its potential usefulness.

This is why, in this text, the focus is very much on an understanding of the general principles – from a management perspective – behind each technique. It is not the intention of the text to turn you into an 'expert' in the use of such techniques, although you will develop skills in the practical aspects of many of these as we progress. Rather it is to enable you to appreciate when such techniques may be useful in your decision-making capacity and to provide you with an insight into how the information generated by such techniques can be evaluated and used.

But don't just take our word for this. Let's look at some documented examples.

- An electricity company in the USA developed a computer-based planning system to help improve forecasts of demand. The result was a reduction of some US$140 million in fuel costs over a seven-year period.
- The UK Royal Air Force developed a simulation model to quantify the number of battle damage repair teams likely to be required to maintain aircraft capabilities in the event of hostilities.
- A computer-based simulation model was developed to help evaluate the strategic options in terms of transporting coal in Canada from its source to power stations – a distance of some 3000 km.
- In Canada the technique of linear programming was applied to the use of ambulances in health care and to the related shift systems. This generated annual savings of around CN$250 000.
- A farming cooperative in Holland implemented an interactive optimisation system to help plan bulk deliveries of its sugar beet crop with a resulting reduction of 7 per cent in its operating costs.
- A New Zealand utility company applied quantitative techniques to its car-pooling procedures with the result that the number of vehicles required was reduced by 35 per cent, which generated annual savings of NZ$55 000.
- Quantitative techniques were applied to the problem of transporting mentally handicapped adults to a training centre in the UK. As a result travel time could be reduced by almost 16 per cent and distance travelled by 12 per cent.
- A quantitative model was developed to assist in the planning of transportation of blood from a regional centre to hospitals. The model generated a reduction of over 12 per cent in the number of units of blood which had reached their expiry date before use compared with the manual planning system.
- American Airlines has developed a number of quantitative models in relation to its airline seat reservation systems. The models are estimated to contribute around US$500 million per year to the company's revenue.
- Hewlett-Packard used quantitative techniques to forecast capacity and to determine locations of stocks and supplies in the context of one of its computer printers. As a result, productivity increased by 50 per cent and incremental revenues of US$280 million in sales were generated.

- Forecasting models are estimated to have saved the mail order company L.L. Bean US$300 000 each year through improved prediction of incoming calls and staffing requirements in its call centres.

- Delta Airlines uses mathematical programming models to help in its assignment of airplanes in its fleet to flight routes. The approach saved the company around US$300 million over a three-year period.

- Kentucky Fried Chicken (KFC) reduced waiting times for customers by half and improved productivity, sales and profit through the application of quality management techniques.

- DEC (Digital) saved an estimated US$100 million by applying linear programming to its global manufacturing and distribution strategy.

- Taco Bell, a chain of popular restaurants, used forecasting to help it predict arrivals of customers through the day and developed a simulation model for planning its personnel requirements. The company saved an estimated US$53 million in labour costs in one year alone.

- UPS, the delivery and logistics company, sees business analysis as critical to its operation performance. Finding the best routes for its delivery drivers to take cut total mileage by over 85 million miles a year, reducing fuel consumption (and costs) and the company's carbon footprint.

That made you sit up and take notice, didn't it?

The appropriate use of quantitative techniques can help the business 'bottom line' – whether that bottom line is increased profitability, reduced costs, improved efficiency or better customer service. Quantitative techniques *work*! And they work best when used by managers.

Mathematics offers business a formula for success

By Clive Cookson, Science Editor

Mathematicians have come up with an impressive multiplication formula for British commerce and industry: spend a few million pounds promoting the use of maths as a strategic tool, and add billions of pounds of value to businesses.

That is the thinking about a new government–industry consortium, the Mathematics Knowledge Transfer Network.

The network aims to boost the use of maths throughout the economy from grocery distribution to banking, telecoms to manufacturing.

The Department of Trade and Industry will make a core investment of £1.5m in the network's infrastructure over three years, with other partners contributing £3.5m.

Industry is expected to increase research and development spending by a further £7m as a result of the project. But Robert Leese, the consortium manager, said the indirect benefits could be hundreds or thousands of times greater.

"It is already recognised that the use of mathematics in the R&D process adds billions of pounds of value to UK business," said Mr Leese, who directs the Smith Institute for Industrial Mathematics in Guildford. "I predict the newly-formed KTN will multiply that value by two, three or perhaps even four times."

Mr Leese added: "I do not think many businesses are fully aware of the benefits that maths can bring. Few companies recognise that they have mathematical expertise in-house, and few universities are promoting their maths departments effectively to industry."

Lenny Smith, an American mathematician with academic appointments at the London School of Economics and Oxford University, said: "The quality of mathematics and the ability to do ground-breaking research in the UK are second to none."

But Prof Smith, who works with industry on both sides of the Atlantic, added that UK companies were slower than their US counterparts to apply mathematical ideas.

Huge savings can be made by applying algorithms – mathematical rules – to existing information, according to Prof Smith. For example, the retailing and logistics sectors could find more efficient ways to move goods around the country. "Maths can help Adnams brewery decide how best to collect its empty beer kegs or Sainsbury's decide where to sell two truckloads of lettuce in Birmingham," he said.

Unilever, one of 12 companies on the network industrial steering committee, has recently made extensive use of maths. It says statistical analysis of the relationships between advertising campaigns, sales and market share has made Unilever advertising campaigns 15 per cent more efficient.

"We are also borrowing mathematical simulation methods used in the film industry and gaming world, such as agent-based methods, to model the psychology of how shoppers choose one brand over another," said Shail Patel, mathematical and psychological sciences leader for Unilever Research. "Mathematics is universal as, unlike most other disciplines, it can add value to any function within Unilever."

Mr Leese is most enthusiastic about the ability of maths to "shine a torch" down possible R&D routes so that managers can decide quickly which are dead ends and which should be pursued. "The whole concept of mathematics 'accelerating' the innovation process is simple to state," he said. "It both provides an earlier return on investment in R&D and cuts down on wasted R&D spend."

Global business has started to wake up to the benefits that quantitative methods can bring.

The role of quantitative analysis in business

It is worthwhile at this stage considering the specific role of quantitative analytical techniques in the wider business decision-making context. Although this text inevitably focuses on a number of common techniques, business decision making is more than simply the application of a technique to a problem. It is worth considering what the overall purpose of such techniques is in relation to the decision maker. Such techniques aim to improve decision making within an organisation.

Those of you with experience of management in an organisation will appreciate that life for any manager in any organisation is becoming increasingly difficult and complex. Although there are many factors contributing to this, Figure 1.1 illustrates some of the major pressures making decision making increasingly problematic. Organisations generally find themselves operating in an increasingly complex environment. Changes in government policy, privatisation, increasing involvement of the European Union, and political and economic changes in Eastern Europe all contribute to this complexity. At the same time, organisations face increasing competition from both home and abroad. Markets that were thought to be secure are lost to competitors. In the public sector, services – local authority, health care, emergency services – are increasingly required to operate in a competitive manner. Also, the markets and customers available to organisations are changing. This combines with increasing and constantly changing pressures from customers in terms of both their requirements and their expectations. The drive for quality and customer satisfaction gathers pace in both the public and private sectors.

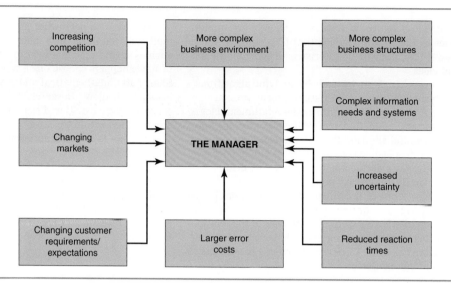

Figure 1.1 The manager and the decision-making environment

Because of the increasing complexity of the business environment in which organisations have to function, the information needs of a manager also become more complex and demanding. With the pace of increasing competition – and with continual improvements in telecommunications – the time available to a manager to assess, analyse and react to a problem or opportunity is much reduced.

Managers, and their supporting information systems, need to take fast – and hopefully appropriate – decisions. Finally, to add to the problems, the consequences of taking wrong decisions become more serious and costly. Entering the wrong markets, producing the wrong products or providing inappropriate services will have major, often disastrous, consequences for organisations.

All of this implies that anything which can help the manager of an organisation in facing up to these pressures and difficulties in the decision-making process must be seriously considered. Not surprisingly, this is where quantitative techniques have a role to play. This is not to say that such techniques will automatically resolve such problems. But they can provide both information about a situation or problem and a different way of examining that situation which may well help. Naturally such quantitative analysis will produce information that must be assessed and used in conjunction with other sources. Business problems are rarely, if ever, tackled solely from the quantitative perspective. Much qualitative assessment must also take place. For example, think about a local authority considering the replacement of some of its refuse collection vehicles. We may well be able to apply a number of quantitative techniques to this situation – using financial analysis principles, examining patterns and trends in refuse collection, comparing one vehicle's performance with other vehicles, forecasting the likely demand for refuse collection over the life of the vehicle and so on. However, before reaching a decision, other factors and information will need to be considered. Is this the right time 'politically' to be making what may be a major capital investment? How will the workforce react to a new vehicle – given this may require some retraining – and to what may be new modes or methods of working? Will the management of this service be able to cope with the problems that such a change will bring? All of these factors and more will need to be taken into account by the manager before reaching a decision. Clearly, quantitative

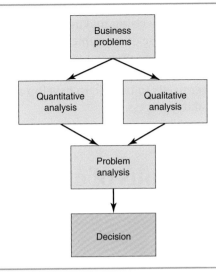

Figure 1.2 The decision-making process

techniques have a potentially important role to play in helping reach a decision but they are not sufficient by themselves. This is illustrated – albeit simplistically – in Figure 1.2. A business situation – at the strategic or operational level – needs to be examined from both a quantitative and a qualitative perspective. Information and analysis from both these perspectives need to be brought together, assessed and acted upon.

However, the techniques we introduce in this text not only are valuable at corporate, strategic level, but they are also particularly useful at the operational level in day-to-day management (although use at this level is rarely publicly reported). We shall be introducing a number of illustrations of this level of use throughout the chapters. In short, knowledge of such techniques, the ability to know when to apply them and the ability to relate the quantitative outputs from such techniques to business decision making is critically important for every manager in every organisation. Not to develop such skills and knowledge will put your own organisation at a critical competitive disadvantage.

Models in quantitative decision making

Throughout the text we shall be introducing what are known as *models* to help develop quantitative techniques in a business context. Models come in a variety of forms in business: they are not just quantitative. A scale model might be constructed of a new office development; a financial model may be developed to assess the impact of budget changes on goods/service delivery; the marketing department may develop a model in terms of assessing customer response to product changes. However, any model, no matter what its form or purpose, has one distinctive feature: it is an attempt to represent a situation in a simplified form. Any model tries to represent the complex real-world situation in a more simplistic and potentially more easily understood form. This is achieved by developing the model so that it focuses on the key aspects of the situation and ignores the rest. By definition, every model is limited in the insights that it provides. It's your job to understand the model outputs and the model limitations when making decisions.

In this text we shall be developing a variety of statistical and mathematical models for use in business decision making. We shall be using such mathematics and statistics to help us make sense of a complex real-world problem, and we shall be utilising techniques to help us focus on what we believe to be the key aspects of the problem. Just as an architect uses a scale model of a new construction or an engineer of some machine, so a manager needs to be able to develop and use quantitative models to help in the decision-making process.

John Hull: Cautious of creating too much complexity

By Bernard Simon in Toronto

John Hull has a confession to make.

As a professor of finance at the University of Toronto's Rotman School of Management, he has won international acclaim for designing and valuing complex financial tools such as options and other derivatives.

But when it comes to managing his own money, Prof Hull has little use for such exotic instruments. His investment portfolio comprises mainly index funds. And while he keeps reminding his students about the importance of hedging risk, his own liabilities are heavily concentrated in Canadian dollars.

Seen from a different angle however, Prof Hull's financial strategy is entirely consistent with the message he hammers home as a teacher, author, consultant and expert witness in derivative-related lawsuits: that is, keep things as simple as possible.

"There's a danger, with all the people with PhDs in physics and maths who have moved into this area, that some of the models become too complicated", Prof Hull says. "There's a tendency for people with that sort of background to just want a really difficult problem to solve. And that's not necessarily what's needed."

Quantitative analysis and analysts have made deep in-roads in trading rooms and financial research departments since two University of Chicago economists, Fischer Black and Myron Scholes, devised a mathematical model for pricing options and corporate liabilities in the early 1970s.

However, the recent turmoil in financial markets has jolted faith in the so-called "quants".

Prof Hull agrees that "there's some ground for concern" that traders and analysts have relied too heavily on mathematical models in their decision-making.

"We need a much more common-sense approach to risk management and must not let quants and traders run free-rein for short-term profits," he says.

The problem, in Prof Hull's view, has been an over-dependence on models that are based chiefly on recent market trends.

Over the past three years, for instance, "we were looking at a period when volatilities were very low", he says, "so values at risk were lower".

"To some extent, that model led to a false confidence on the part of the banks. Somebody should have been saying: 'Let's look at the big picture, what could go wrong? How well will we come out if it does go wrong?'

"In most institutions I don't think anybody was doing that. They were just relying on: 'We're making a lot of money, the value-at-risk model says we're okay'."

But heavy losses since the onset of the US sub-prime mortgage crisis have prompted a good deal of soul-searching among quants, and those who employ them. "I don't think there is a substitute for sound managerial judgment," Prof Hull says.

"In a few companies, however, rather than senior managers letting the traders run loose on this, they sat back and thought about the environment out there; about what could go wrong and how badly they would suffer if it did."

"It's more looking at a situation, coming up with the simplest model that captures the essence of it, and then writing it up in such a way that people will easily be able to understand it."

Models have a useful role to play in business decision making, but they have to be used in combination with management judgement and experience.

QADM IN ACTION

You've got direct mail: the Marks & Spencer '& More' credit card

*Predictive modelling provides a way to increase profitability and customer satisfaction in the financial services sector. **Omar Mohamed** describes the successful use of this technique in recent marketing activities for the M&S '&More' credit card.*

Why use predictive modelling?

The financial services industry is fiercely competitive, with a constant stream of new entrants (e.g. Egg and Virgin) branching out into financial services, and companies must find ways of targeting customers effectively if they are to increase their market share. Knowing which customers are most likely to respond to a particular product offer is invaluable business information. By analysing customers' responses to past offers, businesses can gain insight into which offers individual customers are likely to respond to and decide whether they should be contacted in connection with a particular product offer in future marketing activities.

Effective targeting allows businesses to be extremely cost effective in activities such as direct mail, and also to maintain a good relationship with customers by not bombarding them with offers which do not interest them. This is particularly important because the number of pieces of direct mail the average household receives is constantly increasing.

Predictive modelling is key to effective targeting. Predictive models allow businesses to forecast customer behaviour by analysing the wealth of information stored on large customer databases. These models are used to produce forecasts of customer behaviour commonly known as *scores* or *propensities*, which are then used to decide which customers should be mailed to achieve the most profitable activity or financial target. Customers are usually ranked by their score and then the best customers are selected first until response targets are met.

The challenge

The marketing Credit Card Team wanted to carry out an offer mailing to existing M&S Money customers.

The initial problem was to decide which customers were likely to take up the product, with the goal of reaching the desired number of responders at minimum cost. Since the cost per mailing piece is fairly constant, the only way to reduce the cost of the campaign was to send fewer pieces of mail.

However, since the Credit Card Team wanted to reach a target number of responders, the solution was not simply to send fewer mail pieces. If customers were selected for the offer at random from among all available customers, the number of mail pieces could not be reduced without the risk of falling short of the number of responders required to make the campaign successful. So we needed a targeting tool that could be used to select those customers who were most likely to respond to the offer.

Application of predictive modelling

Creating the model

The first step in producing the predictive model was data selection. This step was key, since a model is only as good as the underlying data. Selecting the best data for the development of the targeting model required a good understanding of the market and the objective, and, not surprisingly, this stage took up the most time and effort, identifying, locating and preparing the data. Since there were no previous campaigns offering this product, the data set was selected from customers who had, and who had not, taken up the product of their own accord.

The model's target variable was the probability that a customer would take up our offer. Customers who had taken up the product were given a value of 1 and customers who did not have the product were given a value of 0.

We then identified and located data, from sources both inside and outside the organisation, that could be used to build the model. This covered:

- demographics, including gender, age, household income, marital status, home ownership and type of dwelling;

- behavioural information, including types and numbers of purchases;
- product holdings, including characteristics describing the products customers already held (e.g. 'holds an M&S Money Mini Cash ISA, previously held an M&S Money loan');
- third-party data, including products customers purchased, their attitudes, beliefs and opinions, geodemographic data, demographic and lifestyle data.

The next stage was the creation of new variables from these raw data. This is a critical element of good model building as data are often more predictive when transformed into descriptive and summary statistics. Behaviour and product data, such as monthly balances, monthly transactions and the loans a customer had in the past were used in the creation of new fields. For example, balances over the last six months were used to create a new field: 'average balance in the last six months'.

At this point we had generated a modelling data set with several hundred variables, including derived and raw data inputs. We next looked at reducing the number of modelling variables from several hundred to the 100 or so most predictive, by selecting those that were most correlated with the target variable. The tools used included descriptive statistics, crosstabs, χ^2-tests and cumulative modelling.

Next came the modelling stage, for which we separated the modelling data set into a training data set and a validation data set. The training data set was used to develop the model and the validation data set was held back to check that the model was robust.

Stepwise logistic regression was then used for the development of the response model, although other statistical techniques were also investigated. The 100 variables identified as being the most predictive in the previous stage were used for modelling the training data set. This was an iterative process, resulting in several variants of the final model that all performed well. These were compared against each other using a variety of diagnostic tools in order to select the best performing model.

The final model was then validated by running fresh data through it to see how well it performed. The results were very consistent with the results seen in the training stage so we were confident that the model would perform well when implemented.

Implementing the model

The model was then used to produce scores for all available customers on the customer database (a score of 100 meaning that a customer was most likely to take up the product and a score of 1 meaning that the customer was least likely to take up the product).

Customers were then sorted into descending order according to their score. First a small random sample of customers was selected so that the model's performance could be compared against results for a non-targeted campaign, and then a group of the best customers was selected to achieve the required number of responders for the campaign.

The benefits

When the responses had come in, we could see how the predictive model performed.

The mailing carried out to a selection of our best customers achieved approximately three times the number of responders we would have received had we mailed a random selection of the same size.

Figure 1.3 shows the total mailed population, ranked according to their model score along the x-axis (highest likelihood to respond to lowest likelihood to respond from left to right). The y-axis shows the cumulative captured responses, as percentages of the total response to the campaign. The straight line represents the results of a non-targeted campaign within the mailing population; the dotted curve shows the actual response to the campaign.

Table 1.1 further illustrates the efficiency of the model and the benefit to the business. The first column describes the mailing population split into deciles, the second the cumulative percentage of customers who responded, the third the cumulative percentage of customers who did not respond, the fourth the cost per response relative to the overall cost per response and finally the model efficiency, this last being the rate at which responding customers are found in the targeted population.

It can be seen that the model was most efficient at the first decile and least efficient at the bottom decile. In the first decile the cost per response was only 36 per cent of the overall cost per response for the targeted mailing, showing that the cost of acquisition could have been further reduced if we had not needed to meet a target number of respondents.

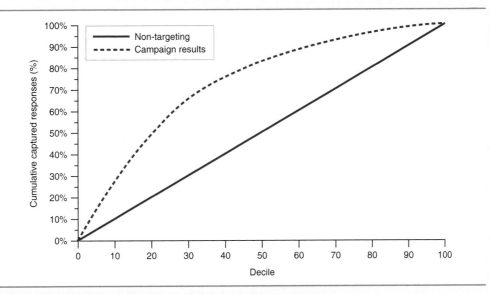

Figure 1.3 Cumulative capture by decile within mailing population

The development and successful implementation of the predictive model had two main benefits. The first was a cheaper and more effective campaign; the second was a reduction in mailing volume.

Overall, the reduction in costs and number of customers mailed was good news from both a financial and a customer relationship perspective.

Table 1.1   Efficiency of the model

Cumulative decile	% of responding customers	% of non-responding customers	Cost per response as % of overall cost per response	Model efficiency
1	27.8	9.4	36	278
2	49.2	19.0	41	246
3	65.7	28.8	46	219
4	75.5	38.8	55	189
5	82.1	48.9	61	164
6	88.2	59.1	68	147
7	93.4	69.2	75	133
8	95.6	79.5	84	120
9	98.3	89.7	92	109
10	100.0	100.0	100	100

Use of computers

Readers will probably be aware already that computers and information technology in general have had a fundamental effect on most business organisations. The same applies to the quantitative analytical techniques that we shall be introducing in the text. It used to be the case that 'solving' quantitative problems – in the sense of completing the mathematics and statistics required – restricted the use of such techniques to large-scale problems, which were analysed by the quantitative analysis specialist. Over the past few decades, however, advances in technology – such as smart devices – have revolutionised both the areas to which techniques are applied and the type of person using such techniques. Software such as spreadsheets or the more common statistical and mathematical packages as well as simulation models now make such analysis readily available to any business decision maker. In the authors' view, this has been one of the major factors behind the explosion of interest in such techniques (mirrored of course by virtually all business undergraduate and postgraduate students being forced to undertake at least one course in such techniques). Naturally the use of such software presupposes that you are able to interpret the computer output that can be generated, not only in a strictly quantitative way but also in terms of assessing its potential to help business decision making. Many of the end-of-chapter exercises, however, are eminently suited for further analysis using either a spreadsheet package or some statistical software, and we would encourage both students and tutors to take advantage of this wherever possible.

Using the text

As we've said, the text is aimed primarily at those students who have a clear interest in management and business decision making but who also appreciate the potential that quantitative analysis brings to the management process (or at worst find themselves required to complete a course in this area). Deliberately we have kept the focus throughout the text on developing a conceptual, rather than a mathematical, understanding of the principles of each topic and on the potential application of the techniques to typical business problems.

At the same time we need to stress that one of the worst ways in which such techniques can be seen by a manager is in terms of the 'toolbox' approach, where the focus is often on finding a technique to fit the problem rather than on focusing on an appropriate method and methodology to help resolve the problem under investigation. It is all too tempting to look at a business problem briefly and assume that it is one of stock control, forecasting or whatever. Once designated as, for example, a stock-control problem, it is tempting then to ignore other quantitative – and qualitative – ways of examining the problem. This can result in the technique being forced to fit the problem and generating information and results that are at best incomplete and immediate and at worst downright misleading to the manager. Business problems rarely, if ever, fit into nice neat compartments labelled 'stock control' and the like. What may on the surface appear to be a problem in the stock department may well turn out to be a problem in production or sales or related to quality management.

Each chapter in the text follows a similar general format. First, we provide an introduction to the focus of that chapter. Then we introduce the relevant topics and place them in a typical business context. An example problem is then introduced and thoroughly investigated and discussed in terms of both determining a solution to the problem and the wider business applications of the technique. Within each chapter you will also find a number of Progress Check activities. These are tasks for you to complete at that point in your reading of that chapter. Although you may be tempted to 'skip over' an activity we would strongly encourage you not to do so. The activities are an integral part of the learning process and will typically lead you into the next part of that chapter. Solutions to these activities appear either in the next part of the chapter or in Appendix F. Most chapters conclude with a fully worked example showing how to approach a particular problem or question using the techniques introduced thus far. Finally, we present details of actual business applications, illustrating how the techniques introduced in that chapter are used in the real world to help business decision making. We have tried to provide you with the most recent case studies. However we value the relevance and educational richness of a case study more than its publication date. Where a case study appears old by its date of publication but is still highly relevant we have not hesitated in using it.

Summary

It will by now be evident that the topics and techniques that we introduce in this text are not merely of academic interest. They are all techniques that are actively – and profitably – used by a variety of business organisations and, perhaps more importantly, they are being used by the managers of these organisations as well as the 'experts'. Developing your own awareness and understanding of these techniques as well as skills in their use will be a worthwhile investment, not only as part of your current studies but also in terms of your management career.

QADM IN ACTION   British Telecom

British Telecom (BT) is one of the largest UK-based organisations in terms of both employees (over 200 000 at the time this application was undertaken) and financial size (a market capitalisation of over £30 billion in mid-2001). It is also an organisation that was one of the first to be converted from a state organisation controlled by the UK government to a private sector company. Along with other privatised organisations this has led to a fundamental change in attitudes and approaches to customers where customer care, responsiveness to customer requirements and high-quality customer service are seen as critical items on the organisation's strategic agenda.

At the time this application was being conducted, BT was looking at ways of improving the initial interface with customers, the so-called Front Office. This was seen as a single point of contact for the customer, so any customer telephoning the company to make enquiries, to seek assistance or just to obtain service information would be dealt with by the Front Office. The intention was that the customer experience of being transferred from one person in the organisation to another (something that most of us will have experienced at some time with some organisation) could be minimised and, potentially, removed. A specialist team within the company was given the task of looking at ways of delivering this service.

The first step – as is often the case – involved basic data collection and building up a picture of the situation under investigation. In this context, the team first needed to assess the typical pattern of calls received during the day and during the week, shown in Figures 1.4 and 1.5, in order to assess likely demand on the Front Office.

Using simple presentation techniques, it can readily be seen that there are classic resource implications to the patterns exhibited. From Figure 1.4 we note that the maximum number of calls is around 300 in any one 30-minute period – an indication of current maximum demand on the Front Office. Similarly, we see from Figure 1.5 that Monday is the peak day with around 5000 calls having to be dealt with in total. It is evident, though, that the number of calls not only

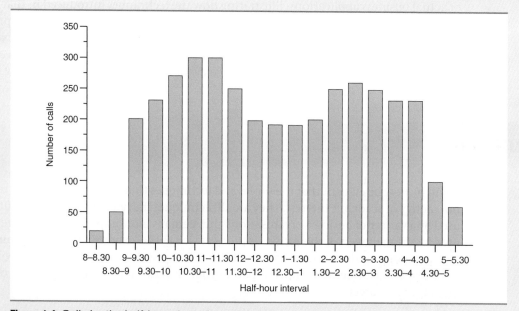

Figure 1.4 Calls by the half-hour throughout the day

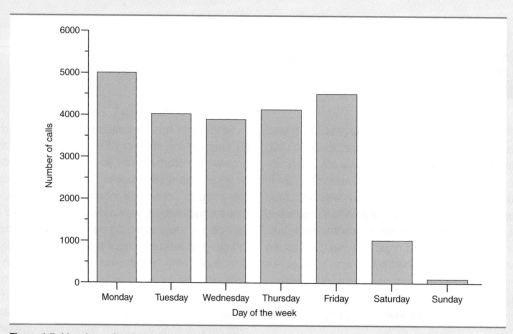

Figure 1.5 Number of calls by day of the week

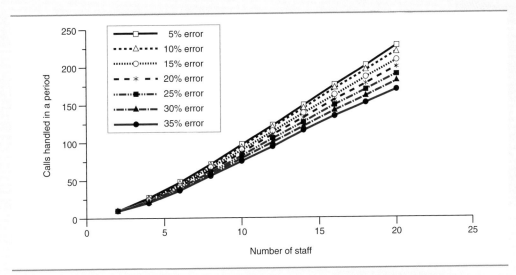

Figure 1.6 Maximum number of calls handled reduces as the forecast error increases

fluctuates during each day, it varies considerably across days of the week. The obvious implication of this fluctuation is in terms of staffing – having people available to respond to the calls. The manager's dilemma is evident. On the one hand the company is keen to have prompt responses to customer calls so that customers will not be kept waiting for the phone call to be answered. From Figure 1.4 this implies a maximum capacity of about 300 calls in a 30-minute period and having enough staff available to deal with this capacity. On the other hand, the company will also want to minimise staff costs associated with this part of its activities, and it is evident that for most of the time this capacity will not be needed, as the number of calls will be less than 300. If the manager provides dedicated staff to deal with the maximum capacity, they will not all be needed at other times of the day and will represent an unnecessary cost, unless the situation can somehow be managed in terms of rotas and shift patterns or ensuring these staff are multi-skilled so that they can undertake other productive work during a quiet period. As if this were not enough of a problem, such call patterns are not likely to remain static: they will change over time as the size of the business changes. As BT's customer base grows the demand on the Front Office is also likely to increase.

Accordingly, the team used a number of forecasting techniques to try to predict future call levels and also carried out some 'what if' analysis around these forecasts, recognising that any particular forecast cannot be 100 per cent guaranteed. In conjunction with this work, the team developed a computer simulation model to simulate staff workloads in a typical Front Office and to assess the impact on staffing levels and performance of different call levels occurring. The call level forecasts, the what-if analysis and the staffing simulation could then be put together to help assess the staff required to deal with particular call levels, as shown in Figure 1.6. The team made great efforts to ensure the results of their analysis would be available in a readily accessible form to the managers taking the actual decisions. Managers in any organisation are, understandably, reluctant to act on information that they do not properly understand, and the team developed a user-friendly computer program based around this analysis to help managers take decisions about staffing the Front Offices for which they were responsible. As the team concluded, '[this] offers managers, for the first time, the ability to understand the full implications and potential consequences of staffing decisions'.

Source: Based on Richardson, C. (1991) Staffing the front office, *Operational Research Insight*, 4 (2), pp. 19–22.
© 1991 Macmillan Publishers Limited.

2

Tools of the Trade

Learning objectives

By the end of this chapter you should be able to:

- work with fractions, percentages and proportions
- explain the principles of rounding and significant figures
- use common mathematical notation
- use mathematical symbols and equations
- construct and use graphs
- explain what is meant by the term 'real' value

As we said in Chapter 1, the main focus throughout the text is on the practical uses of quantitative analysis in business and management decision making. However, before we can start introducing the more common techniques used by managers, we have to make sure that we have the basic quantitative knowledge and skills we will need. So, in this chapter, we shall be covering the concepts and skills forming the 'tools of the trade' that we will be using throughout the text. Many of you will remember from school some, if not all, of the material we are covering in this chapter. However, don't just skip over it because it looks familiar. Try one of the associated Reality Check activities just to make sure you do know how to do what that section is covering. Also, if later on in the text some of the calculations we're doing are causing you difficulty, come back to this chapter and re-read the relevant section.

Some basic terminology

Like any other academic subject, quantitative analysis has its own jargon. The following sections introduce some of the basic terminology that we shall be using.

Variables

The term *variable* refers to a characteristic we are investigating or analysing. So, for example, the variable in question might relate to company profits, number of employees, salaries, length of service, customer attitudes and so on. In general, a variable may fall into one of three types.

Discrete

A discrete variable is one which can only take certain fixed numerical values. The number of cars sold globally by Toyota in 2020 can only be a whole number. The amount of money in my savings account will be a certain number of pounds and pence. Typically the value of a discrete variable is determined by counting.

Continuous

A continuous variable is one which – in principle at least – can take any numerical value and typically comes from measuring rather than counting. The length of a piece of sheet steel used in the vehicle manufacturing process can be measured to any required degree of accuracy – centimetres, millimetres, hundredths of a millimetre and so on.

Attribute or categorical

An attribute variable is one which is not normally expressed in numerical terms. The gender of the person buying a Toyota car will fall into one of two categories – male or female. For purposes of analysis, however, we may assign an arbitrary numerical value to such a variable. Many of you will have seen and completed personal questionnaires where you are asked to indicate your gender. You may recollect that there is often a numerical value printed alongside the possible responses – for example, Male = 1 Female = 2 – which will allow the computer system being used to quantify the number of responses in each category.

Progress Check 2.1

Consider the following and determine what type of variable each best represents:

(a) the number of private houses built last year
(b) the average price of a house
(c) the number of people employed in the construction industry
(d) the number of tonnes of concrete used in house construction
(e) the different types of houses constructed.

Solution is given on p 569.

Primary and secondary data

It is always important in business to assess the source of the data which is being analysed and upon which decisions might be based. We distinguish between *primary* data and *secondary* data. Primary data is data which has been collected at first hand for the purposes of some specific analysis. Secondary data, on the other hand, relates to data which has been collected for some purpose other than the analysis currently being undertaken. It's second-hand data. Consider the Finance Department of a local authority with the responsibility for collecting a local tax from residents in its area. It may well construct a database of those residents who have not paid the tax this year. Clearly for the department this will be primary data: collected by the department for its own use. This database, however, may then be used by the Economic Development Unit in the local authority, which is investigating income and poverty levels in the area and evaluating strategic options to try to alleviate these. Although the database may well be useful for their purposes, it is now a secondary source of data. In principle we would need to be more cautious about analysing and using such information from secondary data. Since we would not have been involved in the initial data collection, we may be uncertain about the precise logistics used to obtain this data. Its quality, therefore, on a secondary basis, must be suspect – guilty until proven innocent. It's worth noting that much of the business data you're likely to encounter in your day job will be secondary and it's worth getting into the habit of asking a few questions about such secondary data – and any analysis based on it – before reaching any conclusions and certainly before making any decisions. This is ever more important when more and more data is available on the internet. Consider the following questions when evaluating any secondary data.

Who collected it?

Your assessment of the reliability of data can be affected by knowing who collected it – their background, qualifications, credibility etc. Data from a government agency is likely to be more reliable than data found on a personal website for example and may be more reliable than that published by a company's marketing department.

What was the purpose in collecting the data?

Why was this data collected – what was the intended purpose? There may be a biased reason for posting the data. Commercial businesses, political groups, lobby groups, marketing departments post data that might represent their own interests but may not be 100 per cent accurate or reliable. Knowing the purpose of data collection will help you evaluate the quality of the data and assess the potential level of bias (or spin!).

When was the data collected?

Timeliness is one of the most important aspects of accuracy, reliability and usefulness. If you're researching the hottest food trends for your start-up restaurant, then analysis from a few years ago probably won't help – and may even lead you to make inappropriate decisions.

How was the data collected?

Is it clear how the data was collected and how reliable and representative it is? This won't always be directly available but you should be able to find out if the data is from a reputable source. Asking a cross-section of the general population whether they use Facebook or Twitter may not be the best approach given that some age/demographics groups (e.g. older people) are more/less likely to be users. Does the data relate to what you're interested in?

Is the data consistent with data from other sources?

Do the numbers make sense? Is this data consistent with that from other sources or is it markedly different? If you happen to see data and 'facts' varying from source to source, you need to do some research as to which are most reliable.

It's also important to realise that primary data can take considerable time to collect accurately, it requires expertise and it can be very costly to collect. Secondary data on the other hand is available immediately and is effectively 'free'. Bear in mind that secondary data will never be perfect for your own requirements. The key question though is: is it reliable and helpful enough for me to use?

Fractions, proportions, percentages

> ### Reality Check 2.1
>
> Take a look at the following question to see if you're familiar with fractions, proportions and percentages. If you are, you don't have to read this section – although you might still find it interesting.
>
> Which is bigger: 1/6, 30%, 0.35?

The 30 per cent struggle

In their book, Michael Blastland and Andrew Dilnot comment on a survey which found that 30 per cent of people struggle to understand what '30%' actually means!

Source: Blastland, M. and Dilnot, D. (2007) *The Tiger That Isn't: Seeing through a World of Numbers*. London: Profile Books.

Fractions, proportions and percentages are all around us. Sale items at half-price, a 20 per cent reduction on original prices, a discount of 0.05 if you buy at least £100 of goods, an internal e-mail saying that your department is facing budget cuts (sorry, 'efficiency savings') of 10 per cent next year. We assume that everyone understands what these mean and the implications. Perhaps surprisingly, there are levels of numerical ignorance around that people/managers are, understandably, reluctant to admit to. After all, it's almost like admitting you can't read and write.

Fractions are simply a way of expressing amounts which are, literally, less than one (in whatever units of measurement we are using). Consider monetary measurement. The pound sterling (£) is made up of 100 pence. If we insist on our units of measurement being pounds, however, then any amount less than this will need to be shown as part of a pound – a fraction. So, for example, 50p is less than one unit (£1) and since we are insisting on units of measurement being in pounds, it cannot be shown as 50p. Instead, it can be shown as a fraction: $£\frac{1}{2}$. Similarly, 25p would be $£\frac{1}{4}$ as a fraction of a pound. Any number can be shown as a fraction simply by taking that number and dividing by the number that makes up one unit. So for 50p we would have:

$$\frac{50}{100}$$

since 50 is the number we require the fraction for and there are 100p making up one unit (£1). Clearly this does not look like $\frac{1}{2}$. The reason is that 50/100 can be simplified through some basic arithmetic. We note that both numbers are in terms of 10s (five tens and ten tens respectively), so it can be rewritten:

$$\frac{5}{10}$$

These numbers are in turn seen to be in units of 5 (one on top, two on the bottom) so we have $\frac{1}{2}$ as the final fraction. It is important to realise that it really does not matter which of these fractions you use $\left(\frac{50}{100}, \frac{5}{10}, \frac{1}{2}\right)$ since they are the same. Which you use is up to you in terms of whichever you find easiest.

The fraction we have, $\frac{1}{2}$, can also be expressed as a decimal proportion: 0.50. To add to the confusion, if we multiply a proportion by 100 we have a percentage:

$$0.50 \times 100 = 50\%$$

(that is, 50p is 50 per cent of £1). Although it does not matter whether we use fractions, proportions or percentages in terms of the calculations, it may well affect how we view the information that is generated. Perceptions differ, but consider what reactions you might get from employees if you told them that they would receive a salary increase next year of either 1/10, 0.10 or 10 per cent. Do you think that everyone would immediately view these as being identical in terms of the impact on their salary?

We must also be careful when using percentages in terms of how we comment on or explain the results, as not everyone understands them. Consider the following example. We are told that inflation in the UK last year was 5 per cent (that is prices went up on average by 5 per cent). This year inflation is 6 per cent. A typical comment in the press might then be: 'the rate of inflation has increased by 1 per cent'. In fact it has not. To be technical, the rate of inflation has increased by 1 percentage *point* (since our initial unit of measurement is in percentage terms) and by 20 per cent (1/5). It is also easy to become confused over percentage increases and decreases. Consider the following. A manufacturer sells a product for £10 inclusive of a government tax. Because of cost pressures the company increases the price by 15 per cent. Some time later the government reduces the tax on this product, bringing the price down by 15 per cent. It is tempting to conclude that the price will once again be £10 but some simple arithmetic illustrates the error in this conclusion.

Original price: £10 Price increase: 15% = 15%(£10) = £1.50

New price: £11.50

Tax decrease: 15% = 15%(£11.50) = £1.72

New price: £9.78

We see that after these changes the new price is actually lower than the original.

Progress Check 2.2

Calculate the following percentages and fractions of 12 098 and 139.5:
25%, 33%, 90%, 5%, 1/3, 1/8, 3/8

Solutions are given on p 569.

Rounding and significant figures

Take a look at the following calculation to see if you're familiar with rounding and significant figures. If you are, you don't have to read this section.

Round 6.3467 to three significant figures.

It is often useful to abbreviate – or round – numbers to make them easier to understand and use. For example, if we are out shopping and we see some item on sale for £9.99 most of us would view this as £10 – mentally we round the original figure to the nearest whole number. Similarly, being told as a manager that you have a budget for a particular project of £124 784 doesn't really help you remember what your budget allocation is. If we rounded this to £125 000, however, it becomes much easier to remember (although technically less accurate).

The principle of rounding numbers is based largely on common sense. First, we determine how many *significant figures* we require. The term significant figures relates to the number of digits in the number that are precise and accurate. So, our exact budget figure of £124 784 contains six significant digits (all six numbers are accurate).

The rounded number of £125 000 contains only three significant figures (the last three zeroes are not accurate). Having decided we want the number to be rounded to three significant figures, we then take the last four digits of the original number and round to the nearest whole number: thus 4784 becomes 5000. (The reason for taking the last four digits is that we start with six significant figures, we require only three, so that the last (3 + 1) digits need to be rounded.) The only slight note of caution comes when rounding the number five. For example if we had had 6500, should we round this to 7000 or to 6000? The answer is that it depends on which convention you use. Our preference is to round fives to the nearest *even* number – in this case to 6000, although we should note that it is just as acceptable to round upwards to the nearest whole number.

A company reports a profit figure for last year of £1 078 245.67. Show this figure with:

(a) 8 significant digits

(b) 6 significant digits

(c) 4 significant digits

(d) 2 significant digits.

Solutions are given on p 570.

What does matter, though, is the degree of accuracy you imply in any calculations you produce using rounded numbers. Consider the following two numbers: 3.4 and 6.23. We know that each number has been rounded to two and three significant digits respectively. If we multiply these two numbers we have:

$$3.4 \times 6.23 = 21.182$$

which appears to imply five significant digits (and a relatively high level of accuracy). However, the result of this arithmetic cannot be accurate to more than two significant digits (the lower of the two original numbers), hence we should report the result as 21. To see why, consider the two original numbers: 3.4 could originally be anywhere between 3.35 and 3.45, and 6.23 anywhere between 6.2251 and 6.2349. The smallest possible value from this multiplication would then be 20.854085(3.35 × 6.2251) and the largest 21.510405 (3.45 × 6.2349). Hence only the first two digits should be seen as significant.

Let us illustrate with another example. Consider the company with an annual profit of £1 078 245.67. This may well have been reported in the local press as a profit of £1.1 million. The company has an agreement with the workforce that 10 per cent of the profit will be distributed equally among the firm's 100 employees. The arithmetic appears to be:

$$\frac{£1.1 \text{ million } \times 10\%}{100} = £1100$$

which is what each member of the workforce may well expect to see in their next pay packet. The actual amount, however, will be £1078.25. A simple misunderstanding may well lead to industrial relations tension. The message is clearly to round numbers *after* completing the arithmetic and not before and to ensure that results which have been rounded are acknowledged as such.

ING cuts 5,000 jobs in branch cull

Belgian and Dutch networks hit low interest rates, regulation and online rivals cited

By Jim Brunsden in Brussels

Dutch bank ING yesterday announced a significant scaling back of its branch network in Belgium and the Netherlands, with the loss of more than 5,000 jobs, and gave a stark warning of the challenges facing the industry.

The lender said that the equivalent of 3,150 full-time jobs would be lost in Belgium by 2021, close to a third of the total in the country. In the Netherlands, 2,300 jobs are to be shed, equivalent to about 15 per cent of full-time staff.

Source: Brunsden, J. (2016) ING cuts 5,000 jobs in branch cull: Belgian and Dutch networks hit low interest rates, regulation and online rivals cited, *Financial Times* (UK), 4 October, Section: Companies & Markets, p 15.
© The Financial Times Limited. All Rights Reserved.

Rounding numbers can change the impact

The headline shows 5000 job losses although the actual number in the article is 5450. Which is easier to remember? Which has most impact?

Common notation

One aspect of quantitative analysis that many students encounter in the early stages of their studies relates to the use of mathematical 'shorthand' – the use of mathematical notation in analysing and presenting results. Tell people that the average salary of a group of employees is £23 500 and there is no problem. Tell them that the arithmetic mean for a random sample taken from the statistical population is 23 500 and the eyes glaze over and the mental shutters start to come down. Clearly this is a barrier we must break if we are to progress through the text, since we require this shorthand frequently.

Symbols

The first thing to get accustomed to is the use of symbols rather than descriptive text. We might use the symbol S to represent the salary of an individual, for example. This makes it much more convenient when we need to indicate that S = 12 000 rather than having to spell out that 'the salary of an individual is £12 000'. Similarly we might use D to denote taxes and other salary deductions, with T representing take-home pay for the individual. A simple equation then becomes:

$$T = S - D$$

That is, take-home pay is salary minus deductions, which is much easier to note and use than its verbal equivalent.

Arithmetic operators and symbols

You will already be familiar with the more common mathematical operators: $+, -, \times, \div$. Some of the other operators and symbols that we shall be using include:

- $<$ less than
  - <10 implies all numbers taking a value less than 10.
- $>$ greater than
- $\leq$ less than or equal to
  - So, for example, ≤10 means any number up to and including 10 but excludes all numbers greater than 10.
- $\geq$ greater than or equal to
  - ≥10 implies all numbers of 10 or more.
- $\neq$ not equal to
  - So $\neq10$ implies all values which are different from 10.

Reality Check 2.3

Take a look at the following question to see if you're familiar with arithmetic operators. If you are, you don't have to read this section.

What's $(58 - 3) \times 10 + (42 + 6) / 20$?

The sequence of calculation when there are several operators in an expression is also important. For example, consider:

$$10 + 3 \times 6 - 3 \times 2$$

Arithmetic operators have an established order of priority and this order must be followed to obtain the correct numerical result. The logic is generally straightforward. We use the convention in terms of using different operators that we evaluate in the priority of: $\times$, $\div$, $+$, $-$. That is, we perform:

- any multiplications
- then any divisions
- then any additions
- then any subtractions.

Multiplying (3×6) first, and then (3×2) we have:

$$10 \mid 18 - 6$$

And then we complete the arithmetic as:

$$28 - 6 = 22$$

We will frequently encounter expressions which also involve brackets. Consider the expression:

$$(10 + 3) \times 6 - (3 \times 2)$$

The approach is as before in terms of priority but we must first evaluate all expressions *inside* brackets. This gives:

$$(13) \times 6 - (6) = 78 - 6 = 72$$

It is also worth noting that computer logic acts in exactly the same way when it comes to undertaking some assigned calculation. Spreadsheets, for example, will tend to calculate the expression in the same way and same order as we do.

Note also that we may frequently omit the multiplication symbol, $\times$, in complex expressions. We might have, for example:

$$10 \times (6 - 4)$$

although this would normally be shown as:

$$10 \, (6 - 4)$$

Progress Check 2.4

Work out the following expressions:

(a) $100.2(34 - 7)/13$
(b) $0.5 - 0.8 \times 13 + 3$
(c) $(100 \times 2) - (5/2) \times 10$

Solutions are given on p 570.

Powers and roots

Frequently we may be involved in arithmetic that requires one number to be multiplied by itself some number of times. For example, we may want:

$$3 \times 3 \times 3 \times 3 \times 3$$

The shorthand way of writing this is as 3^5 (read as three to the power of five). The superscript number (5) is known as the *exponent* and simply shows that we take the actual number (3) and multiply it by itself five times. So, we would have:

$$3^5 = 3 \times 3 \times 3 \times 3 \times 3 = 243$$

As with most mathematics there is an opposite to taking the power of a number. This is known as taking the *root* of a number. For example, we might have:

$$10^2 = 100$$

and then require what is known as the root of 100, which we would denote as:

$$\sqrt{100}$$

where $\sqrt{}$ is the root symbol. A root implies that we require a number such that when we square the number (raise to the power 2) then we will obtain 100. Clearly in this case we have:

$$\sqrt{100} = 10 \text{ since } 10^2 = 100$$

This example is known as the square root of 100. Other roots – the third, fourth, etc. – are possible. So we might have:

$$\sqrt[5]{243} = 3$$

since as we saw earlier, $3^5 = 243$. (We'll see how to work out the answer of 3 shortly.) To make matters worse, however, it is possible to denote roots as fractional powers. Thus:

$$\sqrt{100} \text{ can be written as } 100^{1/2} \quad \text{or} \quad 100^{0.5}$$

and

$$\sqrt[5]{243} \text{ as } 243^{1/5} \quad \text{or} \quad 243^{0.2}$$

It is worth remembering that whenever you see a number raised to a fractional power it is simply another way of writing a root expression. We should also note two special cases. Any number raised to the power 1 simply equals that number:

$$10^1 = 10$$

and any number raised to the power zero equals 1:

$$123^0 = 1$$

(Don't ask why! Just remember it!) And if you think only statisticians are interested in square roots have a look at the next FT case study!

Multiple answers to Europe's maths problem

By Wolfgang Munchau

What is a fair voting system for the European Union? It looks as though, thanks to Poland, European leaders will be forced to debate this difficult question at their summit this week.

Since the simplified draft treaty is substantively identical to the old and rejected constitution – minus some cosmetics – the voting system proposed is going to be the same one: passage of legislation requires a coalition of countries representing at least 55 per cent of the member states and 65 per cent of the population. The Poles have threatened a veto unless the second of those two numbers is based on the square root of the population size – to reduce Germany's influence. It sounds arbitrary, but the Poles have a point. Mathematics is on the side of Poland.

To an uninitiated observer, this does not appear immediately obvious. Does it not seem fair that the voting power of a country in an international organisation should be proportional to its population size? The answer is no. In fact, it is totally unfair. The reason is that effective voting power in multi-nation settings such as the EU depends not on voting size but on the ability to form winning coalitions. Large countries are better placed than their relative population size would suggest.

The original, six-member Community is a good example of this counter-intuitive idea. Germany, France and Italy each had four votes in the council of ministers, the Netherlands and Belgium had two and Luxembourg one vote. Germany then had more than 100 times the population of Luxembourg, yet only four times the number of votes.

Intuition might suggest that tiny Luxembourg was surely over-represented. In truth, the opposite was the case. The threshold for a majority was set at 12 votes.

Since every member except Luxembourg had an even number of votes, Luxembourg was never in a position to cast a make-or-break vote. Despite being numerically over-represented, Luxembourg in effect had zero voting power. That would have been different if, for example, an odd number had been chosen as the threshold.

So how do you measure effective voting power? Lionel Penrose, the British mathematician and psychiatrist who developed a theory of voting power in the 1940s, concluded that votes in international organisations should be based on the square root of the population. This is where the Poles got their idea. . . .

Is Poland's square root solution the only alternative? Of course not. EU leaders could, for example, raise the threshold for population size and number of countries from their 55 and 65 per cent respectively or introduce some complicated new formula – perhaps with a square root in it. There is a quite a bit a leeway left without creating Nice-style gridlock. Professors Baldwin and Widgrén propose another simple and effective solution: drop the voting rules of the constitution and just repair the Nice rules by reducing some of the high thresholds.

The Poles have put their finger on an important issue, though their own answer is not as compelling as they think. If and when EU leaders set out to amend the rules, they should heed the lessons of the past. Any new system needs to fulfil two parallel goals: it needs to make the voting system more effective and it needs to be fair. The Nice system is fair and ineffective. The constitution is effective but unfair.

If they get this wrong again, they will be back at the negotiating table not too long from now. But if they get it right, they will have managed to create the one and only substantive change from the original treaty.

Politics and a square root! You may want to find out if the idea was adopted.

Logarithms

It may have occurred to you that using power and roots notation is all very well but how do we actually work out the answer? Consider:

$$\sqrt[4]{365.3}$$

How do we actually determine what the fourth root of 365.3 is? To obtain such a result we must turn to the use of logarithms. You will find it useful to have a calculator with logarithmic facilities available for this next section. We have already seen that the exponent of a number indicates the power to which it is to be raised. Let us consider the number 10. We then might write:

$$10^2 = 100$$
$$10^3 = 1000$$
$$10^4 = 10\,000$$

and so on with the exponents being 2, 3 and 4 respectively. We can describe the logarithm of a number as the exponent of 10 which equates to that number. That is, we say that the logarithm of 100 is 2 (since $10^2 = 100$), the logarithm of 1000 is 3, of 10 000 is 4 and so on. In fact any number (not just those involving 10) can be expressed in logarithmic form. For example, from a pocket calculator:

$$\log(13) = 1.11394 \text{ since } 10^{1.11394} = 13$$
$$\log(540) = 2.73239 \text{ since } 10^{2.73239} = 540 \text{ and so on.}$$

Calculators vary but there should be a key marked 'log'. Press the log key, key in 13 and then press the = key and you should get the same answer as us −1.11394. Effectively with logarithms what we are doing is converting all numbers to a common base of 10 (with the exponent allowing us to use 10 raised to some power to denote any other number). But how do we use such logarithms? Suppose you were asked to calculate:

$$3^2 \times 3^4$$

With a little thought you might realise that this would be 3^6 (since it is actually $3 \times 3 \times 3 \times 3 \times 3 \times 3$). That is, if we require to multiply two numbers together that have a common base (3 in our example) we can simply *add* their exponent parts together to get the result. With logarithms that is exactly what we do, given that logarithms use the base 10. So, for example, if we wanted:

$$13 \times 540$$

we use the principle of logarithms:

$$10^{1.11394} \times 10^{2.73239} = 10^{3.84633}$$

or just using the logarithms:

$$1.11394 + 2.73239 = 3.84633$$

But how do we get back to 'sensible' numbers (like 13 and 540)? The answer is that we reverse the logarithmic process and take the *antilog* of the logarithm (again using a pocket calculator, where the antilog key is often shown as 10^x). The antilog of 3.84633 is 7019.9, which, if you check the multiplication of 13×540 directly, is different from the 'true' answer of 7020 only because we rounded the logarithmic values. In fact we can generalise logarithmic arithmetic into some simple rules:

Multiplication of numbers

- Convert the numbers into logarithms.
- Add the logarithms together.
- Take the antilog of this total to get the answer to the original multiplication.

Division of numbers

- Take the logarithm of the number on top of the division.
- Take the logarithm of the number on the bottom.
- Subtract this second number from the first.
- Take the antilog of the result to get the answer to the original division.

Obtaining powers

- Take the logarithm of the number to be raised to some power.
- Multiply the logarithm by the exponent.
- Take the antilog of the result to obtain the answer to the original power.

Obtaining roots

- Take the logarithm of the number for which the root is required.
- Divide the logarithm by the required root.
- Take the antilog to obtain the required result.

We shall illustrate with our original example. We required the fourth root of 365.3. Following the rules we have:

$$\log(365.3) = 2.562648672$$

(Note the number of significant digits used to ensure accuracy.)

$$\frac{2.562648672}{4} = 0.640662418$$

$$antilog(0.640662418) = 4.3718 \text{ (rounded)}$$

which is the fourth root of 365.3. To check, multiply 4.3718 by itself four times and you will get 365.3. Logarithms are very useful ways of performing complex calculations.

Note that we've employed logarithms using base 10. These are often referred to as *common* logarithms. There are also what are known as *natural* logarithms, which use not 10 as the base but 2.718 instead (don't ask!). Your calculator may have a key like 'ln' to work in natural logs. Natural logs are also known as base *e* logs.

Progress Check 2.5

Perform the following calculations using logarithms:

(a) 1098.2×34
(b) $345.6/23.7 \times 109.3$
(c) 12.569^5
(d) $156^{1/8}$

Solutions are given on p 571.

QADM IN ACTION

Google and logarithms

Internet search engines. We all use them – searching for websites we're interested in, products that we want to buy, concerts that we want to go to. As users of a search engine like Google we want the search to throw up the most relevant websites for our search. But if we're an advertiser or supplier of products or services on the web then we want a search engine to put our details and website at the top of the search results list.

For example, you might have used a search engine to search for quantitative analysis textbooks. A Google search done when we were writing this edition revealed around 2 million webpage hits.

So how do search engines like Google decide where to present each webpage in their results? The answer is – no one really knows except a few people in the company! Search engines keep most of their methods – their algorithms – secret for competitive reasons and also to try to prevent webmasters manipulating the system to put their page at the top

of the list. However, some details of one of the algorithms are known publicly, for the PageRank algorithm invented by Google founders Larry Page and Sergey Brin when they were graduate students in Computer Science at Stanford University. Its details were published when they were granted a US patent. PageRank effectively measures the probability that you would end up on a given webpage if you clicked links randomly while surfing.

Google assigns a numeric weighting for each webpage on the internet, effectively showing a webpage's importance in the eyes of Google. This PageRank score is derived from a theoretical probability value on a logarithmic scale.

And when Google started planning to sell shares through an IPO (initial public offering) in 2004 it valued itself at $2 718 281 828. Some commentators realised that the value quoted was exactly 1 billion times the value of the natural logarithm base e, or 2.718281828!

Logarithms are – probably – the key to Google's approach to prioritising web pages.

Summation and factorials

Reality Check 2.6

To check whether you're OK with summation and factorials try these:

What's Σx for $x = 3$ to 7?

What's 5!?

We frequently need to undertake repetitive calculations on a set of numbers and it is useful to be able to summarise such calculations. There are two such calculations that we shall require. The first of these is *summation*. Consider if we have the salary levels of a number of employees and we wish to add these together to get the total salary cost. Clearly we would add the first figure to the second to the third and so on. If we denote the salary figures with a suitable symbol such as S then we can summarise the required calculation as:

$$\Sigma S_i \quad \text{where} \quad i = 1, ..., n$$

This simply indicates that we have some number (n) of salary figures and that we are to add them together, that is, we're adding S_1 to S_2 to S_3 and so on. The Σ symbol (pronounced sigma) is the conventional symbol for summation. Here we would simply say that we required the sum of all the S values, with the expression i = 1 to n indicating that we take each S number in turn from the first in the data set to the nth. We may for convenience remove the i notation where it is clearly understood. Frequently we may want to use the symbol in more complex formulae and care must be taken to evaluate these properly. For example, suppose the organisation is adding a £50 annual bonus to everyone's salary. The corresponding total would then be:

$$\Sigma(S + 50)$$

That is, we would first add £50 to each of the individual S values and then we would add these together to give the total. This would be different from:

$$\Sigma S + 50$$

which implies we are adding £50 to the total salary cost.

The second type of calculation for which we require a shorthand notation is the *factorial*. We shall see the uses of such a calculation later in the text, but assume that we require a calculation such as:

$$7 \times 6 \times 5 \times 4 \times 3 \times 2 \times 1$$

That is, a sequence of numbers multiplied together where the sequence changes by one each time. We would denote such a calculation as 7! (pronounced 7 factorial).

Progress Check 2.6

We have the following data:

    Y: 10, 12, 14, 18
    X: 2, 3, 7, 9

Calculate:

(a) ΣX (d) $(\Sigma X)^2$ (g) $10!$

(b) ΣY (e) ΣYY (h) $3!$

(c) ΣX^2 (f) ΣYX (i) $10! - 3!$

Solutions are given on p 571.

Equations and mathematical models

We shall be expressing relationships between variables frequently in the form of an equation and using such equations to develop business mathematical models. An equation is simply any expression where we have an equals sign (=). Consider a store selling an item for £9.99. For any given level of sales the firm can calculate its sales income. If the store sells 100 items then its income is readily calculated as £999. But if we are interested in a more general expression – allowing us to calculate income for any level of sales – we will benefit from an equation. The income, or revenue, the firm gets from selling this item can be expressed as a simple equation:

$$R = P \times Q \quad \text{or} \quad R = PQ$$

where R denotes the revenue from sales, P the selling price and Q the quantity, or number, of items sold. Clearly this is a generic equation (it will fit any such situation). For this firm the corresponding equation would be:

$$R = 9.99Q$$

since the selling price is fixed at £9.99. All this equation does is to define numerically the exact relationship between the two variables R and Q. In simple terms it allows us to calculate R for any value of Q. So, if $Q = 1000$, R will be 9990 (9.99 × 1000); if $Q = 5000$, $R = 49\,950$ and so on. Such equations can be used with others to develop simple mathematical models.

Let us expand the problem. The firm actually buys these items from a supplier at £6.99 each and has calculated that, on an annual basis, its overheads are £45 000 (made up of rent, staff costs and various fixed costs). In the same way as with revenue we can derive an equation showing the firm's costs:

$$C = 45\,000 + 6.99Q$$

where C is costs. These costs are made up of two elements: a fixed cost and a variable cost. We see clearly that fixed costs are independent of Q (that is, if Q changes, the fixed cost element will not). The variable cost *is* affected by Q, however. We can go one step further. The firm wishes to quantify the profit it will have earned for any level of sales. In simple terms profit (F) will be the difference between revenue (R) and costs (C). So we have:

$$F = R - C$$

but we know that C = 45 000 + 6.99Q and R = 6.99Q, so substituting these for C and R we have:

$$F = 9.99Q - (45\,000 + 6.99Q)$$

Note we have enclosed 45 000 + 6.99Q in brackets to make it clear that *all* of this must be subtracted from 9.99Q. If we multiply everything in the brackets by the minus sign in front of the bracket we get:

$$F = 9.99Q - 45\,000 - 6.99Q$$

We now have two terms involving Q on the right-hand side of the equation and so to simplify we can bring them together. We have +9.99Q and −6.99Q. This gives an equation for profit of:

$$F = -45\,000 + 3Q$$

Effectively, this equation allows us to determine the profit we would achieve for any given level of Q.

Progress Check 2.7

How many items must the firm sell before it breaks even (i.e. where its profit is exactly zero)?

Such an equation becomes useful when we wish to carry out some business analysis such as determining the break-even level of sales. It is evident that the profit equation consists of a negative element (−45 000) and a positive one (+3Q). It will also be evident that when Q takes low values the calculation for F will turn out to be negative (since the (−45 000) part will more than outweigh the +3Q part). This means that the firm will make a negative profit (i.e. it will make a loss). Conversely, if Q is sufficiently high, profit will become positive. The break-even point by definition is where we are about to move from a loss situation into one where we earn a positive profit. What we require is a value for Q where this will happen. Also, by definition, at the break-even point F = 0. So we have:

$$F = -45\,000 + 3Q = 0$$

or

$$-45\,000 + 3Q = 0$$

We now have just one variable, Q, and should be able to work out its numerical value. To do this we use a simple procedure. We can alter the left-hand side (LHS) of the equation in some way, as long as we alter the right-hand side (RHS) in exactly the same way. This will mean we still have the exact relationship specified in the original equation, even though the resulting (new) equation might look different. Let us add 45 000 to the LHS. This gives:

$$-45\,000 + 3Q + 45\,000$$

which simplifies to 3Q since the two other numbers cancel out. But we must now alter the RHS in the same way to keep the relationship as per the original equation. This would then give a new equation:

$$3Q = 45\,000$$

Let us now divide the LHS by 3, remembering that we must do the same to the RHS. This will give:

$$Q = \frac{45\,000}{3} = 15\,000$$

We have now 'solved' this equation. For the firm to break even it must sell 15 000 items. If it does this, profit will be exactly zero. The implication is that if it sells less, profit will be negative, if it sells more, profit will be positive. The potential use of such equations and the models they can be built into should now be clear. They offer a convenient way of both describing and analysing more complex situations – to those who can understand and use them. To expand on this, consider the following:

- The firm's overheads look as if they will increase by 15 per cent next year. How will this affect the break-even sales figure?
- The firm's supplier indicates that the cost of the item will increase by £1.50. How will this affect profit?
- The firm is considering increasing its selling price to £11.99. How will this affect profits and break-even?

All of these questions can readily be investigated through the use of the appropriate equations.

The equations we have examined in this section are all technically known as *linear* equations. They can be recognised as such since they involve only variables of the first power – they do not involve variables which are squared, cubed, rooted, etc. Such equations are referred to as linear because they can be represented as a straight line on a graph. Other types of equation are *non-linear*, since they will not show as a straight line.

Mobiles aid Africa's women farmers

By Margaret O'Connor

Mobile airtime is as precious to Lucia Njelekele as the chicks that are her livelihood. The poultry farmer relies on her mobile phone: for real-time information about demand for her 3,000 livestock from one of Tanzania's biggest supermarkets; to arrange transport; source feed; and consult her vet.

What is more, Ms Njelekele's data trail is valuable. The stream of information left by her consumption of mobile phone airtime, her data purchases, and her social network interactions has persuaded Fanikiwa Microfinance, a local outfit, to provide a loan to expand her business.

The mother of two school-age children recently left a secure job as a secretary to set up the business she runs from home in Imbezi, an hour's walk from downtown Dar es Salaam. She believes that, as an entrepreneur, she will be able to profit more fully from Tanzania's near-7 per cent economic growth.

Despite that growth, Tanzania's female agricultural workers need all the help they can get. The UN found that women in the country earn on average about half what men do and bear the brunt of unemployment. Women form about 90 per cent of the country's agricultural workforce, and wages are low.

But Ms Njelekele has benefited from a credit scoring system designed for consumers without bank accounts by First Access. The social enterprise creates custom-built financial models for lenders such as Fanikiwa to evaluate the creditworthiness of people whose mobile data offer financial information.

Such credit-scoring services could help many more women across rural Africa qualify for loans, the organisation says.

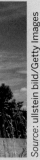

Source: ullstein bild/Getty images

 Source: O'Connor, M. (2014) Mobiles aid Africa's women farmers, FT.com, 7 March. © The Financial Times Limited. All Rights Reserved.

Analytical models crop up where you least expect them.

Graphs

We shall be exploring a number of methods of presenting management information in graphical form in more detail in the next chapter. Before doing so, however, we need to ensure that the basics of graph drawing are understood and appreciated, particularly for equations of the form we have been looking at. It's tempting these days to say: *why bother*? After all, spreadsheets like Excel and other analytical software produce such graphs and charts automatically. Whilst that's true – and we shall be assuming from now on that you're using such software – it's still necessary for analysts and managers to understand what makes for a *good* graph (and a misleading one). And if you don't understand the principles of graph construction it's difficult to assess graphs and charts that appear in reports you're expected to act upon in your day job.

We shall use the profit equation we derived in the last section as our example to illustrate. We want to show the equation in graphical form:

$$F = -45\,000 + 3Q$$

What we require is a diagram like that in Figure 2.1. We see from the graph that profit, F, is shown on the vertical axis and sales, Q, on the horizontal. We also see that the equation line slopes upwards as it moves from left to right indicating that profit increases as sales increase. At the left of the graph we see that when sales are zero, profit is below 40 (000) and we know this will represent fixed costs. Note that we can't see the exact amount of fixed costs at 45 (000) because of the scale. We also see that the equation line crosses zero on the vertical axis when Q is (about) 15 (000). This shows the break-even level of output and the line confirms that at output levels below this, profit will be negative and at output levels above this profit will be positive.

Given that a graph has two axes and two scales, this implies that we must plot one variable on the vertical axis and one on the horizontal. Typically, for an equation the vertical axis (often referred to as the Y axis) is used for the variable on the LHS of the equation (in this case profit), and the horizontal axis, referred to as the X axis, for the variable on the RHS. We can then follow a sequence of stages to construct the graph.

Step 1

Choose an appropriate numerical scale for the X axis. This can be somewhat arbitrary, depending on the context of the problem. Let us assume we wish to plot a graph for sales up to 50 000. Logically, the minimum value for the X scale is then 0. If you are drawing

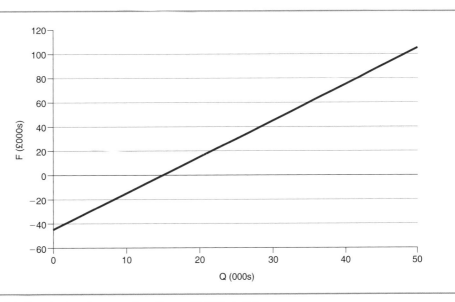

Figure 2.1 Graph showing equation F = −45 000 + 3Q

the graph manually (as opposed to using a spreadsheet) then you will need to determine a suitable number of points to label on the scale. It seems sensible to show steps of 10 000 in this case (i.e. 0, 10 000, 20 000, 30 000, etc.). Where possible keep the number of steps shown on the graph to between 5 and 10.

Step 2

Calculate a suitable scale for the Y axis. Having chosen values for the X axis we can use these in the equation to calculate corresponding values for the Y axis. In fact, in our example we can take advantage of the type of equation we have derived to simplify this. Our profit equation is known as a *linear* equation, which will give a straight line on a graph. To obtain the straight line we need only two points to be able to draw it. Logically, we can determine the Y value corresponding to the minimum and maximum X values. We would then have:

X value	Y value
0	−45 000
50 000	105 000

Using these Y values we can again choose a suitable Y scale, say from −60 000 to 120 000 with intervals of say 20 000.

Step 3

Draw both axes on the graph and both scales. Label each axis with the variable it represents and the units of measurement on each scale.

Step 4

Take the first pair of coordinates (X = 0, Y = −45 000) and plot this as a single point on the graph. Take the second pair (X = 50 000, Y = 105 000) and plot this as a second point. Both points are shown in Figure 2.2 as points A and B.

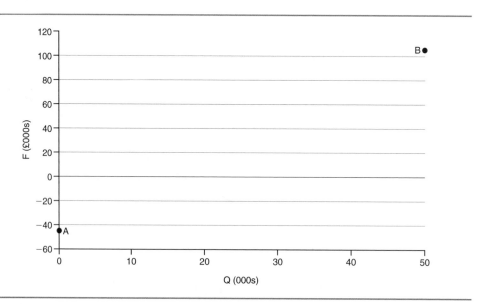

Figure 2.2 X and Y coordinates for $F = -45\,000 + 3Q$

Step 5

Join both points together with a straight line. This line represents the linear equation F = −45 000 + 3Q as shown in Figure 2.1.

It is important to appreciate that the equation and its graph contain exactly the same information, and either or both can be used for analysis purposes. We can, for example, determine the break-even point on the graph, although because of the scale its accuracy is not as good.

Progress Check 2.8

A firm has assessed that sales of its products are linked to the price it charges:

Q = 100 − 5P

where Q is sales (in 000s of units) and P is the price charged in £s per unit sold.

Draw a graph of this equation, known as a demand equation, and from the graph determine the following:

(a) sales when the firm charges a price of £7
(b) the price that was charged if the firm sold 40 000 units.

Solutions are given on p 572.

Non-linear equations

Not all equations, however, will be linear. Many of the more useful quantitative business models involve non-linear equations, as these frequently more accurately represent business behaviour, or may be more useful in a decision-making context. Consider the linear equation in Progress Check 2.8:

Q = 100−5P

This shows the quantity of some product sold at any given price. From the company's perspective, it would also be interested in not just the quantity sold but the revenue or income earned from such sales. Clearly, in terms of simple arithmetic, its revenue (R) will be found by multiplying the quantity sold, Q, by the price charged per unit, P. That is:

R = Q × P

but Q itself can be represented by the linear equation, giving:

R = Q × P
R = (100 − 5P) × P
R = 100P − 5P^2

This revenue equation is clearly not linear (it involves a variable which is not to the power 1 – we now have a P^2 term). The procedure for graphing a non-linear equation is very similar to that of a linear equation.

Step 1

As before, choose an appropriate range for the X scale. Here, it makes sense to choose $P = 0.$ to $P = 20$.

Step 2

For a linear equation we would now find two Y values and then the two points to be plotted to give the straight line. For a non-linear equation we must determine more than two such points, since we no longer have a simple straight line to draw. As a rule of thumb, if we are drawing such a graph manually then we need to find around 10 to 15 different Y values for the non-linear equation. (On a spreadsheet, of course, this can be done very easily and, indeed, you should take advantage of the spreadsheet to plot more points than this to give a more accurate graph.) In our example, it seems sensible to determine values for Y (Q) for $P = 0, 2, 4, 6, 8, 10, 12, 14, 18, 20$. The results are as follows:

P	Q	Equation
0	0	$100 \times 0 - 5(0^2)$
2	180	$100 \times 2 - 5(2^2)$
4	320	$100 \times 4 - 5(4^2)$
6	420	$100 \times 6 - 5(6^2)$
8	480	$100 \times 8 - 5(8^2)$
10	500	$100 \times 10 - 5(10^2)$
12	480	$100 \times 12 - 5(12^2)$
14	420	$100 \times 14 - 5(14^2)$
16	320	$100 \times 16 - 5(16^2)$
18	180	$100 \times 18 - 5(18^2)$
20	0	$100 \times 20 - 5(20^2)$

So we have a total of 11 points of P and Q values that we can now plot on a graph. We can also determine from this series of Q values that the Q (Y) scale would need to cover 0 to 600.

Step 3

Draw both axes on the graph and both scales. Label the axes with the variable it represents and the units of measurement on each scale.

Step 4

We can plot the 11 points we have but this time we join the points together with a curve rather than a straight line (since we know the equation will be non-linear). This produces the graph shown in Figure 2.3.

   As with all such business diagrams it is always worthwhile spending a few moments studying the diagram to ensure the business implications are understood. Here, we see that R (revenue earned) starts from zero (after all setting a price of zero will give you zero revenue no matter what quantity you sell), gradually rises to a maximum of 500 (£000) and then falls away again to zero (since at a price of 20 we know from the demand equation that sales will be zero, hence revenue must be zero also). It is also clear that such a

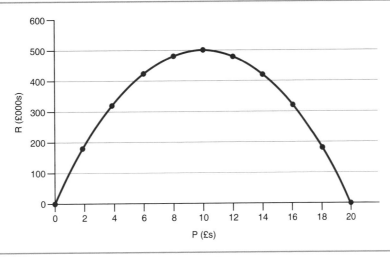

Figure 2.3 Graph showing equation $R = 100P - 5P^2$

diagram reveals something that is not evident from the equation itself. Under such a situation there is clearly an optimal price for the firm to charge if it wishes to maximise the revenue it earns from sales. At a price of 10 the firm clearly will maximise its revenue at £500 000.

And if you think this sort of analysis looks too simplistic for the real business world take a look at the next case study.

QADM IN ACTION

Capgemini – an optimisation model

Capgemini's client is the European corporate arm of one of the world's largest car manufacturers.

The company sells a large range of cars into distinct market sectors in most European countries with the client controlling the market spend budget for the national sales companies in each country. One of the responsibilities of the client is to ensure that each budget is allocated effectively and that total profit across Europe is maximised. Historically, each national sales company would submit a base plan as the basis for its budget allocation. However, the corporate client was interested in seeing whether a model could be developed to suggest alternative budget allocations that would deliver more profit than those submitted in each base plan. The model

would need to be based on its understanding of the economic theory at work in its markets and on the practical constraints facing the business.

Capgemini first developed a detailed understanding of the data which the client had available. A model to represent the economics of the business in Europe was developed and agreed. This model was then used to underpin an optimisation model (we shall develop these ourselves in Chapter 11), which was solved using a specialist computer package. Input and output of the data required by the optimisation model was through Microsoft Excel and an interface created by Microsoft Access.

The model found an optimal solution over three levels of the business: for the country being

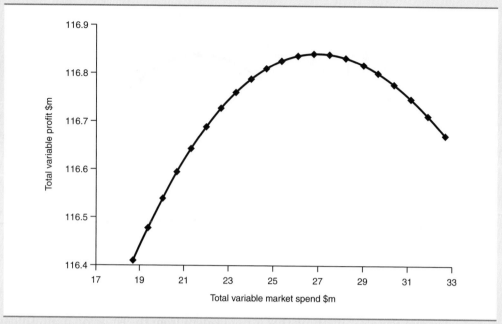

Figure 2.4 Total variable profit vs total variable market spend

analysed, for the model of car being analysed and for the market segment under review. The output for the model was written to a spreadsheet system to help in the easy analysis of results and to enable graphs of key relationships to be shown readily. The results from the model were also stored to allow what-if analysis to be undertaken easily.

Figure 2.4 shows the relationship between total variable profit and total variable market spend for a particular combination of country, car model and market segment. The graph illustrates clearly that there is an optimal market spend if profit is to be maximised.

The benefits were:

● The model provides a rigorous basis for proposing alternative market spend allocations which deliver higher expected profits.

● The client can now easily run additional what-if optimisations, which allow the results of any further proposed actions to be seen easily.

● The client has gained an understanding of the importance of price elasticities in each of their market segments (price elasticity shows the percentage change in sales demand in response to a percentage change in price).

Source: Based on a Capgemini case study, with thanks to Capgemini for permission to use their material.

Real and money terms

Reality Check 2.7

To make sure you understand the difference between real and money terms try this:

An individual's current income in 2020 is £50 000. They've been told that their real income, base 2010, is £47 000. What does this mean?

Education Policy Institute

Third of secondary schools in deficit, finds think-tank

By Andrew Jack

Source: Jeff J. Mitchell/Getty Images

Testing times: austerity policy has had an impact on schools, say critics.

Nearly a third of English state-maintained secondary schools reported deficits last year, up fourfold from 2014. Critics say the study highlights the impact of the government's austerity programme on education.

The think-tank's findings reflect research from the Institute for Fiscal Studies, showing overall school spending fell 8 per cent per pupil in real terms between 2009–10 and 2017–18.

The education department said: ". . . the core schools and high needs budget is rising from almost £41bn in 2017–18 to £43.5bn by 2019–20 . . . "

The distinction between money terms and real terms isn't just of interest to analysts.

In most business organisations we will frequently have to deal with financial information that often covers some period of time. Consider an individual who had an income in 2020 of £25 000. In 2015 this individual's income was £20 000. On the face of it, it appears that the individual is better off (a 25 per cent increase in income over this five-year period). However, as we all know from personal experience, most economies are affected by inflation – the increase in the prices of goods and services that people buy. If over this same five-year period prices (inflation) had risen by more than 25 per cent, the individual would actually be worse off in terms of what the money could buy, even though – at face value – they appear to be better off. Accordingly we frequently make the distinction between a financial value being expressed in *money* terms and being expressed in *real* terms. The two figures we have so far are expressed in money terms. Let us suppose inflation over this period has actually been 10 per cent. The individual's income in money terms in 2020 is still £25 000. In real terms, however – in terms of what the money would buy compared with 2015 – we need to make an adjustment. Between 2015 and 2020 the individual would require a 10 per cent increase in income just to be able to buy the same quantity of products bought in 2015. So to see how the 2020 income really compares with that of 2015 we need to reduce the 2020 income by the amount of inflation. There are different ways we can perform the calculation but we shall do so by using what is known as an *index*.

An index effectively allows us to perform percentage comparisons and calculations. Some index variables may already be known to you: the Retail Price Index, the FT Share Index, the Dow Jones Index. We denote the price level in 2015 as an index with an arbitrary – but convenient – value of 100. The price index for 2020 must be 110 (i.e. 10 per cent higher). The 2020 money income can then be adjusted for inflation:

$$25\,000 \times \frac{100}{110} = £22\,727$$

with the result of £22 727 referred to as *real* income. It can be seen that we have multiplied the 2020 income by a ratio of the two price index numbers: the 2015 figure on top and the 2020 figure below. Effectively the result of £22 727 is the value of the 2020 money income (£25 000) in terms of what it would have bought in 2015 prices. We see that in real terms the individual's income has increased by £2727 after we have taken inflation into account. Such a result would often be reported as £22 727 in 2015 prices or as base 2015. The distinction between money and real values is a critical one for business analysis. The calculation is often referred to as *deflating* the money value. It's worth remembering that whenever you're analysing financial data over time you should deflate the data to see a more accurate picture of what's happening.

Progress Check 2.9

In 2021 this individual's income rose to £26 000. Inflation between 2015 and 2021 was 15 per cent. Calculate the real income for 2021.

Solution is given on p 573.

Worked example

To illustrate some of the techniques introduced in this chapter we'll use a small case study. In the UK, as in many other economies, credit and debit cards are big business. People use them on a routine basis to pay for goods and services and for obtaining cash. As you'll know, a credit card works on the principle that you use the card to pay for purchases, effectively borrowing money from the credit card company. Typically, every month you'll be notified of how much you owe the credit card company with the option of paying off some or all of the outstanding debt. A debit card works differently, being linked to your current/chequing bank account. When you use your debit card to pay for goods or services, the amount is debited from your account. In the UK there has been an increasing trend away from using traditional written cheques.

Consider that you've been asked to do some preliminary analysis to provide an overview of the situation in terms of people's use of credit/debit cards over the last few years in the UK particularly since the credit crunch/financial downturn in the mid-2000s. Table 2.1 shows data for the period from 2005 to 2017 (the latest available when this book was written). The table shows a number of things. First the total number of card

Table 2.1 UK credit and debit card purchases 2005–17

| Year | Total number of transactions millions | Total value of transactions £ millions | of which credit cards | | of which debit cards | | CPI 2005 = 100 |
			Number of transactions millions	Value of transactions £ millions	Number of transactions millions	Value of transactions £ millions	
2005	6095.0	291028.7	2002.0	121678.5	4093.1	169350.2	100.0
2006	6445.3	315534.8	1945.7	119926.2	4499.5	195608.6	102.5
2007	6928.6	347732.0	1955.3	123756.6	4973.3	223975.4	105.0
2008	7447.9	371780.7	1973.1	126121.5	5474.7	245659.3	109.0
2009	7949.3	388949.6	2004.2	125473.8	5945.2	263475.8	111.0
2010	8500.6	416571.9	2003.1	128001.3	6497.5	288516.6	114.6
2011	9471.3	476992.8	2255.8	150888.4	7215.5	326104.4	119.4
2012	10254.5	500941.3	2386.8	153800.9	7867.7	347140.4	122.3
2013	10881.2	531627.0	2532.4	159509.3	8348.8	372117.6	125.9
2014	12062.6	574445.0	2804.3	170587.0	9258.3	403858.0	128.3
2015	13397.3	625285.6	3133.6	181479.9	10263.7	443805.7	128.2
2016	14843.2	647412.4	3349.4	186183.2	11493.8	461229.3	128.8
2017 estimated	15462.5	665817.5	3471.3	192137.5	11991.2	473680.0	132.2

CPI is for June each year
Source: UK Finance;
UK Office for National Statistics

Excel file T2-1

transactions each year (the number of times cards were used to buy something) and then the value of card transactions (i.e. spending) each year (in £ millions). The table shows the split between credit cards and debit cards. So we see, for example, that in 2005 the total number of card transactions was 6095 million; the total value of card transactions was around £290 000 million (or £290 billion – a billion is one thousand million) with about £120 billion on credit cards and the rest, £170 billion, on debit cards. The table also shows the Consumer Price Index (CPI) for this period, measuring inflation. A quick scan of the data in the table shows that since 2005 cards are being used more frequently and the amount spent using cards has been increasing.

Even though we've only looked at the basic 'tools of the trade' so far we can fairly easily think of several types of analysis we might want to do. We'd want to look at:

● trends in the use of credit and debit cards in terms both of how often they're used and how much is spent on them;
● trends in both money and real terms;
● trends in terms of average amounts spent;
● other variables that might link with these trends – people's income for example, debt levels and so on;
● trends in other countries to see if what's happening in the UK is typical.

As we'll see in more detail in Chapter 3, it's often far more helpful to show data visually in the form of a graph or chart. Figure 2.5 shows the number of transactions each year over this period. We can now see that the total number of transactions has steadily increased over this period, with the level of use of debit cards following this trend. Credit card use, however, shows a different picture, with transaction fairly flat from 2005 to 2012 and then showing a modest increase. Note that we've shown the vertical scale in £ millions to be consistent with the table. We might have chosen a scale of £ billions instead (1 billion equals 1000 million).

What about the monetary value of these transactions? Figure 2.6 shows the comparable data. We see similar steady upward trends in transaction values over this period. But in value terms the use of credit cards shows a much more modest increase, perhaps reflecting the economic downturn and consumer uncertainty since the financial crash in 2008.

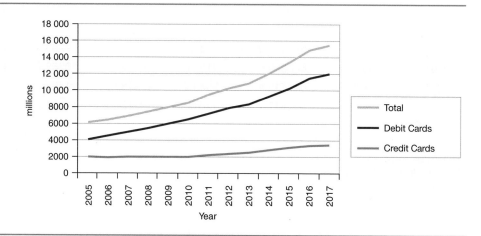

Figure 2.5 UK credit and debit card transactions 2005–17

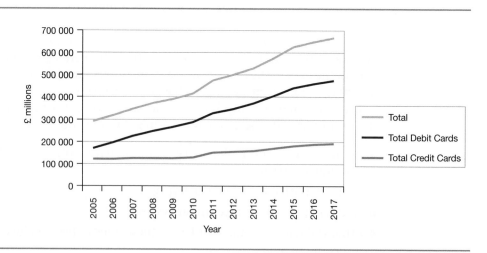

Figure 2.6 UK credit and debit card transactions value 2005–17

However, as we also know, this data is shown in money terms and is potentially being distorted by the effects of inflation. The final column in Table 2.1 is headed 'CPI' and shows the UK Consumer Price Index – a general measure showing how much prices of consumer goods and services generally have changed. We note this is based on 2005. So, for example, prices in 2007 were 5 per cent higher than in the base period of 2005. By 2017 prices generally were almost 30 per cent higher than in 2005. We now use the CPI data to deflate credit card lending and show this in real terms (that is with the effects of inflation removed). Table 2.2 shows the deflated data (you may wish to do these calculations yourself on a spreadsheet for extra practice). Remember that deflated data like this has had the effects of inflation taken out so we're seeing the real value of the three series. From Figure 2.7 we now see that total spending in real terms shows a gradual increase year on year, as does that for debit cards, although both have flattened out somewhat since 2015. For credit cards, however, overall spending is relatively flat over this period once we strip away the effects of inflation.

The relative trends between the three variables can be best illustrated by showing each variable as an index. For each series, we divide each value by the value in 2005 (the first year) and multiply by 100. We then get a series for each variable effectively showing the relative change year on year. Table 2.3 shows the index values and Figure 2.8 shows the graph of these index values. We now see that total spending has risen by around 70 per cent in real terms while that on debit cards has increased by over 100 per cent. Credit card spending, on the other hand, decreased in real terms until 2010 and has remained relatively flat since then. A few simple calculations, a few graphs and you can get a lot out of a few numbers. There's more we could do with this data but we'll leave that for you in the end-of-chapter exercises.

Table 2.2 UK credit and debit card purchases, UK 2005–17, £ millions at 2005 prices

	Total value of transactions	of which credit cards	of which debit cards
2005	291028.7	121678.5	169350.2
2006	307838.8	117001.2	190837.7
2007	331173.3	117863.4	213309.9
2008	341083.2	115707.8	225375.5
2009	350405.0	113039.5	237365.6
2010	363500.8	111694.0	251759.7
2011	399491.5	126372.2	273119.3
2012	409600.4	125757.1	283843.3
2013	422261.3	126695.2	295566.0
2014	447735.8	132959.5	314776.3
2015	487742.3	141560.0	346182.3
2016	502649.4	144552.2	358097.3
2017	503644.1	145338.5	358305.6

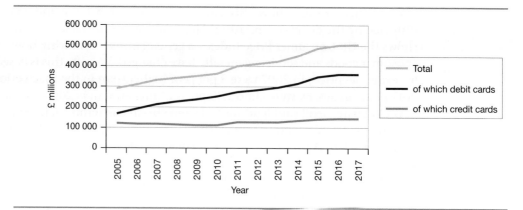

Figure 2.7 UK credit and debit card transactions value 2005-2017

Table 2.3   Index of UK credit and debit card purchases 2005–17 at 2005 prices

	Total value of transactions	of which credit cards	of which debit cards
2005	100.0	100.0	100.0
2006	105.8	96.2	112.7
2007	113.8	96.9	126.0
2008	117.2	95.1	133.1
2009	120.4	92.9	140.2
2010	124.9	91.8	148.7
2011	137.3	103.9	161.3
2012	140.7	103.4	167.6
2013	145.1	104.1	174.5
2014	153.8	109.3	185.9
2015	167.6	116.3	204.4
2016	172.7	118.8	211.5
2017	173.1	119.4	211.6

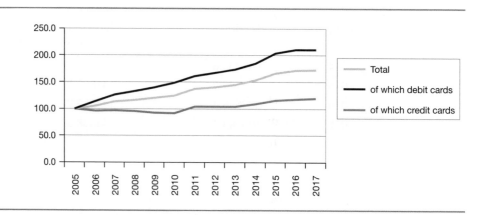

Figure 2.8 Index of UK credit and debit card purchases 2005–17 at 2005 prices

Summary

In this chapter we have introduced the basic mathematical tools that we shall need as we progress through the text. For your own benefit you should ensure you are competent in these before proceeding. If at a later stage in the text you find you are having difficulty with part of the topic, consider returning to the relevant section in this chapter to ensure you understand the basics.

Exercises

1 In the chapter we formulated a break-even problem with:

$$R = 9.99Q$$
$$C = 45\,000 + 6.99Q$$

Find the new break-even level if:

(a) overheads increase by 15 per cent.

(b) costs increase by 1.50 per item.

(c) the selling price increases to 11.99.

2 A couple are thinking of investing £15 000 in a savings fund to pay for their children's college education in future. The fund runs for a 10-year period and is expected to generate a return each year of 8 per cent of the amount invested. All annual returns remain in the fund until the end of the period.

(a) Construct a table showing the value of the original investment each year over this period.

(b) Draw a graph representing this information.

(c) Convert these annual values to logarithms and construct a graph showing the logarithmic values. What comments can you make about this graph compared with the original?

3 A firm finds that the demand for its product can be represented mathematically as:
$$Q_d = 1000 - 5P$$

where Q_d is the number of units of the product demanded by customers and P is the selling price.

(a) Construct a graph for a price between 0 and 200.

(b) Comment on the shape of the graph. Why does the line slope downwards?

(c) If we define revenue as quantity sold times price, obtain an equation for revenue.

(d) Draw a graph of this revenue equation.

(e) What price should the firm charge in order to maximise revenue?

4 Next week you have to travel around parts of the country on business and have decided to hire a car from a car-hire company. You have contacted two companies which offer different services. The first company will rent you a car for £45 per day. The second company will charge you £30 per day but with an additional charge of 5p per mile travelled. You know you will require the car for four days but are unsure of the mileage you will cover.

(a) Determine mathematically what mileage you would need to cover to make the second company's charge cheaper.

(b) Confirm this using graphs.

(c) Both companies now realise that they will need to add VAT at 20 per cent to the charge for the daily hire but not to the charge for the mileage covered. How will this affect your decision?

5 An airline company is considering providing a new daily service between Edinburgh and Copenhagen. The aircraft has a maximum capacity of 200 passengers and each flight incurs a fixed cost of £25 000 (regardless of the number of passengers). In addition, a cost is also incurred of £75 per passenger (to cover such things as catering, booking, baggage handling).

(a) The company is thinking of charging £225 per ticket. How many passengers will the airline need on each flight to break even?

(b) The company knows from previous experience that it is unlikely to sell more than 80 per cent of its seats on any one flight. Assuming it sells exactly this many, what price per seat should it charge to break even?

(c) The company also has the option of accepting a cargo contract with a Danish company. Under this contract the airline will receive £5000 per flight for transporting cargo but, because of the extra weight, it will have to reduce its maximum number of passengers to 190. How will this affect the break-even ticket price?

6 A firm has analysed its sales and profitability and found that its profit can be represented as:

$$F = -100 + 100Q - 5Q^2$$

where F is profit (£000s) and Q is units sold (in 000s).
It has also found that its costs are:

$$C = 100 + 2Q^2$$

where C is costs (£000s).

(a) Obtain a third equation showing the firm's revenue, R.

(b) Using a graph, determine how many units the firm should sell to maximise profit.

(c) What will the firm's costs be at the profit-maximising level of sales?

7 Return to the worked example data shown in Table 2.2

(a) Calculate the percentage of total transactions split between credit cards and debit cards and show the results in a suitable diagram. Comment on what you see. How many significant figures do you think should be used for the percentage data?

(b) Calculate the average spend per transaction each year, split by total, credit card and debit card. Comment on the results.

(c) Show the average spend as a deflated index. Comment on the results.

8   A relatively recent development with credit and debit cards is the introduction of contactless cards. Contactless cards have a chip inside them that emits radio waves. To pay for something with a contactless card, you hold or wave the card near a special payment terminal (known as an RFID reader) and it picks up the signal, communicates with the card and processes the payment. In the UK there is currently a limit of £30 on contactless payments, so they tend to be used for convenience shopping. A major retailer has asked for a short report on the use of such cards in the UK. The relevant data is shown in Table 2.4.

Table 2.4   Contactless cards UK 2014–2017

	Jun-14	Dec-14	Jun-15	Dec-15	Jun-16	Dec-16	Jun-17
Number of Contactless Cards issued (Million)	48.32263	58.70708	70.46748	81.60026	93.53159	102.6726	110.7525
Number of Debit Contactless Cards issued (Million)	28.79702	36.88161	46.12864	55.13853	63.73298	70.1071	74.17533
Number of Credit Contactless Cards issued (Million)	19.52561	21.82547	24.33884	26.46173	29.79862	32.56548	36.57718
Monthly spend in the UK on Contactless Cards (£ Million)	158.5033	380.7969	567.1315	1200.979	1882.809	3370.581	4335.489
Monthly spend in the UK on Contactless Debit Cards (£ Million)	138.284	343.5734	496.1247	1055.343	1648.282	2964.841	3744.887
Monthly spend in the UK on Contactless Credit cards (£ Million)	20.21933	37.22351	71.0068	145.6362	234.5268	405.7395	590.6015
Number of monthly contactless transactions (Million)	23.83091	46.10969	81.22997	140.1532	218.8667	353.9378	469.5789
Number of months Debit card transactions (Million)	20.67773	40.5334	70.68194	123.0448	191.6229	312.467	407.9896
Number of monthly Contactless Credit card transactions (Million)	3.153173	5.576293	10.54803	17.10849	27.24375	41.47081	61.58926
Number of Bank Owned Contactless Terminals	190642	215380	259074	309706	393032	450554	506110

Source: UK Finance

Excel file T2-4

9 Scotland is home to almost 800 offshore islands and, for the communities that live on them, a reliable ferry service between the islands and with the mainland is critical. Not only do the communities themselves rely on the ferry service, so do the tourists that visit. The island of Arran, for example, can only be reached by sea and it has two ferry services. The island is home to around 5000 people but in 2017 attracted over 900 000 tourists and over 250 000 vehicles. Recently, however, there has been increasing concern across the Scottish ferry network about the reliability of the ferries in operation, with an ageing ferry fleet. Data has been collected for the first seven months of 2018 and is shown in Table 2.5. The data shows the number of scheduled ferry sailings across Scotland each month together with:

- cancelled sailings: the number of scheduled sailings that were cancelled;
- cancelled sailings due to ferry mechanical problems;
- cancelled sailings due to severe weather;
- cancelled sailings for other reasons: these might include medical emergencies, harbour problems etc.;
- additional sailings: the number of additional ferry sailings organised.

The Scottish Minister for Transport has asked for a brief report summarising the data. What other data might you realistically collect to help analyse this situation?

Table 2.5   Scottish ferry statistics 2018

	Scheduled sailings	Cancelled sailings	Cancelled due to mechanical problems	Cancelled due to weather	Cancelled for other reasons	Additional sailings
January	9133	545	19	449	77	44
February	8632	384	14	318	52	98
March	9865	519	118	228	63	119
April	11 843	275	14	224	37	85
May	12 547	224	67	123	34	309
June	13 115	271	62	180	29	169
July	14 068	108	33	48	27	135

Source: The Herald on Sunday newspaper Sept. 2018

Excel file T2-5

3 Presenting Management Information

Learning objectives

By the end of this chapter you should be able to:

- explain the potential for using different methods of data presentation in business
- outline the major alternative methods of data presentation
- choose between the major alternative methods
- explain the limitations of data presentation methods

In this chapter we will look at methods of data presentation typically used by business organisations. You may consider at this stage that such a topic appears somewhat elementary for a manager. After all, why should the busy manager spend valuable time on tables, charts, graphs and other pictorial representations? Why not get straight down to 'hard' analysis of the problem and the 'bottom line'? We shall be addressing this question throughout the chapter, but suffice it to say for the moment that diagrammatic representation of information has over the past few years become increasingly important at middle and senior management level to the extent that the whole area of data visualisation has developed. The old adage that a picture is worth a thousand words is an appropriate one in this context. As we shall see, data presentation can provide a quick and concise insight into some business problems, allowing a manager to identify and focus upon the key elements of the situation. Thanks largely to the advances in computing and business analytics, managers these days have a considerable facility to display information visually and to focus quickly on the key characteristics of a set of data. This is a particularly valuable skill when managers have more and more data coming their way and have to make sense of it quickly but accurately. One of the purposes of this chapter is to allow you to develop an awareness of what is possible and, equally, what is desirable in the context of business data presentation.

A business example

To illustrate the usefulness of diagrams at presenting management information in a concise and user-friendly way, let us consider the following situation. Over the past few years domestic consumers of gas and electricity in the UK have been able to select their energy supplier, unlike the previous arrangements where as a domestic customer you had to buy your gas or electricity from the single supplier operating in your area. A company – perhaps currently operating in the petrol and oil markets – is thinking of entering this business and has asked us to provide an overview of domestic electricity sales in the UK over the last few years. Naturally, we could produce a variety of tables showing patterns and trends in terms of sales (and would certainly want to do so as part of a more detailed analysis). However, we can give a quick overview with Figure 3.1, which shows electricity sales measured in gigawatt hours (a gigawatt is 1 billion watts – enough to power a 100-watt lightbulb for over 1000 years) to UK domestic customers for the period 1995 to 2018 on a quarterly basis. The data is from the UK's Office for National Statistics. We see clearly that domestic sales follow what we can refer to as a seasonal pattern through the year, with sales higher in quarters 1 and 4 (the winter period) and lower in the summer (quarters 2 and 3).

By calculating what is known as a trend (which we will look at in Chapter 9) and superimposing this on quarterly sales, we obtain Figure 3.2. The trend shows the long-term movement in domestic sales and some interesting patterns begin to emerge.

We see that up to 2006 electricity sales showed an upward growth trend – about 15 per cent is what we extrapolate from the data in the diagram. However since 2006 the trend

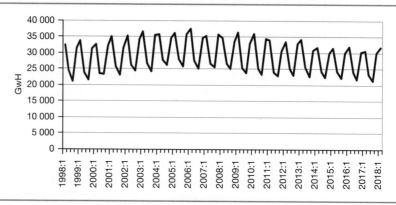

Figure 3.1 UK Domestic electricity sales per quarter GwH 1998–2018

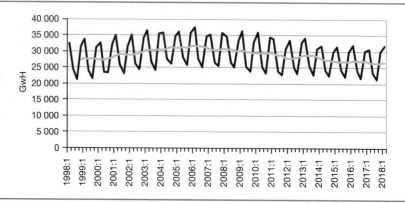

Figure 3.2 Trend in domestic electricity sales per quarter GwH 1998–2018

has been downwards, implying a general decline in electricity sales to domestic customers. Again, a rough estimate from the diagram indicates a reduction of around 15 per cent. Clearly, the diagram does not tell us what caused this phenomenon but it does provide a clear impression of the variable over time. In short, simple diagrams convey general patterns and trends in a way which has considerable impact. We can use such diagrams to convey key conclusions about some analysis that we have undertaken. Naturally, as part of the decision process, such diagrams would not be sufficient by themselves. We would need further detailed analysis and more information but such diagrams do help convey a message quickly and clearly. In part this explains why such business diagrams are both popular and common – appearing in many organisations' annual reports, in the financial and business press and in internal management reports. There are a considerable number of diagrams available and we shall look at some of the more common and useful.

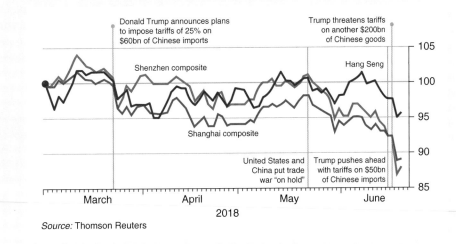

America's trade spats are rattling markets: Donald Trump believes he has the upper hand when negotiating trade deals

Source: America's trade spats are rattling markets, *The Economist*, 20th June 2018.

A time-series plot like this can be helpful in showing patterns and trends easily

It is also worth commenting at this stage that the production of such diagrams to help decision making is often a process of trial and error (fortunately made easier through the use of spreadsheet and graphics software). It is often difficult at the start of some analysis to know exactly which type of diagram will best convey the message you wish to put across. Through trial and error – and experience – it is often a matter of constructing one diagram and assessing whether this conveys the information you want it to. If it does not, then a different diagram can be tried. Realistically, you need to accept that this trial-and-error approach is inevitable.

We shall illustrate a number of the more common diagrams used in business with the following scenario. As part of a wider analysis, a large national supermarket company in the UK is undertaking a strategic review of its product mix – what products it should stock in its stores. As we all know, people's shopping habits change over time and the company is keen to ensure it is keeping up with changes in shopping trends. It has asked for an overview of what consumers have been spending their income on over the last 20 years or so. They have a particular interest in certain product sectors:

- Food: food bought for consumption at home (e.g. groceries).
- Non-alcoholic beverages: tea, coffee, fruit and soft drinks.
- Alcoholic beverages: beer, wines, spirits bought for consumption at home.
- Tobacco.
- Newspapers, books and stationery items.

To help with this, we've obtained some national data from the Office for National Statistics, shown in Table 3.1. The data shows consumers' expenditure (£m) at constant prices (base year 2016) for these expenditure categories in each of three years (1997, 2007 and 2017 was the latest available data when this book was written). So, for example, across the UK people spent just under £8000 million on non-alcoholic drinks in 1997. The 'Total of five categories' data shows the sum of these five categories whilst 'Total household expenditure' refers to all consumer spending in that year. Although the table contains detailed data, we want a quick overview of the data: we want to see key patterns, trends and features of the data set quickly and easily. Obviously the data could be examined in a variety of ways: each year individually, the three years together, the change between the years, the percentage in each year, the percentage change between the years and so on. Let's have a look at the different diagrams we could use with this data.

Progress Check 3.1

Why do you think a company might be interested in such data? What comments can you make about the data as it's presented in Table 3.1?

Solution is given on p 573.

Table 3.1   UK Household consumption expenditure, £m at constant prices

	1997	2007	2017
Food	71 548	82 610	89 356
Non-alcoholic beverages	7 957	11 340	12 078
Alcoholic beverages	12 131	19 099	19 191
Tobacco	39 102	27 886	18 395
Newspapers, books and stationery	15 335	17 199	11 595
Total of five categories	146 073	158 134	150 615
Total household expenditure	804 714	1 122 979	1 249 286

Source: Office for National Statistics
Excel file T3-1

Bar charts

Bar charts are probably one of the most popular types of business diagram, examples of which are found in the annual report of almost every large public and private sector organisation. They come in a number of forms, all of which are relatively straightforward to produce and to interpret from a management perspective. There are a variety of bar graphs that can help provide this overview of the data. Once again, we reinforce the point that very often we produce a particular diagram on a trial-and-error basis – not knowing until we see it whether it will be helpful at providing this overview. Figure 3.3 shows a bar chart of the data. For each of the categories in each year we have simply drawn a bar, where the height of that bar represents consumers' expenditure on that category in that year. From the graph we can readily see that:

● The Food category is by far the largest.

● Non-alcoholic beverages has the lowest expenditure.

● Trends over the period varied:
  ■ Food, Non-alcoholic beverages and Alcoholic beverages all saw an increase in spending.
  ■ Tobacco saw a decrease in spending.
  ■ Newspapers etc. fluctuated with an increase in 2007 followed by a decline in 2017.

We might also decide to rearrange the order in which the categories are shown, as in Figure 3.4, where the categories have been ordered from highest in 1997 to lowest. We did say you need to experiment with diagrams to see which conveys the key messages better.

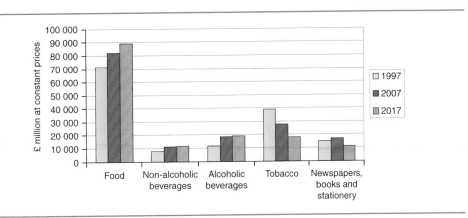

Figure 3.3 Multiple bar chart: consumers' expenditure

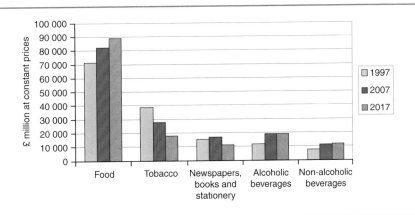

Figure 3.4 Expenditure ranked by 1997 category size

It is worth knowing that a number of different types of bar graph are available. The diagram we have produced is technically known as a *multiple* bar graph since it shows more than one bar in each category (one for each year in our case). *Simple* bar graphs, as the name suggests, show just one bar in each category, which would have been the case if we had graphed only the 2007 data, for example. A *component* bar chart (sometimes known as a *stacked bar*) for this data is shown in Figure 3.5.

It is evident that we now have a single bar for each year, with the height of the bar representing the total of the five categories. The bar is then subdivided to show each element – or component – as a proportion of the total. So for 2007, for example, we see that the Food category made up just over £80 billion of the total of around £160 billion (note that throughout the text we are adopting the convention of denoting a billion as one thousand million or 1 000 000 000). From the component bar chart we can see that:

- Food is the largest category by far and has shown a steady increase over the period.
- Tobacco has shown a steady decline.
- Spending on alcohol has increased steadily.
- Total spending on these five categories increased between 1997 and 2007 but then fell between 2007 and 2017 (remember the financial crisis that happened in the UK and other economies from around 2008).

Although such component bar charts are common, they should be used with caution. They are typically useful only where we have a relatively small number of categories. It can be difficult to see the changes between categories if there are too many in the bar itself. Note also that we've drawn each component bar starting with the largest category at the bottom, then the next largest and so on rather than simply use the data in the order presented in Table 3.1. This tends to give a better picture of what's happening.

A related bar chart can be produced using the *percentage component bar chart,* as shown in Figure 3.6. In this case, each category is shown as a percentage of the total for that year and, accordingly, the height of each bar is the same – corresponding to 100 per cent. Although we lose any impression of the change in the total expenditure over this period, we gain a different comparison between the different categories. We see that:

- Food is around 50 per cent of all expenditure in these categories and increasing.
- Tobacco has gone from around 25 per cent to around 8 per cent.
- Alcoholic beverage has increased although it's difficult to tell how much.
- Non-alcoholic beverages have also increased but again it's difficult to tell by how much.

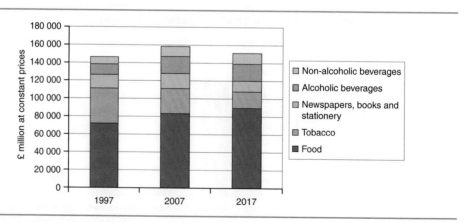

Figure 3.5 Component bar chart of expenditure

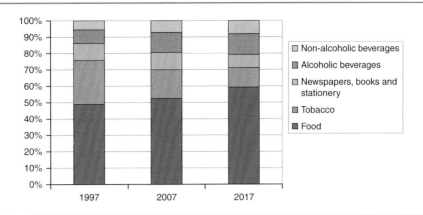

Figure 3.6 Percentage component bar chart of expenditure

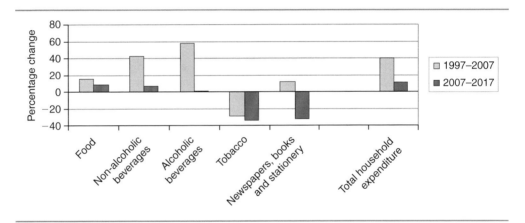

Figure 3.7 Percentage change in each expenditure category

Note that it's difficult to say what's happening to Newspapers as its part of the column moves up and down as other categories change (and this is one of the problems with this type of bar chart). Finally, we might use a simple bar chart to show the percentage change in expenditure over these categories, as in Figure 3.7.

We've also included Total household expenditure to act as an overall benchmark. We see that overall Total expenditure increased by around 40 per cent between 1997 and 2007 and by around 10 per cent between 2007 and 2017. Four out of the five categories showed an increase between 1997 and 2007, with Alcoholic drinks the greatest at almost 60 per cent. The Food category (the largest of the five in money terms) showed a below-average increase of around 15 per cent. Tobacco expenditure fell by around 30 per cent over the period. From 2007 to 2017 Tobacco showed a further decline in sales at around 35 per cent. The Newspapers category also declined by around the same amount, perhaps affected by the increasing availability of the internet and online media sources. Growth in sales in the other three categories was much more modest and below average compared with Total expenditure.

Progress Check 3.2

From the analysis we've done so far on this data, draft a short report summarising the key findings that would be relevant to the retail organisation. Which of the bar charts would you include in the report?

Datawatch

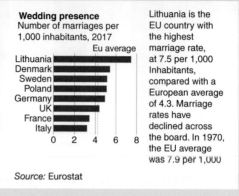

Wedding presence
Number of marriages per
1,000 inhabitants, 2017

Lithuania is the EU country with the highest marriage rate, at 7.5 per 1,000 Inhabitants, compared with a European average of 4.3. Marriage rates have declined across the board. In 1970, the EU average was 7.9 per 1,000

Source: Eurostat

A simple bar chart like this can be effective at showing comparisons – in this case marriage rates across parts of the EU.

Global card spend to hit $45 trillion

Value of card payments by region
$tn

- Middle East and Africa
- Europe
- Latin America
- North America
- Asia-Pacific

Source: RBR

What does the chart show?
It shows the rise in worldwide card spending from 2011 to 2017, including forecasts suggesting card payments will reach $45tn by 2023.

Payment cards were used for purchases totalling $25.1tn in 2017, a 13 per cent increase on the previous year.

Analysis from RBR, a retail banking research consultancy, shows the Asia Pacific Region spent the most via payment cards in 2017 at over $12tn, a 205 per cent rise on 2011.

A stacked bar chart like this can look impressive but it can be difficult to draw many conclusions for comparison.

Companies turn to secured loans as Fed rates freeze deters loan investors

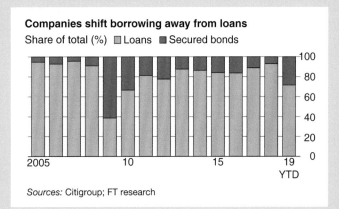

Companies shift borrowing away from loans

Share of total (%) ☐ Loans ■ Secured bonds

Sources: Citigroup; FT research

A stacked – component – bar chart can be effective at showing how data is split across different categories. In this case we see the source of US companies borrowing split between loans and corporate bonds.

Alphabet: the algorithm section

Google's owner invested heavily last year. Its capital spending was nearly twice as high as the year before. It is also spending heavily on research and development. This pushed operating margins lower, but it will help protect its towering market position in advertising revenues.

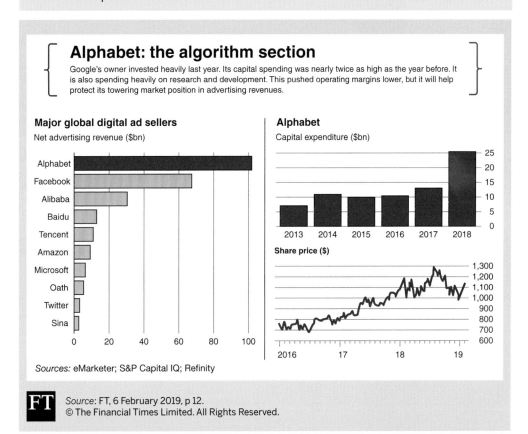

Major global digital ad sellers

Net advertising revenue ($bn)

Alphabet

Capital expenditure ($bn)

Share price ($)

Sources: eMarketer; S&P Capital IQ; Refinity

Different types of chart can be combined effectively as with these looking at Alphabet's (aka Google) performance

Pie charts

Very often data shown in bar charts can also be shown in the form of a pie chart. Again, these are quite a common method of visually presenting some types of data, although actually quite limited in their ability to convey useful management information. Figure 3.8 shows a pie chart for the 2017 consumer expenditure category data. A pie chart is readily – if somewhat tediously – constructed manually, although anyone in their right mind will use a spreadsheet instead, which will do all of this for you automatically. We draw a circle to represent the total expenditure for all categories then proportion the 'slices' of the pie to represent the percentage of this total made up by each category. Given that a circle (the pie) has 360 degrees, we simply apportion the circle to the component categories according to their relative importance. In 2017 the Food category, for example, comprises around 59 per cent of the total spent in these five categories. Given that the total of the circle is 360 degrees, then this 'slice' has to cover 214 degrees (59 per cent of 360). A pie chart allows for a quick overall view of relative sizes of categories but offers little potential for comparison – with another year, for example. As with bar charts, pie charts should be constructed, and used, with caution, ensuring they provide useful information rather than simply looking pretty.

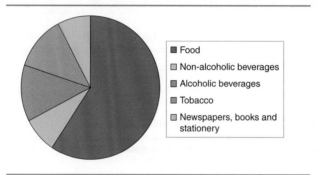

Figure 3.8 Pie chart of consumers' expenditure 2017

Steel industry addresses challenge of cutting CO_2

Total industry CO2 emissions
By subsectors (%)

Pie charts can be useful if they don't have too many slices, as with this one showing CO_2 emission of the global steel industry compared with other industrial sectors

Frequency distributions

The next aspect of data presentation we shall consider relates to the *frequency distribution*. To illustrate this – and a number of related areas – we shall introduce a detailed example to which we shall return over the next few chapters. Consider the following scenario. A large retail organisation operates a great number of high street convenience stores. These are small stores with limited stock where passers-by can pop in to buy a few items. As part of an ongoing process to monitor costs and efficiency and to boost profitability, individual stores within the company have been organised as profit centres. It was felt by senior management that such a move would help the organisation become more profitable and more efficient. Each profit centre has its own manager, who has full operational responsibility and authority. Effectively each profit centre operates as an individual business but, naturally, is linked to the central business organisation.

As part of this strategic change in a number of these profit centres, performance-related pay (PRP) is being considered by senior management. In simple terms, the more profit a store earns, the more PRP the manager responsible earns. To try to assist this decision it has been decided to examine a sample of profit centres in two different regions of the country. In Region A, 113 stores operating as profit centres were chosen for analysis, as were 121 stores in Region B. As far as possible, both samples were carefully chosen as a suitable cross-section of all centres of that type, and great care has been taken to ensure that the two categories are comparable – in terms of size, geographical location, type of products and so on. Tables 3.2 and 3.3 show weekly profits achieved by each centre in each region.

It does not take an analytical genius to realise that the data in this form is worthless. It provides little, or no, information about the situation we are investigating. The only features of any value that we note are that there is considerable variability in the data and that some are positive and some negative (the latter indicating that a centre operated at a loss in that year). Clearly the data must be manipulated or processed in some way in order to be useful in managerial terms. It is, for example, far more meaningful to show this data in the form of Table 3.2, known as a frequency table.

Table 3.2 Weekly profit for stores in Region A (£s)

42 130	6 320	38 470	−320	3 650	7 770	4 310	4 530	−2 690	3 220	9 030	−2 590
6 390	84 330	47 230	11 780	4 310	5 270	9 730	5 480	62 480	−1 510	13 920	2 130
17 480	7 210	15 620	55 310	−1 160	12 620	−490	3 390	24 390	7 510	7 670	12 590
41 470	8 040	2 150	4 760	−1 570	10 800	5 530	14 730	14 970	15 170	16 070	13 310
93 050	5 460	6 610	33 610	5 300	8 560	−1 120	4 590	2 300	66 990	5 430	5 980
3 630	10 530	8 010	38 920	−740	3 530	32 070	42 200	13 820	17 730	4 760	1 450
5 200	9 860	11 350	−270	18 360	3 300	30 880	1 760	16 730	−13 070	9 060	2 440
7 230	1 270	−270	10 010	43 060	25 460	570	6 620	10 780	6 330	3 480	5 000
16 050	3 870	7 760	12 870	−3 850	4 740	21 110	29 070	3 570	1 760	4 720	6 600
3 160	6 840	34 100	−6 480	20 230							

Data available in file T3-2

Table 3.3   Weekly profit for stores in Region B (£s)

4280	2340	−2470	3400	9170	46620	560	−2340	91400	3470	13030	2800
−4130	1800	8690	28000	36240	21300	8580	82880	11680	3930	13140	1710
7360	2610	5350	5040	7540	9760	12980	67780	5490	38210	4600	38360
−3200	7440	500	23580	11620	1230	26990	13350	11800	20080	8460	3810
8740	32890	3650	180	43530	36800	62510	12520	14950	42170	120	4600
6080	13600	42640	7390	2010	2610	14290	23870	12540	14020	1560	13320
11050	72660	50400	98800	4400	3640	35390	13140	25570	15010	8560	17700
3030	770	31260	8250	25000	24100	3240	47730	1360	4600	22680	27310
44910	4020	35970	6800	43530	17720	9580	37600	1540	31700	2360	6510
30100	5870	4360	6250	14080	22740	12140	6570	1850	7750	28040	730
5640											

Source: Company accounts

Data available in file T3-3

This frequency table shows the distribution of the individual data items in the two data sets, Region A and Region B. We have chosen a number of profit intervals (eight in this instance) and then counted the number of centres of each type falling into each interval. So, for example, we see that there was one Region A centre making a loss of more than £10000 compared with none for the Region B group.

Progress Check 3.3

What observations can you now make about profits in the two years, based on Table 3.2?

Clearly such tabulation allows us to begin the process of identifying the key characteristics of the two data sets, comparing and contrasting. We see that in both cases the bulk of stores fall into the profit category of £0 to £10000. At the extremes of the distribution, however, the two regions appear to differ. At the lower end of profitability, Region B stores appear to be fewer in number, whilst there are more of them at the higher profit levels. Clearly, we shall wish to investigate the data in other ways, but the frequency table is a start in the process of examining a data set to determine its key features. The construction of such a table from a set of raw data is straightforward – particularly if using computer software to do the hard work. Like much of this chapter, the construction follows a set of 'rules' that are a mixture of common sense and things that have been found to work. We must make two decisions:

- the number of classes, or intervals, to be used;
- the size of these intervals.

The two decisions are interrelated and typically subject to trial and error. Fortunately, with appropriate computer technology it is generally a matter of a few moments to 'experiment' with these two features to see which combination of those available gives the 'best' distribution. One useful rule of thumb is that between 5 and 15 classes will usually prove suitable (with a smaller number of classes for a smaller set of data). In Table 3.4 we have eight classes. More than eight and a number of these would contain few, if any, observations. Fewer than eight and we would lose sight of some of the patterns becoming apparent. The class width(s) must then be chosen. Ideally, class widths should be the same for all the classes. Frequently, however, this is impractical and would lead to a large number of classes. Note also that we have two open-ended classes at the start and end of the table. Once again, this is quite a common way of dealing with one or two individual extreme values. Technically we could have 'closed' each of these classes by using, respectively, the minimum and maximum values in the data set. It is arguable, however, whether this would help our understanding of the data distribution. You should also note that the lower and upper limits of each of the classes are clearly and unambiguously defined. We know categorically into which class any one individual observation will have been placed. A common error is to present classes in the form:

0 to 10 000

10 000 to 20 000

20 000 to 30 000

and so on. This is inappropriate since it is not evident into which class an observation taking a value, say, of 10 000 would be placed. Having decided on the number of intervals to be used and their size, it is then a straightforward matter to count the number of data items falling into each interval. In Excel, or similar spreadsheets, the FREQUENCY function can be used to count the number of observations in each interval and create a frequency table.

Table 3.4 Frequency table

Profit interval			Region A	Region B
Lower class limit (£s)		Upper class limit (£s)	No. of stores	No. of stores
less than		−10 000	1	0
−10 000	<	0	13	4
0	<	10 000	56	58
10 000	<	20 000	22	21
20 000	<	30 000	5	13
30 000	<	40 000	6	11
40 000	<	50 000	5	7
50 000 or over			5	7
Total			113	121

Percentage and cumulative frequencies

It may also be appropriate to show the frequency distribution in the form of percentages of the total or of cumulative frequencies (or cumulative percentages). The reasons for this are self-evident. Percentage comparisons are often more revealing, whereas cumulative frequencies have their own special uses that we shall explore in more detail later in this chapter. In Table 3.5 a number of these calculations have been performed: the percentage of observations in each interval and the cumulative total up to and including that interval

We can now see readily that for Region A some 12.4 per cent of stores were operating at a loss, compared with only 3.3 per cent of Region B stores. Similarly, some 8.8 per cent (100 – 91.2) of Region A stores had a profit of £40 000 or more compared with 11.6 per cent of Region B's. What the analysis does not reveal, of course, are the causes of such differences.

Table 3.5   Frequency table: percentages and cumulative figures

Profit interval			Region A				Region B			
Lower limit		Upper limit	Frequency		Cumulative frequency		Frequency		Cumulative frequency	
(£s)		(£s)	no.	%	no.	%	no.	%	no.	%
less than		−10 000	1	0.9	1	0.9	0	0	0	0
−10000	<	0	13	11.5	14	12.4	4	3.3	4	3.3
0	<	10000	56	49.6	70	62.0	58	47.9	62	51.2
10000	<	20000	22	19.5	92	81.5	21	17.4	83	68.6
20000	<	30000	5	4.4	97	85.9	13	10.7	96	79.3
30000	<	40000	6	5.3	103	91.2	11	9.1	107	88.4
40000	<	50000	5	4.4	108	95.6	7	5.8	114	94.2
50000 or over			5	4.4	113	100.0	7	5.8	121	100.0
Total			113				121			

Histograms

Naturally, given the orientation of this chapter, we would expect to be able to show the data from the frequency table in the form of a diagram. In fact, a variety of these are available. The first is a simple representation of the frequency distribution in the form of a *histogram*. Figure 3.9 shows such a diagram for the Region A stores. Effectively, a histogram is a type of bar chart but the bars are adjacent to each other rather than with a gap between them as in a bar chart. The reason for this is that the histogram (and frequency table) shows data which is continuous, whereas a bar chart is dealing with data which is discrete.

For each interval in the table a bar has been drawn where the height represents the frequency of observations in that interval. For example, the second interval, stores making

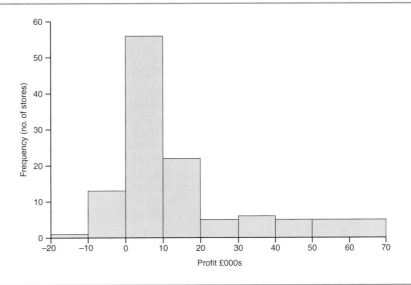

Figure 3.9 Histogram showing profits for Region A

a loss of up to £10 000, has a frequency of 13, which corresponds to the height of the bar in the histogram. But what about the two open-ended intervals? Remember that we have two intervals: less than −£10 000 and £50 000 or over. To draw each interval on a histogram we must close these to give, respectively, lower and upper limits. Ideally, we could close these intervals to make them the same width (10 000) as all the others. This would give a lower interval of −£20 000 < −£10 000. For the upper interval, however, it might seem a little misleading to set the upper limit at £60 000, since we know from visual inspection of Tables 3.2 and 3.3 that there are stores exceeding this. Obviously a compromise is necessary. We could set the upper limit at £100 000, which would ensure we properly include all values. The trouble is this would give us one interval much wider (five times) than any of the others, although it would include all the data. However, it is worthwhile remembering why we are bothering with a diagram at all. Its purpose is to give a quick – and reasonably accurate – overview of the data we are examining. We do not pretend the diagram allows us to see all the fine detail of the data. As long as it is not downright misleading, it will have served its purpose. Let us choose, therefore, an upper limit of £70 000 as a compromise figure.

Effectively, this interval is now double the width of the others and it would not be 'fair' to show the height of this (extra-wide) interval as five, the actual frequency. If we were to do this, it would make this (wider) interval look too 'important' relative to the others. (If you are unsure of this point, you should try drawing this last interval on the histogram without the adjustment we are about to calculate.) Accordingly, we must adjust the actual frequency of the observations in this interval to compensate for the different width. If we denote the standard interval as having width SW and the width of the interval we need to adjust as AW, then the actual frequency can be adjusted by:

$$\text{Adjusted frequency} = \frac{\text{Adjusted frequency}}{\text{AW/SW}}$$

$$= \frac{5}{20\,000/10\,000}$$

$$= \frac{5}{2} = 2.5$$

Broadband speed map reveals Britain's new digital divide

Access to fast internet broadband is increasingly important both to individuals and to organisations and can be a key component in competitive edge. In the UK generally there is concern that more remote rural areas may be left behind in the race to improve broadband speeds. The *Financial Times* makes available an interactive chart allowing users to compare broadband speeds in their area compared with those for the UK as a whole. The chart below shows how broadband speeds in Scotland compare with those for the UK.

The data is broken down by postcode area with broadband speeds shown on the horizontal axis (in interval of 2MB/S) and the percentage of postcodes falling into each speed interval shown on the vertical. Although the two distributions have similar profiles there are a couple of key differences. Scotland has a higher number of postcode areas with slower broadband speeds (2–6 MB/S to the left of the chart) and a lower number in the middle speeds (34–76 MB/S)

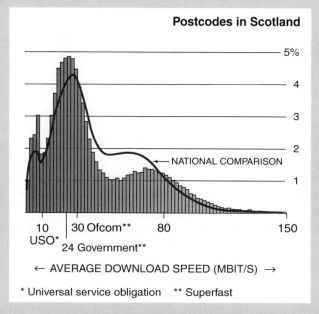

 Source: Based on: Smith, A., Fildes, N., Blood, D., Harlow, M., Nevitt, C. and Rininsland, A. (2018) Broadband speed map reveals Britain's new digital divide, *Financial Times*, 18 July.

Histograms and frequency polygons are useful in making distribution comparisons like this one.

That is, the frequency to be plotted on the histogram for this interval is 2.5 not 5. You will probably have realised that we have effectively scaled the actual frequency down by a factor of two (given that the interval width is two times the standard). It is important to bear this point in mind when constructing histograms – either manually or using computer software – particularly as many commercial software programs do not automatically adjust the frequencies of unequal intervals. It reinforces the point that, wherever possible, we should construct frequency tables with equal class widths to avoid the problem.

However, leaving aside the technicalities, consider your own reaction to the diagram. As a manager wanting a quick and easy overview of profits from the Region A stores, would you prefer the histogram or the frequency table?

Progress Check 3.4

Draw a comparable histogram for profits for Region B stores and compare it with Figure 3.9. What comments can you make about this distribution compared with that of Region A?

Solution is given on p 573.

Histograms in percentage form

We could just as well have drawn the histograms not in terms of frequency – the actual number of stores in each interval – but in terms of the percentage of total stores falling into each interval. A percentage histogram is often useful where the total number of observations makes direct comparison from one interval to another difficult: we might prefer to use percentages in our example given the (albeit slight) difference in total number of observations between the Region A and Region B groups.

Excel has a histogram function in the Data Analysis add-in pack that will produce a histogram using specified intervals. Note that by default the histogram will be shown as a bar chart with gaps between the intervals. The gaps can be set to zero by using Chart Options.

Frequency polygons

Although a histogram shows the overall distribution of the variable, it can be problematic when we wish to compare two, or more, such distributions. (You may have already experienced difficulty in making detailed comparisons in the last Progress Check.) An alternative method is to construct a *frequency polygon*. Such a diagram differs from a histogram only in that rather than drawing a bar for the frequency in each interval we use points. We mark the frequency in each interval with a point drawn at the appropriate frequency height in the middle of the interval width. These points are then joined using lines as in Figure 3.10, which shows a frequency polygon for Region A. There appears little benefit from showing the data in this way until we superimpose the data for Region B stores onto the same diagram, now shown in Figure 3.11. The polygons now make a visual comparison between the two sets of data much easier. We see that the two distributions follow a broadly similar profile and that the major differences in the two distributions occur at the two ends of the distribution – in the middle intervals the two groups of stores are more or less the same. The Region B polygon tends to be below that for Region A stores at low profit levels and above it for high profit levels, indicating fewer low-profit stores and more high-profit stores. Note that the frequency polygons intercept

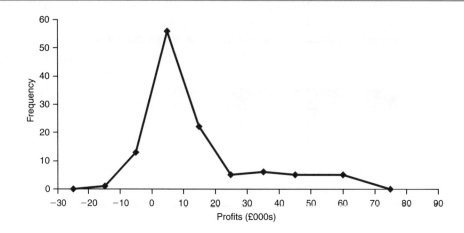

Figure 3.10 Frequency polygon for Region A stores

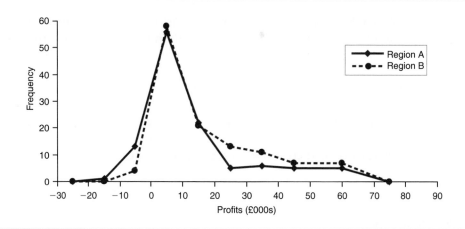

Figure 3.11 Frequency polygons for Region A and Region B

the horizontal axis at either end. This is done by finding the midpoint for the interval preceding the first in the frequency table and for the interval after the last in the table. For Region A, for example, the preceding interval is from −30 to −20 and 70–80 for the final interval. The easiest way to construct a polygon in a spreadsheet is as a scatter diagram with the interval midpoints on the X axis and the frequencies on the Y axis.

Ogives

You will remember that in Table 3.5 we calculated the cumulative frequencies as well as the individual ones. The visual presentation of these cumulative frequencies – either the actual values or the percentages – takes the form of an *ogive* (pronounced oh-jive). Such a diagram is easily constructed. We have the intervals as usual on the horizontal axis and the cumulative values on the vertical axis. We plot the cumulative value for each interval against the upper limit of each interval and then join the points together with straight lines.

To see how this is done – since it sounds more complicated than it is – let us return to the data in Table 3.5. Figure 3.12 shows the cumulative percentage frequencies for Region A stores, using the data in Table 3.5. So, for example, there are 0.9 per cent of stores with a profit less than −£10000, 12.4 per cent of stores with a profit less than £0 (obviously including the 0.9 per cent in the previous interval) and so on. The ogive is now constructed by marking the right-hand end of each bar with a point (also shown in Figure 3.12) and then joining each pair of these points together with a straight line to give the ogive shown in Figure 3.13.

The diagram may take a little getting used to. Remember that the vertical scale shows the cumulative percentage frequencies. The figure of 30, for example, relates to 30 per cent of all stores in Region A. The ogive starts from 0 per cent and goes up to 100 per cent. Any point we choose on the line will show the percentage of stores falling below a given profit figure and, by default, the percentage lying above that profit figure. For example, assume management regard a profit of £25 000 as a critical performance measure. Locating this value on the horizontal axis, drawing a line upwards until it intersects the ogive and then extending the line along until we intersect the vertical axis will give 84 per cent. This implies that 84 per cent of stores in Region A have a profit of up to £25 000 while the remainder, 16 per cent (100 − 84), have a profit greater than £25 000. The ogive is readily used to examine the distribution of data over a given range and to compare one data set with another in terms of its distribution. As with polygons, the easiest way to construct an ogive in a spreadsheet is through a scatter diagram.

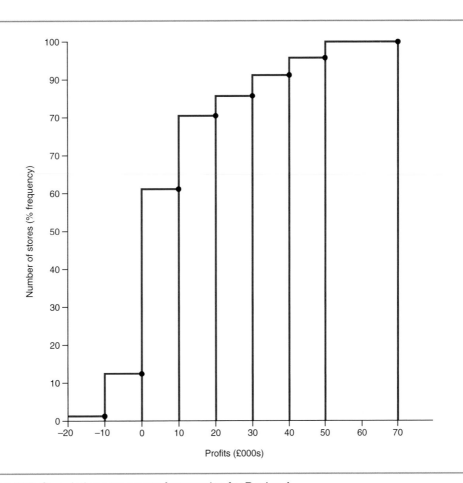

Figure 3.12 Cumulative percentage frequencies for Region A

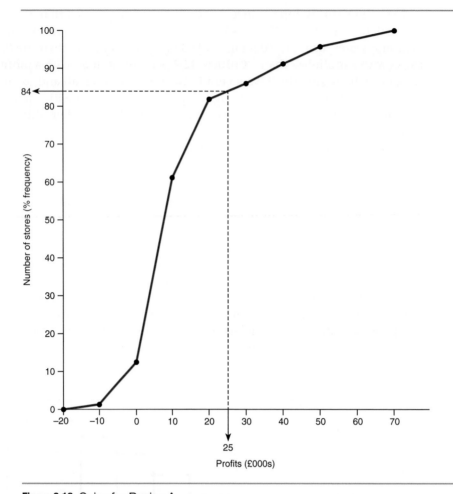

Figure 3.13 Ogive for Region A

Progress Check 3.5

Draw an ogive showing profits for Region A and Region B on the same diagram. Comment on the differences.

Solution is given on p 574.

Lorenz curves

Similar in principle to an ogive is the *Lorenz curve,* sometimes known as a *Pareto diagram.* An ogive plots cumulative percentage frequencies against the class intervals. A Lorenz curve plots cumulative percentage frequencies against cumulative percentage class totals and is often used to measure equality of distribution. This sounds far more complicated than it is. Let us return to the Region A stores. This time we shall consider only those which showed a profit greater than zero. The results we shall be using are shown in Table 3.6.

Table 3.6   Region A stores with a positive profit

Profit up to (£s)	Frequency	%	Cumulative %	Total profit (£s)	%	Cumulative %
10 000	56	56.6	56.6	289 150	19.2	19.2
20 000	22	22.2	78.8	307 290	20.4	39.7
30 000	5	5.1	83.8	120 260	8.0	47.7
40 000	6	6.1	89.9	208 050	13.8	61.5
50 000	5	5.1	94.9	216 090	14.4	75.9
70 000	5	5.1	100.0	362 160	24.1	100.0
Total	99			1 503 000		

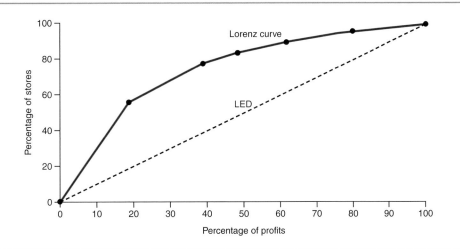

Figure 3.14 Lorenz curve for Region A and line of equal distribution

The table shows the distribution of stores (restricted to those earning a positive profit) in both frequency, percentage and cumulative percentage terms. Of the 99 Region A stores making a positive profit, 56 of them – 56.6 per cent – earned a profit of up to £10 000, 22.2 per cent earned a profit between £10 000 and £20 000 and so on. In the final three columns, however, we have added new data. We now show – for the stores in each interval – the total profit that they earned. So, for example, these 56 stores earned a combined profit of £289 150, which in turn represents some 19 per cent of total profit for the 99 stores. You may begin to see where we are going. We have a situation where some 57 per cent of stores contribute only 19 per cent of total profit – a somewhat disproportionate result. On the other hand, we have (the top) 5 per cent of stores contributing some 24 per cent to total profit. Effectively, we are comparing the percentage distribution of stores against the percentage distribution of profit. If we do this visually with the cumulative values, we get a Lorenz curve as in Figure 3.14. On the diagram we have plotted the cumulative percentage values for the number of stores on the vertical axis and the cumulative percentage profit on the other to give the Lorenz curve. Also on the diagram is the line of equal distribution (LED). This is a line showing what the distribution would be if it were perfectly equal: if 10 per cent of stores earned 10 per cent of profit, 20 per cent of stores earned 20 per cent of profit and so on. The LED acts as a reference point to allow us to assess actual 'inequality' in the distribution. The further away the Lorenz curve is from the LED the more unequal is the distribution of profit. It will probably be evident that we could now compare inequality in the Region A group with that of the Region B group. While this is left as an exercise, the potential importance of the diagram is evident. Given the relative importance of a small number of stores in terms of their profit contribution, management should be focusing attention on these stores to ensure continuing profitability. Equally, the large number of stores which contribute relatively little to overall profit need to be examined in the context of the organisation's strategy. Would we be better merging some of these stores to make them more viable or even getting rid of some of them altogether?

Lorenz curves are a fairly specialist diagram but quite useful in certain circumstances. Typical uses relate to income distribution, distribution of value among stock (inventory) items, distribution of earnings/profits and distribution of faults/failures in a manufacturing process. One local authority in the UK, for example, was investigating the outstanding debt owed by housing tenants in terms of rent on the properties. The total amount of such rent which had not been paid by tenants was around £2 million, a substantial sum given the financial restrictions under which local authorities operate. Management were considering a number of options in terms of trying to recover this debt, but the issue was a sensitive one due to the economic recession and general levels of income of the tenants. However, the application of a Lorenz curve to the data revealed that around 72 per cent of the outstanding debt was owed by only 9 per cent of those in arrears. Rather than considering options to recover arrears from all tenants, management realised that by focusing effective measures on only a small group most of the outstanding debt could be recovered.

The man who helped Japan's quality revolution

By Richard Donkin

Joseph Juran, who died last week at the age of 103, was the last of the great statistical gurus who established the quality movement in business and helped to transform Japanese production after the second world war.

Perhaps his best known contribution to the workplace – and not unrelated to this casino observation – was what he called the "Pareto Principle" now better known as the 80/20 rule. This holds that most effects come from relatively few causes. Later, he acknowledged that the influence for this rule had less to do with Vilfredo Pareto, the Italian economist after whom it was named, and more to do with the work of Max Otto Lorenz, whose "Lorenz curve" displayed the deviation of a sample from the standard. Juran used this observation when tackling waste, arguing that it was more important initially to concentrate on the "vital few" operations in manufacturing, rather than the "trivial many".

 Source: Donkin, R. (2008) The man who helped Japan's quality revolution, FT.com, 6 March. © Richard Donkin, www.richarddonkin.com.

Time-series graphs

Frequently we may wish to examine the behaviour of some variable in which we are interested over a period of time. Our interest may lie in production figures, costs, manpower levels, sales, profits and the like, and we wish to gain some impression as to how the variable of interest has altered over a given period. A *time-series graph* shows such patterns.

In fact, we have already seen a time-series graph at the start of this chapter in Figure 3.1. Their construction is straightforward, with time being displayed on the horizontal axis and the value of the variable on the vertical, and they are useful for showing major trends over some period. Frequently we may wish to show two or more series on the same graph. Consider, for example, Table 3.7, which shows motor vehicle registrations in Great Britain. Figures are included for 'All vehicles' and for three particular categories: 'Private cars', 'Goods vehicles' and 'Motor cycles'. Data such as this is of interest to managers in government and the private sector as new vehicle sales are seen in many economies as an important economic indicator. Individuals and companies will delay the purchase of a new vehicle if they are concerned about the economic future and if confidence is low. And if they delay the purchase of a new vehicle now they may well cut back on consumption of other products in the near future.

From the table, it's difficult to see what's happening over this period. We get the sense that total vehicle registrations have fluctuated over this period from 2 million to over 3 million; private car registrations seem to take up a large part of the total; goods vehicles have changed relatively little; and motor cycles have gone up and down. The use of time-series graphs can make patterns and trends much more obvious. Figure 3.15 shows new registrations for all vehicles. We now see that since 1980 registrations peaked in 1989 then fell sharply (this coincided with an economic recession in the UK). From 1992 registrations climbed back up, reaching their 1989 level again in 2000. Registrations continued to climb, reaching a new peak in 2003. Then registrations declined (again the financial crisis hit in 2008) but started to increase again in 2012 and 2013.

Figure 3.16 shows vehicle registrations by category. We can see that registrations of private cars closely follow the overall total during this period, with private cars taking up a smaller percentage of the total from around 1998 onwards. However, it's difficult to see what's happening with the other two categories, as the vertical scale we've had to use compresses these two series. One solution to this is to use two vertical axes, as shown in Figure 3.17 (often referred to as a 2Y time-series graph). All vehicles and private cars are shown on the left axis and motor vehicles and goods vehicles on the right axis. Using this scale, we now see that registrations of motor cycles show a sharp decline from 1980 until 1993 followed by a steady increase up to 2000 then a further steady decline followed by a sharp increase in 2015. By contrast, registrations of goods vehicles have been fairly stable, with a decline coinciding with the recessions of 1989 and 2008. Although this type of time-series graph is quite common, considerable care needs to be taken over the choice of scales on both axes to avoid misleading the user, and it should always be made clear on the diagram that two different scales are being used. Although we have shown time-series graphs here on an annual basis, they can be used for any time period – quarters, months, days, even hours and minutes, if that is appropriate. All of them are equally relevant for trying to highlight patterns and trends over time.

Table 3.7   New vehicle registrations Great Britain, 000s

Year	Total	of which: Private cars	Goods vehicles	Motor cycles
1980	2155.8	1699.2	54.9	312.7
1981	2030.3	1643.6	39.9	271.9
1982	2103.9	1745.5	41.2	231.6
1983	2307.5	1989.1	46.6	174.5
1984	2238.9	1932.6	49.6	145.2
1985	2309.3	2029.5	51.7	125.8
1986	2333.7	2070.7	51.4	106.4
1987	2473.9	2212.6	54.0	90.8
1988	2723.5	2437.0	63.4	90.1
1989	2828.9	2535.2	64.5	97.3
1990	2438.7	2179.9	44.4	94.4
1991	1921.5	1708.5	28.6	76.5
1992	1901.8	1694.4	28.7	65.6
1993	2073.9	1853.4	32.8	58.4
1994	2249.0	1991.7	41.1	64.6
1995	2306.5	2024.0	48.0	68.9
1996	2228.5	2093.3	45.5	89.6
1997	2407.7	2244.3	41.8	121.7
1998	2740.0	2367.0	49.0	144.0
1999	2766.0	2342.0	48.0	168.0
2000	2871.0	2430.0	50.0	183.0
2001	3137.7	2431.8	48.6	177.1
2002	3229.0	2528.8	44.9	162.2
2003	3231.9	2497.1	48.4	157.3
2004	3185.4	2437.4	48.0	133.7
2005	3021.4	2266.3	51.2	132.3
2006	2913.6	2160.7	47.9	131.9
2007	2996.9	2191.5	41.1	143.0
2008	2672.2	1891.9	47.0	138.4
2009	2371.2	1765.5	27.0	111.5
2010	2417.8	1765.3	27.0	97.1
2011	2381.5	1663.8	36.9	96.2
2012	2469.8	1784.1	38.0	96.6
2013	2716.1	1988.1	48.1	94.2
2014	2973.7	2438.3	38.5	108.3
2015	3212.0	2602.1	49.1	123.4
2016	3296.0	2665.3	51.3	138.2
2017	3102.9	2509.33	50.7	113.6

Source: UK Department for Transport

Data file T3-7

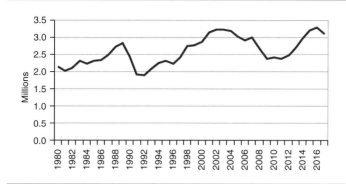

Figure 3.15 Total new vehicle registrations GB

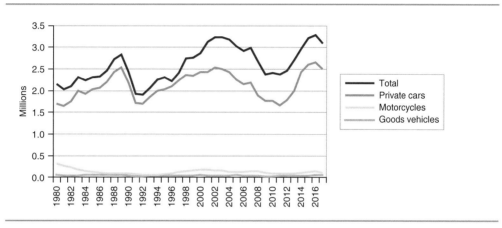

Figure 3.16 New vehicle registrations by category

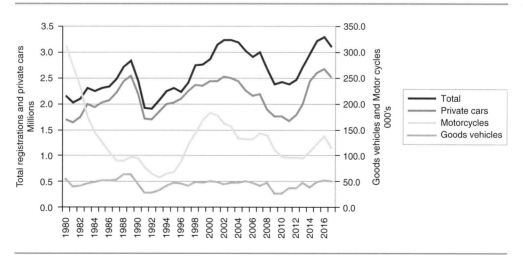

Figure 3.17 New vehicle registrations by category: 2Y chart

Z charts

The next type of diagram we introduce is the *Z chart,* so called because the final diagram looks like the letter Z. The other types of diagram we have introduced are effectively concerned with looking back over time to assess patterns and trends that have occurred. The Z chart is more an operational diagram and concerned with current patterns and trends. Consider the data shown in Table 3.8.

The data relates to the number of roof repairs completed on social housing in a particular local authority area in 2020. The authority has set a target for 2021 of 1800 repairs to be completed, and the manager responsible wants a simple method of monitoring performance over the year. We can visualise that at the end of each month the authority's management information system would provide details of the number of repairs completed during that month and the manager periodically during the year requires a quick and easy way of seeing how this relates to the annual target. This is precisely the function a Z chart serves.

A Z chart looks and sounds complicated to begin with but at the end of the construction process you should be able to see how easy it actually is to use. The first task is to establish a monthly target profile like that shown in Figure 3.18. Note that the line representing the target starts at 0 in December 2020 given that the X axis relates to end-of-month figures, and ends at the end-of-year target for 2021 of 1800. We have assumed for simplicity that the target of 1800 is split equally over the 12 months. We could also have drawn a target line which showed differing, non-equal monthly targets to allow for changing work patterns through the year. Consider the situation later in the year when we have the number of repairs completed in the first four months, as shown in Table 3.9.

In the second column, marked 2021 total, we have the actual number of repairs completed during each of these first four months. In the next column – 2021 cumulative total – we have the running total to date for 2021, and in the last column – last 12 months – we have the total for the last 12-month period. So, at the end of April the authority had

Table 3.8 Number of repairs completed

	2020
January	150
February	133
March	147
April	126
May	124
June	131
July	140
August	132
September	144
October	153
November	155
December	188
Total	1 723

Source: Works Department

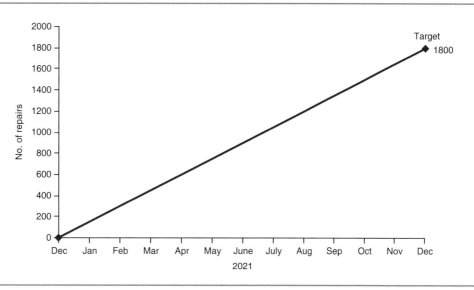

Figure 3.18 Target line

Table 3.9 Number of repairs to council housing completed as at end April 2021

	2020 total	2021 total	2021 cumulative total	Last 12 months
January	150	119	119	1692
February	133	108	227	1667
March	147	127	354	1647
April	126	116	470	1637
May	124			
June	131			
July	140			
August	132			
September	144			
October	153			
November	155			
December	188			
Total	1 723			

completed 116 repairs during that month, 470 in the year to date (January to April inclusive) and 1637 since the previous April. The last figure is simply the total of the previous 12 months' figures (May 2020 to April 2021). The reason for having each of these series needs comment. The actual number in each month is obvious. The cumulative total shows us how close we are to the end-of-year target of 1800. The figure for the last 12 months gives us an idea as to the general long-term trend in the number of repairs being completed, since it indicates performance on an annual rather than a monthly basis. This could be upwards, downwards or constant. Each of these three series can now be superimposed on the Z chart, as shown in Figure 3.19. This shows us that our cumulative total is already below the target for the first four months of the year and has consistently been below target since January. The moving total confirms a downward trend

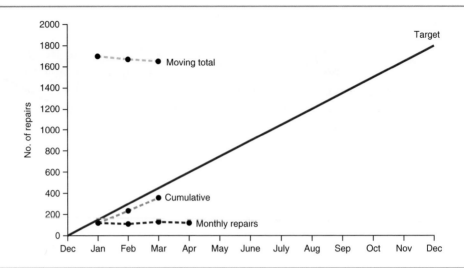

Figure 3.19 Z chart for March

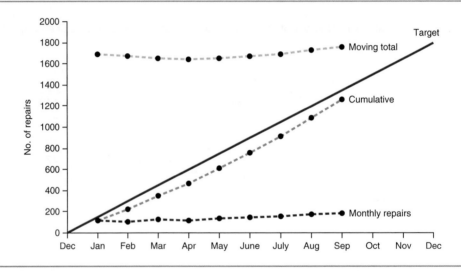

Figure 3.20 Z chart for September

in performance. Action obviously needs to be taken if we are to achieve the target set by the end of the year. Consider now the use of the Z chart on an ongoing monthly basis. When the next monthly figures are produced, the chart can be updated and a monthly check on progress maintained to see when managerial action is required.

Some of you may have wondered why it's actually called a Z chart. The answer becomes clear if we examine Figure 3.20, which shows the state of play later in the year – at the end of September. We see that we're still below the overall target for this time of year although improvement has been made. We see that the number of repairs each month has been slowly increasing and we see from the moving total that the trend is upwards. It is also evident that by the time we get to the end of the year our three series will have combined to form the shape of the letter Z! Z charts are, again, a relatively specialised diagram but extensively used in those situations where it is applicable. Almost every organisation will wish to monitor on a regular basis some variable: housing repairs, number of customers, production of a product, sales of a product, number of patients treated, budget expenditure and so on. It may be appropriate to monitor this on a monthly basis or on a weekly or daily basis, all of which are readily done on this type of diagram.

Scatter diagrams

The next type of diagram we examine in this chapter is known as a *scatter diagram* (also known as an XY plot). All the situations we have examined so far have been concerned with evaluating one variable at a time – profits, sales, spending, housing repairs. Frequently, however, managers may wish to consider whether some relationship exists between two variables. Examples of this might be:

- the price of a product and the quantity sold;
- people's income and their spending patterns;
- levels of production and costs.

It is not too difficult to add to the list with pairs of variables which we might think are in some way connected. A scatter diagram is simply a way of showing the data for two variables together. Consider the data in Table 3.10, which returns us to the retail organisation investigating profitability of stores in two regions.

For 20 of the stores in Region A, the table shows the weekly sales in that store together with profit achieved by that store.

Progress Check 3.6

In what way do you think these two variables might be connected? What would you expect to happen to one store's profit as its sales increased/decreased?

Table 3.10   Sales and profits for 20 stores in Region A

Sales (£s)	Profit (£s)
748 820	42 130
140 776	6 320
702 109	38 470
41 536	−320
96 846	3 650
166 926	7 770
109 048	4 310
263 915	4 530
50 842	2 690
90 077	3 220
190 590	9 030
91 750	−2 590
141 571	6 390
377 044	24 390
198 690	13 920
62 775	2 130
265 284	17 480
91 802	7 210
231 600	15 620
548 307	33 610

Data file T3-10

Clearly there would be reasonable logic in expecting the profits of a store to rise as its sales rose and to decrease as its sales decreased. Whether it would be reasonable to assume this pattern for all the different stores is more problematic. However, it seems reasonable to examine this data graphically and to assess whether there appears to be any evidence of such a relationship. The scatter diagram for this data is shown in Figure 3.21. On the diagram we have, literally, shown the scatter of data for these 20 stores. On the bottom axis we have shown sales and on the vertical axis, profit. For each store we can then locate its actual sales–profit combination and mark its position with a suitable symbol. Repeating this for all the data points, we begin to build up a picture of the overall relationship between the two variables.

Progress Check 3.7

Do you think we have any evidence regarding the relationship between sales and profit that we assumed earlier? Is this relationship exactly the same for all stores? Are there any stores that appear to differ from the norm?

The diagram appears to indicate that, for most of the stores, a relationship between the two variables exists, indicating that as sales increase so do profits. Clearly this relationship is not exactly the same for all the stores; indeed it would be unreasonable to expect this. Profit in any one store will not depend entirely on sales but on other variables also – the location of the store, the number of customers, their income levels and so on. Equally, we are able to identify those stores which are clearly different from the others in the context of this relationship. We see that there is one store which lies away from the general relationship and, given its low profit level, appears to have particularly high sales. Consider carefully what this means. It implies that this store has sales which ought to be generating higher profits given the performance of the other stores. In other words, we can regard this store as being 'abnormal' and worthy of management attention. Its

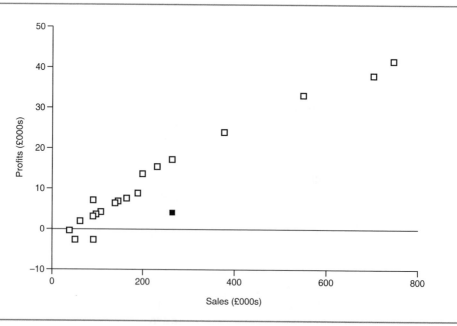

Figure 3.21 Scatter diagram

performance is clearly at odds with that of the other stores, even after we allow for variability in the sales–profit relationship. A scatter diagram, then, enables us not only to see whether there is any relationship between two variables but also to identify those observations which lie away from such a relationship. Clearly, from a management perspective, we would now wish to quantify the nature of the relationship we have observed, but this will have to wait for a later chapter.

Radar charts

The last type of chart we look at is the radar chart (also known as a spider chart). Radar charts are useful when we want to look at several variables simultaneously and we want to plot groups of values. Let's look at a simple scenario. A company has a national sales force who visit clients to negotiate sales. The company is in the process of providing the sales staff with the latest smartphone which, as well as having normal smartphone functionality, will also enable them to log sales information directly through a dedicated app. Two alternative smartphones are under consideration: the Global and the Constellation. A small number of each has been tested by some of the sales staff and each phone has been assessed out of a maximum score of 100 against several criteria. The test results are shown in Table 3.11. It's difficult to get any real sense of how the two models compare. We could try showing the data in some sort of bar chart to help comparison but we'll use a radar chart instead, as shown in Figure 3.22.

Table 3.11 Smartphone test scores

	Global	Constellation
Cost	90	70
Ease of use	90	75
Reliability	85	85
Battery life	65	90
Screen size	70	90

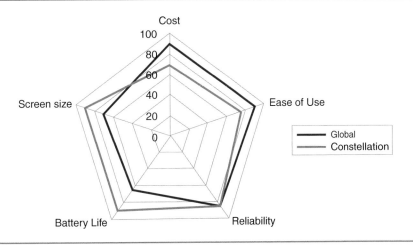

Figure 3.22 Radar chart

Each of the five criteria (variables) is provided with an axis – like the spokes on a wheel – that starts from the centre of the chart. All the axes are arranged radially, with equal distances between them, while maintaining the same scale between all axes. Grid lines that connect from axis to axis are often used as a guide as in this case. Each variable value is then plotted along its individual axis and connected together with the other variable values to form a polygon. We can now more easily see similarities and differences between the two phones. The Global scores better on Cost and Ease of use while the Constellation scores better on Screen size and Battery life. Radar charts are a useful way of comparing multiple quantitative variables and seeing which variables are scoring high or low within a dataset, making them helpful for displaying comparative performance.

Which chart to use

With such a variety of charts – and with more becoming available through spreadsheets and graphics packages – it can be difficult to decide which type of chart to use in a report or presentation. It can be helpful to ask yourself what you're mostly interested in showing in a particular diagram:

- Do you mostly just want to *comment* on the data?
- Do you want mostly to *compare* the data with other data?
- Do you want mostly to highlight *change* in the data?
- Do you want mostly to show how this data *connects* with another data set?

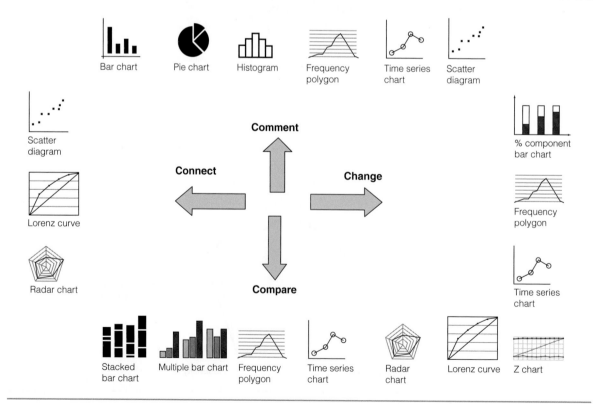

Figure 3.23 Choosing charts

Clearly, there will be times when you want to do several of these but it can be helpful in deciding which type of chart to use to consider Figure 3.23. This shows suggested diagrams depending on the focus of your analysis and can be helpful in deciding which charts to try with your data.

General principles of graphical presentation

In this chapter we've introduced a number of the more common types of business diagram. When you're busy or short on time it's tempting to use the default settings in a spreadsheet or visualisation package when creating a chart. Some of the time this will be fine. However, it's always worth checking that the diagram is as you want it to be. There's no magic formula that works every time but there are some general principles to try and follow.

- Remind yourself of the key message that you're trying to get across in a particular diagram and keep checking that the diagram you're working on still gets this message across clearly. As we've said a number of times, you may need to try different types of chart before you get one that's right.
- Keep it simple. Just because a spreadsheet has 57 different colours, multiple fonts and 3D options doesn't mean you have to use them. However, simple use of colour can help highlight the points you're trying to make.
- Don't try to put too much information on one diagram. Two simple diagrams are often better than one complicated one.
- Make sure that the technical details of the chart are correct:
  - there's a self-explanatory title;
  - axes are clearly and sensibly labelled;
  - the scales are clear and sensible. Simplify large numbers to make them easier: 40 000 000 takes up a lot of space but 40 with an axis scale in millions doesn't and is easier on the eye;
  - different variables are labelled clearly;
  - ask whether all of the above are really necessary or some can be removed to make the chart simpler.
- Try sorting your data into order. Don't necessarily show the data in the order in which you got it.
- In most cases start the Y axis at 0 to avoid misleading.
- Ask yourself – if someone just saw this chart what message would they see – and is that what I want them to see?

Worked example

One of the changes seen in the labour market in many countries has been the increase in the number of self-employed workers. This has happened for a variety of reasons: the loss of many traditional industries; an increasing tendency for organisations to outsource work; the move to less permanent employment; the rise of the gig economy. We've been asked by a major recruitment company to put a short informal report together highlighting what's happened in this context in the UK. Data has been collected as shown in Table 3.12. This displays the July–September quarter each year from 2000 to 2018 (the latest available when this text was being produced) the total number of employees in the UK is split by gender and the number of self-employed is also split by gender. You may want to stop at this point and consider what diagrams you might use to analyse the data shown.

Clearly we have a time series where we would want to look at any changes over time but we also have data by gender, so we could make comparisons. Let's start with a simple time-series graph showing employees and self-employed over this period (Figure 3.24). We see that both variables have shown a fairly steady increase over this period although Employees took a dip in 2008 for a few years (probably linked to the job losses after the financial crisis). However, it's difficult to make much of a comparison because of the differing scales. To get round this let's try displaying both series as an index to make direct comparison easier. Figure 3.25 shows the two series as an index base 2000. We now see quite clearly that although both variables have increased over this period, the growth in self-employment has outstripped that of employees with an increase of almost 50 per cent. We could also review the year-on-year change in both series to assess how stable these increases have been. Figure 3.26 shows the results. It's not a particularly useful chart although it does reveal that the annual change in self-employed numbers is quite erratic.

Table 3.12   Numbers of employees and self-employed 000s

	Employees	Men	Women	Self-employed	Men	Women
2000	24 156	12 534	11 621	3 267	2 359	909
2001	24 296	12 583	11 714	3 328	2 444	884
2002	24 492	12 615	11 877	3 372	2 464	908
2003	24 492	12 613	11 879	3 664	2 678	986
2004	24 816	12 741	12 075	3 598	2 655	943
2005	25 170	12 877	12 293	3 673	2 684	989
2006	25 318	12 989	12 329	3 774	2 733	1 041
2007	25 490	13 109	12 381	3 831	2 758	1 073
2008	25 676	13 131	12 545	3 816	2 766	1 050
2009	25 105	12 686	12 419	3 880	2 747	1 133
2010	25 204	12 781	12 423	4 045	2 863	1 182
2011	25 062	12 680	12 381	4 121	2 896	1 225
2012	25 340	12 832	12 508	4 231	2 971	1 260
2013	25 660	13 028	12 632	4 240	2 943	1 297
2014	26 139	13 230	12 909	4 523	3 113	1 410
2015	26 633	13 515	13 118	4 566	3 111	1 455
2016	26 890	13 664	13 226	4 775	3 204	1 571
2017	27 159	13 739	13 420	4 799	3 214	1 585
2018	27 584	13 995	13 589	4 750	3 171	1 579

Source: Office for National Statistics

Data file T3-12

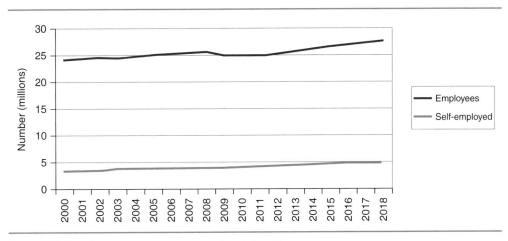

Figure 3.24 Number of employees and self-employed

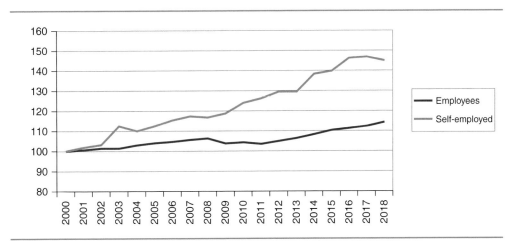

Figure 3.25 Index of employees and self-employed

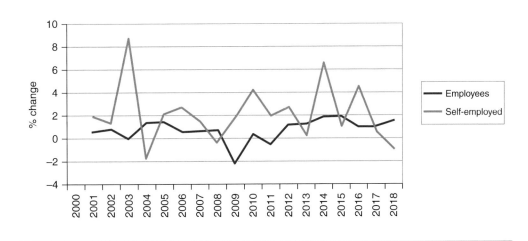

Figure 3.26 Annual percentage change employees and self-employed

Let's now look at this data split by gender. Again there are different ways we could do this. Figure 3.27 shows a 2Y graph for employees and self-employed split by gender. It's not a helpful chart as it's quite difficult to see what's happening given the two scales. Again, we'll try a chart showing the data as a series of indices, base 2000 as in Figure 3.28. The diagram takes a bit of effort to understand. However, we can see that for employees the trends for male and female are fairly similar. However, the number of women classed as self-employed has been increasing at a faster rate than for men. A different perspective can be gained through the use of a component bar chart, as in Figure 3.29. For three specific years – 2000, 2010 and 2018 – this shows the percentage of men/women in the employee and self-employed categories. For employees the gender split is around 50/50 and has remained fairly stable over time. For the self-employed, however, we see a different pattern. Males in this category account for around 70 per cent of the total, although the percentage of females is increasing over time. A few diagrams and some basic calculations allow us to highlight patterns and trends quite effectively. We'd probably include Figures 3.24, 3.25, 3.28 and 3.29 in the report.

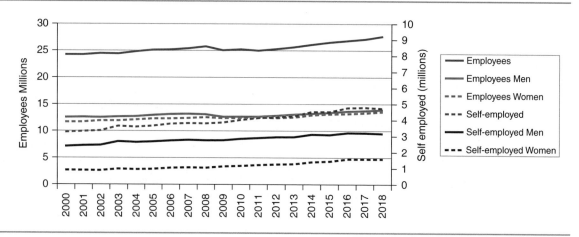

Figure 3.27 Employment and self-employment by gender

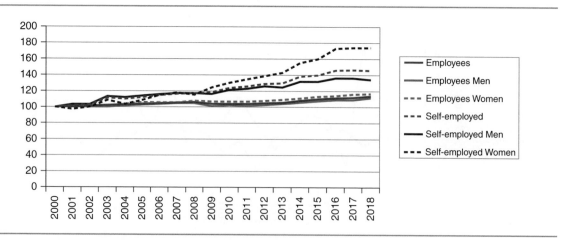

Figure 3.28 Index of employees and self-employed by gender

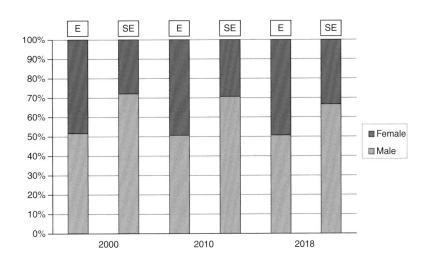

Figure 3.29 Percentage of employees and self-employed by gender

Summary

Now we have completed this chapter we hope you are convinced that the production of diagrams and graphs is a useful skill for any manager to develop. Every manager should be spending some time assessing the current situation in the context of their own area of responsibility, keeping an eye on performance, changing circumstances and the like. Diagrams – particularly when supported with computer-based information systems and suitable graphical software – are a quick and easy way to examine data for such patterns and trends. Equally, managers are frequently called upon to present information to other managers or to employees. Skills in developing an appropriate presentation are obviously essential.

However, we cannot end this chapter without a reminder of the danger of relying solely on graphical presentations. As you will be aware, graphs can give a misleading picture of the situation – either accidentally or deliberately. This might be because we have chosen the wrong sort of diagram or the wrong numerical scale. We should remember that such diagrams are intended only as the first step in the business analysis approach.

QADM IN ACTION

Cowie Health Centre, Scotland

The National Health Service (NHS) in the UK has been in existence since 1948 and at some time or another provides a service to every person in the country. It has a budget of over £30 billion and directly employs over 1 million people with countless private sector companies dependent on doing business with some part of the NHS – from catering to high-tech medical equipment. Expenditure on the NHS has grown considerably since its creation in 1948 and the range and quality of services provided have expanded beyond the imagination of its creators.

Perhaps not surprisingly, given the size of its annual budget, there has been increasing concern expressed by the government at the services provided in terms of their range, their extent, their quality and their value for money. Since the 1980s, the government has initiated a number of major (and minor) changes in the way parts of the NHS operate, are funded and provide a service to the public. One particular area has been one aspect of service in the primary care sector. For most people, their first contact point with the NHS when seeking some treatment or diagnosis will be their family doctor: the GP or general practitioner. All citizens are registered with a specific GP, who may provide a service on an individual basis or on a group basis with other GPs. In many cases GPs form the front line in terms of health care, providing treatment or some medical service directly to the patient or referring the patient to another part of the NHS system where appropriate. The financial funding that GPs receive for providing such treatment and medical services arises from a complex system. To oversimplify, GPs receive an annual per capita amount for every patient registered (regardless of what that patient requires in terms of treatment through the year) and also payments for specific treatments provided to individual patients.

One area of medical service provided by GPs relates to cervical screening in adult women. The purpose of such screening is to monitor any changes occurring in the cervix. This facilitates the detection of cancers at an early stage when they are most treatable, although it must be remembered that the incidence of such cancers in the general female population is relatively low (around 15 per 100 000) and that the majority of such cancers are treatable. The screening process typically involves a short consultation with the GP, when a sample of cells will be taken from the surface of the cervix. These cells are then placed onto a specimen slide, which is sent to a specialist laboratory for examination. The slide is examined by laboratory staff and the results reported back to the GP. Any reported abnormalities require further examination to be undertaken, whereas normal results are reported back to the patient, who is advised to attend for another screening test in three to five years' time. Naturally such a screening process should be carried out on a mass basis to be properly effective and, in the past, concern has been expressed at the take-up rate among women of such screening facilities. Typically, as with this type of health care service, such a screening facility tends to attract those who are least at risk, whereas those who could benefit most from the service tend to have low usage rates. It has been reported, for example, that nine out of every ten women who die from cervical cancer have never had such a smear test conducted, while a study in inner London revealed that around 50 per cent of women were too frightened to come forward to be tested.

To try to encourage a higher take-up of the screening service among women, GPs have been offered incentives to publicise such services and attract more women to them. Such incentives have taken the form of a 'bonus' payment to GPs when at least 80 per cent of eligible women on the GP's register have been screened in this way. GPs who do not meet this target simply receive a per capita fee for each screening test conducted.

Cowie Health Centre in Scotland is a GP practice with four GPs providing a health-care service to a population of over 3000 in a large village and the immediate surrounding area. The catchment area for the practice is one with relatively high levels of social deprivation and is affected by the problems that come with this. In such an area the take-up of preventive health-care initiatives – such as cervical screening – tends to be lower than average. The staff in the centre had expressed concern about the take-up rate for the cervical screening service provided, and in early 1991 a more rigorous system was put into place to try to improve the take-up rate. The new system took advantage of regular computer printouts supplied by the local health authority responsible for undertaking the examination of the cell samples. These printouts provided details of those patients who had had a test conducted and those who should have had a test conducted (on the basis of the test being repeated every three to five years) but had not. Combined with this, the centre instituted its own monitoring system and began sending reminder letters to patients who should be having a test conducted over the next few months. Figure 3.30 shows the number of screening tests conducted from April 1990 to March 1993 on a monthly basis. (The 'year' begins in April for the centre. It should also be noted that the figures have been adjusted by a constant value to maintain confidentiality. This does not affect the overall patterns and trends observed.)

The centre felt that the new approach and systems were gradually having an impact in terms of increasing the number of patients who were attending for their next screening test. With the introduction of financial changes in terms of payments

→

systems, however, it also became important for the centre to monitor the number of tests conducted in relation to the annual target of 80 per cent required to trigger the bonus payments. The use of a Z chart through the year enables their monitoring to be conducted effectively. Figure 3.31 shows the target line from the Z chart for 1992/93 and Figure 3.32 shows the Z chart at the end of January. It is clear from the Z chart at this date that there is a danger of the overall target not being achieved. In the first few months of the year the number of tests was slightly under target. This was followed by several months where performance improved and by October all looked well. However, from the top line of the chart it is evident that October saw the beginning of a downward trend in the monthly number of tests. Clearly, as of January, a concerted effort would have to be made to achieve the annual target, an aspect of performance clearly highlighted by use of the Z chart.

The centre did, in fact, meet its target by the end of the year.

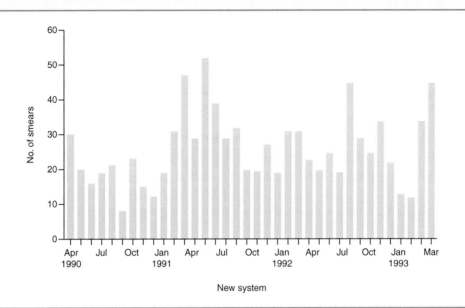

Figure 3.30 Number of cervical screenings April 1990–March 1993

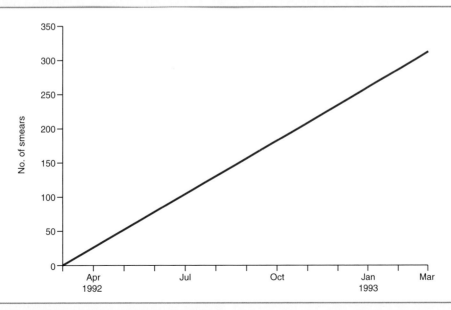

Figure 3.31 Target line for cervical screenings 1992/93

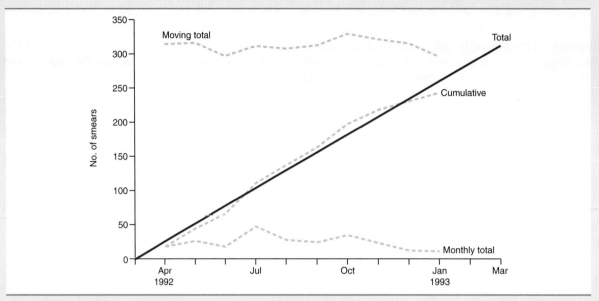

Figure 3.32 Z chart for January

The authors are grateful to the doctors and staff at Cowie Health Centre for the information supplied for this QADM in action.

Exercises

1 Like many countries, Scotland is facing challenges in terms of providing health care to a demographically changing population. Health-care provision and planning is organised largely on a regional basis. Two of the regions have commissioned a short report highlighting the key demographic changes expected over the next couple of decades. Dumfries & Galloway is a largely rural region and one of the smallest in population terms; Greater Glasgow & Clyde is primarily urban and the largest region. Table 3.13 shows data that has been collected on the latest population estimates and population forecasts for 2020 and 2030. Draft a short report for senior health managers highlighting the major changes affecting their region. Use suitable diagrams and additional calculations.

2 You also obtained supplementary information about the financial costs typically involved in providing health care for people of different ages. On a per capita basis the costs are as shown in Table 3.14. Although this data is an estimate only for 2013/14 (the latest available), the managers feel it would be useful to consider the financial implications of expected demographic patterns, given the absence of such financial information for Scotland. You are required to present a second briefing outlining the financial implications of the demographic changes.

3 Table 3.15 shows the UK expenditure on bilateral aid from 2009 to 2017 by geographical region of the recipient country. Using appropriate diagrams, draft a short report highlighting key patterns and trends.

Table 3.13 Population by age group

		Under 5	5 to 14	15 to 64	65 to 74	75 and over	Total
Scotland	2012	295 871	557 138	3 534 840	507 265	418 486	5 313 600
	2020	299 664	587 310	3 507 166	585 019	495 232	5 474 391
	2030	301 245	611 333	3 433 637	676 632	658 274	5 681 121
Dumfries & Galloway	2012	7 480	15 419	93 592	18 859	15 478	150 828
	2020	7 310	14 940	86 917	20 706	18 869	148 742
	2030	7 110	14 816	77 739	21 736	24 274	145 675
Greater Glasgow & Clyde	2012	68 404	124 729	828 900	103 849	91 143	1 217 025
	2020	70 464	131 098	821 844	117 087	99 731	1 240 224
	2030	68 822	138 105	795 981	145 201	125 438	1 273 547

Source: General Registrar's Office

Table 3.14 Estimated per capita costs for health-care provision

Age group	Estimated spending per person (£s) in 2013/14
Under 5 years	1 080
5 to 15	675
16 to 64	1 300
65 to 74	3 800
75 and over	6 300

Source: King's Fund

Table 3.15 UK total expenditure on bilateral aid £m

	2009	2010	2011	2012	2013	2014	2015	2016	2017
Total	3 323	3 447	3 589	3 744	4 620	4 569	5 066	5 606	5 901
Africa	1 803	1 990	2 126	2 171	2 494	2 637	2 759	2 858	2 996
Americas	87	82	102	164	148	73	159	242	346
Asia	1 399	1 334	1 339	1 372	1 949	1 818	2 084	2 344	2 330
Europe	31	37	19	32	24	34	55	156	223
Pacific	4	5	2	6	5	7	8	6	6

Source: DFID

Data file 3X-3

4   Table 3.16 shows motor vehicle production from 2000 to 2017 for selected countries and the global total. Using appropriate diagrams and any additional calculated statistics, comment on the trends in production over this period.

5   Table 3.17 shows selected labour market statistics for 2018 for each region of the UK. Draft a report highlighting key patterns.

Table 3.16   Global vehicle production; all figures in 000s

Total global	2000 Cars	2000 Commercial vehicles	2007 Cars	2007 Commercial vehicles	2013 Cars	2013 Commercial vehicles	2017 Cars	2017 Commercial vehicles
production of which:	41 216	17 159	53 201	20 065	65 462	21 892	73 457	23 846
Brazil	1 352	330	2 391	586	2 723	989	2 269	430
Canada	1 551	1 411	1 342	1 237	965	1 415	749	1 450
China	605	1 464	6 381	2 501	18 085	4 032	24 807	4 209
France	2 880	469	2 551	465	1 458	282	1 748	479
Germany	5 132	395	5 709	504	5 439	278	5 646	0
India	518	283	1 713	540	3 156	742	3 953	830
Italy	1 422	316	911	373	388	270	743	400
Japan	8 359	1 781	9 945	1 652	8 189	1 441	8 349	1 346
Mexico	1 279	656	1 209	886	1 772	1 283	1 900	2 168
Russia	969	236	1 289	371	1 928	265	1 348	203
South Korea	2 602	513	3 723	363	4 123	399	3 735	380
Spain	2 366	667	2 196	694	1 755	409	2 292	557
UK	1 641	172	1 535	216	1 510	88	1 671	78
USA	5 542	7 258	3 924	6 856	4 369	6 698	3 033	8 157

(Several countries/manufacturers do not provide production figures for heavy vehicles anymore due to legal constraints.)

Source: OICA www.oica.net.

Data file 3X-4

Table 3.17   Employment activity rates by region, seasonally adjusted, September to November 2018

UK regions	Employment rate (%) aged 16 to 64 years	Unemployment rate (%) aged 16 years and over	Inactivity rate (%) aged 16 to 64 years
UK	75.8	4	21
England	76	4.1	20.6
North East	71.7	5.5	24
North West	75.2	4	21.7
Yorkshire and The Humber	74.1	5	21.9
East Midlands	75.4	4.6	20.9
West Midlands	73.2	5.2	22.6
East	78.6	3.1	18.8
London	74.9	4.5	21.4
South East	78.8	3.2	18.5
South West	79.1	3.1	18.2
Wales	75.8	3.9	21
Scotland	75.3	3.6	21.9
Northern Ireland	69.6	3.4	27.9

Source: Office for National Statistics

Data file 3X-5

6   Table 3.18 shows data on employment rates by gender for EU countries and for selected other countries for 2007 and 2017. Analyse the data using appropriate diagrams. Employment rate is the number of people in paid employment as a percentage of the population of working age.

7   Table 3.19 shows data on the distribution of incomes before and after tax in the UK in 2015/16. Using Lorenz curves, and any other analysis you think relevant, analyse the data shown.

Table 3.18   Employment rate by gender

	Females		Males	
	2007	2017	2007	2017
EU (28 countries)	62.1	66.5	77.7	78
Belgium	60.3	63.6	75	73.4
Denmark	74.7	73.7	83.2	80.2
Germany	66.7	75.2	79.1	83.1
Ireland	65.8	67	84.2	79.1
Greece	51.7	48	80.1	67.7
Spain	58.6	59.6	80.6	71.5
France (metropolitan)	64.9	67.2	75.1	75
Italy	49.9	52.5	75.7	72.3
Latvia	70.3	72.7	80.5	77
Lithuania	69.1	75.5	76.6	76.5
Hungary	55.2	65.7	69.8	81
Netherlands	70.7	72.8	84.8	83.3
Austria	66.2	71.4	79.5	79.4
Poland	55.5	63.6	70.2	78.2
Portugal	66.3	69.8	79.1	77.3
Romania	57.9	60.2	71	77.3
Slovenia	67.1	69.7	77.5	76.9
Slovakia	58.7	64.7	76	77.5
Finland	72.5	72.4	77.2	75.9
Sweden	77.1	79.8	83.1	83.8
United Kingdom	68.4	73.1	82.2	83.4
Iceland	81.4	84.5	91.5	90.5
Norway	77.5	76.2	84.3	80.2

Source: Eurostat

Data file 3X-6

Table 3.19

Range of total income (lower limit) £	Total				Male				Female			
	No. of taxpayers 000s	Total income before tax £ million	Total tax paid £ million	Total income after tax £ million	No. of taxpayers 000s	Total income before tax £ million	Total tax paid £ million	Total income after tax £ million	No. of taxpayers 000s	Total income before tax £ million	Total tax paid £ million	Total income after tax £ million
10600	1960	22000	248	21800	851	9560	115	9450	1110	12400	133	12300
12000	4310	58100	2230	55900	1970	26600	1040	25500	2340	31600	1190	30400
15000	6160	107000	7830	99300	3150	54800	4020	50800	3010	52300	3810	48500
20000	8050	197000	21200	176000	4710	116000	12500	103000	3340	81400	8640	72800
30000	6990	266000	35800	230000	4530	173000	23500	150000	2460	92800	12300	80600
50000	1780	103000	20100	83100	1270	73500	14500	58900	516	29800	5640	24200
70000	919	76100	18600	57500	680	56400	13900	42400	239	19800	4710	15000
100000	467	55700	16600	39000	358	42700	12800	29900	109	12900	3780	9160
150000	162	27700	9240	18400	131	22400	7490	14900	31	5300	1750	3550
200000	111	26700	9510	17100	90	21700	7780	13900	21	4930	1730	3190
300000	65	24500	9210	15300	54	20500	7710	12800	11	4050	1500	2550
500000	36	24900	9630	15300	31	21500	8330	13200	5	3410	1300	2110
1000000	19	46600	18100	28500	17	41500	16300	25300	2	5010	1840	3180
Total	31000	1040000	178000	858000	17800	680000	130000	550000	13200	356000	48300	307000

Source: HMRC
Data file 3X-7

8   A local authority operates a leisure centre for its citizens, offering a swimming pool, squash courts, badminton and other facilities on a single site. Last year the authority was concerned about the relatively low number of people using the leisure centre on a daily basis and as a result started to advertise the facilities more widely in the local media. Data was collected before the media campaign on the number of people using the facilities each day over an eight-week period. A similar data collection exercise has taken place after the campaign. The results are shown in Tables 3.20 and 3.21. You have been asked to draft a short report, highlighting the key changes in users that have occurred, using frequency tables and related diagrams.

9   Table 3.22 shows per capita income in the UK and consumers expenditure on a number of categories. For each category, analyse the relationship between income expenditure using scatterplots.

Table 3.20   Daily number of users before the media campaign

213	225	237	262	281	299	173	208
221	229	255	276	295	179	173	179
312	189	204	214	228	189	231	226
248	262	186	302	204	206	221	227
255	276	295	214	173	197	189	204
214	228	174	231	252	237	262	281
278	317	208	221	229	255	276	295

Table 3.21   Daily number of users after the media campaign

299	317	337	363	381	281	262
255	276	295	312	334	359	377
284	272	259	241	228	214	204
208	223	238	249	270	287	301
313	329	262	255	204	208	223
214	276	281	299	295	228	238
249	241	311	316	262	312	214
270	287	301	313	314	300	301

Note: The data in both tables are in no meaningful order and have been taken for two eight-week periods which are directly comparable.

Data available in file 3X-8

Table 3.22   UK per capita income and per capita consumer expenditure on selected categories, £ at constant prices

	Income	Restaurants and hotels	Communications	Electricity, gas and other fuels	Non-alcoholic beverages, mineral water and soft drinks	Alcoholic beverages
1995	13769	1700	147	621	102	176
1996	14130	1788	154	654	101	196
1997	14611	1792	171	639	100	209
1998	14894	1830	188	625	102	202
1999	15374	1825	212	598	109	230
2000	16253	1857	249	633	113	234
2001	16956	1858	287	638	119	254
2002	17287	1900	294	624	127	272
2003	17641	1907	316	630	135	287
2004	17802	1926	341	672	140	310
2005	18014	1896	368	640	147	327
2006	18181	1858	369	638	152	325
2007	18526	1857	384	623	148	329
2008	18217	1798	401	633	146	320
2009	18493	1635	391	603	142	308
2010	18526	1664	391	648	140	316
2011	17990	1672	381	571	144	308
2012	18257	1684	372	594	141	311
2013	18119	1721	385	596	145	307
2014	18254	1735	376	509	144	307
2015	18770	1742	395	526	142	313
2016	18930	1772	414	536	149	319

Source: Office for National Statistics

Data file 3X-9

4 Management Statistics

Learning objectives

By the end of this chapter you should be able to:

- explain the need for management statistics
- calculate the more common types of statistics
- understand and explain the principles of such statistics
- assess the management information such statistics provide

In Chapter 3 we saw the usefulness of presenting information visually in the form of tables and a variety of diagrams. Such methods allow the manager to gain a quick impression of the key characteristics of the data under examination. It will be apparent, however, that these presentation methods are not by themselves sufficient for business decision making. Having gained an impression of the overall characteristics of some set of data, we must examine the data in more detail – to develop a more precise, quantitative description of the data. In this chapter we begin this process of closer examination by introducing a number of management statistics.

A business example

In the last chapter, we covered a detailed example relating to a sample of profit centres in a retail organisation taken from two different regions. We saw through a variety of diagrams that there are differences in the two sets of data and we began to describe what those differences are. However, our comments have been fairly general and somewhat imprecise. We concluded that with Region B stores there were relatively fewer at the bottom of the profits range and relatively more at the top of the range. For management purposes this is somewhat imprecise, to say the least. Given the management interest in this variable, we clearly need to more precisely quantify the differences between the two samples. For this reason we must turn to statistical rather than diagrammatic measures to describe the data.

The overall purpose of this chapter is to introduce some of the more common management statistics, not with the intention of turning you into a statistician but to enable you to assess the usefulness – or otherwise – of such statistical information in a decision-making context. After all, if you are presented with statistical information relating to a business problem you need to be able to assess its relevance to the decisions you may have to take. Depending on your experience, you may have already encountered this situation. Production comes to you with the latest monthly production data; finance comes to you with the monthly budget data; marketing comes to you with the latest sales figures; HR comes to you with sickness and absence statistics for different parts of the organisation; IT comes to you with the latest figures on website traffic following the website redesign. Somehow, as an effective manager, you need to be able to look at the data – or the few statistics that have been calculated and presented to you – and decide what to do (and what not to do!). It must be said, however, that the only real way of being able to assess the potential usefulness of statistical information is to have an understanding of how such statistics are calculated. Furthermore, today, such statistics are produced using appropriate computer technology so that, increasingly, a manager does not need to apply some poorly understood statistical formula to obtain a numerical result. However, the computer system cannot (as yet) interpret or evaluate such statistical information on your behalf. We shall return later to our continuing example of retail stores' performance. For the time being, however, we shall illustrate the principles of the statistics we need with a different – and smaller – example.

Consider the following. A National Health Service (NHS) hospital in the UK is under increasing pressure to improve its performance. On the one hand the hospital is expected to increase the number of patients receiving treatment in order to reduce waiting times and waiting lists, and on the other it is expected to maintain or improve the quality of health care provided to patients. To make the management task more difficult, it is expected to achieve this with – at best – the same quantity of resources: staff, finance, equipment and so on. The hospital manager has been examining one particular area of medical care provided by the hospital – that is, treatment for one particular illness. The exact area of care is irrelevant for our purposes but let us assume that it requires patients to be admitted to hospital for an operation, the operation to be carried out, and the patient to be looked after in hospital until they are well enough to be discharged and return home. Last month the hospital's business analyst investigated the patients who had been discharged from the hospital during that month and calculated that these patients – 11 in total – had an average length of stay (LOS) in the hospital of 10 days. That is, on average, a patient would spend 10 days from entry into the hospital to discharge back home. This month, after a concerted effort by the hospital to improve performance in this area, the analyst has calculated that for patients discharged this month – again 11 in total – average LOS has fallen to eight days.

Progress Check 4.1

Why do you think a reduction in LOS would be seen, in management terms, as an improvement in performance, all other things being equal? Based on these statistics would you conclude that, in this area of health care, the hospital has 'improved' its performance?

Why are management statistics needed?

In general terms you can probably see that – all else being equal – a shorter LOS implies that the hospital will require fewer resources to treat an individual patient and, with a shorter LOS, has the potential for treating more patients with the same resource base. After all, for every day a patient spends in the hospital this implies a hospital bed is being used (which could be used by a newly admitted patient), staff resources are devoted to caring for this patient, catering resources are being used and so on. Equally, it is probably the case for most patients that they would prefer to be in and out of the hospital as quickly as possible, so a shorter LOS would most likely be seen as an improvement in 'quality' from their perspective. It is also tempting to conclude that the hospital has improved performance given that LOS has fallen between the two months by two days on average.

However, on reflection, we might wish to be a little more cautious. Exactly what do we mean by an average? Are we implying that last month *every* patient had an LOS of exactly 10 days and that this month *every* patient had an LOS of 8 days? Clearly these are important questions, given that the statistics may be used by the manager to make important decisions, and it is not an ideal situation for the manager to have to rely on the analyst's evaluation of this information. You will probably realise that the averages by themselves are likely to make us ask more questions rather than answer existing ones. In particular, one aspect to the average that we need to resolve relates to how well it represents what happened to the typical patient. In fact, in statistical terms, there are usually two aspects to such descriptive statistics we need to consider:

● some measure of an average value;
● some measure of variability around this average.

Consider the hospital manager's position. The manager may well be thinking about using this information for resource allocation purposes. Assume, for example, that the cost of keeping one patient in the hospital for one day is £1000 – the cost of providing medical and nursing care, drugs and medicine, catering provision, laundry and so on. If we anticipate an average LOS of eight days then this implies that we should allocate £8000 per patient to this part of the hospital. However, since we are not (yet) sure whether all patients stay exactly eight days – and this seems unlikely – we would need to make some allowance for possible variation in the LOS. After all, if one patient stays two or three days longer than the average this will increase health-care costs, so an average by itself is of little use. We also need some way of assessing the variability of patients' stay around the average. If we know the average is eight days, can we somehow determine what a typical variation around this average was? Did patients typically have an LOS that varied from this average by only, say, one day or was the variability five days? The difference in management terms is obviously important.

Housebuilders bet on listings portal start-up

Rummage4Property plans to charge a tenth of Rightmove's prices

By Judith Evans

Some of the UK's largest housebuilders are backing a new property portal that will launch next year in the latest attempt to challenge the two dominant market leaders, Rightmove and Zoopla. . . .

Rummage4Property, headed by a former analyst at Jefferies, will seek to compete with the two biggest portals, which command the majority of both listings and consumer clicks. Portals have become crucial to matching consumers with homes in the digital age, but the existing players have been criticised by some agents for their subscription fee levels.

Average revenue per advertiser at Rightmove rose 8.3 per cent year on year to £987 a month, according to filings for the six months to June. . . .

Anthony Codling, chief executive of Rummage4 Property, said: "The key selling point is that it is much cheaper than Rightmove, Zoopla and OnTheMarket plc." He added that Rummage4Property would begin by charging a flat fee of £100 a month and would link any changes to house price inflation. . . .

OnTheMarket, another challenger portal, listed on London's junior market in February and has reported average revenue per advertiser of £235 a month.

 Source: Evans, J. (2018) Housebuilders bet on listings portal start-up: Rummage4Property plans to charge a tenth of Rightmove's prices, *Financial Times* (UK), Tuesday, 4 December, Section: Companies & Markets, p 21.
© The Financial Times Limited. All Rights Reserved.

Averages and other management statistics are used frequently to try to describe company performance. But it's important to understand how they're calculated and what they actually show.

Measures of average

The arithmetic mean

We shall first examine the concept of an average in the context of our example. Consider the data shown in Table 4.1.

This (fictitious) data relates to the NHS hospital for Month 1 and shows how long each of the 11 patients who were discharged that month had been in the hospital. We see, for example, that two patients had been in the hospital for five days before discharge, three for six days, one for eight days, four for nine days and one for 38 days. Clearly the patient who was discharged after 38 days in hospital had been admitted in the previous month, not the current month.

Progress Check 4.2

Calculate an average LOS for these 11 patients. How 'good' an average is this?

Most people know how to calculate an average without any knowledge of statistics. What you probably did was simply to add the 11 numbers together and divide by 11 to get an average of 10 days:

$$\text{Total number of days} = 110$$

$$\text{Number of patients} = 11$$

$$\text{Average LOS} = \frac{110}{11} = 10 \text{ days}$$

Table 4.1   Duration of stay (days): Month 1

5	9	6	6	9	8	9	6	38	5	9

In fact a statistician would refer to this average as the *arithmetic mean*, for, as we shall see soon, there are different averages that can be calculated for the same set of data. In short, we can express this calculation as a simple formula. If we denote x as the individual numbers – the items of data – and n as the number of data items, then our calculation becomes:

$$\text{Mean} = \frac{\Sigma x}{n}$$

where Σx refers to the summation (total) of all the x values (go back and read the section on summation in Chapter 2 if you're not sure what this means). However, on reflection, you have probably realised that the mean value of 10 days is not a particularly 'good' measure of average in this case. From Table 4.1 we can see that 10 out of the 11 patients were in fact discharged *before* the mean LOS and it is the one patient who had a long LOS that is dragging the average above the majority of values. This is an important point. If the hospital manager only has a single statistic – the mean LOS (i.e. the number 10) – there is no way of knowing from this whether it is a typical or representative value. We are only able here to comment on its 'reliability' because we have access to the original data and can see how the original figures compare to the mean of 10 days. Frequently this will not be the case and we obviously require supplementary statistics to allow us to come to the same conclusion. We shall introduce these shortly. Consider now Table 4.2, which shows comparable data for Month 2.

The mean would be:

$$\text{Mean} = \frac{\Sigma x}{n}$$

$$= \frac{88}{11}$$

$$= 8 \text{ days}$$

Once again, however, the mean is not really representative of the data in the set. This time 9 out of 11 patients stayed *longer* than the average, although it must be said that most of the actual LOS figures appear closer to the mean for Month 2 than is the case in Month 1. However, consider our original question: has the hospital improved performance as measured by LOS between Month 1 and Month 2? The mean values by themselves imply that it has, although access to the original data indicates that we need to be more cautious about our conclusion.

It can be tempting, when faced with data like that in Table 4.1, to consider removing 'outliers' – like the patient who was 38 days in the hospital. We may try to rationalise this by saying: that one patient is distorting the average LOS and is very untypical of what's happening. However, we should be very cautious before removing such data from the data set. After all, that patient *did* spend 38 days in hospital. We should only remove such outliers if we're convinced – using data from other sources – that they are extreme and unusual occurrences.

Table 4.2 Duration of stay (days): Month 2

1	10	9	10	9	9	10	9	1	10	10

The median

The arithmetic mean is, therefore, not necessarily a representative indication of an average for a set of data. As we mentioned earlier, there are other measures of average that can be calculated for the same set of data. One of these is the *median*. The median is a measure of average representing the middle value of a set of data which has been ordered (ranked from lowest value through to highest). Frequently the median will differ in value from the mean and this difference may tell us something about the variability within the data. To determine the median for Month 1 we must rank the data. This would give:

5 5 6 6 6 8 9 9 9 9 38

We are seeking the middle value which, since we have 11 items, must correspond to item 6 in the array. The middle value in this array then corresponds to eight days, which we now call the median. Consider what we can now infer about the set of data – even if we have not seen the original data. Given that the median LOS is eight days, this implies we had an equal number of patients (five in this case) below the median value as above. We know, therefore, that 5 of the 11 patients were discharged before the median LOS and 5 of the 11 discharged after (although without the raw data we do not know how much before or after the median). This is something of an improvement over the mean, which gives no indication of how many of the data items fall above or below the mean value. Consider also for this set of data that the median – at 8 days – is less than the mean – at 10. What can we infer from this? We know that the mean by definition includes all the data items – including any extreme values. The median, however, simply counts along the ordered data until it gets to the middle. Extreme high values are therefore ignored. Since the mean is above the median and since the mean must include all the data, it follows that there must be (at least) one extreme value in the data set to pull the mean above the median.

Progress Check 4.3

Consider the data item of 38 days. Assume this is a clerical error and should be 48 days. What would you expect to happen to the mean and median values? Determine the median for Month 2. Comparing the two medians as measures of average, what would you now say about the hospital's performance in Months 1 and 2?

Solution is given on p 574.

The median for Month 2 is nine days and we begin to see why, in some ways, statistics has the reputation it does. We could legitimately say that the hospital's performance has improved, since average LOS has fallen by two days (from 10 to 8 if we use the mean). We could equally say it has worsened, since average LOS has increased (from 8 to 9 days if we use the median). Of course, we now know that we should really refer to the statistics as the mean and median rather than the average, and that they show slightly different aspects of the same data.

Doctor's orders

By Gavin Jackson

In news that will delight statisticians everywhere the distinction between the mean and the median finally has the political profile it deserves.

Yesterday Sir Andrew Dilnot, chair of the UK statistical authority, wrote a letter clarifying an ongoing debate between Labour and Conservative politicians on waiting times in accident and emergency rooms. It began at Prime Minister's question time on the 2nd July when David Cameron claimed that the "average" waiting time was 30 minutes, down from 77 minutes under Labour.

The week after Jeremy Hunt, the Secretary of State for Health, referred to the median in a statement to the House of Commons: "NHS staff are working incredibly hard to see and treat these patients within four hours, and it is a tribute to them that the median wait for an assessment is only 30 minutes under this Government, down from 77 minutes under the last Government."

Andy Burnham, the shadow Health Minister, referred the Prime Minister's initial answer and Jeremy Hunt's later statement to the UK statistics authority. Andrew Dilnot's letter clarifies that the 30 minute average is actually the mean and suggests that Jeremy Hunt might want to take advice on whether he ought to correct the parliamentary record.

The median is lower at eight minutes. The mean is calculated by adding up all waiting times and dividing by how many they are, the traditional average. The median is the middle – half wait less than the median and half wait longer. Both the mean and median are summary statistics, they summarise across the whole distribution of waiting times rather than giving us the exact distribution. Extreme values can make the mean unrepresentative as a few people who wait an extremely long time push it upwards.

Fortunately, we don't need to limit ourselves to just one measure and the chart below, from Sir Andrew's letter, shows both for initial assessment, treatment and departure. The median has been broadly stable for the last five years. But the gap between the mean and the median has fallen, perhaps indicating that the number of extremely long waits has fallen.

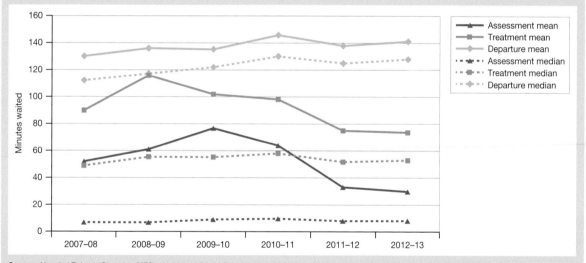

Sources: Hospital Episode Statistics (HES), Health and Social Care Information Centre.

Statistics such as mean and median aren't just of academic interest. They can affect political and management careers.

Measures of variability

We now realise that averages by themselves are potentially misleading and that we require some measure of variability around the average as well to give us an idea of how 'good', or typical, that average is. Consider the hospital manager who knows that the mean LOS is 10 days per patient in Month 1. For planning and management purposes this statistic is inadequate by itself (notwithstanding that the median may well show a different average value). The manager will also want some indication as to how much this LOS is likely to vary from one patient to another. Is a typical variation likely to be one day or two or three or . . . ? The importance of knowing likely variability should not be underestimated. Such an average figure may well be used to set staffing levels, number of beds, number of doctors and other trained staff, patient admission rates and so on. We clearly need to consider measures of variability and we shall introduce several.

The range

The first of these measures is the *range*, which is simply the difference between the maximum value and the minimum value in a data set. By simple inspection of Tables 4.1 and 4.2 we see that we have:

Month 1: Maximum $= 38$

Minimum $= 5$

Range $= 38 - 5 = 33$ days

Month 2: Range $= 9$ days $(10 - 1)$

We see that for Month 1 the range was much larger (almost four times) than for Month 2. This implies potentially more variability in the first set of data compared with the second. The range is a fairly crude, but effective, measure of variability. One common use is in the quotation of stock market prices, where the minimum and maximum share price during the year are shown in published data.

The standard deviation

A far more important – and more widely used – measure of variability is the *standard deviation*. Consider what we require. Just as we have calculated the mean as a statistical measure of average, so we wish to calculate a measure of variability around this average: typically how much do the items in the data set differ from the mean value? Is there a typical variability around the mean LOS of one day, two days, three days . . . ? A logical first step, therefore, would be to determine the individual differences between the actual data and the mean. We show the results for this for Month 1 in Table 4.3.

The final column simply shows the difference – the deviation – of the mean from each actual data value. For the first patient, therefore, the actual LOS was five days less than the mean (hence -5 as the deviation). However, we require a statistic showing variability from the average for *all* the data, not for each item individually. It seems logical, therefore, to consider taking the individual deviations and finding an average deviation for all the 11 patients.

Table 4.3   Deviations from the mean

Actual LOS	Mean	Deviation
5	10	−25
5	10	−25
6	10	−24
6	10	−24
6	10	−24
8	10	−22
9	10	−21
9	10	−21
9	10	−21
9	10	−21
38	10	+128

Progress Check 4.4

Calculate an average (mean) deviation for the whole data set. How do you explain your result?

On performing such a calculation we find that the total of all the individual deviations is zero and that if we proceeded to find an average or mean deviation this would be zero also. Clearly this doesn't look right as we know that there is considerable variation simply on inspection of the raw data. In fact, the sum of the individual deviations will always total to zero for any data set. This must be the case since by trying to calculate an average deviation for the whole data set we are effectively saying: by how much on average do the numbers in the first column deviate from those in the second? The answer must be zero since the numbers in the second column are effectively the same (although they look different) as those in the first (think about how we worked out the mean of 10 days in the first place). So the obvious calculation does not work.

We can still proceed, however, if we reconsider what we require. We are searching for a statistic that indicates the typical difference between all the actual data items and the mean. Since our interest is primarily in this difference – particularly whether it is large or small – then the sign of the individual differences is irrelevant. That is, it does not matter whether an individual deviation is positive or negative but rather whether it is large or small. Since it is the signs of the individual deviations in Table 4.3 that are causing the current difficulty, we can remove them. The way in which this is done by the standard deviation calculation is to square the individual deviations. This will have the effect of converting all values into positives (remember when multiplying, two minuses make a plus). The calculations are shown in Table 4.4.

Table 4.4   Squared deviations from the mean

Actual LOS	Deviation	Squared deviation
5	−5	25
5	−5	25
6	−4	16
6	−4	16
6	−4	16
8	−2	4
9	−1	1
9	−1	1
9	−1	1
9	−1	1
38	+28	784
Total	0	890

This produces a total of 890 (notice also that the squaring has the effect of increasing the importance of the larger deviations in the total). This is a number we can now average over the whole data set. That is, we can now divide by 11 to find an average squared deviation.

Progress Check 4.5

If we were to perform this calculation, what units of measurement would the resulting number have?

Since we squared the individual deviations (measured in days) we must also have squared the units of measurement (think about measuring a room for a carpet). We therefore must have a number, 890, whose units of measurement are 'square days' – a meaningless unit of measurement. To revert to something sensible we must therefore reverse the squaring process by taking the square root and thereby also reversing the units of measurement. We then have:

$$\sqrt{\frac{890}{11}} = 8.99 \, \text{days}$$

That is, the standard deviation for Month 1 is approximately nine days. But how is this interpreted? What does it mean? Remember that we were trying to calculate a statistic which indicates variability around the mean (of 10 days); that is, how much actual lengths of stay vary from the mean LOS. This measure of variability – the standard deviation – is nine days and is an indication of the typical, or standard, difference of the actual data items from the mean we have calculated. Given that the mean is 10, the value for the standard deviation implies (relatively) high variation from the mean within the original set of data. That is, if we are simply told the mean and standard deviation we can infer that the mean is not really a 'typical' value, given the standard deviation is relatively large. Some care must be taken when interpreting the standard deviation but, as we shall see, it is an important statistic in other quantitative areas.

Progress Check 4.6

What do you think the minimum value for the standard deviation can be for any data set? What does this imply? Calculate the standard deviation for Month 2 and compare it with that calculated for Month 1.

Solution is given on p 575.

With some thought it becomes evident that the minimum value the standard deviation can ever take for a set of data is zero – implying that all the individual data items take the mean value, and hence there is no variability from this average value. At the other end there is, in principle, no upper limit to the value the standard deviation can take: higher values simply imply more variability. But how do we compare two (or more) standard deviations? The answer must be 'carefully'. The reason for this is that in a data set the standard deviation is calculated around the mean value. If, in another data set, the mean value is different, then we could well get a different value for the standard deviation, even though the actual variability is the same. If this sounds unconvincing you should attempt Exercise 1 at the end of this chapter now, to confirm the point. Consider Month 2, where the standard deviation works out at 3.3 days. What can we say about variability of LOS in Month 1 compared with Month 2? We can conclude that, in absolute terms, the variability in Month 2 is less (about a third of that in Month 1). This can be confirmed by recollecting that 9 out of 11 observations in Month 2 were of either 9 or 10 days with a mean of 8. However, the means themselves differ and this might be the cause of (at least some of) the difference in the standard deviations. For this reason it is usually advisable to calculate a related statistic – the coefficient of variation – which we shall examine shortly.

Formula for calculating the standard deviation

The calculations we have completed for the standard deviation can be summarised into an appropriate formula:

$$SD = \sqrt{\frac{\Sigma (x - \bar{x})^2}{n}}$$

where x refers to the individual data items, $\bar{x}$ (pronounced 'x bar') is the mean and n the number of data items in the data set. The formula is simply the square root of the sum of the squared deviations divided by the number of items in the data set. All we have done in the formula is express the step-by-step calculations we performed earlier. The formula indicates that we subtract the mean from each data value, square these, sum these for the entire data set, divide by the number of data items and then take the square root. Earlier we calculated $\Sigma (x - \bar{x})^2$ as 890 and n as 11 so we have $\sqrt{(890/11)} = 8.99$. You will sometimes also find reference to the term *variance*. The variance is the square of the standard deviation or

$$\frac{\Sigma (x - \bar{x})^2}{n}$$

Strange days for goldbuggers

By Cardiff Garcia

A bloodbath for gold this week but especially today, when it was off more than $100 at its lowest point before rallying a bit. Reuters analyst John Kemp pointed out earlier in the day that this is more than a four-standard deviation move:

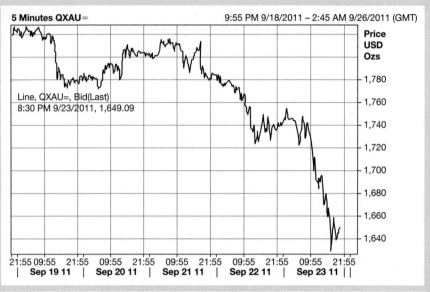

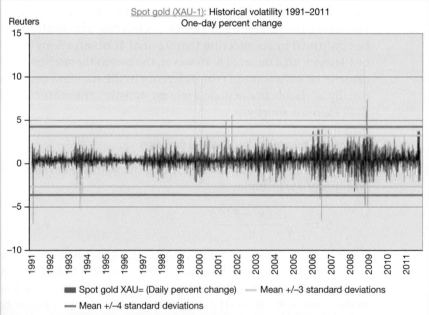

Standard deviation is frequently used to show volatility in share price movements – or in this case the price of gold. The higher the standard deviation the higher the volatility. A four standard deviation move implies exceptional volatility.

Populations and samples

It is worthwhile at this stage making the distinction between sets of data which represent a statistical population and those which represent a sample from a population. A *population* relates to the entire set of data that is of interest to us. A *sample* is a selected part of that population. For the example we were using in the last chapter on stores in two regions, we indicated that we had collected data on a sample of stores. This implies that our data is technically incomplete – that we are analysing only a part of the total population, which, in this case, would consist of all stores within each region. The reasons for obtaining and analysing data on only a sample from the population are usually self-evident – particularly in a business context. It may simply not be feasible to collect data for the entire statistical population: it may be too expensive, it may be too time-consuming. For whatever reason, in a business environment we are usually investigating a sample of data rather than the population. Why does this matter?

It matters because, in principle, our data – and thereby our analysis – is incomplete. Potentially, the conclusions we come to, based on our analysis of a sample – of only part of the population – might be different from those we would have reached had we examined the whole population. A considerable area of statistics is devoted to trying to assess how 'accurate' the sample analysis is in the context of the (missing) population data, and this is also an area we will touch on later. For the moment it is sufficient to note the potential problem. We must also begin to distinguish our statistics in terms of whether they relate to the sample or the population, and there is some standard terminology to facilitate this. Typically in statistics, calculations which relate to the population are denoted by a character from the Greek alphabet. Thus:

Population mean $= \mu$ (pronounced 'mew')
Population standard deviation $= \sigma$ (pronounced 'sigma')

The equivalent sample statistics are typically denoted with letters from the standard alphabet:

Sample mean $= \bar{x}$ (pronounced 'x bar')
Sample standard deviation $= s$

In the context of the sample standard deviation, it is also important to note that the formula for its calculation is slightly different from that of the population standard deviation:

$$s = \sqrt{\frac{\Sigma (x - \bar{x})^2}{n - 1}}$$

with the divisor in the equation being n–1, not n (the reason for this can only properly be explained using some detailed mathematics). This is particularly important when analysing data using a computer package. Spreadsheet programs have in-built statistical functions which allow you to specify a range of data and ask for certain statistics, such as the mean, median or standard deviation, to be calculated automatically without the need for the intermediate calculations (i.e. finding the deviations, squaring them, summing them, dividing by n, etc.). In the case of the standard deviation, however, spreadsheets will usually have two such in-built functions: one to work out the standard deviation assuming it represents the population, and another assuming it represents a sample. You should check carefully which function does which in your own spreadsheet program.

Excel has several different statistical functions for calculating a standard deviation. Make sure you're using the right one!

The coefficient of variation

We have seen that it is not always easy to compare and interpret two or more standard deviations. Sometimes when comparing different sets of data it can be helpful to compare their relative variability rather than the absolute variability (as measured by the standard deviations). We can do this through the statistic known as the *coefficient of variation* (CV).

The coefficient of variation is a statistic using the mean and standard deviation:

$$CV = \frac{\text{Standard deviation}}{\text{Mean}} \times 100$$

So for Month 1 we have:

$$CV = \frac{8.99}{10} \times 100 = 89.9\%$$

That is, the standard deviation is approximately 90 per cent of the mean value. For Month 2 the CV works out at 42 per cent. This implies that, even after allowing for differences in means, relative variation in Month 2 is approximately half that of Month 1. You will probably also realise that potentially the coefficient of variation is a useful statistical measure in those situations where consistency is important (and remember that consistency and variability are effectively the same). We may be producing some product, for example, where we need to ensure (perhaps for trading standards purposes) that the quality of the product is consistent and maintained. Monitoring the variability through the standard deviation may not help if the mean value itself is altering, but using the CV will.

Consider the following scenario. A manufacturing company produces a product in two sizes: a 1000 ml bottle and a 500 ml bottle. The machinery filling the bottles fills an average (mean) of these amounts but, because of mechanical variability, there is a standard deviation of 5 ml and 4 ml respectively. Although the machine filling the smaller bottle has a lower standard deviation – and lower absolute variability – the CVs would indicate that it is the machine filling the larger bottle which is *relatively* more consistent. The CV for the larger bottle would be $5/1000 \times 100 = 0.5$ and for the smaller bottle would be $0.4/500 \times 100 = 0.8$.

Quartiles

The standard deviation is a common measure of variability. However, by definition it measures variability around the mean – only one of the measures of average. As we have seen, the median will occasionally be a more representative measure than the mean and we may wish to calculate an appropriate measure of variability without the mean. We can do this through the use of *quartiles*. We know already that the median is the middle item in an ordered data set. We can describe the median in terms of its percentage position in the data set. The median is the 50th percentile, given that this would be in the middle of the data set. Two other common percentiles are the lower and upper quartiles, often denoted as Q_1 and Q_3 respectively. The lower quartile is the 25th percentile and the upper quartile is the 75th. This implies that a quarter of the items in a data set will have a numerical value up to the lower quartile value, and that a quarter will have a value equal to or higher than the upper quartile value. What this effectively implies is that a distribution can be neatly categorised as shown in Figure 4.1. For any set of data, a quarter of the items will fall below the lower quartile, a quarter between the lower quartile and median, a quarter between the median and upper quartile and a quarter above the upper quartile.

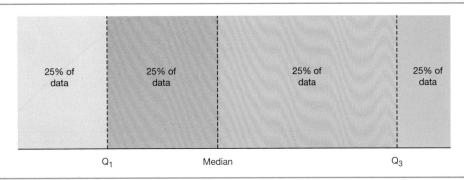

Figure 4.1 Quartiles

Note that the two quartiles will not necessarily be equidistant from the median. One of the quartiles may be further away than the other from the median value, typically if the overall shape of the data distribution is not symmetrical.

Calculating the quartiles

Calculating the quartiles is, in principle, the same as calculating the median. The data can be sorted and then the item a quarter of the way through found, the lower quartile, and then three-quarters of the way through, the upper quartile can be found. In practice, for any large set of data, a computer package will obtain these values.

The interquartile range

Another measure of variability that can be used in relation to the quartiles is the *interquartile range* (IQR). This is simply the difference between the upper and lower quartiles:

$$IQR = Q_3 - Q_1$$

and, as can be seen from Figure 4.1, always encloses the central 50 per cent of the data. Other things being equal, a lower value for the IQR implies less variability in the central part of the data set. Literally, the lower the IQR value, the closer Q_1, and Q_3 must be to each other. Note, however, that the IQR ignores the data in the bottom and upper quarters of the distribution.

Coefficient of skewness

The final statistical measure that we introduce before putting all of them to use is the *coefficient of skewness*. Such a statistic tries to provide an impression of the general shape of the data distribution in the context of its overall symmetry. Consider Figures 4.2-4.4. Figure 4.2 shows a reasonably symmetrical distribution, with the bulk of the data in the middle and two reasonably balanced extremes. However, Figure 4.3 shows a distribution which is decidedly unsymmetrical, with the 'hump' towards the lower end of the X axis scale and a long 'tail' of relatively high values to the right. Figure 4.4 shows the reverse pattern to this, with the 'hump' now on the right-hand side. Figures 4.3 and 4.4 are said to show 'skewed' distributions. Given the focus of this chapter on statistical – rather than diagrammatic – descriptions of a set of data, we require some quantitative method of assessing whether the data we are examining fits into one or other of these patterns. Such a measure is given by the coefficient of skewness (more formally known as *Pearson's coefficient of skewness*), which is calculated as:

$$SK = \frac{3\,(\text{Mean} - \text{Median})}{\text{Standard deviation}}$$

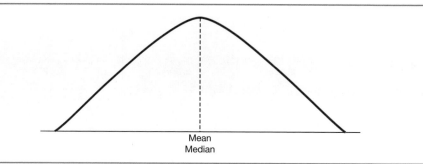

Figure 4.2 Symmetrical distribution

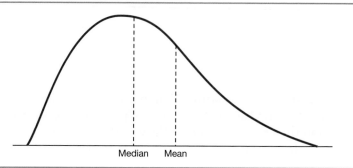

Figure 4.3 Positive skew

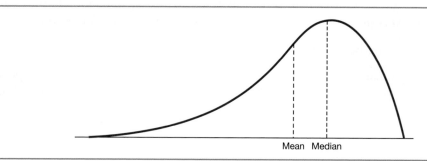

Figure 4.4 Negative skew

By reference to Figures 4.2 to 4.4, where the mean and median values are shown, you should be able to see the logic of this. In Figure 4.2 (the symmetrical distribution) the values for the mean and median will be the same, since there are no extreme values on the one side to pull the mean value away from the bulk of the data. The coefficient, therefore, will take a zero value. In Figure 4.3, however, the mean will tend to be pulled upward by the relatively high values in the tail. Thus, the mean will take a higher value then the median. The skewness formula, therefore, will generate a positive result, since the expression on top must be positive, as must the standard deviation (by definition). Such a distribution is said to be positively skewed, with a larger value implying more skewness (i.e. the distribution being further away from the symmetrical distribution in Figure 4.2). By comparison, Figure 4.4 will be negatively skewed, with the mean taking a lower value than the median and the expression on top of the skewness formula taking a negative value. Thus, simply by knowing the value for the skewness coefficient, we can infer the general shape of the distribution without resorting to a diagram.

Pressure over pay gap set to increase: Gender remuneration reporting has been an unsettling experience for both the public and private sectors

By Barney Thompson

There have been other surveys showing how, on average, Britain pays men more than women, but none has shone a spotlight quite as fiercely on individual companies, charities and public organisations — or sparked as much debate.

The UK government's year-long, mandatory gender pay gap reporting exercise has been an uncomfortable experience for many employers, who have been forced to reveal their internal statistics rather remain anonymous in sweeping national or sectoral studies.

Many left reporting their pay gap data up until the last minute — or slightly beyond, in the case of Unite, the country's largest trade union, which filed its report on Thursday, several hours after Wednesday's midnight deadline.

Hundreds more missed it entirely, according to the Equality and Human Rights Commission, which is responsible for policing the reporting.

The task for British public and private employers alike will now be to show how they will respond to the huge pressure to improve their figures — especially since they will be required to publish their gender pay gap each year.

"This has put the issue on the table so companies could not fail to address it," said Alison Jefferis, head of corporate affairs at Columbia Threadneedle

Investments and a board member of the Women in Finance initiative.

Tulip Siddiq, a Labour MP and member of the Commons women and equalities committee, said she hoped the pay gap reports would mark a "watershed moment in the battle against pay inequality in Britain". She added that while the figures would "always be open to some degree of interpretation ...the scale of the problem is self-evident".

Petra Wilton, director of strategy for the Chartered Management Institute, said organisations needed to acknowledge they had a problem and pledge to do something about it. "This can be reputation-enhancing or it can have a shaming effect, which is in fact a really good incentive to act," she said.

Some groups have a greater gap to close than others. The filings revealed striking differences between certain sectors, with construction, financial services energy and professional services among those with far higher median gender pay gaps than the national figure of 9.7 per cent. Arts and entertainment, hospitality and healthcare all fared better — though men were still paid more than women overall.

Ms Wilton said data showing the proportion of men and women in each pay quartile were particularly revealing, illustrating the lack of women in top

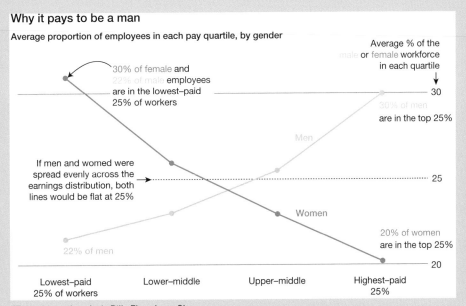

Why it pays to be a man

Average proportion of employees in each pay quartile, by gender

Average % of the male or female workforce in each quartile

30% of female and 22% of male employees are in the lowest–paid 25% of workers

30% of men are in the top 25%

Men

If men and womed were spread evenly across the earnings distribution, both lines would be flat at 25%

Women

20% of women are in the top 25%

22% of men

30

25

20

Lowest–paid 25% of workers | Lower–middle | Upper–middle | Highest–paid 25%

FT graphic and analysis Billy Ehrenberg-Shannon;
Source: Gov.uk
@FT

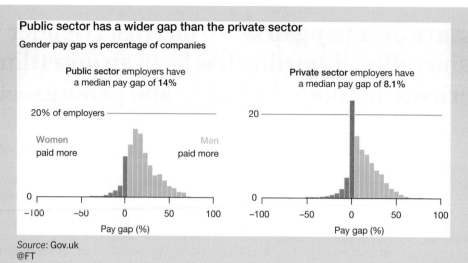

Public sector has a wider gap than the private sector

Gender pay gap vs percentage of companies

Public sector employers have a median pay gap of **14%**

Private sector employers have a median pay gap of **8.1%**

Source: Gov.uk
@FT

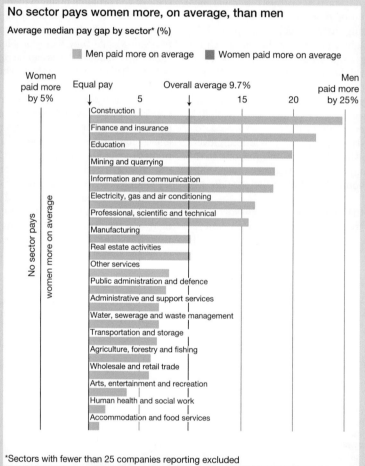

No sector pays women more, on average, than men

Average median pay gap by sector* (%)

Men paid more on average   Women paid more on average

*Sectors with fewer than 25 companies reporting excluded

FT graphic and analysis Alexandra Wisniewski, Billy Ehrenberg-Shannon
Source: Gov.uk
@FT

roles — something she called the "glass pyramid". "Averages are blunt instruments but [the gender pay gap exercise] is a realistic representation of where organisations are across society, both the worst-offending sectors and those that are doing well," she said.

But the figures also point to broader social issues, including the subjects boys and girls are expected to take at school and careers advice they receive, the jobs men and women traditionally choose, and the availability of good-quality, affordable childcare.

"This is not something employers can solve on their own," said Charles Cotton of the CIPD, the professional body for human resources. "Government and society also have a role in challenging assumptions about what is man's work and what is woman's work." Neil Carberry, managing director of people and infrastructure at the CBI, the employers group, agreed. "We need to make sure there is not an outsourcing of responsibility on to employers only," he said. "This is about much more complex societal and workplace issues."

Nevertheless, the exercise has presented companies with opportunities as well as embarrassment. "This should make forward-looking companies think about what they are doing with their best talent," said Philip Hampton, non-executive chairman of GSK and co-chair of the Hampton-Alexander review into improving gender balance in the leadership of FTSE groups. "The more data you get, the more you can understand [the issue] and the more you can take steps to deal with it."

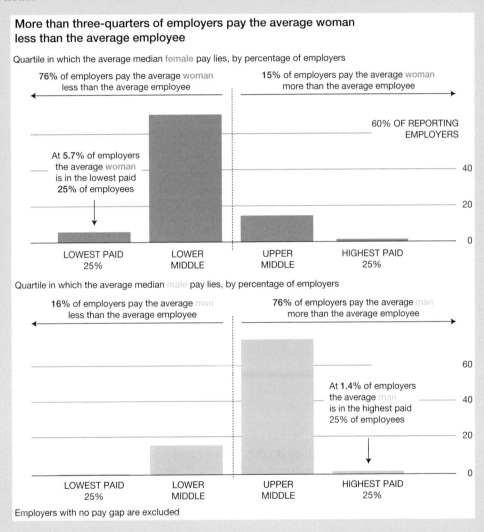

More than three-quarters of employers pay the average woman less than the average employee

Quartile in which the average median female pay lies, by percentage of employers

76% of employers pay the average woman less than the average employee

15% of employers pay the average woman more than the average employee

60% OF REPORTING EMPLOYERS

At 5.7% of employers the average woman is in the lowest paid 25% of employees

40

20

0

LOWEST PAID 25% | LOWER MIDDLE | UPPER MIDDLE | HIGHEST PAID 25%

Quartile in which the average median male pay lies, by percentage of employers

16% of employers pay the average man less than the average employee

76% of employers pay the average man more than the average employee

60

At 1.4% of employers the average man is in the highest paid 25% of employees

40

20

0

LOWEST PAID 25% | LOWER MIDDLE | UPPER MIDDLE | HIGHEST PAID 25%

Employers with no pay gap are excluded

FT graphic and analysis Cale Tifford Billy Ehrenberg-Shannon
Source: Gov.uk
@FT

UK companies now have to report on the gender pay gap by showing data not only on mean and median pay but also for the four quartiles.

Index tracking: information – a double-edged sword

By Jim Pickard

Information is very hard to come by in many property markets. Try buying a building in Dubai, for example, and you will find that working out comparative pricing for recent deals is a tricky task. Investors in the US and the UK – and a growing number of other markets – should consider themselves lucky. In these places transparency has improved over the years thanks to the efforts of researchers.

In the UK, a company called Investment Property Databank (IPD) has long provided the backbone for the entire asset class by collating all the pricing, rental and total returns data from most of the big fund managers and property companies. IPD has also established a presence in 19 other countries including Germany, France and South Africa.

"The IPD has done more for the UK property fund management industry than any other single initiative," says Stuart Beevor, managing director of Grosvenor Fund Management. "Their indices are the best in the world."

This increase in transparency, however, is seen by many as a doubled-edged sword because of its impact on fund management. Rather than go their own way,

fund managers are becoming more likely than before to hug the benchmark by buying the same proportional allocations as everyone else. By doing so, they are unlikely to underperform and miss their targets – and therefore bonuses. The same trend has long been established in equity markets, where fund managers do not fear for their jobs even if they lose money so long as everyone else is in the same boat.

Performance figures for the industry over recent years certainly show a thinning of the gap between best and worst – a fact that many attribute to benchmark-hugging. The spread of returns from "core" fund managers within the IPD universe – termed the "interquartile range" – has narrowed in recent years, says Robin Goodchild, head of European strategy at LaSalle Investment Management.

"If you went back 10 or 15 years it would have been much wider," he says. "Now, fund managers are not going to stray a million miles from the index. So they will all have some industrial, some retail and some offices and within that it's a question of where they take their bets."

Here the interquartile range is used to identify 'core' fund managers – ignoring the best and worst 25 per cent of fund managers.

Using the statistics

We are now in a position to consider the use of all the statistics we have introduced in a management context. To do this, we will return to our earlier example in Chapter 3 of a sample of stores in Region A and Region B. Remember that we have already examined the data visually. We now wish to compare the two samples statistically and consider the two data sets. If you have access to a suitable computer package you may wish, at this stage, to calculate the statistics we have introduced for both of these data sets. You should duplicate the results shown in Table 4.5, which shows the output from a typical statistical package in terms of a number of the statistics we have developed for profits of stores in Region A and Region B. From summary statistics such as these we can tell a reasonably accurate story of what's happening without looking at the detailed data.

Progress Check 4.7

Take a few minutes to consider the statistics shown in Table 4.5. What conclusions can you make about similarities and differences between the two sets of data? How might such statistics be used in a business context?

Table 4.5 Profits for stores in Region A and in Region B

	Region A	Region B
Sample size	113	121
Minimum	−13070	−4130
Maximum	93050	98800
Range	106120	102930
Mean	12981.2	17168.8
Median	6840	9580
Standard deviation	17476.3	19688.1
Coefficient of variation	134.6%	114.7%
Lower quartile	3530	3930
Upper quartile	15170	25000
Interquartile range	11640	21070
Skewness	1.0	1.9

Table 4.5 allows us to make a considerable number of comments about the data. Remember the purpose of statistics: to try to provide a reasonably accurate description of a data set in a concise way. We can start first of all by looking at the more obvious statistics. Mean profit for stores in Region A is around £13000 and for Region B around £17000. So – on average – stores in Region A make around £4000 more profit per year. However, this isn't the full picture. Are the mean profit figures typical, or representative, of stores in the two regions? The answer from the other statistics is no.

From the minimum values we see that at least one store in each region is running at a loss (we don't know from this data how many stores are loss making but could determine this from the primary data) and at least one store in each region is making considerably more profit than the average: around £93000 in Region A and almost £99000 in Region B. The standard deviations also indicate considerable variation around the means with the coefficients of skewness high at 135 per cent and 115 per cent respectively. Given the means are not really typical of what's happening to stores' profitability, are the medians more helpful?

We see that in both regions the median profit is considerably lower than the corresponding mean. In Region A the median is around £6800 (compared to the mean of £13000), implying that half of stores earn a profit less than this amount and half earn a higher profit. In Region B we have a similar picture, with the median around £9600 compared to the mean of £17000. In both regions the median is only around half of the mean value. The lower quartiles in the two regions are quite similar – £3500 and £3900. However, the upper quartiles are considerably different: £15000 for Region A and £25000 for Region B.

Let's look at the quartiles and median more closely. The lower quartile represents the least profitable stores in both cases. We see that the lower quartiles are quite similar, implying that the 'worst' stores are quite similar in both regions. With the medians, Region B is about £2700 higher than Region A. So Region B stores in the middle of the data are around £2700 more profitable than their counterparts in Region A. Finally, if we look at the upper quartiles, Region B is around £10000 higher. In this case, the 'best' Region B stores are outperforming their counterparts in Region A by this amount. We also see that the coefficient of skewness is higher in Region B, confirming more of a skew in store profits in this region.

To summarise, stores in Region B tend to be more profitable than those in Region A. However, in both regions there is considerable variability in profitability. Clearly we do not know the reasons for these differences. It could be that stores in Region B are better managed; or have a higher turnover; or are located in a more affluent area. Although we can use management statistics to paint a detailed picture, such analysis typically raises questions that require further data collection and further analysis to answer. Such statistics, however, do help management decide on the questions they want answered.

Progress Check 4.8

In Exercise 8 at the end of Chapter 3 data was provided for two samples in respect of users of a sports centre before and after a media campaign. The data is contained in filename 3X–8.Using the raw data, calculate appropriate statistics and use these to highlight key changes that have taken place since the media campaign.

Try not to refer back to the diagrams you produced for this data but use only the statistics.

Solution is given on p 575.

Calculating statistics for aggregated data

The methods we have developed for calculating management statistics have all been applied to a set of raw data – where we had access to the individual values in the data set. Frequently this will not be the case; we may only have data which has already been aggregated in some way. This often occurs when we are using secondary data. Consider the frequency distribution we developed in Chapter 3 relating to Region A stores, which we reproduce as Table 4.6.

Assume that this data has simply been presented to us as managers. We do not have access to the raw data but, for obvious reasons, we wish to obtain a statistical description of the distribution. Clearly, the formulae we have developed will not work, since they were based on the availability of the raw data. For the mean, for example, we cannot now add all the individual data items together and divide by 113 as we do not know the individual data values. We must adapt our formula accordingly.

Table 4.6   Frequency tabulation: stores' profits

Interval			
Lower class limit (£s)		Upper class limit (£s)	Region A stores frequency	Region B stores frequency
−20 000	<	−10 000	1	0
−10 000	<	0	13	4
0	<	10 000	56	58
10 000	<	20 000	22	21
20 000	<	30 000	5	13
30 000	<	40 000	6	11
40 000	<	50 000	5	7
50 000	<	70 000	5	7
Total			113	121

The mean

Since we do not know the individual values, we must make a simplifying assumption to allow the calculation of this statistic: that the observations in a particular class or interval all take the same value and that that value is the mid-point value in the interval. This may sound unreasonable until you realise that, particularly for intervals with a large frequency, we can logically expect items with a value at the bottom of the interval to be compensated for by those with values at the top. So, for the last interval, for example, the mid-point will be £60000. Since we are assuming all data items (five) in this interval take this value, the sum of these five items will then be five times £60000 or £300000. We can duplicate this arithmetic for the other intervals, as shown in Table 4.7.

So our estimated total of all the values in the data set is £1390000. Given that we have 113 data items, the mean can then be estimated as:

$$\text{Mean} = \frac{1\,390\,000}{113} = 12\,300.88$$

Notice that this is an *estimate* of the actual value of £12981.2 calculated from the raw data. This calculation can be summarised as the formula:

$$\text{Mean} = \frac{\Sigma fm}{\Sigma f}$$

where m is the mid-point for each interval and f the frequency of observations in that interval.

Progress Check 4.9

Using this formula, calculate the mean for the Region B data shown in Table 4.6.

Solution is given on p 576.

Table 4.7 Calculations for the mean

Interval			Region A		
Lower class limit (£s)		Lower class limit (£s)	Frequency	Mid-point	Mid-point x frequency
−20000	<	−10000	1	−15000	−15000
−10000	<	0	13	−5000	−65000
0	<	10000	56	5000	280000
10000	<	20000	22	15000	330000
20000	<	30000	5	25000	125000
30000	<	40000	6	35000	210000
40000	<	50000	5	45000	225000
50000	<	70000	5	60000	300000
Total			113		1390000

The standard deviation

A similar formula can be developed for calculating the standard deviation for aggregated data:

$$\sqrt{\frac{\Sigma fm^2}{\Sigma f} - \left(\frac{\Sigma fm}{\Sigma f}\right)^2}$$

The formula looks complex but simply requires us to square the interval midpoint (m^2) and multiply by the frequency. Note that the second part of the expression (to be subtracted) is simply the mean value squared. Using Table 4.7 and calculating Σfm^2 as 45500000000, we obtain the standard deviation for Region A as 15853.8. Again we note that this is an estimate of the actual value for the raw data.

Progress Check 4.10

Calculate the standard deviation for Region B using the aggregated data.

Solution is given on p 576.

It must be remembered that such statistics based on aggregated data are only estimates of the 'true' figures based on the raw data and should be used with a degree of caution. In this case we have calculated such statistics from the aggregated data even though we have the raw data available. We have done this to emphasise the differences that will occur. In practice, of course, you would not do this. If you have the raw data then you will use it for any statistical calculations. Frequently, however, you may not have the raw data but only the aggregated data (perhaps because it has been obtained from published sources, where raw data is not available) and will have to use the frequency table to estimate the statistical measures you are interested in.

The median and quartiles

The median and quartiles can also be estimated from the frequency table. In this case we require the *cumulative* frequencies as shown in Table 4.8.

We then need to determine the interval which will contain the middle value. Given that technically we require data item 57 (since this is the middle of 113 numbers) we see from the cumulative frequencies that this will fall somewhere in the interval 0 < 10 000. We can then apply a formula to estimate the median value:

$$\text{Median} = \text{LCL} + (\text{MI} - \text{CF})\frac{\text{CW}}{\text{F}}$$

where:

LCL   is the lower class limit of the interval in which the median item occurs;

MI   is the median item;

CF   is the cumulative frequency up to the median item interval;

CW   is the width of the median item interval;

F   is the frequency of observations in the median item interval.

Table 4.8   Cumulative frequency

Interval			Region A	
Lower class limit (£s)		Upper class limit (£s)	Frequency	Cumulative frequency
−20 000	<	−10 000	1	1
−10 000	<	0	13	14
0	<	10 000	56	70
10 000	<	20 000	22	92
20 000	<	30 000	5	97
30 000	<	40 000	6	103
40 000	<	50 000	5	108
50 000	<	70 000	5	113
Total			113	

The corresponding numerical values will then be:

$$\text{Median} = 0 + (57 - 14)\,\frac{10\,000}{56}$$

$$= 0 + 7679 = 7679$$

giving a median value of £7679. Once again this is only an estimate of the actual value based on the raw data. If the formula appears to be nothing more than black magic just consider what we are actually doing. We know the median value occurs in this interval, which is of £10 000. We know therefore that the median must be at least equal to the lower value of this interval (£0). But there are 56 data items in this interval. One of them represents the median. Once again, given that we do not know the actual data items, we assume that they are equally spread over the interval (hence 10 000/56). To determine which of these items we require we must take into account the items from earlier intervals (since the median is found in principle by counting along the data from the first item). Hence the (57 − 14).

Progress Check 4.11

Estimate the median for Region B and compare it against the value for the raw data calculated earlier.

Solution is given on p 576.

The same formula is readily adapted to estimate the lower and upper quartiles for an aggregated data set. Since the lower quartile occurs 25 per cent of the way through an ordered data set we need to locate the lower quartile item rather than the median item. Otherwise the procedure outlined for using the median formula can be used in exactly the same way. Naturally, the upper quartile can also be found by adapting the formula.

Progress Check 4.12

Use the adapted formula to estimate the lower and upper quartiles for Region A.

Solution is given on p 577.

Index numbers

Finally, in this chapter we return to the idea of an average and look at a special type of average: an *index*. In its simplest form an index is a different form of a percentage. Consider a product that you might be thinking of buying, say, a new car. Last year the showroom price of the car might have been £18 750. This year the same car – assuming the same model, features and so on – would cost £19 250.

Progress Check 4.13

By how much has the price of the car changed? What is this change as a percentage?

While you can pull out the calculator and determine both the absolute and percentage change in the price, it would be useful to be able to see this at a glance. Constructing a *simple* index of the price will enable us to do this. Let us take last year's price as our reference point – known in index number terms as the base period. We arbitrarily set the price in this year to 100 (not £100 or 100% but simply 100, without units of measurement). The price in the second year can then be expressed as a proportion of the base-period price. We have:

$$\frac{19\,250}{18\,750} = 1.027 \text{ (to 3 decimal places)}$$

We then multiply this by 100 to provide an index of 102.7. What does this index value mean? It indicates that from an index of 100 last year the car price has increased to an index of 102.7 this year. Effectively the price of the car has increased by 2.7 per cent (hence the reason for choosing 100 as the base index value). A simple index then allows a ready comparison of percentage change in the variable. Clearly we could calculate an index for the price in Year 3, Year 4 and so on simply by taking the price in that year, dividing by the price in the base period and multiplying by 100. One point to note is that we chose to base our index in the first year. Although this is common practice, the choice of base period can be somewhat arbitrary. We could equally have chosen to set the base period in the second year. This would give an index for the base of 100 and an index for the first year of:

$$\frac{18\,750}{19\,250} \times 100 = 97.4$$

We would now conclude that the price of the car in the first year is 2.6 per cent below that in the second (you will appreciate, of course, why the two percentages are different for each choice of base year: if you don't, go back and read the appropriate section in Chapter 2). It should also be noted that the choice of base period can distort a long time series of index calculations. If the period we chose as base was abnormal or untypical in some way, we might produce a distorted view of the index trends over time.

Main equity markets

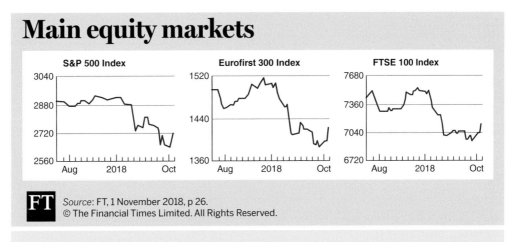

Share price indices, like these, are very common and receive considerable media exposure.

Deflating using index numbers

One of the common uses of index numbers which measure price changes is to *deflate* a financial time series. You may remember that in Chapter 2 we stressed the importance of the difference between money value and real value.

Table 4.9 shows average weekly earnings for those in employment in the UK from 2000 to 2017 (the latest available at the Main equity markets time this book was published). We see that earnings were £313 in 2000 rising to £507 by 2017, an increase of over 60 per cent. However, as we all know, prices also rise over time – inflation – so the money we have won't necessarily buy as much. From a management perspective the effects of inflation on financial time series can be distorting and misleading. For this reason, it is usually necessary to adjust financial data to allow for inflation. This is known as *deflating* a time series.

Table 4.9 also presents the consumer price index (CPI) as a composite or aggregate index showing the general level of retail prices. We'll look at aggregate indices in the next section. The CPI for the UK is currently set with a base period of the year 2000 (with the index taking a value of 100). We note that prices have risen between 2000 and 2017. Effectively we wish to calculate the real value of the average income figures (that is, to adjust them for inflation over the period). The calculation is:

$$\text{Real value} = \text{Money value} \times \frac{100}{\text{Price index}}$$

If we perform the calculation for 2001, for example, we then have:

$$\text{Real value} = 329 \times \frac{100}{101.2} = £325$$

Progress Check 4.14

Provide an interpretation of this result in the context of the problem.

Table 4.9 UK Average weekly earnings and the CPI

Year	Earnings £s	CPI 2000 = 100
2000	313	100.0
2001	329	101.2
2002	340	102.5
2003	350	103.9
2004	366	105.2
2005	382	107.4
2006	400	109.9
2007	420	112.5
2008	436	116.5
2009	435	119.1
2010	445	123.0
2011	455	128.5
2012	461	132.2
2013	466	135.5
2014	472	137.6
2015	484	137.6
2016	495	138.5
2017	507	142.2

Some care should be taken in terms of interpreting such calculations – they are a frequent source of misunderstanding and confusion. The figure of £325 is interpreted as the real value of the money sum of £329. That is, the money sum of £329 that we had in 2001 was actually 'worth' £325 in terms of what it would have bought in 2000 (the base period we are using). We are saying that the £329 in 2001 and the hypothetical sum of £325 base 2000 are effectively the same in terms of their purchasing power.

Progress Check 4.15

Compare the real value of 2000 income with the income shown for 2005. Calculate the real value of each of the other years' money income.

Table 4.10 UK Average weekly earnings and the CPI

Year	Earnings £s	CPI 2000 = 100	Real AWE £s
2000	313	100.0	313
2001	329	101.2	325
2002	340	102.5	332
2003	350	103.9	337
2004	366	105.2	348
2005	382	107.4	356
2006	400	109.9	364
2007	420	112.5	373
2008	436	116.5	374
2009	435	119.1	365
2010	445	123.0	362
2011	455	128.5	354
2012	461	132.2	349
2013	466	135.5	344
2014	472	137.6	343
2015	484	137.6	352
2016	495	138.5	357
2017	507	142.2	356

Source: Office for National Statistics

We begin to see the use and importance of such deflated data when we examine Table 4.10, which shows both the money income series and the real income series over this period. The money income series shows a generally increasing trend, implying a steadily rising income. From the money income series earnings have risen consistently over this period, showing an increase of almost £200 in money terms from 2000 to 2017. However, Table 4.10 also shows that, at 2000 prices, earnings rose only by about £40 over the same period in real terms. Without deflating the data we might have developed an incorrect view of what has actually happened.

If we are examining any financial series over time then the only reliable way of examining such data is by deflating using an appropriate price index. We will discuss shortly what is meant by 'appropriate'. We should also note that all the real values are now expressed in terms of 2000 prices (since this was the base year for the price index). A different base period would lead to different real values (although the relationship between them would be unchanged).

House of Lords takes aim at Statistics Authority's failure to fix UK prices index

Government swapping between RPI and CPI creates winners and losers, says report

By Delphine Strauss in London

The UK Statistics Authority risks breaching its statutory duty by publishing a widely used measure of inflation that it admits is flawed but refuses to fix, a parliamentary inquiry has concluded. Michael Forsyth, who chairs the Lords economic affairs committee, said that well-documented problems with the way the retail price index was calculated were not merely a "technical debate" but were creating winners and losers by boosting payments to holders of index-linked gilts by £1bn a year, at the exchequer's expense, while pushing up the cost of rail fares and student loans.

UKSA's decision to treat RPI as a legacy measure and make no further improvements to its methodology was "untenable" when the index remained in widespread use and would be embedded in contracts for many years, the committee said in a report published on Thursday. A gap between RPI and the consumer price index — the measure of inflation used for the Bank of England's inflation target — has widened since 2010, an unintended consequence of a tweak in the way the Office for National Statistics collects clothing prices, which exacerbated the RPI's existing upward bias.

In the latest figures, for December, the RPI shows annual inflation at 2.7 per cent, while the

CPI records it at 2.1 per cent. A third measure, the CPIH (which, in common with RPI but unlike CPI, includes a measure of owner occupier housing costs) put annual inflation at 2 per cent. This divergence has encouraged governments to indulge in "index shopping", the committee said, with benefits, tax thresholds and public sector and state pensions all now uprated using the lower CPI measure. RPI is still used, however, to uprate many payments made by the public, including air passenger, alcohol and tobacco duty, regulated rail fares and interest rates on student loans.

The government's chief statistician has argued that, while RPI is acknowledged to be a poor measure of inflation, any proposal to fix its most glaring deficiencies would by law require consultation with the Bank of England and approval from the chancellor, as it would be detrimental to bondholders. . . .

The committee acknowledged the lack of consensus among statisticians on the best way to measure inflation, but said the government should take advice and decide within five years which of the three main indices to adopt as its single official measure in order to bolster public confidence in statistics.

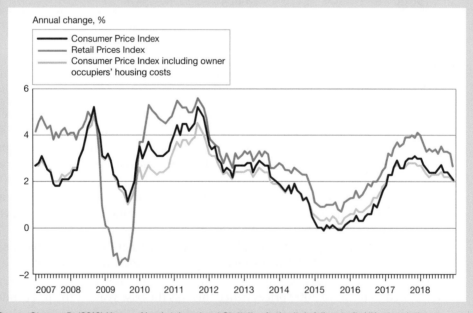

Annual change, %
— Consumer Price Index
— Retail Prices Index
— Consumer Price Index including owner occupiers' housing costs

Source: Strauss, D. (2019) House of Lords takes aim at Statistics Authority's failure to fix UK prices index: government swapping between RPI and CPI creates winners and losers, says report, *Financial Times*, 17 January.
© The Financial Times Limited. All Rights Reserved.

Inflation is an important national and management statistic but its measurement is not straightforward.

Aggregate index numbers

We introduced the idea of an index with the simple index that we calculated for two prices. Another type of index is available: the *aggregate* or *composite index*. In fact we have already encountered such an index: the consumer price index we used in Table 4.9. This is an index of a group of items – a typical basket of goods and services purchased by an average household in this case – rather than a single variable. Such indices are frequently useful in decision making.

Consider the following example. In 2015 an organisation decided to restructure its business by making more use of part-time staff in certain areas: cleaning, catering and secretarial. Over the past few years the finance director has expressed concern about the way the costs associated with these groups of staff appear to have increased. In her view this may have been caused by lack of central management responsibility in negotiating suitable pay scales with part-time staff. You have been asked to investigate and have collected the data shown in Table 4.11 for 2015, when these services were converted to a part-time staff basis, and for 2020, which is the latest year available.

In both cases you have data showing the hourly rate paid to the three types of staff and the number of hours worked by these staff in that year.

Progress Check 4.16

Is there any evidence that the finance director's suspicions are correct and that costs have escalated?

It is clearly difficult to reach a conclusion based on the data as shown. On the one hand hourly rates have increased, but then so have the number of hours worked. We can readily calculate the total cost in each of the two years by multiplying pay rates by the hours worked for the three types of staff:

2015: Total cost = £124 000
2020: Total cost = £169 950

The problem is that, although we conclude part-time wage costs have increased, it is impossible to disentangle the two possible causes: a rise in pay rate and a rise in hours worked. Clearly, from a management perspective, these two possible causes may require different solutions and different control mechanisms. However, if we consider constructing an aggregate index for pay rates this might enable us to determine how important

Table 4.11 Hourly rates and hours worked: part-time staff

	2015		2020	
	Hourly pay rate (£s)	Total hours worked	Hourly pay rate (£s)	Total hours worked
Cleaning	8.00	4000	9.90	5500
Catering	8.50	2000	10.00	2100
Secretarial	12.50	6000	13.50	7000

this factor was in the cost escalation. You should be able to see that simply averaging pay rates for 2015 and comparing this average with that for 2020 would not be appropriate, since a simple average would fail to take into account the differing importance of the three types of staff. Accordingly, we need a *weighted* average. In fact there are two common methods of calculating an aggregate index: the Laspeyres index and the Paasche index.

The Laspeyres index

The first of these is the *Laspeyres index* (pronounced 'Lass-pairs'), which is technically known as a base-date weighted index. Remember that we require an index for pay scales and that we must weight the pay scales by the respective hours worked. The problem is that there are two possible weightings from the table: we could use hours worked in 2015 or hours worked in 2020. The Laspeyres index uses weights from the chosen base period, and here we will choose 2015 as the base. The calculation is then:

$$\frac{\sum P_n W_0}{\sum P_0 W_0} \times 100$$

where:

P	is the variable for which we require an index (pay scales);
W	is the weight we are using (hours worked);
subscript 0	relates to the chosen base year (2015);
subscript n	relates to the year for which we are calculating the index (here 2020).

You see from the formula that we are using the same set of weights to calculate both the top and bottom part of the expression. Any change in the index over time, therefore, must be caused by a change in P between the two periods, since the weights used in the calculation are constant.

A shopping trip with the inflation experts from the ONS

By Chris Giles, Economics Editor

Wild bird seed has been added to the shopping basket to measure inflation, with wallpaper paste removed, but how does the Office for National Statistics make these decisions that reflect the state of Britain today?

Working out the items that should be included in the national shopping basket is a full-time job throughout the year for the statisticians in the commodity review team of the ONS. Some elements of the work are automatic. To measure inflation, statisticians need to know how much people spend in broad categories such as food or leisure pursuits. These weights tally up with the expenditure patterns in the national accounts, and much of the information comes from the annual Living Costs and Food survey, which asks about 5,000 households annually to complete a two-week diary of everything they have bought.

This is high-level stuff, and does not help the statisticians in Newport get to the real nitty-gritty. For example, are the price movements of a kilogram of lamb shoulder sufficiently representative for measuring a leg of lamb or even a fillet of beef? Cost prevents measuring everything. To make these judgments, the commodity review team analyses every part of the shopping basket in detail at least once every five years. The members have to follow some basic rules. If spending on a particular item is more than £400m – equal to about £1 in every £2,000 spent by UK households – there have to be extremely good reasons for it not to appear in the basket. Likewise, few items where spending is lower than £100m appear. Where low-value items appear, it has to be because they represent wider spending categories pretty well. As an example, power drills represent the wider category of electrical tools.

"The selection of these representative items is judgmental," the ONS says, and it is the committee that decides, using information about how easy it is to collect prices for individual items, market research and press reports as an indicator of the current zeitgeist. The decisions are reached by consensus by a small number of statisticians in the commodity review team on the basis of reports written about different sectors throughout the year. The reports bring in outside voices from market research, the people who collect prices every month, and external auditors who examine the price collection process. But the final decisions are taken by the statisticians in the ONS.

Source: Giles, C. (2014) A shopping trip with the inflation experts from the ONS, FT.com, 13 March.
© The Financial Times Limited. All Rights Reserved.

The collection of prices and weights to measure inflation is complex but critical to the reliability of inflation statistics.

Progress Check 4.17

Calculate a comparable index value for 2020 using the formula. Comment on the result.

The calculation becomes:

$$\frac{\sum P_n W_0}{\sum P_0 W_0} \times 100 = \frac{140\,600}{124\,000} \times 100 = 113.4$$

That is, the pay scale index for 2020 is 113.4. Given that by default the index for 2015 is 100 then this implies that – on average – pay scales have risen by 13.4 per cent over this period. In 2020 we would have paid 13.4 per cent more for the same number of hours that we did in 2015. It is important to appreciate exactly what this figure shows – and what it does not. Given its method of calculation, we can interpret this value in the following way: if we had kept the hours worked at the 2015 level then, in 2020, the pay cost would have been 13.4 per cent higher than in 2015. The pay scales have been weighted by the relative importance of the three categories.

Updating the Laspeyres index

Naturally, having gone to the trouble of calculating a pay index for 2020, it seems likely that we will wish to use the index to keep track of pay costs over time. Consider that in 2021 pay scales are: cleaning £10.00; catering £10.50; secretarial £14.00.

Progress Check 4.18

Calculate a Laspeyres index for 2021.

The formula indicates that all we need to do is to calculate a new weighted total for 2021:

$$\frac{\sum P_n W_0}{\sum P_0 W_0} \times 100 = \frac{145\,000}{124\,000} \times 100 = 116.9$$

and we see that the pay index for 2021 is 116.9 (again based on the assumption that hours worked is at the 2015 level). Updating the Laspeyres index is then relatively straightforward – calculating a new weighted total for the current year. One final point about the Laspeyres index: we chose 2015 as the base year; in practice any year can be chosen as the base – it is not necessary for this choice to be the first year in the series. We could have chosen 2020 as the base: this would then have been the base period which supplied the set of weights we would have used in all the calculations.

The Paasche index

The Laspeyres index used a set of base weights in the calculations. It will be evident that, over time, these base weights may become less and less representative of the situation. It seems sensible, then, to consider using more up-to-date weights for the pay-scale index. Such a calculation is available through the Paasche (pronounced 'Pash') index, which uses *current* rather than base weights. The appropriate formula is now:

$$\frac{\Sigma P_n W_n}{\Sigma P_0 W_n} \times 100$$

Notice that once again it is the P variable that is allowed to change in the calculation while the weights remain constant – this time for the current year. The calculation is then:

$$\frac{\Sigma P_n W_n}{\Sigma P_0 W_n} \times 100 = \frac{169\,950}{149\,350} \times 100 = 113.8$$

and we have a pay scale index of 113.8 for 2020. Note that this is a slightly different result from the Laspeyres. The reason is that we are now using the 2020 weights (hours) for the 2015 calculation. The result implies that, based on the 2020 staffing levels, pay costs have risen by 13.8 per cent since 2015. The Paasche index has the advantage of showing the index based on the current (2020) hours worked. However, one of the drawbacks of the Paasche appears if we now move to 2021 and wish to calculate the appropriate index. First of all – given that 2021 is now the current year – we require weights for 2021. Second, to perform the calculation we must now recalculate both the top and bottom part of the equation.

You may well be left with the question: which type of index should I calculate? As ever, the answer will depend on circumstances. However, we can categorise the general features of the two methods:

● The Laspeyres index is easier to calculate for a long series of data. This is because it uses a single set of weights in all the calculations, whereas the Paasche requires the calculation for each period to use that period's weights.

● The Laspeyres tends to be easier in terms of data collection since it requires only one set of weights. The Paasche is relatively 'data-hungry', requiring a set of weights for each period in the series. For more complex series this can be both time-consuming and costly.

● The weights used in the Laspeyres series will gradually become out of date and hence the series will be less and representative of the current situation. This will affect some variables more than others. Consider a consumer price index. This will need to reflect as accurately as possible actual consumer purchases. Think back only a few years and you will note that a number of items that would appear today in such patterns would not have been available: Kindle e-readers, tablet computers and smartphones would not have appeared in the weights used.

● Linked to the weights, the Laspeyres method will tend to overestimate the effect of price increases. The reason for this is simple. In terms of price increases, consumers (other things being equal) will buy less of a product that experiences such an increase.

The relative importance of such an item in their consumption will decrease and hence the lower will be the weight of this item. However, the Laspeyres method uses base period weights, which do not change over time and hence will not reflect this pattern.

Overall, then, the Laspeyres method is easier, quicker and less costly but potentially less accurate, particularly in times of rapid change. Finally, we should also point out that although our examples have been in terms of prices, it is possible – and common – to produce other types of index numbers. One frequent example is an index of quantity rather than price (in a production organisation, for example). In such a case the variable to alter in the formulae would be quantity and we would choose some appropriate weight for the problem.

Worked example

Finally, in this chapter let's look at a worked example to bring together some of the techniques we've looked at. Table 4.12 shows individual income before tax for selected tax years in the UK (2016 was the latest available when this edition of the textbook was being produced). We've been tasked with producing a short summary report highlighting what's happened to individual income over this period.

The first thing we notice is that inflation over this period has been around 40 per cent so we need to deflate the data using the CPI figures to show real income otherwise our analysis may be distorted by inflation. Table 4.13 shows the results (you may want to confirm the calculations for yourself for extra practice).

From Table 4.12 we get the impression that individual incomes have generally risen – although at different rates depending on which part of the distribution we look at. Mean income, for example, has risen by around 22 per cent over the period while median income has risen by around 18 per cent. However, looking at the deflated data in Table 4.13 gives a different picture. We see that in real terms mean income has risen but by only 12 per cent once we strip out the effects of inflation and median income by around 9 per cent. We can also comment on what's happened to individuals in different parts of the distribution. In summary:

● Individual incomes, in money terms, have generally increased over this period although at different rates in different parts of the distribution.

● Taking inflation into account, individual incomes show a much more modest increase over this period, typically around 1 per cent a year.

Table 4.12   Individual income before tax

Tax Year ending	Lower quartile	Median	Upper quartile	Mean	CPI 2000 = 100
2000	£9 260	£14 400	£22 300	£19 600	100.0
2006	£10 800	£17 100	£27 400	£24 300	109.1
2011	£12 700	£19 500	£30 900	£27 400	127.5
2016	£16 100	£23 200	£35 600	£33 400	138.6

Source: Office for National Statistics

Data file T4-12

Table 4.13   Individual income before tax at 2015 prices

Tax year ending	Lower quartile	Median	Upper quartile	Mean
2000	£9 260	£14 400	£22 300	£19 600
2006	£9 897	£15 670	£25 108	£22 267
2011	£9 959	£15 291	£24 231	£21 486
2016	£11 617	£16 740	£25 687	£24 100

- Lower quartile incomes show the largest increase in real terms.
- Real incomes actually fell between 2006 and 2011.
- Income distribution in each period is positively skewed, with a relatively small number of individuals on high incomes.

Summary

In this chapter we have introduced some of the more common management statistics available. We have tried to develop an understanding of how such statistics can be used in a management context by examining their methods of calculation as well as their direct interpretation. It is once again important to appreciate that such statistics are potentially valuable sources of information about some situation or variable but they do have the capacity to mislead if not evaluated and interpreted in the correct manner. In practice it may be appropriate to calculate a variety of statistics for some problem and then to consider which of these presents a reasonably fair and accurate description.

Exercises

In addition to the exercises shown here you should return to the exercises in Chapter 3 and, where appropriate, calculate the statistics introduced in this chapter for each data set. Compare the information obtained from the statistics with that obtained from the diagrams produced for Chapter 3.

1   For the two data sets shown below calculate the mean and standard deviation and comment on the relationship.

Set 1	Set 2
10	100
20	200
30	300
40	400
50	500

2   For the data in Table 4.01, plot the real and money values over time on the same graph. Comment on the potential for misleading the user of money values.

3 In the Laspeyres index in this chapter we used 2015 as the base year. Choose 2020 as the base year instead and recalculate the Laspeyres series for 2015, 2020 and 2021. Comment on these values compared with the index base 2015.

4 Consider the consumer price index which is published by your own government (or its statistical agency). Find out:

(a) what weights are used in the calculation of the price index;

(b) how these weights are obtained;

(c) whether the calculations follow the Laspeyres or Paasche method.

How 'reliable' do you think the price index is as a measure of how inflation is affecting the consumer over time?

5 Table 4.14 shows the age distribution of males and females in England and Wales at the time of their marriage, from 1981 to 2015 (the latest available when this book was written).

Using the data calculate for each gender:

(a) the mean

(b) the median

(c) the standard deviation

(d) the lower and upper quartiles

(e) the IQR

(f) the coefficients of variation and skewness.

Use these statistics to comment on similarities and differences between the genders and over time. Comment on the implications for the business strategy of a bridal/wedding company.

Table 4.14 Age distribution at marriage, England and Wales

Age at marriage	Males					Females				
	1981	1991	2001	2011	2015	1981	1991	2001	2011	2015
16–19	18542	4632	1945	850	512	63343	17738	6896	2924	1516
20–24	136042	75331	24651	19318	13419	149052	107028	45317	34154	24153
25–29	85391	100891	67934	62456	57772	58183	87244	73799	74927	71187
30–34	42696	50403	61409	59579	58437	30122	38425	51865	53944	54481
35–39	22612	25132	36397	35785	32812	17174	19591	29144	28862	26964
40–44	13700	17881	20475	24380	21908	10837	14164	16528	19519	18076
45–49	9755	11503	12782	17274	17864	7637	9587	10523	14293	15793
50–54	7107	7426	10167	11346	14171	5205	5304	7548	9308	12045
55–59	5647	4938	5860	7327	9264	3509	2679	3552	5205	6982
60–69	7126	5877	5408	8147	9554	5182	3507	3018	4725	6000
70–79	2923	2309	1819	2178	2707	1598	1290	851	1076	1575
80 and over	432	433	380	486	570	131	199	156	183	211
Total	351973	306756	249227	249126	238990	351973	306756	249227	249120	238983

Source: ONS

Data file 4-14

6 The leisure services committee of a local authority has seen its budget decline over the last few years and is currently having to consider closing a number of its leisure facilities – sports halls, small parks, museums and so on. One closure being considered is that of a small branch library in an outlying village. As a preliminary aspect of the decision some data has been collected on the number of people using the library and its facilities:

No. of people using the library per day	No. of days
fewer than 10	5
10 < 20	12
20 < 30	28
30 < 40	44
40 < 50	50
50 < 75	30
75 or more	8

Calculate suitable measures of average and dispersion for this data. Comment on the usage of the library.

7 The data shown in Table 4.15 shows average weekly earnings for all adults, weekly rate of unemployment benefit for single adults and the consumer price index for the UK for the period 2000–17.

Table 4.15   Earnings, unemployment benefit, retail price index: UK 2000–17

Year	Average weekly earnings £s	Weekly unemployment benefit	CPI 2000 = 100
2000	321	52.20	100.0
2001	329	53.05	101.2
2002	340	53.95	102.5
2003	350	54.65	103.9
2004	366	55.65	105.2
2005	382	56.20	107.4
2006	400	57.45	109.9
2007	420	59.15	112.5
2008	436	60.50	116.5
2009	435	64.30	119.1
2010	445	65.45	123.0
2011	445	67.50	128.5
2012	461	71.00	132.2
2013	466	71.70	135.5
2014	472	72.40	137.6
2015	484	73.10	137.6
2016	495	73.10	138.5
2017	507	73.10	142.2

Source: Office for National Statistics, DWP.

Data file 4-15

Using this data comment on any trends in earnings and benefits. Do you think the CPI is the most appropriate index for deflating the unemployment benefit series?

8   A retail organisation has recently been investigating customer spending patterns at two of its stores, Store A and Store B, and has obtained the following data:

	Store A (£s)	Store B (£s)
Mean spending per customer	12.25	30.05
Median spending per customer	10.88	29.91
Standard deviation	7.79	7.77
Lower quartile	6.34	25.04
Upper quartile	17.43	35.32

Using these statistics, and any others you can derive, draft a short management report summarising the implications of this data. The Store A figures were based on a representative sample of 500 customers and the Store B figures on 350 customers.

9   The data below shows quartile and median income for UK taxpayers before and after paying income tax for selected years. Analyse and comment on the data.

Tax year	Total income before tax			Total income after tax		
	Lower quartile £	Median £	Upper quartile £	Lower quartile £	Median £	Upper quartile £
1999–00	9260	14400	22300	8490	12500	18800
2000–01	9280	14800	23000	8510	12900	19400
2001–02	9910	15500	24300	9120	13600	20600
2002–03	10000	15800	24700	9230	13800	20900
2003–04	10100	16000	25100	9290	14000	21100
2004–05	10300	16400	26100	9470	14400	22000
2005–06	10800	17100	27400	9930	14900	23100
2006–07	11200	17700	28400	10300	15400	23800
2007–08	11800	18500	29500	10800	16100	24800
2008–09						
2009–10	12900	19600	30900	11800	17200	26300
2010–11	12700	19500	30900	11700	17100	26300
2011–12	13500	20300	32100	12500	18000	27500
2012–13	14200	21000	32900	13200	18700	28200
2013–14	15000	21900	33900	14000	19500	29300
2014–15	15500	22400	34500	14500	20000	29900
2015–16	16100	23200	35600	15100	20800	30900

Source: Office for National Statistics

Note: Data for 2008–9 is not available

10 A local residential community has been complaining to the chief of police about speeding traffic through their area. Residents have complained that vehicles driving through the community have not been observing the speed limit, which officially is 50 kilometres per hour (kph). The police force undertook a vehicle speed survey to check the residents' claims. Recently they launched a major anti-speeding campaign in the residential area and they also undertook a vehicle speed survey after the anti-speeding campaign. The results from the two surveys are shown in the table.

	Survey results before the anti-speeding campaign	Survey results after the anti-speeding campaign
No. of vehicles in the sample	311	409
Mean vehicle speed (kph)	63.2	54.8
Standard deviation (kph)	15.2	11.7
Median vehicle speed (kph)	59.2	54.1
Lower quartile vehicle speed (kph)	48.1	47.4
Upper quartile vehicle speed (kph)	75.3	64.6
Minimum vehicle speed (kph)	45	44
Maximum vehicle speed (kph)	111	112

(a) Using the statistics in the table, highlight the key differences in vehicle traffic speed before and after the anti-speeding campaign. Explain your results in detail.

(b) What information would you want about the two surveys?

(c) Has the anti-speeding campaign been successful at reducing speeding traffic? Explain your answer.

5

Probability and Probability Distributions

Learning objectives

By the end of this chapter you should be able to:

- explain the basic rules of probability
- apply probability to typical business problems
- use the Binomial distribution
- use the Normal distribution

This chapter is concerned with introducing the basic principles of probability and discussing how such principles relate to business and to management decision making. Regardless of the organisations with which you are familiar and regardless of the nature and extent of your own management experience, you will appreciate that all business organisations operate in an uncertain environment. Uncertainty exists in a variety of forms: will the company's new product be popular with customers; will we win the new contract; will we gain the export order we have bid for; will our employees take industrial action next week? Doubtless you can add to the list of typical uncertainties yourself. *Probability* is a way of trying to quantify such uncertainties and we shall begin to see in this chapter how probability can be used as an aid to management decision making. For it is in the area of decision making that such uncertainties cause problems for the manager. If we knew for certain what the outcome(s) of a particular managerial decision would be, then we could rationally choose between the alternative decisions available to us. Consider a firm assessing the price to charge for one of its products. The manager responsible knows that, other things being equal, a price reduction is likely to attract more customers and that, logically, the larger the price reduction the larger the likely number of customers attracted to the product. The difficulty for the manager lies in assessing these likelihoods – they are not guaranteed outcomes. There are too many other factors which might impact on the outcome to offer such guarantees: the effect of advertising, customer attitudes, fashions, competitors' strategies.

Somehow, the manager has to assess such likelihoods and reach an appropriate decision. In many cases the principles of probability will help. Equally, probability lies at the heart of market research – an important activity for most organisations today. Private sector organisations frequently commission market research in the context of customer attitudes to price, design, availability, quality and so on. Public sector organisations are increasingly involved in market research: what do patients think of the health services provided, what do local authority 'customers' think of the refuse collection services, the municipal leisure facilities and so on. The principles of such market research are that we collect data on a sample – of customers perhaps – and analyse this using some of the techniques already introduced. So, for example, we might undertake market research on a sample of our customers and determine that, say, 40 per cent of our customers would increase their purchases of our product if we reduced the price by 10 per cent. The difficulty for the manager is that this information relates only to the sample. What the manager is primarily interested in is the population – all customers in this instance. Somehow we have to be able to transfer our conclusions based on the sample analysis to the entire population. This can also be achieved through the application of the probability principles that we shall introduce.

The concept of probability and its basic calculation often seem straightforward and no more than common sense. For example, suppose I asked you to guess my birthday – that is on which day of the year my birthday occurred – and I wanted to figure out how likely it was that you'd guess correctly. Some simple logic would be: there are 365 days in the year and my birthday falls on one of them. In the absence of any other information you'd simply have to guess which day in the year was my birthday and given you only get one guess then the probability of guessing correctly would be 1/365. However, for decision making we're rarely interested in situations that are so simple. The problem is that when we're calculating more complex probabilities the end result often appears intuitively 'wrong' and as a result managers not familiar with probability may not use this information in their decision making, with the obvious consequences. Consider a slightly different scenario. You're in a group of 50 people (perhaps your office where you work or one of the classes you're taking). What's the probability that two (or more) people in the room share the same birthday – their birthdays are on the same day of the year?

Common sense might run as follows. There are still 365 days in the year but we now have 50 people (and potentially 50 birthdays) so the probability is something like 50/365 (or 0.14 or 14 per cent) – pretty low. In fact, the answer is 97 per cent! That is, in a group of 50 people there's a 97 per cent chance that at least two of them have the same birthday (you'll be able to work out the answer yourself after this chapter). Tell that to most people and they won't believe you – it simply doesn't look 'right'. Let's look at a business problem to appreciate the implications. A company manufactures a tablet laptop that comprises 100 different parts or components. Its suppliers guarantee that the probability of any one part failing in the first 12 months is no more than 1 per cent, or 0.01. What percentage of tablet laptops will be returned by customers in the first 12 months because they've developed a fault? Think about this for a few moments.

You may have said 1 per cent (many people would) – after all there's a 99 per cent probability that each component will be OK. In fact the correct answer (again as we'll see later) is 37 per cent – that is over a third of tablet laptops will be returned as faulty in the first year. Doesn't seem 'right' does it? And as a result many managers wouldn't believe the result and wouldn't act on it. But the implication is major – the company will incur large costs in terms of replacements or repairs; the company's reputation will suffer; it's likely to attract adverse media coverage, and market share may be hit. And all of this was avoidable if only we'd acted upon the probability answer.

Terminology

Like most topics, probability has its own terminology and to help introduce this we'll use a simple scenario. A large organisation has realised that as part of its overall strategy it needs to change the organisational culture in the context of customers and service quality. Bluntly, the organisation has realised that many of its staff are not fully committed to providing a quality service to the customer on time and every time. Accordingly, the organisation is considering an organisation-wide training and development programme to raise the awareness of staff in terms of the importance of quality service. However, the organisation is concerned about the reception such a programme might get from staff and has decided to pilot the programme amongst a small number of employees to gauge their reaction before introducing the programme throughout the organisation.

It is important, though, for a cross-section of employees to be exposed to the pilot programme. It is also important that attendance on the pilot programme is not restricted to those who can be spared for a few hours from their normal duties. Accordingly, it has been decided to choose a small number of employees to attend the pilot programme at random from all those employed by the organisation. The words 'at random' imply a selection which is unpredictable and without any particular pattern or guidance. The organisation's employees can be categorised by gender and by age, as shown in Table 5.1.

Experiments, outcomes, events

An *experiment* is some activity that takes place. In our example the experiment would relate to the selection of an employee at random from all those employed by the organisation. An *outcome* is one of the possible results of the experiment. In this example there are outcomes representing the possible characteristics of the person chosen – we would identify six different outcomes, the six combinations of gender and age group. Note that the definition of the outcomes may vary even though the experiment does not. We might, for example, define just two outcomes: the gender of the person chosen. Finally, an *event* is the specifically defined outcome(s) that is of particular interest to us. We might define the specific event of interest as selecting a female employee under 25 years of age.

Table 5.1   Employees by gender and by age

	Age (years)			
	< 25	25 < 46	45 or over	Total
Male	132	297	206	635
Female	108	152	311	571
Total	240	449	517	1 206

Measuring probability

By definition, a probability is the likelihood or chance of a defined event occurring and can take a value between zero and one. Zero indicates literally that the event has no chance of occurring, while a probability of one indicates that it is certain to occur. In general, there are three ways of obtaining such a probability. The first is theoretical, where, using mathematics and/or logic, we can calculate or derive a probability. The second is empirical, where we directly observe a probability. The third is subjective, where we have an opinion, or hunch, about the chance of something happening. Consider the experiment of rolling a dice which has six sides, with each side showing one number from one to six and each side showing a different number.

Progress Check 5.1

If we define an event as the number six showing, what is the probability of this event happening? How do you know? Would you class this as theoretical, empirical or subjective?

Solution is given on p 577.

In its most basic form a probability can be calculated as:

$$P(\text{Event}) = \frac{\text{Number of ways the event could occur}}{\text{Total number of outcomes}}$$

where P(Event) is the standard form of notation indicating that we require the probability of the event defined. In the context of our Progress Check example we would have:

$$P(6) = \frac{1}{6}$$

That is, there is a probability of 1/6 that when throwing a die we would get a six. Consider carefully the implications of this. It does not mean that if we were to throw such a die six times then on exactly one of those occasions we would throw a six. It is, rather, an indication of a theoretical probability – one that in the long run we would expect to observe (and note that we do not define exactly what is meant by 'long run' in this context). In our organisation example, comparable probabilities are also obtained. If we require, for example, the probability of selecting at random an employee who is male we have:

$$P(\text{Male}) = 635/1206 = 0.527 \text{ (to 3 decimal places)}$$

Mutually exclusive events

Two events are said to be *mutually exclusive* when they cannot occur simultaneously. For example, we define the experiment of choosing an employee at random. We define three events: Event A the person is male; Event B the person is female; Event C the person is under 25 years. It is clear that Events A and B are mutually exclusive: they cannot happen simultaneously. However, Events A and C are *not* mutually exclusive: they could happen at the same time (as could B and C).

Independent and conditional events

An *independent* event is one where the probability of the event occurring is not affected by other events. A *conditional* event is one whose probability is so affected. It seems reasonable to suppose, for example, that the probability that a person buys this book is independent of the probability of the person being left-handed. That is, the probability of a person buying this book is independent of whether they are left- or right-handed. The probability of a person buying this book, however, may well be conditional on which type of course they are taking at college or university. That is, the probability of a person buying this book is affected by the type of course they are taking. We shall see shortly why it is important to distinguish between conditional and independent events.

Collectively exhaustive events

A group of events are said to be *collectively exhaustive* if they encompass all possible outcomes from the experiment. Consider the experiment of choosing an employee at random. We define two events: the person is male, the person is female. Clearly the two events are collectively exhaustive since one of the two events must occur. This is frequently useful in probability calculations. We know that:

$$P(\text{Male}) = 0.527$$

and because they are collectively exhaustive we know that:

$$P(\text{Male}) + P(\text{Female}) = 1$$

Hence

$$P(\text{Female}) = 1 - P(\text{Male}) = 0.473$$

This is known as the *complement* of the defined event.

Most of us are highly likely to get probability wrong

By John Kay

The Monty Hall problem is named after the host of a 1970s quiz show, *Let's Make a Deal*. The successful contestant chooses from three closed boxes. One contains the keys to a car and the other two a picture of a goat. The choice made, Monty opens one of the other doors to reveal – a goat. He taunts the guest to change the decision. Should the guest switch to the other closed box?

When the solution was published in an American magazine, thousands of readers – including professors of statistics – alleged an error. Paul Erdös, the great mathematician, reputedly died still musing on the Monty Hall problem. But the answer is, indeed, yes: you should change.

This is not the only case where intuition does not correspond to the mathematics of probability. One person in a 1,000 suffers from a rare disease. A friend has just tested positive for this illness and the test gives a correct diagnosis in 99 per cent of cases. How likely is it that your friend has the disease? Not at all likely. In random groups of 1,000 people an average of 10 would display false positives and only one would be correctly diagnosed with the disease. But most people, including most doctors, think otherwise. "The human mind," said science writer Stephen Jay Gould, "did not evolve to deal with probabilities."

Last month, the General Medical Council struck off Professor Sir Roy Meadow, the paediatrician, from the medical register. He had given misleading evidence in the criminal prosecution of Sally Clarke, whose two infants died in their cots. When Mrs Clarke was charged with their murder, Sir Roy told the jury that the chances of two successive cot deaths in the one family was "one in 73m".

But although the disciplinary committee heard evidence from distinguished statisticians, it does not appear that they understood the application of probability theory to such cases any better than Sir Roy. The committee found that he had underestimated the incidence of cot deaths, and that he had not taken account of genetic and environmental factors that mean a household that experiences one cot death is more likely than average to suffer another. But even if you recognise these effects, his key conclusion remains valid. It is unlikely that such an accident would have happened at all. It is very unlikely indeed that such an accident could have happened twice in the same family.

Of course it is unlikely. The events that give rise to criminal cases are always unlikely, otherwise the courts would be unable to deal with the backlog. If Osama bin Laden is ever brought to justice, the question will not be "is it likely that two aircraft hit the World Trade Center on September 11?" – to which the answer is no – but "given that two aircraft did hit the World Trade Center on September 11, is it likely that bin Laden was responsible?" Confusion of these two separate issues has become known as "the prosecutor's fallacy".

A cot death in a family increases the probability that there will be another, but a murder in a family may well increase the probability of another murder by even more: wicked parents may continue to be wicked. Sir Roy might have been right to conclude that two cot deaths were more suspicious than one. But the Court of Appeal, releasing Mrs Clarke, was certainly right to have concluded that this statistical evidence could never, on its own, establish guilt beyond reasonable doubt.

You should not trust doctors, or lawyers, with probabilities; and be very hesitant about trusting yourself.

Understanding probability isn't as easy as it looks as this article explains.

The multiplication rule

We have seen how we can calculate a simple probability. Frequently we require the probability not of one event but of some sequence or combination of events occurring. Consider the experiment of selecting two employees at random for the pilot programme. Let us assume that the selection is to be computer-based by using the personnel records of all employees held on the computer network. Let us consider the probability of the first person chosen being male, $P(M1)$. This, as we know, is 0.527. Let us now consider the probability that the second person chosen is also male, $P(M2)$.

To determine this we must consider whether the two events, M1 and M2, are independent. This in turn depends on the sample selection process itself. We might consider the scenario where the computer system could select the same person twice (after all, having been selected once their name will still be on the computer file for selection a second time). In this case the two events will be independent and P(M2) will be 0.527 also, since from a total of 1206 employees on file, 635 will be male. Assume we now require P(M1 and M2), that is the probability that both selections are male. The calculation is straightforward, applying what is known as the *multiplication rule*:

$$P(M1 \text{ and } M2) = P(M1) \times P(M2)$$

$$= 635/1206 \times 635/1206 = 0.2772$$

That is, there is a probability of 0.2772 that we choose two males when choosing two employees at random. (Note that when calculating this probability we used the data from the table rather than the rounded probability value we had earlier. This ensures appropriate accuracy in the result.) The rule is readily extended to longer sequences – for example choosing three males or four. However, the rule as currently formulated only applies to events which are independent – as we supposed these two are.

For conditional events the rule must be modified. Consider the following. We now decide to amend the computer program which is selecting names at random from the personnel file. The program is changed so that if a person has been chosen once in any given experiment, they cannot be chosen again. Once more we require the probability P(M1 and M2) – that both people chosen are male. However, this time Event M2 is conditional upon Event M1. Consider P(M1). Given that 635 out of 1206 employees are male this will be 635/1206. Now consider Event M2. Its probability will depend on Event M1 – whether we chose a male the first time or not. Assume that we did (after all the required probability relates to both selections being male). If the first selection was male this implies that of the remaining 1205 employees, 634 are male, hence $P(M2) = 634/1205$. Technically we should now refer to the probability of Event M2 in a different way, since we have specified that Event M1 must have happened first. The notation for doing this is to denote the probability of Event M2 as:

$$P(M2|M1) = \frac{634}{1205}$$

where $P(M2|M1)$ is referred to as the probability of M2 *given that* Event M1 has occurred. So technically we now have:

$$P(M1 \text{ and } M2) = P(M1) \times P(M2|M1) = \frac{635}{1206} \times \frac{634}{1205}$$

$$= 0.2770$$

The difference between the two results may seem trivial. It is, however, important to ensure the appropriate calculation is being performed. In practice the resulting difference can be critical.

It is also worth noting that for two independent events, A and B, then $P(B|A) = P(B)$ – if the events are independent then by definition Event A cannot affect the probability of Event B.

Progress Check 5.2

The training manager is concerned that using this method of selection for the pilot training programme we might just by chance choose four people at random and that all four are aged under 25.

Can we provide any reassurance to the training manager that this is highly unlikely to occur? Assume that if a person is chosen for the programme their name is removed from the personnel file.

We would then have:

$$P(4 \text{ under } 25) = \frac{240}{1206} \times \frac{239}{1205} \times \frac{238}{1204} \times \frac{237}{1203}$$

$$= 0.00154$$

That is, a chance of less than 2 in a 1000 that such a set of events could happen. We can inform the training manager that such a sequence of selections is very unlikely but not zero.

The addition rule

The second important rule is the *addition rule*. Whereas the multiplication rule is concerned with situations where we require two or more events to occur, the addition rule is concerned with situations where we require only some of a group of events to occur. Consider the following. We select an employee and define two events: Event A where the person is under 25, Event B where the person is 45 or over. We require the probability of *either* Event A *or* Event B occurring – P(A or B). Simple logic indicates that this would be:

$$P(A \text{ or } B) = P(A) + P(B)$$

$$= \frac{240}{1206} + \frac{517}{1206} = \frac{757}{1206} = 0.628$$

In this case, however, the two events are mutually exclusive. Consider the same Event A but a different Event B: that the person is female. If we now apply our rule we have:

$$P(A \text{ or } B) = \frac{240}{1206} + \frac{571}{1206} = \frac{811}{1206} = 0.672$$

On reflection, however, you may realise that we have effectively double counted: there are some people who are under 25 who are also female. Clearly we have two events which are not mutually exclusive and the rule must be amended:

$$P(A \text{ or } B) = P(A) + P(B) - P(A \text{ and } B)$$

P(A and B) will be 108/1206 so we will then have:

$$P(A \text{ or } B) = \frac{240}{1206} + \frac{571}{1206} - \frac{108}{1206} = \frac{703}{1206} = 0.583$$

This is the correct probability. As with the multiplication rule you will realise that P(A and B) for mutually exclusive events will be zero.

The general form of the two probability rules will be:

Multiplication rule: $P(A \text{ and } B) = P(A) \times P(B|A)$

Addition rule: $P(A \text{ or } B) = P(A) + P(B) - P(A \text{ and } B)$

QADM IN ACTION

The National Lottery

Gambling in Britain has been transformed by the National Lottery. The small pink ticket from the newsagent's electronic outlet offers temptation of wealth beyond the dreams of avarice. **John Haigh** *examines a bet that, statistically, not one of our readers will live to win.*

The main game in the UK National Lottery has run since November 1994. Sales figures no longer reach those touched in January 1996, when two separate draws both passed the £100 million mark, but over £50 million worth of tickets are still sold every week. Some 90 per cent of UK adults have played at least once, despite the low rate of return – in most draws, only 45 per cent of proceeds are returned as prizes.

The UK format is to select six numbers from a list of 49, with a prize if you match three or more winning numbers. This is similar to many other lotteries, and teachers worldwide have found them a useful resource for illustrating ideas of probability and statistics. I offer a few here.

Counting tells us that the UK format gives almost 14 000 000 different selections. If they are equally likely, the chance of winning a share of the top prize by matching all six numbers is $p \sim 1/14\,000\,000$. To appreciate how tiny this is, suppose the chance that a particular man has a heart attack within the next year is 1 in 1000: if heart attacks occur at random, then p represents the chance that he has a heart attack within the next 40 minutes. Thus, if he buys his lottery ticket before 7.20 p.m., he is more likely to have a heart attack before the 8.00 p.m. draw than to have selected the winning numbers.

Indeed, if you spend £5 per week, you can expect to wait about

- 10 weeks to win the fixed £10 prize for matching 3 numbers;
- 4 years to win a Match 4 prize (around £62);
- over 200 years to win a Match 5 prize (perhaps £1500); and
- some 9000 years to win a bonus prize (some £100 000).

So forget about winning the jackpot (average £2 million).

In their efforts to increase the chances of winning the jackpot, punters have stooped to absurd levels of irrationality. In the USA players have driven great distances to buy their tickets at the "lucky" store that sold the winning ticket on the Powerball game. Just as irrational is the belief that we statisticians should be better than average at forecasting the winning numbers. Your dog would do equally well.

Dr John Haigh, Reader in Statistics at Sussex University, is author of *Taking Chances: Winning with Probability* (Oxford University Press).

Source: Haigh, J. (2006) Reflections on the UK National Lottery, *Significance*, 3 (1), pp 28–9.
© 2006 John Wiley and Sons.

A business application

Let us consider a typical business application at this stage to reinforce what we have covered. A manufacturer of computer hardware buys microprocessor chips to use in the assembly process from two different manufacturers. Concern has been expressed from the assembly department about the reliability of the supplies from the different manufacturers, and a rigorous examination of last month's supplies has recently been completed with the results shown in Table 5.2.

On the face of it, it does look as if the assembly department is correct in expressing concern. Manufacturer B is supplying a smaller quantity of chips in total but more are found to be defective in some way compared with Manufacturer A. However, let us consider this in the context of the probability principles we have developed. Let us consider the total of 9897 as a sample. Suppose we had chosen one chip at random from this sample. The following events and their probabilities can then be obtained:

Event A: the chip was supplied by Manufacturer A

Event B: the chip was supplied by Manufacturer B

Event C: the chip was satisfactory

Event D: the chip was defective

and

P(A and C) supplied by A and satisfactory

P(B and C) supplied by B and satisfactory

P(A and D) supplied by A and defective

P(B and D) supplied by B and defective.

Progress Check 5.3

Calculate the probabilities of the events defined.

We then have:

$$P(A \text{ and } C) = 5828/9897 = 0.589$$
$$P(B \text{ and } C) = 3752/9897 = 0.379$$
$$P(A \text{ and } D) = 119/9897 = 0.012$$
$$P(B \text{ and } D) = 198/9897 = 0.020.$$

Table 5.2   Reliability of silicon chip supplies

	Manufacturer A	Manufacturer B	Total
Chips found to be:			
Satisfactory	5828	3752	9580
Defective	119	198	317
Total	5947	3950	9897

Table 5.3 Joint probability table

	Manufacturer A	Manufacturer B	Total
Chips found to be:			
Satisfactory	0.589	0.379	0.968
Defective	0.012	0.020	0.032
Total	0.601	0.399	1.000

These probabilities are empirical – they have been observed to occur – and are known as joint probabilities for the obvious reason. In fact, we can construct a joint probability table as in Table 5.3.

Note that, as they must, the joint probabilities sum to 1.000 (since all the joint events are collectively exhaustive). But how does this help, given that these probabilities simply express in another form the data we had in Table 5.2? Let us begin to apply the principles of conditional probability that we have developed. Suppose we wanted to know: given that a chip comes from Manufacturer A then what is the probability that it is defective? Using our standard notation this probability would be $P(D|A)$. From Table 5.2 we can derive this probability directly. Some 119 out of the 5947 chips supplied by Manufacturer A were defective, hence $P(D|A) = 0.02$. But as we know, it's more useful to have a general rule to work out such a probability rather than having to resort to direct observation of values in a table. Let's do some simple maths to get this. We have:

$$P(D|A) = \frac{119}{5947} = 0.02$$

Let's divide both the numerator (the number at the top) and the denominator (the number at the bottom) by 9897, the total number of chips checked. By dividing both numbers by 9897 we're not actually changing anything. We then get:

$$P(D|A) = \frac{119/9897}{5947/9897} = 0.02$$

But 119/9897 is 0.012 which, from Table 5.3, is P(D and A) while 5947/9897 is 0.601 or P(A). So we actually have:

$$P(D|A) = \frac{119/9897}{5947/9897} = \frac{P(D\ and\ A)}{P(A)} = 0.02$$

giving a general rule for any two events X and Y that:

$$P(X|Y) = \frac{P(X\ and\ Y)}{P(Y)}$$

Progress Check 5.4

Using the general rule calculate the probability that, if the chip was supplied by Manufacturer B, it is defective. Compare the two probabilities.

The same logic can be applied to Manufacturer B:

$$P(D|B) = \frac{P(D \text{ and } B)}{P(B)} = \frac{0.020}{0.399} = 0.05$$

Consider what we have determined. If a chip is supplied by Manufacturer A then the probability that it will be defective is 0.02. On the other hand, if the chip comes from Manufacturer B then the probability that it will be defective is two-and-a-half times as high at 0.05. Effectively, we have concluded that the Event D and the source of manufacture are *not* independent events – if they were, then conditional probabilities would be the same. Clearly, we cannot conclude, based solely on this evidence, that Manufacturer B has a worse record than Manufacturer A. Many other factors would need to be taken into account: the price charged, design, availability and the fact that we have taken only one month's sample. However, we do have sufficient evidence to warrant a further investigation. We also have a planning tool to quantify the difference in quality between the two manufacturers and to take this into account in the assembly process so that the quality of the finished product is not compromised.

QADM IN ACTION

Microsoft Research

Spam – unsolicited commercial e-mail – is a complex and growing problem, and threatens to derail the internet revolution. **Joshua Goodman** *and* **David Heckerman** *of Microsoft Research describe some statistics-based methods for blocking spam, first by distinguishing it from wanted mail, and then by constructing puzzles they propose to use to challenge suspected spammers.*

Some statistics about spam

Spam is a huge problem. A few statistics can tell us just how huge.

- Brightmail has reported that over 50% of mail on the internet is now spam.
- A recent Infoworld poll identified spam as the number 1 "information technology disaster of the past year".
- From a report by the United States Federal Trade Commission[1]:
  - 66% of spam had false information somewhere in the message;
  - 18% of spam advertises "adult" material.

- From a report by the Pew Internet and American Life Project[2]:
  - 25% of e-mail users say that spam has reduced their use of e-mail;
  - 12% of users spend half an hour or more per day dealing with spam.

Statistics also help to explain why spam is such a problem.

- It costs only about 0.01 ¢ to send spam.
- 7% of e-mail users say they have bought a product advertised in unsolicited e-mail[2].

Given the tiny costs of spamming, even a tiny response rate makes spam economically viable.

Identifying spam – harder than it looks

Around a year ago, MSN's Hotmail service proposed blocking all spam entering their system that was allegedly from Hotmail. Spammers often fake the address that their mail is from, including pretending that such mail is from Hotmail itself. Because there are no standards on the internet to

→

say which IP addresses are allowed to send mail from which domain names, we usually cannot tell when a sender's address has been faked. (Recent proposals such as Microsoft's Caller-ID standard will help to fix this problem in the future.) The one exception today is that Hotmail knows its own valid internet addresses, and knows that mail from outside those addresses that says "From Hotmail" is fake. It sounded reasonable to block all such deceptive mail.

There are, however, a few cases where this faking may be legitimate. For instance, when your friend sends you an on-line birthday card via e-mail, the "From" address has your friend's e-mail address (perhaps at Hotmail), even though the e-mail actually originates on the greeting card company's servers, and comes from their internet address. Fortunately, we had acquired a data set of spam and good mail. We could show that, for every four spams allegedly from Hotmail that would be blocked, one good message would be lost – the exceptions were not as rare as had been thought. A 4-to-1 trade-off is not close to tolerable. This simple analysis was key to preventing an unacceptably large number of deleted good messages, including those birthday cards.

Although there are no hard-and-fast rules for marking mail as spam – even a faked "From" address is only moderately bad – by combining different indicators together, we can often be almost certain that mail is spam, and safely delete it, or very confident that it is spam, and place it in a junk folder. The question is how to combine these indicators.

One of the most popular techniques for stopping spam is the *naïve Bayes method*[3], often mistakenly simply called *Bayesian spam filtering*. In the naïve Bayes method, we try to determine the probability that a given message is spam, or good. We start by using the Bayes rule, which in this case tells us that

$$P(\text{spam}|\text{message}) = \frac{P(\text{message}|\text{spam}) \times P(\text{spam})}{P(\text{message})}$$

where:

$$P(\text{message}) = P(\text{message}|\text{spam}) \times P(\text{spam})$$
$$+ P(\text{message}|\text{not spam}) \times P(\text{not spam}).$$

$P(\text{spam})$ is simply the prior probability that any given message is spam. For instance, if half the messages you receive are spam, $P(\text{spam}) = 1/2$, and similarly for $P(\text{not spam})$. Also, we need to compute $P(\text{message}|\text{spam})$ and $P(\text{message}|\text{not spam})$ – these are respectively the probability of receiving any of the billions of possible spam messages and the probability of receiving any particular good piece of e-mail, of the infinite possibilities. Again this is difficult, if not impossible. However, we can make some approximations. In particular, we shall assume that the probability of every word in the message is independent of every other word, conditioned on knowing whether the message is spam. For instance, we assume that the probability of "click" is independent of the probability of "here", given that the message is spam. Clearly, this approximation is not a great one, which is why the technique is called naïve. However, once we have made this assumption, it is easy to compute the message probabilities. In particular,

$$P(\text{message}|\text{spam}| = P(\text{firstword}|\text{spam})$$
$$\times P(\text{second word}|\text{spam})$$
$$\times \ldots P(\text{last word}|\text{spam})$$

$$P(\text{message}|\text{not spam}| = P(\text{firstword}|\text{not spam})$$
$$\times P(\text{second word}|\text{not spam})$$
$$\times \ldots P(\text{last word}|\text{not spam}).$$

What is the probability of a particular word given spam? For each word, e.g. "click", we simply count the number of times the word occurred in all spam messages in a "training corpus" (a set of message known to be spam or good) and how many spam messages there were overall. The ratio is an estimate of the probability that any particular spam word is the word "click". We can do the same for words in non-spam messages.

Naïve Bayes is just one of many machine learning techniques, often used because it is the easiest to implement. It can be surprisingly effective, despite the simplicity of the model. If you are willing to label carefully thousands of your messages as spam or good to train the model, it can result in excellent performance for you on your own mail. However, the independence assumption in naïve Bayes limits its effectiveness. A naïve Bayes model will tend to be confused by common spam phrases like "click here to unsubscribe" that sometimes also occur in good mail, because naïve Bayes does not model the fact that these words occur together. If each word is 10 times as likely in spam as in good mail, a naïve Bayes model will think any such message is 10 000 times more likely to be spam than good ($10 \times 10 \times 10 \times 10$) – a large overestimate of the true ratio. Other model types, such as neural networks, graphical models, logistic regression and support vector machines all make fewer assumptions and can model these kinds of relationships between words implicitly or explicitly, at the expense of more complexity. At Microsoft, we use these more complex model types.

Conclusion

Spam is an extremely complex topic, and no single article can hope to describe all the ways to fight it. We have described here those techniques that rely most heavily on statistics, but we are exploring and pursuing many other ideas as well[4]. For example, we are currently exploring new industry standards that can help to stop spam. In particular, our challenge–response systems are expensive for very large legitimate senders. We are exploring standard ways for these senders to become certified as non-spammers.

No single solution will stop spam. New laws will be one part of the solution. Improved filters using better statistical analyses will be another part. Finally, all legitimate senders will be able to bypass any filter mistakes: large senders through certification; smaller senders through low variance computational puzzles. We anticipate a future in which the vast majority of spam is stopped, and all legitimate mail is delivered.

References

1. US Federal Trade Commission (2003) *False Claims in Spam*. Washington DC: US Federal Trade Commission.
2. Fallows, D. (2003) Spam: how it is hurting email and degrading life on the Internet. *Pew Internet and American Life Project.*
3. Sahami, M., Dumais, S., Heckerman, D. and Horvitz, E. (1998) A Bayesian approach to filtering junk e-mail. *American Association for Artificial Intelligence Workshop on Learning for Text Categorization, Madison, July 27th.*
4. Goodman, J. (2004) Spam technologies and policies. Microsoft Research. (Available from http://www.research.microsoft.com/~joshuago/spamtech.pdf.)

Joshua Goodman is a Researcher in the Machine Learning and Applied Statistics Group at Microsoft Research. He has been on loan to Microsoft's Anti-Spam product team since its inception. His previous work was on language modelling (predicting word sequences) and fast algorithms for logistic regression.

David Heckerman is founder and manager of the Machine Learning and Applied Statistics Group at Microsoft Research. Since 1992 he has been a Senior Researcher at Microsoft, where he has created applications including junk mail filters, data mining tools, handwriting recognition for the Tablet PC, troubleshooters in Windows and the Answer Wizard in Office. His work includes Bayesian methods for learning probabilistic graphical models from data. David received his doctorate from Stanford University in 1990 and is a Fellow of the American Association for Artificial Intelligence.

Probability distributions

So far we have been considering the probability of one particular event occurring. We may also be interested in determining the probabilities of all outcomes from some experiment. In such a case we might want to evaluate the probability distribution that applies to the problem under investigation. Consider the following. Assume we have two normal dice, each with six sides and each showing the number one through to six. We have an experiment where we throw both dice together and we note the total of the two numbers showing. So, for example, if we threw two sixes then the total (the outcome) would be 12. However, rather than consider one specific event, we are interested in all the possible outcomes and their probabilities.

Progress Check 5.5

Calculate the probability for each outcome from the experiment.

We can start by determining all the possible outcomes

Total
2
3
4
5
6
7
8
9
10
11
12

But we note that some of these outcomes can occur in different ways. For example, the outcome of a total of three could occur in two ways: the first die showing one and the second die showing two, or the reverse, with the first die showing two and the second die one. It is important to realise that these are two distinct and different ways in which the outcome could occur. If we determine the number of ways each outcome could occur we obtain Table 5.4. There are a total of 36 individual outcomes (6×6), which can be grouped into the 11 different categories. Logically, each outcome has the same probability of occurring – 1/36 – so multiplying the number of ways the outcome can occur by this probability will give the probability of that specific outcome occurring. Table 5.5 summarises the results. So, the probability of throwing two dice and them show a total of nine is 4/36 or 0.111. Technically, what we have produced is the probability distribution for this experiment – the probability associated with each and every outcome. As ever, we can show this visually as in Figure 5.1. The diagram simply shows the probability on the vertical axis and the outcomes on the horizontal.

Table 5.4 Outcomes

Total	No. of ways outcome can occur
2	1
3	2
4	3
5	4
6	5
7	6
8	5
9	4
10	3
11	2
12	1
Total	36

Table 5.5 Outcome probabilities

Total	No. of ways outcome can occur	Probability of each way occurring	Probability of each outcome	Probability as a decimal
2	1	1/36	1/36	0.028
3	2	1/36	2/36	0.056
4	3	1/36	3/36	0.083
5	4	1/36	4/36	0.111
6	5	1/36	5/36	0.139
7	6	1/36	6/36	0.167
8	5	1/36	5/36	0.139
9	4	1/36	4/36	0.111
10	3	1/36	3/36	0.083
11	2	1/36	2/36	0.056
12	1	1/36	1/36	0.028
Total	36		36/36	1.000

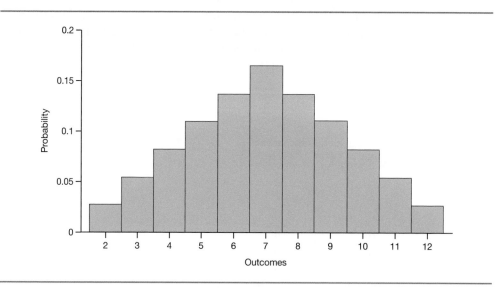

Figure 5.1 Histogram of probability distribution

This is all very well, but what has it to do with management decision making? The answer is that there are a number of theoretical probability distributions which can be of considerable use to managers. We shall be investigating two of these. However, such distributions can be quite difficult to apply when we have to resort to a calculation of the probabilities as we have so far. They are far more useful if we are able to use the

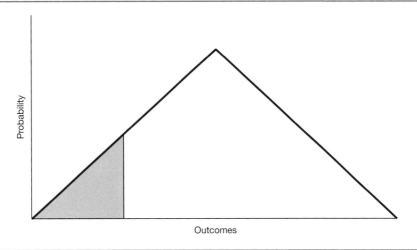

Figure 5.2 Probability polygon

features of the distribution as shown in Figure 5.1. This is no more than a histogram for the probability distribution. It is easily converted into a frequency polygon, as in Figure 5.2.

From Figure 5.2 we can now begin to see the potential of such a probability distribution. So far, in order to obtain a probability, we have had to calculate it using an appropriate formula. We now have the possibility of obtaining a probability from the graphical probability distribution. In principle if we wanted, say, the probability of the two dice showing four or less, we could obtain this from Figure 5.2. If we define the total area under the polygon as equal to one (as with probability) then if we were to measure the area under the polygon to the left of four we could express this as a proportion of the total area and hence derive the probability rather than calculate it. It should be evident that the table of probabilities and the probability distribution in Figure 5.2 show the same information. Either could be used to obtain a specific probability.

Naturally, for the simple problems we have examined so far there is no real advantage in doing this: the calculation method is simple enough. However, for some areas of probability the calculation method is not effective and we have to resort to the graphical distribution method instead.

The binomial distribution

The first common theoretical probability distribution is the *Binomial*. Consider the following example. On an assembly line, concern has been expressed over the quality of the final item produced. A large-scale investigation has recently been completed to assess the percentage of final output which is defective in some way and must be scrapped. The analysis revealed that on average 5 per cent of output was deemed to be defective in some way. The company – somewhat old-fashioned since it has never heard of total quality management principles – has now set up an inspection system at the end of the production process to monitor the quality of the output produced – specifically to monitor the defect rate of 5 per cent.

Georgian life

By Chris Cook

Charles, William, George. If all goes to plan, and God does, indeed, save our Kings, Britons now know the names of the men who will be head of state for the 21st century. But Ben Goldacre, the science writer, asked a good (if morbid) question: what chance does any one of us have of being alive when George finally takes to the throne? Thanks to Matthew Fletcher, a senior consultant at Towers Watson, a global actuarial firm, we now know.

First, there is the likely probability distribution about when he will get under the crown. This makes a few assumptions that the royals age much like the rest of us, will not abdicate and that culottes-free Britons won't storm Sandringham any time soon.

Again, assuming no chopping and changing, he also worked out the probability

- that George follows on straight from Elizabeth – 0.1 per cent
- that George takes over from Charles – 4.7 per cent
- that George follows William – 88.6 per cent
- that George is never king – 6.6 per cent

And there is the probability that any given 10-year-old, 20-year-old and so on will be alive when he takes the reins:

Probability, given your age now, that you'll be alive at the coronation

Current age	Men	Women
0	88%	90%
10	82%	86%
20	70%	76%
30	51%	58%
40	30%	35%
50	14%	17%
60	6%	7%
70	2%	2%
80	0%	0%

Source: Anwar Hussein/Getty Images

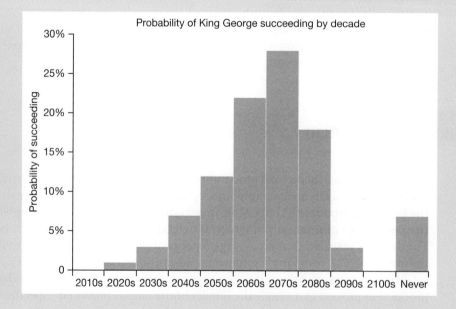

And a graph of the same:

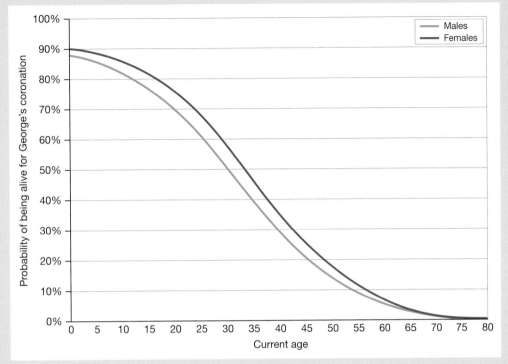

God save the Kings!

An interesting application of probability and probability distributions! Are you likely to be alive when George becomes king?

Progress Check 5.6

The inspector chooses one item at random from the production line. What is the probability that it will be defective?

Using the simple probability principles we have developed, the probability will be 5 per cent or 0.05. Similarly, suppose the inspector took two items at random. What is the probability that at least one of them is defective? To calculate this we must first assess independence: are the two events statistically independent? It seems reasonable to assume that as long as the output total is a large one then the two events can be deemed to be independent (if the factory produced only 100 items, for example, this assumption would be questionable). Defining Event A: the first item chosen is defective, and Event B: the second item chosen is defective, we then have the following possible sequences:

Progress Check 5.7

Calculate the probability of each of these four sequences.

- first item defective, second item not defective;
- first item not defective, second item not defective;
- first item defective, second item defective;
- first item not defective, second item defective.

Calculating the probabilities gives respectively:

$$0.05 \times 0.95 = 0.0475$$
$$0.95 \times 0.95 = 0.9025$$
$$0.05 \times 0.05 = 0.0025$$
$$0.95 \times 0.05 = 0.0475$$

and this gives a distribution of:

No. of defective items	Probability
0	0.9025
1	0.0950
2	0.0025

We require the probability of at least one defective item from the two chosen and this will consist of the last two probabilities to give 0.0975. That is, with a 5 per cent defect rate overall there is a probability of 9.75 per cent that at least one of the two items chosen will be defective in some way. However, this is a somewhat tedious calculation, even for two items. Consider the situation if the inspector had taken a sample of 100 items and we wished to determine the probability that, say, no more than five were defective. Clearly we need some general method of addressing this type of problem. This is where the Binomial distribution comes in. In fact, we can identify the key features of the experiment we have just described (choosing items at random from the assembly line and checking to see if they are defective).

- The experiment consists of a number of trials (choosing two items in our example).
- Two outcomes are possible in each trial (defective, not defective; win, lose; succeed, fail).
- The probabilities of the outcomes in each trial do not change.
- The trials are independent.

If these factors apply then we have what is known as a Binomial experiment. Under such conditions we can use the Binomial formula to calculate directly the probabilities we have determined using logic. The formula can be expressed as:

$$^{n}C_{r}\, p^{r}\, q^{n-r}$$

where

$^{n}C_{r}$ is the term for determining the number of different ways the event can occur;

p is the probability of the outcome from the trial under investigation;

q is $(1 - p)$, the probability of the specified outcome from the trial not occurring;

n is the number of trials;

r is the specified number of outcomes we are looking for.

This sounds complex but is in fact no more than we have done already. In our example we would have:

$p = 0.05$ (the probability of an item being chosen that was defective)

$q = 1 - 0.05 = 0.95$ (the probability of the item chosen not being defective)

$n = 2$ (the number of trials)

$r = 0, 1$ or 2 (the number of defective items chosen).

The only term still to explain is the ^nC_r term. This is a shorthand way of referring to the number of ways an event can occur. It is calculated as:

$$^nC_r = \frac{n!}{r!(n - r)!}$$

where ! is a factorial (which we introduced in Chapter 2). If we specify $r = 1$ (we want the number of ways we can obtain one defective item from a sample of two) then we calculate:

$$^nC_r = \frac{n!}{r!(n - r)!}$$
$$= \frac{2!}{1!(2 - 1)!} = \frac{2}{1} = 2$$

That is, there are two different ways of choosing one defective item from a sample of two items.

Progress Check 5.8

How many different ways are there of choosing five items from a sample of 50?

Here we would have $n = 50$ and $r = 5$, which would give:

$$^nC_r = \frac{n!}{r!(n - r)!}$$
$$= \frac{50!}{5!(50 - 5)!} = \frac{50!}{5!45!} = 2\,118\,760$$

That is, there are over 2 million different ways of choosing five items from a sample of 50. You might have a pocket calculator which has a factorial function built into it (often shown as x!). If you don't you might have had a problem with this activity because otherwise the arithmetic is very long. We can short-circuit the arithmetic we need to do. Remember that 50! is actually $(50 \times 49 \times 48 \times 47 \ldots)$ and that 45! is $(45 \times 44 \times 43 \ldots)$. This means that:

$$\frac{50!}{5!\,45!}$$

is actually the same as

$$\frac{(50 \times 49 \times 48 \times 47 \times 46)}{5!}$$

since the rest of the factorial calculation on the top is actually 45!, the two would cancel (one on top and one underneath). Returning to our probability problem, the calculation would then be:

$$P(1 \text{ defective item}) = {}^{n}C_{r}\, p^{r}\, q^{(n-r)}$$
$$= (2)(0.05^1)(0.95^1) = 0.095$$

which is the same as in our earlier calculated distribution. We could equally have set r to 0 or to 2 and used the formula again, but it hardly seems worth it for the current problem. However, for larger problems it may well be.

Consider the following scenario. On another assembly line the inspector has taken a sample of 50 items and checked to see whether or not they are defective. The inspector has been told that the defect rate on this assembly process last week was 6 per cent. The sample results indicate that five items were found to be defective from the sample of 50, i.e. a defect rate of 10 per cent. Does this mean that the defect rate has got worse?

Consider the logic of our situation. We know that from our sample of 50 items no more than three (6 per cent) should have been defective if the overall defect rate has not worsened since last week. We found five. But we could equally argue that the sample is a fairly small one. Perhaps, just by chance, we happened to pick an extra couple of defective items even though overall the defect rate is still 6 per cent. Perhaps, if we repeated the sample, we might find the next one showed only three items defective. Again, how can probability help? The answer is that we have a Binomial situation and can apply the formula we have introduced. The calculation will not *prove* whether the defect rate is still 6 per cent or not but it will provide additional evidence that might help us reach a decision (bearing in mind that our decision, like any, may turn out to be wrong).

Progress Check 5.9

Determine the probability of choosing 50 items and finding five of them to be defective. Consider your result in the context of having to make a decision about the actual defect rate.

The calculation is straightforward using the formula. We have:

$${}^{n}C_{r}\, p^{r}\, q^{(n-r)} = (2\,118\,760)0.06^5 0.94^{45} = 0.102$$

That is, a probability of 0.102 of choosing 50 items at random from the assembly line and finding that five were defective. Let us consider the implications of this in a management context. There is one critical assumption behind this calculation: that the actual defect rate is *still* 6 per cent. Our result implies that *if* this assumption is true then there is approximately a 1 in 10 chance of having five defective items in the sample (even though on average we would expect only three). To evaluate this position consider a different scenario. Suppose someone passes you a six-sided die and bets £100 that you will throw six sixes. You roll the die six times. Each time it shows a six and you lose the bet.

What is your conclusion? Effectively you have two choices: either the die is fixed or tampered with in some way or a highly unlikely sequence of events has actually happened. Given that the probability of rolling six sixes with a fair die is 0.00002 (the multiplication rule, remember?), it is tempting to conclude that the die has been tampered with in some way. However, based on this evidence alone we have no hard proof of this. It is a subjective assessment based on the (very low) probability of the event.

Let us return to our example. We are now in the position of having to assess this result and decide whether the actual defect rate is still 6 per cent or whether it might have worsened. We might argue that a 10 per cent probability is a reasonable one and that we cannot therefore say the defect rate has altered from its level of 6 per cent. On the other hand, we might argue that the probability of 10 per cent is too high to be likely to relate to the original actual 6 per cent defect rate. Like many situations we cannot prove one way or the other what has happened to the defect rate. Our assessment of the sample result must to some extent be subjective. As a compromise we might suggest that if the defect rate is of critical importance to the organisation – perhaps because of its quality policy or its costs – then we should repeat the sample and assess the second sample result. You should be able to see the logic of this. The only reason for rejecting the evidence of the first sample is to say that, by chance, we took more than a proportionate share of defective items from the assembly line. However, if we repeat the sample – particularly if we increase its size – then the chances are we should not repeat this 'bias': we would expect a new result closer to the three defective items we ought to be getting. If, on the other hand, we are still finding a higher number of defective items, this strengthens the case for concluding that the actual defect rate has worsened. A detailed investigation would then be needed to ascertain why this has happened and what corrective action could be taken.

Binomial tables

There is another method of obtaining Binomial probabilities: we can use pre-calculated tables and obtain the required probabilities directly. Then why, you ask, did we bother with the formula we have just introduced? The answer is that the tables typically only show the probabilities for certain combinations of n and p. If the required application falls outside these combinations we will need the formula in any event.

Typical tables are shown in Appendix A and we shall examine them shortly. To illustrate their use we shall introduce another typical situation. You may be aware that airlines operating passenger flights typically book more passengers onto a flight than there are seats available. They do this because experience has shown that not all passengers booked will actually turn up – they become 'no-shows'. Obviously, if the airline did not take this into account then the flight would typically depart with empty seats (and lost revenue). On the other hand, the airline does not wish to be in the embarrassing position of having too many passengers for a given flight (although this does happen). It is not only airlines who operate on this sort of basis: many organisations providing direct customer services operate on the same principle.

Assume the airline is operating a short-haul flight from Manchester to Edinburgh on a 16-seat aircraft. The typical passenger is an executive going to some business meeting and returning the same day. The airline knows from past experience that 15 per cent of passengers booked on their early morning flight will not appear. They have therefore adopted the practice of taking a maximum of 20 bookings for this flight. The customer service manager, however, is concerned about the likelihood of passengers booked on the flight not having a seat because more passengers than expected turn up for the flight. We have been asked to assess the probability of this happening. As usual we must make assumptions to apply the Binomial principles. We clearly have a sequence of 20 'trials': passengers booked on the flight. The probability of any one passenger not showing is 0.15, and to apply the Binomial we must make the assumption that the trials are independent. This implies that, for example, no two passengers are booked together (and hence will 'not-show' together). We then require the probability that there will be no more than three 'no-shows' (implying that we will have at least 17 passengers for 16 seats). Clearly this requires:

$$P(0\,\text{no shows}) + P(1\,\text{no shows}) + P(2\,\text{no shows}) + P(3\,\text{no shows})$$

That is, we will need several parts of the appropriate probability distribution. Obviously we could use the Binomial formula to work out each of these individual probabilities and the total (and you should do this later to practise the use of the formula approach). However, we can instead use the table in Appendix A, part of which is duplicated here for ease of reference.

Binomial distribution

n	r ≥	p = 0.15
20	0	1.0000
	1	0.9612
	2	0.8244
	3	0.5951
	4	0.3523
	5	0.1702
	6	0.0673
	7	0.0219
	8	0.0059
	9	0.0013
	10	0.0002

The table will require a little explanation. First, take note that it shows cumulative rather than individual probabilities, hence ≥. We shall explore this in a moment. Second, the table is segmented for various combinations of n, p and r, and we are interested in the combination of n = 20 and p = 0.15 with the values of r relating directly to our problem. The probabilities in the table are straightforward in their application. For example, we have:

$$P(r \geq 0) = 1.0000$$

$$P(r \geq 1) = 0.9612$$

$$P(r \geq 2) = 0.8244 \text{ and so on.}$$

In the context of our problem – where r effectively equates to a 'no-show' – we have a probability of 0.9612 that there will be at least one no-show, a probability of 0.8244 that there will be at least two and so on.

Progress Check 5.10

Using the table, determine the probability that more passengers arrive for the flight than there are seats available.

Applying some simple logic it is evident that directly from the table we can derive:

$$P(r \geq 4) = 0.3523$$

That is, there is a probability of 0.3523 that there will be at least four no-shows and, therefore, we will have sufficient seats for the remaining passengers. It follows then that we must have:

$$P(r < 4) = P(r = 0) + P(r = 1) + P(r = 2) + P(r = 3)$$
$$= 1 - 0.3523 = 0.6477$$

as the probability that there will not be enough no-shows to avoid an excess of passengers over seats. That is, a probability of 0.65 (approximately) that the airline will have overbooked. If the airline has not yet had complaints from irate passengers who have booked but couldn't get a seat, it soon will have!

Note also that, although the table relates to cumulative probabilities, it can be used to derive individual probabilities. Suppose we had actually wanted the probability of exactly three no-shows: $P(r = 3)$. From the table we have:

$$P(r \geq 4) = P(r = 4) + P(r = 5) + \cdots + P(r = 20) = 0.3523$$
$$P(r \geq 3) = P(r = 3) + P(r = 4) + \cdots + P(r = 20) = 0.5951$$

Hence we must have:

$$P(r = 3) = P(r \geq 3) - P(r \geq 4)$$
$$= 0.5951 - 0.3523 = 0.2428$$

Mean and standard deviation of a Binomial distribution

It may have occurred to you that the Binomial distribution (or indeed any other probability distribution) is just a special example of distributions in general, like those we looked at in Chapter 4. For those distributions we were able to calculate a number of summary statistics such as the mean and standard deviation. It seems logical that we should be able to calculate comparable statistics for the Binomial distribution. In our airline example, the mean would indicate the mean number of no-shows on each flight, and the standard deviation would show the variability around this mean. We could calculate the mean and standard deviation using the formulae from Chapter 4 with the probabilities as the frequencies and the outcomes as the interval values. However, there is a more direct method. Without proof we state that for a Binomial distribution:

$$\text{Mean} = np$$

$$\text{Standard deviation} = \sqrt{npq}$$

Here we would have:

$$\text{Mean} = 20(0.15) = 3$$

$$\text{Standard deviation} = \sqrt{20(0.15)(0.85)} = 1.597$$

The mean and standard deviation for a Binomial problem can be interpreted and used as with any other set of data. We can expect a mean number of no-shows of three per flight with a standard deviation of 1.6 (the mean confirms that with a 16-seat aircraft available and 20 seats sold the airline is heading for trouble). We could also calculate the mean number of no-shows for a range of ticket sales (17, 18, 19, 20, 21, etc.) to assess the likely impact on overbooking.

Progress Check 5.11

You work for a mail-order retail company which advertises special promotions on the internet. Customers who respond to the promotion asking to buy the product are offered it on a sale-or-return basis. That is, the company sends the product to the customer together with an invoice. If the customer is happy with the product they will pay the invoice. If they are not happy, they can simply return the product to the company and do not have to pay the invoice. Obviously, in the latter case, the company has incurred costs which it cannot recoup (postage, handling, etc.). For past promotions the company has noted that 12 per cent of customers return the product. For the next promotion 50 000 customer orders are expected. Calculate the mean and standard deviation and comment on how this might be used by management.

Solution is given on p 577.

Binomial probabilities in Excel

Excel, and other spreadsheet packages, have built in statistical functions to calculate binomial probabilities directly. The function is:

$$\text{BINOMDIST}(r, n, p, \text{cumulative})$$

Where:

r is the specified number of outcomes we wish to calculate for

n is the number of trials

p is the probability of the outcome in each trial

cumulative is a logical value that is set to be either TRUE or FALSE. If the logical value is set to TRUE then Excel calculates the cumulative probability up to and including r. If the logical value is set to FALSE then Excel calculates the probability of exactly r outcomes.

So, with the airline example from the previous section we had $n = 20$ and $p = 0.15$. Using the function as:

$$\text{BINOMDIST}(4, 20, 0, 15, \text{TRUE})$$

then Excel would return a value of 0.6477 as the probability of $r \leq 4$. On the other hand, using the function as:

$$\text{BINOMDIST}(4, 20, 0, 15, \text{FALSE})$$

Excel would return a value of 0.1821 as the probability of $r = 4$.

The normal distribution

We now turn to the second theoretical probability distribution – the *Normal distribution*. The Normal distribution is widely used in business and management decision making and underpins the area of statistical inference that we shall be examining in detail in Chapter 7. It is instantly recognisable graphically, as shown in Figure 5.3. The Normal distribution is symmetrical – often referred to as bell-shaped – and this general shape remains the same no matter what problem we are examining where the Normal distribution applies. This has important consequences, as we shall see shortly. What will vary from one application of this distribution to another is not the general shape but two key characteristics of that shape:

● the mean value;
● the variability as measured by the standard deviation.

Figure 5.4 illustrates two such distributions where the means vary and Figure 5.5 where the standard deviations vary.

We could build up an entire family of such distributions depending on the specific values of the mean and standard deviation. So how do we determine the appropriate probabilities for such a distribution? For the Binomial we saw that we could either apply a formula or we could use pre-calculated tables. In the case of the Normal distribution

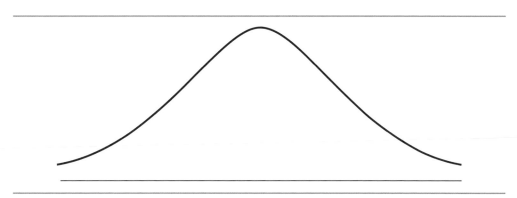

Figure 5.3 The Normal distribution

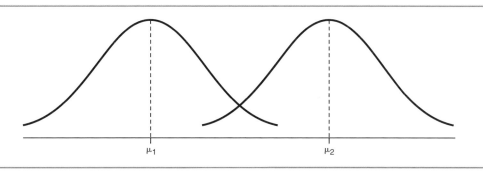

Figure 5.4 Two Normal distributions: differing means

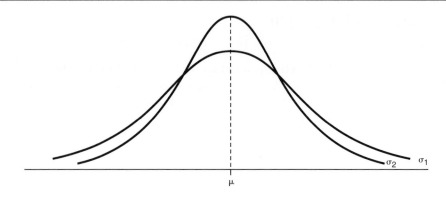

Figure 5.5 Two Normal distributions: differing standard deviations

the only feasible method is to use tables. The reason for this may become evident if we examine the formula behind the Normal distribution:

$$P(x) = \frac{1}{\sqrt{2\pi}\sigma} e^{-\frac{(x-\mu)^2}{2\sigma^2}}$$

where:

μ is the mean

σ is the standard deviation

$\pi = 3.14159$

$e = 2.71828$

and x the value for which we require a probability.

Fortunately for all of us, tables of probabilities have been pre-calculated! However, before we can utilise them we must consider the issue of varying means and standard deviations in the family of Normal distributions. Remember for the Binomial distribution certain combinations of n and p gave rise to specific probability values. The number of combinations was fairly limited, partly because the Binomial deals with combinations of n and r which take only discrete values. We could always return to the Binomial formula if a particular combination did not appear in the tables. For the Normal distribution this problem is compounded. The number of possible combinations of mean and standard deviation we might require is much larger, since it is a continuous distribution, and if the particular combination we do require is not available the prospect of returning to the formula is not a happy one. However, we can take advantage of the fact that all Normal distributions follow the same general shape to use what is known as the *Standardised Normal distribution*.

The Standardised Normal distribution

Let us consider the following problem. A large retail organisation has recently been receiving a number of complaints from customers about one of its products: bottles of own-brand hair shampoo. Customers have complained that they think the actual contents of the shampoo bottles are sometimes less than they are meant to be according to the printed contents label on each bottle. The organisation currently sells two bottle sizes: one at 490 ml and one at 740 ml. The shampoo is actually manufactured and bottled by a subsidiary company, and an investigation into the bottling process is currently under way. The process is such that two production lines are in use – one for each bottle size. On each line a computer-controlled machine fills the bottle with shampoo automatically. However, management recognise that the machine is not 100 per cent reliable and some variability inevitably arises in the exact volume of shampoo put into each bottle. Further analysis has revealed that on one line the machine is calibrated to deliver 500 ml of shampoo into each bottle but that the actual process is normally distributed with a standard deviation of 10 ml. This implies – remember Figure 5.3 – that the mean of the distribution is 500 ml but that some bottles will contain less than this and some more. So some might actually contain 495 ml, others 505 ml and so on. Similarly, from the shape of the distribution, it is clear that the further away from the mean we get then the fewer the number of bottles we are considering. On the second line a similar situation applies but with the machine set to deliver a mean amount of 750 ml with a standard deviation of 15 ml, and again the distribution of amount filled is Normally distributed.

Clearly we have two Normal distributions under examination and although both have the characteristic shape, they differ in both their mean and their standard deviation. To determine relevant probabilities it might appear that we need two sets of tables. However, if we examine Machine 1 we can determine a number of possible values for the amount filled, as shown in Table 5.6.

In the table we show a number of possible amounts filled, varying from 470 ml to 530 ml. However, we can express these amounts in a different way, showing not the absolute amount filled but how much the amount differs from the mean – expressed in ml. This difference in turn can now be shown in a relative way by expressing the difference from the mean in terms of the number of standard deviations (which you will remember was 10 ml). So, an amount of 470 ml is effectively three SDs below the mean, 480 ml is two SDs below and so on for this variable. There appears little benefit from performing such calculations, however, until we do the same for our second distribution.

Table 5.6   Machine 1

Amount filled (ml)	470	480	490	500	510	520	530
Difference from mean amount (ml)	−30	−20	−10	0	10	20	30
SDs from mean	−3	−2	−1	0	1	2	3

Progress Check 5.12

Construct a similar table for Machine 2 showing amounts filled that vary from three SDs below the mean to three SDs above.

Table 5.7 shows results for both machines.

It now becomes evident that although the two Normal distributions vary in terms of their means and standard deviations, we can transform both with a common yard-stick – the number of standard deviations away from its mean that a particular value is. But what is the point of all this? Remember that we wanted to be able to use probability tables for the Normal distribution but realised that the number of such tables required – given we need one for every possible combination of mean and standard deviation – would be enormous.

We can now resolve this problem. Instead of analysing each specific Normal distri-bution – with its own mean and standard deviation – we can effectively standardise all such distributions by converting them to this yardstick measure. This means, for exam-ple, that in the case of our two distributions we now recognise that a value of 470 ml for Machine 1 and 705 ml for Machine 2 are effectively at the same point in their own distributions, since both values are three SDs below their own mean. What this means is that rather than use the specific – and often unique – Normal distribution that applies to the problem under investigation we can actually use just one Normal distribution for every problem – once we have transformed the problem values into SDs from the mean.

This particular distribution is known as the Standardised Normal distribution and the process of performing the calculations shown in Table 5.7 is known as calculating a *standard score* – usually denoted as a *Z score*. Such a Z score is readily found from the standardising formula:

$$Z = \frac{X - \text{Mean}}{\text{SD}}$$

where Z is the standard score, X is the specific value we are examining and Mean and SD are the mean and standard deviation respectively of the specific distribution we are look-ing at. Without proof we state that the Standardised Normal distribution has a mean of 0 and a standard deviation of 1. Pre-calculated tables of probability relating to the Stand-ardised Normal distribution are readily available and one is shown in Appendix B.

Table 5.7   Machines 1 and 2

Machine 1							
Amount filled (ml)	470	480	490	500	510	520	530
SDs from mean	−3	−2	−1	0	1	2	3
Machine 2							
Amount filled (ml)	705	720	735	750	765	770	785

Progress Check 5.13

Calculate the Z score for the following values:

Machine 1	Machine 2
X = 475 ml	X = 745 ml
X = 505 ml	X = 725 ml
X = 518 ml	X = 759 ml

Solutions are given on p 578.

Using Normal probability tables

We can now start to use the Normal probability tables that are available to help us assess our current situation. Remember that for Machine 1 the equipment was calibrated to fill the bottle with an average of 500 ml, SD 10 ml and that the bottles were actually labelled as containing 490 ml. We now wish to assess the probability that any one bottle will actually contain less than 490 ml (and thereby give customers legitimate grounds for complaint). We already have the relevant Z score ($Z = -1$). Turning to Appendix B (reproduced here for convenience) we see that the table of probabilities is shown by row and by column. Both row and column actually refer to the Z score value. The rows refer to the first two digits of the calculated Z score – ranging from 0.0 through to 3.0. The columns across the top of the table refer to the second decimal digit. So, looking at the first row (0.0) and then moving across the columns, we effectively have Z scores of 0.00, 0.01, 0.02 and so on. Conventionally, Z scores are calculated to two decimal places. Our score is technically $Z = -1.00$. However, searching for this in the row/column combination we appear to have a difficulty since no negative Z scores are shown.

The reason negative values are not shown is that they are not actually needed. Remember that by definition a Normal distribution is symmetrical around its mean. This implies that the two halves of the distribution are mirror images of each other and effectively the same. So, in probability terms, a Z score of -1.00 and $+1.00$ are identical. If we now look for $Z = 1.00$ we read a value from the table of 0.1587. To understand what this shows, we consider Figure 5.6. This shows the Standardised Normal distribution together with the Z score of -1.00. The area to the left of the Z score is effectively the area we are seeking (to represent the proportion of all bottles which have contents less than 490 ml). This is also what the figures in the table show – the area under the curve to the left of the Z score line (or to the right if we had a positive Z score). So, the figure of 0.1587 implies that some 15.9 per cent of all bottles will contain less than 490 ml of shampoo. Used in this way the

Areas in the tail of the Normal distribution – part of Appendix B

Z	.00	.01	.02	.03	.04	.05	.06	.07	.08	.09
0.0	.5000	.4960	.4920	.4880	.4840	.4801	.4761	.4721	.4681	.4641
0.1	.4602	.4562	.4522	.4483	.4443	.4404	.4364	.4325	.4286	.4247
0.2	.4207	.4168	.4129	.4090	.4052	.4013	.3974	.3936	.3897	.3859
0.3	.3821	.3783	.3745	.3707	.3669	.3632	.3594	.3557	.3520	.3483
0.4	.3446	.3409	.3372	.3336	.3300	.3264	.3228	.3192	.3156	.3121
0.5	.3085	.3050	.3015	.2981	.2946	.2912	.2877	.2843	.2810	.2776
0.6	.2743	.2709	.2676	.2643	.2611	.2578	.2546	.2514	.2483	.2451
0.7	.2420	.2389	.2358	.2327	.2296	.2266	.2236	.2206	.2177	.2148
0.8	.2119	.2090	.2061	.2033	.2005	.1977	.1949	.1922	.1894	.1867
0.9	.1841	.1814	.1788	.1762	.1736	.1711	.1685	.1660	.1635	.1611
1.0	.1587	.1562	.1539	.1515	.1492	.1469	.1446	.1423	.1401	.1379
1.1	.1357	.1335	.1314	.1292	.1271	.1251	.1230	.1210	.1190	.1170
1.2	.1151	.1131	.1112	.1093	.1075	.1056	.1038	.1020	.1003	.0985
1.3	.0968	.0951	.0934	.0918	.0901	.0885	.0869	.0853	.0838	.0823
1.4	.0808	.0793	.0778	.0764	.0749	.0735	.0721	.0708	.0694	.0681
1.5	.0668	.0655	.0643	.0630	.0618	.0606	.0594	.0582	.0571	.0559

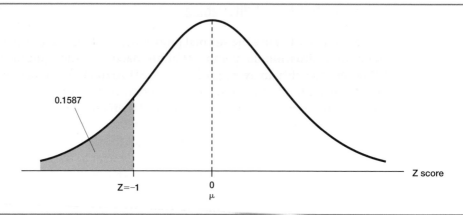

Figure 5.6 Standardised Normal distribution

Normal distribution tables allow us to calculate the proportion of the distribution that falls in any given area. Management would now need to evaluate their position given this new information. Should they carry on regardless and run the risk of customer complaints (and possible violation of consumer protection regulations); should they change the label on which the contents are shown; should they change the setting of the mean amount filled by the machine? All of these are options which would need to be carefully considered based on all the other information pertaining to the problem. You should be able to see by now, however, the importance of applying these probability situations to such a set of circumstances. Such principles do not 'solve' the problem but they do supply the manager with additional information that, arguably, could not have come from any other source. It will be worthwhile at this stage reinforcing the use of the tables with a few worked examples.

Progress Check 5.14

Determine for Machine 1 the proportion of bottles:

(a) that will contain more than 515 ml;
(b) that will contain less than 475 ml;
(c) that will contain between 520 and 525 ml;
(d) that will contain between 490 and 480 ml.

Until you gain practice it may well be worthwhile sketching the Normal curve and highlighting the area you are trying to determine with the tables, as we did with Figure 5.6. For (a) we require the area to the right of the corresponding Z line. Here we have:

$$Z = \frac{X - \text{Mean}}{\text{SD}} = \frac{515 - 500}{10} = 1.5$$

and from the table this gives a value of 0.0668, i.e. 6.7 per cent of bottles will contain over 515 ml. For (b) we require the area to the left of the Z score:

$$Z = \frac{Z - \text{Mean}}{\text{SD}} = \frac{475 - 500}{10} = -2.5$$

giving a value of 0.0062 from the table or 0.62 per cent of bottles. Parts (c) and (d) are a little different and a sketch is definitely worthwhile to confirm what we require. Figure 5.7 shows the two X values (520 and 525), and the area in between these two lines is the one we require, which corresponds to values between 520 and 525 ml.

The method of calculation is a little more complicated this time. If we find the area to the right of 520 and then subtract the area to the right of 525 this must, logically, give us the area we actually require. The relevant calculation is then:

$$Z_1 = \frac{X - \text{Mean}}{\text{SD}} = \frac{520 - 500}{10} = 2.0$$

$$Z_2 = \frac{X - \text{Mean}}{\text{SD}} = \frac{525 - 500}{10} = 2.5$$

with the two probabilities from the table being 0.0228 and 0.0062 respectively. This then gives:

$$Z_1 - Z_2 = 0.0228 - 0.0062$$

$$= 0.0166$$

or 1.66 per cent of bottles will contain between 520 and 525 ml. Part (d) follows a similar logic and you should be able to confirm that we obtain a result of 13.6 per cent.

As a final example, let us return to the management problem in hand. Management have now decided that, for a variety of reasons, the situation cannot continue with almost 16 per cent of output below the advertised contents. Accordingly they have decided that Machine 1 will continue as before (delivering a mean content of 500 ml, SD 10 ml) but that a new label will be produced showing the new minimum contents and guaranteeing that no more than 1 per cent of output will fall below this minimum figure. The problem is now to determine what this new minimum figure on the label should be – 480 ml, 470 ml or what?

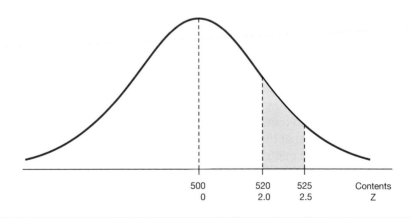

500	520	525	Contents
0	2.0	2.5	Z

Figure 5.7 P(520 < x < 525)

Progress Check 5.15

Can you provide any advice to management on what the new minimum contents figure should be?

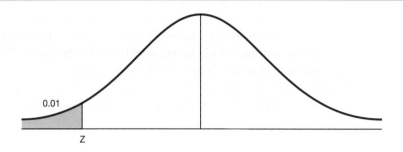

Figure 5.8 Finding X value given 1 per cent probability

We need to approach this from a different angle than previously. Up to now we have known the X value in the Z score formula and wanted to determine the Z score and then the probability. Now we know the required probability – 1 per cent – and require to determine what the X value must be to ensure this. Figure 5.8 illustrates this.

Given that we require a probability of 1 per cent we should be able to search through the table and determine what the associated Z score must be. If we do this we eventually find a value in the table of 0.01 (1 per cent probability) corresponding to a Z score of 2.33. It is important to remember, however, that we are actually examining the left-hand side of the Normal distribution, so technically this Z score is −2.33. If we now re-examine the Z score formula we have:

$$Z = -2.33 = \frac{X - \text{Mean}}{\text{SD}}$$

$$-2.33 = \frac{X - \text{Mean}}{\text{SD}} = \frac{X - 500}{10}$$

and rearranging gives:

$$-23.3 = X - 500$$

$$X = 500 - 23.3 = 476.7$$

That is, the new advertised minimum contents to meet the required 1 per cent target must be 476.7 ml. We could always check this is correct by finding the probability of a bottle containing less than this.

It's worth remembering when you're faced with a Normal problem – particularly in an exam – that there's only one formula, the Z score formula. So we have to use the same formula no matter whether we're asked to work out X, the mean, the standard deviation or a probability.

Normal probabilities in Excel

Excel, and other spreadsheet packages, have built in statistical functions to calculate Normal probabilities directly. The function is:

NORMDIST (X, mean, sd, cumulative)

Where:

X is the specified value for which we require a probability

mean is the mean value for the distribution

sd is the standard deviation of the distribution

cumulative is a logical value that is set to be either TRUE or FALSE. If the logical value is set to TRUE then Excel calculates the cumulative probability up to and including X

So, with the shampoo bottle example from the previous section we had one bottle with a mean of 490 ml and a standard deviation of 10 ml. If we wish to determine the probability that X ≤ 480
we have:

NORMDIST (480, 490, 10, TRUE)

And Excel would return a value of 0.1586 as the probability that X ≤ 480.

Tails of the unexpected

By Claire Jones

The events of the past years have shown that economic and financial systems are prone to so-called "tail risks", which are the sorts of events which the standard suite of models predict will happen very rarely indeed. However, these tail-risk events, many of which have proven catastrophic for the global economy, have been uncannily common in recent years. Remember this famous line from David Viniar, Goldman's CFO, in 2008:

"We were seeing things that were 25-standard-deviation events, several days in a row."

25-standard-deviation events are exceptionally, exceptionally rare. And if you're seeing them day after day, then chances are that your model might not correspond to reality – or even be a fair approximation of it. In a fascinating paper out today, the Bank of England's executive director Andy Haldane and Bank economist Benjamin Nelson argue that the models that banks and economists – among them the world's monetary authorities – were using were indeed deeply flawed. The paper criticises risk models' reliance on the so-called "normal distribution":

"The normal distribution provides a beguilingly simple description of the world. Outcomes lie symmetrically around the mean, with a probability that steadily decays. It is well-known that repeated games of chance deliver random outcomes in line with this distribution: tosses of a fair coin, sampling of coloured balls from a jam-jar, bets on a lottery number, games of paper/scissors/stone."

But the economists believe we have been fooled by randomness into thinking that these "tail risks of the unexpected" are far less normal than they actually are. As the research notes, the world in recent years has not conformed to what we think of as normal to a degree that suggests events that were once seen as tail risks should "not be unexpected, for they are the rule". These events may become even more common in the years to come.

"As the world becomes increasingly integrated – financially, economically, socially – interactions among the moving parts may make for potentially fatter tails. Catastrophe risk may be on the rise."

The normal distribution can be very useful – but you need to be sure it's appropriate to the situation you're analysing.

Worked example

At this stage, the material we have introduced on probability and probability distributions can seem very mechanical and of little relevance to management decision making. Let us introduce a scenario where we might apply such principles to assist management. A power company has been examining its long-term strategy in terms of customer loyalty, particularly amongst domestic customers where there's considerable competition in the energy market. It is concerned that as the power markets become more competitive, it is in danger of losing some of its customer base to its competitors and hence its revenue and profit stream. It is considering introducing some sort of discount or loyalty scheme for some of its domestic electricity customers. Senior management are not yet clear as to what such a scheme would entail, or exactly which customers would be targeted. However, they are currently thinking of offering a price discount to relatively large users of electricity (since larger users are by and large more profitable and hence more valuable to the company). We have been asked to undertake some initial analysis and offer what guidance we can to senior management as to how we might target which group of customers to offer such a price discount to. The company currently has around 2.5 million domestic electricity customers and charges domestic customers 6.7p per kilowatt hour (kWh) used, no matter how much they use. We have done some initial data collection from the computerised customer records files and have obtained electricity usage of a representative sample of 1500 customers for the past 12 months. The results are shown in Table 5.8.

You may want to stop reading at this point and see whether you can suggest how we might approach this situation in terms of analysis and recommendations.

Although this is a chapter on probability, we should not forget some of the techniques we introduced earlier. Clearly we have a frequency distribution and we can obtain a histogram from this, as in Figure 5.9.

We gain a visual impression of a symmetrical distribution which, with a little imagination, takes the shape of the Normal curve. In other words, it seems reasonable to say,

Table 5.8   Electricity usage of domestic customers over the last 12-month period (kWh)

Lower limit (kWh)		Upper limit (kWh)	No. of customers
3000	<	4000	11
4000	<	4200	24
4200	<	4400	69
4400	<	4600	141
4600	<	4800	225
4800	<	5000	292
5000	<	5200	281
5200	<	5400	218
5400	<	5600	132
5600	<	5800	71
5800	<	6000	26
6000	<	7000	10
Total			1500

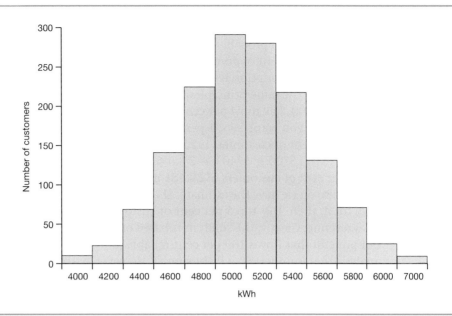

Figure 5.9 Distribution of a sample of electricity usage

based on this sample, that electricity consumption is Normally distributed. Given this assumption, we can determine the mean and standard deviation of this distribution. These are calculated from the table as:

$$\text{Mean} = 4996 \text{ kWh}$$
$$\text{SD} = 424.4 \text{ kWh}$$

and by also calculating the median we can determine that the coefficient of skewness is −0.03, as close to zero as makes no difference, again confirming that we have a symmetrical distribution. Given that we can assume we have a Normal distribution, we can use it to do some 'what-if' analysis to try to help senior management. First of all, we can estimate total annual revenue from domestic electricity sales. Assuming this sample is representative, we know that mean sales are 4996 kWh per customer per 12 months. The company has 2.5 million domestic customers and sells at 6.7p per kWh. This gives annual revenue from sales as:

$$\text{Sales revenue} = 4996 \times 2\,500\,000 \times 0.067 = £836\,830\,000 \text{ or } £836.83 \text{ million}$$

We have little guidance from senior management as to which customers they wish to target but let us, for the moment, assume that it is the top 5 per cent of customers, in terms of their usage – probably a realistic assumption since these will generate most revenue and probably most profit. Using the principles of the Normal distribution we can estimate the annual electricity consumption level that will mark this top 5 per cent. We require the top 5 per cent of the customer distribution. From the Normal distribution table we see that this equates to a Z score of 1.645 (interpolating between 1.64 and 1.65). We know that the mean consumption level is 4996, standard deviation 424.4, so we have:

$$Z = 1.645 = \frac{X - 4996}{424.4}$$

giving X = 5694. That is, to be in the top 5 per cent of electricity users we would need to have an annual electricity consumption of over 5694 kWh. For practical operational purposes we would probably want to round this to 5700 kWh. So, if we wanted to target the top 5 per cent of domestic users, we would have a cut-off of at least 5700 kWh per year as a consumption level. Can we estimate the sales revenue from this customer group? Using the same principles, we know that the top 5 per cent have consumption levels over 5700. The top 4 per cent will have consumption levels over 5740 (check the arithmetic if you want). So, 1 per cent of customers will use between 5700 and 5740 kWh; 1 per cent of customers is 25 000, so we have 25 000 customers using an average of 5720 kwh ((5700 + 5740) ÷ 2) at 6.7p per kWh, giving an estimated revenue from this 1 per cent of customers of £9.581 million. Using the same logic for the next 1 per cent and so on we have the estimates shown in Table 5.9.

In total, then, this top 5 per cent of customers will generate almost £50 million in sales revenue. Clearly, this analysis is based on a number of assumptions and we would not pretend that it was 100 per cent reliable (and this is typical of much quantitative analysis that is undertaken by business). However, with some key assumptions (which are not too unrealistic) we can provide some information to senior management. The top 5 per cent of customers are clearly important in terms of company revenue – and we have been able to estimate what they are 'worth' in that sense. We might be able to go one stage further and undertake some market research to estimate the probability of these customers taking their business to a competitor and the probability of them *not* moving to a competitor if we offered a price discount. This would then allow us to calculate the likely loss in revenue if we did not offer a discount, and the impact on our customer base and revenue if we did.

Table 5.9   Estimated revenue

Customer group (kWh)	No. of customers	Estimated revenue (£m)
5700 < 5740	25 000	9.581000
5740 < 5800	25 000	9.664750
5800 < 5870	25 000	9.773625
5870 < 6000	25 000	9.941125
6000 < 6200	25 000	10.217500

Note: Customer group consumption figures have been rounded.

Summary

In this chapter we have examined the idea of probability and introduced two common distributions – the Binomial and the Normal. Both distributions – as well as others we have not considered – find frequent use in management decision making and are based on relatively simple principles. The Binomial distribution requires a number of key characteristics to be satisfied before it can safely be applied to a problem. The Normal distribution, on the other hand, requires only that the variable we are investigating is Normally distributed. A surprising number of variables in practice do follow a Normal distribution – or at least come sufficiently close. However, as we shall see in a subsequent chapter, a far more important use of the Normal distribution lies in its application to the areas of statistical inference.

Some useful numbers to remember for the Normal distribution

For any Normally distributed variable:

- 68.26 per cent of the data (about two-thirds) will be within ± 1 standard deviation of the mean.
- 95.44 per cent (call it 95 per cent) of the data will be within ± 2 standard deviations of the mean.
- 99.7 per cent of the data will be within ± 3 standard deviations of the mean.

Exercises

1 Return to the example of Machine 2 in the shampoo bottle problem. Assume that management likewise wishes to ensure that the advertised contents satisfy some specific criteria. Determine what the advertised contents should be if management:

   (a) require no more than 1 per cent of bottles to be under the advertised contents;

   (b) no more than 5 per cent of bottles to be under the advertised contents.

2 The finance department of a large organisation has responsibility for monitoring costs in other departments of the organisation. A photocopier facility is available for one department's use and data has been collected which reveals that the number of photocopies made on the machine on a daily basis follows the Normal distribution; the mean of the distribution is 380 copies per day with a standard deviation of 35. The cost per copy is estimated at 6p.

   (a) Determine the probability that daily costs incurred on the photocopier machine will be:
   - more than £25;
   - less than £22.50;
   - between £24 and £26.

   (b) Explain the basis of your calculations in a short memo to the finance director.

3 A large retail store buys an item from a supplier in batches of 100. Because of the delicate nature of the item some are inevitably damaged in transit between the supplier and the store and the price the store pays to the supplier reflects this. Over the past few years an average of four items are damaged in each batch of 100. Recently the supplier has used another transport company to deliver supplies. The store has recently checked a total of 25 items and found that three were damaged in transit. As manager of the store, how might you use this information?

4 A small firm has recently purchased a new PC system comprising a colour monitor, a CPU, a laser printer and a keyboard. The supplier of the equipment states that the chance of any one of the components developing a fault in the first year is 1 per cent. What is the probability that the firm will have to have its PC repaired in some way during the first year? What assumptions have you made to work out your result?

5 On average last year a local leisure centre had 230 customers per day, standard deviation 27, and the distribution of customers was found to be Normal. Determine the probability that on any one day the centre has:

   (a) more than 270 customers;

   (b) less than 210 customers;

   (c) between 225 and 250 customers.

6 An auditor is checking invoices that have been paid to see if they contain any errors. Historically around 7 per cent of all invoices are expected to contain some error. The auditor takes a random batch of ten invoices. Calculate the probability distribution of errors for this batch of ten. What assumptions have you made?

7 An enterprising MBA graduate who has been unable to find gainful employment has taken to visiting an office block in town each lunchtime with an array of freshly made sandwiches for sale. The graduate reckons that he has a 90 per cent chance of selling a sandwich to any of the people working in the office block. He visits one office with 12 employees.

(a) Calculate the probability distribution of sandwich sales.

(b) Calculate the mean number of sales.

(c) How might the graduate use this information to improve the profitability of his activities?

8 A supermarket sells one particular item in its store on a regular basis. It currently has 750 units of this item in stock and no deliveries are expected until next week. The manager knows that average weekly sales of this item are 625, standard deviation of 55, and that sales are Normally distributed. Calculate the probability that the firm will not have enough stock to meet sales. How much stock should be kept if we want the chance of *not* having enough stock to be no more than 1 per cent?

9 A firm is involved in manufacturing high-quality electrical equipment. Each item produced costs £6000 and total annual output is 500 items. At the end of the production process each item is individually tested for quality and safety. If the item is defective in any way it is scrapped at a complete loss to the firm, since it has been found not cost-effective to repair such items. Historically, one item in 1000 is found to be faulty in some way.

(a) Determine the probability that the firm will produce zero faulty items in a year.

(b) Determine the probability that the firm will produce no more than three faulty items in a year.

(c) The firm is considering employing a quality inspector at an additional cost of £1000 per year. The inspector, however, will be able to prevent any item from being defective. Suggest how the firm might evaluate whether employing the inspector would be cost-effective.

10 Return to the example used in the chapter of two machines filling bottles of shampoo. One machine had a mean of 500 ml, SD 10 ml, the other a mean of 750 ml, SD 15 ml. For each machine calculate the lower and upper amounts (in ml) between which:

(a) 90 per cent of all output will fall;

(b) 95 per cent of all output will fall;

(c) 99 per cent of all output will fall.

11 Return to the Worked Example in this chapter. After conducting market research we have found that the possibility of a customer in the top 5 per cent group switching to a competitor is 0.85 if we do not offer a price discount and 0.15 if we do. Consider how you could use this information to determine the appropriate level of the price rebate to be offered.

6

Decision Making Under Uncertainty

Learning objectives

By the end of this chapter you should be able to:

- calculate and explain expected value
- construct and use decision trees
- explain the difference between uncertainty and risk
- assess the value of perfect information

As we concluded in the previous chapter, much of business decision making takes place under conditions of uncertainty. Frequently we must take decisions with incomplete knowledge or knowing that the outcomes of these decisions are at best uncertain. Although there is no magic solution for the dilemma facing a manager in these uncertain situations, there are ways of examining these decision problems that can help clarify how decisions can be made. This is the area of decision making under uncertainty. In this chapter we shall be exploring the issues involved in making decisions under such conditions and seeing how probability can be used as part of the decision-making process.

The decision problem

We shall illustrate the principles of using probability to help reach management decisions with the following example. A small company has established a niche for itself in the computer market. It specialises in assembling and selling specialist tablet computer systems for use by family doctor practices throughout the UK – a market which, since the reform initiatives in the National Health Service, has proved particularly lucrative. The tablets can be networked together and can be used by medical staff in the practice itself or when visiting patients at home. The tablet is specially programmed for the user by the medical staff and has a number of in-built apps. The company is developing a new tablet which it intends to market under its own brand name next year. At present the company is trying to decide on the manufacturing and assembly process to be used. It has decided that it faces three alternatives:

● It can manufacture/assemble the tablet itself.
● It can buy the tablet from a domestic manufacturer.
● It can buy the tablet from a manufacturer in the Far East.

The problem is that each of these options has different costs and benefits associated with it. To manufacture/assemble the tablet itself, the company would require major investment in new production equipment as well as extensive training of the workforce. It is felt that such an investment is only likely to be cost-effective if sales of the new product are particularly good. Buying the tablet from a domestic supplier will involve the company in less up-front expense and will be safer if large sales do not materialise in the future. Buying from an overseas supplier offers better quality but with the risk of disruptions in supply if there are problems in the supply chain. In other words, there is uncertainty as to which decision to take because there is uncertainty over future sales. To help simplify the situation, the company is planning for one of three possible sales levels in the future: low, medium or high.

This problem typifies many situations that organisations have to face in real life. The company is faced with a range of alternative decisions over which it has control (i.e. it can choose between them) and it also faces an uncertain future in terms of sales, over which it has less control. This future position is generally referred to as the possible *states of nature*: these states, future sales levels, are outside the direct control of the company but they do include all the possibilities and only one of them can actually occur. So, the basic decision to be made is: which of the three supply options do we go for, given the uncertainty we face as to the state of nature that will actually occur? How do we decide what to do *now* given that we do not know the level of sales we will achieve in the *future*?

Progress Check 6.1

If you were making this decision, what additional information would you like to have?

In order to progress we clearly need additional information to help us assess the alternatives. One of the key pieces of information would relate to the financial consequences of each combination of decision and state of nature. That is, how would the company be affected financially if, for example, it decided to manufacture the tablet itself and future sales turned out to be low? What would the financial outcome be if sales were medium or high and so on. We shall assume that such information is available to the company in the form of the profit contribution that would be made to the company's activities in terms of each decision/state of nature combination. This information is presented in Table 6.1.

The table is usually referred to as a *pay-off table* since it shows the financial consequences – or pay-offs – in terms of the alternative decisions that can be made and the alternative states of nature that might result. If we examine the decision option to manufacture the tablet in-house we see that the pay-off could vary from a loss of £15 000 through to a profit of £55 000. This implies that if this decision is taken and future sales

Table 6.1 Pay-off table: profit contribution (£000s)

Decision	Future sales level		
	Low	Medium	High
Manufacture	−15	10	55
Buy abroad	10	30	25
Buy domestic	5	20	40

are low, the decision will adversely affect profitability to the tune of £15 000 – presumably because the firm has had to make a major investment, which will not be recouped due to low sales levels. On the other hand, if sales turn out to be high the company stands to generate a profit contribution of some £55 000. Equivalent pay-offs are shown for the other two decision alternatives.

What could possibly go wrong?

By Emma Jacobs

Source: © Anna Gordon

When Trevor Maynard travels, he turns up at the airport a couple of hours before most people would. "Just in case the taxi breaks down or [is] attacked by a swarm of frogs," he says. This is not the sign of a worrier, he insists, but a rational response to risk. "Let the data speak for itself. It's not about being overcautious." As head of the exposure management and reinsurance team at Lloyd's of London, the insurer, thinking of worst-case scenarios and calculating the likelihood of a disaster is his job.

Despite being mired in death and catastrophe, the grey-haired 42-year-old is not, he says, gloomy but entirely "sensible". A trained actuary who studied mathematics, he applies data to every area of his life: even childcare. "It's not about scaremongering or being overcautious. It's about being aware of the true risk and then acting in accordance with it. People do run into the road, so you don't let a three-year-old play in the front garden unattended, but you do let a 16-year-old."

However, not every disaster can be planned for. "Clearly, some things are too big . . . asteroids killed the dinosaurs: so, you're not going to care if your insurance is paid off." Based since 2005 in the inside-out office designed by "starchitect" Richard Rogers, he took over the team in March 2011, just two days after the earthquake and tsunami hit Fukushima in Japan. "We have modelled the impact of earthquakes in Japan for some time. The 2011 Japanese event was a surprise in several ways. Firstly, the magnitude of an event at that location was outside our expectations; secondly, the chain of events that led to the severe damage at the Fukushima nuclear reactor was not commonly modclled."

When disaster happens on an unprecedented scale or unravels in an unexpected way, he checks it against the mathematical models his department runs to see if there was something foreseeable they should have included. Despite the severe financial losses to Lloyd's that year – 2011 proved to be full of disasters, resulting in a loss of £516m for the insurer as a big earthquake in New Zealand and severe floods in Thailand followed the Japanese quake – he does not believe his team was at fault. "Scientifically, people didn't expect a quake of that magnitude [in Japan], so that was a surprise. I don't think that implies an error. It just implies that there's a lot about this planet that we don't fully understand.

"Most things that happen, people describe as exceptional, and I'm trying always to say 'no they weren't, they were absolutely predictable'." Superstorm Sandy was seen by many as exceptional. But it was entirely foreseeable, he insists. "With climate change, sea level [rising], warmer pools of water, you absolutely would expect Sandy situations to occur." He warns against hyperbole: "Don't describe that as exceptional, because you won't be prepared for the next one."

Sandy, which hit the Caribbean and North America in October 2012, resulted in a £1.4bn payout. Yet Lloyd's still made pre-tax profits of £2.77bn last year. There is a danger in painting a catastrophe as unusual, he says.

"People have very short memories. And things that are very rare are either fixated on and given too much weight, or they're totally ignored. Usually what happens is, when it's new, people fixate on it and then very, very quickly it just gets forgotten, and then it gets completely overlooked." He adds: "The danger is that the risk hasn't gone away. Sometimes it could be growing."

While some see beauty in numbers, he sees solutions. "Solving [maths] problems is important. Some people think it's an art rather than a science, and it has a lot of artistic elements to it. But for me solving a problem [is] part of the appeal."

His job is not just about mapping risk, he insists. It is also about influencing policy makers. His team recently submitted research to the US's Federal Energy Regulatory Commission on the risk of magnetic storms from the sun that could melt electricity transformers, which take months to rebuild. "We'd actually rather the risk is managed; therefore, the insurance cost goes down; the premium would be less." He denies talking up risk to scare businesses into taking out insurance. He views the industry as a force for good. "Insurance helps pick people up after disaster. Your GDP could be severely harmed by a major event like an earthquake, and it can set you back 20 years. Whereas if you've got insurance in place, then very rapidly you get an injection of capital, and can move on from that."

So far, he has put a brave face on the catastrophes he deals with on a daily basis, but one threat does concern him: climate change. "People think this is tomorrow's problem," he says. They do not probe the knock-on effects on their business. "There might be more political tension in some parts of the world, because food's going to be more expensive. Before you know it, you've put together a scenario where you can see there's actually quite a lot of stress on your business." He pauses for breath. "With increasing globalisation and supply chain issues, then you start to see that climate changes in some parts of the world that are far removed from you are actually having a big impact on your locally based business."

Uncertainty, risk and probability are all around us at both a personal and a business level. We need to be able to deal with these.

Progress Check 6.2

Considering the information in Table 6.1, which of the three alternative decisions would you recommend?

The answer has to be: it depends. It will depend on a number of factors: how reliable you think the information is, how risky the various options are, how critical the decision is to the company's future and so on. One of the key factors, however, will depend on your own attitude to these future states of nature. In the absence of any other information on the likelihood of each state of nature actually occurring we can consider a number of common attitudes and we shall examine each in turn.

The maximax criterion

Let us assume for the moment that you have a very optimistic view of the future. If this were the case you would tend to choose the decision which could generate the highest possible pay-off. Such an approach is known as the *maximax* criterion, since we are searching for the *maxi*mum of the *maxi*mum pay-offs. In this problem our maximax decision would be to manufacture the tablet ourselves since this generates the highest of all potential pay-offs at £55 000 (compared with the best pay-off of £30 000 for buying abroad and of £40 000 for buying domestically). In general, for this approach, we determine the maximum pay-off for each decision and then choose the largest of these. This approach has the advantage of focusing on the best possible outcome. In summary, such an approach follows two steps.

- For each possible decision, identify the maximum possible pay-off.
- Comparing these pay-offs, select the decision that will give the maximum pay-off.

The maximin criterion

However, we are not all optimistic about the future. There is something to be said for examining the worst-case scenario – being pessimistic about future outcomes. In such a situation we can apply the *maximin* criterion, since we search for the *maxi*mum of the *min*imum pay-offs. For each possible decision we determine the minimum (worst) possible pay-off and then choose the best of these. In this case this would lead us to choose the option of buying abroad, since this is the largest of each of the minimum pay-offs at £10 000 (the minimum pay-offs being −£15 000, £10 000 and £5000 respectively). While such an approach has the logic of ensuring that we are in the best possible position if the worst happens, the approach does obviously ignore the potentially larger profit contributions that can be made by the other two decisions. The summary of the approach is:

- For each possible decision, identify the minimum possible pay-off.
- Comparing these pay-offs, select the decision that will give the maximum pay-off.

The minimax regret criterion

A third approach is possible using the concept of opportunity loss or regret. Let us assume we take a decision to buy abroad. Having committed ourselves to this course of action we later observe that sales levels were actually high. Clearly – with hindsight – this was not the best decision given what actually occurred. The optimal decision would in fact have been to manufacture ourselves – generating a profit contribution of £55 000 rather than £25 000. Effectively we have 'lost' £30 000 by taking our original decision. This figure is referred to as the opportunity cost – or regret – of the decision for that situation. Clearly we can calculate the opportunity loss, or regret, associated with each possible decision and the various circumstances. This is summarised in Table 6.2, which is derived from Table 6.1.

We take each column (situation) in Table 6.1 in turn and determine, for that situation, what the optimum decision would be if we knew for certain what would actually occur. So, if sales turn out to be low, the optimum decision would have been to buy abroad. If we had actually taken this decision, our 'regret' in financial terms would be zero since it was the best decision. On the other hand, if we had decided to manufacture, the regret would be £25 000 since we could have had a profit contribution of £10 000 but actually incurred a loss of £15 000. Similarly, if we had decided to buy domestically, the regret would be £5000. We can perform similar calculations for the other two columns.

Progress Check 6.3

Calculate the maximum regret for each of the other possible decisions. Using this information, which decision would you recommend?

For each of the decision options we can now determine the maximum of these regret values and these are shown in the last column in Table 6.2. The logic we apply is simple. We consider each decision in turn and the maximum regret value shows the maximum opportunity cost associated with this decision on the assumption that the worst happens. Effectively we are saying, suppose we take a particular decision, what will it cost us (in opportunity cost terms) if the worst then happens in terms of future sales? Clearly we would then wish to take the decision where this maximum regret was minimised. This would be the decision to buy domestically, since this has the lowest maximum regret at £15 000.

To summarise this approach:

- Calculate the regret table for the problem for each situation.
- For each decision option determine the maximum regret value.
- Select the decision option that gives the minimum of these maximum regrets.

It is worth noting that in this simple example the three different approaches have led us to three different decisions. In itself this is no bad thing since it reinforces the view that – without certain knowledge of the future – there is no one ideal decision. The decision we take will, under these circumstances, depend on the decision maker's view of the future.

Table 6.2 Pay-off table: regret or opportunity loss (£000s)

| Decision | Future sales level | | | |
	Low	Medium	High	Maximum regret
Manufacture	25	20	0	25
Buy abroad	0	0	30	30
Buy domestic	5	10	15	15

However, one of the potential benefits of this type of approach is that it forces decision makers to consider and justify explicitly their view of future circumstances. One of the main drawbacks of this approach is that we have treated the three situations as being equally likely. In the last approach, for example, the process would lead us to the decision to buy domestically, even though in two out of three situations the decision to buy abroad has a zero regret. Clearly it is often more appropriate to view these circumstances as having differing probabilities in terms of their happening. Thus we might feel that medium sales has a higher chance of happening than low sales. We need to be able to incorporate such information into the decision-making process.

Decision making using probability information

Let us assume that the company has been able to quantify the likelihood of each of the states of nature occurring by attaching a probability to each. Such probabilities may have been derived from market research, from sales forecasting, or may simply be a 'guesstimate' based on some hard evidence and the experience of the decision maker. The probability of low sales is assessed at 0.2, medium at 0.5 and high at 0.3. Note that, as they must, the probabilities sum to 1 to include all possible outcomes. Clearly we now need to be able to use this additional information to help us reach a decision. The approach we can develop is to calculate the *expected value* for each of the alternative decisions. Let us consider the decision to buy domestically. For this decision there are three possible states of nature, each with a financial outcome, and for each state of nature we now have a probability. It seems reasonable to use these probabilities to calculate a weighted average outcome for this decision. There's a 20 per cent chance of earning £5000, a 50 per cent chance of earning £20 000 and a 30 per cent chance of earning £40 000. That is:

$$(£5000 \times 0.2) + (£20\,000 \times 0.5) + (£40\,000 \times 0.3)$$

to give a figure of £23 000. This result is known as the expected value (EV) of this decision: the alternative financial outcomes weighted by the respective probabilities. Care needs to be taken in terms of what the EV represents. It is not a guaranteed financial outcome if we were to take this particular decision. Rather it is a measure taking into account both the outcomes and their likelihood – recollecting that probabilities themselves should be seen as long-term averages. The overall purpose of EVs is to facilitate comparison.

Progress Check 6.4

Calculate the EV for each of the other decision alternatives. Based on this information, which decision would you recommend?

The EVs for all the decisions are then:

Manufacture	£18 500
Buy abroad	£24 500
Buy domestically	£23 000

Based on this information we would logically recommend that we buy the tablet abroad since it has a higher EV. Once again, we must stress that taking such a decision does not guarantee better profitability. What actually occurs will generate for this decision a profit of £10 000, £30 000 or £25 000. Overall, however, this decision option is to be favoured since the weighted combination of outcomes and probabilities is higher than that for the other two options.

John Kay: Is insurance worth paying for? Probably

By John Kay

Scott Fitzgerald claimed that the mark of first-rate intelligence was the ability to hold two contradictory ideas in mind at the same time, and still function. Thinking in terms of probabilities is a technique for managing Fitzgerald's problem.

Probabilistic thinking is particularly relevant to insurance and investment. While it is vexing to have your television stolen, or to lose your bag on holiday, insurance will not bring back either. The financial loss from a stolen television or lost bag is probably smaller than you will incur on a bad day on the stock market. So you should think probabilities when you take out insurance. But so does the insurance company, which knows the probabilities well. It has estimated the expected value of claims and, if the expected value was not less than the premiums, it would not stay in business. Worse still, much of the premium on policies that insure against these minor contingencies goes not to pay policyholders but to the administrative costs of small claims.

So insure only those things you cannot afford to lose. You need insurance against your house burning down, but not for replacing the bedroom carpet. You need insurance against being hospitalised in the US, but not for an extra night's accommodation because your plane is delayed. Many people struggle with this advice. Insurers find their customers have little appetite for policies that rarely pay out, even though low probability risks are those most appropriate for insurance. Policyholders like the reassurance of occasional small cheques even if such cheques add up to much less than their premiums.

You will be financially better off if you can be detached and learn to control these emotions. But even people educated in intelligent investment find it hard to exercise such control. If you can't refrain from kicking yourself, or your spouse can't refrain from kicking you, when an uninsured television set is stolen, then you should take out the policy. This strategy is, however, likely to cost you considerably more in premiums than you received in claims.

The stock market throws up similar probabilities. Last week, I wrote about Robb Caledon, a bankrupt shipyard in the 1970s. Its shareholders would receive £1 per share if the company was nationalised, but otherwise would lose their money. Its shares were standing in the market at 40p. These shares were a good buy if you thought the nationalisation bill would succeed. But they were also a good buy if you thought the nationalisation bill might not succeed. The expected value of a gamble such as an investment in Robb Caledon is measured by multiplying the possible outcomes by their probabilities. If you thought the probability that the bill would pass was 0.5, then the expected value of a share was 50p – 10p more than the market price.

In spite of the name, the expected value is not what you should expect, and the expected profit is not the profit you should expect, either. A year after a purchase, you would either have lost your whole investment or made 60p of profit. Still, if you use expected values, you will sometimes win, sometimes lose. But over time, the overall outcome will approach the expected value. In the long run, using probabilities and calculating expected values is likely to leave you better off.

So think probabilities and be detached. It's hard advice to follow. That is why the financial services industry is better off than its customers.

Moral: Don't expect to get the expected value – it's a decision-making tool not an outcome.

Risk

Clearly, one aspect of the problem that we have ignored relates explicitly to the decision maker's attitude to risk. Consider the following scenario. Your lecturer or tutor offers you a simple game of chance. A coin will be tossed in the air. On landing, if it shows heads you have lost and must pay the tutor £1. If the coin shows tails you have won and the tutor must pay you £2. The simple question: would you play (assuming your tutor isn't cheating)? The answer must be 'yes', since you have a 50 per cent chance of winning £2 and a 50 per cent chance of losing £1, implying in the long run that you ought to make a profit (the EV would be 50p). However, suppose the rules change slightly. Now if you win the tutor will pay you £20 000 but if you lose you will pay the tutor £10 000. Would you still play? There is now probably some hesitancy on your part. The odds of your winning are still the same. What has changed is the amount you stand to lose. If you could not afford to lose £10 000 on the first throw you would probably decline to take part. Consider if the stakes went up to £100 000, or £1 000 000. The recommended decision – based on the approaches we have introduced – would not be affected by this. What will be affected is our attitude to the risk that we face.

Returning to our business problem, consider the decision option to manufacture. In principle this could lead to the highest profit contribution −£55 000. But equally it might lead to a loss of £15 000. If the company's cash flow is poor or it already has large debts it might decide – on a risk basis – not even to consider this option but to play safe and take another decision which leads to a surer – if smaller – profit.

Decision trees

It is also possible – and frequently useful – to represent the type of problem we have been examining in graphical form by constructing what is known as a *decision tree*. The tree diagram shows the logical progression that occurs over time in terms of decisions and outcomes and is particularly useful in sequential decision problems – where a series of decisions need to be made with each, in part, depending on earlier decisions and outcomes. The tree diagram for our tablet problem is shown in Figure 6.1. The construction starts from the left-hand side and gradually moves across to the right. A box is used to indicate that at this point we must take a decision (the box is technically known as a *decision node*), and the three alternatives branch out from this node: to manufacture (M), to buy abroad (BA) or to buy domestically (BD). Logically we can only move down one of these branches but we do not yet know which one. Each of these branches leads to a *chance* or *outcome node* (indicated by a circle), which represents the possible states of nature: these are outcomes over which the decision maker has no control and we will only know in the future which branch we will follow. In our simple example this node along each decision branch is the same: sales could turn out to be low (L), medium (M) or high (H). At the end of each branch originating from a chance node we have a pay-off. We see, therefore, that there are a total of nine possible pay-offs of this problem. The next stage is to add to the tree the relevant information on what the pay-offs are, what the probabilities of the chance branches are and the EVs of each decision branch.

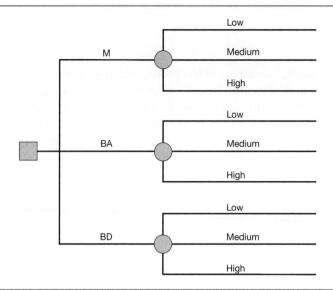

Figure 6.1 Decision tree I

This has been done in Figure 6.2. It can be seen that the relevant information has been added: pay-offs, probabilities and expected values. The decision maker now sees clearly the potential pay-offs from each combination of decision and situation. Also, the EVs for each decision can be identified and used to assist in the decision-making process, as we have just discussed. Based on this information we would recommend, other things being equal, that we choose the BA branch, although we recognise from the tree that the eventual outcome of this decision is as yet unknown.

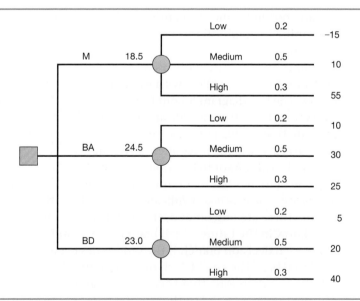

Figure 6.2 Decision tree II: pay-off values in £000s

'Risk Savvy: How to make good decisions', by Gerd Gigerenzer

Review by Clive Cookson

How many people did the 9/11 terrorists kill? According to Gerd Gigerenzer, more than 4,500 died as a direct result of the attacks. Besides the almost 3,000 slaughtered in the airliners and their targets on the ground, an additional 1,600 lost their lives in US road accidents during the year that followed because they chose to drive rather than risk flying.

Gigerenzer's statistical analysis of the increase in road traffic during 2001/02 – and its fatal consequences – is one of many powerful examples in *Risk Savvy* of the way people make bad decisions because they misunderstand risk.

 Source: Cookson, C. (2014) 'Risk savvy: How to make good decisions', by Gerd Gigerenzer, FT.com, 23 May.
©The Financial Times Limited. All Rights Reserved.

Understanding risks is not easy and can lead to poor decision-making at a personal level as well as managerial.

QADM IN ACTION Capgemini – risk management modelling

Capgemini's client was a major US oil exploration and production company. As part of a major change programme, the client wanted to promote improved decision making amongst its employees through a better understanding of risk management techniques. The client was unsure as to the level of risk the company was exposed to in the different geographical regions in which they operated. Similarly, they were unsure as to the effect that the interrelationships between its different assets had on the overall level of risk. Given the nature of their business, many of their activities were subject to considerable uncertainty. The economic life of an oilfield can be predicted but not with certainty. The economic viability of the field will itself be affected by future world oil prices, which, again, are uncertain. Similarly, changes in technological efficiency and development will be uncertain. All of these factors and more will have a significant impact on key business decisions.

The initial approach was to develop a clear understanding of the client's business and the nature and structure of the risks involved in the different parts of the business. The team then developed a financial model (we shall look at these in Chapter 15) using Microsoft Excel. Uncertainty and risk were built in using a simulation approach (we shall look at simulation modelling in Chapter 14).

A variety of risk models were developed for the business. These simulated financial investment performance by geographical region and provided management information on the risk and return by type of asset, by area and by region. The models helped managers identify and understand the key uncertainties they faced with such decisions. The models also helped identify the potential impact of global risks such as major oil price changes and loss of production due to hurricane activity. A set of training modules based on the risk management modules were developed for use across the company.

The figure below relates to part of the risk management modelling looking at the uncertainty involved in the quantity of oil reserves. The distribution should look familiar!

A number of benefits were realised by the client:

- Improvements in the decision-making process itself.

- An increased understanding of risk by managers in the business.
- Improved information on business assets.

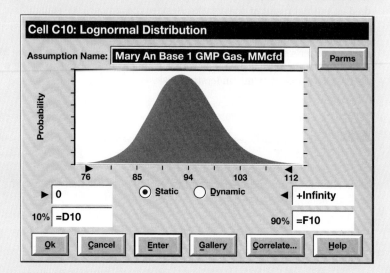

Source: Based on a Capgemini case study, with thanks to Capgemini for permission to use their material.

Such decision trees are useful ways of showing the outcomes and potential consequences of alternative decisions. They are particularly useful in situations where a series of decisions over time may need to be taken which could not easily be shown in tabular form.

We can illustrate this by adding an extra factor to our existing problem. The company is still evaluating its options in terms of the tablet decision. One of the management team has now suggested that *if* the decision to manufacture is taken and *if* sales turn out to be low then the company should consider a marketing campaign to try to boost sales. Such a marketing campaign would largely be based on adverts in magazines and trade journals, together with mailshots to family doctors advertising the new system. Such a marketing exercise would cost an estimated £10 000. It is felt that such a campaign would have an 85 per cent chance of being successful. If it were successful then the gross pay-off (before subtracting the campaign cost) would be £40 000. On the other hand, if the campaign were not successful, it would still have raised sales sufficiently for the pay-off to be break-even, i.e. £0, before the campaign costs have been taken into account. While the company would like to defer the decision on the marketing campaign option, the advertising agency which would handle the campaign wants to know *now* if its services would be required so that it can ensure it has staff and resources available at the right time.

You can picture the firm's dilemma. The campaign appears to offer an additional option but only *if* the decision is taken to manufacture and *if* sales turn out to be low. We won't know whether this will happen until some time in the future. But the company cannot delay its decision on the marketing campaign. It needs to decide *now* before sales are known.

Progress Check 6.5

Amend the decision tree we have for this problem to incorporate the new option.

Referring to Figure 6.2 we see that the only part of the tree that would be affected would be the very top branch relating to a combination of manufacture decision and low sales. Effectively, if we ever got to this part of the tree we would face another decision (and hence would require another decision node) relating to whether we undertook the marketing campaign (MC) or did not (NMC). If we did launch the campaign, two circumstances might arise: the campaign could be successful (S) or a failure (F). We can now incorporate this information into the decision tree, shown in Figure 6.3.

At the top right of the tree we have added another decision node with two alternatives: launch the marketing campaign (MC) or do not (NMC). If we launch the campaign then two outcomes are possible: the campaign will be successful (S) or it will not (F). We can then add the new pay-offs, the probability information and the new calculations for EV. Starting at the very right-hand side of the tree we see that the pay-off if the campaign is launched and is successful is £30 000 (the gross of £40 000 less the campaign costs). If the campaign is launched and is not successful, the pay-off will be −£10 000. The pay-off if we do not have a marketing campaign obviously stays the same as before (−£15 000). The probabilities of 0.85 and 0.15 have been added to the appropriate branches. We can then calculate the EV of the two new alternative decisions. The decision to launch the campaign has an EV of £24 000, while the decision not to launch has an EV of −£15 000 (remember that the pay-off of −£15 000 is 100 per cent certain if we do not have a campaign). Clearly

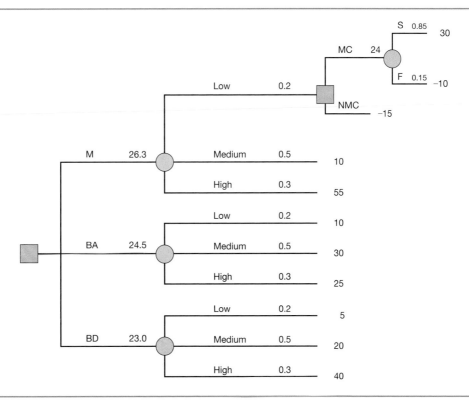

Figure 6.3 Completed decision tree: pay-off values in £000s

if we found ourselves in the position of having manufactured the tablet with resulting low sales, our subsequent decision would be to launch the marketing campaign since this has a higher EV than the alternative of doing nothing. We can then use the EV of this decision to work backwards to the left and calculate the new EV for the manufacture decision. This figure – originally £18 500 – must change since the pay-off linked to low sales has changed. The new EV is £26 300. Other things being equal, our initial decision would now be to manufacture the tablet ourselves. However, we now know one of our future decisions. Given that we now decide to manufacture the tablet, we also know that if future sales turn out to be low we will be launching a marketing campaign. We cannot, at this stage, tell the marketing company that their services are definitely needed (after all, low future sales are not a certain outcome) but we can confirm their services will be needed if sales are low. Consider also the timescale for this decision. Once we receive information that sales have indeed been low, we shall not need to spend time considering our options. We have already decided what our future decision would be if we found ourselves in this situation. We would launch the campaign (always assuming of course that at that time in the future the information relating to probabilities and pay-offs has remained unchanged). The speed of decision making can potentially be improved through this approach, as it allows us to assess in advance our decisions under different scenarios.

Police attempt to collar crooks before they offend

Durham force puts algorithm through its paces to assess chance of recommitting crime

By Patricia Nilsson in Durham

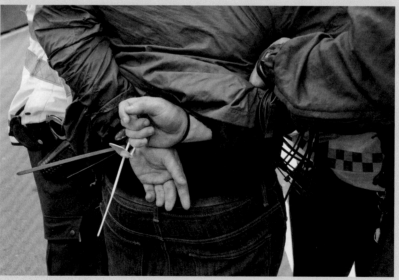

Source: Janine Wiedel Photolibrary/Alamy Images

With 25 years' experience in the police force, Inspector Jason Meecham reckons he can tell whether someone under arrest can be safely released on bail or whether they will commit another crime as soon as they are out of custody. "I think I have a good gauge of risk," Mr Meecham said.

But he and his colleagues at Durham Constabulary have spent the past three years testing a computer program, the Harm Assessment Risk Tool (Hart), that claims to take a data-based approach to predicting whether an arrested person will reoffend.

Durham is the first UK police force to use an algorithm to predict the behaviour of an individual, although other police forces have experimented with trying to predict where crimes are likely to occur and with trying to predict which households might be vulnerable to cases of domestic and child abuse.

Durham police use Hart to target support for offenders seen as most likely to commit further crimes. Outside the UK, tools similar to Hart have been used by courts to inform sentencing or decisions on parole. The program, developed by the police force's own engineers in collaboration with academics at Cambridge University, is built on five years' worth of data on people taken into custody in Durham, and whether they reoffended within two years of release. It makes predictions based on 33 different metrics, including previous offence history, age and postcode.

The model uses a machine-learning technique called "random forest". It is made up of 509 decision "trees", essentially questions, that branch out to other relevant trees, one after the other, before arriving at a prediction.

The accuracy of Hart, which suggests to officers whether an arrested person is at low, medium or high risk of reoffending, will be evaluated when its trial period wraps up in April.

Decision trees can crop up in the most unexpected places.

The value of perfect information

We shall illustrate one further use of this type of approach. The company has been considering extending its activities to the economies of Eastern Europe. With the political and economic changes that have taken place over the last few years the company feels that the time might be ripe for a move into these markets. After some initial analysis and a fact-finding visit to three of the East European economies by the company chief executive, the pay-off table shown in Table 6.3 has been constructed.

The company is considering three options. The first is to launch the product in one or two key geographical areas as a pilot programme and to postpone a final decision as to whether to market throughout the whole of Eastern Europe until the results of the pilot programme are known. The second option is to go ahead straight away with a major product launch. The third option is to establish a joint venture with key trading partners already operating in these economies. The financial outcomes of these decisions will, in part, depend on the level of market growth achieved over the next three years. For simplicity this has been categorised as zero, low or high. The local chamber of commerce has indicated that, in its opinion, the chance of each of these three growth levels being

Table 6.3 Pay-off table: Eastern Europe (£000s)

	Market growth		
	Zero	Low	High
Pilot programme	10	50	150
Major product launch	−300	100	500
Joint venture	−200	200	350

realised is 0.5, 0.4 and 0.1 respectively. However, the reliability of this opinion is not very high, as the chamber readily admits. If we apply the principles of expected value we obtain the following:

Pilot programme	EV = £40 000
Major product launch	EV = −£60 000
Joint venture	EV = £15 000

Based on this information, we would recommend a pilot programme since it has the higher EV. So far this is no different from what we have done previously. However, let us add a twist to the business problem. A market research firm specialising in forecasting in Eastern European economies has approached the company, offering to undertake research into the company's intended markets. The purpose of this research would be to try to provide a firmer view of likely market growth – that is, to try to predict with increased accuracy whether the future growth will be zero, low or high. The key question for the company is: what is this information worth?

Progress Check 6.6

How much would you be prepared to pay the research company for such information?

From the company's perspective, the whole point of having such additional information is to reduce – and ideally eliminate – the chance of taking a wrong decision based on the limited information currently available. Consider the situation where the research firm *guaranteed* that it could predict with 100 per cent certainty the future market growth. If this were the case the company would, based on this prediction, take the optimum decision. If the prediction were of zero growth, the optimum decision would be to pilot. On the other hand, if the prediction were for low growth, we would decide on a joint venture, and if the prediction were for high growth, we would opt for a major product launch. In short, with *perfect information* about the future we would make the perfect decision each time. But how does this help? If we now summarise these 'perfect' decisions incorporating both the pay-off and the probability of that situation we have:

$$(0.5 \times 10) + (0.4 \times 200) + (0.1 \times 500) = £135(000)$$

as the EV of having perfect information about the future circumstances. Compare this with the EV of £40 000 under the existing conditions. It is then clear that to the company such perfect information has a maximum worth of £95 000 (135 − 40). If the research firm is willing to guarantee its prediction then the company would be wise to pay up to this amount for the perfect information. But what if – as is usual – such information is not perfect in terms of predicting the future? Suppose the research firm offers only a 90 per cent chance that it will get the prediction right? In principle it is then possible to evaluate the worth of such imperfect information using a similar approach. The technicalities of doing this, however, take us beyond our remit for this text.

Worked example

A company specialises in establishing local, privately run leisure centres throughout the country. Typically, the company will undertake considerable demographic analysis and assess the potential for establishing such a centre in a particular area. Areas targeted are typically those with a high proportion of middle-income families (young age profiles, parents with professional occupations, car owners) and with poor or non-existent public leisure facilities. The centres offer a range of sporting and related leisure facilities: squash, badminton, swimming, gym, sauna together with a cafe and bar. The centre facilities are offered on an annual membership basis. After some initial analysis the company is considering building one such centre in a particular area. Detailed planning permission has already been obtained and financial support from the company's bank has been approved. On this particular site the company is considering a range of options:

- *Option A*: Build a large centre offering the full range of facilities.
- *Option B*: Build a medium-sized centre now with a selected range of facilities. Over the next two to three years assess whether the centre should be further expanded to the full range of facilities.
- *Option C*: Delay a decision about the size of the centre until more detailed market analysis has been completed (expected to take a further 12 months). At that time a decision would be taken to build either a large centre or a medium-sized centre. This extra market analysis would cost an additional £150 000.

To help in its analysis, the company has commissioned forecasts of the likely levels of use of the centre and undertaken a financial assessment of the various options/outcomes. Preliminary market research indicates that for Option A the chance of demand for the centre's facilities being high is 0.7, and of demand being low is 0.3. With high demand the company stands to make an estimated £950 000 profit. With low demand it would generate a loss of £700 000. For Option B the probabilities of high and low demand remain the same. If demand does turn out to be low then the company has already decided it would not expand the centre any further. Projected profit is £100 000. However, if demand turns out to be high, the company has a further option of expanding the centre, although it has not yet decided if it should do this. Such an expansion might be successful and generate an estimated profit of £650 000 but if it is not successful the company will lose £100 000. The chance of a further expansion being successful has been put at 0.9.

If more detailed market analysis is undertaken in Option C the probabilities of high and low demand change to 0.8 and 0.2 respectively, since the company will be able to target its marketing and advertising more precisely. However, after such analysis has been completed the company will still have to decide whether to build a large centre (as in Option A) or a medium-sized centre (as in Option B), although in this latter case it would not subsequently be worthwhile expanding the medium-sized centre any further. For a large centre the financial outcomes are a profit of £950 000 if demand is high and a loss of £700 000 if demand is low. If a medium-sized centre is built the company estimates a profit of £700 000 if demand is high but a profit of only £100 000 if demand is low.

What should the company do? Clearly the company faces a range of decisions and possible outcomes so a decision-tree approach seems appropriate. The company faces three initial choices (Options A, B, C), with two of these options involving further decisions at a later date. The decision tree for this situation is shown in Figure 6.4. The tree

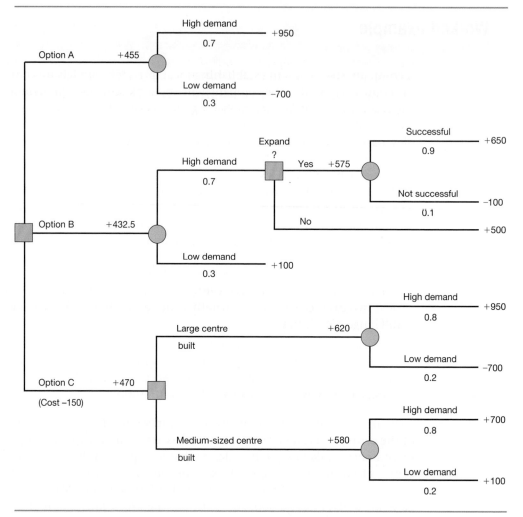

Figure 6.4 Leisure centre decision tree (figures shown in £000s)

is quite complex and will need careful study. We start on the left with the three basic options available to the company. Option A is the easiest to assess since there are two possible outcomes from the decision. We see the expected value from this decision as +455 (+£455 000). Option B is more complex. If the company builds a medium-sized centre and demand turns out to be low then no further decision is required. However, if demand is high (something we will not know until some time in the future) the company must then decide whether or not to expand the centre. If it does not expand it earns a profit of £500 000. If it does expand, the expansion could be successful (with a probability of 0.9) or it might not be (with a probability of 0.1, or 1 − 0.9). We see that the two expected values are +575 for expansion and +500 for no expansion.

Clearly, based on this information, the logical decision would be to expand the centre if demand turns out to be high. So we already have one benefit from this approach. We know *now* whether we should expand or not in the future if we go ahead with Option B and if demand is high. However, what about Option A versus Option B? Continuing with the Option B branch, although we see that the centre expansion is preferable to no expansion, we also calculate the EV for the whole of Option B as +432.5 – lower than that for Option A.

Option C, however, generates an even higher EV at +470 and would be the preferred option. Effectively, by delaying the decision 12 months and collecting more information we are delaying the decision as to which size of centre to build and also increasing the probability of high demand associated with the decision. We see that the logical decision for Option C would be to build the large centre (since this has the higher EV at +620 compared with +580). From this EV, however, we must subtract the additional cost incurred under Option C of £150 000 for undertaking more analysis. This gives a final EV for Option C of +470.

Clearly, decisions would not be taken based on this information alone. However, the implications of the three options become clear and can be assessed analytically. The company could also use this approach to do some sensitivity analysis. Would the decision change if some of the probabilities changed (since we might influence the probability of high demand, for example, by more extensive advertising and marketing)? Would the decision change if some of the financial data altered? Equally, we can assess the value of additional information. Without Option C, our decision would have been Option A with an EV of 455. Under Option C the EV is 470, an extra £15 000. This is the 'value' of the additional information we have collected over and above the cost we incurred of £150 000. We could advise the company that if the cost of completing additional analysis under Option C is likely to rise its maximum 'worth' to the company would be £165 000 (£150 000 + £15 000).

Summary

In this chapter we have considered the decision-making process in the context of trying to evaluate alternative decisions under alternative states of nature given the ever-present problem of uncertainty. We presented a number of different approaches to trying to reach a suitable decision under such circumstances, both with and without information relating to the probabilities of the different situations occurring. We also introduced the decision tree both as a method for summarising this information and for analysing more complex decision scenarios. While we cannot pretend that such approaches solve the uncertainty problems facing the decision maker, they do encourage a logical consideration of such uncertainty and a methodical investigation into the alternative decisions and their possible consequences.

QADM IN ACTION   Gulf Oil

The oil exploration and production industry is characterised as one with huge initial investments, often to be taken on very limited information, leading to potentially high returns on that investment or equally high losses and where uncertainty over the outcomes of decisions is particularly high. For an oil company the related decision-making process is a lengthy and difficult one. Typically, a national government will offer areas, or blocks, of the seabed for investigation and development. Such blocks are usually offered for sale through some form of sealed-bid auction process. A company wishing to bid for a particular block, or group of blocks, therefore has to decide:

● whether to bid

● how much to bid if it decides to do so.

The decision problem is compounded by two major factors. The first relates to the information available to an oil company at this stage about the economic and financial prospects for the blocks. Typically, this is extremely limited and very uncertain. Usually relatively detailed information will be available on the geological structure itself. A decision must then be taken on the likelihood of such a structure revealing substantial hydrocarbon (gas and oil) deposits. A decision must then be made on the likely nature of the deposits that may be found in terms of the grades of deposits revealed and their quantity. Next an evaluation of the likely cost of exploiting the deposits is required together with some estimate of production costs once the development is in production. Since such deposits may have an economic life lasting ten to twenty years or more, some judgemental view must also be taken on likely revenue from such production – which requires an assessment of future world oil and gas prices, tax regimes and the like. The uncertainties surrounding each of these areas are, understandably, high.

The second factor compounding the problem for an oil company is that such sealed-bid auction processes are competitive. Competing oil companies are simultaneously assessing the same blocks and will reach their own views on what their own bids should be. On the outer continental shelf (OCS) of the United States the difference between the winning bid for one block and the second highest bid has exceeded 100 million US dollars. As a further complication, any single company will naturally have limited capital resources available for such a bidding process. The question then arises as to the priorities in terms of bidding and, indeed, whether a single company should bid in isolation or should consider some joint venture with another oil company, in terms both of pooling resources and spreading the inherent risk. In the early 1980s Gulf Oil Corporation developed a lease bidding strategy system (LBSS). This was part of a longer-term effort designed to assist management make the best use of the limited capital resources at their disposal for US offshore oil and gas block sales. Historically, the company undertook an economic evaluation of a block, or

blocks, when they were placed at auction. Such an evaluation took into account the geological prospects for the block, the chance of finding recoverable deposits, assumptions about the size and quality of the deposit and estimates of development and production costs. Together with forecasts of future prices and market conditions, this led to estimates of the financial return for the block. However, such estimates were typically point estimates: a single figure produced in terms of expected return rather than a range of figures incorporating different assumptions and different likelihoods of occurrence. It was also felt at the time that a number of managers in the company were unfamiliar with quantitative business techniques in general and with techniques for dealing with uncertainty in particular. An overview of the structure of the LBSS designed to try to improve this decision-making process is shown in Figure 6.5.

The historical database was, as the name suggests, data and information relating to previous auction sales and bids and the information made available at the time for each block. A number of sub-models were then designed. The first of these was the POW (probability of winning) model, which provided an indication of the probability of Gulf winning the bid for a given block based on a bid amount. This model was developed on the basis of the patterns from previous auction sales between the economic evaluation produced by Gulf and competitor behaviour. The model also took into account, when providing a probability estimate, the economic evaluation for the current blocks on offer. The performance model then provides information on the likely performance outcomes arising from any specific bidding decision in the context of sales and revenue performance. Feeding into this model were also the data relating to the economic evaluation for the blocks under consideration as well as management preferences in terms of performance criteria (for example, was the preference for minimising risk, maximising production, maximising revenue, or maximising the number of blocks won). The final part of the system was then an optimisation model (discussed in detail in Chapter 11), which sought the optimum bidding policy for the blocks currently for auction, subject to a variety of constraints.

Figure 6.6 shows the simplified structure to part of this modelling process in the form of a decision tree. The tree relates to the bidding process for a single block being auctioned. The amount bid for the block by Gulf is denoted as b and the POW

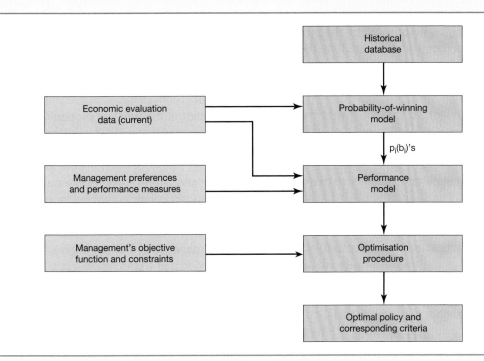

Figure 6.5 Schematic representation of the LBSS

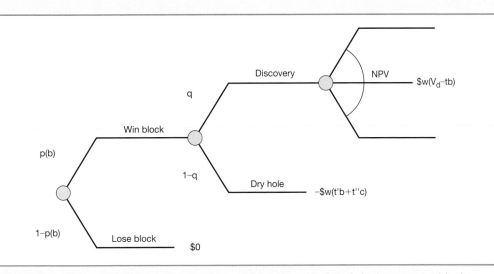

Figure 6.6 Tree diagram showing outcomes from bidding on an isolated single-prospect block

model generates a numerical value for $p(b)$, the probability that the amount bid for the block will be successful. By definition, the probability of that bid being unsuccessful is $1 - p(b)$. Naturally, if the bid is unsuccessful the financial outcome is \$0. If the bid is successful at auction, Gulf will then have to invest further in the exploration of the block to determine whether hydrocarbon deposits in economically viable quantities are to be found. The probability of such deposits being found is quantified as q. If such deposits are not found then the block is designated as a 'dry hole', with a probability S1of $(1 - q)$ of occurring. The financial outcome of a dry hole is a combination of b, the amount bid for the block, and c, the exploration costs incurred. In total the financial outcome is shown as:

$$w(t'b + t''c)$$

t' adjusts the amount bid to compensate for the tax regime and t" adjusts for the timing of the exploration costs since, typically, such costs may be incurred over a period of several years (the principles of such adjustments to cash flows are detailed in Chapter 15). The term w is used to represent Gulf's share in this block, since it may be a joint venture. The larger Gulf's share the closer w will be to 1: the smaller its share the closer to 0. Naturally, for this branch of the tree this financial outcome is negative. The top part of the tree represents an outcome where economically recoverable deposits are located. In such a case the financial outcomes are much less certain (depending on future costs, revenues, oil prices and the like). However, a range of likely outcomes can be developed (an indicative three branches are shown at this point). The financial outcome for any branch is shown as:

$$w(V_d + tb)$$

where V_d represents the net return on the block over its economic lifetime (calculated using the principles of net present value discussed in Chapter 15) and t adjusts the bid cost for taxes and time. The value that V_d takes will vary depending on which branch of the tree is being considered. Also relevant to each branch for this part of the tree is a probability representing the likelihood of that particular outcome over time.

The introduction of such a modelling system and the related techniques into the company was not an easy, or short-term, task. Some parts of management needed considerable evidence that the LBS system would be worthwhile 'under fire', and the development team spent considerable time convincing management of the improvements in decision making that would result. It is also worth noting that a number of spin-off benefits were later realised, notably the need for more detailed and comprehensive information to be fed into the model and the need for a rigorous feedback and analysis procedure following both successful and unsuccessful bids. As with other applications, the introduction of the model into the decision-making process was seen as a long-term activity and one which had to be able to adapt itself to changing business circumstances.

Source: The above application is based on the article: Keeper, D.L., Beckley Smith, F., Jr and Back, H.B. (1991) Development and use of a modeling system to aid a major oil company in allocating bidding capital, *Operations Research*, 39 (1), pp 28–41. I am grateful to the Operations Research Society of America for permission to reproduce the figures shown in this section.

Exercises

1   For the pay-off table shown in Table 6.3 construct a decision tree to confirm the decision without perfect information. If the pay-off for pilot/zero growth was now changed to −£10(000), how would this affect the potential value of perfect information for the company?

2   Consider the pay-off in Table 6.3 *without* the probability information. How could you now evaluate suitable decisions?

3   A manufacturing firm has decided to capitalise on its existing success by building an extension to its production plant to come on stream by 2022. The firm has evaluated the decision and calculated that its profitability will improve by £650 000 if the extension is completed on time. If, however, the extension is delayed then, because of contractual production commitments, the firm stands to lose some £350 000. The firm has invited tenders for the construction work and two contractors have been shortlisted. Contractor A has indicated that it would undertake all the work itself and that it has a track record such that 75 per cent of previous jobs have been completed on time. Contractor B, on the other hand, has a track record of

95 per cent of jobs being completed on time where Contractor B has done all the work. However, Contractor B occasionally subcontracts work to other companies – some 30 per cent of jobs have a subcontract element in them. The company's completion rate on jobs involving subcontractors is less impressive, with 40 per cent of such jobs not being completed on time.

Required:

(a) Draw a decision tree for this situation.

(b) Using this information, recommend which of the two shortlisted contractors should be given the job.

(c) In practical terms how useful do you think the technique would be for the firm? What other information might you take into account?

4   A large multinational oil company is considering its strategy in the North Sea. The UK government has announced that a new drilling site in the North Sea will be offered for sale on a competitive tender basis, the site going to the company making the highest bid. Provisional exploration of the site indicates that, over its life, it can be expected to generate revenue of around £1500 million if the oil reserves turn out to be high, but only £500 million if they turn out to be low. Seismic tests have indicated that the probability of high reserves is 0.60.

If the company is successful in its bid, it will also have to decide whether to construct a new oil rig for the site or to move an existing oil rig which is currently operating at an uneconomic site. The costs of the new rig are around £250 million and for moving the existing rig around £100 million. A new rig would be able to boost production by £150 million if reserve levels turned out to be high. The company has decided that if it is to bid for the site, the maximum bid it can afford at present, because of its cash flow situation, is £750 million. In the past, 70 per cent of the company's bids for such sites have been successful.

However, the company is also under pressure to refurbish some of its existing rigs for both efficiency and safety reasons. The £750 million could be used for this purpose instead. If the money is used for refurbishment, there is a 50 per cent chance of increasing efficiency to generate a return on the £750 million of 5 per cent, and a 50 per cent chance of generating a return of 10 per cent. If the decision to refurbish takes place after the bid has been made and failed, only £500 million will be available.

(a) Construct a decision tree for this problem.

(b) Using the decision tree, suggest a suitable decision for management.

(c) Determine the value of perfect information about the size of the reserves on the new site.

5   A small engineering firm is under increasing pressure from foreign competitors and is considering a number of strategic options. One of these relates to changing over from the existing production process to one which is completely automated. The firm has narrowed down its choices regarding this option to two possibilities.

The first, System I, is that the firm could install a production process using computer-controlled production equipment purchased from the Far East. This system is expected to have a marked impact on the firm's operating costs. However, the system would take three years to design and install and would cost some £2.5 million. The projected cost savings are around £1 million a year once the system is operative. The system is expected to have a useful life of 10 years. However, the Far East company which would design and supply the equipment is new to the engineering company and it has been assessed that this course of action has a probability of only 55 per cent of performing satisfactorily.

The second possibility is that the firm could collaborate with the production engineering department at the local university, which is at the leading edge of research in this field. This production system, System II, would be designed to run in parallel with the first, System I, and would cost £1 million to design and develop.

However, System II would take three years to implement. The university estimates that it has a 75 per cent chance of coming up with an appropriate system. The problem is that System II is basically for 'insurance' in case System I fails to perform as required. If System I does work satisfactorily, the expenditure on System II will have been for nothing. To complicate the issue the decision to develop System II does not need to be taken now: it can be taken at any time during the 10-year life of System I but bearing in mind that System II takes three years to develop. Ignoring the time consequences of expenditure and cost savings, construct a decision tree for this problem and advise the company on a suitable course of action.

6 A small company finds itself in the position of having to complete a contract for a large customer or pay high financial penalties for failing to deliver. The firm finds itself with a problem. The stocks of one particular component used to assemble the product have been exhausted and the contract cannot be completed. The company has contacted a number of possible local suppliers of this component. The company needs some 10 000 units of the component, which cost £1 each. The quality of the component is very variable, however, and in the past the company has found that 55 per cent of components are acceptable, 30 per cent are of poor quality and the remainder are sub-standard. Poor components can be improved to standard at a cost of 25p per unit while sub-standard components can be rectified at a cost of £1 per unit.

Because of the short timescale for completion of the contract, the company has decided to visit each supplier in turn. A small sample of the component will be inspected and if the components look acceptable, 10 000 will be purchased from that supplier. If the first supplier's sample is not acceptable the company will inspect a sample from the second supplier, and so on. If, however, the company gets to the fourth and final supplier, it will have to purchase all 10 000 items from this supplier regardless of quality.

Construct a decision tree for this problem and evaluate the likely financial consequences for the company of its situation.

7 Market Research and Statistical Inference

Learning objectives

By the end of this chapter you should be able to:

- explain the difference between a sample and a population
- explain the principles of a sampling distribution
- calculate and explain a confidence interval around a sample mean and a sample percentage
- calculate a variety of common hypothesis tests

We have been exploring some of the principles and applications of probability over the last two chapters. We now introduce one of the key areas to which probability is applied by business – that of market research and statistical inference. Many organisations frequently commission or undertake basic market research into their products, their services and their customers. Production organisations will frequently test-market new products before launching them nationwide. Service organisations seek to assess the public's expectations, perceptions and views on their products and services. Increasingly public sector organisations are trying to assess customers' views on the services provided – whether the customer is a patient in a hospital or a citizen in a local authority area. Such information, from a management perspective, is potentially very valuable. It can provide an insight into areas of uncertainty and may help the manager assess both strategic and operational options for future change. However, such 'research' tends to have one thing in common, no matter which organisation it is for and the purposes for which it is undertaken. The common factor is that such investigations invariably focus on a *sample* rather than on the statistical *population* – that is on part rather than on the whole. We shall explore the reasons for this shortly but the obvious consequence is that the manager must then – somehow – assess the reliability of the results. It is in this area that we can apply the principles of what is known as *statistical inference*.

SAP is buying survey software maker Qualtrics for $8bn just before the US company was set to go public.

By Shannon Bond in San Francisco

The German business software group said it would pay cash to acquire all outstanding Qualtrics shares and had secured €7bn in financing to cover the purchase price and acquisition costs. The deal, expected to close in the first half of next year, has been approved by both companies' boards of directors and by Qualtrics shareholders. . . .

Qualtrics sells market research and survey software to more than 9,000 customers, from Coca-Cola to the US Air Force and Walt Disney. Competitors include SurveyMonkey, which went public in September in an initial public offering that valued it at $1.25bn, a steep discount to its last private valuation.

Market research is big business these days.
According to one report the global market research industry was worth around US$80 billion in 2018 (Esomar: Global Market Research Report)

Populations and samples

We made the distinction between samples and populations in Chapter 4. In a statistical sense a population relates to the entire set of items under consideration, whereas a sample is a subset (or part) of that population. The most common example relates to opinion polls which attempt to determine voting patterns at a forthcoming election. Clearly in an ideal world the organisation undertaking the survey would like to contact all voters to determine their intended voting behaviour. From a practical perspective this is unrealistic. The cost of doing this, the resources required, the organising needed, the time required would all make such an approach infeasible. Instead the organisation is likely to choose a subset of the population – a small cross-section of voters from the entire electorate. In the UK, such a sample is likely to consist of around 1000 people – compared with over 20 million voters. Most organisations wishing to collect data to help in their decision making are likely to find themselves in a similar position – forced to consider a sample of data rather than the entire population. An organisation thinking of launching a new product would like to ask all potential customers their opinions but will have to restrict itself to only a sample. A hospital assessing the quality of the health-care services delivered would like to ask all patients but will have to satisfy itself with asking only a sample. A production organisation which mass-produces some item would like to be able to check every item for quality but will have to restrict itself to only a sample. The list of examples is endless.

However, from the manager's perspective, although this is understandable, it does cause problems. At the end of the data collection – whether it is an opinion poll, a survey of customers or a quality check – the manager will be presented with data relating to a sample. Based on this sample data, the manager must somehow try to decide how this applies to the whole statistical population – which after all is what the manager is really interested in. In statistical jargon the manager will be trying to infer key characteristics of the population based on sample data.

Consider this example. A restaurant has recently opened on a prime retail site in a large city. The restaurant has deliberately focused on a particular market niche and specialises in fusion cuisine in a fine dining experience. The manager is interested in trying to determine the profile of customers: their age, gender, socio-economic group, income, preferred foods and so on. The reasons for this should be self-evident: such information will, potentially, assist the manager in matching products/services to customers' needs, in matching advertising to the client base, in matching menus with likely demand and so on. As we have already established, the manager is unlikely to be able to carry out a full study of the entire population – all the customers using the restaurant – but will have to be satisfied with collecting and analysing data on only a sample of customers. However, based on the sample data, the manager will be interested in trying to determine the equivalent characteristics of the (unknown) population. Let us focus on a particular example. The manager has decided to try to obtain information about the income levels of customers. The manager feels that, given the nature of the restaurant's menu, customers are more likely to come from middle to higher income groups. The sample data is intended to throw some light on the income profile of customers.

Suppose, for example, the manager has taken a sample of customers and found that the mean income of the sample was £42 000. What does this imply about the mean income of the customer population (on whom we have no actual data)? Would it be appropriate to conclude that the population mean income was also £42 000? Or about £42 000? Clearly some method of transferring our sample findings to the statistical population would be highly desirable. It is this process that is generally referred to as statistical inference – the ability to *infer* the population characteristics based only on sample data.

Before we proceed, however, we must introduce an important note of caution. The whole basis for statistical inference is built on two key assumptions about the sample data:

- The sample is a properly representative subset of the statistical population. In the context of the restaurant, for example, results are unlikely to be reliable if the sample consists predominantly of male customers. The sampling process must ensure that a proper cross-section of customers is obtained. In practice, this is easier said than done.

- The data collected is reliable and accurate. Once again this is a critical assumption, particularly when the statistical sample consists of people. We have to be realistic and accept that people will not always give an 'honest' answer to a question. Consider asking a customer their income level as part of the survey. Although many people might give a reliable response there are likely to be those who 'inflate' their actual income, giving rise to a sample result which is 'inaccurate'. Frequently there is no way of properly assessing the validity of some responses, although careful survey design can help minimise the possibility.

These two assumptions must be remembered when we are applying inferential principles.

Don't shoot the statisticians

By John Kemp

Modern societies have made a fetish of official statistics, particularly the national income and production accounting (NIPA) system developed by Nobel Laureates Simon Kuznets and Richard Stone during the 1930s and 1940s. NIPAs, especially the top-line figure for gross domestic product (GDP), as well as monthly employment data such as U.S. nonfarm payrolls, have become the arbiters of economic policy and the success and failure of politicians.

In a strange way, Britain's ONS (Office for National Statistics), and similar agencies like the Bureau of Labor Statistics (BLS) and Bureau of Economic Analysis (BEA) in the United States, hold the fate of politicians in their hands because they help write the political narrative. It is only a slight exaggeration to say BEA is one of the most powerful agencies in the US government. It may not have as many tanks as the Pentagon, but by measuring the success and failure of economic policies, it can make and break presidencies, as President George H.W. Bush could confirm and Barack Obama fears.

Yet most statistics users (businesses, economists, politicians, voters) neither know nor care how they are put together. If there is an image of how statistical agencies work, it is of armies of faceless bureaucrats carefully counting things, rather like an audit of widgets in a warehouse. The reality is more complicated. If statistics agencies were to count every car, computer and hospital operation they would have to be as large as the economy itself. Britain's Statistical Authority employed the equivalent of just 2,995 full time staff at the end of February 2012, plus 250 contractors, to produce a wide range of stats, not just on the economy. In the United States, BEA has around 600 staff, of whom less than 200 work on the national economic accounts.

So, all statistics agencies rely on surveys and sampling. The approach introduces both sampling and non-sampling errors. Some degree of sampling error is unavoidable because the sample will not precisely match the characteristics of the whole population, but agencies take great care to ensure samples are as representative as possible to avoid systematic bias. Non-sampling errors include human error, data entry and sample design.

In the United Kingdom, ONS GDP data are based on a very large sample of firms, including 8,000 in the construction sector, which is a far larger and more detailed sample than the surveys conducted by the Chamber of Commerce and other business lobby organisations.

The most important lesson is to treat all economic statistics with appropriate scepticism. Statistics are always subject to some uncertainty, which is why ONS and BEA label them 'preliminary estimates'. It is not possible to measure growth to one decimal place – which is why announcements that analysts at XYZ bank have cut their GDP forecast by 0.1 or even 0.2 per cent should draw a wry smile. It is time to have a more grown-up debate about what statistics actually mean and how they should be used, rather than criticise the statisticians who produce them. On balance they do a good job with few resources.

Sampling is necessary for effective data collection and timely analysis – but it can be contentious.

Sampling distributions

Let us return to the sample of customers for the restaurant. For simplicity let's assume that the restaurant has a number of regular customers and that a sample of 100 of these has been taken and the results analysed (bearing in mind what we have just said about assumptions). The restaurant found that the mean income of the sample was £42 000 with a standard deviation of £5000. In symbolic form this would be:

$$\bar{x} = 42$$
$$s = 5$$
$$n = 100$$

where n refers to the size of the sample, and we have the results in £000s. Note that we use the appropriate symbols for the sample (and not the Greek character symbols, which relate to the population as we discussed in Chapter 4). However, in principle this sample is only one of many that we could have chosen. A second, and different, sample of 100 customers could have been taken (and bear in mind that we would technically only need to change one of the customers in the sample for it to be a different sample).

Progress Check 7.1

If we took a second, and different, sample would you expect to get a sample mean of £42 000? Why? Or why not?

In principle there is no reason why we should obtain a second sample mean of exactly £42 000 since, technically, we have a different sample of customers. However, it does seem reasonable to expect the second sample mean to be similar to the first on the assumption that both are representative of the statistical population. If, for example, the second sample mean had been £18 000 we might have been both surprised and suspicious given the difference between the two sample results. The principle then is that we would expect different samples taken from the same population to generate similar, but not necessarily arithmetically identical, sample means.

QADM IN ACTION

Capgemini – sampling for perfect modelling

Capgemini's client was a major UK utility company. The client had contracted with a third party organisation for receiving and processing over-the-counter payment of bills by its utility customers. The contract between the client and the third party service provider specified standards that had to be achieved in terms of the elapsed time between payment by the utility's customers and the receipt of the transaction data tapes at the client's site. Clearly, the longer it took for the client to actually receive the payment made by its customers to the third party organisation then the worse the effect on its cash flow. Effectively, the client wanted to ensure that the third party's performance met the contractual obligation. However, one of the key difficulties was that there was no electronic capture of the date and time of payment, only a paper record date stamped at payment time. The client wanted a method for monitoring performance that would be cost-effective and would also be acceptable to the third party service provider.

In order to establish a cost-effective monitoring system it was clear that it would have to be based on a sample basis. Statistical sampling principles were used to ensure that robust and representative samples of data were chosen for monitoring purposes. The third-party service provider proposed that it should be responsible for operating the monitoring process but that the client would undertake strict audits from time to time to ensure compliance with agreed procedures. Initial audits were conducted by Capgemini to ensure that the sample results were both fair and accurate and that the monitoring operation conformed to recommended procedures.

Rules were developed for regular selection of samples of payment vouchers from all those processed by the third party service provider. The information to be extracted from the sample vouchers was identified. Procedures were then established to determine the elapsed times for processing these vouchers and to convert these into measures of performance.

Capgemini provided initial training to the third party service provider, which, it had been agreed, would be responsible for sampling, data collection and routine monitoring. Capgemini also carried out a series of audits to establish that the sampling system gave a fair picture of the performance of the third party service provider. Monitoring procedures were refined following these initial audits.

Analysis by payment centre is as follows:

% of national	Adjusted % delivered on time
11.5	93.8
14.1	90.8
13.2	90.0
12.1	92.5
13.7	95.0
12.3	100.0
12.8	97.5
10.3	93.3
100	94.1

Source: Based on a Capgemini case study, with thanks to Capgemini for permission to use their material.

The benefits are as follows:

- A method for monitoring standards of service was developed that was agreed as fair both by the client and by the third-party service provider.
- The provision of robust, cost-effective monitoring information ensures that there is a continuing focus on payment processing performance by both the client and the third party service provider.
- As a by-product of the initial audits conducted by Capgemini, a number of apparent anomalies in the payment process were identified. These were drawn to the attention of the client and the service provider for remedial action.

Now consider the following scenario. We take repeated, but different, samples of 100 customers from the population and calculate the mean of each sample. We continue this until all possible samples have been taken from this population. (A word of caution: do not think about actually doing this! There are over six million million million million million million different samples of size 100 that could be taken from a population of just 1000!) So – in principle – we have a very large number of sample means. Obviously some of these sample means will take the same value; others will differ. Effectively then we have a data set consisting of sample means, which we could analyse in the same way as any other, using principles introduced in earlier chapters. In principle, for example, we could now construct a histogram and frequency polygon for the sample means. What would this histogram look like?

The Central Limit Theorem

To answer this question we must turn to what is known as the Central Limit Theorem. While such a theorem can only be 'proven' using mathematics, the principles can be seen using some simple logic. We have taken all possible samples from the population and for each sample calculated its mean. Logically, there will be one sample – and only one – which contains the 100 customers in the statistical population with the lowest incomes. The mean of this sample therefore must be the lowest sample mean. There will be a number of samples, however, which contain 99 of the lowest-income 100 customers. These will have sample means slightly above the lowest sample mean. A larger number still will contain 98 of the lowest income customers, yet more with 97 and so on. The majority of samples will, reasonably, contain a cross-section of incomes from lowest to highest. Clearly the same logic applies at the other end of the distribution – customers with the highest incomes. It seems reasonable, then, to conclude that the distribution of all these samples means would look like that shown in Figure 7.1. That is, the

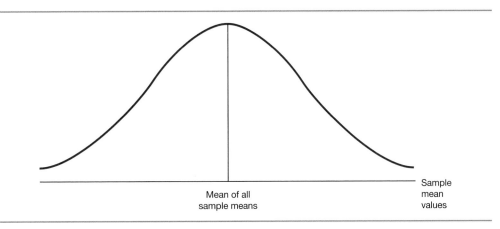

Figure 7.1 The sampling distribution

distribution of all possible sample means will be Normal. The implications of such a distribution are that we have a symmetrical distribution of sample means, with only a few results at each of the extremes and the bulk of results in the middle of the distribution. This distribution is known as *sampling distribution*. In fact this is what the Central Limit Theorem concludes:

> *If we take random samples of size n from a population, the distribution of sample means will approach that of the Normal probability distribution. This approximation will become closer, the larger is n.*

This is a particularly important conclusion and underpins much of statistical inference. We need to consider its implications. It implies that – no matter what type of population we are examining – when we take random samples, the distribution of the means of these samples will approximate to the Normal distribution. Similarly, the larger the sample sizes we use, the closer this approximation will become. Consider our example. We do not know what form our population distribution (of customer incomes) actually takes. It could be Normal or it could be skewed (more likely, given both demographic patterns and the type of business). However, it really doesn't matter because the sampling distribution will approximate to the Normal distribution as long as we take sufficiently large samples. ('Sufficiently large' is generally accepted to be a sample size of at least 30.)

But so what? How does this help our search for inferences that we can make about the population based only on a sample? After all, we do not have all these sample results that make up the Normal sampling distribution. We only have the result from *one* sample. To see how we can progress we need to examine further characteristics of the sampling distribution.

Characteristics of the sampling distribution

We have already seen that, under certain conditions relating to sample size, the sampling distribution will approximate to the Normal. Can we say anything else about this distribution?

The sampling distribution – like any other Normal distribution – can be summarised with two statistics: its mean and standard deviation. Let us consider the mean first. Remember that the sampling distribution is made up of all the possible sample means. Suppose we were to take all the individual sample means making up the distribution (in fact to treat them just as any normal data set) and calculate the mean. This is where English gets cumbersome but this effectively requires us to calculate the mean of all the sample means. You should be able to see that if we were to do this then the mean we actually calculate must be the same as the mean of the population since the sampling distribution by definition covers all the data in the population. So the mean of the sampling distribution is actually μ, the population mean. What about the standard deviation? This is more difficult and we can only state that the standard deviation of the sampling distribution is given by:

$$\frac{\sigma}{\sqrt{n}}$$

where σ is the population standard deviation and n the sample size. In practice, because σ is generally unknown, we can approximate the standard deviation with:

$$\frac{s}{\sqrt{n}}$$

where s is the standard deviation of the sample. So, we are able to describe the sampling distribution in terms of its mean, μ, and its standard deviation, given by $s/\sqrt{n}$. Before seeing how we can use this information, it might be useful to summarise our statistics given that we are starting to talk about different means and different standard deviations. Remember that we are actually talking about three different groups: the sample, the population and the sampling distribution of sample means. Each of these will have a mean and a standard deviation:

	Mean	SD
Sample	$\bar{x}$	s
Population	μ	σ
Sampling distribution	μ	$s/\sqrt{n}$

The standard deviation of the sampling distribution is more frequently referred to as the *standard error* and we shall be using this terminology from now on. To summarise, so far we have established that when we take a sample from a population, the mean of this sample will form part of a distribution which will be approximately Normal with a mean, μ, identical to that of the population and a standard deviation calculated by $s/\sqrt{n}$. But how does this help us evaluate the sample result in the context of the population? To answer this, we now introduce the concept of a confidence interval.

Confidence intervals

We know that our sample mean forms part of a distribution which is Normal: our sample mean of 42 (£000) lies somewhere in the Normally shaped sampling distribution in Figure 7.1. However, we have no way of knowing *for certain* whereabouts in this distribution our mean actually occurs. The sample mean could, for all we know, be identical to the population mean or considerably lower or considerably higher. However, although we cannot know *for certain* where the sample mean lies in relation to the population mean, we can use probability to assess its *likely* position in relation to the population mean. The sampling distribution is made up of all possible sample means and, given that the sampling distribution is Normal, we can use the principles we developed in Chapter 5. Let us examine Figure 7.2. The figure shows the sampling distribution and we have set a value such that we wish to determine the relevant Z scores, Z_1 and Z_2, to encompass the central 95 per cent of values (which in this case are sample mean values).

Progress Check 7.3

Determine the relevant Z scores for Figure 7.2.

We require the area in each of the two tails of the distribution to be 2.5 per cent, i.e. a total area of 5 per cent to be outside the designated central area (this 5 per cent value is generally denoted as α). From the Normal table in Appendix B we note that this equates to a Z score of 1.96. So, a pair of Z scores of -1.96 standard errors and $+1.96$ standard errors will encompass the central 95 per cent of sample means.

Progress Check 7.4

What is the probability that a sample mean will fall within this central part of the sampling distribution?

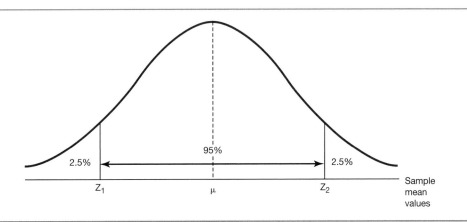

Figure 7.2 Sampling distribution: 95 per cent limits

Clearly the answer to the question must be 0.95 since, in total, 95 per cent of all sample means must fall in this area. Following from this we can then ask: what is the probability that our sample mean – at 42 (£000) – falls in this area? Again it must be 0.95 or 95 per cent. So, although we do not know for certain how close our sample mean is to the population mean, we now know that there is a 95 per cent chance that it is no further away than ± 1.96 standard errors from μ, the population mean. However, since we can calculate the standard error, we can actually quantify this distance:

$$\pm 1.96 \text{SE} = \pm 1.96 \frac{s}{\sqrt{n}}$$

$$= \pm 1.96 \frac{5}{\sqrt{100}}$$

$$= \pm 1.96 \,(0.5) = \pm 0.98 \,\text{£000}$$

That is, there is a 95 per cent probability that the sample mean and population mean are no further apart than 0.98 (£000), or £980.

In other words, the population mean income is likely to be between £41 020 and £42 980.

In fact, what we have calculated is generally referred to as a *confidence interval*. We have taken the sample mean and calculated an interval, $\pm£980$, around this statistic, such that we can state that we are 95 per cent confident that the actual population mean lies within £980 of the estimated mean (which is the sample mean). The confidence interval calculation can be summarised as:

$$95\% \text{ CI} = \pm 1.96 \frac{s}{\sqrt{n}}$$

Based on such an interval there is a 95 per cent probability that this interval contains the (unknown) population mean, μ. This means that, based on sample information, we can infer, for a given level of probability, a likely value for the population mean. It will be worthwhile reiterating what we've done here and what we've achieved. The arithmetic involved in calculating a confidence interval is fairly simple. However, it can be difficult to figure out what's actually going on in the calculation – and explaining it to others. We started with a requirement that for business planning purposes we wanted to know the mean income of the restaurant's customers. We decided that realistically it would not be cost-effective to collect and analyse the data for all customers (the statistical population) but that we would look at a random sample of customers. From the random sample of 100 customers we calculated the sample mean income to be £42 000 (with a standard deviation of £5000). Using the Central Limit Theorem and probability, we calculated a confidence interval of plus/minus £980 – that is, an interval from £41 020 to £42 980. The interval is a range of values that we can be 95 per cent certain contains the mean of the population. So, we can inform the restaurant that – based on a sample of only 100 customers – we're 95 per cent confident that the mean income of all restaurant customers is between £41 020 and £42 980. Such a conclusion is made possible only by the Central Limit Theorem. You shouldn't underestimate the importance of what we've been able to do here. Based on limited sample data we're able to conclude on a likely population mean at a high level of probability.

A confidence interval is often also referred to as the *margin of error* (MoE). In some ways, this is potentially a misleading name as it suggests we've made a mistake somewhere. We haven't. The term simply indicates that whenever we have a sample statistic (like the sample mean income) we cannot assume this precisely represents the population statistic. We have to allow for a margin of (sampling) error in the sample results. The margin of error is the statistical way of showing how well the sample statistic reflects the population statistic. It does have very important management implications. If you're given statistics that are based on a sample you *must* factor in the margin of error to help assess the 'true' (population) statistic. If you're not given the margin of error you need to be very cautious about using the sample results.

- A sample of customers finds that 62 per cent would buy our new product. This may look good but unless we know the MoE it tells us nothing about the true percentage.

- We checked productivity in a sample of our manufacturing and found a 2.6 per cent increase in productivity compared with last year. Unless we know the MoE it tells us nothing about the true change in productivity.

- A sample of patients in a health centre found that 81 per cent were happy with their treatment. Unless we know the MoE it tells us nothing about the true percentage that was happy.

- A survey of a sample of our employees found that 79 per cent felt our organisation was a good employer. Unless we know the MoE it tells us nothing about the true percentage.

- A check of a sample of our production showed that less than 1 per cent failed the quality assurance check. Unless we know the MoE it tells us nothing about the true percentage.

Doubt grows over official migration data as cabinet splits over direction of policy

By Helen Warrell, Alan Smith and Keith Fray

Amber Rudd, the home secretary, has proposed new limits on overseas students in response to official figures showing that large numbers are overstaying illegally after their studies have finished. But underlying the debate is a growing concern that the net migration figures from the Office for National Statistics are unreliable.

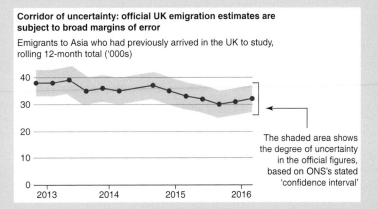

Corridor of uncertainty: official UK emigration estimates are subject to broad margins of error

Emigrants to Asia who had previously arrived in the UK to study, rolling 12-month total ('000s)

The shaded area shows the degree of uncertainty in the official figures, based on ONS's stated 'confidence interval'

Official statistics are published with confidence intervals that express the margin of error. In the case of the IPS, these intervals become proportionally larger for more detailed estimates — such as the numbers of workers, or students — because they are based on much smaller samples than the headline net migration figure.

Looking in detail at one group, for example, the data on Asian emigrants returning after a period of study in the UK have a confidence interval of 10,000 for an estimated figure of 40,000.

Confidence intervals aren't just of academic interest as this article extract illustrates. The confidence interval has been relabelled in the diagram as the 'corridor of uncertainty'!

Other confidence intervals

But why did we choose to use a 95 per cent probability in calculating the interval? The answer is that this was an arbitrary – but common – choice. We could actually have established a confidence interval for any probability figure: 10 per cent, 50 per cent, 90 per cent. Naturally, knowing what we do about the Normal distribution, we realise that changing the probability figure will cause the confidence interval itself to change. In general, our CI formula can be rewritten as:

$$CI = \pm Z_{\alpha/2} \frac{s}{\sqrt{n}}$$

where Z is the Z value from the Normal table associated with the chosen probability value. The term $\alpha/2$ needs clarification: α denotes the area in the two tails of the distribution which delimit the confidence interval (5 per cent in our example). However, given that we require a central CI, this implies that the area in each of the two tails must be $\alpha/2$ (5%/2 or 2.5 per cent) and this provides the value for Z that we seek in the Normal table. In practice, although any level of probability could be chosen to calculate a CI, three tend to be used: 90 per cent, 95 per cent and 99 per cent.

Progress Check 7.5

Calculate a 90 per cent and a 99 per cent CI for this problem. Provide an explanation as to what these actually are. What do you observe about the size of the CI as the chosen probability increases?

We would obtain:

$$90\% \text{ CI} = 42 \pm 0.82 \quad (Z = 1.64) \text{ i.e. between £41 180 and £42 820}$$
$$95\% \text{ CI} = 42 \pm 0.98 \quad (Z = 1.96) \text{ i.e. between £41 020 and £42 980}$$
$$99\% \text{ CI} = 42 \pm 1.29 \quad (Z = 2.58) \text{ i.e. between £40 710 and £43 290}$$

We see that as we require a higher probability we must accept a wider CI. The logic of this is clear. If we wish the probability of the CI containing the population mean to increase then we must accept a wider interval within the sampling distribution. In practice, the combination of probability and size of CI is a trade-off and we must compromise in our choice.

Confidence intervals for proportions

So far we have examined CIs in the context of a mean value. There are numerous situations where we may have a sample result expressed not in terms of a mean value (like £42 000) but rather as a proportion or percentage. Consider a company sponsoring market research into a new product and the impact of an internet-based advertising campaign designed to launch the product. A sample of the public was selected and asked whether they had seen the recent online adverts for this product. Clearly their response would be either yes or no (we shall discount the don't knows). At the end of the survey we should be able to calculate the proportion – or percentage – of respondents who saw the adverts. But to talk of a mean in this context would make no sense. Let us say we found that 63 per cent of a sample of 250 people saw the adverts. Exactly the same problems arise in trying to evaluate this sample result vis-à-vis the statistical population as when we had a mean. Can we calculate a comparable CI for this type of problem? The answer is 'yes' but in a slightly different way. The same logic applies. This sample proportion is only one of those which make up the sampling distribution (of all sample proportions) and again this distribution will be approximately Normal. So, if we can calculate the standard error of this distribution, we can then calculate a CI. However, you may appreciate that while we could calculate a standard deviation for a problem with a sample mean, we cannot do this for a sample proportion. Remember that the standard deviation is a measure of variability around the mean (in the last problem we had a mean of 42 and a standard deviation of five). But it clearly doesn't make sense to ask: what's the standard deviation around a 'yes' response? However, we can still calculate the standard error of the sampling distribution using an appropriate formula (which we simply present here as given).

QADM IN ACTION

Capgemini – estimating energy consumption through sampling

The client, supplying gas and other energy products throughout the UK, is required to produce auditable financial accounts each month. However, individual customers' gas consumption may only be known when gas meters are read and consumption recorded and for some customers this may occur only – at best – at quarterly intervals. The client must therefore rely on estimates of customer consumption, which need to be as accurate as possible but also to be as cost-effective as possible. In addition, the independent industry regulator requires the estimated monthly accounts for customers to be within 4 per cent of the real bill value.

A panel of customers who read their meters on a weekly basis was established. Capgemini then developed a fully integrated IT system which provided database storage of the panel meter readings, full analysis of the panel data and a process for 'boosting' the panel to replace panel members who withdraw from the scheme. A graphics element to the system allowed users to store and analyse data without accessing the actual database.

Capgemini provided a methodology for collecting information on customer consumption patterns over time. The data could then be used for a range of analyses, forecasts and estimates of gas consumption. Clearly, it was essential that the panel was representative of the population. A stratified sampling procedure was used to select panel members and it was estimated, based on the panel size, that the accuracy of the panel results was within ± 2 per cent.

- A cost-effective process for collecting sufficient data was established. The stratified sampling approach that was used meant that a smaller panel size could be used to achieve a given confidence interval than would have been the case with simple random sampling. This in turn meant that the costs of data collection were much reduced.

- An accurate estimate of the volume of gas consumed each month could be produced.

- Accurate data became available that could be used for medium- and long-term planning.

Source: Based on a Capgemini case study, with thanks to Capgemini for permission to use their material.

$$\text{SE of a proportion} = \sqrt{\frac{p(1-p)}{n}}$$

where p is the sample proportion. The formula for the CI can then be given as:

$$CI = p \pm Z_{\alpha/2}\sqrt{\frac{p(1-p)}{n}}$$

or as:

$$CI = p \pm Z_{\alpha/2}\sqrt{\frac{p(100-p)}{n}}$$

if we express the sample result as a percentage rather than a proportion. Interpretation and use of such a CI is exactly as before.

Progress Check 7.6

Calculate a 90 per cent, 95 per cent and 99 per cent CI for the online advert survey.

We would have for a 90 per cent CI:

$$90\% \ CI = p \pm Z_{\alpha/2}\sqrt{\frac{p(100-p)}{n}}$$

$$= 63 \pm 1.64\sqrt{\frac{63(100-63)}{250}}$$

$$= 63 \pm 5\%, \text{ i.e. between 58\% and 68\%}$$

and:

$$95\% \ CI = 63 \pm 5.98\%, \text{ i.e. between 57\% and 69\%}$$
$$99\% \ CI = 63 \pm 7.88\%, \text{ i.e. between 65\% and 71\%}$$

The 95 per cent CI, for example, indicates that there is a 95 per cent probability that the sample percentage and the population percentage are no further apart than six percentage points, i.e. a CI of 57 per cent to 69 per cent. That is, we're 95 per cent confident that the true percentage of people who saw the advert is between 57 per cent and 69 per cent.

Hyundai hit with lawsuit over fuel efficiency

By Simon Mundy in Seoul

Hyundai Motor has been hit by a lawsuit in South Korea over an alleged misstatement of its vehicles' fuel efficiency, deepening the carmaker's embarrassment over an issue that has already saddled it with a nine-figure compensation bill in North America. About 1,500 Hyundai customers on Monday filed a complaint with the Seoul Central District Court over the company's mileage claims for the diesel-fuelled model of its Santa Fe sport utility vehicle, according to Yeyul, the law firm representing them.

Last month the transport ministry announced the results of tests showing that the overall and urban mileages for the vehicle were respectively 6.3 per cent and 8.5 per cent lower than had been claimed by Hyundai, breaching the 5 per cent margin of error allowed by the government.

Source: Bloomberg/Getty Images

Hyundai responded to a request for comment by highlighting a statement last month in which it said it "thoroughly manages its fuel economy measurement process in many ways, including conducting numerous tests at government-authorised facilities in Korea starting from almost a year before new products are launched, while also having the company's own test equipment verified annually by an authorised government agency". Hyundai admitted in March overstating the fuel mileage of the latest model of its Sonata sedan, which it had stressed as a key selling point of the vehicle.

Angela Hong, an analyst at Nomura, said Hyundai had one of the most serious problems in the automotive industry where fuel efficiency statements were concerned. In November 2012, the company and its affiliate Kia announced a compensation offer for the owners of more than 1m vehicles in the US and Canada, after admitting overstating their fuel mileage, with payments to be spread over several years. They settled a subsequent lawsuit last year by offering a lump-sum payment option to unhappy customers, with the total cost expected to reach several hundred million dollars. Ms Hong said some South Korean customers had been "grumpy" that a similar scheme had not been introduced in Hyundai's domestic market, which accounted for 15 per cent of its retail vehicle sales last year, measured by unit sales.

Hyundai's shares fell 1.1 per cent on Monday, with the broader Seoul market down only 0.2 per cent, and Ms Hong said that the mileage controversies were of concern to investors. "If there's a court decision that the company has to compensate, the burden will be huge."

Hyundai has pointed out that tests by the industry ministry endorsed its mileage claim, and expressed irritation at the "confusion and disorder" caused by having two government-mandated tests on fuel efficiency. The government has responded to this controversy by promising to "consolidate" these tests, though it has not yet decided on how to do so.

Margins of error and confidence intervals are used frequently in the area of consumer protection to check companies' claims and advertising about performance. Getting it wrong can prove expensive.

Interpreting confidence intervals

Although the calculation of a confidence interval for a given problem may be straightforward, interpreting and commenting on the result may be less so. Care needs to be taken in terms of how the result is explained. The following two comments are appropriate in the context of our last CI example.

● I am 95 per cent confident that the percentage of people who saw the TV adverts is between 57 per cent and 69 per cent.

● I am 95 per cent confident that my estimate of the population percentage (63 per cent based on a sample of 250 people) is within 6 per cent of the actual population percentage.

The following statement is not appropriate, even though it is commonly made.

● There is a probability of 0.95 that the population percentage is between 57 per cent and 69 per cent.

You can see why this last statement is inappropriate. The population percentage is a fixed, constant value, i.e. it is one number. The population value either will or will not fall into this interval. The probability that it does must, therefore, either be zero (it does not) or one (it does). It cannot be anything in between. We also need to highlight a few further points.

The first is that some people will misinterpret a confidence interval (particularly students in the exam!). If we go back to our restaurant example where we had the 95 per cent confidence interval of £40 020 to £42 980, some will give an interpretation along the lines: '95 per cent of customers have an income between £40 020 and £42 980'. This is wrong. We've no idea, based on the information given, what individual customer incomes are. The Central Limit Theorem focuses on sample *mean* income, not individual incomes.

A second point relates to comments often made by managers who don't understand the principles of sampling variation. Again using our restaurant example, you'll hear comments along the lines of: 'but your conclusion is only based on a sample of 100 customers out of hundreds (or thousands or millions). You just can't be sure it's that accurate based on only 100 people'. Such comments show ignorance of the statistical principle behind the confidence interval calculation. Yes, in this case, our conclusion is based on a sample of only 100 people. And yes, our sample result can't be guaranteed as 100 per cent accurate as an estimate of the true population. However, the Central Limit Theorem allows us to quantify precisely what the margin of error is for any specific situation. I'm 95 per cent certain that the mean income of our restaurant customers is between £41 020 and £42 980 even though it's based on only 100 customers.

A third point relates to the sample size. *Common sense* (!) suggests that for a sample to be an accurate estimate of the statistical population, the sample size should be a relatively large proportion of the population. 'Surely', people will argue, 'the sample should be at least 10 per cent of the population or 20 per cent to be reliable.' Again, we refer back to the Central Limit Theorem. The key aspect from the theorem that allows us to calculate a confidence interval is that the distribution of sample means (or percentages) will approximate to the Normal distribution – as long as the sample size is large enough. And we stated earlier that 'large enough' is generally taken to be a sample size over 30 items from the population. The Central Limit Theorem does not require the sample size to be a given proportion of the statistical population – simply to be over 30.

The final point relates to this. Again, you'll hear managers who don't understand the principles argue about the sample size. 'Surely', they'll say, 'a sample size of 200 is more accurate than a sample size of 100 and 300 would be better than 200 and so on.' They're right in part but the relationship between the size of the confidence interval and the sample size is not a direct one. Look back at the standard error formula we've used (which is used in calculating the confidence interval) and you'll see that it appears as $\sqrt{n}$. So changing the sample size will change the size of the confidence interval but not in proportion. Let's see what happens with our restaurant example. Given the data with a sample mean of £42 000, a sample standard deviation of £5000 and a sample size of 100 we calculated the confidence interval as +/−£980. Let's recalculate the confidence interval assuming sample sizes of 50, 200, 500 and 1000. The results (check them yourself) are:

Sample size	Confidence interval
100	+/−£980
50	+/−£1386
200	+/−£693
500	+/−£438
1000	+/−£310

Doubling the sample size (from 100 to 200) does reduce the size of the interval but by less than half. Similarly, increasing the sample size by 10 fold (from 100 to 1000) only reduces the size of the interval by two-thirds. Clearly from a management perspective there's a trade-off between increased accuracy (a reduction in the size of the confidence interval) and the extra costs of increasing the sample size. In the market research industry, surveys and opinion polls are often conducted with a sample size of around 1000, giving a margin of error of +/−3 per cent, which is seen as a reasonable compromise in most circumstances between cost and accuracy.

Scottish polls: margin call

By Gavin Jackson

Polls for the Scottish independence referendum come with a margin of error. Usually this is about three percentage points, which means that for all of this week's polls, both 'Yes' and 'No' fit into this margin of error.

In some ways polling on the independence referendum is a lot like figuring out whether a coin is fair or not. Toss a coin once and you'll get a single head or tail; ask someone how they'll vote in the independence referendum – assuming they will and they've made a decision – and you will get a single yes or no. One result is not enough to make a judgement in either case. But do it a thousand times and you'll have a pretty good idea. Of course, it's unlikely the coin will come down on heads exactly 500 times out of a thousand even if it is fair. Likewise, if Scots are split perfectly down the middle and you randomly interview a thousand of them, it's unlikely you'd end up getting exactly 500 in each camp just because it is a random sample.

Now imagine if we did the interviews a hundred times. If the Scots were split down the middle: we should expect that, in 95 out of the 100 times we did

the poll, we would get a 'Yes' value of between 47 and 53 per cent. Only in five times would we get a response outside of this 6 per cent range. This is the so-called 95 per cent confidence interval: the size of the margin of error is half of it, 3 per cent, which can be either added to or taken from the poll's headline result. So what do this week's polls tell us about the likely outcome of the referendum?

Polling ought to follow a normal distribution, commonly called a bell curve.

For the latest ICM poll, which was released on Friday, I've plotted this curve. The headline result was a 51-49 split in favour of 'No'. Both a 'Yes' and 'No' result in the actual referendum are consistent with the poll, as both are within the margin of error.

So, what do the polls tell us? First, a 'Yes' and 'No' outcome are both within the margin of error; neither is inconceivable. Second, this doesn't mean that we are stumbling around in the dark: the majority of polls have put 'No' in the lead which means that it ought to remain the favourite by some distance. However, the polls could systematically be wrong. Their predictions could be incorrect due to more than mere randomness. As the first election of its kind, there's no way at all to judge how reliable they are. With a record turnout expected, 16- and 17-year-olds voting for the first time, as well as some concerns of 'shy no voters' unwilling to admit that they intend to vote against independence and a significant number of Scots reporting they still haven't decided, there are plenty of sources of uncertainty.

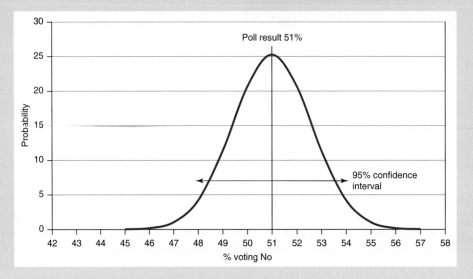

Opinion polls like these often have a sample size of around 1000, giving a margin of error of about 3 per cent around the result – assuming you have a random representative sample and assuming people are telling the truth!

This has been a tough section but one that's critical for many analytical approaches to decision making. We'll use one more example to reinforce what we've been doing. A company is reviewing the performance of its call centre and wanting to ensure it has adequate staffing levels to meet customer demand at peak times. As part of this, the company is trying to ascertain the typical duration of an incoming call. A random sample of 1000 recent incoming calls has been obtained and it's been calculated that the mean duration of a call is 130 seconds with a standard deviation of 40 seconds. We've been asked to estimate the population mean duration and explain the result. Try this yourself before reading further.

It's clear that we're in a confidence interval situation and given we're dealing with a mean we can perform the necessary calculation:

$$130 +/- 1.96(40/\sqrt{1000}) = 130 +/- 2.5 \text{ seconds}$$

That is, we're 95% confident that the mean duration of calls coming into the call centre is between 127.5 seconds and 132.5 seconds. Although this is based on only 1000 calls we can attach a high probability to our conclusion thanks to the Central Limit Theorem. Note that we don't have to make any assumptions about the distribution of individual call durations but we do have to assume that the sample is randomly taken from all calls received.

Hypothesis tests

Our investigation so far into sample data has focused on the calculation of a confidence interval. Although these are useful in quantifying an interval in relation to the population parameter, there are frequently occasions when we wish to assess whether a *specific* value for the population is likely (rather than a range of values, as in the CI approach). Imagine the reaction of the CEO or Marketing Director or Finance Director to your explanations about sampling variation, confidence intervals and margins of error. 'That's all very well', says the CEO 'but what I want to know is: have our average unit costs come down; has our social media marketing campaign improved our brand image; has productivity improved; have customer response times decreased?' In other words, has something we're interested in changed? A confidence interval won't tell us this directly. We need to carry out what is known as a *hypothesis test*. Fortunately, we have all the information we need.

Consider the following. The company undertaking the online advertising to support its new product has decided that the cost of such an online advert campaign can only be justified if more than 55 per cent of target customers see the adverts. We are now no longer interested simply in calculating a CI for the sample result but wish to assess whether, based on the sample data, this criterion is being met across the statistical population. In such a case we must approach the problem from the perspective of a *hypothesis test*. Fortunately, this uses exactly the same principles that we have already established for the CI, although in a slightly different way. We shall examine a number of the more common forms of hypothesis test in the remainder of this chapter. Most of these follow exactly the same approach as we shall follow. Carrying out a hypothesis test follows a logical sequence.

- Formulate the null and alternative hypotheses.
- Determine a significance level.
- Identify the rejection area.
- Determine the critical statistical value.
- Calculate the test statistic value.
- Choose between the two hypotheses.

Let us examine these in turn for our online advert problems. The actual information we have is from the sample:

$$p = 63\%$$
$$n = 250$$

We wish to use this information to assess whether the population percentage was more than 55 per cent. On the face of it, it appears that we have met this target, since the sample result, at 63 per cent, is higher than 55 per cent, but we also know we must allow for what we can call *sampling error* or *sampling variation*: a possible – but legitimate – difference between the sample result and the population result. As we've said before, the term 'sampling error' is a little unfortunate since it implies we have made some sort of mistake. Sampling error indicates that no matter how carefully we have selected and analysed the sample, we must allow for the fact that the sample result may differ from the population result simply because it is a sample – only part of the population data set. Let us show the population parameter with the symbol π (pi). We wish to assess whether π could take a value of more than 55 per cent, given that the sample result was 63 per cent.

Formulate the null and alternative hypotheses

The first step is to formulate appropriate hypotheses that we can test statistically. We must specify two hypotheses: the null and the alternative. What we're effectively doing by setting up two hypotheses is putting ourselves into an either/or position where we must decide – using probability principles – which of the two hypotheses is more likely. It's often easier to start with the alternative hypothesis, which always focuses on the situation we are trying to assess or 'prove'. In our example, we could verbally state the hypothesis we're trying to 'prove' as:

'More than 55 per cent of target customers saw our online ads.'

We denote the alternative hypothesis as H_1. The null hypothesis is then formulated as the 'opposite' of the alternative hypothesis. We would express the null hypothesis as:

'No more than 55 per cent of target customers saw our online ads.'

We denote the null hypothesis as H_0. Given that we're using π as the population percentage viewing the online ads we can show the two hypotheses as:

$$H_0 : \pi \leq 55\%$$
$$H_1 : \pi > 55\%$$

The null hypothesis, H_0, states that π is no greater than 55 per cent (i.e. it does not meet the required target audience) and H_1, the alternative hypothesis, states that π is over 55 per cent. Note that, in probability terms, the two hypotheses are collectively exhaustive: they encompass all possible values for π. A common failing in formulating hypotheses is that they do not encompass all possible values. For example, the formulation:

$$H_0 : \pi < 55\%$$
$$H_1 : \pi > 55\%$$

would be technically incorrect since it does not allow for p taking a value of exactly 55 per cent. The order in which we formulate the two hypotheses is also important (and again often the cause of error). The general principle is that H_1 should be formulated in the context of whatever value(s) we wish to test. Our criterion here is whether the adverts were seen by more than 55 per cent of target customers. This minimum figure then becomes the basis for H_1, and H_0 must be formulated to ensure all other possible values have been included. We have two hypotheses and only one of them can be chosen. We must decide which is correct (or more precisely which is most likely to be correct) based on the information we have available. And the information we have available is based on our sample set of data – '63 per cent of 250 people saw our online ads'. But we know that this information is sample-based and therefore cannot be taken at face value and assumed to be 100 per cent correct – we need to take sampling variation into account when making our decision about the two hypotheses.

The basis for our test is now as follows. We start from the premise that our null hypothesis is the appropriate one for our problem. Only if we can amass sufficient statistical evidence will we accept the alternative hypothesis. In the jargon of hypothesis testing, at the end of the test we will have come to one of two conclusions:

● either we will reject H_0 (and thereby accept H_1)

● or we will fail to reject H_0.

The terminology may sound odd but it is carefully logical. If we fail to reject H_0 we are not concluding that H_0 is correct but rather that insufficient evidence was available to reject H_0. The analogy that is often used to try to explain this logic relates to criminal law practice in many countries. If you are charged with some criminal act you will be asked how you plead. In many countries the choice is either 'not guilty' or 'guilty' and by presumption you are not guilty until proved otherwise. In such a situation, the null hypothesis, H_0, is that you are not guilty and the alternative hypothesis, H_1, is that you are guilty. The null hypothesis is assumed to be the case unless the prosecution can bring sufficient evidence to persuade the judge/jury to reject the null hypothesis and if they reject the null hypothesis they have to accept the only alternative – H_1, guilty. However, if the prosecution *fails* to convince the judge/jury to find you guilty then we say that we fail to reject H_0. This doesn't mean that H_0 is 'proven', simply that we can't reject it based on the evidence available. In the court situation finding you not guilty is *not* the same as saying you're innocent – that you didn't actually commit the crime – it says simply you weren't found guilty on the evidence available. This is exactly the same as in our test. Unless we can bring sufficient evidence, we have no reason to reject H_0. It is also worth noting that the hypotheses we use will fall into one of three categories:

(a) $H_0: \pi \leq x$
$H_1: \pi > x$

(b) $H_0: \pi \geq x$
$H_1: \pi < x$

(c) $H_0: \pi = x$
$H_1: \pi \neq x$

where x is the appropriate numerical value we wish to test. The first two are technically referred to as *one-tail* tests and the last a *two-tail* test. A one-tail test indicates that we want to decide if the parameter (π) is greater than a specific value (in the case of example (a)) or is less than a specific value (as in example (b)). A two-tail test indicates we want to determine if the parameter has changed (and we're not bothered whether the change is upwards or downwards). Which of the three categories we choose will depend on the specific problem. In our example we have a one-tail test (of type (a)) given that we want to know if the population viewing figures are greater than 55 per cent.

Determine a significance level

Having formulated the hypotheses we must now choose a level of significance associated with the test. To explain this we need to consider that, whatever our conclusion at the end of the test, we may actually have reached the wrong conclusion about the population based on the sample evidence. Once again, the legal analogy is useful. In your trial, let us assume that you are in fact not guilty (H_0) but that the jury finds you guilty on the evidence presented. Alternatively, let us assume that you are in fact guilty (H_1) and that the jury mistakenly finds you not guilty. In both cases an 'error' has occurred but of two different types. We can distinguish two different possible 'errors' in our test.

Type I error	We reject H_0 when in fact it is correct. In this case what is called a Type I error would occur if we rejected H_0 when in fact the population percentage was no greater than 55 per cent.
Type II error	We should reject H_0 but fail to do so. In our case a Type II error would occur if the population percentage was actually over 55 per cent but we failed to reject H_0 based on the evidence available.

Table 7.1   Decisions and errors

Decision	Actual situation	
	H_0 is true	H_0 is false
Do not reject H_0	Correct	Type II error
Reject H_0	Type I error	Correct

We can summarise the possibilities in tabular form as in Table 7.1.

A Type I error is denoted as α and a Type II error as β. Although we would like the chance of making either error to be as low as possible, in practice the two errors are inversely linked. That is, other things being equal, the lower the probability of making a Type I error, the higher the probability of making a Type II and vice versa. In most hypothesis tests we are able to control directly the probability of making a Type I error. We do this by specifying the maximum allowable probability of making a Type I error. Typical values for α are 0.05 and 0.01 and the choice of α will, in part, depend on the consequences of making a Type I error (i.e. incorrectly rejecting the null hypothesis).

Progress Check 7.7

Consider the analogy of your being tried for murder in a court of law (a crime which in fact you did not commit). Would you want the probability of a Type I error being committed to be low or high?

Naturally you would wish the probability of the jury reaching the wrong decision in the context of H_0 to be as low as possible, hence you would choose α at 0.01 rather than 0.05. The less obvious implication of a low choice for H_0 – but particularly important in the context of the test – is that if H_0 were not rejected based on the evidence available there would be a high probability (0.99) of this being the correct decision. However, in other cases we may prefer to see the Type II error probability minimised (with the implication that α will be higher at 0.05).

Consider the situation facing a medical consultant who is examining you for some serious disease. The null hypothesis will be that you do not have the disease (and hence require no treatment). The alternative is that you do have the disease and require treatment. The consultant's decision may, in part, be based on some medical test that has been undertaken. But like any test, the results cannot be 100 per cent guaranteed in terms of their accuracy and reliability. Consider the consultant's position in terms of committing a Type I and II error. A Type I error is committed if the consultant decides incorrectly that you have the disease and provides the appropriate treatment. All this means is that you are subjected to a course of treatment which is actually unnecessary (and hopefully harmless). However, if you do actually have the disease, the consultant would quite naturally wish to minimise the probability of a Type II error – that you do actually have the disease but that the consultant decides you do not and therefore does not provide treatment. In this case the consequences are potentially more severe: i.e. you failed to receive treatment which you actually needed.

Progress Check 7.8

Consider our problem of the online advertising. Which choice of α would you recommend?

All of this may sound unduly complex but actually condenses to a simple choice of either $\alpha = 0.01$ or $\alpha = 0.05$, depending on whether we wish to minimise the chance of a Type I error or a Type II. In many business applications the choice is actually quite arbitrary. The principles are important, however. At the end of the test, whatever conclusion we have come to we must remember there is a possibility that we have made the wrong decision based on the available data.

In the case of the online advert problem it would seem sensible to choose α at 0.01 – to minimise the chance of a Type I error. H_0 by implication means that the online advert campaign should be halted as it is not reaching what is seen as a sufficient percentage of viewers. We would not wish to go ahead with such an expensive campaign if there was any reasonable doubt that it would not be effective in terms of reaching over 55 per cent of viewers. This implies that we wish to minimise the potentially high cost of a Type I error. On the other hand, it might be the case that the new product's sales success depends on the online campaign and that the cost of not advertising might be high in terms of lost sales and overall company performance. In this case we might legitimately wish to minimise the cost of a Type II error and choose $\alpha = 0.05$. This simply reaffirms that such a decision cannot be taken as an integral part of the test but rather in the context of the wider decision-making problem. It also reaffirms that such decisions should not necessarily be left to the statistician/analyst, who may be unaware of the wider picture. However, let us stick with our first logical position and require $\alpha = 0.01$.

Identify the rejection area

The next stage is to identify the relevant rejection area. Consider Figure 7.3. This shows the sampling distribution for our problem. Note that the population parameter, $\pi \leq 55$ per cent, is based on the assumption that our null hypothesis is not rejected. The rejection area is shaded and corresponds to $\alpha = 0.01$: the rejection area equates to 1 per cent of the total area under the Normal curve. The logic of the rejection area is straightforward. We are trying to decide whether to reject H_0 based on the sample evidence. For the sake of

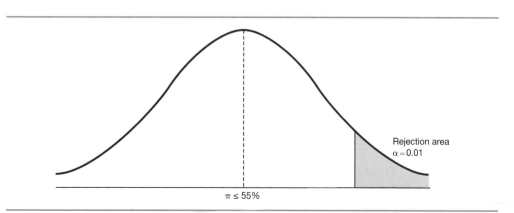

Figure 7.3 Sampling distribution showing rejection area

argument, let us assume that H_0 is in fact correct and that π is no greater than 55 per cent. We can then apply our knowledge of the sampling distribution in a logical way.

Progress Check 7.9

Assuming H_0 is correct, what is the probability of taking a sample from this population and finding a sample percentage that falls in the rejection area? What conclusion would you come to if this were actually to happen?

Clearly the probability of any one sample result falling in the rejection area is 0.01 (or 1 per cent) based on the assumption that H_0 is actually correct. However, consider our position if we did in fact take a sample from this population and found that it fell in the rejection area. We would have to conclude:

- either that a highly improbable event had occurred (actually obtaining a sample result that far away from the population percentage)
- or that our assumption that H_0 was correct is unlikely.

These are the only two possibilities, and the reason for identifying the rejection area now becomes clear. It will allow us to determine whether the sample result we have does fall in the rejection area or not. If it does then we shall be forced to conclude that the assumption that H_0 is correct is unlikely. If it does not fall in the rejection area then we shall have no reason to reject the null hypothesis.

It is worth noting that the rejection area itself will depend on which of the three general types of hypothesis we actually formulate (illustrated in Figure 7.4). For type (a), where H_1 takes the $>$ form, the rejection area will be in the right-hand tail of the distribution (as in our example). For type (b), where H_1 takes the $<$ form, the rejection area will be in the left-hand tail. For the third type (c), where H_1 takes the form not equal to, then we require the two tails each with an area $\alpha/2$ at either end of the distribution. For this reason the first two types of test are known as *one-tail tests* and the last type as a *two-tail test*. With practice you will find it is not necessary to sketch the rejection area each time, although it is advisable to do so to begin with just to confirm which area you are classing as the rejection area.

Determine the critical statistical value

Using the rejection area and our choice of α we must now obtain a critical statistical value that is associated with this rejection area. In other words, we must find the Z value associated with this area.

Progress Check 7.10

What is the Z value for the rejection area if we set $\alpha = 0.01$ for a one-tail test?

From the Normal table we see that an area in one tail of 0.01 has a Z value of 2.33. Consider carefully what this implies. It implies that, if H_0 is correct, then 99 per cent of all samples from this population should result in a percentage viewing figure no further away from 55 per cent than 2.33 standard errors. If we put this another way, it implies

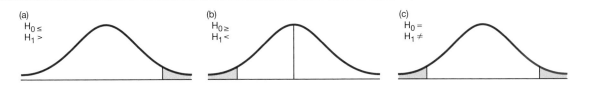

Figure 7.4 Rejection area

that the probability of any one sample occurring more than 2.33 SEs above 55 per cent is only 0.01, but again on the assumption that H_0 is correct. The critical Z value, in other words, simply marks out the rejection area in terms of standard errors. This value is usually denoted as:

$$Z_\alpha = 2.33$$

Calculate the test statistic value

Having obtained the critical Z value appropriate to our test we must now calculate a Z value for the actual sample result. We do this in exactly the way we developed in Chapter 5, when we were introducing the use of the Normal distribution. Our calculated statistic becomes:

$$Z_{Calc} = \frac{p - \pi}{\sqrt{\dfrac{\pi(100 - \pi)}{n}}}$$

where you will note that the denominator of the equation is just the formula for calculating the standard error for a percentage. The calculation is then:

$$Z_{Calc} = \frac{63 - 55}{\sqrt{\dfrac{55(100 - 55)}{250}}}$$

$$= \frac{8}{3.15} = 2.54$$

Progress Check 7.11

How would you interpret this figure? What are the units of measurement?

What we have actually done is to calculate how many standard errors the sample result of 63 per cent is away from the (assumed) population value of 55 per cent. We find that the sample result of 63 per cent is 2.54 SEs away from the (assumed) population value of 55 per cent. We can now tackle the last step in the test.

Progress Check 7.12

Would you reject or fail to reject the null hypothesis in our problem?

Choose between the two hypotheses

We are now in a position to choose between our two hypotheses. The null hypothesis was formulated on the assumption that we had not reached our target audience figure of more than 55 per cent of viewers. If the null hypothesis is correct then we would expect a sample result to be no more than 2.33 standard errors above the assumed population value of 55 per cent. However, based on the sample information that we have, the sample viewing percentage of 63 per cent is 2.54 standard errors above the target of 55 per cent – *above* the critical Z figure of 2.33. We have found that the sample result, at 63 per cent, is inconsistent with what we would expect a sample result to be based on the null hypothesis. We are therefore forced to reject the null hypothesis and accept the alternative: based on the sample result we are 99 per cent confident that the target audience figure of more than 55 per cent of viewers has been reached.

In practice the decision rule for comparing the critical with the calculated Z value is readily summarised. If we take the absolute values for any Z values (that is we ignore any minus signs) then we have a simple decision rule:

- If $Z_{Calc} > Z_\alpha$ then we must reject H_0.
- If $Z_{Calc} > Z_\alpha$ then we cannot reject H_0.

We can summarise the various stages we have followed for this test in a concise manner:

$$H_0: \pi \leq 55\%$$
$$H_1: \pi > 55\%$$
$$\alpha = 0.01$$
$$Z_\alpha = 2.33$$
$$Z_{Calc} = 2.54$$
$$\text{Reject } H_0 \text{ (since } Z_{Calc} > Z_\alpha).$$

We have deliberately taken a lengthy approach to this hypothesis test to discuss the stages we follow and the rationale behind each stage. With practice, of course, the whole analysis is much quicker and more straightforward and can be completed in a few moments – provided you understand what you are doing. Once again, it is worthwhile summarising what we have been able to do. Through this test we have been able to assess – based on limited sample information – a particular numerical value or values for the statistical population. We have not been able to do this with certainty – indeed the only way to do that would be to collect data on the entire population – but we have been able to quantify the likelihood of our conclusion being the appropriate one. We must also bear in mind the caveats we raised earlier about the reliability, accuracy and representativeness of the sample data.

We must also conclude that no manager in their right mind would base any critical decision solely on a hypothesis test. Such tests – and their conclusions – are but one more piece of information available to the manager. Such information – like that from all other sources – must be assessed in the context of the decision to be taken and not in isolation.

Tests on a sample mean

The test we have just completed is technically known as a test on a sample percentage (proportion). A considerable variety of other tests are available (you will find textbooks available with encouraging titles such as '100 Common Statistical Tests') and we shall examine some of the more common. Fortunately, all follow exactly the same process as our first test, with only slight differences occurring. Let us first consider a test on a sample mean. The first difference that occurs is that the two hypotheses must be formulated in terms of the population mean, μ, not the population percentage, π. The second difference is in the formula for calculating the Z statistic. The appropriate formula is now:

$$Z_{Calc} = \frac{\bar{x} - \mu}{\frac{s}{\sqrt{n}}}$$

where the denominator of the expression relates to the standard error of the sampling distribution for the sample mean. Apart from this, the test is conducted in exactly the same way as before.

Let us consider an example. A local authority has one of its administrative centres located out of town and the majority of employees drive to work. As part of the authority's 'green' policy (with the authority wanting more environmentally friendly initiatives and activities) various efforts have been made to encourage employees to car-share: that is for several people to travel to work in one car rather than each use their own. The authority is trying to assess the impact of these measures on car-sharing. Last year, in a comprehensive exercise, the authority found that the number of cars parked in the staff car park each day averaged 220. This year, based on a sample of 75 days' observations, it has calculated that the mean number of cars parked in the staff car park is 205, with a standard deviation of 32.

Progress Check 7.13

Based on this data can we comment on the impact of these measures on car-sharing? What assumptions have you made in assessing this data?

We can summarise the test:

$$H_0: \mu \geq 220$$
$$H_1: \mu < 220$$
$$\alpha = 0.05$$
$$Z_\alpha = -1.64$$
$$Z_{Calc} = \frac{205 - 220}{32/\sqrt{75}} = -4.06$$

Reject H_0.

The null hypothesis is formulated on the assumption that there has been no change in car-sharing as measured by the mean number of cars in the car park – that the mean number of cars is still 220 or more. The alternative hypothesis is that the mean number of cars has fallen. The choice of α is arbitrary in this example but we have chosen 0.05. From the Normal table this gives a critical Z value of -1.64 (since our rejection area will lie in the left-hand tail of the sampling distribution we get a negative Z score). Calculating the Z value for the sample data gives a result of -4.06, hence using the decision rule we must reject the null hypothesis, which states that there has been no reduction in cars parked. We are forced to conclude, based on the sample evidence, that the mean number of cars has reduced.

Once again it will be worthwhile to reinforce the logic of what we have done. We start with the hypothesis that the mean number of cars has not decreased since last year. Based on this assumption we can calculate the maximum expected variation of a sample mean from this (assumed) population mean. This is expressed in SEs as the Z_α. We then calculate how far the observed sample mean actually is from the population mean. In this case it is further away than we would expect on the basis of the assumed population mean. It seems more likely, therefore, that the population mean has decreased, based on the sample evidence, and we are forced to accept H_0.

Apart from the usual assumptions relating to the statistical logic underpinning the test, it is also important to be aware of other assumptions – often implicit – that we are making. The key assumption is that all other factors that might impact on the number of cars parked have remained unchanged since last year: the number of people working at the centre, the type of staff employed, working patterns, income patterns and so on. We should also remember that we have not 'proved' that the measures introduced by the authority have increased car-sharing. Other factors may well have affected behaviour: fuel prices, public transport prices/availability and the like. Nevertheless, we should not underestimate the usefulness of such statistical inference in management decision making.

Tests on the difference between two means

Our next two tests are concerned with assessing the difference between two samples rather than comparing a sample result with an assumed population value. First, we shall examine the difference between two sample means. For this we shall return to the situation we were examining in Chapters 3 and 4. Remember that a retail organisation had collected and analysed data on a sample of its stores in two regions, A and B. The variable measured was the profit achieved by profit centres in each of the two regions. The available information is shown again in Table 7.2.

Mean profit of the sample of stores was £12 981.2 in Region A and £17 168.8 in Region B. We wish to determine, based on this data, whether there is a statistically significant difference in mean profit between the two samples of profit centres. Once again, the logic of the test process can be applied. In this case, however, we are testing not one mean but two, and we need briefly to discuss the principles of the test we are about to undertake. We can treat each sample as if, in principle, it came from a separate and distinct population. That is, our Region A sample represents one statistical population while the Region B sample represents a second and potentially different population. The difference between the two populations relates to their mean values. Given that we have two populations then we also have two population means, μ_1 and μ_2. Effectively what we wish to test is whether there is any difference between these two populations' means.

Table 7.2 Profit achieved in Regions A and B

	Region A sample	Region B sample
$\bar{x}$	£12 981.2	£17 168.8
s	£17 476.3	£19 688.1
n	113	121

Our two hypotheses then can be formulated in terms of $(\mu_1 - \mu_2)$. As you might expect, the rest of the test procedure is as before, with the exception of the calculation for the Z statistic. This then becomes:

$$Z_{\text{Calc}} = \frac{(\overline{X}_1 - \overline{X}_2) - (\mu_1 - \mu_2)}{\sqrt{\dfrac{s_1^2}{n_1} + \dfrac{s_2^2}{n_2}}}$$

The formula looks horrendous but is actually straightforward to calculate. The denominator is once again the standard error of the relevant sampling distribution and you may be able to see that it is effectively an average of the standard errors of the two individual populations; that is, we use the standard deviations of the two samples, s_1 and s_2.

Progress Check 7.14

Calculate the standard error. Complete the appropriate test to determine whether there is a significant difference in mean profit between the two regions. How do you explain your conclusion given that the difference between the means of the two samples is over £4000?

We are required to test to see if there is a difference between the two groups (not whether one is larger than the other), hence a two-tail test is appropriate:

$$H_0: (\mu_1 - \mu_2) = 0$$
$$H_1: (\mu_1 - \mu_2) \neq 0$$
$$\alpha = 0.01$$
$$Z_\alpha = -2.58$$
$$Z_{\text{Calc}} = \frac{(12\,981.2 - 17\,168.8) - 0}{\sqrt{\dfrac{17\,476.3^2}{113} + \dfrac{19\,688.1^2}{121}}} = -1.72$$

Do not reject H_0.

A two-tail test requires $\alpha/2$ to determine the critical Z value, hence Z_α at -2.58. Note also that we have chosen $\alpha = 0.01$ given the potential importance of the conclusion. The test does not provide us with sufficient evidence to reject H_0 so we cannot conclude that there is a significant difference between the two groups. We would conclude, based on this sample data, that there was no evidence of a significant difference in the mean profit of stores in Region A compared with stores in Region B. If we had been thinking, for example, of offering some financial bonus to managers in Region B to reward their 'better' performance then this test indicates we have no evidence to conclude that mean profits in Region B are any different from those in Region A. To people unfamiliar with hypothesis testing such a conclusion may seem odd given that numerically there is a difference of over £4000 between the two sample means. Noting that, in the case of both samples, the sample standard deviation is relatively very large, we might comment that although there is a large numerical difference between the two sample means, once we allow for the variation we might expect in the sampling process, this difference cannot be said to be statistically significant.

Two final points can be made about this test. The first is that the formulation of the hypotheses can test for any numerical difference between the two means not just, as in our case, zero. Thus, if we had wanted to see if there was a difference of at least £4000 between the two groups, we could have formulated H_0 as $(\mu_2 - \mu_1) > £4000$. This would be rewritten as:

$$H_0: (\mu_2 - \mu_1) - £4000 > 0$$

for the purposes of carrying out the test. The second point to note about the test is that for the test to be valid, the two samples must be obtained independently. This is the case in our example: sample 1 and sample 2 are not connected (apart from the fact that all the profit centres are part of the same organisation). However, consider a different scenario. Suppose we had collected data on only one region's stores for last year and for this year with a view to assessing where profits had changed. In such a case, the two samples would not be independent (since each sample would contain exactly the same profit centres). The test we have just conducted would not be appropriate for testing to see whether there was a difference in profit. If we did want to conduct such a test, the easiest way would be to calculate the difference in profit between the two years for each profit centre and then to find this mean difference. This mean could then be tested (against zero) using the one-sample test we completed in the last section.

Tests on two proportions or percentages

Given that we can conduct a test on two means it seems logical to consider an equivalent test on two proportions or percentages. Let us illustrate with the following example. An organisation operates on two different sites and both sites have support services available – personnel, training, finance and so on. On Site A the Finance Department still operates on a largely manual basis, whereas in Site B they have invested in computerised cloud-based accounts and invoicing systems. Management concern has recently been expressed about the number of invoices the organisation receives which are not properly checked against goods and services received. For example, if someone in the organisation orders a computer, a copy of the order is sent to Finance. When the computer supplier has delivered and installed the computer, then an invoice for the appropriate amount should be passed to Finance for payment authorisation. There are concerns, however, that the Finance Department receives – and pays – invoices which do not exactly match the goods supplied. For example, the original order may have specified a laptop with a touchscreen but a laptop without a touchscreen was actually supplied and the invoice still detailed the original order and payment. Accordingly, a detailed investigation has been carried out at each of the two sites into a sample of recently paid invoices to determine the percentage of these where an overpayment occurred, i.e. where the organisation paid the supplier more than it should (management are less concerned about underpayment). At Site A, 250 invoices were checked and it was found that 13 per cent represented overpayments. At Site B, 200 invoices were checked and only 8 per cent were overpaid. Is there any evidence of a difference in overpayments at the two sites? Once again, we can assume two independent samples, each, in principle, representing a different statistical population. Our hypotheses this time are formulated in terms of $(\pi_1 - \pi_2)$ using π since we are dealing with percentages.

$$H_0: (\pi_1 - \pi_2) = 0$$
$$H_1: (\pi_1 - \pi_2) \neq 0$$
$$\alpha = 0.05$$
$$Z_\alpha = 1.96$$

The calculated value for the Z statistic can once again be obtained, but for this test we need to explain as we progress. According to our null hypothesis there is no difference between the two population percentages. If this is the case then $\pi_1 = \pi_2$ and we can average the two sample results to provide one estimate of the population percentage.

$$p = \frac{n_1 p_1 + n_2 p_2}{n_1 + n_2}$$

$$p = \frac{250(13) + 200(8)}{250 + 200} = 10.78\%$$

You will see that this is effectively a weighted average of the two sample results. We can now use this value of 10.78 per cent to calculate the standard error for the relevant sampling distribution and obtain a figure of 2.94.

$$SE = \sqrt{p(100 - p)\left(\frac{1}{n_1} + \frac{1}{n_2}\right)}$$

$$= \sqrt{10.78(89.22)\left(\frac{1}{250} + \frac{1}{200}\right)}$$

$$= \sqrt{8.66} = 2.94$$

Our calculated Z value then becomes:

$$Z_{Calc} = \frac{(p_1 - p_2) - (\pi_1 - \pi_2)}{2.94} = \frac{(13 - 8) - 0}{2.94}$$
$$= 1.70$$

Since $Z_{Calc} < Z_\alpha$ we have no reason to reject the null hypothesis based on this data. That is, we have no evidence that there is a significant difference in the percentage of invoices overpaid. Once we allow for sampling variation, we cannot conclude that the two samples come from statistically different populations.

You may also remember that for the two-sample test on means it is possible to formulate the two hypotheses so that we do not assume the populations are equal but rather that one is greater than the other or that the difference between them exceeds some numerical value. The same applies to this test. In such a case it would not be appropriate to use the two sample results to find an average estimate of the population percentage (since we are now not assuming they are the same). The SE formula would then be:

$$SE = \sqrt{\frac{p_1(100 - p_1)}{n_1} + \frac{p_2(100 - p_2)}{n_2}}$$

Tests on small samples

The next test we introduce is one relating to small samples. You will recollect the basis of our being able to use the Normal distribution in the test process: the Central Limit Theorem indicates that as long as we take sufficiently large samples then the sampling distribution will approximate to the Normal. For our purposes we defined a sufficiently large sample size as over 30. But what if the sample size is not sufficiently large?

Suppose our sample has only a few observations? Can we carry out a hypothesis test on small samples? The answer is a qualified 'yes'. The qualification is needed because we cannot carry out the tests we have looked at so far, since they are based on the Normal distribution. Instead we must base our test for a small sample on something known as the t distribution. The t distribution is similar in appearance to the Normal distribution – that is, it is symmetrical and bell-shaped. However, its exact shape will depend on the sample size. The larger is n, then the closer the t distribution becomes to the Normal. The smaller is n, then the worse the approximation to the Normal distribution. The general relationship is shown in Figure 7.5, where the Normal distribution and two t distributions are shown. Notice that the t distributions follow the general shape of the Normal but tend to be flatter and have wider tails. This feature is further exaggerated as the sample size for the distribution decreases. In Figure 7.5 distribution t_1 has a smaller sample size than t_2 and is 'flatter'. The implications of this are that if the sample is sufficiently large then for our purposes there are no practical differences between the Z and t distributions. Once the sample gets smaller, however, we must be careful to use the t distribution in our tests. In effect there is such a t distribution for each possible sample size. That is, the t distribution for a sample size 10 will be slightly different from that of sample size 11, 12 and so on. Once again, such tables have been pre-calculated and are shown in Appendix C. The table contains much the same information as the Normal but is presented in a slightly different way. The rows of the table relate to what is known as degrees of freedom, shown as v. This is defined as $(n-1)$, one less than the size of the sample. Across the top of the table we distinguish columns in terms of the appropriate level for α (the significance level) that we are using for the test in question. These range from 0.10 to 0.005.

Progress Check 7.15

Assume a sample size of infinity (∞). For $\alpha = 0.05$, 0.025 and 0.005 determine the t value from the table. Compare this with the equivalent Z values from the Normal table. What conclusion do you come to about the t and Z tables?

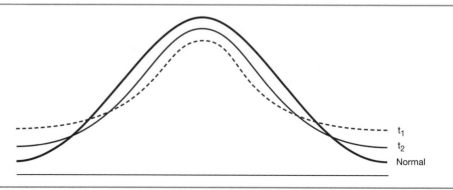

Figure 7.5 Comparison of the Normal distribution and two t distributions

From the table we see that for an infinite sample size the t values are identical to those we would obtain from the Normal table, implying that for large samples there is no difference between the two distributions. If we follow the $\alpha = 0.05$ column upwards we see that as the degrees of freedom decrease, the area in the tail gradually gets larger (which is what we showed in Figure 7.5). Apart from this we can conduct a t test on a sample mean in exactly the same way. Consider the following problem. A manufacturing company has recently completed a retraining programme for some of its assembly-line staff to try to improve quality, productivity and performance. Fifteen employees performing the same task on the assembly line went through the training programme and the time it took them to perform an assembly operation was noted before the training and again afterwards. The result was that on average these 15 employees were able to complete their tasks 1.6 minutes faster after the training (with a standard deviation of 0.34 minutes around this mean). Can we conclude that the training has been effective?

Progress Check 7.16

Carry out the appropriate test for this situation.

Our test follows the usual procedure. We have:

$\bar{x} = 1.6$ (where $\bar{x}$ is the mean time saved)

$s = 0.34$

$n = 15$

and the test is then:

$H_0: \mu \leq 0$

$H_1: \mu > 0$

$\alpha = 0.01$ d.f. $= 14$

$t_{\alpha,14} = 2.624$

$$t_{Calc} = \frac{\bar{x} - \mu}{\frac{s}{\sqrt{n}}} = \frac{1.6 - 0}{\sqrt{\frac{0.34}{15}}} = 10.63$$

Reject H_0.

The null hypothesis is formulated such that we assume that the mean time saved has not improved; therefore μ is no greater than zero. The degrees of freedom is 14 (n − 1) and for the one-tail test the critical t value from the tables is found to be 2.624 (compared with 2.33 if this had been a large-sample Z test). Calculating the t value gives a value which forces us to reject the null hypothesis and conclude that there has been a significant reduction in time taken to complete the task after the training programme. It is important to realise that a t test automatically makes allowances for the fact that any conclusion we come to about the hypotheses is based on only a small sample. You will frequently encounter the criticism from other managers along the lines of 'but it's based on only 15 employees!' The allowance for the fact that we have only a small sample is built into the critical t statistic that we use in such tests by default. Effectively, the

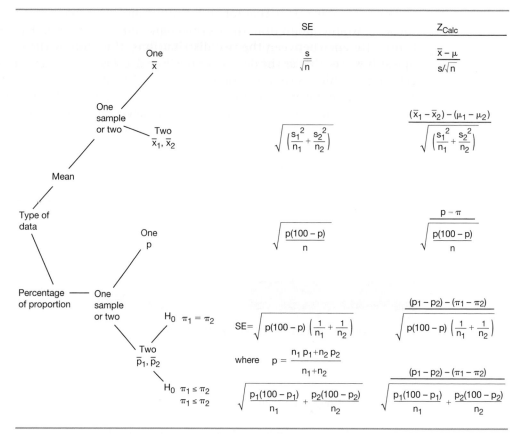

Figure 7.6 Large sample tests

critical t statistic will be larger than its Z counterpart. This implies that we must have 'stronger' evidence from a small sample before rejecting the null hypothesis we have formulated.

One large caveat must be made, however, for a t test. With the Central Limit Theorem we were able to say that as long as sample sizes were sufficiently large then the sampling distribution will approximate to the Normal no matter what the original population distribution. For the t distribution, however, this is not the case. For the t test to be valid we must make the assumption that the population from which the sample was taken is Normal. In practice this is often an assumption impossible to assess and we must carry out the t test anyway. We must remember though that the test conclusion is suspect unless we are confident that the population is Normally distributed.

Although the t test demonstrated here relates to a test on a mean, the t test can also be applied to percentages/proportions and to tests on two means (t tests on two percentages or proportions are not usually undertaken, since the standard error is often too large to make the test worthwhile). Be warned, however, that in the case of a t test on two means the calculations for the standard error become complex and there are further critical assumptions that apply. Use the more advanced tests only with considerable caution and, preferably, supported by a friendly and comprehensible statistician. Figures 7.6 and 7.7 summarise the key tests on both large and small samples, together with the relevant standard errors and calculated Z or t statistics.

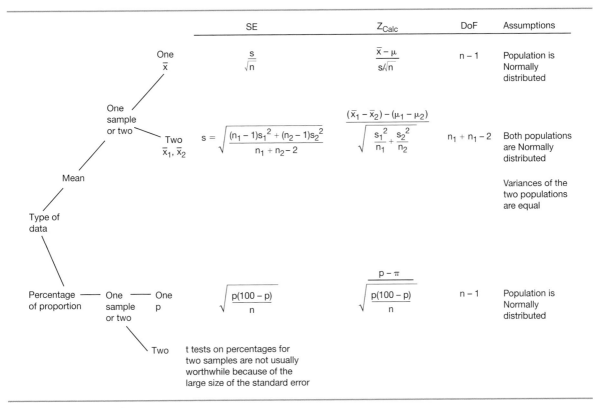

		SE	Z_{Calc}	DoF	Assumptions
	One $\bar{x}$	$\dfrac{s}{\sqrt{n}}$	$\dfrac{\bar{x} - \mu}{s/\sqrt{n}}$	$n - 1$	Population is Normally distributed
One sample or two	Two $\bar{x}_1, \bar{x}_2$	$s = \sqrt{\dfrac{(n_1 - 1)s_1^2 + (n_2 - 1)s_2^2}{n_1 + n_2 - 2}}$	$\dfrac{(\bar{x}_1 - \bar{x}_2) - (\mu_1 - \mu_2)}{\sqrt{\dfrac{s_1^2}{n_1} + \dfrac{s_2^2}{n_2}}}$	$n_1 + n_1 - 2$	Both populations are Normally distributed
					Variances of the two populations are equal

Mean

Type of data

Percentage of proportion	One sample or two	One p	$\sqrt{\dfrac{p(100 - p)}{n}}$	$\dfrac{p - \pi}{\sqrt{\dfrac{p(100 - p)}{n}}}$	$n - 1$	Population is Normally distributed
		Two	t tests on percentages for two samples are not usually worthwhile because of the large size of the standard error			

Figure 7.7 Small sample tests

Gig economy is a man's world, data show

Male workers outnumber women by two to one, Ipsos-RSA survey finds

By Sarah O'Connor, Employment Correspondent

Britain's "gig economy" is a man's world where male workers outnumber females by roughly two to one, according to new research into this small but growing part of the workforce. Gig economy companies vaunt the flexibility of their online labour platforms, which often allow people to log on to work whenever they want. Yet while part-time or flexible work is often assumed to appeal more to women, data suggest the gig economy is powered by men.

There are roughly 1.1m people working in Britain's gig economy and 69 per cent of them are male, according to a face-to-face survey of 8,000 people by Ipsos Mori and the Royal Society for the encouragement of Arts, Manufactures and Commerce, or RSA.

The RSA's survey should be treated with some caution since it is based on a small sample of 243 people who reported they had done gig economy work. But the think-tank said all the comparisons were statistically significant. Because the sample size is small, the proportion of gig workers who are men could be between 62 and 76 per cent.

It's often necessary to use small sample data but as the article points out small sample size results should be treated carefully. The article helpfully provides the confidence interval around the headline result.

Table 7.3 Computer output

Two-sample analysis results				
		Region A	Region B	Pooled
Sample statistics:	Number of obs.	113	121234	
	Mean	12981.2	17168.8	15146.5
	Variance	3.0542E8	3.8762E8	3.47937E8
	Std. deviation	17476.3	19688.1	18653.1
	Median	6840	9580	8025

Difference between means = −4187.61

Conf. interval for diff. in means:		95 per cent		
(Equal vars.)	Sample 1 − Sample 2	−8996.47	621.252	232DF
(Unequal vars.)	Sample 1 − Sample 2	−8976.99	601.772	231.4DF

Ratio of variances = 0.787937

Conf. interval for ratio of variances: 0 per cent

                 Sample 1 Sample 2

Hypothesis test for H_0: diff = 0   Computed t statistic = −1.71609

                vs ALt: LT   Sig. Level=0.0437404

                at Alpha = 0.01   so do not reject H_0

Inferential statistics using a computer package

Increasingly, inferential analysis is based around the output from some suitable computer package: EXCEL, MINITAB, STATGRAPHICS, SPSS, SAS. Although the structure and format of such packages varies, they all typically provide many of the statistics we have introduced in this chapter (as well as others that we have not introduced). Table 7.3 shows the output produced when analysing the mean profit levels of stores in Region A and Region B (remember the test on two means that we carried out). The raw data was analysed by the package and the one-tail test on two sample means conducted. Summary details of the two samples are provided (n, the mean, the sample standard deviation) and the difference between the two means shown (−4187.61). The results of the test are shown at the bottom of the table.

In this example, we have set up the null hypothesis for a one-tail test (that Region A $\geq$ Region B) and for $\alpha = 0.01$. We see from the output that H_0 is set up as diff = 0 with the alternative hypothesis (ALT) that Region A is less than (LT) Region B. The calculated Z statistic is shown at −1.71609 (we worked it out earlier as −1.72) and the package conveniently interprets the result for us, telling us, with this sample data, that we do not reject H_0.

p values in hypothesis tests

It will be evident that in any hypothesis test the choice of α is to some extent arbitrary. In the previous illustration we set α at 0.01. We could just as easily have set it at 0.05 or indeed 0.001 or 0.005. With some thought you should realise that different choices of α

may lead us to different conclusions about whether or not to reject the null hypothesis, H_0. At one level of α we might reject H_0, whereas at another level of α we do not reject it. It is partly for this reason that, with tests typically being generated through some computer package rather than a manual calculation, common use is made of something known as the *p value*. The p value in a test is the smallest value for α for which the sample results become statistically significant. In the case of the test in Table 7.3 this is reported close to the bottom right of the table as:

```
Sig. Level = 0.0437404
```

That is, for any α value up to this value of 0.0437404 we would decide not to reject H_0. For any α value above 0.0437404 we would reject H_0 and accept H_1. The p value removes the need to establish an α value first and, importantly, allows others using our results to see precisely at what significance level a null hypothesis would be rejected.

Evidence-mongers rush in where angels fear to tread

The importance of knowing your unknowns

By Martin Sandbu

Last month the American Statistical Association published a critical statement on the use of p-values, a measure of the statistical solidity of relationships found in data. Loosely speaking. . . the p-value is the probability that a relationship you find between variables in the data would appear (or appear even more strongly) in your sample if in reality the variables are unrelated. A broad convention – including for much of economics – treats a p-value of 5 per cent as the threshold for "statistical significance". In practice, that also means low-enough p-values have become a threshold for publication in academic journals, and thus keys to the gates of academic careers.

This creates huge problems both for what is filtered through the academic publication process to join the received body of knowledge, and for the policymakers who, with the best intentions, try to shape "evidence-based policy".

One problem is that a "statistically significant" relationship between variables does not mean "important" in any other sense that matters for policy, such as economically substantial or useful in terms of our normative goals (nor does it mean "true"). An even more basic problem is that even statistical "significance" is not what it's cracked up to be. Christie Aschwanden at fivethirtyeight.com explains the statistical problems with p-values. More intuitively, we should expect p-values below 5 per cent to occur about 5 per cent of the time in completely unrelated data — which is why it has been said that "most published research is wrong". That does not stop it from influencing public debate and public policymaking.

A science journalist showed this by simply concocting a spurious result with standard statistical methodology, and quickly got the global press to report his "finding" that chocolate helps with weight loss. The trick was to include enough variables that something would come up with a "significant" p-value.

p values are useful but they need to be understood and used in context.

χ^2 tests

The last test we shall introduce is known as the χ^2 test (pronounced 'kai square'). This is an example of something known as a *non-parametric test* (of which there are many different sorts, just as we have Z and t tests). The tests we have conducted so far have, in fact, been on key parameters of the data set we have examined – on the mean or the percentage. Effectively we have been conducting various *parametric tests* up to now. There are frequently times, however, when we are interested not in a specific parameter of a data set – such as the mean – but on the whole set of data. Consider the following scenario. The Education Department of a large local authority has been concerned for some time about traffic accidents that occur immediately outside schools. Frequently such locations are very busy and often quite chaotic as parents arrive in cars to deliver or collect their children and as other traffic becomes congested. Over the last few months data has been collected on the number of accidents that occurred and noting the day of the week the accident occurred. This is given in Table 7.4.

Clearly we have a distribution and could work out the mean number of accidents, but to what point? Our interest in this data is in the entire distribution, not simply in one of its parameters, the mean. In this case it appears there is some sort of variation in the number of accidents occurring on a daily basis: the numbers on a Monday and Friday appear higher than those on the other days. However, since we are dealing with a sample set of data we must somehow try to take sampling variation into account. In other words, our question must be: is there a statistically significant difference in the number of accidents on a daily basis? It is in this type of situation, where we are interested in the distribution of the data, that we can apply the χ^2 test.

Let us apply some logic to the situation in Table 7.4. If there were no particular pattern in the distribution of accidents on a day-by-day basis then it would be logical to expect the same number of accidents each day. This then becomes our null hypothesis, H_0. Since we have observed the total number of accidents at 75 over this sample period then we would expect, given H_0, that there would be 15 accidents each day (75/5). Clearly, from Table 7.4, there are not exactly this number each day. However, given that we are dealing with a sample set of data we must make allowances for the sampling variation that exists between the number of accidents actually observed each day and those expected.

Let us show the observed frequencies as O and the expected as E. If the null hypothesis, H_0, is correct then we would expect there to be no significant difference between O

Table 7.4   Traffic accidents involving schoolchildren

Day of week	No. of accidents
Monday	20
Tuesday	13
Wednesday	12
Thursday	12
Friday	18
Total	75

and E. If, however, there were a significant difference we would be forced to reject H_0 and conclude that there was some difference in the number of accidents on a daily basis. To perform such a test we use something known as the χ^2 distribution, where:

$$\chi^2 = \sum \frac{(O - E)^2}{E}$$

We will look at the calculations involved in a moment. Like the Binomial, Normal and t distributions this is a probability distribution and like our other tests we can obtain two χ^2 values: one we calculate (from the formula above) and one from tables (shown in Appendix D). As with the t distribution, there are many different χ^2 distributions – each one varying with the degrees of freedom. As with the other tests, we have a simple decision rule. If the calculated χ^2 (obtained from the sample data using the above formula) is greater than the critical χ^2 (obtained from the table) we must reject the null hypothesis. One good thing about a χ^2 test is that the null hypothesis is always the same: that there is no significant difference between the observed frequencies and the expected.

Let us perform the test on this data. The relevant calculations are shown in Table 7.5.

This calculation gives a calculated χ^2 at 3.74. The calculation itself deserves a little explanation. We are interested in whether the differences between the observed and expected frequencies are significantly different from zero (if they were zero it would imply the distribution was exactly as expected). However, there is little point summing the $(O - E)$ figures, as they will always sum to zero (remember the standard deviation calculation in Chapter 4?) So, as with the standard deviation, we square them. However, we must also divide each by its respective E value and then total. The division by its respective E value is necessary since, in some applications, the E values themselves may differ within the distribution. Consider for example if we had had a simple situation where:

O	E	$(O-E)$	$(O-E)^2$	$(O-E)^2/E$
50	75	−25	625	8.33
50	25	25	625	25.00

Table 7.5 χ^2 test calculations

	Observed	Expected	$(O - E)$	$(O - E)^2$	$\frac{(O - E)^2}{E}$
	20	15	5	25	1.67
	13	15	−2	4	0.27
	12	15	−3	9	0.60
	12	15	−3	9	0.60
	18	15	3	9	0.60
Total	75	75	0		3.74

The (O − E) deviation is the same in both cases (so the (O − E)^2 figure must be also). However, it is evident that this deviation is proportionally more important for the second category (with E at 25) than for the first (with E at 75). In fact, the second category's deviation is effectively three times that of the first (with the two Es at 75 and 25 respectively). Dividing the (O − E)^2 values through by E keeps this relative relationship (25 to 8.33).

Following the standard test methodology we now have:

● Formulate the hypotheses:

H_0 is that there are the same number of accidents each day of the week (O = E). H_1 is that the number of accidents varies between the days of the week (O ≠ E). (Note in H_1 we are not saying which days are higher.)

● Determine a significance level:

Let us set this at $\alpha = 0.01$.

● Determine the critical statistical value:

For a χ^2 test we must determine the relevant degrees of freedom. For this type of test it is defined as:

$$\text{d.o.f.} = (\text{no. of classes or categories in the distribution}) - 1$$

Here we have five classes or categories (days of the week) so we have four degrees of freedom. From Appendix D, with $\alpha = 0.01$ and four degrees of freedom, the critical χ^2 is 13.3 (the situation is illustrated in Figure 7.8).

The critical value at 13.3 relates to the null hypothesis and the calculated statistic from the sample. Although we would expect some difference between a sample and some hypothesised population in this case (with four degrees of freedom and α at 0.01) we would expect the sample result to generate a calculated statistic of no more than 13.3 *if* the null hypothesis is not to be rejected. If we found that our sample generated a statistic of more than 13.3, we would have to reject H_0.

● Calculate the test statistic value:

We have already done this at 3.74.

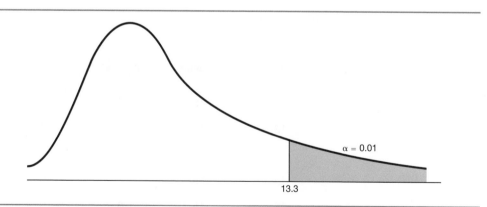

Figure 7.8 χ^2 test: rejection area

● Choose between the two hypotheses:

We apply the same decision rule as before: if the calculated statistic exceeds the critical, we reject H_0. In this case it does not, so we cannot reject the null hypothesis. Effectively we conclude that the number of accidents is the same each day. Any variation on a particular day is purely random, arising from the sampling process.

Progress Check 7.17

The local chamber of commerce has commissioned some market research into the spending habits of the local adult population. A random sample of 500 adults has been selected as follows:

Age group (years)	Number in sample
18 < 21	54
21 < 30	63
30 < 45	167
45 < 60	85
60 and over	131
Total	500

From government census statistics it is known that the local adult population has the following distribution:

Age group (years)	% of population
18 < 21	13
21 < 30	12
30 < 45	38
45 < 60	15
60 and over	22
Total	100

What comment can you make about the age profile of the selected sample compared to that of the population?

Solution is given on p 578.

This type of test involving χ^2 is known as a *goodness of fit test* because we are testing whether an observed distribution fits some expected distribution (as defined in the null hypothesis). It is worth noting that the test can also be applied to determining whether an observed set of data fits some theoretical distribution like the Binomial or the Normal. If we were wanting to see whether a set of data fitted a Binomial or Normal distribution then the process is as before but now calculating an appropriate Binomial or Normal distribution for the expected values. The degrees of freedom associated with a test on the Binomial or Normal are then:

Binomial
d.o.f. = (no. of classes/categories in the distribution) − 2
Normal
d.o.f. = (no. of classes/categories in the distribution) − 3

Tests of association using χ^2

There is a second application of the χ^2 tests known as the test of association, sometimes known as a *contingency table* test. To illustrate, consider the following scenario. A local health clinic currently operates a no-appointments system if a patient wishes to see a doctor. That is, a patient wishing to see a doctor turns up at the clinic and waits until the doctor is free. This may take a few minutes or an hour or more depending on how many other patients are waiting. Some patients have indicated that they would prefer to have an appointment at a specific time rather than simply turn up, and the clinic has recently completed some basic market research. A representative sample of patients were asked whether they would prefer the clinic to move to an appointments system or not. The results are shown in Table 7.6.

So, for example, out of 153 male patients 106 were in favour of an appointments system, 27 were against and 20 had no preference either way. Simple observation of the survey results appears to indicate that there is a divergence of opinion by gender. Males appear to be in favour, whereas females appear to be against. However, this is only a sample and again we must allow for sampling variation. Clearly our interest lies in trying to answer the question: do men and women have different views about an appointments system? The reason Table 7.6 is referred to as a contingency table is that we are effectively asking the question: is opinion about the appointments system contingent (or dependent) upon gender?

To undertake a χ^2 test we need a set of expected frequencies as well as the observed. What is less clear is where these expected frequencies are to come from. The answer begins to appear if we consider the last question posed: is opinion about the appointments system dependent upon gender? The word 'dependent' has a clear meaning in a probability context (as we discussed in Chapter 5). Let us for the moment assume that the two characteristics – gender and response to the question – are independent. *If* they are independent then we can use basic probability to calculate the expected frequencies.

Table 7.6   Patient responses

| Patient gender | Patient view on appointments systems | | | |
	For	Against	No preference	Total
Male	106	27	20	153
Female	97	166	34	297
Total	203	193	54	450

Progress Check 7.18

How could we use probability to determine the expected number of males who were for the new system?

We see that there was a total of 153 males in the sample (out of 450 people). The probability of someone in the sample being male is then:

$$P \text{ (Male)} = 153/450 = 0.34$$

Similarly, the probability of someone in the sample being for the new system, regardless of gender is:

$$P \text{ (For)} = 203/450 = 0.451$$

So *if* gender and response to the new system are independent we have:

$$P \text{ (Male and For)} = 0.34 \times 0.451 = 0.15334$$

and hence we would expect 69 males (0.15334×450) to have responded 'For' *if* the two characteristics are independent. The calculation can be summarised as:

$$\frac{153}{450} \times \frac{203}{450} \times 450$$

which simplifies to:

$$\frac{153 \times 203}{450}$$

or in general:

$$\frac{\text{Row total} \times \text{Column total}}{\text{Sample total}}$$

Clearly we can calculate the expected frequencies for the other cells in the table in exactly the same way.

Progress Check 7.19

Calculate the rest of the expected frequencies for Table 7.6.

The calculations are summarised in Table 7.7.

For each cell in the table (Male–For, for example, or M–F) the expected frequency is shown, and these total, as they must, to 450. We can now complete the test in the usual way.

The null hypothesis is that the two characteristics – gender and response – are independent (which is how we worked out the E frequencies). *If* they are independent, we can determine from Appendix D the maximum χ^2 we would expect from the sample results. If we set $\alpha = 0.01$ we can determine the critical χ^2 if we have the relevant degrees of freedom. For a contingency table test this is calculated as:

$$\text{d.o.f.} = (\text{No. of rows} - 1) \times (\text{No. of columns} - 1)$$

Table 7.7 Expected frequencies

Table cell	O	E	(O − E)	(O − E)^2/E
M–F	106	69.02	36.98	19.81
M–A	27	65.62	−38.62	22.73
M–NP	20	18.36	1.64	0.15
F–F	97	133.98	−36.98	10.21
F–A	166	127.38	38.62	11.71
F–NP	34	35.64	−1.64	0.08
Total	450	450		64.69

where the number of rows and columns in the table *excludes* the totals. Here we have:

$$d.o.f. = (2 − 1) \times (3 − 1) = 2$$

From Appendix D we see a critical χ^2 of 5.99. The calculated χ^2 at 64.69 is greater than the critical, so we must reject H_0 – effectively rejecting the hypothesis that the view of a patient on the new system is independent of gender. We conclude therefore that the patient's view *is* dependent on gender – that male and female patients have different views on an appointments system.

As with other tests, computer-based statistics packages will perform the various calculations for you. Typical output for the problem we have examined would look like this:

```
Chi-Square  D.F.  Significance  Min E.F.  Cells with E.F.<5
64.69        2     .0000         18.36     None
```

We see the calculated χ^2 at 64.69 with the degrees of freedom (D.F.) at 2. The Significance figure shows the p value indicating that we should reject H_0 – there is a significant difference between the observed and expected frequencies.

In summary, the χ^2 test is particularly useful where we require a non-parametric test either in terms of goodness of fit or as a contingency table. There are three other points to note about the use of the test:

● The test can only be used on frequencies/counts. It cannot be used where the observed data shows percentages or proportions.

● Technically, the test should be applied only where all E frequencies are at least five in value. As a rule of thumb, the test can still be applied as long as no more than 20 per cent of E values are less than five. If there are more E values than this it might be possible to combine classes/categories together. When using computer output like that shown earlier, you are often told what the minimum calculated expected frequency for the problem was (18.36 for the computer output shown above) and told how many expected values were less than five (none in our example).

- In the event of a test which has only one degree of freedom (for example on a 2×2 contingency table) then something known as Yates' correction must be applied to the calculated statistic, which becomes:

$$x^2 = \sum \frac{(|O - E| - 0.5)^2}{E}$$

Again, a statistics package will normally perform this adjustment for you.

Worked example

In Great Britain, in addition to paying income tax, households also have to pay a council tax, which is effectively a local tax levied on a residential property. The amount of tax to be paid is, in part, dependent on the value of the residential property and all properties in England are classified into one of eight value groups, Band A to Band H, with Band A corresponding to the lowest value category and Band H to the highest. A household in a Band A house, for example, would pay less council tax than a household living in a Band B house. One local authority has recently completed a survey of 2500 residential properties in its area in terms of which band they fall into, and has been investigating how this compared with the England average. The results of the survey are shown in Table 7.8, together with the percentage distribution in England for the 2017 financial year.

So, for example, we see that the local authority found 734 out of a sample of 2500 residential properties fell into the lowest band, A. For England as a whole around 25 per cent of residential properties fall into this band. The local authority has asked us to assess whether the local distribution of residential properties between the bands is

Table 7.8 Council tax bands of residential properties

Band	England percentage	District number
A	24.5	734
B	19.6	505
C	21.9	490
D	15.4	413
E	9.5	187
F	5.0	98
G	3.5	45
H	0.6	28
		2500

England percentages are taken from Office for National Statistics

different from that for England as a whole since, if it is, this might have implications for the amount of council tax the authority is able to collect. If, for example, lower bands are over-represented in the local authority's area compared with England then the local authority may be able to collect less tax because these properties pay less than higher-band properties. Can we help in determining whether there is a significant difference?

Clearly we have an observed distribution from the survey carried out by the local authority, and if we can obtain an expected set of frequencies, we can conduct a χ^2 test. We can readily obtain an expected set of frequencies. We know the England percentage distribution and if we use these percentages multiplied by 2500 (the sample size) this will give us the distribution we would expect based on the England averages. We can then compute a χ^2 test in the usual way. The relevant calculations are shown in Table 7.9.

The E column shows the expected number of properties in each band based on the hypothesis that they follow the England percentages (613 is obtained from 0.245 × 2500). None of the expected frequencies is less than 5, so we can proceed to perform the necessary calculations as shown in the final column. This gives a calculated χ^2 value of 81.12. To conduct the test we need a critical value for χ^2 from tables in Appendix D. Setting $\alpha = 0.01$, we have seven degrees of freedom (8 bands − 1). From Appendix D we obtain a critical χ^2 of 18.48. The null hypothesis is that there is no significant difference between the observed and expected frequencies. However, since the calculated statistic at 81.12 exceeds the critical statistic at 18.48, we are forced to reject the null hypothesis and conclude that there is a statistically significant difference between the observed and expected frequencies. We conclude, therefore, that based on this sample the local distribution of residential properties among council tax bands in this local authority area is significantly different from the England average. The test does not, however, tell us what the difference is. By simple inspection of the data, though, we realise that the O values for the first four bands (A, B, D) are higher than the E values, while the reverse is true for the higher bands (E, F, G). It seems reasonable to conclude, then, that this local authority has more properties in the lower tax bands than England as a whole and fewer in the higher tax bands.

Table 7.9 χ^2 test calculations

Band	England (%)	District O	District E	$(O − E)^2/E$
A	24.5	734	613	24.1
B	19.6	505	490	0.46
C	21.9	490	548	6.04
D	15.4	413	385	2.04
E	9.5	187	238	10.74
F	5.0	98	125	5.83
G	3.5	45	88	20.64
H	0.6	28	15	11.27
Total	100.0	2500	2500	81.12

Summary

In this chapter we have explored the ideas behind statistical inference and introduced a number of formal tests to allow us to assess the characteristics of some statistical population based on sample information. The potential behind such tests is apparent. Most managers and decision makers find themselves in situations where decisions must be taken on limited and often incomplete information. In those situations where sample data can be collected and analysed, the tests we have covered offer a valuable aid to the manager in evaluating options and alternatives. All the tests we have introduced are based on similar principles even though the exact calculations may vary slightly. Such tests do not offer a guaranteed solution to a manager's problems but they do offer a cost-effective method of supplementing the information available. Such information, however, needs to be carefully evaluated alongside that from other sources. This can only be done properly with an adequate understanding of the basic principles behind inferential techniques. It should also be remembered that we have only touched upon some of the more common tests available. A whole barrage of additional tests exists and details can be found in the relevant references.

Exercises

1   Return to Exercise 6 in Chapter 4. Calculate the mean and standard deviation if you have not already done so. Given that this data is a sample, calculate the 90 per cent, 95 per cent and 99 per cent confidence intervals around the mean. Provide a management interpretation of these in the context of the problem and explain why the interval gets larger.

2   Return to Exercise 6 in Chapter 4. The Finance Department in the local authority has estimated that at least 45 people per day on average need to use the local library to justify the cost of keeping it open – costs relate to staff wages, heating, lighting, cost of periodicals and so on. You have been asked to evaluate the data collected on the mean number of people using the library in the context of this minimum figure.
    Draft a report to the committee (most of whom have low levels of numeracy) evaluating the information available. If you had been given the task of collecting data on the number of users how would you have done this and how would you try to ensure you had a representative sample?

3   Several years ago a new chief executive was appointed to a group of firms. On appointment the CE expressed concern about the quality of the senior management in one of the major companies in the group. She felt that this group of managers was by and large out of touch with new technology, new market opportunities and so on and, in spite of boardroom opposition, the CE has tried over the past few years to encourage a younger age structure among these senior managers via an active promotion and recruitment policy. Data has been provided on the age structure of these senior managers in 2010. The group had a mean age of 53 years. A sample of 20 senior managers this year finds an average age of 46, standard deviation 4.6 years. Can the CE conclude that her policies have had an effect in terms of reducing the mean age of senior managers?

4 In the Worked Example in Chapter 5 we had a distribution of a sample of customers' electricity consumption. Test whether this distribution is Normal.

5 A small engineering firm manufactures high-precision components for the aeronautical industry. In order to ensure quality, the production equipment has to be regularly maintained. One particular component in the production equipment must be replaced regularly. At present the component is supplied by a Japanese company and has a mean life of six months. A French company has approached the firm claiming to supply a comparable component at lower cost. The French company has supplied six of the components for testing and the life of the components has been found to be, in months:

6.2; 7.6; 6.5; 7.4; 6.3; 6.3

Recommend whether you think the engineering firm should switch suppliers based on this information.

6 A local authority has a pool of cars available for staff to use on official business. One particular make and model of car, of which the authority has a considerable number, claims to give a miles per gallon (mpg) performance of 52 mpg for simulated out-of-town driving. For a sample of 20 cars the transport manager has calculated that the actual mpg for such driving has been 47 mpg, standard deviation of 7 mpg.

Based on this information would you conclude that the car manufacturer's claimed mpg is unrealistic? What assumptions have you had to make to reach a conclusion?

7 A local hospital is trying to assess its performance vis-à-vis national performance. The Department of Health has recently indicated that, nationally, for a particular hospital-based treatment the mean length of stay of patients in hospital was 8.6 days. The local hospital has checked the records of 150 of its patients who have recently been discharged from hospital having received this treatment and found the mean LOS was 7.5 days, standard deviation 1.1 days. The hospital manager is keen to contact the local media to publicise that the hospital is performing better than the national average in this treatment area. Would you recommend her to do this?

8 A local training agency is trying to get government support for its activities – which relate to the provision of industrial and commercial training for the local labour force – on the basis that unemployed workers who are better skilled have a better chance of finding new employment than unskilled workers. A group of people who have recently been unemployed but now found work has been investigated. One group, the skilled, comprised 120 people who had been unemployed for a mean of 16.2 weeks, standard deviation 1.3 weeks, before finding employment. The second group, 150 unskilled workers, had been unemployed for an average of 24.9 weeks, standard deviation 2.1 weeks. Is there any evidence that the training agency argument is valid?

9 An organisation is trying to evaluate which of two PC computer systems to standardise on within the organisation. In terms of price, specification and performance there is little to choose between the two models being considered, Model A and Model B. However, the computer services manager is concerned about the possible maintenance and repair costs of the two models. Based on a sample of 40 of each type, the annual maintenance costs have been estimated at £45.60 for Model A, standard deviation £4.20, and at £39.65 for Model B, standard deviation £6.52. Would this information help the organisation choose between the two models?

10 Historically it has taken a local council an average of 18 weeks to reach a decision about planning applications for building development work submitted by construction companies. The companies have complained that decisions are taking too long and delays are costing them money. The chief executive of the local council has initiated a streamlined system for such applications with the intent of reducing the time taken to reach a decision. After a few months' operation, a sample of 250 planning applications has been analysed and a mean time of 15 weeks found, with a standard deviation of 5.2 weeks. Has the streamlined system led to a reduction in mean time taken?

11 The government has introduced a self-assessment system for tax payments whereby citizens themselves calculate the amount of tax to be paid on income each year. Naturally, the revenue department checks such self-assessments, although it does not have the resources to check them all each year. At the start of the new system, it was felt that at least 90 per cent of such self-assessed tax returns would be correctly completed by the citizen (with the remainder containing errors which are either accidental through miscalculation or deliberate as the result of an attempt to defraud). Some months after the start of the new system a sample of 1750 self-assessments has been rigorously checked; 11.8 per cent were found to be incorrect in some way. Comment on the initial view that at least 90 per cent would be correctly completed.

12 A company employs largely part-time staff, and in the past has found staff turnover to be 23 per cent each year (that is 23 per cent of staff in any one year leave the company). This is felt to be too high, with implications for morale, motivation and costs (since new staff have to be recruited and trained). The company has recently put into place a performance management system intended to improve productivity, morale and staff retention. The latest figures based on a sample of 20 teams of staff in the company indicate staff turnover is 18.6 per cent, standard deviation 1.7. Is there any evidence that staff turnover has fallen?

13 An international company routinely rotates its senior managers every five to six years around its activities worldwide. Staff are financially compensated for such moves but with many staff buying a house in their new location, there are concerns about relative house prices. The company has recently surveyed house prices in two cities where it is based:

	Mean price (£)	Standard deviation	Sample size
City A	235 000	12 750	132
City B	261 000	15 680	161

Prices are for comparable houses and have been adjusted for exchange rates. Is there any evidence of a difference in mean house prices between the two cities?

14 Recent legislation requires adherence to detailed and complex food-labelling requirements on products sold to consumers. A recent survey examined whether the food labelling on supermarket own-brand products met these requirements. The results were categorised as:

- Complete compliance with legislation.
- Satisfactory compliance, indicating that some minor irregularities occurred.
- Unsatisfactory compliance, implying that major breaches of the legislation had occurred, with the supermarket liable to a fine as a result.

Table 7.10 Number of items complying with legislation

Supermarket	Compliance			Total
	Complete	Satisfactory	Unsatisfactory	
A	80	23	9	112
B	121	32	17	170
C	105	27	12	144
D	172	58	12	242
Total	478	140	50	668

The results of the survey were as shown in Table 7.10.

Do the supermarkets have the same performance in the sense of compliance with this legislation?

15 An airline operating between London and Aberdeen knows that a large part of its customer base represents business executives. The airline is considering offering a limousine service to/from the airport to be included in the airline ticket price, which would have to increase as a result. A survey has recently been completed on a number of flights of 10 executive passengers asking if they (or their company) would be willing to pay 10 per cent extra for their flight if this service was included. The responses were:

No. responding Yes from 10 surveyed	No. of flights
0	6
1	12
2	15
3	13
4	9
5	3
6	2
Total	60

Estimate p as the total number responding yes/total number surveyed.
   Determine whether these responses follow the Binomial distribution.
   Why do you think the airline might be interested in whether responses follow the Binomial distribution?

16 Return to Exercise 8 in Chapter 4. Test to see whether there is a significant difference between mean customer spend in the two stores. Draft a short report explaining your conclusion in non-technical terms for the store managers.

8 Quality Control and Quality Management

Learning objectives

By the end of this chapter you should be able to:

- understand the importance of quality management for all business organisations
- construct statistical process control charts
- apply Pareto charts to quality issues
- construct and use an Ishikawa diagram
- understand the concept of six sigma and its link to the above

For many years quality of goods and quality of services were not seen by most businesses as a key part of their overall business strategy. Rather their focus historically was on cost reduction, improving efficiency, increasing sales, maintaining and increasing profit margins. Importantly this focus was often short-term. Today the focus has changed dramatically. Most major business organisations now accept that, literally, their long-term business survival may be at stake if they do not improve the quality of the goods and services they provide to compare favourably with some powerful overseas economies. Manufacturing companies in the late 1970s gradually began to realise that quality products were essential if they were to survive in a global market. Gradually this focus on quality has extended to the service sector and increasingly into the public sector, where the ideas of quality, standards and customer satisfaction are becoming more widespread. Many areas of the UK public sector economy are engaged in major programmes to improve the service provided to their customers through quality initiatives. In fact, in the UK, central government is now requiring many public sector organisations to take the issue of quality of customer service very seriously and to publish their criteria for 'good' or quality service.

Historically, this relatively new emphasis on 'quality' took root in the manufacturing sector – largely thanks to the ever-increasing success of Japanese companies in the world market. In this chapter we shall explore some of the issues relating to quality management and some of the techniques available to the manager to help monitor and improve quality of goods and services.

The importance of quality

What makes quality important to any organisation is that, if the organisation provides goods or services which more than satisfy the customer, then that business is likely to be successful, other things being equal. Organisations which do not provide quality goods and services are likely to fail. Obviously this is a gross oversimplification: many other factors will contribute to an organisation's success or failure. Increasingly, however, quality is seen as a critical factor in the success/failure position of a business organisation. Any business organisation is constantly searching for what a business strategist would call its competitive advantage: what allows one organisation to compete successfully against other organisations. What distinguishes this organisation – particularly from the perspective of the customer – from others?

Organisations which identify and then exploit their competitive advantage are well on the way to success and continued survival. One popular way of examining the principles of business strategy is to consider different possible sources of such a competitive advantage: how an organisation can establish and maintain such an advantage. As a generalisation, such competitive advantage can be exploited through one of two broad strategies: cost or differentiation. Quality has a potential impact on both of these.

Through a cost focus, an organisation tries to secure its advantage by ensuring that the cost of producing the good or supplying the service is lower than for its competitors. All its strategic focus is on ensuring that this cost advantage is maintained. In the UK, for example, it is estimated that between 30 per cent and 40 per cent of effort in business may be spent detecting errors, problems and poor quality and in taking the necessary corrective action. Consider the cost savings if an organisation gets quality right first time. Consider translating these costs into a competitive advantage in relation to competing organisations.

On the other hand, a differentiation focus implies that an organisation is trying to ensure that its goods/services are seen by customers as different in some meaningful way from those of its competitors. Differentiation can be achieved in a variety of ways: through the range of goods or services offered; through the availability of the goods/services; through the standard of goods/services offered; through quality.

In both cases – cost and differentiation – a quality focus can help establish and maintain the organisation's competitive advantage. On the cost side, quality procedures and processes can ensure that quality of output is kept high and therefore the costs associated with faulty output are kept low. Equally, on the differentiation side, high quality can differentiate a good/service from that of competitors.

Techniques in quality management

Naturally, quality management is more than just the application of techniques to the quality problem in an organisation. Quality management is also concerned with organisational structure, organisational culture, interpersonal relationships, links between customers and suppliers, motivation, team building and the like. However, it is widely acknowledged that a number of common 'tools' have an important part to play in any organisation's search for improved quality. These tools can be applied at different stages of the quality process, which can be simplified, according to Juran[1], as:

- planning for quality;
- controlling for quality;
- improving for quality.[1]

IHI Corporation: cratering credentials

Life imitates art imitating life. Poor quality control in an aero engine plant is the subject both of an Arthur Miller play – *All My Sons* – and the latest Japanese corporate scandal. The great American, shocked by wartime malpractice, dramatised the ebbing of trust. IHI Corporation, a supplier to Boeing, Airbus and General Electric, must deal with that problem for real. The engineering group has apologised for misconduct that included uncertified employees signing off engine repairs with the names of qualified colleagues. A random spot check by Japan's Ministry of Transportation discovered some of the suspect practices. These have come to light before. The ministry is pondering what action to take. Japanese carmakers and air bag producer Tanaka have had problems with quality control lately too. This is surprising in a country famed for its attention to detail. Misguided loyalty to the corporation may be the culprit. Scrutiny of IHI's standards and governance could unsettle other units, especially those involved in defence. IHI produces engines and electronics for military aircraft. The company's share of defence spending may shrink. IHI's core business is the aircraft engine operations unit. This works for Japan Airlines, All Nippon Airways and other budget carriers. It is a big chunk of the company's aerospace and defence business, bringing in more than three-quarters of operating profits of ¥77bn (£705m). Ebitda margins are tolerable at 9.3 per cent, but perhaps not for much longer. A new factory is scheduled to start operations this year. Orders could take a knock as customers obsessed with safety re-assess their contractor. Shares in IHI have fallen by a third from recent highs. The company's enterprise value is about five times forward Ebitda, just a fraction above all time lows. Yet there has been no dip worth buying into in response to the latest bad news. Investigations may uncover worse. Full disclosure is needed before a sober inspection can pass the shares as fit to fly.

Source: IHI Corporation: cratering credentials, FT.com, 6 March 2019.
© The Financial Times Limited. All Rights Reserved.

The costs of poor quality service are often hidden – but always high.

Given that a central part of the modern quality philosophy relates to the prevention of quality-related problems rather than their detection and correction, the planning and improving phases of the process take on an increased importance. We shall introduce three techniques commonly used in quality management: control charts, Pareto charts and Ishikawa diagrams. We will see how these techniques relate to each other and can complement each other later in this chapter.

Statistical process control

We shall illustrate the first of these quality-related techniques with reference to a production environment. An organisation produces and packages a range of soft drinks. One of the product lines has recently been launched on the market and consists of a

---

[1] J.M. Juran (1986) 'The Quality Trilogy: A Universal Approach to Managing for Quality', paper presented at the ASQC 40th Annual Quality Congress in Anaheim, California, 20 May.

tropical fruit fizzy drink sold in cans. The production line operates in such a way that several hundred thousand cans are processed each day. The automated machinery is set to fill each can with an average (mean) content of 400 ml. Naturally, we expect some variation in this mean amount and this has been quantified as a standard deviation of 10 ml. It is also known that the distribution of filled contents is Normal. Clearly, from a quality management perspective, we would wish to establish some quality inspection process to check that the mean quantity filled does meet these specifications. Over time we would expect to have to maintain, adjust and repair the automated machinery delivering this mean amount. Naturally, we would not want large quantities of the product which were underfilled to be distributed and sold as this would violate consumer protection legislation. Equally, we do not want large numbers of cans to be overfilled, as this will add to our costs. We would require some quality control procedure to monitor the quality of output on a regular basis so that substandard quality can be detected at an early stage and the production process adjusted or repaired as necessary to bring the production process back to the required quality level.

Given the volume of production each day, management will require some easy and cost-effective method of quality control. Clearly we cannot afford to check the entire production batch each day; nor can we afford to halt production while we check output quality. It is evident that in this type of situation we shall require some sort of sampling process to be undertaken: to select a random sample of output to check for quality. However, this sampling process will bring its own difficulties. If we take too large a sample then the physical task of checking quality will be both time-consuming and expensive. On the other hand, too small a sample and our conclusions based on the sample evidence might be suspect. Consider also the dilemma of the manager if the sample evidence appears to reveal that quality problems are occurring in production. Knowing what we do about statistical inference, we know that such a conclusion based on sample evidence cannot be guaranteed: it will be based on some stated significance level derived from probabilistic distribution principles. If such sample evidence appears to reveal production problems, the manager is faced with a major dilemma:

- to accept the sample evidence and stop production to rectify the problem and suffer the consequences of this lost production; or
- to hope that the sample evidence is wrong and continue production.

The other side of this picture is equally worrying. Suppose that the sample leads us to conclude that production quality is acceptable when in fact it is not? That is, that the sample fails to reveal a production problem. The dilemma faced by the manager in this context can be summarised as shown in Table 8.1.

The manager is faced with two alternative decisions based on the sample evidence: to continue production or to stop production. There are also two alternative states of nature (and remember that the manager has no immediate control over which state of

Table 8.1 Decisions and outcomes

	State of nature	
Decision	Quality level acceptable	Quality level not acceptable
Continue production	Correct decision	Type II error
Stop production	Type I error	Correct decision

nature occurs): the quality level of production is acceptable or the quality level is unacceptable. Clearly there are two situations where the correct decision will have been taken and two where it will not.

Social media and big data come into play

By Maija Palmer

Statistical process control – where big data allows companies to monitor the manufacturing process more precisely than before – is also helping save money.

Coty, the beauty and perfume company, for example, saved more than $250,000 by avoiding overfilling its perfume bottles. The company spent $47,000 on a system from manufacturing intelligence company InfinityQS and in two years saved $270,000 simply by being more exact about the amount of liquid in each bottle.

 Source: Palmer, M. (2014) Social media and big data come into play, FT.com, 24 June.
© The Financial Times Limited. All Rights Reserved.

Simple applications of SPC can make a big difference to the bottom line.

Using the terminology we introduced in Chapter 7, we can refer to these as Type I and Type II errors respectively. If we base our logic around the null hypothesis that the quality level is acceptable, then a Type I error occurs when we decide to stop production based on the sample evidence and the quality level is actually acceptable. A Type II error occurs when we should have taken the decision to stop production but did not do so. In the terminology of quality management, the situation of the quality level being acceptable is referred to as *the process being in control* and that of the quality level being unacceptable as *the process being out of control*. So, a Type I error occurs when we decide to adjust a process which is actually still in control and a Type II error occurs when we allow an out-of-control process to continue. We can use the statistical principles we have developed in earlier chapters to help in the quality management area.

Control charts

We clearly need some technique to allow us to assess whether a situation is in control or not. Such a technique is available through the use of *control charts*. These are a graphical method of monitoring such a process on a regular and frequent basis and helping to evaluate whether it is in control or not. The principles of control charts were actually developed in the 1920s but saw a resurgence of interest in the 1980s and continue to be used extensively. It is important to stress that such charts can be applied to any situation where we are 'measuring' quality and not just to production situations, as in our example.

The logic behind such charts is straightforward and based on the principles of the sampling distribution that we introduced in Chapter 7. We know that in some particular process – like that of our production line example – there will be some inherent variation around the quality target. In our example, we know the production line is meant to put 400 ml into each can (our quality target) but we also know that there is some inherent variability around this target; after all, this is what the standard deviation of 10 ml indicates. However, it is also possible over time that additional variability will occur, perhaps because of incorrect machine settings, the need for equipment maintenance and repair or because of human error. In other words, there may be more variability in the production process than we expect. We can denote the one type of variation as *process variation*: the variation we would normally expect in such a process (as measured by the standard deviation); and we can denote the other type of variation as *assignable variation*: variation which is not normally expected and which, once we know about it, we would try to assign to particular factors which can be controlled or corrected (like the need for machine maintenance or repair).

It should also be clear that in many such situations we would want to be checking our quality target – and trying to determine whether the process was in control or not – on a frequent and regular basis. In other words, we would be taking frequent samples from the production line and checking the sample to make inferences about the population variability. This, obviously, is where we return to the sampling distribution concept. Suppose we take a sample of size n from the production line. We know from our understanding of the sampling distribution concept that we would expect 95 per cent of all sample means to lie within 1.96 standard errors of the population mean. That is:

$$\mu \pm 1.96 \frac{\sigma}{\sqrt{n}}$$

This is obviously no more than a 95 per cent confidence interval that we have examined and used elsewhere. For convenience, in control charts we round this to +/−2 standard errors. For use in control charts we also calculate a second interval, this time relating to +/−3 standard errors, which, from Normal tables, would relate to 99.7 per cent of sample means.

We now have the basis for a simple and straightforward sampling approach to check periodically whether the production process is still in control: i.e. the observed variation is within predicted limits. The logic is straightforward. The 2 SE interval is used to establish what are referred to as *warning limits* for the process. On the assumption – the null hypothesis – that the process is properly in control, 95 out of every 100 sample means should lie within these calculated limits. If a sample mean falls outside these limits, we take it literally as a warning that the production process *may* be out of control – exhibiting more variation than the process itself contributes. However, such evidence is not seen as definitive but as a warning only. The 3 SE interval is used to establish what are known as *action limits* (in some cases these are the only control limits – meaning, no warning limits – and are simply referred to as upper and lower control limits). We would expect 997 out of every 1000 sample means to fall within these limits. If a particular sample mean does not, then the probability that the process is still in control is no more than 0.3 per cent and we would be justified in taking action – perhaps even to the extent of stopping the production process until the source of the assignable variation has been traced and corrected.

All this means, of course, that we are simply applying the principles and concepts of sampling and confidence intervals from the previous chapter. In diagram form we have the situation as shown in Figure 8.1, with the sampling distribution Normal as predicted by the Central Limit Theorem and the two confidence intervals we are now referring to as the warning and action limits.

Let us stop and reflect on what we have here. Effectively, the warning and action limits that we can calculate give us a decision tool. We want to know, based on sample evidence, whether we have a quality 'problem' with some process, in this case our production line. Fundamentally, from time to time management will ask the question: is the production line still in control in the sense that production is in line with the target set? If we take a sample of production, measure the mean contents of the sample items and then plot the sample mean on Figure 8.1 (after we have substituted precise numerical values for the action and warning limits), we can decide at a given probability level whether the production process is in control or not. If the sample result is inside the warning limits, we need do nothing. If the sample mean is outside the action limits we should take immediate action to stop production, as we have evidence that something is wrong – the process is exhibiting more variation than we would expect. If the sample mean is in between the warning and action limits, we investigate to see whether this is some sort of fluke event even though the process is still in control or whether the process genuinely is going out of control.

On a practical note, given that we will want to take samples repeatedly over time and not just once, it is more helpful to turn Figure 8.1 on its side, as in Figure 8.2. If we then remove the Normal curve, since we used this simply to show the derivation of the limits, we have the control chart in Figure 8.3. Anyone in the organisation, from managing director through to shop floor, can then use this control chart to check whether a particular process is in control and whether action needs to be taken. They do not even need to understand the principles of statistical inference to use the chart.

Using the control chart

Let us illustrate the use of the chart with the following scenario. Returning to the production example, we have decided to take a sample of 10 items from the production line every 15 minutes and for each sample calculate the sample mean to enable us to

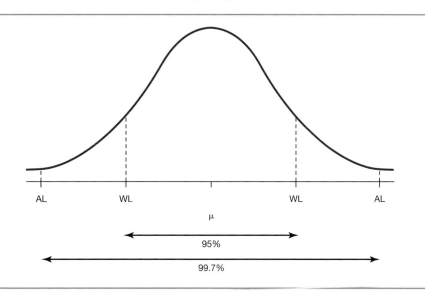

Figure 8.1 Warning and action limits

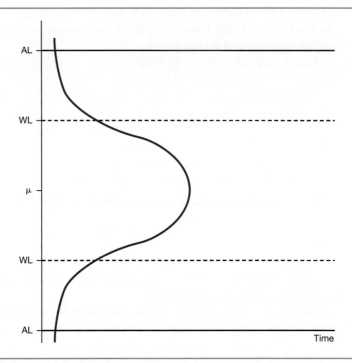

Figure 8.2 Figure 8.1 turned on its side

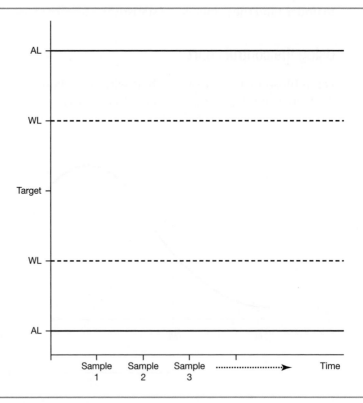

Figure 8.3 Control chart

check whether the process is still in control. You may consider that the number of items sampled is small. The purpose of control charts, however, is to allow a quick and cost-effective sampling process to be undertaken frequently over a short period. We could, in principle, take samples of 100 items rather than 10 each time. The potential problem is that such sample sizes might take some time to assess in terms of calculating the sample mean. Therefore, in principle, while this calculation is under way we could still be operating a production process that is no longer in control, with all the related costs and problems. 'Do it quickly and do it often' is the principle behind such control charts. However, with a given sample size we are now able to quantify the action and warning limits.

Progress Check 8.2

Calculate the action and warning limits for this problem.

With n at 10 and σ at 10 ml we have:

$$+2(10/\sqrt{10}) = +6.3 \text{ ml}$$
$$+2(10/\sqrt{10}) = -6.3 \text{ ml}$$

and with the mean μ, at 400 we have:

Upper WL = 406.3
Lower WL = 393.7

Action limits:

$$+3(10/\sqrt{10}) = +9.5 \text{ ml}$$
$$+3(10/\sqrt{10}) = -9.5 \text{ ml}$$

giving:

Upper AL = 409.5
Lower AL = 390.5

The control chart is shown in Figure 8.4.

Over a period of time we would take samples of 10 items from the production line, calculate the mean of each sample and plot this mean on the control chart. Gradually, over time, we would build up a picture of successive sample means taken from production. If the process is in control then we would expect a series of sample means like that shown in Figure 8.5. The series of sample means taken 15 minutes apart are all within the limits of process variation that we have calculated – within the warning limits. Although there is variability in production, this is within the predicted limits and no action is required. It is important to realise that a chart such as this would not be seen solely after sample 10 had been calculated but would rather be in continuous use over this entire period so that any trends or patterns can be identified.

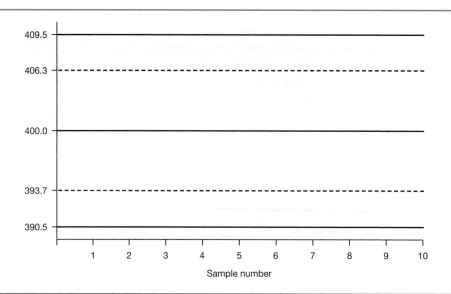

Figure 8.4 Control chart limits

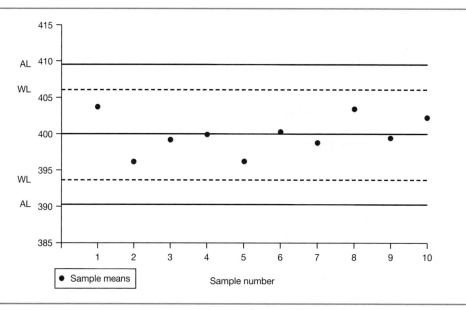

Figure 8.5 Control chart: process in control

The chart can also be used to track potential problems, as shown in Figure 8.6. We see here that from sample 3 onwards a trend in variability is clearly developing. By the time we take sample 9 we breach the upper WL and this should indicate cause for concern about the assignable variation. Sample 10 clearly confirms the process is out of control and that the cause of the increase in assignable variation needs to be identified and corrective action needs to be taken.

In practice, after sample 9 when the UWL has been breached, another sample should be taken immediately, rather than waiting for the appropriate time. The reason for this is based on the logic of the chart: such a sample mean should not have occurred if the process is still in control but we do not have sufficient evidence to stop the process. Rather than wait for the next sample to be taken at its allotted time – and run the risk of

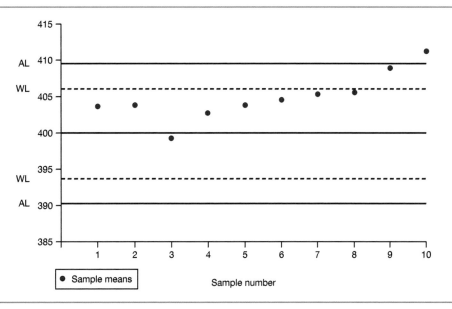

Figure 8.6 Control chart: process not in control

continuing an out-of-control process in the meantime – it is advisable to take another sample immediately to check the sample 9 result. Control charts can be used to monitor the process, and investigations or actions should take place when we observe:

● any result outside the action limits;
● a series of means in one particular direction;
● a series of means on one side of the population mean;
● more than 5 per cent of sample means lying above the WLs but below the ALs;
● any other apparent non-random pattern.

Control charts are easy to construct and easy for any employee in an organisation to use and understand – even if the principles of statistical inference are unheard of. Although a manufacturing production example has been used to illustrate the principles, their applicability to a wide range of service areas goes a long way to explaining the recent resurgence of interest in them as part of a wider quality management policy. Such charts can be used in almost any management situation where some quality target is appropriate – telephone answering times, customer complaints, absenteeism, financial performance, the list of applications is extensive.

QADM IN ACTION

Capgemini – control charts for a call centre

Over the last decade or so, call centres have sprung up everywhere. A key issue in operational terms is measuring the performance of staff working in such a centre. Capgemini were involved in establishing a suitable performance measurement system for a

call centre operating in the travel and transport sector. The client required a performance measurement system that was based on measures that were relevant to call centre staff's jobs, were easily understood, helped identify areas for improvement, were

flexible enough to cope with changing business circumstances and which would recognise sustained
performance improvement.

Capgemini identified core business processes
within the call centre and discussed these with all staff
involved to determine a complete set of measures.

Given the nature of the client's business, the fundamental purpose of the call centre was to increase
sales. Staff in the call centre were accordingly measured on revenue generated per hour from their activities. In addition, a number of contributory drivers
(or factors) that helped explain the revenue per hour
achieved were established. These drivers included
measures such as average call duration and the conversion rate (effectively the proportion of calls resulting in a sale). Using methodology developed in-house
from a proprietary system called iChart, Capgemini
were able to introduce statistical process control
charts as the method for recording and monitoring
performance at all levels through the call centre.

Statistical process control charts were used to
track performance at different levels in the call centre: for the call centre as a whole, for families of
teams, for teams, for individual members of staff.
The charts were found to be simple to understand
and staff were able to visualise changes in performance easily. Charts were produced for revenue per
hour and for five key contributory drivers, allowing
changes in the main performance indicators to be
monitored and understood.

The benefits are as follows:

● Call centre staff were motivated to improve their
performance as their improvement is highly visible through the use of SPC.

● Staff morale improved as there was an agreed
and fair measurement system in place.

● Overall improvement in performance as attention
was focused on prioritised areas for improvement.

● Performance improvement initiatives could be
evaluated on a sound, rigorous basis in terms of
their impact over time on the key performance
indicators.

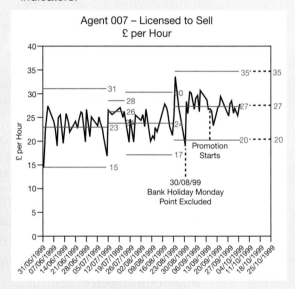

Source: Based on a Capgemini case study, with thanks to Capgemini for permission to use their material.

Control charts for attribute variables

In some instances we may monitor the quality of goods or services in terms of percentages rather than means. Consider the following example. A large organisation has
recently expressed concern over the number of incorrect invoices it receives for goods/
services and over the fact that many of these invoices are paid without proper checking. Such invoices cause problems because the firm finds it is consistently paying more
than it should: goods invoiced but not yet delivered, an invoice for goods delivered to a
different specification and so on. As part of a quality drive, the Finance Department has
calculated that last year 5 per cent of invoices were overpaid, and a determined effort is
being made this year to reduce this percentage through improved staff training and better systems. On a weekly basis a sample of 100 invoices paid is taken and the percentage
overpaid is calculated. A control chart can be used in such a situation even though we

have no mean and standard deviation. Remember that in Chapter 7 we gave the standard error of such a percentage as:

$$\text{SE} = \sqrt{\frac{\pi(100 - \pi)}{n}}$$

and we can again calculate warning and action limits:

$$\begin{aligned} \text{WL} &= 5 \pm 2\sqrt{\frac{\pi(100 - \pi)}{n}} \\ &= 5 \pm 2\sqrt{\frac{5(100 - 5)}{100}} \\ &= 5 \pm 4.4 \end{aligned}$$

and

$$\begin{aligned} \text{AL} &= 5 \pm 3\sqrt{\frac{\pi(100 - \pi)}{n}} \\ &= 5 \pm 3\sqrt{\frac{5(100 - 5)}{100}} \\ &= 5 \pm 6.5 \end{aligned}$$

Note that in this case the lower WL and AL would probably be omitted from the control chart. The reason for this is that a reduction in the percentage of invoices overpaid would be seen very much as an improvement and not as a problem.

Progress Check 8.3

A local supermarket knows that, on average, it receives 12 customer complaints a day about poor-quality service, damaged goods and so on. The standard deviation around this average is 5. The supermarket manager wants to set up a control chart to monitor this aspect of performance, with results compiled for each two-week period (the store is open seven days a week).

Calculate warning and action limits for this situation.

The first seven sets of results are:

     13.4, 11.3, 14.2, 12.5, 11.1, 10.7, 9.5

Comment on the store's performance in this context.

Solution is given on p 579.

Specification limits versus control limits

In some situations we are aware – based on market research or customer survey/feedback – that the customer considers only certain measurements of a product to be within the acceptable range or target (a screw thread to be not too weak and not too strong – a range – or a pack of cod fillets to weigh at least a certain limit – a target – for a certain price). The production line aims to meet these specifications while making sure that the process is in control. Here therefore we have two types of limits: *upper and lower specification limits* and upper and lower control limits.

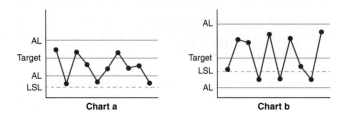

Figure 8.7 Control charts with specification limits

It is important to understand and differentiate the idea behind the specification limits and control limits. Specification limits indicate when the product is not acceptable to the customer. Control limits indicate when the process is out of control. The specification limits are set by knowing customers' expectations (or by internally set targets). The control limits are set by measures of probability distributions based on process variation. The specification limits and control limits may not necessarily aim for the same sample size of the product.

For the above reasons and to avoid confusion there is a recommendation that the specification limits and control limits should not be illustrated on the same chart. While appreciating the advice, here for educational purposes we look at some examples of control charts with specification limits to see how they can be interpreted. The control charts in Figure 8.7 show upper and lower action limits (control limits) along with a lower specification limit. This is the illustration of a situation where the market research reveals that customers expect a minimum limit of measurement for one of the features of a product. We assume that the same samples are used for investigating both kinds of limits.

Neither of the charts is carrying good news! Although chart 'a' does not show any samples violating the specification limit, the samples are clearly showing that the process is out of control. This means that despite the fact that for now the product seems acceptable, the production line cannot be trusted. The process is not stable as it contains variations that should not be there. Technically we say that the process is capable (at least at present) but is out of control.

Chart 'b' shows an even worse situation. Here the process is in control but a number of samples are below the specification limit. Technically we can say that the process is in control but not capable. In fact there is a fundamental problem with chart 'b'. The specification limits should normally be outside of the action (control) limits. This way we can make sure that if the process is in control then it is also capable. The situation that is presented in chart 'b' practically makes the lower action (control) limit redundant. This may happen when the customer expectations are unrealistic or when the processes in place are not good enough to produce for the target market. Again, as explained above, it is highly recommended to use two different charts for the control limits and specification limits. Here for illustration purposes we used one for both.

Pareto charts

We introduced Pareto charts in Chapter 3 as a general method of data presentation. They have a particularly useful role to play in quality management. Let us develop the scenario we had above. Let us assume that the large firm checking its invoice payment performance has found that performance has worsened: the percentage of overpaid invoices has increased. Clearly the use of control charts will help the firm identify that the problem exists at an early stage. What the control chart will not do, however, is identify the causes of the problem or possible solutions. In practice a 'quality' problem is likely to have a number of contributory factors. What management must do is identify these causes and prioritise them, since it is unlikely that all the problem's causes can be resolved simultaneously. Assume that an investigation into factors contributing to the worsening performance in the context of overpaid invoices has been completed, with the results as shown in Table 8.2.

A variety of factors are contributing to the problem: some internal, such as clerical errors, and some external, such as those originating with the supplier. A Pareto diagram like that in Figure 8.8 of these factors will help management prioritise which of these should be investigated first. Clearly, and in line with the Pareto principle, the first two factors – delivery not as per invoice and wrong price charged by supplier – account for

Table 8.2   Causes of overpayment of invoices

Factor	Percentage frequency
1 Wrong price charged by supplier	20
2 Incorrect price discount calculated	6
3 Incorrect quantity delivered	10
4 Initial order changed	8
5 Delivery not as per invoice	36
6 Goods returned to supplier	2
7 Clerical error by Finance Dept.	18
Total	100

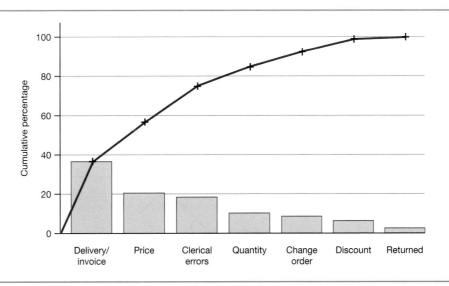

Figure 8.8 Pareto chart

over half of the errors in the overpaid invoices and, other things being equal, should be investigated first in detail. Pareto charts can help put into context the management priorities in terms of the factors contributing to the quality problem.

Ishikawa diagrams

The topic of this book is quantitative analysis. However, the discussion on quality will be very short-sighted here if we do not also look at a qualitative technique that is popular in quality management and can work very closely with the quantitative techniques that have been covered in this chapter. It is in fact the complex nature of quality that requires both quantitative and qualitative techniques to reach valid decisions.

The topic that we are looking at here is the Ishikawa diagram – alternatively known as the cause–effect diagram or the fishbone diagram. Such diagrams can help management focus on the specific problem faced in a quality management context and identify the factors contributing to that problem. The general format of the diagram is shown in Figure 8.9. We start with the observed 'effect'. This is the characteristic or factor that we are focusing on in a quality context. Typically, this might be the particular problem that needs to be resolved. The major causes, or contributory factors, to this effect are then identified and used to label the ends of each major branch as shown. Factors which in turn contribute to these major causes can then be determined in turn and used to label each branch coming from a main cause branch. In effect, the Ishikawa diagram is a method of focusing on the major factors causing a particular quality effect. It seems very simple and straightforward but is deceptively powerful when used in the right way. Clearly a team approach is likely to be needed to develop a complete diagram for some designated effect, since most processes and activities will involve a group of people rather than one individual.

It should be noted that the exact format of the diagram depends entirely on the nature of the application. How many main cause branches there are and how many sub-branches depends entirely on the context of the problem. The main principle is that the diagram should include all suspected causes. In a manufacturing context, the major causes may well be categorised as the five Ms: Manpower, Materials, Machinery, Methods and Measurements (or Information) as shown in Figure 8.10. This can provide a very useful and focused structure to the investigation.

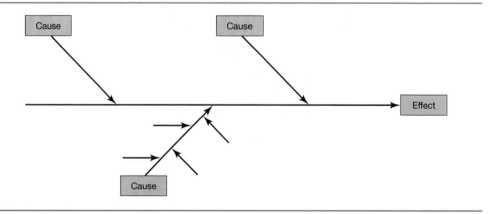

Figure 8.9 Ishikawa diagram

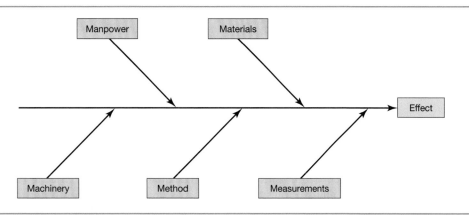

Figure 8.10 The five Ms

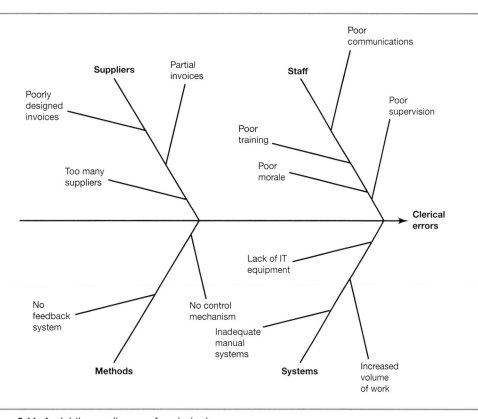

Figure 8.11 An Ishikawa diagram for clerical errors

In a service context, as one might expect, the structure will be far more variable. To illustrate, let us return to the example in the section on Pareto diagrams. Let us assume that management have decided to investigate in detail one of the factors contributing to the overpayment of invoices: clerical errors. Although this does not have the highest priority in the Pareto diagram, we may assume management have decided to investigate this factor because it is internal to the organisation and may, therefore, be more amenable to a prompt solution than factors contributing to the problem from outside the organisation. Figure 8.11 illustrates the diagram we might produce. In this case the effect is the clerical errors and four major causes have been identified: Suppliers, Staff, Methods and Systems.

Note: Just as there are famously 5Ms as causes for effects in a manufacturing context, there are also famously 4Ss in a service context. These are Surroundings, Suppliers, Systems and Skill. As you see the causes identified in Figure 8.11 are very close to these 4Ss.

Under Suppliers, factors contributing to this major cause are: poorly designed invoices used by suppliers, which cause problems for the clerical staff; partial invoices submitted by suppliers; and too many different suppliers, making it difficult to keep track of different goods. On the Staff cause, we have: poor training of clerical staff; poor supervision of clerical staff, poor communications with clerical staff, who are unsure who to contact in the event of queries or problems; and poor morale of staff. On the Methods cause, we have: no feedback system to allow clerical staff to monitor the quality of their own work; and no control mechanism to monitor the quality of performance in this area on an on-going basis. Finally, on the Systems cause, we have: lack of IT equipment for staff to use; manual systems in use are inadequate; and staff have seen a marked increase in the volume of work recently. Although the diagram is illustrative, it clearly demonstrates the potential. Having identified causes, management can now consider solutions to some, or all, of these factors. For example, we could consider requiring all our suppliers to use a common invoice form that has been designed in-house; we could introduce a focused training programme for clerical staff; we could invest in additional IT equipment. Whatever the possible solutions, the diagram allows management to assess the impact each solution could be expected to have on the effect. This by itself can be a valuable conclusion to reach. Improving staff training, for example, we now realise will not solve the entire problem, given that there are other factors contributing to the problem that will not be solved by this initiative.

Equally, although the diagram is readily applied to quality 'problems', it can also be applied to quality 'success'. If one feature of a good or service is seen as particularly successful, this method can be a useful mechanism for identifying the key factors that have contributed to this success, with a view to replicating these factors for other goods/services.

Six sigma

The quality management techniques we've looked at in this chapter have been used by many different organisations as part of their drive to improve quality and standards. Over the last couple of decades, however, a number of organisations have taken these techniques further by developing a structured approach to quality management known as *six sigma*. Six sigma began in 1986 as a statistically based approach to reduce production process variation in Motorola in the USA. Today, six sigma has developed into a business performance improvement methodology and has effectively become a brand in its own right, applied across public and private sectors alike. It's also become big business, with a number of consultancy companies providing six sigma training and consultancy.

In statistical terms, the purpose of six sigma is to reduce process variation so that virtually all the goods or services provided meet or exceed specification (or, more statistically speaking, there are no more than 3.4 defects per million opportunities). The 'six sigma' title obviously refers to the $+/-3$ SE principle that we examined earlier. The concept of six sigma, however, goes far beyond a mere statistical goal. It is really a management philosophy that looks at different ways and methods to improve operations by reducing variation, leading to minimising defects.

There are three basic elements to six sigma:

1 Process improvement
2 Process design/redesign
3 Process management

The focus of *process improvement* is to eliminate the root causes of deficiencies in existing processes. These may be causing specific problems for the organisation, or may be preventing it from working as efficiently as it could. *Process design/re-design* starts from the basis that sometimes existing processes may no longer be fit-for-purpose and tinkering with them will not deliver the required level of performance. New processes need to be designed or existing processes need to be fundamentally redesigned. *Process management* focuses on ensuring that a structured approach to managing processes is in place. This often requires a fundamental change in the way an organisation is structured and managed. In general, process management consists of: defining processes, key customer requirements and process owners; measuring performance against specification and customer requirements; analysing data to measure and improve processes; controlling process performance by monitoring process inputs, process operation and process outputs.

The main approach to carry out six sigma is summarised as DMAIC. This stands for Define, Measure, Analyse, Improve and Control. Define the problem in hand, collect data and decide on the Measure to be used to compare the situation before and after the improvement project, Analyse to find what needs to be changed, Improve the situation by implementing a solution to the problem and finally Control to maintain and sustain the change. As Figure 8.12 shows, DMAIC is an improvement cycle that is supposed to continue to identify more operational problems and improving them by finding solutions based on analysis.

Figure 8.12 DMAIC cycle in six sigma

A number of quality management tools are used to achieve the goals of six sigma. All the techniques that we have introduced in this chapter, while being stand-alone tools, are also labelled as six sigma tools. If you remember, we used the same scenario (the organisation that was struggling with wrong invoices in the system) as an example to illustrate the use of control charts, Pareto analysis and Ishikawa diagram. The sequence was intentional.

Six sigma can conveniently accommodate these three tools, in the same sequence, as a step towards minimising defects. As Figure 8.13 shows, the control charts assist us to find what features of the product are difficult to control. Once these features are statistically identified a technical team can look at the production, including operations as well as the supply chain, to identify factors that result in such large variations and

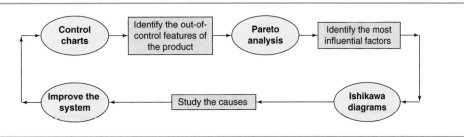

Figure 8.13 One of the strands of a six sigma campaign

defects. Pareto analysis will recognise what factors are the most influential ones. A more in-depth study will then take place to explore what elements in the work, management and the business environment are causing these most influential factors. This in-depth study can be done using Ishikawa diagrams. The results of this study can then lead to some effective improvement decisions. Once some improvement is achieved we can see if the control charts are giving us a better result. This whole improvement project will be just one strand of the six sigma campaign in an organisation.

Worked example

A health clinic has a no-appointments system for patients wishing to see one of the doctors. This means that if a patient wishes to see a doctor they attend one of the available clinics and wait their turn until the doctor is free to see them. In the past there has been considerable criticism from patients about the length of time they have had to wait. Some months ago a number of initiatives were put into place to try to improve the situation. The clinic has found that under the new arrangements the average (mean) waiting time is 12 minutes with a standard deviation of 7 minutes. The doctors at the clinic are keen to ensure that these initiatives have a long-term effect on reducing waiting times and want to monitor the situation to ensure that the problem does not reoccur.

We have been asked to draft a report to the doctors explaining how, with samples of 25 patients, you could set up an effective monitoring system to assess whether waiting times comply with this level of performance in the future.

Your report might run as follows:

The clinic has established a performance level of 12 minutes for average patient waiting time. Clearly this does not mean that every patient will wait exactly 12 minutes before seeing the doctor. Some will wait more, some will wait less. However, it is an indication of the average time a patient might expect to wait. Naturally, on a day-by-day or week-by-week basis there will be some variation around this average due to the inherent variability of the clinic's activities (since we cannot guarantee that every patient will require exactly the same time with the doctors). If, in one week, the average time is found to be 13 minutes, this does not necessarily mean we are failing to meet the 12-minute target in the long term. However, it is important that we monitor our performance in this context to ensure the waiting time of 12 minutes does not worsen. Everyone in the clinic is clearly very busy, so we need an easy-to-use monitoring system to enable us to check waiting time performance. We are proposing that this is done cost-effectively based on a sample of 25 patients each week. The clinic reception staff should then take a random sample of 25 patients each week as they enter the clinic (spread over the days the clinic is open and also spread during each day to give as representative a sample as possible). Each of these patients should be given a small card noting their arrival time as they enter the clinic and asked to leave the card with the doctor. The doctor can then note the time they actually saw the patient on the card. At the end of the week the reception staff can work out the average waiting time for the sample of patients and plot it on the attached chart.

The idea behind the chart is a simple one (although supported by some complex statistical theory). Using some statistical principles, we know that our weekly monitoring is based only on a sample of 25 patients (out of several hundred we might see each week), so we must make allowance for this. Using these same statistical principles we can calculate how much variation, in minutes, from the target of 12 minutes we might normally get for each sample of 25 patients. These allow us to construct what are known as warning limits and action limits, shown on the chart (Figure 8.14).

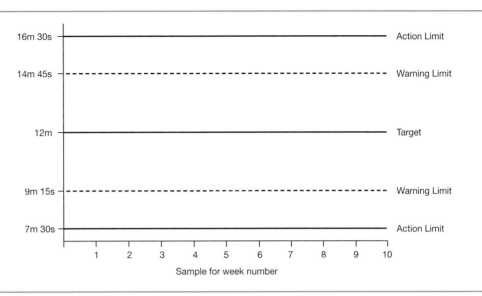

Figure 8.14 Control chart for health clinic

If that week's result is above the upper line marked Action Limit it is highly likely the average waiting time in the clinic as a whole is higher than the target of 12 minutes (even though our result is based on only 25 patients). In fact we would be over 99 per cent sure if this were to happen that we were no longer meeting the overall target of 12 minutes. Action will then need to be taken to find out what has happened that week to cause substandard performance. If the week's result is above the upper line marked Warning Limit but below that marked Action Limit, this should be taken as an indication that average waiting time might be higher than the target of 12 minutes. It is recommended if this happens that another sample be organised as soon as possible to confirm, one way or another, whether the target is still being met. There are also action and warning limits shown below the target time. Although sample results falling below these lines are not a problem in the sense of patients waiting longer than the average of 12 minutes, they do indicate a fundamental change in the average waiting time. The situation should be investigated to see what has occurred to cause waiting times to fall.

The task for the reception staff each week is a fairly easy one of handing time cards to 25 patients, collecting the cards back in and at the end of the week working out a simple average from the 25 times recorded. They then need to plot this time on the chart. If the time for that week is within the two warning limits, no further action is needed. If it is outside the warning or action limits then the reception staff need to bring this immediately to the attention of the clinic manager.

Adventures in six sigma: how the problem-solving technique helped Xerox

Like many other US companies, Xerox was introduced to six sigma through its interactions with General Electric. The financial services to biotechnology conglomerate adopted the metrics-mad process improvement technique in the mid-1990s. Thanks to its size and influence, it has served as an effective missionary.

Anne Mulcahy's conversion came as she was negotiating the outsourcing of Xerox's troubled billing and collections operation to GE Capital. She recalls: "I remember sitting there and watching the discipline with which [the GE team] defined the problem, scoped the problem and attacked it from a six sigma perspective. I remember feeling for the first time that the problem would be fixed."

The precise definition of six sigma quality is an error rate of 3.4 per million. More important than the exact number, however, is an approach to problem solving that emphasizes small teams, measurement and economic return.

Quality improvement techniques were by no means new to Xerox. In the 1980s, it was one of the first US companies to adopt Total Quality Management (TQM) as it fought to turn back the tide of Japanese competition.

As an up-and-coming manager, Ms Mulcahy experienced TQM first hand. "The financial metrics were not as precise with TQM," she recalls. "six sigma is very rigid and very disciplined by comparison. Every project is managed with economic profit metrics. There is none of the squishy stuff."

The "squishy stuff" is the emphasis in TQM on consensus building that, while part of an earnest desire

to replicate the best of Japanese management, did not always play well at US companies.

Ms Mulcahy is also at pains to point out that Xerox practises Lean six sigma, a variation that asks managers to think not only how processes can be improved but also how waste can be reduced: "Lean is an important nuance. The leaning process begins with taking out waste, working out where value gets added and where it does not. For big companies, this is very important."

While companies generally adopt six sigma to improve efficiency, converts insist that there are other benefits. The introduction of a company-wide approach to project management is reckoned to break down barriers between departments, and make it easier to work with suppliers and customers. Ms Mulcahy says: "The reality of our business is that in order to compete you have to find ways to deliver 8, 9, 10 per cent productivity improvements every single year. You only get there if you have a systemic approach."

 Source: Adventures in six sigma: how the problem-solving technique helped Xerox, *Financial Times*, 23 September 2005. © The Financial Times Limited. All Rights Reserved.

The 'sigma' in six sigma refers to the standard deviation which is used to measure the variability around the mean of the process. The error rate of 3.4 defects per million comes from Normal probability calculations.

Summary

In this chapter we have introduced a number of techniques that can readily be applied to the area of quality management in both manufacturing and service organisations. The track record of these techniques, in terms of the range of organisations that have found them of considerable benefit, is considerable and none of the techniques requires any great quantitative knowledge as such, which is one of their considerable strengths. In the quality area more than any other, though, it must also be stressed that quality management is about more than the application of these types of technique to problems and issues. This is illustrated with the six sigma approach adopted by many organisations, which in itself utilises many techniques, including the ones that have been discussed here.

QADM IN ACTION
OBGYN and application of six sigma, Pareto and Ishikawa analysis

A Kuwaiti private hospital and gynaecology clinic (OBGYN) faced problems with outpatient waiting times. The outpatients were facing the longest waiting times compared to other clinics. A team of consultants were recruited to help with this. The team

adopted a DMAIC method to approach the problem. At the Define stage a questionnaire was handed out to 150 patients to understand their experience of waiting at OBGYN. The response rate was 100% and the results show that more than 70% of the

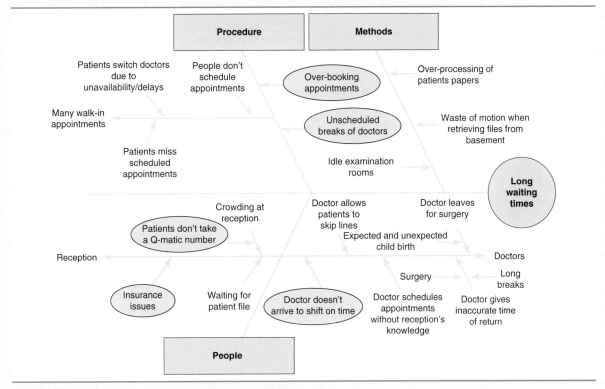

Figure 8.15 Ishikawa diagram for waiting time in OBGYN

patients were not happy with their waiting time. In fact 63% entered the clinic as walk-in patients because they found that patients with appointments did not have any priority.

For the Measure stage it was decided to focus on the service waiting time since other waiting times were within the hospital's standards. For eight working days data was collected between two to five hours per day. In total 168 patients were observed. It was found that walk-in patients and patients with appointments were waiting an average time of 54.3 minutes and 59.6 minutes respectively. A number of statistical tools were then used to understand the process variations and capabilities.

In the Analysis stage an Ishikawa analysis was carried out with waiting time as the 'effect'. The main causes were identified as 'procedure', 'people' and 'method'. Second and third level causes were then explored for each of these three main causes. Once the Ishikawa diagram was developed

(Figure 8.15) the causes were grouped into controllable and uncontrollable. It was found that 9 out of 14 causes were related to the problems in the system and were controllable while the other 5 causes were occurred by chance and could be categorised as uncontrollable.

In the next stage of the analysis a Pareto chart was developed for the controllable causes to identify the most influential ones among them. This was based on both historical data and observations (Figure 8.16). The most influential factors were found to be 'overbooking appointments', 'unscheduled break times', 'doctors not arriving on time', 'insurance processing' and 'patients not taking ticket numbers'.

In the Improvement stage, simulation software was used to test potential solutions. A number of solutions were tested and studied. Output analyser was used to study the effect of each solution on the waiting time. It was found that the solution with the largest effect on reducing waiting time was

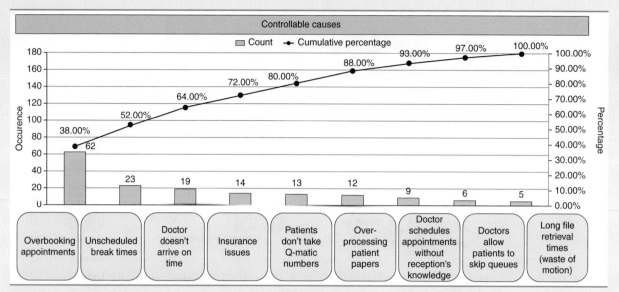

Figure 8.16 Pareto chart for factors influencing waiting time in OBGYN

'rescheduling doctor's working hours and breaks'. This solution provided a 49.15% improvement in the waiting times. It was also decided to use signs to guide patients to take ticket numbers as this would help with organising patients and avoiding conflict.

In the Control stage, the improved system was compared with the original one and a checklist and a set of recommendations were made to establish the improvement measures and to ensure continuous improvement.

Exercises

1   To try to illustrate how effective the Ishikawa diagram can be, focus on one particular problem that you are having in your studies. The problem might be a general one, it might relate to one subject or it might relate to one topic in a subject area. Apply the fishbone principles to try to determine the factors contributing to that problem. Such factors might include lack of study time, poor teaching, a poor textbook and domestic pressures. When you have constructed the diagram, use it to try to identify how the problems might be resolved.

2   A large manufacturing firm is concerned about lost production: that is, production capability that was not utilised for a variety of reasons. One of the causes of such lost production has been identified as employees taking time off work because of illness. Last year the firm estimated that around 53 000 units of production were lost each week due to this cause, with a standard deviation of 4800. The Personnel Department has decided to monitor, on a weekly basis, a small sample

of 15 employees on the production line in terms of their attendance at work and to translate this into a weekly production loss figure for the company. For the first eight weeks the results are as follows:

Estimated lost production (000 units)	
Week 1	50.3
Week 2	53.9
Week 3	55.6
Week 4	51.2
Week 5	51.0
Week 6	50.9
Week 7	48.7
Week 8	49.3

(a) Using this information construct a control chart for Personnel to use.

(b) Draft a short report outlining the potential for using control charts on a regular basis in this context.

(c) Explain what is meant by Type I and Type II errors in this context.

3   A hospital laboratory has the task of screening blood samples of patients and producing a summary report for clinicians. Because of the limitations of equipment, staff training and time, the laboratory manager knows that there is an error rate involved in the production of such reports. It is estimated that 4 per cent of such reports produced are incorrect in terms of their results. Over the past few months the lab has been under increased pressure from clinicians to reduce the turnaround time in the production of the test reports. The manager is concerned that this improvement has been at the expense of an increase in the error rate. Accordingly,

Error rate	Percentage
Day 1	6.9
Day 2	4.3
Day 3	6.6
Day 4	5.2
Day 5	6.8
Day 6	8.5
Day 7	8.9
Day 8	9.5
Day 9	9.8
Day 10	11.5

using the principles of statistical process control, it has been decided on an experimental basis to take samples of 50 reports a day and double-check them to monitor the error rate. The results for the first two weeks are as follows:

(a) Construct a suitable control chart for use by the lab.

(b) Do you think that control charts would be useful and reliable in this context?

4   You are working as a consultant for a private hospital. Your client is hoping to benefit from your analytical skills in managing the customer waiting time at the reception of the X Ray department. Based on consultancy work that was done a couple of years ago in this department, control charts are used to study the variations in the waiting times. The control charts also include lower specification limit for the waiting time. The client seems to have the impression that as long as the samples of waiting times are within the specification limit there shouldn't be any concerns about the operations. Write a short brief with some examples to politely prove him wrong.

5   A public transport organisation has had a reputation for many years of caring little for its customers – the passengers it carries. In particular, the enquiry office has had a particularly poor reputation. New management have decided to try to improve the office's performance and image, and staff have recently been sent on a series of training programmes to help develop a customer focus. The organisation has a formal complaints procedure and, before the training programme, the enquiry office typically received around 15 complaints a week, about its service, staff attitudes and the accuracy of information given to passengers. The office manager has asked for advice on how the office's performance can be monitored on a regular basis. Draft a short report outlining some of the options that are available in terms of monitoring this aspect of performance.

9 Forecasting I: Moving Averages and Time Series

Learning objectives

By the end of this chapter you should be able to:

- understand the different approaches to forecasting that can be applied in business
- calculate a trend using moving averages
- calculate and interpret seasonal components
- calculate and interpret seasonally adjusted data

Business organisations put a high value on reliable information about the future: future sales, future costs, future patterns of consumer demand, future prices of supplies. As we have seen in earlier chapters, many management problems arise simply because the future is unknown or has a high degree of uncertainty about it. Not surprisingly, considerable attention has been focused on methods of trying to predict future values of some key business variable. In this chapter we will look at the general principles of forecasting and introduce a number of common techniques. In the next chapter we shall extend the coverage of forecasting to include the technique of regression. As we shall see in this chapter, many important business variables follow some regular, and potentially predictable, pattern over the period of a year. From a management perspective it is important to be able to quantify such a pattern to help efficiency, performance and forward planning.

The need for forecasting

To some extent the question as to why business organisations need to forecast should be largely rhetorical at this stage in the text. The increasing complexity of the environment in which organisations have to function and survive, together with changing demands and expectations, implies that every organisation needs to establish some view as to future values of key variables, even though these key variables are different for each organisation. As with other techniques, forecasting is primarily concerned with trying to reduce the uncertainty that exists about some part of the future. Managers in an organisation hope that by applying forecasting techniques they can generate additional information about the future that may help them assess the future consequences of existing decisions and to evaluate the consequences of alternatives. What is likely to happen to sales if we maintain our current pricing policy? What is likely to happen if we increase the price by 5 per cent, or 10 per cent? Will a hospital be able to provide an effective and efficient health-care system with existing staff levels given future demographic changes? How will altering the staffing mix affect the level of service that we can provide?

It is important to appreciate the role of forecasting in the wider decision-making process. Figure 9.1 illustrates this. At the centre of this process lie the decisions that the manager must make. These will be strongly influenced by the organisation's chosen strategy with regard to its future direction, priorities and activities. Such decisions logically lead to the establishment of a planned performance – what the organisation is expected to achieve in the way of goods/services provided, together with all the concomitant results. However, influencing such decisions will also be the information generated from the forecasting methods adopted by the organisation. Given that, in principle, these are designed to tell us something about the future then we would expect management decisions to take such forecasts into account along with all other factors influencing such decisions. Depending on the variables being forecast, the methods adopted for forecasting and the perceived accuracy of the forecasts, such information may also affect the strategy formulation process itself. The organisation will clearly need to establish some monitoring system to compare planned with actual performance. Where, inevitably, some divergence between the two occurs then this should be fed back into the forecasting process. Given that predicted performance was not achieved – no matter whether the divergence was large or small and no matter the causes of such divergence – new forecasts will need to be produced which begin the whole cycle again. As we shall see, there is no one ideal approach to forecasting for any organisation. Alternative methods and approaches exist and a manager needs to be aware of what is possible as well as what is feasible in this context.

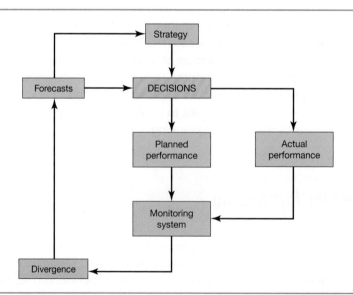

Figure 9.1 Forecasts and decision making

Economists' 2018 forecasts show high level of accuracy

By Chris Giles, Economics Editor

As the year comes to a close, many economists would be justified in feeling a sense of pride. Their key forecasts for the economy in 2018 have proved to be broadly accurate.

Economic growth met expectations in a year that was notable for marking an end to a squeeze on living standards because rises in workers' pay started to outpace increases in prices. . . .

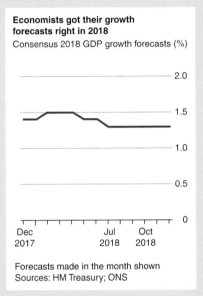

Economists got their growth forecasts right in 2018

Consensus 2018 GDP growth forecasts (%)

Forecasts made in the month shown
Sources: HM Treasury; ONS

Jagjit Chadha, director of the National Institute of Economic and Social Research, a think-tank, said: "If we try to ignore the political traumas of the autumn, the subdued performance of the economy was very much in line with forecasts." . . .

The accuracy of these growth predictions is all the more remarkable given the UK has experienced much more weather-related volatility than normal in 2018. As the Beast from the East cold snap of the first quarter gave way to the joint hottest summer on record, quarterly growth varied between 0.1 per cent and 0.6 per cent. . . .

Economists are now busy producing multiple growth forecasts for different Brexit outcomes, ranging from implementation of Mrs May's withdrawal agreement to a no-deal exit. The average of forecasts by independent economists who participated in a regular Treasury survey suggests the economy will expand by 1.5 per cent in 2019. Few think the slowing rate of growth towards the end of this year and the clouds on the global economy's horizon spell trouble for the UK in 2019. But most are clear that if the UK crashes out of the EU, Britain is heading for a recession. George Buckley at Nomura said: "Brexit is now the big unknown and, in the event of a no-deal, will probably be responsible for accelerating the onset of a sizeable recession."

Accurate and reliable forecasting is important at both the macroeconomic and microeconomic levels

Approaches to forecasting

It will be useful at this stage to provide an overview of the general approaches that can be adopted to forecasting. Figure 9.2 summarises some of the more common ones. One of the most basic distinctions is between forecasting approaches which are primarily *qualitative* as opposed to those which are primarily *quantitative*. The distinction is sometimes misleading since some of the qualitative approaches will generate numerical results and some of the quantitative approaches will be based on subjective, qualitative assumptions.

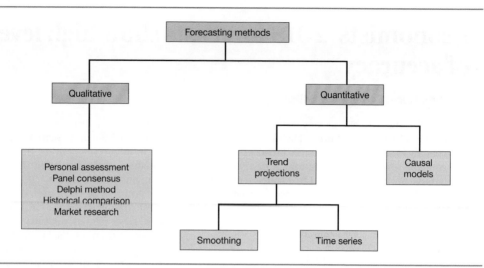

Figure 9.2 Forecasting methods

Qualitative approaches

A number of different approaches fall under this heading and, because they typically involve a considerable element of subjective assessment, they are often categorised as judgemental methods.

Personal assessment

This is probably the most widely used method in practice although this is not necessarily an argument supporting its reliability. Based on their own judgement, an individual produces some forecast of the future situation. In some circumstances, such an assessment can be relatively reliable and accurate. It is particularly appropriate in an operational environment when asking the 'front-line' staff their view of the immediate future: whether a particular machine will need repair or maintenance in the next month; whether stock levels are likely to last until the next delivery takes place; whether the appointments system in a health clinic will be adequate for the number of patients next month.

> ### Progress Check 9.1
>
> What difficulties do you see arising from such a forecasting approach?

The problem with such personal assessments, however, is that as well as relying on an individual's experiences and knowledge (which can be very variable) they are also affected by that person's prejudices and ignorance. The machine operator may not be aware of problems that have arisen with other machines of the same type and age; the stock control assistant may be unaware of a planned increase in production which will deplete stock levels rapidly next week; the health clinic receptionist may be unaware of a health education campaign about to be launched which will increase demand for appointments. Nevertheless, such personal assessments should not be arbitrarily discounted. They have their place, particularly in short-term, operational areas. They can also serve a useful function in cross-checking forecasts produced by other methods. Having developed some extensive and expensive computer-based forecasting model, it is frequently worthwhile checking the results produced by such a model against such personal assessments to help validate the more sophisticated approach.

Panel consensus

To try to take advantage of personal experience in the forecasting process and, at the same time, reduce the prejudices and ignorance that may exist in one person's view of the future, it may be possible to develop a panel consensus view of the future value of some variable. Such an approach collects together a group of individuals and in a structured format tries to develop a shared idea of the view among the group, encouraging them to share information, opinions and assumptions. Such an approach can be particularly productive in areas where the organisation has little comparable historical data: for example, where an organisation is launching a radically different product, or service, or moving into an untested part of the market. The difficulty with such an approach, however, is that it is very dependent on group dynamics and frequently requires a skilled facilitator to 'manage' the process of developing a consensus.

Delphi method

The Delphi method adopts a similar approach to the panel consensus by once again attempting to use the collective experience and judgement of a group of experts. The difference, however, lies in how the group consensus is reached. In the Delphi method the experts never actually meet and, typically, do not know who the other panel members are. Each expert is given an initial questionnaire to complete relating to the area under investigation. A summary is then produced from all the questionnaires and this summary distributed to each expert, who is given the opportunity of revising the responses to the questionnaire in the light of this summary of the group's views. This process is repeated until either an adequate consensus is reached or an agreed number of iterations have been completed. Typically, the Delphi method is used to produce a narrow range of forecasts rather than a single view of the future.

Historical comparison

Under limited circumstances it may be possible to produce forecasts based on observed patterns of some similar variable in the past. Many goods and services, for example, will tend to follow the life-cycle process illustrated in Figure 9.3. A new product, for example, follows a well-defined series of phases: the introduction phase, where customers and the market are becoming familiar with the product/service; the growth phase, where, if the product is successful, rapid growth will be experienced in terms of demand for the product/service; a saturation phase, where demand stabilises as the market reaches saturation point; and a decline phase, as demand enters a period of relatively rapid decline.

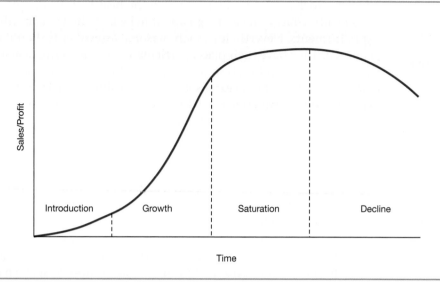

Figure 9.3 Product life cycle

Consider an organisation which has launched a new product and is trying to predict future sales. If product sales have reached the saturation phase of the life cycle then it would be foolhardy to predict that future sales will continue at this plateau level: they are likely to decline at some stage in the future. The trick, of course, is to try to predict accurately when this downturn will occur. It may be possible to do this by turning to a similar product which has already reached the decline phase and, using this historical data, assess the likely pattern of demand for the existing product. To illustrate, consider the problem facing a local authority. The manager of leisure services has noticed a recent explosion in the number of young people in the area with rollerblade roller skates. Because of pressure from parents, elected representatives and the police about the dangers of youngsters rollerblading on the roads and highways, the manager is under pressure to provide off-road facilities for these youngsters. The difficulty the manager faces is trying to assess, given a declining budget, whether this is just another fad that will pass with time or whether it is likely to be a continuing feature of young people's leisure patterns in the future. What the manager may be able to do is assess the future with reference to some comparable historical analogy, for example the skateboard 'boom' in the 1980s or that of BMX bikes in the 1990s. These leisure products followed a typical life-cycle pattern and the manager was under comparable pressure then to provide off-road skateboard and BMX facilities. Assuming that adequate data was kept, it might be possible to track the skateboard and BMX phenomena over their life-cycle timings and assess the current rollerblade position.

Market research

The final qualitative approach is that based around market research. We have discussed the potential for such an approach in general terms already in Chapter 7. It is evident, however, that for the examples used so far in this chapter, market research could have provided information to help assess the future situation.

Davos drops its obsession with financial risks

By Gillian Tett

What are the biggest risks stalking the world today? A cynic might gripe that the list is so depressingly long that it is pointless even to try to choose: populism, cyber attacks, trade wars, weather shocks and global debt are all on the rise.

However, during the past decade the World Economic Forum has asked its members to rank their worries in terms of likelihood and impact, ahead of its annual meeting in Davos. And while this poll is limited in scope – WEF members are drawn, of course, from the global elite of corporate executives, government officials, NGO activists and the media – the results are nevertheless thought-provoking.

This year's "worry" list, for example, is dominated by climate change concerns: Davosians apparently fear that extreme weather events are becoming more common, and that the world has no effective mechanism to respond. Climate issues account for three of the five risks deemed most likely to materialise in 2019 – and four of the top five risks that could cause the most damage. The only other topics cited are weapons of mass destruction and cyber risks. . . .

But what is more striking is how this worry list has changed since the WEF started its survey. A decade ago, what worried Davosians was the economy and the

financial system. . . . The environment was not mentioned at all.

These economic issues continued to dominate in subsequent years. But in 2015 the risk of social strife and intergovernmental conflicts (i.e. war) jumped on to the worry list, partly displacing economic concerns. Then, in 2018, climate change issues and cyber problems suddenly dominated. And this year the swing has gone further — so much so that economic issues do not appear in the top five at all.

To put it another way: a decade ago the WEF elite were apparently so obsessed with the fear that finance would melt down that they did not have time to worry about the environment. Now they are so alarmed that the planet and/or the internet will collapse that the economic risks are less prominent. . . .

Perhaps the most practical conclusion from the poll is that it signals where policy action may next heat up. Think about it. The explosion of concern about finance in 2008 led to significant financial reform. Rising fears about migration in 2016 triggered a political response. Cyber hacking fears jumped on to the list as the cyber security industry boomed.

On that basis, the key conclusion from the Davosian list might be that investors should now look for more climate action.

Source: Tett, G. (2019) Davos drops its obsession with financial risks, *Financial Times* (UK), Friday, 18 January. © The Financial Times Limited. All Rights Reserved.

Qualitative forecasts such as these have a role to play.

Quantitative approaches

Quantitative approaches tend to fall into two general categories: *trend projections* and *causal models*. The rest of this chapter will focus on common methods of trend projections, while causal models will be the focus of Chapter 10. Suffice it to say for the present that trend projections are concerned with taking some observed historical pattern for some variable and projecting this pattern into the future using a quantitative approach. Simply, we take the trend in the variable we have observed in the past and project it into the future. Such an approach does not attempt to suggest why the variable in question will take some future value. This is left to the application of a causal model, which tries to identify factors that influence the variable in some way or cause it to behave in some predictable manner.

Trend projections

Trend projections methods themselves fall into two broad categories: smoothing, or moving average, methods and time-series decomposition. We shall begin by looking at moving average methods.

Moving averages

Given that we are concerned with observing the movement of some variable over time and trying to project this movement into the future, it seems logical to try to smooth out any irregular pattern in the historical values of the variable and use this as the basis of a future projection. The simplest way of doing this is to calculate a series of moving averages. Consider the data in Table 9.1 and the corresponding graph of the data in Figure 9.4.

The data relates to the weekly sales of some low-value product. It can be seen from the graph that sales have been relatively stable over this 15-week period (showing no marked upward or downward pattern) but have fluctuated erratically on a week-by-week basis. The method of simple moving averages attempts to smooth out these irregularities to calculate the underlying trend and uses this smoothed value as the forecast. For example, suppose we are currently at the beginning of Week 3 and are trying to provide some numerical estimate of that week's sales.

Progress Check 9.2

How would you suggest we estimate sales in Week 3, given we have actual data only for Weeks 1 and 2?

Table 9.1   Weekly sales

Week	Sales units
1	246
2	256
3	255
4	248
5	263
6	254
7	256
8	258
9	249
10	257
11	259
12	243
13	255
14	251
15	253

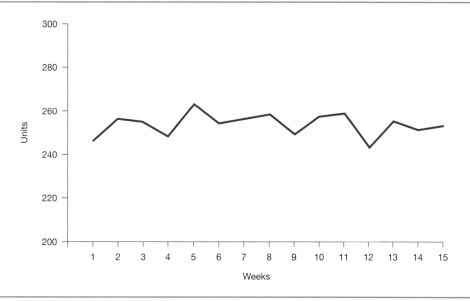

Figure 9.4 Weekly sales

The logical thing to do would be to average the data we have on actual sales for Weeks 1 and 2 and use this as our forecast for Week 3. This would give:

$$\text{Forecast} = \frac{246 + 256}{2} = 251$$

which, when compared with the actual figure for Week 3 of 255, is reasonably accurate. Clearly, we could proceed in this way on a week-by-week basis. That is, for Week 4 we could produce a forecast which was an average of the first three weeks' sales, for Week 5 an average of the first four weeks' sales and so on. The problem with this approach is that over time it uses a lot of data (all the previous weeks' sales figures that are available) and it is not particularly responsive to recent changes in demand. For example, assume an 11-week period where, for the first 10 weeks, sales were all 250 units per week. In Week 11 sales jump to 5000. The forecast for Week 12 would be heavily weighted by the 10 weeks where sales were much lower than the last week's. For this reason, it makes more sense to calculate a moving average rather than a simple average: that is, an average where we use a given number of the most recent weeks. For example, suppose we decided that each forecast would be an average of the two previous weeks' sales. The forecast series would then be that shown in Table 9.2. The forecast for Week 3 is the average of Weeks 1 and 2. The forecast for Week 4 is the average for Weeks 2 and 3 and so on through the series. You will also appreciate from the calculation why we refer to this as a *moving* average. In mathematical form the calculation is given as:

$$F_{t+1} = \frac{\Sigma(D_t + D_{t-1})}{n}$$

where F refers to the forecast and D to the actual data (sales). It will be worthwhile explaining the subscript notation we are using, as this is a common way of representing a moving-average calculation. We denote the time periods using the variable t, which in our example could take a value from 1 to 15. We require a forecast for the *next* time

Table 9.2 Weekly sales and a two-week moving average

Week	Sales	Two-week average forecast
1	246	–
2	256	–
3	255	251
4	248	255.5
5	263	251.5
6	254	255.5
7	256	258.5
8	258	255
9	249	257
10	257	253.5
11	259	253
12	243	258
13	255	251
14	251	249
15	253	253
16		252

period, denoted as $t + 1$. The current period is then denoted as t and the previous period as $t - 1$. So, in our first calculation we would have:

$t + 1$	Week 3
t	Week 2
$t - 1$	Week 1

and the first moving average would be found using the actual sales for Weeks 1 and 2 and dividing by $n = 2$. Clearly, as we progress through the series t changes its numerical value. In this example we have $n = 2$. In other cases we might wish to average the series over a different number of periods: 3, 4, 5 . . . In other words, n could take any numerical value. The expression for the moving average would then become, in general:

$$F_{t+1} = \frac{\sum(D_1 + D_{t-1} + D_{t-2} + \cdots + D_{t-n+1})}{n}$$

The results of the forecasts are shown in Figure 9.5, together with the actual values. The forecasting method appears to perform reasonably well on a period-by-period basis, although there are one or two periods where our forecasts are relatively inaccurate. It will also be evident that in this example we used a moving average of $n = 2$ with no real justification as to why this particular average should be used. In practice this is quite a common situation: the choice of n is to some extent arbitrary. A larger value for n will base the forecast on a larger number of actual values but will also make the forecast relatively unresponsive to recent changes. On the other hand, a smaller value for n will make the forecast more responsive but may be oversensitive to random fluctuations in the variable from one period to the next.

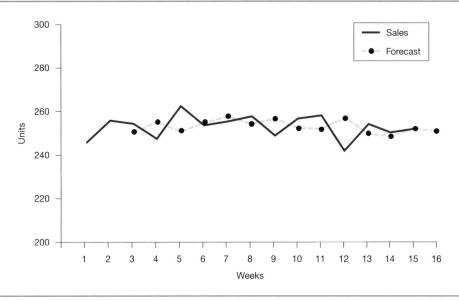

Figure 9.5 Weekly sales and forecast

Oil prices slide after robust supply data and softer Washington line on Iran sanctions

By Myles McCormick and David Sheppard

Source: Robert Gerhardt/123RF

Oil prices tumbled more than 3 per cent yesterday to their lowest since August as traders bet that the market would remain well supplied despite US sanctions on Iran's crude exports starting next week.

Brent crude fell below $73 a barrel, extending a price slide to more than 15 per cent since it peaked above $86 a barrel at the start of last month.

The international benchmark saw losses accelerate after breaking below its 200-day moving average – a key technical indicator – for the first time since September last year.

Moving averages are a common way of assessing change and trends.

Forecast errors

It will also be evident that we will need some method of assessing the overall accuracy of the forecasting method. The 'error', e, involved in the forecast can be defined as:

$$e_{t+1} = D_{t+1} - F_{t+1}$$

where the error is simply the difference between the actual value of the variable (once it can be observed) and the forecast. The error of the forecast for Week 3 is +4 (255−251) and that for Week 4 is −7.5 (248−255.5). Typically, we wish to assess the accuracy of the forecasting method over the entire period and there are two common methods of calculation: the *mean absolute deviation* or the *mean squared error*.

UK sees steep increase in winter deaths

By Emily Cadman

Last year's cold winter saw the number of excess winter deaths jump by nearly a third, according to official data. The Office for National Statistics estimates that there were 31,000 excess winter deaths in England and Wales in 2012–13, a rise of 29 per cent on the previous year.

Last March was the coldest since 1962, with an average temperature of 2.2 °C, and the second coldest since 1910. The majority of the excess deaths, 25,000, occurred among those aged 75 or above. While cold weather is linked to an increase in the number of deaths, hypothermia is not the main cause. The majority of deaths are linked to strokes and heart and respiratory diseases.

Looking at the five-year moving average – which smooths out short-term fluctuation – there has been a long-term steady decline in the number of deaths, but a slight rise in the past seven years. Countries such as Finland and Germany have substantially lower rates of winter deaths than England and Wales despite having significantly colder winters.

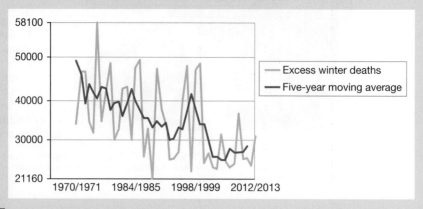

Moving averages like this can highlight long-term trends.

Mean absolute deviation

This method takes the absolute value of each individual error and averages these absolute errors over the entire period. The absolute value of a number is simply that number without a positive or negative sign. An absolute value is usually denoted with the symbol | X | (known as a modulus) and would be pronounced 'the absolute value of X'. So, for example:

$$|-10| = |+10| = 10$$

that is, the absolute value of -10 and $+10$ is the same at 10. The calculations for our example are shown in Table 9.3.

The total of the absolute deviations is 68.5, giving a mean absolute deviation (MAD) of 5.27 (68.5/13). On average, then, the forecast is 5.27 units away from the actual value. The MAD calculations can be summarised as:

$$\text{MAD} = \frac{\sum |e|}{t} \text{ where t is the total number of forecast errors.}$$

Progress Check 9.3

For this data series calculate a four-week moving average. Calculate the MAD of these forecasts and compare it with that of the two-week moving average.

Table 9.3 Mean absolute deviation

Week	Sales	Forecast	Error	Absolute deviation
1	246	–	–	–
2	256	–	–	–
3	255	251	4	4
4	248	255.5	−7.5	7.5
5	263	251.5	11.5	11.5
6	254	255.5	−1.5	1.5
7	256	258.5	−2.5	2.5
8	258	255	3	3
9	249	257	−8	8
10	257	253.5	3.5	3.5
11	259	253	6	6
12	243	258	−15	15
13	255	251	4	4
14	251	249	2	2
15	253	253	0	0
16	–	252	–	–
Total				68.5

Table 9.4   Four-week moving averages

Week	Sales	Four-week average forecast	Error	Absolute deviation
1	246	–	–	–
2	256	–	–	–
3	255	–	–	–
4	248	–	–	–
5	263	251.25	11.75	11.75
6	254	255.5	−1.5	1.5
7	256	255	1	1
8	258	255.25	2.75	2.75
9	249	257.75	−8.75	8.75
10	257	254.25	2.75	2.75
11	259	255	4	4
12	243	255.75	−12.75	12.75
13	255	252	3	3
14	251	253.5	−2.5	2.5
15	253	252	1	1
16	–	250.5	–	–
Total				51.75

Table 9.4 shows the forecasts produced by a four-week moving average and the corresponding error. The MAD in this case is 4.70 (51.75/11), a marginal improvement over the two-week forecast. A four-period total seems to give slightly more accurate forecasts than a two-period model over the entire forecasting period.

Mean squared error

The MAD method produces a forecast error that is relatively straightforward to understand but it attaches no particular importance to large forecast errors. From Table 9.4 we see that there are large errors in Weeks 5 and 12. It may well be, from a management perspective, that we want to 'punish' a forecasting model that produces relatively large errors like these. As far as management is concerned, one such large error might be far more costly to the organisation than a series of smaller errors. Consider a scenario where one method produces a weekly absolute error of two units over, say, 10 weeks. Another method produces a weekly absolute error of zero units for nine weeks and 20 units for one week. Which is the better forecasting method? Clearly the MAD will be the same in both cases. Depending on circumstances, we might prefer a method which has smaller individual errors. This is why, under some circumstances, we might prefer a different method of assessing forecasting accuracy: the *mean squared error*. Rather than taking the absolute value of each error, the errors are squared before summing and averaging. Table 9.5 shows the calculations for both moving-average models.

Table 9.5 Mean squared error

Week	Sales	Two-week average forecast	Error	Squared error	Four-week average forecast	Error	Squared error
1	246	–	–	–	–	–	–
2	256	–	–	–	–	–	–
3	255	251	4	16	–	–	–
4	248	255.5	−7.5	56.25	–	–	–
5	263	251.5	11.5	132.25	251.25	11.75	138.0625
6	254	255.5	−1.5	2.25	255.5	−1.5	2.25
7	256	258.5	−2.5	6.25	255	1	1
8	258	255	3	9	255.25	2.75	7.5625
9	249	257	−8	64	257.75	−8.75	76.5625
10	257	253.5	3.5	12.25	254.25	2.75	7.5625
11	259	253	6	36	255	4	16
12	243	258	−15	225	255.75	−12.75	162.5625
13	255	251	4	16	252	3	9
14	251	249	2	4	253.5	−2.5	6.25
15	253	253	–	0	252	1	1
16		252			250.5		
Total				579.25			427.8125

We then have:

MSE two-week model: 44.56 (579.25/13)

MSE four-week model: 38.89 (427.8125/11)

Note that the larger errors in both models have become more 'important' in the calculation. Effectively this error calculation penalises larger errors. Once again, the four-week model appears to perform better than the two-week one. Note that we cannot compare the MAD with the MSE for one particular model.

It is important to realise that moving-average models are unlikely to generate highly accurate forecasts by their very nature. However, this is relatively unimportant as long as such models are applied to problems where high accuracy is not the sole criterion. Consider the scenario of a supermarket with an in-store bakery. Each day the bakery supervisor must decide on that day's production, since unsold bakery items must be disposed of at a loss at the end of the day. Clearly in such a situation a number of criteria would apply to the use of a suitable forecasting model. It would need to be:

● simple to use;
● quick to use;
● easy to understand;
● low cost;
● reasonably accurate.

Given that such a model will be in use each day – and will be used to support decisions that must be made quickly – forecast accuracy is only one feature of a suitable model. The managerial consequences of forecast error in such a scenario are relatively minor. If the model produces a 'large' forecast error at the end of one day, the supermarket will not go out of business. On a daily basis accuracy should be reasonable. On the other hand, on a long-term basis we could not afford to use a model which repeatedly produced large errors as this would affect profitability.

QADM IN ACTION

Capgemini – improving forecasting accuracy

Capgemini's client was a major UK mail order retailer. The client launches two mail-order catalogues each year with the majority of products shown in the catalogue being new each season. As a result, little previous sales history is available to develop sales forecasting and to support purchasing decisions (i.e. how many items of a particular product should the client contract to purchase from its suppliers). To compound the problem, there are relatively long lead times involved in the business and consequently contracts for large volumes of stock have to be negotiated well in advance of each season. The client already used a number of statistical forecasting models to predict sales demand. However, the client also knew that even small percentage improvements in the accuracy of these models could lead to large savings both by reducing lost sales (because a customer wanted to buy an item that was now sold out) and by reducing excess stock holdings.

By applying a combination of additional forecasting and quantitative techniques Capgemini were able to segment the client's catalogue. Essentially, this enabled Capgemini to identify groups of similarly behaving products. This in turn enabled the development of more accurate forecasting models for each of the different product groups.

Capgemini worked closely with the client's own modelling group. They developed a number of models to forecast demand at an individual product level for different parts of the catalogue. The models were developed using data from one previous season's sales and then used to forecast the following season so that actual demand could be compared with the statistical forecasts and the forecast errors identified. A business case was also made for integrating

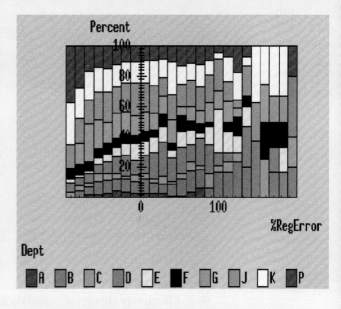

the new forecasting methods into the existing purchasing and stock management systems.

The initial models indicated a 3–5 per cent improvement in forecasting accuracy, which translated to between £8m and £15m in profit. A second phase of development indicated further improvements in accuracy of 2–3 per cent (worth c. £6m) from using new input variables.

The graph shows forecasting errors by product type. Such errors helped to identify groups of products which could be modelled separately to improve forecasting accuracy.

The benefits are as follows:

● Improved forecasting accuracy leading to a reduction in lost sales and in excess stock.

● Knowledge transfer to the client's own modelling team.

Source: Based on a Capgemini case study, with thanks to Capgemini for permission to use their material.

Exponential smoothing

The moving-average model developed in the previous section poses the manager two questions regarding its use and development.

● How many periods should be used in calculating the average?
● Is it logical in the context of the problem for each item used to have an equal weight in the calculation?

Answers to both these questions must be largely subjective. Daily data might use a seven-period average, weekly data a four-period average and so on. The second question may need some explanation. If we consider, say, a four-period moving average the formula:

$$F_{t+1} = \frac{\sum(D_t + D_{t-1} + D_{t-2} + D_{t-3})}{4}$$

can be rewritten as:

$$F_{t+1} = 1/4D_t + 1/4D_{t-1} + 1/4D_{t-2} + 1/4D_{t-3}$$

Each item in the average is given the same weight. In some circumstances it may seem more reasonable to allocate larger weights to more recent items, since the 'older' an item gets the less it reflects the current situation. Such a method is provided using *exponential smoothing*, a widely used moving-average method. The forecast formula for this method is given by:

$$F_{t+1} = \alpha D_t + (1 - \alpha)F_t$$

where α is a weight taking a value between 0 and 1. The method looks deceptively simple: the forecast for period $t + 1$ is some proportion (α) of the latest data item, D_t, plus some proportion ($1 - \alpha$) of the forecast produced for the previous period, F_t. To appreciate the formula fully it will be worthwhile exploring the mathematics which develops it. Consider what we require: a moving average where more recent items are given larger weights. This can be represented as:

$$F_{t+1} = w_1 D_t + w_2 D_{t-1} + w_3 D_{t-2} + \ldots + w_n D_{t-(n+1)}$$

where w represents the weights to be used. We impose two restrictions:

$$\sum w = 1$$
$$w_1 > w_2 > w_3 > \ldots$$

That is, the sum of the weights must total to 1, and each weight is larger than the weight immediately preceding it (to give more importance to more recent data items). From a management perspective we clearly have one important difficulty: how do we establish what the weights should be? The method used by this model is to use weights which follow what is known as an exponential pattern. Such exponential weights are denoted as a, with a taking α value between 0 and 1. The exponential pattern is illustrated with a = 0.2 in Table 9.6, which shows the weights for the first 20 periods.

Table 9.6   Exponential pattern: $\alpha = 0.2$

Period			Weight	Cumulative
t	α	0.2	0.2	0.2
t−1	$\alpha\,(1-\alpha)$	0.2(0.8)	0.16	0.36
t−2	$\alpha\,(1-\alpha)^2$	0.2(0.8)^2	0.128	0.488
t−3	$\alpha\,(1-\alpha)^3$	0.2(0.8)^3	0.1024	0.5904
t−4	$\alpha\,(1-\alpha)^4$	.	0.08192	0.67232
t−5	$\alpha\,(1-\alpha)^5$	.	0.065536	0.737856
t−6	$\alpha\,(1-\alpha)^6$	.	0.052428	0.790284
t−7	$\alpha\,(1-\alpha)^7$	.	0.041943	0.832227
t−8	$\alpha\,(1-\alpha)^8$	.	0.033554	0.865782
t−9	$\alpha\,(1-\alpha)^9$	.	0.026843	0.892625
t−10	$\alpha\,(1-\alpha)^{10}$	.	0.021474	0.914100
t−11	$\alpha\,(1-\alpha)^{11}$	.	0.017179	0.931280
t−12	$\alpha\,(1-\alpha)^{12}$	.	0.013743	0.945024
t−13	$\alpha\,(1-\alpha)^{13}$	.	0.010995	0.956019
t−14	$\alpha\,(1-\alpha)^{14}$	.	0.008796	0.964815
t−15	$\alpha\,(1-\alpha)^{15}$	.	0.007036	0.971852
t−16	$\alpha\,(1-\alpha)^{16}$	.	0.005629	0.977482
t−17	$\alpha\,(1-\alpha)^{17}$	.	0.004503	0.981985
t−18	$\alpha\,(1-\alpha)^{18}$	.	0.003602	0.985588
t−19	$\alpha\,(1-\alpha)^{19}$	.	0.002882	0.988470
t−20	$\alpha\,(1-\alpha)^{20}$	0.2(0.8)^{20}	0.002305	0.990776

In the first period the weight used is equal to α at 0.2. In the second period the weight is a proportion of the first. Given that $\alpha = 0.2$ then $(1-\alpha) = 0.8$, with a resulting weight of 0.16. This second weight is less than the first (as required by the exponential-smoothing model). The third weight is then a proportion of the second and so on through the series. It can be seen that the individual weights gradually decrease over time, whereas the total of all the weights to that period, the cumulative, gradually increases and approaches 1.0, again as required by the model. Figure 9.6 shows the graph of the individual weights over time, with the decreasing pattern clearly visible. It is apparent that, had we continued our calculations past $t - 20$, further weights would have become smaller and smaller and the cumulative weight gradually closer to 1.0. But how does this help? Let us return to the general formula we had earlier and express it in terms of the exponential weights:

Equation 1

$$F_{t+1} = \alpha D_t + \alpha(1 - \alpha)\,D_{t-1} + \alpha(1 - \alpha)^2\,D_{t-2} + \alpha(1 - \alpha)^3\,D_{t-3}$$
$$+ \cdots + \alpha(1 - \alpha)^{n-1}\,D_{t-(n+1)}$$

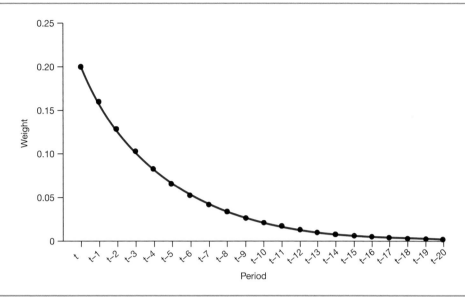

Figure 9.6 Exponential weights

This hardly seems to fit the criteria we established for the application of a moving-average model: simple, easy to use, etc. Let us consider some simple rearrangement of this formula. The term $(1 - \alpha)$ is common to all parts of the RHS of the equation except for the first term. This means that we can rewrite Equation 1 as:

Equation 2

$$F_{t+1} = \alpha D_t + (1 - \alpha)\,[\alpha D_{t-1} + \alpha(1 - \alpha)\,D_{t-2} + \alpha(1 - \alpha)^2\,D_{t-3}$$
$$+ \cdots + \alpha(1 - \alpha)^{n-2}\,D_{t-(n+1)}$$

Study Equation 2 carefully. It is exactly the same as the previous one except that we have taken the common term, $(1-\alpha)$, out of the expression and reduced each subsequent weight accordingly.

Progress Check 9.4

Obtain a formula for producing a forecast for period t comparable to Equation 1.

The formula for the forecast for period t would be:

Equation 3

$$F_t = \alpha D_{t-1} + \alpha(1 - \alpha)\,D_{t-2} + \alpha(1 - \alpha)^2\,D_{t-3} + \alpha(1 - \alpha)^3\,D_{t-4}$$
$$+ \cdots + \alpha(1 - \alpha)^{n-2}\,D_{t-(n+1)}$$

Consider what this formula represents. F_{t+1} is the forecast for the next period: what we can regard as the new forecast. F_t is then the old forecast: what we forecast in the previous period for the current period. However, on inspection we can see that Equation 3 is identical to that part of Equation 2 that was in the square brackets []. So, the formula for F_t in Equation 3 can be substituted into that for F_{t+1} in Equation 1 to give:

$$F_{t+1} = \alpha D_t + (1 - \alpha)F_t$$

which was what we stated the exponential-smoothing model to be in the first place. This diversion into the mathematics underpinning the model is important. On the face of it the model we have derived looks too simple. After all, it represents a forecast which is made up of a proportion of the latest item of data and a proportion of the previous forecast. However, by returning to the derivation of this formula we see that implicit in the calculation is the use of *all* historical data: every single D value is actually incorporated into the forecast calculation and each of them has a decreasing weight. So we have derived a moving-average model that actually uses all the available data even though it does not require this data for the calculation. We can make the model even easier to use, however. We have:

$$F_{t+1} = \alpha D_t + (1 - \alpha)F_t$$

Let us expand the term involving F_t to give:

$$F_{t+1} = \alpha D_t - \alpha F_t + F_t$$

and rearranging gives:

$$F_{t+1} = F_t + \alpha(D_t - F_t)$$

Progress Check 9.5

In non-mathematical terms what do the term F_t and the term $(D_t - F_t)$ represent?

F_t is clearly our 'old' forecast: the forecast we produced in the previous period for the current period. The term $(D_t - F_t)$ is the difference between the actual value of the variable in the current period and what we forecast it would be: the forecast error, in other words. So, our sophisticated exponential-smoothing model, underpinned by some complex mathematics, actually simplifies to a method which says that:

New forecast = Old forecast + α(last forecast error)

So we have developed a model which is deceptively simple to use and understand, has considerable managerial logic and yet is underpinned by the appropriate mathematics.

To illustrate the calculations let us return to the unit sales data we had for the earlier moving-average model. We shall use $\alpha = 0.2$ and to begin the process we shall assume that the forecast for Week 1 was the same as the actual at 246. The forecast error for this period will then be zero. The forecast for Week 2 will then be:

$$F_2 = F_1 + \alpha(D_1 - F_1) = 246 + 0.2(0) = 246$$

Clearly with no forecast error from Week 1 there is no reason to alter the forecast since it was 100 per cent accurate. We note that in Week 2 the actual sales were 256. The forecast for Week 3 then becomes:

$$F_3 = F_2 + \alpha(D_2 - F_2)$$

$$= 246 + 0.2(256 - 246)$$

$$= 246 + 2 = 248$$

The logic is clear. The forecast for Week 2 was an underestimate of what actually occurred. Accordingly, the forecast for the next week is increased by a proportion (0.2) of the underestimate. The forecasting model can proceed in this way on a period-by-period basis. In the event of an underestimate the next period forecast is increased and likewise in the event of an overestimate the next forecast is adjusted downward. Similarly, the larger the error, the larger the adjustment. But what of the choice of a at 0.2? a must take a value between 0 and 1 to satisfy the logic of the model. Other things being equal, the smaller the value of α then the less responsive the model becomes to forecast errors. In practice, values of α are typically between 0.15 and 0.35. Too high a value for α and we may be over-responding to a forecast error in one period. In practice we may also be able to gain an insight into an appropriate choice for a by applying varying values to historical data and assessing which gives a 'better' set of forecasts using either the MAD or the MSE that we introduced earlier.

Extensions to the exponential-smoothing model

To illustrate the principles of the model, we have examined a simple, and stable, variable which fluctuates over time but shows no other pattern in terms of either trend or seasonality. In practice many variables do exhibit such patterns. The exponential model can readily be adapted, however, to take such factors into account.

Technical analysis: how to identify your friend the trend

By Vince Heaney

The Chartists were a 19th century working-class movement seeking political reform, but in recent years the name has been applied to those who use technical analysis of price graphs to forecast stock price movements.

While the Chartist political movement ended in failure in 1848, three consecutive years of declining equity markets have bestowed credibility on technical analysis. In a market where the disgraced cheerleaders for the equity bubble have incurred fines from financial regulators and face reforms to curb their conflicts of interest, chartists have emerged as more dispassionate observers. Above all, they have been largely right in their bearish forecasts for equities.

Part of the appeal of technical analysis lies in its lack of bias; unlike long-only fund managers, chartists are not encumbered by the requirement always to be bullish or at worst neutral. The same chart data is available to both retail and professional investors – a far more level playing field than applies to company research.

Technical analysis works on the premise that, in an efficient market, prices will discount all the relevant information about the stock or index in question. History may not repeat itself exactly, but patterns of price development are repeated. Studying these patterns over time can offer insight into their future development.

Technical analysis attracts its fair share of purists – chartists who feel no need to consider fundamental economic factors, because their impact is fully discounted in the price. However, at the risk of causing apoplexy among the purists, I believe technical analysis can be used in conjunction with fundamental analysis. There is a place for macroeconomics and a study of corporate balance sheets. But the charts are useful in establishing the direction of the prevailing market trend and help investors to time entry and exit points through studies of market momentum.

Accepting that markets are not entirely random is one of the basic tenets of charting; in the "A" to "Z" of charting "T" is for trend and identifying the prevailing trend is one of the cornerstones of the approach. Markets do not travel in a smooth linear fashion. An uptrend is characterised by successively higher highs, while the periodic pullbacks form successively higher lows.

The reverse is true of a downtrend. The market reaches successively lower lows while the bear market rallies within the trend form a series of lower highs.

It is important to remember that there is a third possibility when looking for the prevailing trend. Markets spend a lot of time moving sideways in trading ranges. Many of the tools used by chartists are trend-following in nature, and do not perform as well in markets that are stuck in a range. The important lesson is not to try to invent a trend when one is not apparent.

Having established the direction of the prevailing trend the chartist can construct a trendline. In a rising market a line can be constructed underneath the successive lows formed by the pullbacks within the bull move. A valid trendline needs to have at least three points of contact. The larger the number of contact points and the longer it has been in existence, the more significant the line becomes. In a bear market the trendline will be a downward sloping line connecting the tops of the bear market rallies. Some chartists believe that the closing price should be used when constructing trendlines, but I believe it is more valid to include the whole range of the day's activity.

The trendline is a very basic tool, but a powerful one. Pullbacks to an upward sloping trendline in a bull market can be used as buying opportunities by those who have missed out on the initial move. When a trendline is violated, it is an important early signal of a change in the direction of the trend. If the market closes below a trendline – one that has supported the market on repeated occasions over several months of a bull market – it is a signal that the technical trader ignores at his peril.

A further important tool of trend analysis is found under "M" for moving average, one of the most widely used technical indicators. A simple arithmetic mean of a previous run of closing prices is one of the most popular moving averages. The number of closing prices used is at the trader's discretion, but 10, 20 and 50-day averages are frequently used. A moving average smooths the trend, producing a line on the chart that lags behind the price data, but makes the trend more easily identifiable. Linearly and exponentially weighted averages can also be used to give more relevance to the most recent price data.

As well as a visual guide to the prevailing trend, moving averages are used to generate buy and sell signals. In a bull market, when the current price drops below the chosen moving average, a sell signal is generated. A shorter-term average follows the price data more closely, but will generate more false signals. To smooth out some of the false signals, two moving averages can be used, such as the 10-day and the 50-day. In the bull market example, the sell signal is generated when the shorter-term average crosses below the longer-term one.

A brief article can provide only a glimpse into technical analysis, but hopefully can provide the spark for further research into a powerful trading tool. If the "trend is your friend", you have to identify it first.

A variety of moving averages are used to try to predict stock price movement.

Time-series models

The issues of trend and seasonality take us logically to the next group of models, which are expressly concerned with forecasting under such conditions. Consider the data shown in Table 9.7 and the corresponding graph in Figure 9.7. The data refers to quarterly electricity sales to domestic customers in the UK from 1998 to 2018 (we looked at this in Chapter 3). Such electricity sales are used by domestic customers for lighting, cooking, heating and running electrical appliances in the home. Unsurprisingly given the UK's climate, we see a clear pattern in the data each year. Within each year we see high sales in Quarters 1 (Jan–March) and 4 (Oct–Dec), with lower sales in Quarters 2 (April–Jun) and 3 (Jul–Sept). Such a pattern is not difficult to explain given that the middle of the year tends to be lighter and warmer with the reverse for six months over the winter. A time series such as this can be analysed in terms of a number of components.

Table 9.7 Quarterly electricity sales to UK domestic customers 1998–2018: giga-watt hours (GwH)

UK Domestic electricity sales 1998–2018	GwH	UK Domestic electricity sales 1998–2018	GwH
Year	Domestic	Year	Domestic
1998:1	32 347	2008:2	26 549
1998:2	24 361	2008:3	24 990
1998:3	21 159	2008:4	33 578
1998:4	31 543	2009:1	36 388
1999:1	33 850	2009:2	25 324
1999:2	23 679	2009:3	23 872
1999:3	21 556	2009:4	32 957
1999:4	31 224	2010:1	36 083
2000:1	32 638	2010:2	25 075
2000:2	23 638	2010:3	23 215
2000:3	23 363	2010:4	34 459
2000:4	32 203	2011:1	34 085
2001:1	35 045	2011:2	23 956
2001:2	25 650	2011:3	22 881
2001:3	23 111	2011:4	30 664
2001:4	31 532	2012:1	33 506
2002:1	35 203	2012:2	25 157
2002:2	26 286	2012:3	23 164
2002:3	24 396	2012:4	32 836
2002:4	34 129	2013:1	34 302
2003:1	36 631	2013:2	25 468
2003:2	26 563	2013:3	22 708
2003:3	24 238	2013:4	30 934
2003:4	35 568	2014:1	31 731
2004:1	35 703	2014:2	24 128
2004:2	27 771	2014:3	22 347
2004:3	26 176	2014:4	29 870
2004:4	34 549	2015:1	31 546
2005:1	36 149	2015:2	24 148
2005:2	27 941	2015:3	22 174
2005:3	25 815	2015:4	29 896
2005:4	35 807	2016:1	31 904
2006:1	37 467	2016:2	24 014
2006:2	27 489	2016:3	21 831
2006:3	24 994	2016:4	30 222
2006:4	34 754	2017:1	30 629
2007:1	35 226	2017:2	23 384
2007:2	26 645	2017:3	21 423
2007:3	25 484	2017:4	29 960
2007:4	35 721	2018:1	31 816
2008:1	34 683		

Source: Office for National Statistics
Data file 9-7

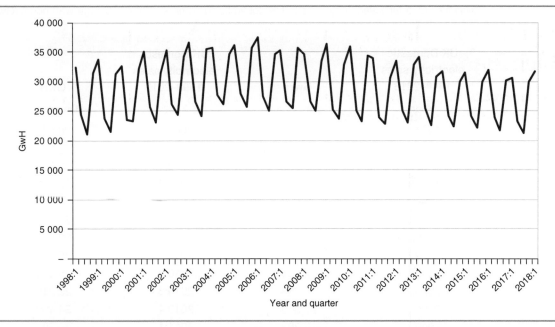

Figure 9.7 UK Domestic electricity sales per quarter GwH 1998–2018

Components of a time series

In general we can distinguish three components of a time series:

- the trend;
- the seasonal components;
- the random element.

The *trend* in a time series is the long-term, underlying movement in the variable. For electricity sales we see a relatively flat trend over this period, with slight growth up to 2006 and then a slight long-term decline since that time. The trend is an indication of the long-term direction of the variable. The *seasonal components* refer to the variability that occurs in the series within the year and that typically repeats itself each year. It is worth mentioning that some variables may exhibit 'seasonal' patterns in a shorter timescale than one year. Demand for electricity in the UK, for example, follows a predictable pattern within each week and within each 24-hour period as well as a seasonal pattern through the year as a whole. Finally, the *random* element refers to the difference between the actual series and what we would have expected the series to be, based on the trend and the seasonal component. It relates to random, unpredictable events which will cause the actual series to deviate from what would normally be expected. Given that by definition such an element is unpredictable, its future impact on the variable cannot be determined. Random elements may relate to features such as unexpected weather patterns (severe storms for example); to labour disputes; to outbreaks of hostilities; or to any 'shock' event, depending on the variable we are looking at.

The overall purpose of time-series analysis is to try to quantify the trend and seasonal components of a variable. Such information can then be used both to assess current performance and to predict the future. Consider the Domestic Electricity Sales data. Analysis of long-term trends will help planning of future generation and supply and may help assess the impact of various energy saving initiatives on electricity consumption. Analysis of seasonal patterns within a 12-month period will help us with short-term planning, with the planning of routine maintenance and power outages and with capacity management through the year. Seasonal analysis will also help with financial planning and quantifying short-term revenue projections.

Some like it hot but heatwave proves mixed blessing

Non-food retail sales fall as shoppers desert the high street for beaches and beer gardens

By Gavin Jackson in Southend-on-Sea

Source: Danny Lawson/PA

Cool customers: ice cream sales are soaring as temperatures rise

The hottest July on record has been a mixed blessing for Charlie Bird, the director of sales at Rossi Ice Cream in Southend-on-Sea. The heatwave has boosted revenues, but played havoc with his freezers. A combination of hot air and low water pressure blew out a freezer component earlier this week at Rossi, a business started by Italian immigrants in 1932, leading to a race against time to fix it before the ice cream melted. Now the company has shifted production to the evening so the equipment can better keep up with demand.

The heatwave may be boosting Rossi's bottom line but it is having a mixed effect on the wider economy as spending and working patterns shift. The streets of Southend offer a snapshot of how this is affecting different sectors.

Official measures of retail sales suggest the high street benefited from a combination of the heatwave, the World Cup and the royal wedding during the second quarter of 2018.

But as these events have provided an alternative to going shopping at the weekend, non-food retail sales such as fashion fell in June.

The impact can be seen in the sales of John Lewis, the department store and supermarket group, which provides weekly performance updates. At its groceries brand, Waitrose, barbecue meat sales were up by 40 per cent last week compared with the same week last year; sales of ice were up by 130 per cent.

But sales of home furnishings in the department stores were down by 6.3 per cent compared with the same week in 2017.

Andrew Wharton, a senior statistician working on economic growth at the Office for National Statistics,

said that typically shoppers bought their summer wardrobes and headed out to garden centres when the sun emerged. Then Britons shifted away from the high street, petrol sales went up and people headed to the beach and beer gardens.

The "displacement from the high street into catering" was a normal summer pattern but the recent heatwave had condensed this pattern over the past three months, he said.

"Usually it's a more gradual process."

On a baking hot afternoon in July, Royals Shopping Centre, near the centre of Southend, bears out the data. The air-conditioned halls are empty compared with the bustle outside as Londoners arrive at the station and head for the beach. The heat is also putting people off walking Southend's pier – the longest in the world at 1.33 miles, according to the woman who operates the ticket office. But the bar outside the pier's Royal Pavilion is doing a brisk trade as visitors cool off with a beer.

The warm weather could change holiday spending. Those who have not already booked trips abroad may decide to stay in the UK, and others will have gone on spontaneous day trips, said Howard Archer, chief economic adviser to the EY Item club.

Economists fret that if the summer sun unleashes a wave of spending, it will lead to a further drop in saving or a squeeze on consumption later in the year.

Last year, British households became net borrowers for the first time since 1988, according to the ONS, as prices rose faster than wages. On average each household spent £900 more than it earned in 2017, borrowing a total of £25bn.

In the countryside around Southend, farmers are also borrowing. With the fields yellowing and grass scorched, dairy farmers were having to "dip into feed supplies" said Anand Dossa, an economist with the National Farmers Union.

These supplies are normally kept for the winter months and while there has been no impact on milk production yet, it was "likely to come under pressure in the rest of the year," Mr Dossa said. That meant farmers, like shoppers, may have to borrow even more to make it through the winter.

"The financial impact [of the heatwave] will be with us for quite some time," he said.

Much of what happens in the economy is affected both by seasonal patterns and by one off events like the heatwave in 2018 or the World Cup or a Royal Wedding.

QADM IN ACTION	Capgemini – forecasting retail sales

Capgemini's client was a major UK newspaper distributor wanting to improve demand forecasts at a retailer level. Under-forecasting leads to a loss in sales; over-forecasting leads to higher costs in wasted copy. The problem was compounded by the fact that demand fluctuates through the year along with a regular weekly pattern and is also affected by holidays. Historical data was obtained on demand, holiday periods and on the timing of promotional activity by publishers. Analysis was then undertaken to look at relationships between the variables to build models that would accurately forecast daily and weekly demand.

Total demand fluctuates throughout the year, with a regular weekly pattern and holidays (particularly Christmas) visible on the demand graph.

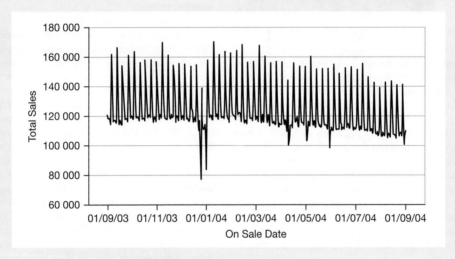

Source: Based on a Capgemini case study, with thanks to Capgemini for permission to use their material.

Time-series decomposition

The process of quantifying the components of a time series is often referred to as *time-series decomposition*. In general, we can identify a model such that:

$$D = T + S + R$$

where:

    D refers to the data series

    T to the trend

    S to the seasonal components

    R to the random element.

We wish to quantify the T and S elements of the model. To do so we use a two-step process: first using moving averages to estimate the trend and then using the trend to estimate the seasonal factors.

Estimating the trend

By definition the trend is the underlying, long-term movement in the variable. It seems logical then to consider estimating the trend using the principles of simple moving averages. Further, since the seasonal components fluctuate during the year, it seems logical, in this example, to calculate a four-quarter moving average for the trend, since this average will cover a 12-month period and must, by definition, include all the seasonal components. Consider the data in the first four quarters of Table 9.7. If we total these and average we get 27 353 – average electricity sales per quarter for the period from 1998:1–4 inclusive. Later in the calculation we shall wish to compare this average with the actual value to begin to estimate seasonality. At the moment, however, we have difficulty in doing so. Which quarter of the year does the figure of 27 353 correspond to? The logical answer would seem to be the middle of the year to which it corresponds. But the middle of the year does not correspond to one particular quarter: rather it falls 'between' two quarters – 1998:2 and 1998:3 in this case. So, to align these moving averages with specific quarters we must adopt a process known as *centring the trend*.

Progress Check 9.6

Calculate the second moving average for the period 1998:2 to 1999:1.

The corresponding moving average for this second period of four quarters is 27 728. We have the same problem of assigning this to any particular quarter. The centring process resolves the problem by taking the two moving averages and averaging them in turn, as shown in Table 9.8.

The average of the two moving averages – at 27 540 – can then be centred on the third quarter of 1995. This figure still contains an equal number of the four quarters of the year to include the different seasonal components. This average then becomes the estimate of the trend value. The calculations for the entire series are shown in Table 9.9 and the graph of the actual series, together with the trend, is shown in Figure 9.8.

The graph clearly shows the longer term trend in the variable over this period – a pattern that was not particularly evident from the original data. We are not yet in a position to forecast this trend into the future: this must wait until later, although even cursory visual inspection of the trend provides valuable management information that is not evident from the original series. The estimation of the trend provides a useful piece of information to the manager, allowing us to quantify the trend changes on a quarter-by-quarter basis.

Table 9.8   Centring the trend

Year	Quarter	Actual	Moving average	Trend
1998	1	32 347		
1998	2	24 361		
			27 353	
1998	3 . . .	21 159	. . .	27 540
			27 728	
1998	4	31 543		
1999	1	33 850		

Table 9.9 Trend calculations

Year	Domestic sales	Four-quarter moving average	Trend	Year	Domestic sales	Four-quarter moving average	Trend
1998:1	32 347					30 390	
				2003:2	26 563		30 570
1998:2	24 361					30 750	
		27 353		2003:3	24 238		30 634
1998:3	21 159		27 540			30 518	
		27 728		2003:4	35 568		30 669
1998:4	31 543		27 643			30 820	
		27 558		2004:1	35 703		31 063
1999:1	33 850		27 607			31 305	
		27 657		2004:2	27 771		31 178
1999:2	23 679		27 617			31 050	
		27 577		2004:3	26 176		31 106
1999:3	21 556		27 426			31 162	
		27 274		2004:4	34 549		31 183
1999:4	31 224		27 269			31 204	
		27 264		2005:1	36 149		31 159
2000:1	32 638		27 490			31 113	
		27 716		2005:2	27 941		31 271
2000:2	23 638		27 838			31 428	
		27 961		2005:3	25 815		31 593
2000:3	23 363		28 261			31 757	
		28 562		2005:4	35 807		31 701
2000:4	32 203		28 814			31 644	
		29 065		2006:1	37 467		31 542
2001:1	35 045		29 034			31 439	
		29 002		2006:2	27 489		31 308
2001:2	25 650		28 918			31 176	
		28 834		2006:3	24 994		30 896
2001:3	23 111		28 854			30 616	
		28 874		2006:4	34 754		30 510
2001:4	31 532		28 953			30 405	
		29 033		2007:1	35 226		30 466
2002:1	35 203		29 193			30 527	
		29 354		2007:2	26 645		30 648
2002:2	26 286		29 679			30 769	
		30 004		2007:3	25 484		30 701
2002:3	24 396		30 182			30 633	
		30 361		2007:4	35 721		30 621
2002:4	34 129		30 395			30 609	
		30 430		2008:1	34 683		30 548
2003:1	36 631		30 410			30 486	

Year	Domestic sales	Four-quarter moving average	Trend	Year	Domestic sales	Four-quarter moving average	Trend
2008:2	26549		30218	2013:2	25468		28591
		29950				28353	
2008:3	24990		30163	2013:3	22708		28032
		30376				27710	
2008:4	33578		30223	2013:4	30934		27543
		30070				27375	
2009:1	36388		29930	2014:1	31731		27330
		29791				27285	
2009:2	25324		29713	2014:2	24128		27152
		29635				27019	
2009:3	23872		29597	2014:3	22347		26996
		29559				26973	
2009:4	32957		29528	2014:4	29870		26975
		29497				26978	
2010:1	36083		29415	2015:1	31546		26956
		29333				26934	
2010:2	25075		29520	2015:2	24148		26938
		29708				26941	
2010:3	23215		29458	2015:3	22174		26986
		29208				27031	
2010:4	34459		29069	2015:4	29896		27014
		28929				26997	
2011:1	34085		28887	2016:1	31904		26954
		28845				26911	
2011:2	23956		28371	2016:2	24014		26952
		27897				26993	
2011:3	22881		27824	2016:3	21831		26833
		27752				26674	
2011:4	30664		27902	2016:4	30222		26595
		28052				26516	
2012:1	33506		28087	2017:1	30629		26465
		28123				26414	
2012:2	25157		28394	2017:2	23384		26382
		28666				26349	
2012:3	23164		28765	2017:3	21423		26497
		28865				26646	
2012:4	32836		28904	2017:4	29960		
		28942					
2013:1	34302		28886	2018:1	31816		
		28829					

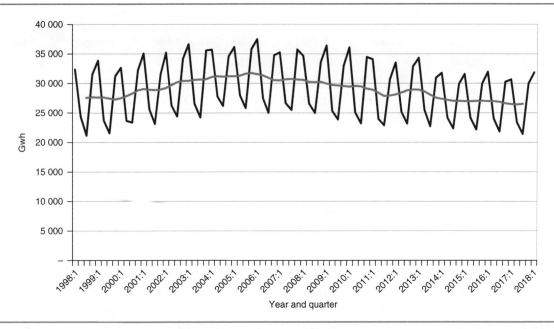

Figure 9.8 Domestic electricity sales and trend

The seasonal components

Using the trend values we can now estimate the seasonal components for each quarter. Remember the basic model:

$$D = T + S + R$$

If we ignore R, since by definition it is random and cannot be predicted, and rearrange we have:

$$S = D - T$$

That is, the seasonal components are the differences between the actual series and the trend. Table 9.10 shows these deviations.

So, for example, we see that in the fourth quarter of 2016 actual sales were around 3627 GwH above the long-term trend whilst in the second quarter of 2017 sales were around 2998 below the long-term trend.

Progress Check 9.7

Why are the deviations in the same quarters of the different years not the same?

To calculate the seasonal component for each quarter of the year, we can average these individual deviations, as shown in Table 9.11, by summing the deviations for a particular quarter and dividing by the number of deviations that were summed.

Table 9.10 Deviations from the trend

Year	Domestic	Trend	Deviation	Year	Domestic	Trend	Deviation
1998:1	32 347			2008:2	26 549	30 218	−3669.28
1998:2	24 361			2008:3	24 990	30 163	−5172.73
1998:3	21 159	27 540	−6381.38	2008:4	33 578	30 223	3354.80
1998:4	31 543	27 643	3900.00	2009:1	36 388	29 930	6457.70
1999:1	33 850	27 607	6242.63	2009:2	25 324	29 713	−4388.95
1999:2	23 679	27 617	−3938.13	2009:3	23 872	29 597	−5724.89
1999:3	21 556	27 426	−5869.77	2009:4	32 957	29 528	3428.89
1999:4	31 224	27 269	3954.84	2010:1	36 083	29 415	6668.28
2000:1	32 638	27 490	5148.31	2010:2	25 075	29 520	−4445.10
2000:2	23 638	27 838	−4200.21	2010:3	23 215	29 458	−6242.90
2000:3	23 363	28 261	−4898.52	2010:4	34 459	29 069	5389.96
2000:4	32 203	28 814	3389.43	2011:1	34 085	28 887	5197.93
2001:1	35 045	29 034	6011.33	2011:2	23 956	28 371	−4414.82
2001:2	25 650	28 918	−3268.60	2011:3	22 881	27 824	−4943.20
2001:3	23 111	28 854	−5743.14	2011:4	30 664	27 902	2762.43
2001:4	31 532	28 953	2578.46	2012:1	33 506	28 087	5418.78
2002:1	35 203	29 193	6009.09	2012:2	25 157	28 394	−3237.52
2002:2	26 286	29 679	−3392.83	2012:3	23 164	28 765	−5601.41
2002:3	24 396	30 182	−5785.75	2012:4	32 836	28 904	3932.35
2002:4	34 129	30 395	3734.03	2013:1	34 302	28 886	5416.71
2003:1	36 631	30 410	6220.82	2013:2	25 468	28 591	−3122.88
2003:2	26 563	30 570	−4007.22	2013:3	22 708	28 032	−5323.40
2003:3	24 238	30 634	−6396.04	2013:4	30 934	27 543	3391.07
2003:4	35 568	30 669	4899.13	2014:1	31 731	27 330	4400.93
2004:1	35 703	31 063	4640.79	2014:2	24 128	27 152	−3024.16
2004:2	27 771	31 178	−3406.07	2014:3	22 347	26 996	−4648.50
2004:3	26 176	31 106	−4929.61	2014:4	29 870	26 975	2894.64
2004:4	34 549	31 183	3366.66	2015:1	31 546	26 956	4589.58
2005:1	36 149	31 159	4990.50	2015:2	24 148	26 938	−2789.63
2005:2	27 941	31 271	−3329.92	2015:3	22 174	26 986	−4811.96
2005:3	25 815	31 593	−5777.86	2015:4	29 896	27 014	2882.56
2005:4	35 807	31 701	4105.69	2016:1	31 904	26 954	4949.80
2006:1	37 467	31 542	5925.36	2016:2	24 014	26 952	−2937.69
2006:2	27 489	31 308	−3818.18	2016:3	21 831	26 833	−5002.81
2006:3	24 994	30 896	−5902.25	2016:4	30 222	26 595	3626.79
2006:4	34 754	30 510	4243.59	2017:1	30 629	26 465	4163.88
2007:1	35 226	30 466	4760.41	2017:2	23 384	26 382	−2998.04
2007:2	26 645	30 648	−4003.51	2017:3	21 423	26 497	−5074.49
2007:3	25 484	30 701	−5217.25	2017:4	29 960		
2007:4	35 721	30 621	5100.21	2018:1	31 816		
2008:1	34 683	30 548	4135.45				

This averaging is necessary because the quarterly deviations include not only a seasonal component but also a random component, which by definition will vary from one year to the next. Such random factors in this case might, for example, include a period of unseasonal weather which will temporarily affect electricity sales or an irregular event like the World Cup which boost TV viewing and therefore domestic electricity consumption. In other situations, a variable may be affected by industrial action, a change in government policy, a media campaign or an event such as the eruption of a volcano affecting regional air traffic. By definition such random factors will not occur every year. We see from Table 9.11 that there is considerable consistency in the variation within each quarter. All the deviations in Quarter 4, for example, are positive and around the same sort of value. If this had not been the case we might wish to check first our calculations for any arithmetical error and then the stability of the seasonal pattern of the data over time. It might be we had a data series without a consistent seasonal pattern.

If we now take the mean deviation for each quarter we obtain the results shown in the final row of Table 9.11. So, on average, sales in the first quarter of the year are around 5300 GwH above trend whilst in Quarter 3 they are around 5500 below trend. However, these deviations typically require a final adjustment before we can refer to them as seasonal components. The sum of these deviations should total to zero, since the sum of the four quarterly seasonal components should cancel each other out over a year. They rarely do, however, and must be adjusted accordingly. If we total the four mean deviations we find they total -4.44 rather than zero. The deviations are in total -4.44 less than they should be. Accordingly, we need to adjust them upwards by this amount. We do this by arbitrarily increasing each quarter's mean deviation by one quarter of 4.44 to give the seasonal components:

	1	2	3	4
Seasonal component	5335.23	-3598.51	-5471.28	3734.56

The interpretation of these results is straightforward. They represent the typical impact of each quarter on domestic electricity sales. In the first quarter of the year, for example, we would expect domestic sales to be some 5335 GwH above the trend or long-term average sales. However, this increase in sales will be temporary, as we expect sales in the following quarter of the year to fall back by some 3600 GwH. Calculating – and understanding – such seasonal factors is a key part of understanding why some important business variable has changed over time. Seasonal change in a given variable has happened because of the time of the year and not because of our own organisation's performance. Without such analysis we might misinterpret such changes and take inappropriate business decisions.

The seasonally adjusted series

The final part of the decomposition process is to produce what is known as the *seasonally adjusted* series. Effectively this is the original series but with the seasonal component removed, thus showing the underlying trend together with random fluctuations. As before, the original model can be rearranged to give:

$$D - S = T + R$$

with $(D - S)$ being the seasonally adjusted series. Table 9.12 shows the calculations and Figure 9.9 the corresponding graph.

Table 9.11   Deviations per quarter

Year	Quarter			
	1	2	3	4
1998			−6381.38	3900.00
1999	6242.63	−3938.13	−5869.77	3954.84
2000	5148.31	−4200.21	−4898.52	3389.43
2001	6011.33	−3268.60	−5743.14	2578.46
2002	6009.09	−3392.83	−5785.75	3734.03
2003	6220.82	−4007.22	−6396.04	4899.13
2004	4640.79	−3406.07	−4929.61	3366.66
2005	4990.50	−3329.92	−5777.86	4105.69
2006	5925.36	−3818.18	−5902.25	4243.59
2007	4760.41	−4003.51	−5217.25	5100.21
2008	4135.45	−3669.28	−5172.73	3354.80
2009	6457.70	−4388.95	−5724.89	3428.89
2010	6668.28	−4445.10	−6242.90	5389.96
2011	5197.93	−4414.82	−4943.20	2762.43
2012	5418.78	−3237.52	−5601.41	3932.35
2013	5416.71	−3122.88	−5323.40	3391.07
2014	4400.93	−3024.16	−4648.50	2894.64
2015	4589.58	−2789.63	−4811.96	2882.56
2016	4949.80	−2937.69	−5002.81	3626.79
2017	4163.88	−2998.04	−5074.49	
2018				
Mean deviation	5334.12	−3599.62	−5472.39	3733.45

Note how the seasonally adjusted series is slightly more irregular than the trend, since it incorporates random changes in the series as well as the trend. If we wish to get a proper sense of underlying performance, then it is the seasonally adjusted data we must examine and analyse. This has had the seasonal effects stripped out so better shows underlying performance, although it does include random factors also. However, at times it is these random factors that we may want to examine. If we return to Figure 9.9 you'll see that one point has been indicated with an arrow. This corresponds to the fourth quarter of 2010. We see from the figure that seasonally adjusted sales for this quarter are higher than we would expect based on the seasonal pattern alone. This implies that this quarter's sales have been pushed higher by some random factor – by some factor not allowed for in our calculations.

In fact this quarter saw two periods of unseasonably cold weather – dubbed the Big Freeze by the media. Temperatures fell below −10 °C on several nights and on

EasyJet proves some airlines are more equal than others

By Matthew Vincent

Source: Pete Pakham/Shutterstock.com

EasyJet said on Tuesday that the load factor on its aircraft increased by 2.1 percentage points in the three months to December 31, to 92.1 per cent. So, with flight capacity increasing by 5.5 per cent, quarterly revenue rose 14 per cent to a forecast-beating £1.14bn.

Source: FT, 23 January 2018.

Passenger load factor is a key performance metric for airlines and is closely watched by financial analysts and investors. It measures the percentage of aircraft seats sold. The higher the load factor the more passengers you're carrying and the more revenue you're earning (and the lower the per passenger carbon footprint of the flight). However, load factors can be very seasonal as both EasyJet and Ryanair – its main rival – know. The chart shows monthly load factors for both airlines from 2011. Both airlines have a similar seasonal pattern – high load factors in the summer and lower load factors in the winter. Interestingly the seasonal variation has reduced over the last few years as the airlines use their marketing and pricing strategies to reduce variation, Ryanair doing better here than EasyJet. Also interesting is that EasyJet started out with higher load factors but has recently been overtaken by Ryanair.

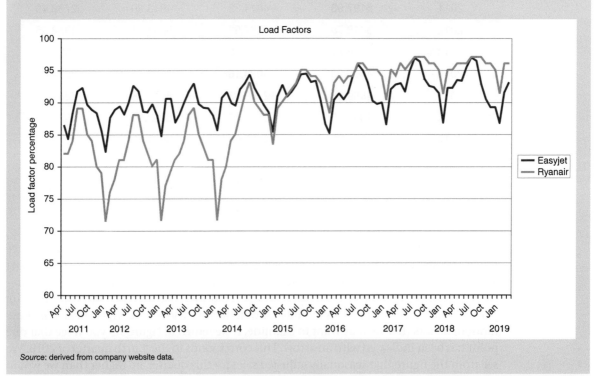

Source: derived from company website data.

Seasonality is an important factor in understanding performance

occasion below −20 °C in northern Scotland. This spell of snow and freezing temperatures occurred unusually early in winter, with the snowfalls seen as the most significant and widespread in late November and early December since late November 1965. Unsurprisingly domestic electricity sales rose during this period as families struggled to cope with the cold. In fact, our analysis allows us to estimate the impact of this weather

Table 9.12   Seasonally adjusted sales: GwH

Year	Domestic sales	Seasonal component	Seasonally adjusted sales	Year	Domestic sales	Seasonal component	Seasonally adjusted sales
1998:1	32347	5335.23	27011.77	2008:2	26549	−3598.51	30147.17
1998:2	24361	−3598.51	27959.51	2008:3	24990	−5471.28	30461.67
1998:3	21159	−5471.28	26630.28	2008:4	33578	3734.56	29843.39
1998:4	31543	3734.56	27808.44	2009:1	36388	5335.23	31052.75
1999:1	33850	5335.23	28514.77	2009:2	25324	−3598.51	28922.41
1999:2	23679	−3598.51	27277.51	2009:3	23872	−5471.28	29343.46
1999:3	21556	−5471.28	27027.28	2009:4	32957	3734.56	29222.18
1999:4	31224	3734.56	27489.44	2010:1	36083	5335.23	30747.70
2000:1	32638	5335.23	27302.96	2010:2	25075	−3598.51	28673.67
2000:2	23638	−3598.51	27236.41	2010:3	23215	−5471.28	28686.61
2000:3	23363	−5471.28	28834.11	2010:4	34459	3734.56	30723.97
2000:4	32203	3734.56	28468.52	2011:1	34085	5335.23	28749.60
2001:1	35045	5335.23	29709.70	2011:2	23956	−3598.51	27554.55
2001:2	25650	−3598.51	29248.08	2011:3	22881	−5471.28	28352.36
2001:3	23111	−5471.28	28582.09	2011:4	30664	3734.56	26929.91
2001:4	31532	3734.56	27797.12	2012:1	33506	5335.23	28171.01
2002:1	35203	5335.23	29867.34	2012:2	25157	−3598.51	28755.21
2002:2	26286	−3598.51	29884.57	2012:3	23164	−5471.28	28635.04
2002:3	24396	−5471.28	29867.69	2012:4	32836	3734.56	29101.37
2002:4	34129	3734.56	30394.80	2013:1	34302	5335.23	28967.05
2003:1	36631	5335.23	31295.78	2013:2	25468	−3598.51	29066.51
2003:2	26563	−3598.51	30161.58	2013:3	22708	−5471.28	28179.61
2003:3	24238	−5471.28	29709.49	2013:4	30934	3734.56	27199.31
2003:4	35568	3734.56	31833.91	2014:1	31731	5335.23	26395.86
2004:1	35703	5335.23	30368.20	2014:2	24128	−3598.51	27726.38
2004:2	27771	−3598.51	31369.94	2014:3	22347	−5471.28	27818.62
2004:3	26176	−5471.28	31647.51	2014:4	29870	3734.56	26135.24
2004:4	34549	3734.56	30814.82	2015:1	31546	5335.23	26210.33
2005:1	36149	5335.23	30813.96	2015:2	24148	−3598.51	27746.50
2005:2	27941	−3598.51	31539.22	2015:3	22174	−5471.28	27645.09
2005:3	25815	−5471.28	31285.95	2015:4	29896	3734.56	26161.89
2005:4	35807	3734.56	32072.00	2016:1	31904	5335.23	26568.87
2006:1	37467	5335.23	32131.95	2016:2	24014	−3598.51	27612.93
2006:2	27489	−3598.51	31087.91	2016:3	21831	−5471.28	27301.94
2006:3	24994	−5471.28	30464.89	2016:4	30222	3734.56	26487.50
2006:4	34754	3734.56	31019.16	2017:1	30629	5335.23	25294.10
2007:1	35226	5335.23	29890.98	2017:2	23384	−3598.51	26982.18
2007:2	26645	−3598.51	30243.04	2017:3	21423	−5471.28	26894.10
2007:3	25484	−5471.28	30955.14	2017:4	29960	3734.56	26225.48
2007:4	35721	3734.56	31986.87	2018:1	31816	5335.23	26480.81
2008:1	34683	5335.23	29347.78				

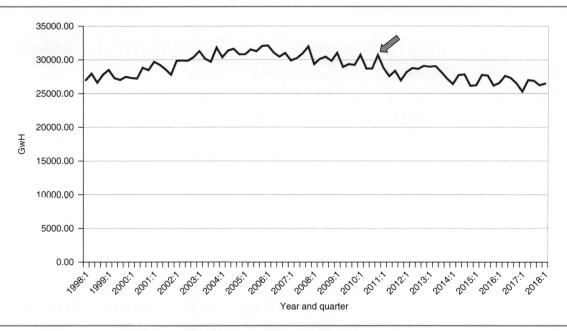

Figure 9.9 Seasonally adjusted domestic electricity sales

on sales. We know that the mean seasonal component for the fourth quarter of a year is 3735 GwH. However, we see from Table 9.9 that in 2010:4 the actual deviation from the trend is 5390 GwH – 1655 GwH above the norm for this time of year. So, we have a pretty good estimate of how much this cold period affected electricity sales. This information will be useful to the power companies who have to manage electricity generation and supply when abnormal conditions occur.

Forecasting with a time series

Forecasting a time-series variable such as ours requires two separate elements to be forecast:

- the trend;
- the seasonal components.

It is usual to assume that the seasonal components will remain unchanged, so we are only required to forecast the trend. The actual mechanics of forecasting the trend must wait until the next chapter, when we have introduced regression as a forecasting technique. However, to illustrate the process of developing a forecast for the time series we will take the forecast for the trend as given. In fact, this situation illustrates the potential of such forecasting methods as an aid to decision making.

Assume we are trying to forecast for the last quarter of 2018 to help with our operational planning. Looking at the trend in Figure 9.8 and the seasonally adjusted data in Figure 9.9, we might develop two scenarios. The first (Scenario A) is to use the trend over the period from 2006 onwards to produce a forecast for the future trend. We see that the trend changes from this period onwards. Up to 2005 the trend was generally upwards whilst from 2006 it is generally downwards. An alternative scenario is to say that the downward trend from 2006 seems to change in 2011 with an upturn in sales but then followed by further decline. So we might want to examine Scenario B using trend

Statistical flaw: Black Friday casts pall over reliability of retail sales figures

By Gavin Jackson

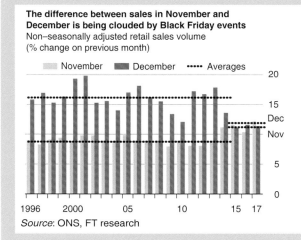

The difference between sales in November and December is being clouded by Black Friday events
Non–seasonally adjusted retail sales volume
(% change on previous month)

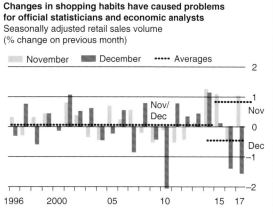

Changes in shopping habits have caused problems for official statisticians and economic analysts
Seasonally adjusted retail sales volume
(% change on previous month)

Source: ONS, FT research

The growth of the Black Friday event has distorted retail sales figures and cast doubt on the official statistics about Britain's huge retail sector. For the past four years, the statistics have shown sharply rising sales in November followed by a slowdown in December, but the Office for National Statistics suggested its seasonal adjustment had been skewed by rapidly changing shopping habits. . . .

Rhian Murphy, senior statistician for retail sales at the ONS, said "five years of a consistent pattern" were usually needed to make these adjustments accurate. But Black Friday has evolved every year since its introduction, growing from a single day of discounts to a weekend, then several weeks. The flawed seasonal adjustment means the figures are not a reliable indicator of the real state of the British consumer this Christmas. Changes in the pattern of demand risk wrongfooting analysts who have been examining retail sales data to understand the impact of higher consumer prices since the Brexit vote.

The miscalculation may have knock-on effects. The ONS uses the seasonally adjusted three-month on three-month growth rate of retail sales, among other data, to calculate quarterly economic growth. Seasonal adjustments are essential, and it is important to smooth out the sharp variations over the festive period to get a better sense of the overall health of the sector.

"As [we produce] a national statistic we influence a lot of policy: things like interest rates are dependent on how the economy is doing," Ms Murphy said. "So we really need to know the underlying growth that isn't influenced by Christmas."

While the ONS has partially managed to adapt to consumers doing more of their Christmas shopping in November, the statisticians have not managed to fully account for the changes, she said.

Since the Brexit vote the volume of retail sales has become a key barometer of how falling consumer confidence and rising prices have affected spending and the overall economy.

Christmas is the most important sales period for retail, which makes up about 6 per cent of national income. About 30 per cent of yearly sales are made in the final three months of the year, according to the unadjusted figures.

These unadjusted figures show the monthly pattern of Christmas spending changed in 2014: the volume of sales has risen more than 10 per cent in November compared with October for the past four years, compared with increases of about 8 per cent in the decade before.

This has been at the expense of growth in December, where monthly increases are down from about 17 per cent to about 11 per cent. These double-digit rises are then adjusted to get to the far lower headline growth rates. These adjusted figures in the same period have shown a consistent pattern of expansion in November, followed by contraction in December, with an average month-on-month increase of more than 0.7 per cent in November compared with October. This has been followed by an average month-on-month contraction of more than 0.4 per cent in December.

Having accurate and reliable seasonally adjusted data is important but it's not easy to get right.

data only from around 2013 when decline occurs again. Naturally, bearing in mind the qualitative approaches we discussed earlier in the chapter, a number of other alternative scenarios could easily be developed and quantified. However, in the context of the two we have put forward, denoted as Scenario A and Scenario B, we can quantify the trend projection for 2018:4 as:

	Trend forecast for 2018:4
Scenario A	25 604
Scenario B	25 709

(Explanation as to how we arrived at these numbers will have to wait until Chapter 10.) To obtain a forecast of the actual domestic sales, we must add in the seasonal factor for Quarter 4 of 3734.56 to give:

	Series forecast for 2018:4
Scenario A	29 338
Scenario B	29 445

Although the mechanics of producing a time-series forecast are straightforward, the two scenarios illustrate the role of such forecasts in the decision-making process. The two forecasts are different: over 100 GwH. However, this information provides a starting point for managers to consider and assess the future.

Models which are not quarterly

There is no reason why we should not wish to apply these principles to variables which show data in a format other than quarterly. Variables which are monthly can readily be analysed in the same way. The only differences would relate to the periods covered by the moving-average calculations – which would now need to be averaged over 12 months rather than 4 quarters – and to the fact that we will derive 12 seasonal factors rather than 4. Indeed, a variable relating to any period within a year can in principle have such a model developed. Data which is daily would be just as suitable, although the calculations become somewhat tedious unless using a specialist package and the quantity of data required becomes cumbersome.

Additive and multiplicative models

The time-series model we have developed is technically known as an *additive* model since the components of the time series are added together: $T + S + R$. The alternative model is known as the *multiplicative* since it denotes the time series as:

$$D = T \times S \times R$$

In practice the multiplicative model is the one more commonly used. The reason for this lies in the trend movement of the variable. The additive model is adequate as long as the trend in the variable is relatively stable. For technical reasons, if the trend shows a marked change over time, either positive or negative, then the multiplicative model will generally be more appropriate. Fortunately, the calculations involved in the multiplicative model are similar to those we have already developed:

- Estimate the trend using moving averages as in the additive model.
- Estimate the quarterly deviation by dividing D by T. Whereas in the additive model we subtracted T from D to find the quarterly differences, for the multiplicative model we calculate a ratio instead. As ratios they will vary about the value 1.0.
- The seasonal factors will then be estimated by ensuring that the four quarterly ratios total to 4.0 and adjusting the average deviations accordingly. A seasonal factor of, say, 1.05 for a data series using this type of model indicates that the data is typically 5 per cent above the trend in this quarter so the average deviations need to be adjusted down by this amount to give the seasonal component values.

We'll see an example of the calculations for the multiplicative model in the worked example. The seasonal factors can be used in exactly the same way as in the additive model, both for analysis and for forecasting.

Time-series decomposition with computer packages

Normally, we would use spreadsheet facilities for performing the calculations required for time-series decomposition. Spreadsheets have in-built functions for calculating moving averages, which can help with this task, although you should check carefully on the exact method your spreadsheet uses (perhaps with a set of data where you already know the results). There are also specialist computer packages available which will perform the time-series decomposition calculations automatically. Such packages usually have sophisticated algorithms for smoothing out the random terms.

Worked example

We have been asked to undertake some analysis on trends in air passenger traffic in the UK. We have obtained the data shown in Table 9.13. This shows, on a quarterly basis, the total number of passengers travelling through UK airports from 1990 to 2018. The first step is to show the data on a time-series graph as in Figure 9.10.

We see a strong seasonal pattern each year, with passenger numbers increasing in Quarters 2 and 3 and falling in Quarters 4 and 1. We also see an upward trend in overall numbers from 1990 to around 2007, with the trend flattening after this. Analysis of such data is clearly of interest to a number of decision makers. Governments will need to consider long-term travel trends to assist in planning for new, or expanded, airports; tax revenue may be affected given taxes levied on air travel; comparisons with other countries may help in understanding the UK's international competitiveness; government agencies responsible for security, immigration and customs will be concerned about planning for staffing requirements; companies responsible for running the UK airports will need to consider issues such as airport capacity, staffing, airport facilities, car parking; individual airlines may want to compare their own passenger statistics to assess changing market share. And this analysis will have to be done to understand long-term trends but also variability through the year. Given the non-stationary trend, the multiplicative model is appropriate. You may want to do the full calculations yourself to confirm our analysis.

Table 9.13   UK air passengers 1990–2018 quarterly

Year	Terminal passengers	Year	Terminal passengers	Year	Terminal passengers
1990.1	20 289 163	1999.4	39 271 250	2009.3	68 015 509
1990.2	27 657 383	2000.1	35 841 660	2009.4	49 699 093
1990.3	33 293 638	2000.2	47 513 866	2010.1	44 022 435
1990.4	22 456 038	2000.3	56 324 086	2010.2	52 865 514
1991.1	17 663 921	2000.4	42 155 274	2010.3	67 963 271
1991.2	24 803 646	2001.1	37 627 234	2010.4	48 493 640
1991.3	31 865 789	2001.2	49 233 970	2011.1	44 284 491
1991.4	22 950 007	2001.3	57 062 199	2011.2	59 151 983
1992.1	20 836 846	2001.4	39 076 743	2011.3	68 842 915
1992.1	28 624 220	2002.1	37 984 761	2011.4	49 834 705
1992.3	34 731 830	2002.2	48 816 747	2012.1	45 183 695
1992.4	23 890 774	2002.3	58 969 804	2012.2	59 389 254
1993.1	21 813 844	2002.4	44 711 949	2012.3	68 169 462
1993.2	29 893 859	2003.1	40 536 305	2012.4	50 738 917
1993.3	36 721 840	2003.2	51 388 971	2013.1	45 500 497
1993.4	25 796 605	2003.3	62 086 369	2013.2	61 576 303
1994.1	23 649 717	2003.4	47 903 657	2013.3	71 434 402
1994.2	32 225 758	2004.1	44 390 941	2013.4	52 815 849
1994.3	40 266 270	2004.2	56 164 286	2014.1	46 891 769
1994.4	28 089 310	2004.3	66 143 405	2014.2	64 731 980
1995.1	24 965 585	2004.4	50 950 860	2014.3	74 161 954
1995.2	34 747 267	2005.1	47 790 049	2014.4	55 565 853
1995.3	41 821 523	2005.2	59 666 982	2015.1	50 376 898
1995.4	29 869 887	2005.3	69 681 481	2015.2	67 368 945
1996.1	27 505 427	2005.4	53 022 087	2015.3	78 220 308
1996.2	35 695 908	2006.1	48 880 997	2015.4	58 588 390
1996.3	42 588 542	2006.2	62 985 095	2016.1	54 275 494
1996.4	32 080 672	2006.3	71 079 230	2016.2	70 759 851
1997.1	29 296 610	2006.4	54 303 524	2016.3	83 282 906
1997.2	38 838 411	2007.1	50 317 670	2016.4	63 171 531
1997.3	46 042 973	2007.2	63 295 108	2017.1	57 979 112
1997.4	34 576 908	2007.3	73 552 123	2017.2	76 999 700
1998.1	31 433 937	2007.4	55 656 557	2017.3	87 682 044
1998.2	42 073 694	2008.1	51 533 621	2017.4	64 988 456
1998.3	50 155 278	2008.2	63 011 826	2018.1	58 979 851
1998.4	37 318 729	2008.3	72 095 685	2018.2	78 873 142
1999.1	34 010 903	2008.4	51 655 981		
1999.2	44 032 553	2009.1	45 094 273		
1999.3	52 749 216	2009.2	58 066 419		

Source: Office for National Statistics
Data file 9-13

The trend is shown in Figure 9.11. We now see that from 1990 to around 2007 there was a strong upward trend in passenger numbers (although with a noticeable slight dip in 2001–02).

After 2008 the trend was negative, showing a sharp decline in numbers. From 2010 the trend has been positive again. Clearly, as with the other forecasting models in this chapter, we do not know the causes of the trend – we simply quantify. However, it's not difficult to speculate that the downward trend from 2008 is probably associated with the financial crash and economic downturn that hit the UK and other economies at this time.

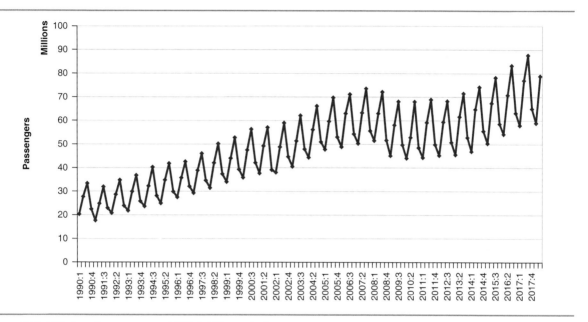

Figure 9.10 UK airport passengers 1990–2018 quarterly

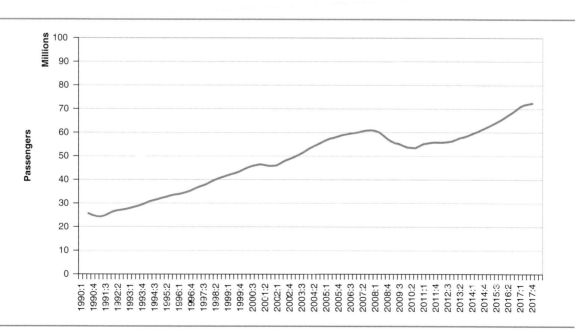

Figure 9.11 UK airport passengers 1990–2018 trend line

The seasonal calculations are:

Quarter	1	2	3	4
Seasonal component	0.8092	1.0514	1.2383	0.9011

So we see that Quarter 3 has a seasonal peak of almost 24 per cent above the trend whilst Quarter 1 has a variation almost 20 per cent below the trend. A few other points can be made. The first relates to forecasting the trend if we wish to estimate the longer-term movement in passenger numbers. In this case we'd probably be better producing a trend forecast for the period from 2010 onwards given the downturn that happened in the few years before. The second relates to examining 'random' events that have occurred during the period. For example, we see from Figure 9.11 there was a temporary drop in numbers around 2001. Examination of Figure 9.10 shows a dip in numbers in Quarter 3 but particularly in Quarter 4 of 2001. It's not difficult to identify the reason. The terrorist attacks took place in the USA on 11 September 2001 (towards the end of Quarter 3). The impact on air passenger travel – initially through mass cancellation of flights and then on passenger confidence in safety – is visible and could readily be quantified. The mean seasonal deviation for Quarter 4 is 0.9011. The actual deviation for Quarter 4 of 2001 was 0.8534 (the calculation is not shown here) some five percentage points lower. Although not evident from the figures, another major 'random' event took place in the second quarter of 2010. Volcanic eruptions in Iceland that started in April of that year caused enormous disruption to air travel across Europe, with knock-on effects around the world. Over 20 countries closed their airspace to commercial air traffic and it has been estimated that this affected about 10 million travellers worldwide. In the UK, analysis of the seasonal calculations (again not shown here) indicate that whilst the normal seasonal variation in Quarter 2 is 1.0514 (i.e. 5 per cent above the trend) the actual seasonal deviation in 2010 was 0.9883 – around 1 per cent *below* the trend. The final point concerns the stability of the seasonal components over time. By averaging seasonal variations we are assuming that the typical variation – per quarter, per month or whatever – will continue in the future. This won't necessarily be the case. We see that the big seasonal peak occurs in Quarter 3 and is almost certainly linked to holidays taken by UK residents flying overseas (and back again) for their annual holiday. Traditionally in the UK annual family holidays – often for two weeks – would take place in July and August. However, if we examine the individual quarter variations (not shown here) we notice that these are changing over time. In 1990 for example, the Quarter 3 variation is calculated as 1.3007 – 30 per cent above the trend. By 2017 this variation had dropped to 1.2171 – 22 per cent above the trend. In other words, There's some flattening out of seasonality over this period. Reasons for this are not difficult to find. An increasing market for short breaks through the year, particularly amongst younger adults and the retired; the increase in cheap budget flights where fares can rise very steeply at peak times. This implies that we'd need to be cautious about extrapolating the historical seasonal variability into the future.

QADM IN ACTION

Retail supermarket, UK

For reasons of commercial confidentiality the organisation used for this application cannot be named. Similarly the data used to illustrate this application have been adjusted by a constant.

A large retail organisation operates a number of retail supermarkets in the UK. These range in size, location and profitability. Some of the stores are relatively small, operating in the high street. Others are located at out-of-town sites, typically as part of a larger retail complex. One supermarket in the group had approximately 15 000 square feet of floor space and formed part of a small retail park that had been established on the fringes of a large market town some 20 years ago. The supermarket had not been purpose-built at the time but had been converted from an existing industrial building. In the late 1980s a larger retail complex had been built on the opposite side of the town. This comprised a number of well-known retail organisations offering furnishings, electrical goods and DIY. On that site one of the company's direct competitors had opened a purpose-built supermarket with almost twice the floor space. This competition had directly affected trading performance of the company's supermarket.

After a major assessment of the situation, the company decided to undertake a programme of varied promotional activities to try to win back customers and improve trading performance. The promotional period lasted approximately 15 months in total. During that time a variety of activities were introduced for short periods: local media promotions, bonus products when a customer spent more than a stated amount, free local bus services to and from the supermarket. At the time, management of the supermarket felt that these initiatives had had a positive impact on trading performance. Towards the end of this promotional period, however, senior management in the company felt that the long run of promotions had probably had all the effect they were likely to have and the promotional programme was halted. Some two years after the end of the promotional campaign a more detailed analysis of the supermarket's performance over this period was undertaken using the principles of time-series analysis.

Figure 9.12 shows the supermarket's turnover over the relevant five-year period. The supermarket operates a reporting system such that the financial year

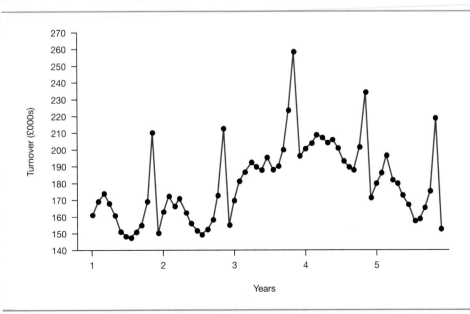

Figure 9.12 Supermarket turnover over five-year period

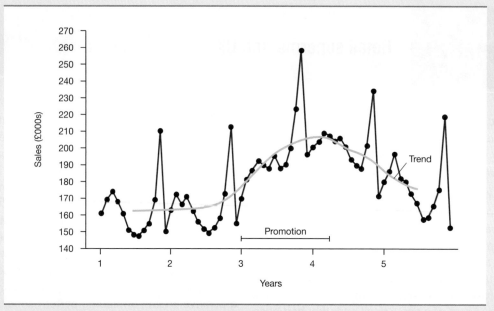

Figure 9.13 Supermarket turnover and trend

begins in February each year and turnover figures are reported on a four-weekly basis. This means that over the year there are 13 four-week reporting periods. From Figure 9.12 a number of points are evident:

- For the first two years of this period turnover was relatively stable but low. The competing supermarket had opened some 18 months prior to Year 1.
- From Year 3 a positive change in turnover begins to appear.
- During Year 4 turnover began to decline.
- The Christmas effect is very marked each year.

A centred moving-average trend was calculated for the data and superimposed on the actual turnover. This is shown in Figure 9.13. The change in trend is evident from the end of Year 2, with strong growth

through Year 3. From the beginning of Year 4, however, the trend reverses into a continuing decline. The duration of the promotional activities is also shown on the diagram. These commenced at the start of Year 3 and continued, at varying rates, until the first quarter of Year 4.

Although cause and effect cannot be established, it is evident from the time-series analysis that the strong upward movement in the trend coincides with the period of active promotion and that when these promotional activities cease the trend moves into decline. The supermarket's manager was convinced that the commencement/cessation of the promotional campaign was a major contributory factor to the trend changes and that, with hindsight, the decision to stop the promotional campaign had been inappropriate.

Summary

In this chapter we have considered some of the issues involved in business forecasting. We have seen that generally two approaches can be adopted: to develop qualitative forecasts or quantitative forecasts. Qualitative methods use opinions, judgements and expertise to develop some numerical forecast about a variable. Quantitative methods that we have introduced in this chapter are built around the principles of moving averages. Such averages can help smooth out random fluctuations in a variable and allow us to produce reasonably accurate forecasts in situations where forecast accuracy is not the sole criterion used to assess a forecasting model's suitability. Such moving averages are also at the heart of time-series decomposition. This is a particularly important technique for analysing, and then projecting into the future, some variable which exhibits a seasonal pattern. Given that many business variables will exhibit such patterns, it is important for a manager to be able to quantify such seasonal variability and to take this into account when trying to assess the underlying movement in some variable.

Exercises

1   Return to the unit sales data used in this chapter. Apply the exponential-smoothing model to this data using values for a of 0.15, 0.2, 0.25 and 0.3. Assess the accuracy of each choice of a and decide which you would use to forecast future values.

2   Consider the two sets of sales data in Table 9.14. Apply the exponential-smoothing model to this data with a variety of values. What do you observe about the accuracy of the model over time in the two series?

3   The following exercises all relate to the development of a suitable time-series decomposition model for the data shown. In each case you should adopt the following procedure:

   (a) Plot the original data as a time-series graph.

   (b) Determine whether an additive or multiplicative model would be appropriate.

   (c) For the model chosen to determine the trend.

   (d) Determine the seasonal components.

Table 9.14   Weekly sales

Week	Sales units	Sales units
1	246	246
2	256	256
3	255	255
4	248	248
5	263	263
6	254	254
7	306	306
8	308	338
9	304	372
10	307	412
11	306	459
12	308	514
13	305	570
14	301	628
15	303	693

Data file 9X-14

(e) Determine the seasonally adjusted series.

(f) Plot the seasonally adjusted series on the same graph as (a).

(g) From the seasonal components try to determine what factors might be causing the seasonal pattern you have estimated and whether the seasonal pattern is likely to remain stable in the immediate future.

You may also want to update the information shown in the tables and see whether the seasonal pattern calculated shows any signs of change over time.

(i) Table 9.15 shows sales of electricity (in TwH) to

- customers in England and Wales (from 2002);
- customers in Scotland (from 2002);
- industrial customers in the UK (from 1995);

Analyse the trends and seasonal patterns for the three sets of data.

Table 9.15   Electricity sales to selected customer segments

| Year | Quarter | Sales of electricity to consumers | | |
		England and Wales	Scotland	Industrial
1995	Quarter 1			25.00
1995	Quarter 2			23.28
1995	Quarter 3			23.53
1995	Quarter 4			23.70
1996	Quarter 1			26.44
1996	Quarter 2			23.86
1996	Quarter 3			24.66
1996	Quarter 4			25.31
1997	Quarter 1			25.55
1997	Quarter 2			23.98
1997	Quarter 3			24.47
1997	Quarter 4			25.03
1998	Quarter 1			25.97
1998	Quarter 2			23.96
1998	Quarter 3			23.40
1998	Quarter 4			24.13
1999	Quarter 1			26.44
1999	Quarter 2			24.05
1999	Quarter 3			24.48
1999	Quarter 4			24.25
2000	Quarter 1			25.08
2000	Quarter 2			25.03
2000	Quarter 3			25.60
2000	Quarter 4			26.32
2001	Quarter 1			27.83
2001	Quarter 2			25.56

Year	Quarter	Sales of electricity to consumers		
		England and Wales	Scotland	Industrial
2001	Quarter 3			24.25
2001	Quarter 4			24.59
2002	Quarter 1	77.83	8.98	26.51
2002	Quarter 2	65.72	6.97	24.35
2002	Quarter 3	63.53	6.36	23.39
2002	Quarter 4	75.02	8.02	24.86
2003	Quarter 1	77.71	8.35	25.50
2003	Quarter 2	67.67	6.67	24.98
2003	Quarter 3	64.99	6.16	24.52
2003	Quarter 4	76.53	8.42	24.28
2004	Quarter 1	80.41	8.18	25.17
2004	Quarter 2	64.02	6.69	22.49
2004	Quarter 3	65.09	6.73	23.66
2004	Quarter 4	76.52	8.52	27.55
2005	Quarter 1	78.90	9.09	27.11
2005	Quarter 2	69.07	7.24	26.67
2005	Quarter 3	65.51	6.39	24.94
2005	Quarter 4	79.18	8.26	27.16
2006	Quarter 1	81.53	8.56	27.24
2006	Quarter 2	67.37	7.03	24.59
2006	Quarter 3	65.91	6.32	25.07
2006	Quarter 4	76.39	8.05	25.51
2007	Quarter 1	78.21	8.49	26.24
2007	Quarter 2	67.52	6.85	25.72
2007	Quarter 3	66.65	6.41	25.53
2007	Quarter 4	79.66	8.04	27.01
2008	Quarter 1	80.71	8.78	28.43
2008	Quarter 2	68.66	7.18	26.41
2008	Quarter 3	66.43	6.57	25.47
2008	Quarter 4	77.38	8.06	27.07
2009	Quarter 1	75.78	8.99	23.97
2009	Quarter 2	65.66	4.48	22.46
2009	Quarter 3	62.48	6.58	22.54
2009	Quarter 4	75.16	6.06	26.04
2010	Quarter 1	79.80	6.71	24.96
2010	Quarter 2	67.00	3.88	23.98
2010	Quarter 3	64.74	4.01	24.09
2010	Quarter 4	78.83	6.01	25.94
2011	Quarter 1	77.05	6.82	25.01
2011	Quarter 2	65.03	3.97	23.27
2011	Quarter 3	62.26	6.14	23.55

(Continued)

Table 9.15 (*Continued*)

Year	Quarter	Sales of electricity to consumers		
		England and Wales	Scotland	Industrial
2011	Quarter 4	70.62	7.93	24.23
2012	Quarter 1	73.72	7.65	23.31
2012	Quarter 2	63.37	6.81	22.88
2012	Quarter 3	61.73	6.45	23.04
2012	Quarter 4	72.88	7.83	24.27
2013	Quarter 1	75.63	7.99	24.34
2013	Quarter 2	62.70	6.88	22.77
2013	Quarter 3	61.15	6.59	23.02
2013	Quarter 4	70.52	7.52	23.38
2014	Quarter 1	70.74	7.94	22.44
2014	Quarter 2	60.81	6.41	21.56
2014	Quarter 3	60.76	6.03	22.19
2014	Quarter 4	67.38	7.07	21.69
2015	Quarter 1	70.37	7.55	23.63
2015	Quarter 2	60.02	6.29	21.90
2015	Quarter 3	59.37	5.78	22.03
2015	Quarter 4	66.30	6.89	20.66
2016	Quarter 1	69.80	7.12	21.49
2016	Quarter 2	59.35	5.94	20.95
2016	Quarter 3	57.94	5.57	21.23
2016	Quarter 4	68.01	6.97	22.09
2017	Quarter 1	67.14	7.10	21.93
2017	Quarter 2	58.07	5.73	20.72
2017	Quarter 3	57.42	5.51	21.68
2017	Quarter 4	67.36	6.85	22.54
2018	Quarter 1	69.41	7.07	22.13
2018	Quarter 2	57.75	5.66	20.92
2018	Quarter 3	57.13	5.46	21.80

Source: Energy Trends
Data file 9X-15

(ii) Table 9.16 shows monthly data for the number of marriages taking place in England and Wales over the last 50 years or so. Draft a report for a company that specialises in providing wedding services.

Table 9.16 Marriages in England and Wales (000s)

Year	Total	January	February	March	April	May	June	July	August	September	October	November	December
2015	245158	6719	9903	12487	16313	27575	24823	32106	41525	28548	20653	11463	13043
2014	252811	6483	9639	13374	19424	28857	25068	30624	44433	28583	19719	13039	13568
2013	240854	6241	8859	15444	18307	25628	26344	26602	40556	28313	18413	13127	13020
2012	262801	5859	9701	15144	20626	25332	34914	29648	37539	34281	19856	13615	16286
2011	249133	6016	8672	10893	19844	24086	28337	35726	36350	31604	20673	13300	13632
2010	243808	6643	8744	11388	17034	26833	25746	34151	36562	30761	21472	11309	13165
2009	232443	6679	9818	10311	15623	25939	23428	29174	38971	28900	19500	11122	12978
2008	235794	5857	9100	12653	14250	25760	24050	28608	43074	28427	18076	12887	13052
2007	235367	6150	8483	12312	14219	21621	30192	32594	36595	32103	16353	10967	13778
2006	239454	6151	8966	10763	17876	21965	26410	34501	37128	34544	16697	10891	13562
2005	247805	7820	10671	11904	17140	23985	27053	36398	37231	31648	19212	11259	13484
2004	273069	8977	13256	12789	19086	27518	28376	39738	40138	33295	22947	12566	14383
2003	270109	7998	11861	14166	18066	28994	28092	32860	46086	32923	20432	14685	13946
2002	255596	6788	10850	14255	15105	24385	31634	31097	43957	30617	18806	14283	13819
2001	249227	6196	9720	12920	16572	23413	30891	31248	38580	35503	17915	12356	13913
2000	267961	7101	11452	12939	20221	24617	29356	37740	39194	39761	19476	12652	13452
1999	263515	7872	10788	13801	17574	28018	27560	37010	37657	34822	23407	13041	11965
1998	267303	7720	12756	12930	18705	29025	27285	33041	43365	33807	23142	12671	12856
1997	272536	7575	11513	15860	17045	29587	30077	33836	45514	33879	20967	14146	12537
1996	278975	7853	12246	16378	19082	27181	34425	33604	46161	34253	20312	14186	13294
1995	283012	8032	11241	14738	22627	26550	32235	39599	38757	41412	20098	12741	14982
1994	291069	8507	12013	16256	23323	28410	32117	39809	39228	39348	24126	13399	14533
1993	299197	9245	11850	15411	22327	32769	33125	41855	40151	39547	25248	13459	14210
1992	311564	8473	15853	15739	22687	33856	32496	37839	49083	41558	26241	13896	13843
1991	306756	8628	12807	20053	21345	30143	38050	34655	47685	39168	23791	16689	13742
1990	331150	9796	14842	22442	26422	32588	42187	37605	42010	47695	24295	15547	15721
1989	346697	10573	14675	23060	28425	31795	37918	44695	42404	51493	27538	17449	16672
1988	348492	10998	14278	21039	30115	31213	37982	46236	43510	45552	32168	17688	17713
1987	351761	12038	17101	19707	27039	36780	37973	41165	50278	44303	31550	17373	16454
1986	347924	10634	14915	25299	24819	35934	37306	39375	51179	42296	28581	20624	16962
1985	346389	10923	14878	25325	27431	31021	42283	38475	51407	41153	26426	20611	16456
1984	349186	11718	16163	26526	29383	30897	41788	38885	42522	47612	25992	18296	19404
1983	344334	12620	16434	25650	32701	29429	34573	42329	39521	42320	30797	18668	19292
1982	342166	13133	16825	24978	31519	31006	33974	41743	39066	41052	30904	18801	19165
1981	351973	15744	21118	26846	31373	34292	32738	36526	43247	39985	31333	19436	19335
1980	370022	14280	19304	34127	30718	35371	35275	37365	47306	40292	30896	24777	20311
1979	368853	14830	19396	35120	29043	28312	39201	36985	40335	47661	30450	22806	24714
1978	368258	15075	19460	36439	29359	26499	33706	43436	40048	46991	29165	22595	25485
1977	356954	17119	20203	31001	34425	23954	33759	40402	37683	39384	32899	21080	25045
1976	358567	18434	22863	32717	27869	27295	30438	40697	37880	42016	34261	20674	23423
1975	380620	16885	21183	43836	25622	30438	32360	36558	47313	43385	33230	25705	24105
1974	384389	17391	21436	38824	30019	26970	38320	36189	47395	43363	32987	26148	25347
1973	400435	18877	22328	41886	32051	27926	39304	38642	41164	51390	33444	23572	29851
1972	426241	21909	22117	36555	38071	30500	37619	47160	43094	55730	35931	25793	31762
1971	404737	20678	20259	30542	34534	34053	38510	46640	41736	48155	40728	23280	25622

(Continued)

Table 9.16 (*Continued*)

Year	Total	January	February	March	April	May	June	July	August	September	October	November	December
1970	415487	20996	22318	38221	30219	34698	38832	40741	50984	48940	40950	22903	25685
1969	396746	16046	20257	41775	32808	31221	35481	36743	48219	48132	36021	25798	24245
1968	407822	14885	22939	80572	17857	15838	32894	30707	42719	55210	45123	24480	24598
1967	386052	14392	20617	69246	26996	17199	25925	32267	32520	62243	42826	17407	24414
1966	384497	17012	22253	62620	30535	16880	26689	32876	31591	50561	52785	16986	23709
1965	371127	15945	22461	60136	27312	17470	28739	32285	31069	50351	47572	17166	20621
1964	359307	12478	20970	64266	22671	18841	26985	27448	35388	48322	44573	16689	20676
1963	351329	12113	19687	65509	16604	13943	33017	26775	36874	47336	38125	19293	22053
1962	347732	12345	18568	70012	16540	13722	32810	26148	29722	51807	34999	15761	25298
1961	346678	12310	18020	54118	32733	16623	26813	31282	30822	50263	31897	15899	25898
1960	343614	15596	21163	52185	30016	13447	29432	33131	29414	41035	36503	15461	26231
1959	340126	15430	18972	67028	20121	17142	26018	27390	35601	39600	32649	15548	24627
1958	339913	12940	20777	68912	21229	17434	27548	27900	37115	36683	24005	19048	26322
1957	346903	13894	19954	76244	19034	12150	34620	28458	38192	36967	21817	18199	27374
1956	352944	13651	19898	73573	21113	15529	32179	30144	34503	42276	21158	15947	32973
1955	357918	17262	22902	60532	31567	16474	26722	38207	30981	37503	26100	16394	33274
1954	341731	16282	21989	57651	28907	14519	30938	38349	30360	35796	23313	15691	27936
1953	344998	15900	20870	56840	30228	18822	28073	32841	38255	34518	23155	15475	30021
1952	349308	13968	22829	69832	22291	17696	29502	31298	37588	34525	20431	18153	31195
1951	360624	14382	17894	77291	14258	17574	34550	33021	35320	42971	21110	15759	36494
1950	358490	15398	21642	49860	31408	18324	30994	37323	35140	42365	21700	16900	37436
1949	375041	21,578	22298	37898	39245	16349	39971	42299	32990	39116	26795	17935	38567
1948	396891	22,958	20630	51855	25729	26577	40516	46248	35343	41566	28248	20142	37079
1947	401210	19866	22347	33028	41602	27578	39966	36388	43277	39761	28283	27395	41719

Source: Office for National Statistics
Data file 9X-16

You may find the following information useful: www.ons.gov.uk/visualisations/marriages/marriages/index.html

(iii) Table 9.17 shows consumers' expenditure in the UK on different categories. How do you explain the difference in seasonal patterns and trends between the series?

4 A large retail organisation is currently investigating a number of areas of its operations with a view to improving performance in terms of efficiency, sales and profits. The organisation has been monitoring the monthly sales of one of its more profitable products for the last few years with a view to trying to forecast future demand. Someone in the organisation has applied time-series analysis to the monthly sales figures and calculated both the trend and the seasonally adjusted sales figures for the first five months of the current year (the latest available). These are shown in Table 9.18. Unfortunately, the person who completed the analysis has left the company and none of the senior managers understands the information provided. You have been asked to provide a short briefing report to management.

(a) Explain in the context of the application what is meant by time-series analysis and why it is important.

Table 9.17 UK household final consumption expenditure, £m at constant prices

	Food & non-alcoholic drink	Alcohol & tobacco	Restaurants & hotels	Clothing & footwear
1988 Q1	35296	7782	13039	7940
1988 Q2	36453	8409	16253	9002
1988 Q3	36975	8687	18080	9389
1988 Q4	37033	9646	18994	12784
1989 Q1	35323	8226	15465	8564
1989 Q2	38033	8759	18072	9578
1989 Q3	37401	8940	20430	9710
1989 Q4	37918	9992	20008	12879
1990 Q1	35035	8553	16669	9171
1990 Q2	38105	9553	19802	9936
1990 Q3	37193	9963	22296	10171
1990 Q4	37934	11158	22010	13535
1991 Q1	35051	9675	17580	9372
1991 Q2	37817	10984	20288	10467
1991 Q3	37560	11321	23179	10872
1991 Q4	38119	12340	22632	14551
1992 Q1	34971	11068	18852	9566
1992 Q2	38214	11597	20866	10977
1992 Q3	38195	11570	23698	11484
1992 Q4	38953	12305	22233	15475
1993 Q1	36687	11607	20068	10121
1993 Q2	38628	12235	22091	11368
1993 Q3	38010	12479	26136	11934
1993 Q4	40243	12961	23755	16663
1994 Q1	37992	12233	20272	10683
1994 Q2	38660	12545	23566	12418
1994 Q3	38774	12660	27080	12947
1994 Q4	39759	13984	25101	17630
1995 Q1	38617	12714	20899	11377
1995 Q2	38722	13218	24798	13105
1995 Q3	38782	13500	28617	13393
1995 Q4	39366	14650	26533	18488
1996 Q1	38673	13835	23000	11786
1996 Q2	39181	14490	27733	13798
1996 Q3	40597	14527	30868	14241
1996 Q4	42358	15722	28488	19597
1997 Q1	39805	14673	23615	12831
1997 Q2	40920	15274	29420	14473
1997 Q3	39753	15261	31691	14788
1997 Q4	42837	16372	29842	19866

(Continued)

Table 9.17 (*Continued*)

	Food & non-alcoholic drink	Alcohol & tobacco	Restaurants & hotels	Clothing & footwear
1998 Q1	40103	15095	25498	13331
1998 Q2	42202	15442	30864	15039
1998 Q3	41471	14862	34134	15615
1998 Q4	42663	15979	32072	20280
1999 Q1	40650	15169	27547	14220
1999 Q2	43973	16064	31979	15761
1999 Q3	43265	16144	34496	16189
1999 Q4	43103	17667	32992	21533
2000 Q1	43195	15574	29099	14823
2000 Q2	44539	16272	33525	16743
2000 Q3	43774	16146	36543	17253
2000 Q4	45584	17541	34986	22998
2001 Q1	43276	15877	30399	15691
2001 Q2	42990	16790	34747	17457
2001 Q3	42551	16693	38747	17986
2001 Q4	46603	18148	36307	23891
2002 Q1	42698	16039	31953	16936
2002 Q2	44200	16794	37233	18802
2002 Q3	43924	16720	41350	19284
2002 Q4	48290	18352	39175	25014
2003 Q1	44019	16226	33261	17786
2003 Q2	46638	16891	38516	19951
2003 Q3	44436	16986	43165	20467
2003 Q4	46930	18743	40282	26372
2004 Q1	46290	16409	35163	19043
2004 Q2	46311	17107	40603	20981
2004 Q3	45220	16883	44195	21037
2004 Q4	49722	18862	41846	27107
2005 Q1	46514	16389	36447	19477
2005 Q2	47955	17325	42424	21580
2005 Q3	46202	17792	45173	21671
2005 Q4	50772	19877	42722	28249
2006 Q1	47500	17409	36504	19778
2006 Q2	48796	18831	43060	22340
2006 Q3	47488	18889	47669	22739
2006 Q4	49957	20060	43586	29451
2007 Q1	47138	17698	38403	20288
2007 Q2	48440	17907	45525	23300
2007 Q3	47228	17704	49146	23757
2007 Q4	50494	19002	45366	30066
2008 Q1	47035	16434	39665	21272

	Food & non-alcoholic drink	Alcohol & tobacco	Restaurants & hotels	Clothing & footwear
2008 Q2	48391	17788	46276	24403
2008 Q3	45961	18253	50031	24885
2008 Q4	47656	20545	44856	30615
2009 Q1	43988	17905	37453	22379
2009 Q2	46416	19237	42541	24249
2009 Q3	45039	19288	46842	24237
2009 Q4	47848	21058	42389	30154
2010 Q1	44529	18358	37031	22315
2010 Q2	47584	19313	45523	24673
2010 Q3	45667	19039	49553	25245
2010 Q4	46837	21558	45901	31710
2011 Q1	44693	19792	40465	23113
2011 Q2	45259	21389	47759	26274
2011 Q3	44829	21630	52617	26562
2011 Q4	47350	23486	49138	33634
2012 Q1	45123	20932	42809	24716
2012 Q2	45471	20944	50078	26823
2012 Q3	45492	21070	55088	27562
2012 Q4	48961	22928	51990	34553
2013 Q1	46294	21066	45442	25397
2013 Q2	45979	20333	52817	27901
2013 Q3	46461	21529	58165	29158
2013 Q4	49516	23150	53926	37202
2014 Q1	46226	21109	47850	26189
2014 Q2	47027	20893	55835	30726
2014 Q3	47422	21438	60290	30840
2014 Q4	50206	23103	55854	39142
2015 Q1	47247	20490	49130	27646
2015 Q2	48014	20414	57134	31953
2015 Q3	48481	20852	62897	32702
2015 Q4	51992	22924	58741	41525
2016 Q1	49412	20214	51064	28975
2016 Q2	49597	20986	60481	31842
2016 Q3	50665	21282	65922	32753
2016 Q4	53646	23103	61959	42519
2017 Q1	50632	20342	54560	30346
2017 Q2	51667	21712	63572	34560
2017 Q3	51852	21695	69457	35317
2017 Q4	54953	23973	64846	44298
2018 Q1	51957	20883	55484	31263
2018 Q2	51967	22389	64763	35167
2018 Q3	52230	22430	70477	35901

Source: Office for National Statistics
Data file 9X-17

(b) Explain why the actual sales figures are of little value by themselves for forecasting purposes.

(c) Explain what is meant by seasonally adjusted sales and how this information could be used.

5 Working with a small group of colleagues, develop a consensus view of private car sales in Western Europe (or another area of your choice) in five years' time. In order to do this, you will need to:

- collect historical data on car sales
- collect data on related variables: population trends, income levels, public transport, etc.
- collect published market research data
- apply quantitative techniques for trend projection
- integrate these projections with likely scenarios.

6 An online retailer has been looking at the number of orders placed online by customers on a daily basis over the last few months. The company offers a next day delivery service for orders placed before 3.00pm (except Sunday) and is looking at the operational implications of this. Table 9.19 shows the data. Analyse the data shown in Table 9.19 and highlight the key findings for management.

Table 9.18 Seasonally adjusted sales figures (£000s)

	Actual sales	Trend	Seasonally adjusted sales
Jan	63	78.50	76.3
Feb	85	80.88	80.7
Mar	100	83.88	84.5
Apr	81	85.88	87.5
May	89	86.47	88.6

Table 9.19 Daily online sales volume

Th	170	W	133	T	82
F	487	Th	167	W	94
S	1704	F	482	Th	143
Su	1168	S	1856	F	419
M	87	Su	1283	S	1408
T	96	M	198	Su	1188
W	85	T	162	M	116
Th	109	W	190	T	97
F	417	Th	307	W	82
S	1591	F	582	Th	147
Su	1163	S	1660	F	456
M	132	Su	1268	S	1718
T	53	M	115	Su	221

M	163	T	147	W	140
T	115	W	134	Th	129
W	175	Th	216	F	475
Th	329	F	612	S	1227
F	753	S	1558	Su	1170
S	1770	Su	1303	M	176
Su	1138	M	514	T	96
M	122	T	5	W	122
T	62	W	20	Th	213
W	121	Th	358	F	559
Th	149	F	835	S	1986
F	459	S	1231	Su	1368
S	1447	Su	1093	M	401
Su	1112	M	168	T	364
M	135	T	71	W	512
T	58	W	121	Th	207
W	143	Th	151	F	121
Th	107	F	526	S	1074
F	397	S	1793	Su	1376
S	1609	Su	1367	M	528
Su	1219	M	134	T	357
M	179	T	78	W	542

Data file 9X-19

10 Forecasting II: Regression

Learning objectives

At the end of this chapter you should be able to:

- explain the principles of simple linear regression
- interpret the key statistics from a regression equation
- explain the limitations of regression in business forecasting
- be aware of the extensions to the basic regression model

In the last chapter we introduced a number of ways of trying to forecast a variable in which we were interested. As we saw, a variety of non-causal models exist for attempting this – models which simply try to predict future changes in the variable without attempting to provide an explanation as to what is causing such change. In this chapter we introduce another method of forecasting, which is to develop a causal model – where we do try to analyse the causes of change in the variable we are trying to forecast. This method is known as *regression* and we shall be examining the basic form of the model, known as *simple linear regression*.

The principles of simple linear regression

To illustrate the principles of simple linear regression we shall return to an example we introduced in Chapter 3, where we were looking at the use of scatter diagrams. The data related to a sample of profit centres in a large company and for each profit centre we had data relating to the centre's profit last year and its sales or turnover figure. Consider a situation where the company is opening a new store with an anticipated initial sales level of £78 000. The Finance Director has asked for a forecast of this store's profit. The data for the existing stores is duplicated in Table 10.1 and the scatter diagram in Figure 10.1. As we saw in Chapter 3, and as is confirmed by the scatter of points on the diagram, for the existing stores there appears to be some definite connection between the two variables in that as one variable takes higher values so does the other. In the context of the business

Art market ripe for disruption by algorithms

The art world and its auctions are becoming more intriguing to applied mathematicians and computer scientists

By John Dizard

As traders and portfolio managers are escorted away from their desks by security, they may plaintively ask which algorithm is replacing them. The guards never know, of course; to them the removal of financial executives is just another task. By now, the automation of securities transactions and investment strategies is widely understood to be a remorseless process.

People in the art world, though, think they are different. Up to now, they have believed what they do is a high-touch, rather than a high-tech business. Art consultants and dealers are convinced they have arcane skills that are difficult, if not impossible, to replicate.

Their clients, though, increasingly wonder if that is true. Some of them, after all, are the same alpha creatures of the financial markets that have been firing MBAs and hiring mathematicians. So while the auctioneers in evening dresses or black tie are droning away in the background, it is only natural for the better-informed collectors to consider how to compress those transaction costs and get that price discovery done more efficiently.

The art world already has transaction databases and competing price indices. The databases tend to be incomplete, since a high proportion of fine art objects are sold privately. The price indices also have their issues, given the (arguably) unique nature of the objects being traded. Sotheby's Mei Moses index attempts to get around that by compiling repeat-sales

Source: Michael Bowles/Getty Images for Sotheby's

data, which, given the slow turnover of particular works of art, is challenging. Other indices, or value estimations, are based on hedonic regression which is less amusing than it sounds. It is a form of linear regression used, in this case, to determine the weight of different components in the pricing of a work of art, such as the artist's name, the work's size, the year of creation and so on. Those weights in turn are used to create time-series data to describe "the art market". . . .

So you can expect the march of the algos to continue, from the investment houses to the art auctions and fairs.

Even the art world isn't immune to regression!

problem this is unsurprising, as we would anticipate that a store with higher turnover would, by and large, generate higher profits. What we seek to establish is the exact numerical relationship between the two variables so that, for any given profit centre, we can try to forecast profit based on some turnover level. This would then allow us to forecast profit for the new store. We begin by clarifying what we believe – or hypothesise – the relationship between the two variables to be:

$$\text{Profit} = f(\text{Sales})$$

Mathematically this indicates that profit is a function of sales (the term $f(\ )$ indicates 'a function of'). We should be clear about the implications of this specification. We are implying in this formulation that profit 'depends' on sales. That is, in some, as yet unspecified, way sales influences or 'causes' profits. Clearly in a business context such a

Table 10.1 Sales and profits for
20 stores in Region A

Sales (£000s)	Profit (£000s)
748.82	42.13
140.78	6.32
702.11	38.47
41.54	–0.32
96.85	3.65
166.93	7.77
109.05	4.31
263.92	4.53
50.84	–2.69
90.08	3.22
190.59	9.03
91.75	–2.59
141.57	6.39
377.04	24.39
198.69	13.92
62.78	2.13
265.28	17.48
91.80	7.21
231.60	15.62
548.31	33.61

Data file 10-1

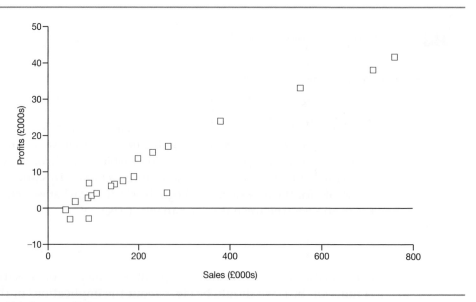

Figure 10.1 Scatter diagram

causal relationship makes considerable sense. In general, we would specify the relationship between any two variables as:

$$Y = f(X)$$

where Y is known as the *dependent* variable and X as the *independent* or explanatory variable. We will also go one stage further and assume that the relationship between the two variables is a linear one: it will result in a straight line if plotted on a graph. This seems reasonable on visual inspection of the scatter diagram. We should note that such an assumption is not always appropriate and will depend much on the context of the problem. This means the general form of our relationship can be specified as:

$$Y = a + bX$$

where *a* and *b* are known as the parameters of the linear equation: the numerical values which give the equation its form. *a* is generally referred to as the intercept of the function and *b* as the slope. Before we consider the implications of this for forecasting we need to ensure that the principles of intercept and slope are clear.

The intercept of a linear function

The intercept of a linear function indicates where that function would cross – or intercept – the vertical, Y, axis. Another way of considering this is to say that the intercept term indicates the value that Y takes when X = 0. Consider the linear equation:

$$Y = 10 + 5X$$

We now know without any graphs or calculations that this equation will cross the Y axis where Y = 10. Equally we can see that if we set X = 0 then Y must take the intercept value of 10. We also realise that a second linear equation:

$$Y = -10 + 5X$$

differs from the first only in its intercept value. In the second instance the intercept equals = −10, so this equation will cross the vertical axis at Y = −10.

Progress Check 10.1

Assume a third linear equation such that:

$$Y = 5X$$

Where would this cross the vertical axis?

The third example has a zero intercept: it could be rewritten as:

$$Y = 0 + 5X$$

implying that it will pass through the origin, where Y = 0. The effect on an equation of a change only in the intercept is illustrated in Figure 10.2.

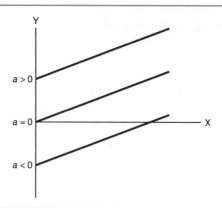

Figure 10.2 Effect of a change in *a*

The slope of a linear function

The slope of a linear function is given by the *b* term in the equation and shows the relationship between a change in the X variable and a change in the Y variable. The *b* term is sometimes referred to as the gradient. It literally indicates the steepness of the straight line representing the function. Let us return to the first function:

$$Y = 10 + 5X$$

Its slope is 5. This indicates that a change in X will bring about a five times change in Y. Let X = 2 and we calculate that Y = 20. If X now changes to 3 (a change of 1) then Y will change to 25: a change of 5 – the *b* value. Note that the same logic applies to a negative change in X. If X reduces from 3 to 2 (a change of –1) then the change in Y must be –5. The *b* term, in other words, provides an indication of the change relationship between the two variables. As with the *a* term, different *b* values are readily compared. A function:

$$Y = 10 + 10X$$

would be twice as steep as the first function: its slope is twice as great. This time a change in X will bring about a tenfold change in Y. As with the *a* term, the *b* value can be negative as well as positive. Consider an equation:

$$Y = 10 - 5X$$

In the first example we saw that with a positive slope a change in X brought about some (multiplied) change in Y: an increase in X was followed by an increase in Y, a decrease by a decrease. With a negative value for *b* the reverse occurs. An increase in X now brings about a decrease in Y. Graphically a function with a negative value for *b* would slope downwards as we look at it from left to right. The effect on an equation of a change in *b* is illustrated in Figure 10.3.

It is important to be able to visualise the implications of different values for *a* and *b* without resorting to a graph or to calculations.

Progress Check 10.2

For the following equations sketch each group of functions on the same diagram. The diagram should be drawn without performing any calculations.

(a) 1. Y = 100 + 5X
   2. Y = 100 + 10X
   3. Y = 100 + 5X

(b) 1. Y = 100 + 5X
   2. Y = 100 + 5X
   3. Y = 5X

Solutions are given on p 580.

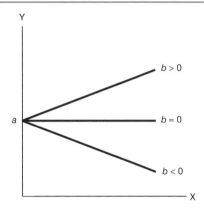

Figure 10.3 Effect of a change in *b*

One final aspect relating to the slope of a linear function needs to be considered. We saw that *a* could take a zero value. What of *b*? If the slope is zero then it implies that as X changes Y remains unchanged. Graphically we would have a line parallel to the X axis: Y would always take the same value regardless of X. More importantly in terms of the functional expression, this would imply that X and Y were *not* functionally related: Y did not depend on X for its value – it was independent of X. This is an important point, to which we shall return later.

Progress Check 10.3

In the case of the profit/sales relationship we had earlier:

   Profit = *a* + *b* Sales

What general numerical values would we expect *a* and *b* to take in this business context: negative, zero or positive?

It is important in this type of analysis to consider carefully the contextual – as opposed to the mathematical – interpretation of the *a* and *b* terms. The exact business interpretation of the parameters will depend on the business context. The *b* term is the slope or gradient of the straight line and, in general, indicates the change in Y that occurs for a given change in X. In our context this would be the change in profit for a change in sales. The *b* term, therefore, will be an indication of the profit margin on sales and we would normally expect this to be positive: as sales increase so do profits. The *a* term is the intercept and indicates, graphically, where the line intercepts the Y axis. It can also be interpreted as the value that Y takes when X = 0. Here, *a* will indicate the profit when sales are zero. Of course, we would never expect to encounter such a situation, but there is an obvious implication. It is unrealistic to expect profit to be positive when sales − 0. At best we would expect profit to be zero also or, more realistically, negative (i.e. representing a loss, since some overhead expenses are likely to have been incurred even when sales are zero). So we might expect a relationship between our two variables such that:

Profit = *a* + *b*X

where $a \le 0$ and $b > 0$. Clearly from a business perspective it would be extremely useful to have such an equation which quantified the relationship between two such variables. Such a linear equation can be estimated using the principles of simple linear regression – so called because we are trying to quantify the parameters of a *linear* equation and because we are dealing with the *simplest* equation, which has only one explanatory variable. We shall see later how the approach can be adapted both to non-linear situations and to situations where we have multiple explanatory variables.

The correlation coefficient

Before we consider the process of estimating such an equation, it will be worthwhile seeing first whether we can measure statistically the strength of the relationship that might exist between the two variables. We might, in general, encounter a situation where there is, literally, no connection between the two variables. Equally, we might encounter a situation where the connection is a particularly strong one. Although the scatter diagram is useful in providing a graphical, but subjective, assessment about the strength of the relationship between two variables, we clearly need an analytical measure. Statistically such a connection is referred to as *correlation* and we can calculate what is known as the *coefficient of correlation* between the X and Y variables. Such a coefficient will take a value between 0 and 1: zero implies literally no correlation between the two variables, while one implies perfect correlation. Anyone in their right mind these days will use a spreadsheet or a statistical package to calculate such a statistic. While we encourage you to do this, we shall introduce and use the appropriate calculation formula, which, because of the mathematics, we simply present as:

$$r = \frac{\Sigma(x-\bar{x})(y-\bar{y})}{\sqrt{\Sigma(x-\bar{x})^2}\sqrt{\Sigma(y-\bar{y})^2}}$$

where r is used to denote the correlation coefficient and the calculations are effectively measuring the difference of x and y values from their respective means. For calculation purposes this is usually rewritten as:

$$r = \frac{\Sigma xy - (\Sigma x \Sigma y)/n}{\sqrt{\Sigma x^2 - (\Sigma x)^2/n}\sqrt{\Sigma y^2 - (\Sigma y)^2/n}}$$

where n is the number of pairs of data items. Although both formulae might look equally horrendous, the second is actually much easier to use for calculation purposes, since all we actually require from the data are the terms:

$$\Sigma x, \Sigma y, \Sigma x^2, \Sigma y^2, \Sigma xy$$

Progress Check 10.4

Using profit as Y and sales as X calculate the totals shown in the last equation and calculate the value for r for this data.

Table 10.2 shows the results of these calculations for our data, with the values of interest being the column totals.

These can be readily substituted into the r formula:

$$r = \frac{\Sigma xy - (\Sigma x \Sigma y)/n}{\sqrt{\Sigma x^2 - (\Sigma x)^2/n}\sqrt{\Sigma y^2 - (\Sigma y)^2/n}}$$

$$= \frac{(104\ 732.59) - (4610.33)(234.58)/20}{\sqrt{1\ 888\ 170.77 - (4610.33)^2/20}\sqrt{6078.73 - (234.58)^2/20}}$$

$$= \frac{50\ 658.03}{\sqrt{825\ 413.63}\sqrt{3327.34}} = \frac{50\ 658.03}{(908.52)(57.68)}$$

$$= 0.97$$

giving a correlation coefficient of 0.97. Interpretation is as follows. First of all we note that the correlation coefficient is positive (it can be negative). This implies a positive relationship between the two variables: as one increases so does the other, and this is exactly what we would expect in a business context for these two variables. A negative coefficient would imply an inverse relationship: as one variable increases the other decreases. Second, we note that on the scale from 0 to 1, the coefficient is very close to one (perfect correlation). This implies that there is a very strong numerical relationship between the two variables. It seems reasonable to conclude that there is a strong positive relationship between profit and sales (although we do not yet know numerically what the relationship is).

However, a few words of caution are necessary about the use of this coefficient. First, the coefficient measures the strength of the relationship between two variables. It does not measure cause and effect. Our choice of which variable to label x and which y was based on logic and the context of the problem, not on statistics. You may be able to see,

Table 10.2 Calculations for r

x	y	x²	y²	xy
748.82	42.13	560731.39	1774.94	31547.79
140.78	6.32	19819.01	39.94	889.73
702.11	38.47	492958.45	1479.94	27010.17
41.54	−0.32	1725.57	0.10	−13.29
96.85	3.65	9379.92	13.32	353.50
166.93	7.77	27865.62	60.37	1297.05
109.05	4.31	11891.90	18.58	470.01
263.92	4.53	69653.77	20.52	1195.56
50.84	−2.69	2584.71	7.24	−136.76
90.08	3.22	8114.41	10.37	290.06
190.59	9.03	36324.55	81.54	1721.03
91.75	−2.59	8418.06	6.71	−237.63
141.57	6.39	20042.06	40.83	904.63
377.04	24.39	142159.16	594.87	9196.01
198.69	13.92	39477.72	193.77	2765.76
62.78	2.13	3941.33	4.54	133.72
265.28	17.48	70373.48	305.55	4637.09
91.80	7.21	8427.24	51.98	661.88
231.60	15.62	53638.56	243.98	3617.59
548.31	33.61	300643.86	1129.63	18428.70
Total				
4610.33	234.58	1888170.77	6078.73	104732.59

on inspection of the coefficient formula, that if we now called profit x and sales y and recalculated the coefficient we would come up with exactly the same numerical value. (If you can't see this then do the recalculation now.) This makes perfect sense, since the strength of the relationship must be the same no matter which variable we label x and y. The second point is that technically the coefficient measures the strength of the *linear* relationship between the two variables. Here we have evidence of a strong linear relationship between profit and sales. In some cases there may be a strong relationship between two variables which is not linear. We need to consider the implications of this for the coefficient.

Consider the scatter diagram shown in Figure 10.4. It is evident that there is a strong relationship between the two variables and equally that this relationship is not a linear one. The correlation coefficient in such a situation would show a value of 0, or thereabouts. We must be cautious then in interpreting the correlation coefficient. It actually indicates the strength of the *linear* relationship between the two variables. A low value for the coefficient implies little evidence of a linear relationship but tells us nothing about other possible relationship forms. However, the calculation for our problem at 0.97 indicates evidence of a strong linear relationship and we now need to progress to see how we can quantify this relationship.

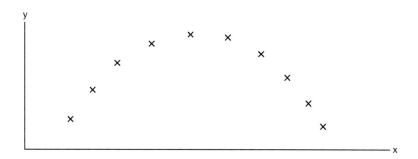

Figure 10.4 Non-linear relationship

The baseline

By John Burn-Murdoch and Gavin Jackson

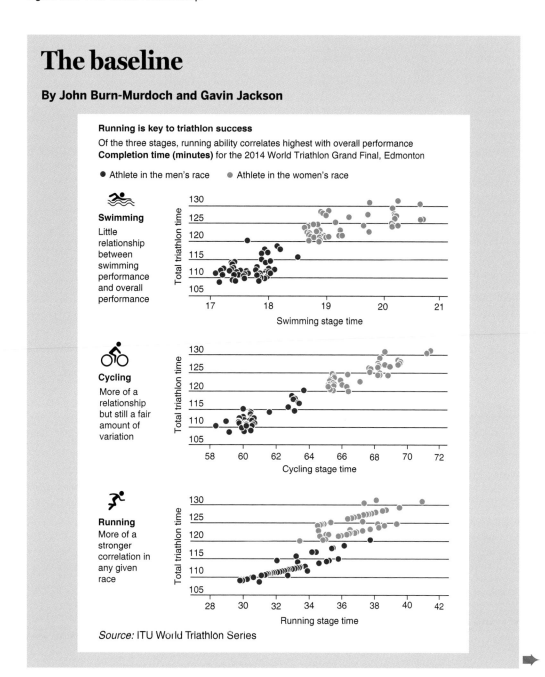

Running is key to triathlon success

Of the three stages, running ability correlates highest with overall performance
Completion time (minutes) for the 2014 World Triathlon Grand Final, Edmonton

● Athlete in the men's race   ● Athlete in the women's race

Swimming

Little relationship between swimming performance and overall performance

Cycling

More of a relationship but still a fair amount of variation

Running

More of a stronger correlation in any given race

Source: ITU World Triathlon Series

The first Olympic-distance elite race of the 2015 ITU World Triathlon Series took place over the weekend in Auckland, with the top men and women each competing in a 1.5km swim, 40km bike section and 10km run. But which of the three disciplines is the key when it comes to elite triathlon success?

Looking at results from every elite race at Olympic-distance since 2009, it is clear that swimming prowess has the weakest statistical relationship to overall triathlon performance, with a correlation coefficient of 0.42. This is partly due to the inherently chaotic nature of open-water swimming, and partly to its favouring of specific body types, which applies much less to cycling and running.

Cycling is more indicative of overall ability, with a coefficient of 0.77, due to its greater emphasis on aerobic fitness, and to aerodynamic factors that lend to splits in the field, making time gains in this phase relatively larger than those in the water.

But at the highest level, running is where the medals are decided – its correlation coefficient with total time is 0.92. The groups formed while on the bike tend to consolidate on foot as athletes tire, and even among the backmarkers, the better overall triathletes almost always complete the final phase quicker than their weaker counterparts.

 Source: Burn-Murdoch, J. and Jackson, G. (2015) The baseline, *Financial Times* (UK), Monday, 30 March. © The Financial Times Limited. All Rights Reserved.

Scatterplots and correlation coefficients are used here to examine links between different aspects of athletic performance in the triathlon.

The line of best fit

We wish to obtain precise numerical values for the *a* and *b* values of the linear equation linking profit to sales. The mathematics underpinning regression is quite formidable and we shall make no attempt to justify it here. However, the general approach can be understood using a little logic and will be worth developing. If we return to Figure 10.1, the scatter diagram, we are looking for an equation that quantifies the linear relationship between the two variables. Such an equation graphically would give us a straight line. However, it is also clear from the diagram that the 20 points we have do not all lie on one straight line (if they did the correlation coefficient would have been 1). It seems sensible though to try to obtain the straight line that comes as close as possible to as many of the points as possible. You can picture that we could try to do this ourselves by drawing on the graph a straight line that we felt came as close to the points as possible. However, such an approach would clearly be quite subjective, with different people drawing (slightly) different straight lines. Mathematically, however, we can do the same thing. The mathematics we shall shortly use calculates the parameters of the straight line that comes closest to these points by minimising the sum of the squared deviations of the pairs of observations from the line. This sounds complex but is in fact based on calculations very similar to those we had for the standard deviation of a set of data. The method often goes under the name of *least squares* for this reason. Remember that we require an equation such that:

$$Y = a + bX$$

where a and b are calculated by:

$$b = \frac{\Sigma xy - (\Sigma x \Sigma y)/n}{\Sigma x^2 - (\Sigma x)^2/n}$$

$$a = \frac{\Sigma y}{n} - b\frac{\Sigma x}{n}$$

The numerical values for a and b can be calculated from the formulae shown. We first calculate the b value and then use this b value to calculate a. You may realise at this stage that we have already calculated all the component parts of the formulae in our correlation coefficient calculations in Table 10.2. The calculations are then:

$$b = \frac{\Sigma xy - (\Sigma x \Sigma y)/n}{\Sigma x^2 - (\Sigma x)^2/n}$$

$$= \frac{104\ 732.59 - (4610.33)(234.58)/20}{1\ 888\ 170.77 - 4610.33^2/20}$$

$$= \frac{50\ 658.03}{825\ 413.64} = 0.0614$$

$$a = \frac{\Sigma y}{n} - b\frac{\Sigma x}{n}$$

$$= \frac{234.58}{20} - 0.0614\left(\frac{4610.33}{20}\right)$$

$$= 11.729 - 14.15 = -2.421$$

giving an equation:

$$Y = -2.0421 + 0.0614X$$

or

$$\text{Profit} = -2.421 + 0.0614\ \text{Sales}$$

This equation is the line of best fit, or the regression equation for our data. We have estimated the numerical relationship between the two variables based on the data available.

Progress Check 10.5

What meaning or interpretation can you give to the *a and b* values we have estimated in the context of this problem?

As we indicated earlier, the *a* term is the intercept of the equation while the *b* term is the gradient or slope. The gradient indicates the change in Y (profit) as X (sales) changes.

Consider a change in sales of one unit. Y would then change by 0.0614 units. Effectively, an extra £1 sales will lead to an increase in profit of 6.14p; hence for these 20 centres there is an average profit margin of 6.14 per cent. The *a* term indicates where the line intercepts the vertical axis. Here it intercepts on the negative part of the axis. This means that for low values of X (sales), Y (profit) will be negative. We can actually calculate when the change from negative to positive profit will occur. Let us set Profit = 0. We then have:

$$\text{Profit} = -2.421 + 0.0614\,\text{Sales} = 0$$

and rearranging gives:

$$0.0614\,\text{Sales} = 2.421$$

$$\text{Sales} = \frac{2.421}{0.0614} = 39.43$$

So, if sales are below 39.43 (£000), profit will be negative, whereas if sales are above this value, profit will be positive. Effectively we have found the break-even position for this group of stores. A store, on average, needs a sales level of around £39 000 before it starts showing a profit. Note also that the numerical values for *a* and *b* are in line with what we initially thought they should be ($b > 0, a \leq 0$). In fact we can superimpose this line of best fit onto the scatter diagram, as in Figure 10.5. This can often help us visualise both the relationship between the variables and the closeness of the various points to the line. We see that a number of points lie on, or close to, the line we have estimated. Although some individual points occur away from the line of best fit, the line does appear to come reasonably close to most of the points shown.

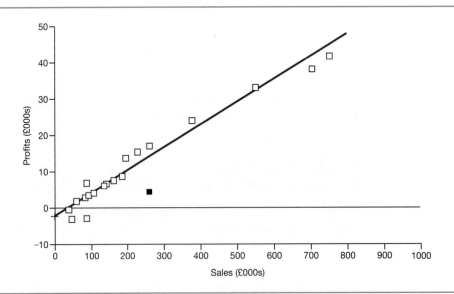

Figure 10.5 Line of best fit

Using the regression equation

In fact the diagram with the line of best fit superimposed helps us see how we can now use the regression equation we have estimated. There are two broad uses. The first is to use the equation directly for forecasting; the second is in terms of performance evaluation.

Forecasting

Forecasting with the regression equation is arithmetically straightforward. We were told earlier that the organisation is thinking of opening another store with anticipated sales of £78 000. Can we predict or forecast likely profit for this store? Using the regression equation all we have to do is to substitute the sales value into the equation to obtain:

$$\text{Profit} = -2.421 + 0.0614(78) = 2.3682(\text{in } £000)$$

That is, on this sales figure, profit would be forecast to be around £2400. Although the derivation of such a forecast is straightforward, we must exercise considerable caution in its evaluation and use. First of all we must note that such a forecast is not a guaranteed outcome. Effectively, what we have done in the regression procedure is to find an average, and historical, relationship between the two variables for the 20 stores in the data set. Like any average – even though the regression calculations make this relatively sophisticated – it is subject to variation within a data set. The forecast clearly is our best 'guess' based on past performance. Also we need to ensure that the other characteristics of this profit centre – its size, its location, its staffing levels, etc. – are reasonably comparable with those of the sample of 20 centres from which we derived the equation. Second, given that the equation is a measure of the past relationship between the two variables, there is no guarantee that this relationship will continue unchanged in the future (which is where we are forecasting). Naturally, we would hope that the past relationship will continue, but once again there are no guarantees and in evaluating the reliability of the forecast we would need to take into account any supplementary information about possible changing circumstances (for example, a major competitor opening up a short distance away from our store). Third, the forecast we have produced is technically known as an *interpolation* – the X value used to produce the forecast is within the observed limits of other X values. That is, the value of 78 is within the range of previously observed X values. Consider, however, if we had used an X value of 900 – for a store with sales of £900 000. This would be outside the previously observed range of X values for this sample of 20 centres. Although we could produce a forecast in exactly the same way – and this would be 52.839 – this would represent an *extrapolation*: a move into unknown territory. Technically, our regression equation was derived by observing behaviour between the two variables when sales was in the range 41.54 to 748.82. We have no way of knowing from this data what happens to the relationship between sales and profit – which is what the regression equation shows – once sales exceeds the maximum observed figure. By using the profit forecast of 52.839 we are extrapolating the historical relationship beyond its observed range and this increases the risk of the forecast being incorrect, since the relationship between the two variables might change in some fundamental way. Stores with larger sales, for example, might have larger profit margins than smaller stores.

However, despite these caveats we have succeeded in producing a forecast which we might regard as reasonably reliable, particularly given r = 0.97, indicating a strong linear correlation between the two variables under consideration.

Performance evaluation

The second use of the regression equation is in the context of performance evaluation of the existing stores. Effectively what the regression line shows us is the profit a particular store *should* have made given its sales level. Stores which have an actual profit figure above the line are 'over'-performing: turning in a profit which exceeds what we would have expected based simply on sales. Similarly, stores which have an actual profit below the line are 'under'-performing. Clearly we would not evaluate performance simply on the basis of this analysis but the estimated equation does provide an insight into relative performance of individual stores. We note from Figure 10.5, for example, that one store, shown as a solid square, with sales of around £264 000, is considerably below the line. In terms of priority and focus we might use the regression equation as a means of assisting management. This store should perhaps be one of the first to be investigated in terms of its profit performance: it appears to be under-performing since its profit is considerably below average given its sales level. Naturally there will be other factors that might emerge from the investigation: the store might recently have been closed for major refurbishment; a large local employer may have closed down, decreasing local income levels; a new competitor might have opened up nearby. Nevertheless, the use of the regression equation to highlight performance at variance with what we would have normally expected should not be underestimated.

A better burger thanks to data crunching

By Robert Matthews

HG Wells foresaw a time when what he called "statistical thinking" would play a key role in the running of society. Those who think of statistics as a way of keeping tabs on Albanian coal output will see this as one of his less inspirational predictions. But for anyone who believes in the power of data to create a better world where evidence reigns supreme, the good news is that the future is already here.

Or at least the foundations are, in the form of data mining: the extraction of insight from data gathered during the operation of everything from airlines and bookstores to supermarkets and schools.

This was all-but impossible before machine-readable records and computing power to crunch the stuff. But now we have both, and it is starting to transform our lives, as Yale Law School econometrician Ian Ayres shows in Super Crunchers, this entertaining, enlightening tour of our data-driven world.

Two statistical techniques lie at the heart of the revolution: regression and randomisation. The former uncovers connections between, say, the chances of people defaulting on their mortgage and factors influencing that risk, such as age, income and type of work.

Airlines, supermarkets, car hire companies and even dating agencies all run computerised "regression analysis" on their raw data to identify the key factors

behind everything from sales of dog food to success in love.

The effects can be felt by consumers, says Ayres, in subtle changes in the way they are treated. For example, when airlines cancel flights, some no longer woo faithful frequent fliers, but focus instead on the customers that regression analysis reveals are most likely never to fly with the airline again. Similarly, credit card users wanting to close accounts are assessed using regression methods – only those predicted to be profitable get the sweet-talk. . . .

Ayres balances his infectious enthusiasm with tales of where data mining can and has gone wrong. Correlation is not causation, and "garbage in" still means "garbage out" – as demonstrated by the salutary story of how honest mistakes led to a spurious correlation between wider gun ownership and lower crime rates – and to several US states changing their laws in line with the "evidence".

As Ayres points out, some people have a visceral loathing of the suggestion that the quality of a wine, a movie script or a relationship can be reduced to mere numbers. Yet those seeking a better world, or just a better burger, may have to get used to the idea that, to paraphrase Churchill on democracy, data mining is the worst possible basis for big decisions – apart from all the others.

The reviewer is visiting reader in science at Aston University, UK

 Source: Matthews, R. (2007) A better burger thanks to data crunching, *Financial Times*, 6 September. © Robert Matthews.

Regression is in more widespread use than you might at first think.

Further statistical evaluation of the regression equation

We can develop the statistical evaluation of the regression equation further. We shall explore this by introducing the coefficient of determination and statistical tests on the equation parameters. To explain the coefficient of determination we need to return to the idea of the regression equation as that of the method of least squares. One way of looking at regression is to say: we have observed some variation within the y values and we can measure this (as we might the standard deviation). We also have observed variation in the x data. Regression is effectively trying to link the variation in the y variable with the variation in the x variable (seeing if the two variations happen at the same time, if you like). We might find that all the variation in y can be associated with the variation in x, or, at the other extreme, that none of the variation in y can be so associated. In fact we can distinguish three types of variation:

- the total variation in y;
- the variation in y associated with variation in x;
- the variation in y not associated with x.

Progress Check 10.6

In terms of the regression equation, given the total variation, would you prefer the variation in y associated with variation in x to be as high or as low as possible?

Clearly the whole purpose of regression is to try to allocate as much of the total variation in y to the variation in our chosen x variable. We would therefore want this variation to be as high as possible. In regression terminology these three types of variation are referred to as total variation, explained variation and unexplained variation respectively. Let us examine Figure 10.6. This shows our line of best fit together with a horizontal line representing the mean of the y values in the data set and one (fictitious) observed point. To help distinguish between the various parts of the diagram we will use the following notation:

y the observed, actual, y value;

$\bar{y}$ the mean of all the y values (pronounced 'y bar');

$\hat{y}$ the value of y predicted by the regression equation (pronounced 'y hat').

You will remember that we said earlier that the regression equation is estimated using the principle of least squares. We can view the difference between y and $\bar{y}$ (between point 1 and point 3 on the graph) as a measure of the total variation: the difference between an individual y value and the mean of all the y values. Of this total variation $\hat{y} - \bar{y}$ (point 2–3) is the variation 'explained' by the regression line, whereas $y - \hat{y}$ (point 1–2) is that part of total variation which is 'unexplained'. Given that we measure variation in terms of squared differences (as with the standard deviations) then for this single observation we have:

Total variation:	$(y - \bar{y})^2$
Explained variation:	$(\hat{y} - \bar{y})^2$
Unexplained variation:	$(y - \hat{y})^2$

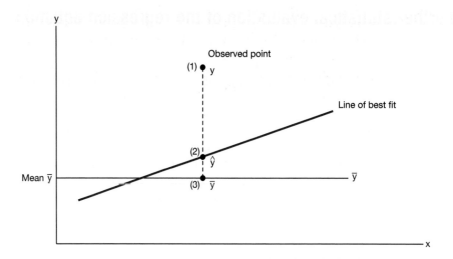

Figure 10.6 Variations

Note that we require the explained variation to be as large as possible in relation to the total variation and that the explained variation will be larger the closer the observed y value is to the estimated (given the line of best fit). In other words, the closer the estimated regression line is to the observed y value, the higher the explained variation will be in relation to the total variation. This applies to our single y value but clearly also applies to all the y values taken together. For all the data set we then have:

Total variation: $\Sigma (y - \bar{y})^2$
Explained variation: $\Sigma (\hat{y} - \bar{y})^2$
Unexplained variation: $\Sigma (y - \hat{y})^2$

If we take a ratio of the explained variation to the total variation:

$$\frac{\Sigma (\hat{y} - \bar{y})^2}{\Sigma (y - \bar{y})^2}$$

we have what is known as the coefficient of determination. This is denoted as R^2 (R squared).

Progress Check 10.7

What are the maximum and minimum values that R^2 could take for any set of data? How would you interpret these?

On reflection you should be able to see that the maximum value R^2 could take would be one, implying that all the variation was explained, or accounted for, by the regression equation. At the other extreme the minimum value would be zero. Typically we would expect the value to be between the two and, preferably, closer to one than zero. As such, the statistic will indicate the percentage of the total variation in y accounted for by the x variable. In practice, such a statistic would normally be computed by the regression software program you were using. In the case of our problem, the R^2 works out at $R^2 = 0.93$.

Ninety-three per cent of the total variation in profit (y) can be accounted for by variation in sales (x). We should also note that r, the correlation coefficient, is the square root of R^2, so either value can be calculated if we know the value of the other. Clearly we have statistical evidence of a strong relationship – as measured by our estimated equation – between the two variables. In fact we can test the estimated equation using the principles of hypothesis testing that we developed in Chapter 7.

Statistical tests on the equation parameters

You will remember from Chapter 7 that it was possible to test a sample statistic, such as the mean, against some hypothesised value for the population. In a variety of ways we can view our estimated regression equation as being a sample: we have used data for only a sample of 20 stores; we have used data for only a sample of years; we might have included data on other explanatory variables and so on. So, we can hypothesise about the population linear relationship and generalise this as:

$$Y = \alpha + \beta X$$

where α (alpha) and β (beta) are the population parameters of the equation (we continue using Greek characters to show population values). Clearly what we now have in our estimated equation $Y = -2.421 + 0.0614X$ is a sample result, and we might wish to test the statistical significance of this result. There are a variety of ways of doing this but we shall consider only one: a test on the b parameter in the estimated equation. Remember that the b term in the equation measures the slope of the line of best fit.

Progress Check 10.8

Suppose we set the H_0: $\beta = 0$. What would this imply for the relationship between X and Y?

The b term quantifies the relationship between X and Y in terms of how Y changes as X changes. If b were actually zero this would imply that Y did not change with X, i.e. there was no connection between the two. Suppose, then, we set up a hypothesis test to determine whether the b term in the equation (which is after all only a sample result) could have come from a statistical population where the slope, β, was actually zero. If we conclude that this has happened then it would imply that there was in fact no statistically significant relationship between the two variables. If we rejected this hypothesis then we would be forced to conclude – based on the sample data – that b was not zero and that there was a significant relationship between X and Y (which is best estimated using the calculated regression line). The principles of such a test are basically as detailed in Chapter 7.

$$H_0: \beta = 0$$
$$H_1: \beta \neq 0$$
$$\alpha = 0.05$$
$$\text{d.f.} = n - 2 = 18$$
$$t_{\alpha,18} = 2.101$$
$$t_{Calc} = \frac{b - \beta}{SE_b}$$

The null hypothesis is formulated such that we assume there is no relationship between X and Y: that $\beta = 0$. This requires us to provide sufficient evidence that there is such a relationship if we want to use the regression equation. The significance level is set at 0.05 and we must use the t distribution for the test, given we technically have a small sample. For a simple linear regression the number of degrees of freedom is given by $(n - 2)$, here 18. From the t table this gives a critical value of 2.101. The calculated t value is then found by taking the difference between the sample value and the hypothesised population value and dividing by the standard error of b. Although the standard error can be manually calculated from the formula:

$$SE_b = \sqrt{\frac{\Sigma(y - \hat{y})^2 (n-2)}{\Sigma x^2 - \left(\frac{\Sigma x}{n}\right)^2}}$$

it is more realistic to assume it will be produced by an appropriate software package. Such a package for our data would produce a result such that $SE_b = 0.003833$ and $t_{Calc} = 16.03$. Given that the calculated t statistic is greater than the critical, we would be forced to accept H_1 at the 95 per cent level and conclude that there is a significant relationship between the two variables (that is, that the slope of the population equation is not zero).

Consider again the logic of the test. We have estimated the slope of the regression line with sample data. We hypothesise that, notwithstanding the numerical result, the 'true' value of the equation for the population is $\beta = 0$: effectively that there is no statistically significant relationship between the X and Y variables. If this is the case we can measure the maximum distance, expressed in SEs, between β and b we would expect at the 95 per cent level. This distance is 2.101SEs: if H_0 is correct then β and b should be no further apart than this. We actually find that b is 16.03 SEs away from the hypothesised value. This is more than we would have expected on the basis of the null hypothesis and we are forced to reject the null hypothesis and accept the alternative instead. We have statistical evidence that there is a significant relationship between the two variables, profit and sales, based on this data, although remembering as we always must with statistical inference the possibilities of a Type I or II error.

It is important to understand that such a test is essential before considering the use of a regression equation in business forecasting. When performing regression we always get the line of best fit for the data being analysed. However, the term 'best fit' can be misleading. Best fit does not necessarily mean 'good fit' in the sense that we have a statistically significant relationship between the X and Y variables being analysed. The only reliable way to assess whether a regression equation is statistically sound is to perform a formal hypothesis test as we have just done. Even then, this is no guarantee that the regression equation will be reliable in a forecasting sense.

Using computer output

These days, regression models are produced via the result of some computer software, whether this is a spreadsheet system or a more sophisticated statistical modelling package. The output from such software varies but the general principles are relatively common. We show the results from one such package in the context of our problem in Table 10.3. The *summary output* shows the key statistical information. The *regression statistics* show the *multiple R* at 0.96663826. This is our correlation coefficient value (note that there are slight differences between the computer output and our manual

Table 10.3   Computer output for regression model

```
SUMMARY OUTPUT

            Regression Statistics
Multiple R                  0.96663826
R Square                    0.934389526
Adjusted R Square           0.930744499
Standard Error              3.482561605
Observations                        20
```

ANOVA

	df	SS	MS	F	Significance F
Regression	1	3109.029944	3109.029944	256.3464394	4.30781E-12
Residual	18	218.308236	12.12823534		
Total	19	3327.33818			

	Coefficients	Standard Error	t Stat	P value	Lower 95%	Upper 95%
Intercept	-2.418465725	1.17779207	-2.053389377	0.05485855	-4.892916958	0.055985509
Sales	0.061372898	0.003833213	16.01082257	4.30781E-12	0.05331961	0.069426187

RESIDUAL OUTPUT

Observation	Predicted Y	Residuals
1	43.53878802	-1.408788025
2	6.221610906	0.098389094
3	40.67205994	-2.202059942
4	0.130964473	-0.450964473
5	3.525499482	0.124500518
6	7.826512199	-0.056512199
7	4.274248842	0.035751158
8	13.77906961	-9.24906961
9	0.701732428	-3.391732428
10	3.11000496	0.10999504
11	9.278594974	-0.248594974
12	3.2124977	-5.8024977
13	6.270095496	0.119904504
14	20.72157187	3.668428127
15	9.77571545	4.14428455
16	1.434524834	0.695475166
17	13.86253675	3.617463248
18	3.215566345	3.994433655
19	11.79549754	3.824502465
20	31.23290817	2.377091825

calculations as we kept the latter simple by rounding values down). Under this we have the *R square* at 0.934389526. At the bottom of the summary output we have the regression equation results. We see an *intercept coefficient* of –2.418465725 and a *sales coefficient* result of 0.061372898, confirming our own calculated regression equation. For each of the equation parameters we also see a *standard error*, a *t stat*, a *p value* and a *lower 95%* and *upper 95%* statistic. We saw earlier that we could undertake a statistical hypothesis test on the *b* value. The output gives us the calculated t value (at 16.01) and also the associated p value. We looked at p values in Chapter 7. Recollect that the p value is a quick way of seeing how likely the null hypothesis is, based on the sample data. The lower the p value the less likely the null hypothesis and if the p value is less than the significance level of the test (where we usually choose to do the test at either the 5 per cent or 1 per cent level) then we reject the null hypothesis. Recollect also that when testing the *b* coefficient in the regression equation the null hypothesis is the *b* = 0. The p value from the output is 4.30781E-12, which seems a very odd number if you're not used to seeing them in this format. This is a standard way in many computer packages of showing very small numerical values. The E term actually represents the number 10 so we have:

$$4.30781\text{E} - 12 = 4.30781 \times 10^{-12}$$

which is 0.000 000 000 004 307 81.

In other words, a very small p value! In this case the p value confirms that the null hypothesis (that *b* = 0) is highly unlikely, implying that we have a highly significant

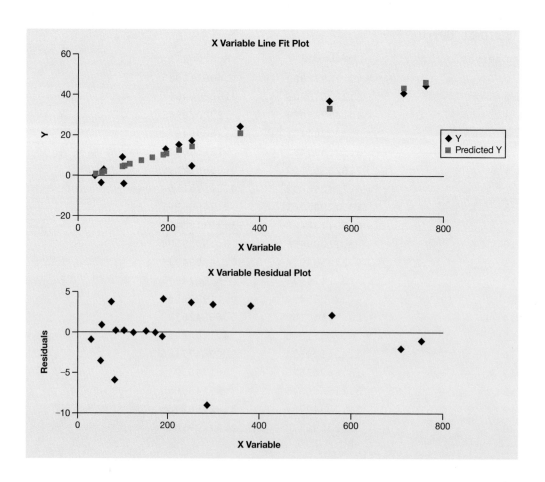

result. The *Lower 95%* and *Upper 95%* statistics give us a calculated 95% confidence interval around the *b* value. Note that the same analysis can be done on the other parameter of the regression equation, the *a* term or intercept. Although less common, it follows exactly the same principles. This test focuses on whether the *a* term is zero, which implies that we think the line of best fit should actually go through the origin on a graph, which may better represent some business situations. Such packages also typically produce additional output as a standard option, here including what is known as Residual output, and can also automatically generate charts of the key results. Note also that additional statistics appear that we have not mentioned. This is an important point for regression modelling. Although in principle regression appears a straightforward technique, the assumptions underpinning the validity of the approach are quite complex. Regression is, arguably, one of the most widely used techniques while simultaneously being the worst understood. These additional statistics – and a veritable array of others – simply underpin the complexity of the technique in terms of its valid application in the business world.

Prediction intervals for forecasts

It may have occurred to you that we have already applied a number of statistical inference principles to the regression analysis. One obvious area of application that we have so far not considered is that of a confidence interval around a forecast produced from the regression equation. Such an interval can be calculated and is known as a *prediction interval*. For the simple linear regression situation a prediction interval around some predicted value of Y, $\hat{Y}$ can be calculated from:

$$\hat{Y} \pm t_{\alpha/2, n-2} S \sqrt{1 + \frac{1}{n} + \frac{(X_F - \overline{X})^2}{SS_X}}$$

where X_F is the numeric X value used to produce the forecast for Y from the regression equation and

$$S = \sqrt{\frac{\sum (Y - \hat{Y})^2}{n-2}}$$

and

$$SS_X = \sum X^2 - \frac{(\sum X)^2}{n}$$

Suppose we want a 95 per cent prediction interval around forecast profit for a store with sales of £400 000. From the regression equation the forecast would be:

$$Profit = -2.421 + 0.0614X = -2.421 + 0.0614(400) = 22.14$$

We then have:

$$\hat{Y} = 22.14 \text{ and } X_F = 400$$

To calculate S we require $\sum (Y - \hat{Y})^2$. Table 10.4 shows the relevant calculations. Thus, from the table, $\sum (Y - \hat{Y})^2 = 218.3091$. This then gives:

$$S = \sqrt{\frac{\sum (Y - \hat{Y})^2}{n - 2}} = \sqrt{\frac{218.3091}{18}} = 3.482565$$

Table 10.4   Calculations for $\Sigma(Y - \hat{Y})^2$

Sales X	Profit Y	$\Sigma(Y - \hat{Y})^2$	Sales X	Profit Y	$\Sigma(Y - \hat{Y})^2$
748.82	42.13	2.0350	91.75	−2.59	33.6684
140.78	6.32	0.0094	141.57	6.39	0.0141
702.11	38.47	4.9220	377.04	24.39	13.4010
41.54	−0.32	0.2021	198.69	13.92	17.1515
96.85	3.65	0.0155	62.78	2.13	0.4848
166.93	7.77	0.0034	265.28	17.48	13.0524
109.05	4.31	0.0012	91.8	7.21	15.9559
263.92	4.53	85.6307	231.6	15.62	14.5982
50.84	−2.69	11.4960	548.31	33.61	5.5921
90.08	3.22	0.0121			
190.59	9.03	0.0631	Total		218.3091

(in fact this S value is found in the summary output table we looked at earlier and is shown as standard error) and from Table 10.2:

$$SS_X = \Sigma X^2 - \frac{(\Sigma X)^2}{n} = 1\ 888\ 170.77 - \frac{4610.33^2}{20} = 825\ 413.63$$

and $\overline{X} = 230.5165$

Substituting, we have:

$$S\sqrt{1 + \frac{1}{n} + \frac{(X_F - \overline{X})^2}{SS_X}} = 3.482565\sqrt{1 + \frac{1}{20} + \frac{(400 - 230.5165)^2}{825\ 413.63}} = 3.6272$$

To calculate the prediction interval we require the relevant t value from Appendix C. With 18 degrees of freedom and $a/2 = 0.025$ we see a t value of 2.101. The prediction interval is then:

$22.14 \pm 2.101(3.6272)$
or 22.14 ± 7.62
or 14.52 ± 29.76

We should note that the sample size (here n = 20) has a large effect on the size of this interval. Realistically, we should be using a larger sample of data for our analysis, which would have the effect of reducing the size of the prediction interval. We should also note that the size of the interval will change as we forecast Y using different values for X. In fact, the size of the interval is smallest as X approaches the value $\overline{X}$ and increases the further away X gets from $\overline{X}$ To illustrate this we have calculated the interval for varying X values as shown in Table 10.5.

The general effect is illustrated in Figure 10.7, confirming again the inherent difficulties of extrapolated forecasts.

Table 10.5 Prediction intervals

X_F	$\hat{Y}$	Interval	X_F	$\hat{Y}$	Interval
50	0.65	7.6372	400	22.14	7.6208
100	3.72	7.5709	450	25.21	7.7031
150	6.79	7.5255	500	28.28	7.8054
200	9.86	7.5016	550	31.35	7.9268
250	12.93	7.4992	600	34.42	8.0665
300	16.00	7.5184	650	37.49	8.2235
350	19.07	7.5591	700	40.56	8.3970

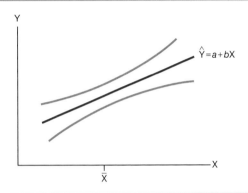

Figure 10.7 Prediction intervals

Estimating a trend using regression

You will remember that in the previous chapter when we were examining time-series models we identified a trend for a time-series variable using moving averages and we produced a forecast of the trend to allow us to forecast the data series we were examining. Regression can be applied to such a trend variable to predict the trend at some future period. Table 10.6 shows the data we were analysing in Chapter 9, domestic electricity sales, together with the trend which we calculated using moving averages.

As far as the trend is concerned, we can view this as a variable which alters over time, that is:

$$\text{Trend} = f\,(\text{Time})$$

We can, in one sense therefore, regard time as an explanatory variable of the trend. If we denote the time variable as T we can then specify a model:

$$\text{Trend} = a + b\text{T}$$

and this model clearly fits into the regression structure we have developed. To obtain a regression line in such a situation we already have numerical values for the trend variable. For T, the time variable, we arbitrarily allocate numerical values of 1 for the first

Table 10.6   Domestic electricity sales GwH

	Domestic sales	Trend	Scenario A	Scenario B		Domestic sales	Trend	Scenario A	Scenario B
2006:1	37 467	31 542	1		2012:2	25 157	28 394	26	
2006:2	27 489	31 308	2		2012:3	23 164	28 765	27	
2006:3	24 994	30 896	3		2012:4	32 836	28 904	28	
2006:4	34 754	30 510	4		2013:1	34 302	28 886	29	1
2007:1	35 226	30 466	5		2013:2	25 468	28 591	30	2
2007:2	26 645	30 648	6		2013:3	22 708	28 032	31	3
2007:3	25 484	30 701	7		2013:4	30 934	27 543	32	4
2007:4	35 721	30 621	8		2014:1	31 731	27 330	33	5
2008:1	34 683	30 548	9		2014:2	24 128	27 152	34	6
2008:2	26 549	30 218	10		2014:3	22 347	26 996	35	7
2008:3	24 990	30 163	11		2014:4	29 870	26 975	36	8
2008:4	33 578	30 223	12		2015:1	31 546	26 956	37	9
2009:1	36 388	29 930	13		2015:2	24 148	26 938	38	10
2009:2	25 324	29 713	14		2015:3	22 174	26 986	39	11
2009:3	23 872	29 597	15		2015:4	29 896	27 014	40	12
2009:4	32 957	29 528	16		2016:1	31 904	26 954	41	13
2010:1	36 083	29 415	17		2016:2	24 014	26 952	42	14
2010:2	25 075	29 520	18		2016:3	21 831	26 833	43	15
2010:3	23 215	29 458	19		2016:4	30 222	26 595	44	16
2010:4	34 459	29 069	20		2017:1	30 629	26 465	45	17
2011:1	34 085	28 887	21		2017:2	23 384	26 382	46	18
2011:2	23 956	28 371	22		2017:3	21 423	26 497	47	19
2011:3	22 881	27 824	23		2017:4	29 960			
2011:4	30 664	27 902	24		2018:1	31 816			
2012:1	33 506	28 087	25						

period, 2 for the second, 3 for the third and so on through to n for the last period. Using these numerical values we can then apply the regression model and obtain the line of best fit, together with the other supporting statistics. You will remember from Chapter 9 that we considered two scenarios for our trend forecast. Scenario A was to use trend data from 2006 onwards for our forecast. Scenario B was to use data only from 2013 onwards. In Table 10.6 we see that the column headed Scenario A starts at 2006 Quarter 1 up to the last available trend data for 2017 Quarter 3 giving T = 1 to 47 for Scenario A.

The appropriate regression results can then be produced, using T = 1 to 47, as shown in Table 10.7.

From the computer output we obtain an equation

$$\text{Trend} = 31\,290 - 109.36T$$

We see that the R^2 is high (at 0.95) and that both parameters in the equation (intercept and slope) are statistically significant (both p values are extremely small) indicating a

Table 10.7   Regression results for Scenario A

```
SUMMARY OUTPUT
            Regression Statistics
Multiple R                  0.974779819
R Square                    0.950195696
Adjusted R Square           0.949088934
Standard Error              347.0721338
Observations                         47
```

ANOVA

	df	SS	MS	F	Significance F
Regression	1	103418489.1	103418489.1	858.5363678	5.91611E-31
Residual	45	5420657.974	120459.0661		
Total	46	108839147			

	Coefficients	Standard Error	t Stat	P value	Lower 95%	Upper 95%
Intercept	31290.16549	102.888942	304.1159222	3.379E-76	31082.93653	31497.39445
X Variable 1	-109.3556569	3.732174192	-29.30079125	5.91611E-31	-116.8726415	-101.8386723

statistically strong result. Interpretation of the results is straightforward. Over this period, the underlying growth in trend domestic electricity sales has been negative – declining by around 110 GwH per quarter. Now by substituting specific numerical values for T into the equation we can forecast future trend values.

Assume we want a trend forecast for Quarter 4 in 2018. According to our arbitrary allocation of numerical values for T this period would take a value T = 52. Substituting $T = 52$ into the regression equation gives a trend forecast of 25 604 GwH.

Clearly we would not necessarily attach a high degree of reliability to such a forecast. After all, it is based on the critical assumption that the growth pattern in the trend evidenced over the period analysed will continue. However, it is easy to see how alternative scenario forecasts could easily be produced and the range of scenario forecasts can then be assessed by management.

Progress Check 10.9

In Chapter 9 we developed a second scenario around the trend forecast for this data. This was to assume that the trend had fundamentally altered from the beginning of 2013. Using the trend from 2013:1 onwards, determine the relevant regression equation and associated statistics. Use the regression equation to obtain a trend forecast for 2018:4.

Statistically, do you think the regression equation for Scenario B is better than that for Scenario A?

Solution is given on p 581.

Non-linear regression

It is also worth noting that regression is readily adapted to situations where we have some non-linear relationship between two variables. Effectively, we can take the actual X and Y data and perform an appropriate mathematical transformation so that a corresponding linear expression can be obtained. The mathematics of this takes us beyond the limits we have set for this subject matter but it is worth being aware that this possibility exists. Clearly if, from the scatter diagram, there is evidence of a non-linear relationship between two variables, this does not necessarily mean that regression must be abandoned as a forecasting approach. It may be possible to adapt the model to a non-linear format, but this will depend on the exact circumstances of the problem and the non-linear relationship between the two variables. Such non-linear transformations are usually available in specialist computer software. An example is shown in Figure 10.8. This relates to work undertaken by British Gas in terms of trying to model and forecast the demand for gas in the UK from industrial customers. From the diagram it can be seen

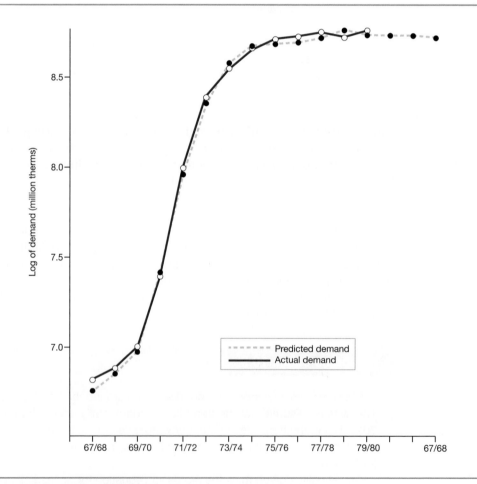

Figure 10.8 Industrial demand for gas

Source: Lang, P. (1988) Energy forecasting made simple, *Operational Research Insight*, 1 (3), pp 5–7.
© 1988 Macmillan Publishers Limited.
Reprinted by permission from Macmillan Publishers Limited, www.palgrave-journals.com.

that the actual demand over the period 1967/68 to 1978/79 was clearly non-linear and any attempt at modelling and then forecasting such demand based on a linear regression model would clearly be worthless. A non-linear model was developed (based on logarithms) and using a number of explanatory variables through multiple regression (which we examine in detail in the next section) and it can be seen from Figure 10.8 that this non-linear model was able to produce highly accurate predictions of industrial gas demand over this period.

QADM IN ACTION

Capgemini – controlling staff costs through regression analysis

Capgemini's client was a major public house operator. The main expense for any of the client's outlets is staff costs. Historically, these had been a predictable percentage of turnover. However, over the last two years staff costs had been increasing whilst, at the same time, the client was moving into a new market by expanding the amount and variety of food that was available across its chain of pubs. The client wanted an analysis of the factors causing staff costs to increase together with possible ways of improving the profitability of its outlets.

The client already had considerable data on factors which influence staff operating costs. It was decided to use a statistical approach to determining categories of variables that influenced staff costs most. Multiple regression was then used using these categories as explanatory variables.

Because of problems with the quality of the data available, *ad hoc* analysis also took place to identify outlets which were outliers in the data set.

The client's existing database was used to collect data on an outlet-by-outlet basis. Because both the type of outlet and the size of outlet are likely to influence staff costs it was important that outlets were categorised accordingly. This was achieved with a combination of questionnaires to a sample of pub managers and by direct data collection on site.

A statistical technique known as factor analysis was used to determine categories of variables that could be interpreted as the main drivers of staff cost. These were then used by a multiple regression analysis that helped identify which of these categories influenced cost. Finally, to prove that the

identified cost drivers could actually be influenced or controlled by pub management, an outlet was chosen to modify the operating procedure.

An example of one of the scatter diagrams used during the project is shown below. Outliers are clearly visible from this approach and can be investigated further.

The benefits are as follows:

- A clear picture of the factors that affect staff operating costs can be obtained.

- The ability to drive down staff operating costs.

- Better management information for pub managers about how they could control staff costs.

- Recommendations about data collection and storage.

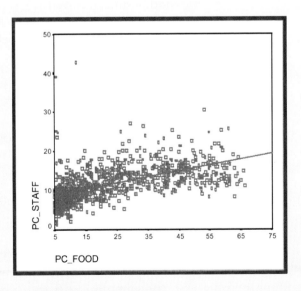

Source: Based on a Capgemini case study, with thanks to Capgemini for permission to use their material.

Multiple regression

So far, we have examined regression in the context of a single explanatory variable. It is unlikely in practice that a business variable, Y, will be influenced by only one other variable, X. We might more reasonably expect a number of explanatory variables to affect the Y variable we are investigating. It is for this reason that *multiple regression* has been developed, where we try to explain some Y variable with several explanatory variables and not just one. An increasing number of regression models in business are based on this approach. In this section we shall introduce the ideas behind multiple regression, although, again, we must comment that in practice the development of such models for business forecasting should be left to those with a detailed statistical understanding of the approach. Multiple regression models are particularly complex in both their structure and the statistical assumptions which underpin them. On the surface, such a model may appear appropriate for forecasting in some business situation, whereas in reality it has some fundamental statistical flaw apparent only to the statistical expert. Hasty use of such models may lead to serious forecasting errors with major – and adverse – business consequences.

However, in this section it is our intention to develop a conceptual understanding of the general approach so that the principles, if not the statistical detail, can be properly understood. In general, then, we can develop a multiple regression model of the form:

$$Y = a + b_1X_1 + b_2X_2 + b_3X_3 + \cdots + b_mX_m$$

with some number, m, of explanatory variables. Clearly this is an extension of the simple regression model. The calculations involved in multiple regression are both complex and tedious and any real application will rely on a suitable specialist computer package. The principles behind the method, however, remain as before. The method of least squares will estimate a relationship which 'best' fits the data across all the X variables and the results can be evaluated in much the same way as before. Consider the simple regression analysis we have just completed, linking profits to sales in a sample of 20 stores. Let us picture a scenario where the company is considering expanding its operations by opening another store. It currently has two alternative sites for the store under examination and is trying to assess the likely profitability of opening a store on the two sites. It might be more realistic to develop a model where we considered additional explanatory variables we felt might logically affect profit. These might include:

- The size of each store measured in thousands of square feet. The larger the store, other things being equal, the more customers and the more profit we might reasonably expect.
- The number of different product lines carried by the store. Again, the more product lines carried, the more 'popular' the store is likely to be with customers.
- The distance from the nearest major competitor measured in kilometres.

Table 10.8 shows the data we shall be analysing collected from 20 existing stores. We can then formulate a model where:

$$\text{Profit} = a + b_1 \text{ Sales} + b_2 \text{ Size} + b_3 \text{ Lines} + b_4 \text{ Distance}$$

Table 10.8   Data for 20 stores

Profit (£000s)	Sales (£000s)	Size (000s sq ft)	Lines	Distance (km)
42.13	748.82	6.0	150	0.1
6.32	140.78	1.4	75	0.1
38.47	702.11	5.0	170	0.5
−0.32	41.54	1.0	75	0
3.65	96.85	1.2	75	0.2
7.77	166.93	1.5	75	0.5
4.31	109.05	1.3	75	0.3
4.53	263.92	1.1	80	0.4
−2.69	50.84	1.1	75	0
3.22	90.08	1.2	75	0.6
9.03	190.59	1.4	80	0.5
−2.59	91.75	1.2	75	0
6.39	141.57	1.4	80	0.3
24.39	377.04	3.5	160	1.2
13.92	198.69	1.5	100	0.7
2.13	62.78	1.3	75	0.1
17.48	265.28	2.1	110	0.9
7.21	91.80	1.3	85	0.3
15.62	231.60	2.5	120	0.9
33.61	548.31	4.5	200	0.5

Data file 10-8

that is, where profit in a particular store is determined not just by sales but by a combination of the explanatory variables. Multiple regression then provides the numerical estimates for the b parameters in the equation. However, there is more to multiple regression than simply feeding numbers into a computer package (and most spreadsheets will perform multiple regression) and getting the numerical results. A common approach is to break the analysis into a number of key stages:

- Determine the expected b values.
- Produce individual scatter plots.
- Produce the multiple regression results.
- Assess the overall fit of the model.
- Assess the individual b parameters.
- Check the multiple regression assumptions.
- Where necessary amend the model and go through another iteration.

It is frequently the case that multiple regression requires an iterative approach. It is unusual to produce the 'best' multiple regression model at the first attempt. Normally, some aspect of the current model will be deemed to be inappropriate and the model adjusted and then reassessed. We shall illustrate with our example.

Determine the expected *b* values

The first stage is to consider the numerical values for the *b* parameters that you would expect, given the business context of the problem. It is important before you start looking at any results that you have a clear view as to the likely results so that you can apply 'common sense' to them before more rigorous statistical analysis.

Progress Check 10.10

What numerical values would you expect for $b_1 \ldots b_4$: positive, negative or zero?

It seems logical in this case to expect all the *b* parameters to take positive values: that is, an increase in any of them would be expected to lead to an increase in profit. Once we produce results, we can check the logical consistency of our results against these expectations.

Produce individual scatter plots

You should understand why it is not possible to produce a scatter plot of the Y variable, profit, against all the X variables on a single diagram: we have only two axes after all and five variables. It is often worthwhile producing a scatter plot of the Y variables against each of the X variables in turn. This then allows us to see the relationship between Y and each X and, importantly, to check visually whether each relationship appears linear. Such a visual check is not particularly rigorous but does help our overall assessment of the model. Figure 10.9 shows the four scatter plots.

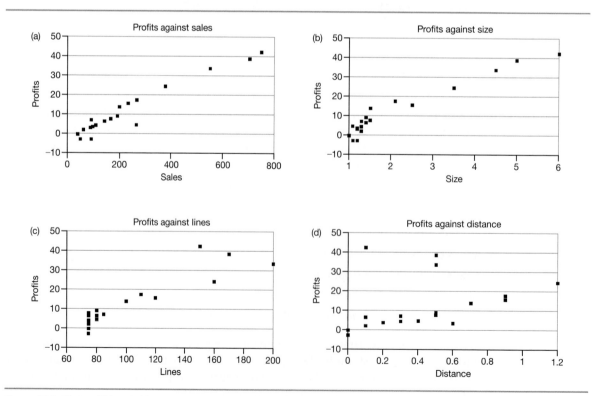

Figure 10.9 Plots of Y variable, profits, against each X variable – sales, size, lines and distance

All four plots appear reasonably linear, although to differing degrees. However, we are not looking for perfect correlations between profit and each X but rather no obvious sign of any non-linear relationships.

Produce the multiple regression results

We have the results from a regression computer package as shown in Table 10.9.

Table 10.9 is typical of such computer output, showing the equation results and something known as an Analysis of Variance table, often referred to as an ANOVA table.

Assess the overall fit of the model

The next stage is to assess the results produced. We do this in several ways, the first of which is to assess the overall fit of the model: overall, how good is the equation we have obtained? The first thing to check is the actual numerical values of the b terms compared with what we expected. It is not uncommon for some of the calculated b values to be different from those expected. If this occurs it should make us reconsider the model itself. It may be that under such circumstances our understanding of the relationships between the variables is incorrect or incomplete; we may have suspect data; there may be a fundamental flaw in our approach. Whatever the reason, we should investigate to try to assess the cause of such an inconsistency.

Table 10.9 Regression results

```
SUMMARY OUTPUT

          Regression Statistics
Multiple R              0.986949961
R Square                0.974070225
Adjusted R Square       0.967155618
Standard Error          2.398292891
Observations                     20
```

ANOVA

	df	SS	MS	F	Significance F
Regression	4	3241.061048	810.265262	140.8713835	1.05404E-11
Residual	15	86.27713186	5.751808791		
Total	19	3327.33818			

	Coefficients	Standard Error	t Stat	P-value	Lower 95%	Upper 95%
Intercept	-7.240858922	2.092137285	-3.460986511	0.003492213	-11.70014673	-2.781571115
Sales	0.025873382	0.010332636	2.504044708	0.024310908	0.003849877	0.047896888
Size	4.549262843	1.773743489	2.564780574	0.021556558	0.768615766	8.32990992
Lines	0.011928598	0.040904073	0.291623731	0.774568575	-0.075256423	0.09911362
Distance	5.844624421	2.085939851	2.801914167	0.013407842	1.398546139	10.2907027

From Table 10.9 we see each of the explanatory variables listed and next to these (labelled 'Coefficients') the estimated numerical coefficient. We also see that the constant term is shown. The estimated equation is then:

$$\text{Profit} = +0.02587\,\text{Sales} + 4.54926\,\text{Size} + 0.01193\,\text{Lines} + 5.84462\,\text{Distance}$$

However, in our example all appears well. Each of the b terms in the estimated equation is positive – consistent with what we initially expected to find. Similarly, although we did not say this earlier, the a term, or constant, which is negative also, takes a logical value given the business context. If all the X variables were set to zero, profit would be negative, implying a store has some break-even position in terms of distance, size, lines and sales.

We can also evaluate the overall fit of the model statistically by examining the R^2 value. However, on inspection we see that the table actually has two R^2 values:

R square at 0.97407 and Adjusted R square at 0.96716

We shall look at the R square value at 0.97407 first. You will remember that we also obtained an R^2 value for a simple regression equation. When we regressed profit only on sales we obtained an R^2 value of 0.93, which was seen as a particularly high value, given that the R^2 for any situation must take a value between 0 and 1. We interpreted this as implying that 93 per cent of the variation in Y (profit) was accounted for by the X variable (sales). For a multiple regression equation we can interpret R^2 in exactly the same way: 97.4 per cent of the variation in Y is accounted for by the variation in the X variables we have used in the equation. Our overall model, then, appears to provide a good fit, with only a small amount of the variation in Y unexplained by the X variables we have chosen. If the R^2 had been lower, say 0.61, we would have been concerned that the X variables were not 'explaining' enough of the variation in the Y variable and that, perhaps, there was some important X variable that we had overlooked and omitted from the analysis.

R^2 can also be confirmed from the ANOVA shown in Table 10.8. Earlier in the chapter we saw that R^2 was the ratio of the explained variation to the total variation. The total variation, logically, is the sum of the explained variation and the unexplained variation. The explained variation is shown in the ANOVA as the *regression sum of squares* at 3241.061048, and the unexplained variation as *residual sum of squares* at 86.27713. The total variation is then 3327.33818 (3241.06105 + 86.27713). This gives R^2 as 3241.06105/3327.33818 or 0.97407, confirming the R^2 shown in the table. However, we can go one stage further. It will be evident that we do not have any rigorous method for assessing whether R^2 is sufficiently high or not. Clearly in this example 0.97 is a high value. Would we have had confidence in the regression equation if R^2 had been 0.87, or 0.77 or 0.67? The method for statistically assessing the overall goodness of fit of the equation is through the application of what is known as an *F test*, effectively a hypothesis test on R^2. With such a test we formulate the same R^2 every time: that the b terms in the equation are not statistically different from zero. That is:

$$H_0: \beta_1 = \beta_2 = \beta_3 = \beta_4 = 0$$

If at the end of the test we reject H_0, it implies that at least one of the X variables is statistically significant. If we fail to reject H_0 it implies that none of the X variables is significant: Y is statistically independent of the X variables and the estimated equation is not reliable. All the details we require for the test are contained in the ANOVA part of the table. The F statistic itself is calculated as:

$$F = \frac{\text{Mean square for regression}}{\text{Mean square for error}} \quad \text{or} \quad \frac{\text{MSR}}{\text{MSE}}$$

MSR is given as:

$$\text{MSR} = \frac{\text{Sum of squares for regression}}{v_1}$$

where $v_1 = m$, that is the number of explanatory variables included in the equation. Here we have:

$$\text{MSR} = \frac{3241.06105}{4} = 810.26526$$

We see from Table 10.9 that all the relevant calculation is in fact given. The mean square is shown at 810.26526 with v_1 at 4, shown as df (or degrees of freedom). MSE in turn is given by:

$$\text{MSE} = \frac{\text{Sum of squares for error (or residual)}}{v_2}$$

where $v_2 = n - m - 1$. Here we have:

$$\text{MSE} = \frac{86.27713}{15} = 5.75181$$

and again we see this figure in the ANOVA. The calculated F ratio is then:

$$F = \frac{\text{MSR}}{\text{MSE}} = \frac{810.26526}{5.75181} = 140.8713$$

and again, this is shown in Table 10.9 for us. Like any hypothesis test, this calculated F ratio is to be compared against a critical F that we obtain from appropriate tables. If the calculated F is greater than the critical we are forced to reject H_0, which in this case means that we would conclude there was a statistically significant relationship between Y and the X variables used. Appendix E shows the relevant table for the F statistic for $\alpha = 0.05$. Note that, unlike the other tests we have conducted, the F statistic has two sets of degrees of freedom associated with it, v_1 and v_2 We have $v_1 = 4$ and $v_2 = 15$ The columns of the table relate to $v_1 = 4$ and we locate the column where $v_2 = 15$ The rows relate to v_2 and we locate the row corresponding to $v_2 = 15$ We read a figure of 3.06. This is the critical F value. If the calculated F is greater than the critical then (like every other test we have done) we reject H_0. If the calculated F is less than the critical then we cannot reject H_0. In this case the calculated F at 140.87 is greater than the critical at 3.05 so we are forced to reject H_0 and conclude that there is a significant relationship between Y and the X variables. As is often the case with computer output, this test has actually been done for us. The term *significance F* shown in the table is in fact the p value associated with the test. That is, it is the probability that we should *not* reject H_0. Given that this is zero, we are being told to reject H_0. The F test is a critical part of the evaluation of a multiple regression model. No matter what the R^2 value, we should conduct such a test to assess the overall goodness of fit of the estimated equation. If we fail to reject H_0 at this stage, there is no point going further in our evaluation. Effectively, the estimated equation is worthless and we would need to reconsider the model we are trying to develop.

Assess the individual *b* parameters

However, in our case, the equation has, literally, passed the test and we move on to the next stage of the evaluation. This is to examine the individual *b* parameters. It is important to realise that the F test we have just conducted assesses the overall equation. It may well be that even though the equation overall is statistically significant there are parts of it that are not. In other words, we have four explanatory variables in the model. How do we know whether each of these by itself is making a statistically significant contribution to the overall equation? For example, if we took out, say, the Size variable, would it really make much of a difference to the R^2? We can answer this by assessing the statistical significance of each *b* term in turn through an individual t test. We have already applied this test on a simple regression equation and the principle is no different. For parameter β_1, for example, associated with the sales variable, we set up the hypothesis test as:

$$H_0 \quad \beta_1 = 0$$
$$H_1 \quad \beta_1 \neq 0$$

That is, could we set β_1 to zero and not affect the overall fit of the model? Note that we have a two-tail test here. In some cases, a one-tail test might be appropriate but the principles do not alter. As with simple regression, the calculated t is found by:

$$t_{Calc} = \frac{b_1}{SE_{b_1}}$$

that is, the estimated coefficient, b_1, divided by its standard error. The standard error is shown in Table 10.8 as SE B at 0.010332636 and we obtain the calculated t as:

$$t_{Calc} = \frac{b_1}{SE_{b_1}} = \frac{0.025873382}{0.010332636} = 2.504$$

which again is shown in the computer output as *t stat*. As before, we must compare this with a critical statistic from the t table. The relevant degrees of freedom is given by:

$$v = n - m - 1$$
$$\text{or } v = 20 - 4 - 1 = 15$$

From Appendix C with $\alpha = 0.05$ we have a critical t of 2.131 (remember it's a two-tail test). As ever, with the calculated t greater than the critical t we reject H_0 and are forced to conclude that β_1 is significantly different from zero. That is, this Sales variable is making a statistically significant contribution to the estimated equation (and hence to the overall R^2). However, once again, the test is implicitly done for us by the computer package. The *p value* figures shown in Table 10.9 are again the p values associated with each test. For β_1 we see a figure of 0.0243, implying that the associated probability of not rejecting H_0 is only just over 2 per cent. With $\alpha = 0.05$ for the test we would decide not to reject H_0 only if the p value was greater than 0.05.

Carry out the tests for each of the other explanatory variables in the estimated equation.

The comparable tests for the other variables lead us to conclude at the 95 per cent level that Size and Sales also are statistically significant (that is, they make a significant contribution to the equation and to the R^2). However, for Lines the test would lead us not to reject H_0. We could not reject the hypothesis for this variable that β_3 equals zero. There is no evidence to conclude that Lines is making a significant contribution to the overall equation. In other words, based on these results, the Lines variable should *not* be included in the equation. This is an important conclusion and one sometimes leading to confusion. The F test we conducted earlier showed that the equation overall was significant. These *b* tests indicate that some of the X variables make a significant contribution to the equation but that the Lines variable does not. So what should we do? The answer is that we go into the next iteration of the regression process. We must drop the Lines variable from the model and recalculate the entire equation and the associated statistics and then re-evaluate the new results.

It is important to realise that by deciding to drop the Lines variable we cannot simply erase it from the existing estimated equation and use the rest of the equation for forecasting. The estimated equation coefficients will be affected by the removal of one variable and the entire equation must be re-estimated before we can proceed. Once it is re-estimated we must evaluate it again – we cannot assume the new equation is statistically sound just because we have dropped one variable at this stage. We must treat the new estimated equation in exactly the same way. The computer output is shown in Table 10.10.

Evaluate the results of this model.

We follow much the same process as before, although clearly we do not need to repeat the stage where we determine the expected values for the *b* terms or produce the scatter diagrams, since these will be unchanged. First we must assess the equation:

$$\text{Profit} = -6.7469 + 0.02562\,\text{Sales} + 4.84849\,\text{Size} + 6.19361\,\text{Distance}$$

Once again, the *b* terms are all positive as we anticipated. Note also that there are slight changes in all the coefficients as a result of removing the lines variable. We see that R^2 at 0.97392 is again high and is, in fact, little changed from our first model at 0.97407. This confirms that we were right to remove the Lines variable – it was adding little to the overall fit of the model. Without the Lines variable we are 'explaining' 97.392 per cent of the variation in profit. With the lines variable we are explaining only another 0.015 per cent. To test the overall fit of the equation we conduct an F test. We see from the ANOVA that the calculated F is 199.19 and the significance F effectively at 0.0000 indicates that

Table 10.10   Regression results: second model

```
SUMMARY OUTPUT

        Regression Statistics
Multiple R              0.98687548

R square                0.973923212

Adjusted R square       0.969033815
Standard error          2.328710628

Observations                  20


ANOVA
                df          SS            MS             F        Significance F
Regression       3     3240.571889    1080.19063    199.1908364    7.05484E-13
Residual        16      86.76629099    5.422893187
Total           19     3327.33818
```

	Coefficients	Standard Error	t Stat	P-value	Lower 95%	Upper 95%
Intercept	-6.746895165	1.192356946	-5.65845252	3.55986E-05	-9.274578402	-4.219211928
Sales	0.02562451	0.009998574	2.562816441	0.020855446	0.004428485	0.046820535
Size	4.84848802	1.404865382	3.451211825	0.003285156	1.870307124	7.826668916
Distance	6.193605355	1.658966238	3.733412538	0.001810049	2.676754829	9.710455881

we reject the null hypothesis and conclude that overall there is a good fit to the model. (You should confirm that the total sum of squares has not altered and also ensure you understand why the degrees of freedom values have altered.)

As before, the F test indicates the equation overall is a good fit, but this does not necessarily imply that each variable is making a significant contribution. However, by looking at the *t stat* values we do in fact confirm that each of the three explanatory variables is statistically significant at the 95 per cent level, since all the p values are less than 0.05. We conclude, therefore, that this equation is statistically significant, not just in overall terms through the F test but also in each of its component parts. Having decided that the equation looks satisfactory so far we move on to the last stage in the analysis.

Check the regression assumptions

There are four key assumptions behind this type of regression model and we need to check as best we can that our results are consistent with these assumptions. Assumptions 1–3 apply equally to simple regression models.

Assumption 1: There is a linear relationship between Y and the X variables.

It is easy to forget in the complexity of some of the analysis that this is a fundamental part of the model. This is one of the reasons we produced the scatter plots at an early stage. There, we saw no evidence of non-linear relationships and relatively strong evidence of linear ones. This assumption appears to hold for our data. To add to the complexity of multiple regression, non-linear models can also be developed as we did for simple regression.

Assumption 2: The regression errors have a constant variance.

The 'errors', e, are simply the difference between each actual Y value and the Y value predicted by the regression equation. You will remember that the variance is simply the square of the standard deviation for a set of data. The implication of this assumption is less clear, but critical. This assumption effectively means that the errors, e, remain relatively constant over the entire range of data. Consider Figure 10.10 for some hypothetical situation where we plot the errors, e, against $\hat{Y}$, the Y values predicted from the regression equation. The variation in the errors remains relatively constant over the $\hat{Y}$ range. Now consider some other situation in Figure 10.11, where we see the errors, e, showing more variation at high levels of $\hat{Y}$ and less variation at lower levels of $\hat{Y}$. In this case we would conclude that the assumption of constant variance of the errors was not being met in the data set we were analysing. Not having constant error variance is often an indication that some important explanatory variable has been omitted from the equation (no matter how high the R^2 of the existing equation might be). Such visual inspection of the errors is often referred to as *residual analysis*, as the errors are frequently referred to as the residuals.

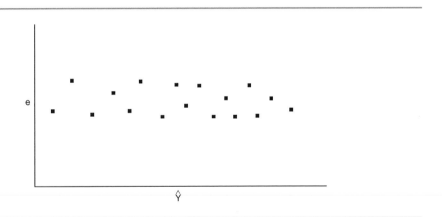

Figure 10.10 Constant variance

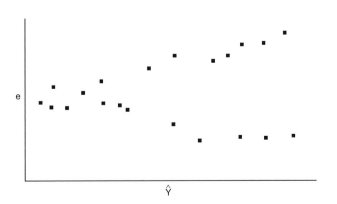

Figure 10.11 Non-constant variance

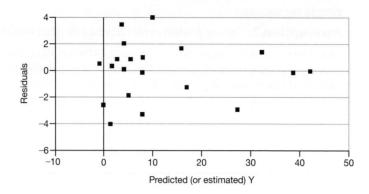

Figure 10.12 Residuals (Model 2)

Figure 10.12 shows plots of the residuals from Model 2 of our analysis, with the residuals plotted against $\hat{Y}$, the predicted Y value. There is no real evidence of any problem with this assumption, although there is a slight hint in the diagram that there might be more variation in the residuals for lower $\hat{Y}$ values than for large (i.e. for stores with lower profits). However, it is difficult to be sure, because the impression may be given from one or two stores with relatively high residuals and the fact that we have only a few stores in the high profit levels. We shall proceed assuming this assumption is not being violated.

Assumption 3: The regression errors are independent of each other.

This assumption implies that each error, or residual, is independent of the errors before it and the errors after it. If this assumption is not met then it is often said that *autocorrelation* exists: errors are strongly correlated with each other. There is a statistical test that can be conducted on the residuals to check for autocorrelation but it is beyond the scope of this text (although for those interested it is referred to as the *Durbin–Watson test* and you will often find a Durbin–Watson statistic on computer output from a regression package). For our purposes, visual inspection of the residuals will often reveal whether any obvious pattern in the e's exists. If it does, the regression equation should not be used for forecasting purposes. Evidence of autocorrelation often indicates that, again, we have omitted some important variable or that the form of the model is inappropriate for the data (perhaps where we should be using a non-linear model rather than a linear one). Autocorrelation is particularly prevalent where we are using time-series data in the equation: that is, where the Y and X variables have some sort of time sequence to them.

Assumption 4: The X variables are independent of each other.

The final key assumption behind multiple regression is that the X variables we have included are each strongly correlated with Y but are independent of each other. If the X variables are not independent then we have a problem of *multicollinearity*. In such a situation the regression equation we have estimated may be unreliable. One worthwhile check of the data being analysed is to calculate what is known as a correlation matrix: the correlation coefficients between all the variables being used in the equation (although this will not always reveal the presence of multicollinearity). Table 10.11 shows the matrix for our data. We note the following. The diagonal elements of the matrix (from

Table 10.11   Correlation matrix

```
Correlations:    PROFIT        SALES         SIZE       DISTANCE

PROFIT           1.0000       0.9666*      0.9673*       0.3937

SALES            0.9666*      1.0000       0.9660*       0.2658

SIZE             0.9673*      0.9660*      1.0000        0.2404

DISTANCE         0.3937       0.2658       0.2404        1.0000

N of cases:    20              1-tailed Signif: * -0.01
```

top left corner to bottom right) are all 1.0000. This is because this coefficient shows each variable correlated with itself. Second, the two halves of the matrix (that below the diagonal and that above) are identical since each shows the correlation between each pair of variables. Third, the package we used to produce this matrix also performs a hypothesis test on each correlation coefficient to assess whether it is significantly different from zero, here at the 99 per cent level.

So, what do we make of this? First, we see that our Y variable, Profit, is significantly correlated with Sales and Size (at 0.9666 and 0.9673 respectively) but less so with Distance at 0.3937. However, more interesting in the context of this assumption is the correlation between the three X variables. We see that Sales and Size are significantly correlated at 0.9660, whereas other pairwise correlations (between Sales and Distance and Size and Distance) are not. On reflection it is no real surprise to see a correlation between sales of a store and its size as we might expect, other things being equal, a larger store to have higher sales. We would conclude here that two of our X variables are correlated and, therefore, our regression equation is suspect.

Multicollinearity is a common problem in business regression modelling since, not unreasonably, many business variables will be correlated with each other. In principle, the solution is straightforward. We can omit one of the two correlated X variables and recompute the regression equation. Statistically, we would probably drop the variable least correlated with Y – here Sales, which has a lower correlation at 0.9666. From a business perspective this seems a logical choice also. Recollect that we are wanting to try to forecast the likely profit from two new stores we are thinking of opening. In such a situation we would certainly know the intended size of each store but not the actual sales levels. So back to the drawing board with our analysis!

Table 10.12 shows the new model. A quick scan of the results (you should be getting used to this by now!) indicates that we have b values for the two explanatory variables which are as expected (both positive and) both statistically significant. The ANOVA indicates the overall equation is significant and we see that R^2 is still high at 0.96. Clearly, we do not need to check for multicollinearity again as the correlation matrix will not have altered.

Figure 10.13 shows the plots of the residuals and again there appears to be little evidence that Assumptions 2 and 3 are being violated. Finally, we produce Figure 10.14, which shows a plot of the observed Y variable against that predicted by the regression equation. We note again that the model appears to be producing quite reasonable forecasts of each store's profits using these two explanatory variables. We conclude, then, that this final model appears to be a reasonably reliable basis for forecasting profit based on the two explanatory variables chosen. Let us return to the scenario where the

Table 10.12   Model 3

```
SUMMARY OUTPUT

        Regression statistics
Multiple R              0.981437031
R square                0.963218645
Adjusted R square       0.958891427
Standard error          2.683106254
Observations                     20


ANOVA
                df          SS              MS              F           Significance F
Regression       2     3204.954174     1602.477087     222.5953488     6.42445E-13
Residual        17     122.3840059      7.19905917
Total           19     3327.33818

                            Standard
            Coefficients     Error        t Stat        P-value       Lower 95%       Upper 95%
Intercept   -8.272705437   1.190300612   -6.950097611   2.34374E-06   -10.78402372   -5.761387157
Size         8.319263423   0.430442355   19.32724168    5.23118E-13    7.411108169    9.227418677
Distance     6.763540333   1.894184772    3.570686679   0.002353989    2.767154213   10.75992645
```

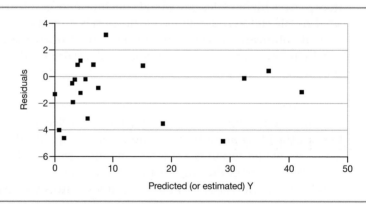

Figure 10.13 Residuals (Model 3)

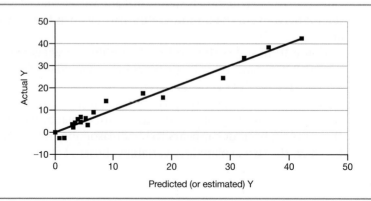

Figure 10.14 Residuals: actual Y against estimated Y

company was considering on which of two sites to open a store. Assume we have the following:

> *Option A*
>
> Floorspace 5.2 (000) sq ft
>
> Distance from nearest competitor 0.5 km
>
> *Option B*
>
> Floorspace 4.8 (000) sq ft
>
> Distance from nearest competitor 0.3 km

Using Model 3 we would obtain the following profit forecasts:

> *Option A*
>
> Profit forecast: £38.37 (000)
>
> *Option B*
>
> Profit forecast: £33.69 (000)

Option A has the higher forecast profit. Clearly we would not base such a strategic management decision solely on the regression analysis. Additional information on site acquisition and construction costs, planning permission, demographic forecasts and market research would all need to be taken into account. However, we are able to quantify expected profitability to help the decision maker in this situation.

We do not want you to go away with the impression that multiple regression is more trouble than it is worth for business forecasting. Used properly it is a particularly powerful statistical model for business forecasting and analysis. Although we have stressed the problems in developing an appropriate model, these problems are not insurmountable in practice and can, in most cases, be overcome. What is required, however, is a complete understanding of the principles behind this model. The saying that 'a little knowledge is a dangerous thing' is particularly appropriate to multiple regression in business.

The forecasting process

Over the last two chapters we have introduced a variety of methods that can be applied to the area of business forecasting. Through the application of such methods information about a possible future can be produced. It is important, however, to realise that the generation of such information is only part of a wider forecasting process which it is frequently advisable to apply to a forecasting activity. This can be summarised in a series of stages.

- Identify at the outset the intended purpose of the forecast.
- Determine the time period we wish to forecast for and how frequently we wish to forecast.
- Select an appropriate forecasting technique.
- Collect appropriate data.
- Produce the forecasts.
- Evaluate the reliability and suitability of the forecasts.
- Monitor the accuracy of the forecasts.

Identify the intended purpose of the forecast

It is important for a manager who is either producing forecasts directly or asking for forecasts to be produced to be clear as to what such forecasts are for and how such forecast information will be used. At one extreme the forecasts may be simply to provide general background information – comfort information – to the decision maker. At the other extreme the forecast information may be used as direct input into the organisation's business plan, with implications for pricing, resource allocation, profitability and the like. Part of the consideration at this stage will be the desired reliability of the forecast information, with the obvious implication that the more important the use of the forecasts then the higher the required degree of reliability.

Determine the time period

This is a two-stage process. First, we must decide how far into the future we wish to forecast. Depending on circumstances, the answer might be that we require a short-term forecast, possibly only a few hours ahead, through to medium-term, say one or two years, to longer-term. The second issue relating to time period is that of the frequency of the forecasts to be produced. We may require such forecasts on a regular basis: daily or weekly for example. Alternatively, such forecasts may be required only once a year as part of the business planning cycle.

Select an appropriate forecasting technique

Part of the consideration of what will be an appropriate forecasting technique to apply to the variable in question will be influenced by our views on the first two issues. As we have discussed, some of the techniques introduced are more appropriate to some circumstances than others. For example, if for stock control purposes a large organisation wanted to produce daily forecasts of demand for a range of several hundred items and these forecasts were to be produced each and every day, then regression models would almost certainly be inappropriate, given the technical complexity and data requirements of such models. On the other hand, if the same organisation is trying to predict demand for some of its key products over the next two to three years for planning and investment purposes then an exponentially weighted moving-average model would certainly be inappropriate. As a crude generalisation, non-causal models tend to be applied to situations which are either very short-term or very long-term, and causal models are applied largely in the medium term (see Figure 10.15).

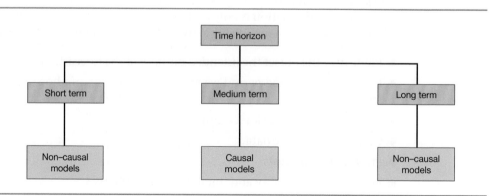

Figure 10.15 Models and the time horizon

The choice of technique will once again be heavily influenced by the foregoing evaluation. The choice of technique will also be influenced by the capabilities of the organisation itself. If no one in the organisation is technically capable of developing, say, a multiple regression model then the choice of technique must match organisational capabilities. This may still apply even if the organisation 'buys in' appropriate expertise to develop and produce technically complex forecasts. Such forecasts may not be capable of being evaluated properly by the organisation's management and may prove more 'dangerous' than simpler, subjective assessments of the future.

Collect appropriate data

Once again, at this stage we cannot determine what data we require in order to produce forecasts of our chosen variable until we have ascertained a suitable technique. The choice of technique will largely determine the data we require. A moving-average model requires data simply on the variable itself. A causal model requires data on explanatory variables as well. It also has to be said that in many organisations the choice of technique may well be affected by availability of data. We might prefer to develop a suitable causal model but if, as is all too common, the organisation historically has not collected data on the model's key variables then we may have to resort to a less preferred technique for which data is available. The non-availability of suitable data is a major problem in the application of forecasting techniques in the real world.

Produce forecasts

This is the easy stage! The technical production of a set of forecasts is relatively straightforward, given computer technology and given our decisions about the earlier stages of the process.

Evaluate the reliability and suitability of the forecasts

Having produced a set of forecasts it will be necessary to evaluate both their potential reliability/accuracy and their suitability for the situation at hand. The evaluation of reliability/accuracy will, of necessity, be a combination of both technical and subjective assessment. We can evaluate a model in terms of its statistical reliability, using MAE, MSE, R^2, as appropriate. But a subjective assessment by the decision maker is still important. The example of forecasting the trend in air passengers illustrates this point particularly well.

Monitor the accuracy of the forecasts

The final stage in the process is to ensure that, at some time in the future, we assess how accurate the forecasts actually were compared with what eventually happened to the variable. It is all too easy in an organisation to use forecasts to assist decision making and then discard the forecasts once used. As part of the evaluation process it is important to monitor their accuracy. The one thing we can almost guarantee about any set of forecasts is that they will turn out to be wrong. From the forecaster's viewpoint, what is of critical importance is to what extent they were wrong – the size of the forecast error – and why they were wrong: were they wrong because of the wrong choice of model, explanatory variables or data used, or because of critical subjective assumptions on which we based the scenario of the future? Only by monitoring in this way can we hope to produce improved forecasts in the future.

Worked example

We have been asked by a leading retailer to provide a short report on consumer spending patterns over the past few years in the UK to help them try to assess which parts of the market they should consider from a strategic perspective. We have collected the latest available data in Table 10.13.

We have data on the following series:

● per capita disposable income;
● per capita expenditure on food and non-alcoholic drink.

We note that all variables are expressed in constant prices so that inflation is removed and will not distort our analysis. It seems reasonable to start by assuming that the expenditure variable can be linked to income through a simple linear regression – people will generally buy more food and drink the more income they have. However, let us first examine the scatter plots shown in Figure 10.16. We see from the scatter plot a generally positive relationship between income and expenditure: that is, as income rises so does expenditure on food and drink . However, we also see a cluster of points to the right-hand side that seem out of line with the other observations. Examination of Table 10.13 reveals that these points are for the period from 2009 onwards. This coincides with the financial crisis that hit the UK and other economies, which led to increased unemployment, pressure on wages and salaries and a general drop in consumer confidence. We see from the scatterplot that expenditure on food and drink post-2008 is lower than we'd historically expect at these income levels. It seems likely that consumers cut back on spending on food and drink perhaps to switch to lower-cost items or perhaps to divert their income to mortgage payments, fuel, heating, repayment of debt etc. The implications for our retail company are clear. The relationship between consumer income and consumer spending on food and drink has altered since 2008 – although we have no way of knowing from this data whether such a change is temporary or permanent.

Clearly, regression analysis on this data is unlikely to be helpful to the retail company but we show the results anyway in Table 10.14. We obtain a line of best fit:

Expenditure $= 947.1 + 0.029*$Income

The equation makes sense in the context of our problem, telling us that 2.9 per cent of extra income will be spent on food and drink. The *a* term, at 947.1, indicates that per capita expenditure if income is zero (people have to eat after all), with food and drink purchases perhaps funded through past savings or through credit. The R^2 value, at 0.53, however, is low, implying that only 43 per cent of the variability in expenditure is accounted for by income even though the two parameters are both statistically different from zero given their t values. A check on the residuals also confirms we have a problem. We see that the residuals are consistently positive in the middle of the period and consistently negative at the end. As we suspected, the line of best fit isn't particularly helpful or reliable given the change in consumer behaviour post-2008. So what can we do?

One possibility would be to estimate an equation for the period up to 2008 and another equation post-2008. However, the latter would only give us nine data points with implications for statistical reliability. An alternative approach is to think about what appears to be happening here. We have one relationship between income and expenditure for the period up to 2008 and another post-2008. Clearly, we don't know if the post-2008 relationship will continue or whether consumers will go back to previous

Table 10.13   Per capita disposable income and per capita 'expenditure
on food and drink (£ at constant prices)

	Income	Expenditure
1995	13769	1302
1996	14130	1344
1997	14611	1361
1998	14894	1383
1999	15374	1416
2000	16253	1462
2001	16956	1442
2002	17287	1466
2003	17641	1483
2004	17802	1520
2005	18014	1540
2006	18181	1548
2007	18526	1532
2008	18217	1486
2009	18493	1431
2010	18526	1430
2011	17990	1399
2012	18257	1412
2013	18119	1427
2014	18254	1436
2015	18770	1461
2016	18930	1505

Source: Office for National Statistics

Data file 10-13

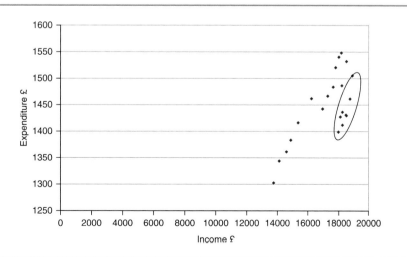

Figure 10.16 Scatter plot: income and expenditure on food and drink

Table 10.14　Regression results

```
SUMMARY OUTPUT

          Regression Statistics

Multiple R                0.726463477

R Square                  0.527749183

Adjusted R Square         0.54136642

Standard Error            45.34256091
Observations                   22
```

ANOVA

	df	SS	MS	F	Significance F
Regression	1	45951.20843	45951.20843	22.35037668	0.000128897
Residual	20	41118.9566	2055.94783		
Total	21	87070.16503			

	Coefficients	Standard Error	t Stat	P-value	Lower 95%	Upper 95%
Intercept	947.1484168	105.7186798	8.959139659	1.94207E-08	726.6231157	1167.673718
X Variable 1	0.028890734	0.006111054	4.7276185	0.000128897	0.016143298	0.041638169

RESIDUAL OUTPUT

Observation	Predicted Y	Residuals
1	1345.0	-42.6
2	1355.4	-11.7
3	1369.3	-8.7
4	1377.4	5.9
5	1391.3	24.8
6	1416.7	44.9
7	1437.0	5.2
8	1446.6	19.7
9	1456.8	26.5
10	1461.5	58.9
11	1467.5	72.5
12	1472.4	75.5
13	1482.4	49.7
14	1473.5	12.6
15	1481.4	-50.7
16	1482.4	-52.7
17	1466.9	-68.2
18	1474.6	-62.9
19	1470.6	-43.5
20	1474.5	-38.4
21	1489.4	-28.4
22	1494.0	11.2

spending patterns when the economy improves in the future. We can, however, picture the shift in consumer behaviour, as shown in Figure 10.17. Before 2009 we have a relationship as shown by the pre-2009 line. After 2008, there appears to have been a fundamental shift in consumer behaviour, pushing the line to the right as shown by the 2009+ line. This is the same as hypothesising that the *a* term in the regression equation has changed (as shown in Figure 10.2 previously) – the whole line has shifted downwards. This implies that at any income level expenditure on food and drink is lower.

You may be wondering how this helps our analysis. It looks as if we'll still have to produce two lines of best fit. In this case, however, we can utilise a regression 'trick'. Effectively the two lines of best fit in Figure 10.16 can be shown as:

pre-2009 $Y = a_1 + bX$

2009+ $Y = a_2 + bX$

where $a_2 = a_1 + d$

that is, where a_2 is equal to a_1 plus a difference, d, that has occurred because of a change in consumer behaviour. We can then write a single equation:

$$Y = (a_1 + d) + bX$$

where $d = 0$ for the pre-2009 period (effectively giving the *a* term as a_1) and d takes some calculated value for the 2009+ period to represent the fundamental shift in consumer behaviour. In this way we only need to calculate one line of best fit and can use the data for the whole period. We do this by introducing what is known as a *dummy variable*. A dummy variable takes a value of either 0 or 1 to represent the absence (0) or presence (1) of an effect like that of a shift in consumer behaviour. Table 10.15 shows the original income and expenditure data together with the dummy variable, D. D takes a value of 0 up to 2008 and a value of 1 thereafter. We can now use multiple regression with income and the dummy variable as explanatory variables. The regression results are shown in Table 10.16.

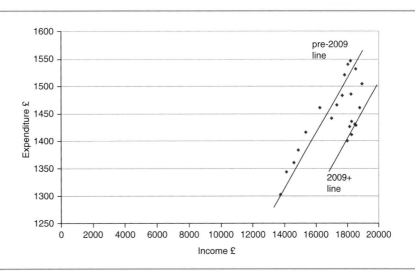

Figure 10.17 Scatter plot: income and expenditure on food and drink

Table 10.15   Per capita household disposable income, per capita consumers'
expenditure on food and drink, dummy variable

	Income	Expenditure	Dummy
1995	13769	1302	0
1996	14130	1344	0
1997	14611	1361	0
1998	14894	1383	0
1999	15374	1416	0
2000	16253	1462	0
2001	16956	1442	0
2002	17287	1466	0
2003	17641	1483	0
2004	17802	1520	0
2005	18014	1540	0
2006	18181	1548	0
2007	18526	1532	0
2008	18217	1486	0
2009	18493	1431	1
2010	18526	1430	1
2011	17990	1399	1
2012	18257	1412	1
2013	18119	1427	1
2014	18254	1436	1
2015	18770	1461	1
2016	18930	1505	1

Data file 10-15

We now have a line of best fit equation:

$$\text{Expenditure} = 693.6 + 0.046*\text{Income} - 96.9*D$$

The interpretation of the b coefficient is as before. Around 4.6 per cent of extra income is spent on food and drink. The a term and the coefficient for D, the dummy variable, need to be considered together. For the period up to 2008 the dummy variable takes a zero value so the regression equation simplifies to:

$$\text{Expenditure} = 693.6 + 0.046*\text{Income}$$

For 2009+ the dummy variable takes a value of 1 so the regression equation becomes:

$$\text{Expenditure} = 693.6 + 0.046*\text{Income} - 96.9*(1)$$
$$\text{Expenditure} = 693.6 + 0.046*\text{Income} - 96.9$$
$$\text{Expenditure} = 596.7 + 0.046*\text{Income}$$

Table 10.16 Regression results with the dummy variable

```
SUMMARY OUTPUT

          Repression Statistics
Multiple R              0.9481841

R Square               0.899053088

Adjusted R Square      0.888427097
Standard Error         21.50821664

Observations                 22
```

ANOVA

	df	SS	MS	F	Significance F
Regression	2	78280.70075	39140.35037	84.60887186	3.45847E-10
Residual	19	8789.464282	462.6033832		
Total	21	87070.16503			

	Coefficients	Standard Error	t Stat	P-value	Lower 95%	Upper 95%
Intercept	693.6435674	58.60329426	11.83625556	3.26644E-10	570.9854631	816.3016717
Income	0.04565146	0.003524573	12.952338	7.05877E-11	0.038274444	0.053028476
Dummy	-96.893306	11.59040828	-8.3597836	8.6666E-08	-121.15230	-72.634302

RESIDUAL OUTPUT

Observation	Predicted Y	Residuals
1	1322.2	-19.9
2	1338.7	4.9
3	1360.7	0.4
4	1373.6	9.7
5	1395.5	20.6
6	1435.6	26.0
7	1467.7	-25.5
8	1482.8	-16.5
9	1499.0	-15.6
10	1506.3	14.0
11	1516.0	24.1
12	1523.6	24.3
13	1539.4	-7.3
14	1525.3	-39.2
15	1441.0	-10.3
16	1442.5	-12.8
17	1418.0	-19.4
18	1430.2	-18.5
19	1423.9	3.3
20	1430.1	6.0
21	1453.6	7.4
22	1460.9	44.3

In other words, the intercept has fallen by around comparing the period from 2009+ with that before. We can interpret this as the per capita reduction in expenditure on food and drink following the 2008 financial crisis – people are spending around £100 per person less on food and drink. How 'good' is our new regression equation?

Well, we have an adjusted R^2 of 0.89 – considerably improved from our first attempt where R^2 was only 0.53. We now have almost 90 per cent of the variability in expenditure accounted for by the regression equation. All three parameters of the equation are statistically different from zero – so all are playing their part. Finally, the residuals still show a little bit of a pattern but are much improved. Overall, our multiple regression equation seems to perform fairly well with the addition that we're able to quantify the per capita reduction in food and drink expenditure that's happened over the last few years. If the retail company is using this information as part of its general analysis we'd be reasonably confident about our results, although more analysis – perhaps looking at additional explanatory variables, perhaps analysing different categories of food and drink expenditure – would be justified if the regression analysis were to be used for important strategic decisions. We might also advise the company that additional market research may be worthwhile to examine a sample of consumers to assess whether the £100 per capita drop in spending is likely to be permanent. This example shows that business forecasting is as much an art as a science!

Summary

In this chapter we have introduced the basic regression model as a method of forecasting. The prime use of regression is as a causal model and such models are of critical importance to any business organisation. The principles of simple linear regression are straightforward although underpinned by rigorous mathematical assumptions. While such a model can be developed and used for relatively simple applications, its development into more complex models is a matter more appropriate for the expert rather than the typical manager. The manager, however, still needs to be aware of the underlying principles applied in order to be able to evaluate the potential use and reliability of the forecasts generated.

QADM IN ACTION   RAC

The UK-based RAC (Royal Automobile Club) is a motoring organisation primarily providing a service to its member motorists whose vehicles have broken down. Members of the RAC who experience a vehicle breakdown will typically telephone a central hotline number, details will be taken by the RAC, and one of its fleet of vehicles will be despatched to provide assistance. The RAC prides itself on reaching members within 60 minutes of receiving a request for assistance. With around five million members the management of this service is a particularly complex task. Predictably, the roadside rescue side of its activities is supported by a considerable IT system, with the roadside operations being managed through CARS (computer-aided rescue service). CARS provides a number of performance measures for the roadside operations, including measures of overall level of service, the rescue patrol attendance rate and the vehicle fix rate. Figure 10.18 shows the key performance measures as well as a number of key terms used.

Although the RAC has a fleet of over 1300 vehicles available to respond to assistance requests, these are distributed throughout the whole of the UK. However, if available resources are already at full capacity when an assistance request is received, the RAC can call on a supplementary fleet operated by contractors. In addition, as one might expect, management of these operations is further complicated by considerable areas of uncertainty and unpredictability: weather patterns, local traffic conditions, the very randomness of vehicle breakdowns. However, to try to help management, a project was initiated to help develop an understanding

AGNT (Agent (Contractor) Go-Not-Tow)	The percentage of contractor rescue jobs that are completed with the vehicle being remobilised.
CARS (Computer-Aided Rescue Service)	The RAC's computer service, used to gather and store breakdown details and report on the various quality and efficiency measures.
Contractor	A complementary resource to the RAC patrols, which are appointed garages approved to act on behalf of the RAC.
Despatcher	A member of staff who allocates an appropriate patrol resource to each service job.
HAT Job (Hire Accommodation Travel Job)	A service job that results in the member receiving a hire car, hotel or accommodation or some form of onward travel.
OLOS (Overall Level of Service)	The percentage of service breakdowns with a resource at the breakdown scene within 60 minutes.
Opportunity	$\text{Opportunity} = \dfrac{\text{Number of Attended Service Breakdowns}}{\text{Number of Patrols}}$
PGNT (Patrol Go-Not-Tow)	The percentage of patrol rescue jobs that are completed with the vehicle being remobilised.
Productivity	$\text{Productivity} = \text{Opportunity} \times \dfrac{\text{Rescue PAR}}{100}$
Recovery Job	A service job which is completed with the vehicle being towed more than 20 miles.
ROLOS (Recovery Overall Level of Service)	The percentage of recovery jobs with a resource at the breakdown scene within 120 minutes.
Recovery PAR (Recovery Patrol Attendance Rate)	The percentage of the recovery jobs completed by patrols.
Rescue Job	A service job which is either completed without a tow or is completed with a tow that is under 20 miles.
Rescue PAR (Rescue Patrol Attendance Rate)	The percentage of rescue jobs completed by patrols. $\text{Rescue Par} = \dfrac{\text{Productivity}}{\text{Opportunity}}$
Service Breakdown	A breakdown where some form of rescue and/or recovery service is provided.
VFR (Vehicle Fix Rate)	The percentage of attended service breakdowns which are fixed.

Figure 10.18 Key terms and performance measures

of the links and interrelationships between the various performance measures and to assess whether the impact of changes in these influence measures on key performance metrics could be reliably predicted. One of the first stages in the project was to develop what is known as an 'influence map', showing the relationships that exist between various parts of the organisation and its key systems. This was felt to be particularly important because the interrelationships between many aspects of performance were complex and not necessarily understood in terms of their detail and logic. Figure 10.19 shows the influence map produced, which gave management a clear, overall view of the complexity of the factors affecting roadside performance. To illustrate the logic and importance of this approach we shall follow through part of the map in detail. At the top of the map we have the number of members, a key parameter if the RAC is to survive and be successful. In part, the number of members is 'influenced' by the proportion of existing members who decide each year to renew membership. In turn, this will be influenced by the level of customer satisfaction a particular member has (since logically the more satisfied a customer is with an organisation, the more likely they are to remain a customer). Although, as can be seen from the map, a large number of factors influence customer satisfaction, one of the key influences is felt to come from OLOS (the overall level of service, defined as the percentage of breakdowns which received roadside assistance within 60 minutes).

Importantly, as the authors of this article point out, the influence map was effectively created by managers and key personnel themselves (and not by the quantitative expert). This provided a sense of ownership among management of the overall approach being developed, and was felt to improve the chances of successful implementation of any performance improvements that might emerge from later analysis. This is a particularly important point, relating to more complex quantitative techniques, which has been mentioned a number of times in this text so far. It may be relatively easy for a quantitative specialist to model and analyse some business situation and then produce a set of performance improvement recommendations based on that analysis. The managers who are then left with the task of deciding whether, and how, to implement those recommendations

may well respond with, at best, a degree of inertia and, at worst, downright disbelief in the validity of the recommendations. Such a response can arise because managers have not been involved in the model development and may feel it has simply been imposed on them and their business by some outside 'expert'.

The next stage was to try to quantify some of these key relationships and then try to develop predictions of key performance variables based on assumed changes in key influences. It was decided to adopt a regression-modelling approach to this analysis. At an operational level the RAC divides the UK into six regions, with each region further split into zones (denoted by a letter). One particular region, Central England, was used to assess whether the modelling approach was feasible and data collected on the 17 zones of this region (denoted as zones A to Q). As is usual with this approach, the data collection process itself was no easy task. Because of previous organisational changes a few years earlier, it was felt appropriate to collect data only for the period after this change (limiting the amount of data that could be used for modelling). The geographical boundaries of some zones had also altered. Some data was available internally from the CARS system, while other data had to be collected externally (weather information, pollution statistics). The influence map was used to identify the key dependent variables of interest and then the potential independent variables influencing each dependent variable. The multiple regression approach that has been described in this chapter was adopted to try to develop appropriate multiple regression models. Scatter plots were used to assess initial linearity (or non-linearity in some cases). R^2 values were assessed, as were residuals, which were examined to test the basic multiple regression assumptions. An iterative approach was adopted until acceptable regression equations had been obtained. A total of 12 equations were developed in this way, with the format of each illustrated in Figure 10.20 (note that for reasons of commercial confidentiality the numerical parameters of the equations are not reported). So, for example, the Customer Satisfaction Index was found to be dependent on five key variables: OLOS (the overall level of service), ROLOS (the recovery overall level of service), VFR (the vehicle fix rate), Jobs/Service breakdown and Rescue PAR.

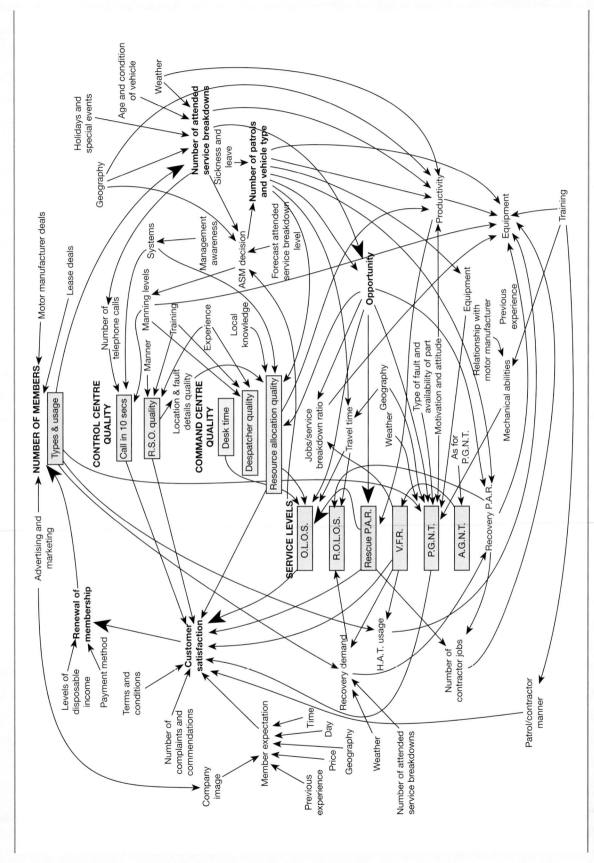

Figure 10.19 RAC roadside operation influence map

Dependent Variable	Explanatory Equation
Central Region Costs	$= a_1$ $+ x_1$ Productivity $+ x_2$ Number of Contractor Jobs $+ x_3$ Number of Hire. Accommodation. Travel (HAT) Jobs $+ x_4$ Jobs/Service Breakdown
Customer Satisfaction Index (CSI)	$= a_2$ $+ x_5$ OLOS $+ x_6$ POLOS $+ x_7$ VFR $+ x_8$ Jobs/Service Breakdown $+ x_9$ Rescue PAR
Jobs/Service Breakdown	$= a_3$ $+ x_{10}$ VFR $+ x_{11}$ Opportunity
Number of Attended Service Breakdowns	$= a_4$ $+ x_{12}$ Weather Index $+ x_{13}$ Number of Individual Members $+ x_{14}$ Number of Motorman Members $+ x_{15}$ Number of Fleet Members
Number of Contractor Jobs	$= a_5$ $+ x_{16}$ Number of Panel Van Patrol Vehicles $+ x_{17}$ Number of Lift and Tow Truck Patrol Vehicles $+ x_{18}$ Number of Attended Service Breakdowns $+ x_{19}$ Recovery Demand $+ x_{20}$ Rescue PAR
Number of Patrols	$= a_6$ $+ x_{21}$ Number of Attended Service Breakdowns $+ x_{22}$ Geography Index
Overall Level of Service (OLOS)	$= a_7$ $+ x_{23}$ Desk Time $+ x_{24}$ Geography Index $+ x_{25}$ Weather Index $+ x_{21}$ (Number of Patrols)^2 $+ x_{20}$ Rescue PAR
Patrol Go-Not-Tow (PGNT)	$= a_8$ $+ x_{28}$ Weather Index $+ x_{8g}$ Number of Individual Members $+ x_{30}$ Number of Fleet Members $+ x_{31}$ Number of Motor Cycle Patrols $+ x_{32}$ Number of Small Van Patrol Vehicles
Productivity	$= a_9$ $+ x_{33}$ Geography Index $+ x_{34}$ Weather Index $+ x_{35}$ Jobs/Service Breakdown $+ x_{36} \dfrac{\text{Number of Attended Service Breakdowns}}{\text{Number of Patrols}}$ $+ x_{37}$ (Number of Patrols)^2
$\log_a$ (Recovery Demand)	$= a_{10}$ $+ x_{38}$ Number of Attended Service Breakdowns $+ x_{39}$ VFR $+ x_{40}$ Geography Index $+ x_{41}$ Number of Motorman Members $+ x_{42}$ Weather Index
Recovery Overall Level of Service (ROLOS)	$= a_{11}$ $+ x_{43}$ OLOS $+ x_{45}$ Recovery PAR
Vehicle Fix Rate (VFR)	$= a_{12}$ $+ x_{45}$ PGNT $+ x_{46}$ Agent (Contractor) Go-Not-Tow (AGNT) $+ x_{47}$ Rescue PAR

Figure 10.20 Multiple regression equations

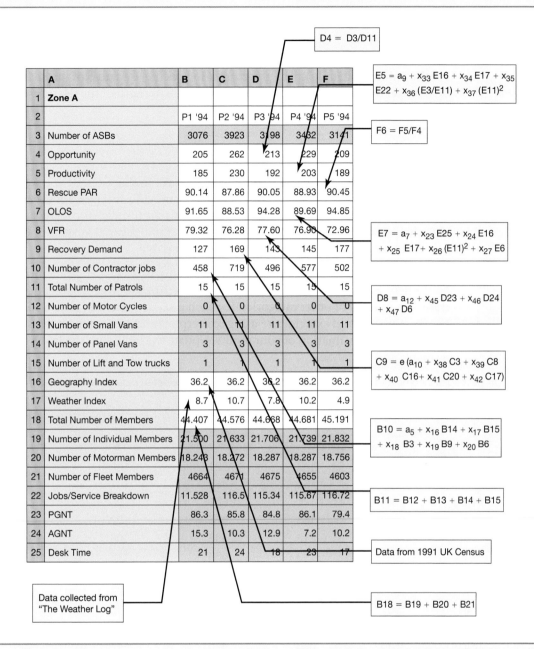

D4 = D3/D11

$E5 = a_9 + x_{33} E16 + x_{34} E17 + x_{35} E22 + x_{36} (E3/E11) + x_{37} (E11)^2$

F6 = F5/F4

	A	B	C	D	E	F
1	Zone A					
2		P1 '94	P2 '94	P3 '94	P4 '94	P5 '94
3	Number of ASBs	3076	3923	3198	3432	3141
4	Opportunity	205	262	213	229	209
5	Productivity	185	230	192	203	189
6	Rescue PAR	90.14	87.86	90.05	88.93	90.45
7	OLOS	91.65	88.53	94.28	89.69	94.85
8	VFR	79.32	76.28	77.60	76.90	72.96
9	Recovery Demand	127	169	143	145	177
10	Number of Contractor jobs	458	719	496	577	502
11	Total Number of Patrols	15	15	15	15	15
12	Number of Motor Cycles	0	0	0	0	0
13	Number of Small Vans	11	11	11	11	11
14	Number of Panel Vans	3	3	3	3	3
15	Number of Lift and Tow trucks	1	1	1	1	1
16	Geography Index	36.2	36.2	36.2	36.2	36.2
17	Weather Index	8.7	10.7	7.8	10.2	4.9
18	Total Number of Members	44.407	44.576	44.668	44.681	45.191
19	Number of Individual Members	21.500	21.633	21.706	21.739	21.832
20	Number of Motorman Members	18.243	18.272	18.287	18.287	18.756
21	Number of Fleet Members	4664	4671	4675	4655	4603
22	Jobs/Service Breakdown	11.528	116.5	115.34	115.67	116.72
23	PGNT	86.3	85.8	84.8	86.1	79.4
24	AGNT	15.3	10.3	12.9	7.2	10.2
25	Desk Time	21	24	18	23	17

$E7 = a_7 + x_{23} E25 + x_{24} E16 + x_{25} E17 + x_{26} (E11)^2 + x_{27} E6$

$D8 = a_{12} + x_{45} D23 + x_{46} D24 + x_{47} D6$

$C9 = e^{(a_{10} + x_{38} C3 + x_{39} C8 + x_{40} C16 + x_{41} C20 + x_{42} C17)}$

$B10 = a_5 + x_{16} B14 + x_{17} B15 + x_{18} B3 + x_{19} B9 + x_{20} B6$

B11 = B12 + B13 + B14 + B15

Data from 1991 UK Census

Data collected from "The Weather Log"

B18 = B19 + B20 + B21

Figure 10.21 Model output and logical relationships for periods 1 (P1) to 5 (P5) of 1994 (shaded cells indicate user inputs)

Further analysis of these equations led to five of the estimated equations being used for what-if modelling purposes, with output from the model equations shown for one zone in Figure 10.21. The authors of the article comment that 'this modelling methodology . . . [stimulated a] new understanding of the business environment', with management now intending to develop a national model using the same fundamental approach.

Source: Based on Clarke, S., Hopper, A., Tobias, A. and Tomlin, D. (1996) Corporate modelling at RAC motoring services, *Operational Research Insight*, 9 (3), pp 6–12.
© 1996 Macmillan Publishers Limited.
Reprinted by permission from Macmillan Publishers Limited, www.palgrave-journals.com.

Exercises

1   For the following data calculate the correlation coefficient and plot the data on a scatter diagram. Do you think it measures the strength of the relationship accurately?

x	1	2	3	4	5	6	7
y	8.25	7	6.25	6	6.25	7	8.25

2   Return to the variables used in Chapter 9, Exercise 3. In that exercise you were required to obtain a trend for each variable using moving averages. For each trend that you obtained, forecast the trend one year into the future using regression. Evaluate the result both statistically and in the context of the variable. Assess how reliable you think such a forecast would be for each variable.

3   In the worked example we analysed the relationship between per capita income and consumers' expenditure on food and drink. Table 10.17 shows consumers' expenditure on a number of other categories. For each category, analyse the relationship between income and expenditure using scatterplots and regression analysis and undertake a full evaluation of your results. Update the table with the latest data available and reanalyse.

Table 10.17   UK per capita income and per capita consumers' expenditure on selected categories (£ at constant prices)

	Income	Restaurants and hotels	Communications	Electricity, gas and other fuels	Non-alcoholic beverages, mineral water and soft drinks	Alcoholic beverages
1995	13 769	1700	147	621	102	176
1996	14 130	1788	154	654	101	196
1997	14 611	1792	171	639	100	209
1998	14 894	1830	188	625	102	202
1999	15 374	1825	212	598	109	230
2000	16 253	1857	249	633	113	234
2001	16 956	1858	287	638	119	254
2002	17 287	1900	294	624	127	272
2003	17 641	1907	316	630	135	287
2004	17 802	1926	341	672	140	310
2005	18 014	1896	368	640	147	327
2006	18 181	1858	369	638	152	325
2007	18 526	1857	384	623	148	329
2008	18 217	1798	401	633	146	320
2009	18 493	1635	391	603	142	308
2010	18 526	1664	391	648	140	316
2011	17 990	1672	381	571	144	308
2012	18 257	1684	372	594	141	311
2013	18 119	1721	385	596	145	307
2014	18 254	1735	376	509	144	307
2015	18 770	1742	395	526	142	313
2016	18 930	1772	414	536	149	319

Source: Office for National Statistics

Data file 10-17

4 A small engineering company has been monitoring its total costs over the last few years on a quarterly basis together with the number of employees and production level. In order to assist the company to evaluate alternative strategic and operational options, the data has been put through a computer package to develop a multiple regression model of the form

$$\text{Costs} = a + b_1 \text{Employees} + b_2 \text{Production}$$

The results of the regression are shown in Table 10.18.

You have been asked to provide a short report to the company chairman explaining both the principles of regression in this context and an evaluation of the results in terms of their potential usefulness in decision making.

Table 10.18 Regression output

```
                  Model fitting results for: Costs

  Independent variable      Coefficient     Std. error      t value
CONSTANT                         63.75         13.7861       4.6242
Employees                      4.02926          0.8587       4.6923
Production                     0.04714          0.0057       8.2702
R-SQ. = 0.9633
24 observations fitted, forecast(s) computed for 0 missing val.
of dep. var.
```

5 The corporate planning department in a large brewing company has been trying to develop a medium-term forecasting model relating to the demand for one of their products: a low-alcohol lager. The method used has been based around multiple regression. The department has collected and analysed data on a monthly basis for the last two years. All data has been seasonally adjusted and is based on constant prices. The variables currently under examination are:

C1   Lager sales, thousands of pints
C2   Number of pubs supplied
C3   Number of supermarkets and off-licences supplied
C4   Price of lager, pence per pint
C5   Price of beer, pence per pint
C6   A time trend increasing by 1 per month.

The results of the latest model are shown in Table 10.19.

You have been asked to summarise the current model for a report to be shown to the managing director, to interpret and evaluate the current model and to suggest possible improvements to the model or alternative methods of trying to forecast this variable.

Table 10.19 Regression output

Variable	Coefficient	Std. error	t value
Constant	24.52	4.609	5.32
C2	1.02	0.357	2.86
C3	2.39	0.699	3.42
C4	-0.59	0.401	1.47
C5	0.082	0.126	0.65
C6	0.98	0.394	2.49
R-SQ. = 0.843			
23 observations			

6 As manager of a local leisure centre you are investigating the frequency of use of the centre by its members. You hope that by understanding some of the key factors that influence how often members use the centre's facilities you will be better able to market the centre and attract more members. Over the last few weeks you have collected data on a representative sample of members. The relevant data is shown in Table 10.20.

Table 10.20 Sample of 20 members

Attend	Travel	Children	Income	Attend	Travel	Children	Income
5	3	2	23	1	8	0	19
4	2	1	34	2	2	0	21
2	3	0	51	2	3	2	45
6	3	3	37	1	9	3	38
7	1	3	29	0	5	0	36
4	3	2	17	2	3	0	19
3	3	1	23	2	4	0	23
4	3	1	28	2	5	0	21
8	2	3	40	1	6	2	46
0	8	1	38	1	7	1	28

Data available in file 10-20

The variables relate to:

Attend   The number of times the member made use of the centre's facilities during a week

Travel   The distance between the member's home and the centre (miles)

Children   The number of children in the member's family (family use of the centre is encouraged)

Income   The annual income of the member (in £000s)

Using the principles of multiple regression, develop a suitable model for forecasting *Attend*.

7   A large retail organisation has a number of home-furnishing outlets in a particular region, selling products such as carpets, curtains, domestic furniture and fittings. The organisation has been affected badly by the downturn in domestic property sales in the region over the last few years, as it has found that much of its business comes from customers redecorating or refurnishing a home they have just purchased. The company has collected and analysed data over the past two years to try to assess the impact that regional property sales have on its business. Two variables in particular have been specified:

- the number of house sales in the region on a monthly basis (000s)
- gross monthly sales in the organisation's outlets in the region (£000 000s).

Data has been obtained for the last 24 months on these two variables and the data analysed using a spreadsheet package applying simple linear regression with the number of house sales as the X variable. The results are:

```
Regression output:
Constant                                    -0.532
Std err. of Y est.                           3.2577
R squared                                    0.83584
No. of observations                         24
Degrees of freedom                          22
X coefficient(s)            0.476
Std err. of coef.           0.380121
```

Explain the principles of simple linear regression in the context of this problem. Assess and comment on the reliability of this analysis for forecasting purposes.

8   A training agency is currently reviewing part of its operations. It runs one particular scheme whereby young people who are unemployed are put through a training course which provides them with a variety of IT skills including word-processing, spreadsheets, database systems, e-mail and the internet. On completion of the training course, participants take a standard test and receive an ability score (from 0 to 40, with 40 being the highest). The training agency then finds them a suitable job with a local company. The agency is trying to assess the wages its trainees receive from the companies they go to work for in relation to the ability test score they received and the number of years of prior, relevant job experience the trainees had. Data has been collected as given in Table 10.21.

Wage   Represents the gross weekly wage (£s) of trainees once they have found employment

Score Represents the ability score they received in the test

Years Represents the number of years of relevant job experience

Analyse the data to assess whether *Wage* could be reliably predicted based on score and years of experience.

Table 10.21　Trainees' wages, ability scores and job experience

Wage	Score	Years
271	37	0
233	29	1
213	24	2
242	32	1
261	36	1
198	27	0
228	31	0
205	22	2
323	38	3
181	21	1
225	30	3
298	34	5
209	28	0
200	25	1
278	33	2
270	35	1
223	29	2
231	34	2
242	32	1
216	26	1
189	25	1
228	31	0
205	22	2
343	38	5
191	21	1
225	30	3
318	34	5
209	28	0
203	24	1
287	34	3

Data available in file 10-21

9　A senior police manager is reviewing manpower allocation of police officers to a number of geographical districts which fall under her responsibility. Data has been collected on a number of variables, as shown in Table 10.22.

Crimes	The number of reported crimes
Officers	The number of full-time equivalent police officers
Support	The number of civilian support staff
Unemployed	The unemployment rate for that area
Retired	The percentage of the local population who are retired

Table 10.22   Policing variables

Crimes	Officers	Support	Unemployment	Retired
860	26	5	6	18.3
890	27	2	7	10.2
852	20	3	5.2	14.7
889	28	3	4.3	13.1
1037	25	4	13.5	7.6
1257	21	6	13.2	8.4
1136	20	3	14.1	8.2
1038	25	4	13.9	8.3
1240	19	4	13.6	7.8
1439	15	5	17.1	4
1126	17	5	8.4	7.1
724	27	3	6.7	18.5
1023	19	6	6.3	7.3
960	22	4	12.3	15.7
890	25	3	8.7	10.2
952	21	4	6.7	9.7
989	26	3	5.3	14.1
1037	25	4	14.5	11.2
1321	20	6	12.3	4.4
1402	16	3	14.1	4.2
1038	25	4	13.9	8.3
941	19	4	8.6	9.8
767	26	5	7.1	17
826	24	5	7.4	16.1
724	27	3	6.7	16.5
823	23	6	6.3	16.3

Data available in file 10-22

(a) Find the most appropriate statistical model for predicting *Crimes* in any given area.
(b) Do you think regression could be used to predict the number of police officers that should be deployed in a given area?

11 Linear Programming

Learning objectives

By the end of this chapter you should be able to:

- understand the principles of constrained optimisation
- explain the relevance of optimisation to business decision making
- formulate a linear programme
- solve a two-variable linear-programming problem
- complete sensitivity analysis on the optimal solution

So far in the text we have developed a variety of different quantitative models. Such models generate information that may be used by the decision maker to help resolve some problem that is faced. Typically, for many of the problems facing a manager, certain restrictions or constraints will exist in terms of what can, and cannot, be done. A manager may see a possible solution to a problem in terms of recruiting extra staff but knows that approval for this will not be given by senior management. A solution to some problem may exist if only the organisation could raise extra capital to replace existing production machinery but the manager knows that this is unlikely in the current economic climate. In short, a manager will be restricted in terms of solutions that can be adopted and yet at the same time that manager is expected not only to solve the problem but, ideally, also come up with the 'best' solution. Not surprisingly, given that so many business problems have these characteristics, a number of quantitative models have been developed to help managers reach such 'best' decisions under the constraints they face. We shall introduce and examine one of these models: linear programming (LP). This is a model that lies at the heart of this type of problem and is typical of optimisation models, often referred to as mathematical programming models.

The business problem

We shall develop a detailed example to illustrate the principles of LP. Assume an organisation manufactures a liquid detergent. The detergent is manufactured from two basic ingredients, both of which are a mixture of appropriate chemicals: Mix A and Mix B. The detergent is packaged and sold to two separate markets: the household market aimed at individual consumers and the industrial/commercial market aimed at large organisations such as hospitals, hotels and local authorities. The exact composition of the detergent sold varies between the two markets and Table 11.1 shows the composition. The two products are sold in five-litre bottles. For the household detergent (H) each five-litre bottle requires four litres of Mix A and one litre of Mix B, whereas the corresponding composition of industrial/commercial detergent (C) is two litres of Mix A and three litres of Mix B. On a weekly basis the company has supplies of no more than 20 000 litres of Mix A available and 15 000 litres of Mix B. In addition, the plastic containers in which the detergents are sold are limited in supply. The company buys these containers from a specialist supplier, who can supply no more than 4000 containers a week for H and 4500 a week for C. The company's accountant has been able to quantify the profit contribution of each product: H contributes 30p to profit per five-litre bottle produced and C contributes 25p. The manager's problem is a simple one: on a weekly basis, what combination of the two products should be produced?

On the face of it, product H appears more profitable than C – 30p as opposed to 25p – and we might be tempted to suggest that production be concentrated on this product. However, it is also evident that there are resource implications of concentrating production on H. For example, this product is relatively costly in terms of Mix A, requiring twice as much per five-litre bottle as product C. Additionally, there is a limit of 4000 to the number of units of H that the company can produce – that is 500 less than the number of units of C that can be produced. Clearly we require some rigorous method of trying to resolve this problem. In fact this problem is an example of what is referred to as *constrained optimisation*. The manager will be searching for an optimum solution – in this case in the sense of maximising profits. At the same time solutions to the problem are constrained by the other characteristics of the problem: limited resource availability and so on. As we shall see, linear programming provides a general-purpose solution method for such constrained optimisation problems.

Table 11.1 Chemical composition of detergents per five-litre bottle

	Household detergent (H)	Industrial/commercial detergent (C)
Ingredient		
Mix A	4 litres	2 litres
Mix B	1 litre	3 litres

Private users: how shops use the information

By Simon Briscoe

Census data can be used as a basis for mathematical models that predict the level of customer trips between residential zones and retail outlets or centres.

Retail location models, more accurately described as gravity or spatial interaction modelling, are used by the UK's leading supermarket and high street retail chains for planning store networks and predicting expected revenues for new sites.

The growing popularity of gravity modelling, which tries to simulate the trip-making behaviour of consumers within the market, owes much to the advantages it has over traditional statistically based models, such as multiple regression. Whereas multiple regression models and their variants provide the answer to one question – what is the expected revenue at each outlet, gravity models provide additional information about market performance, such as the impact that a new site or a closure has on existing outlets, including those belonging to competitors, and the shape and size of each outlet's expected catchment area and the degree of overlap between catchments.

As Steven Halsall of GeoBusiness says, companies will want to avoid opening a profitable outlet which, due to impacts on existing outlets, results in a net loss to the company. Similarly, in a franchise situation, gravity models can be used to estimate the impact of planned outlets on existing franchisees. So successful have the modelling techniques been that more recently they have been extended to retail financial services and to the leisure and health market sectors.

Retailer location – WHSmith

When WHSmith needed to understand how current stores interacted with each other and how to fill holes in their network coverage, they commissioned a bespoke sales prediction model, built by CACI, to help understand the likely turnovers of new stores and the impact these stores will have on their existing portfolio. This capability was all the more relevant given their stated aim of expanding the high street store network and the potential move into factory outlet centres and edge-of-town locations.

"What if?" scenarios were run and the results mapped using CACI's Geographical Information System – InSite – to view the likely catchment of a new store. Demographic reports were generated comparing the new store catchment with the national average and with WHSmith average customers. In addition the model identified likely cannibalisation of the existing portfolio from new store openings, giving a clear view of the real value of a new store.

The process also provides performance measures for the existing store network. A key output from the model is a prediction of "expected" sales from each WHSmith store based on its current size. This measure reflects the potential for WHSmith in that location, given the current size of store, based on the catchment and retail profile. A benchmark based on external factors is invaluable in measuring store performance. Dina Dawes, Estates Manager at WHSmith, said that sales predictions have been borne out by recent store openings.

Cinema site planning – Odeon Cinemas

The UK cinema market has never been so competitive, with many of the key operators fighting for a decreasing number of prime sites. Location decisions have to consider a range of complex factors in order to arrive at some estimate of trading level. According to Steven Halsall of GeoBusiness Solutions, these factors relate to the proposed site in question (quality, accessibility, size, and mix), the competitive offer in the local market, and the satisfied and unsatisfied levels of demand – especially the number of 25–34 year olds – in the market. The use of GIS software, data and modelling techniques can help to make sense of such intricate local markets.

Mr Halsall says the basic system itself comprises the GIS software usually coupled with drive time functionality and a demographic reporting tool and any externally available data. The external data usually consists of: background context mapping (roads, rail, urban sprawl, locations); census or demographic information by small area (census counts, geodemographic or lifestyle profiles); administrative geography (postcodes, postal sector boundaries, TV regions); and competitor locations (quality and location of competitive outlets, open or planned), and if possible, trading levels.

The main source of competitive advantage in such a system is that of internal data – the information held by an organisation that is not generally available to competitors. One significant source of internal data is that about the company's own customers. Odeon Cinemas generate a large amount of local market knowledge from the collection of customer information through their call centre or by box office surveys. For example, gathering postcode information allows Odeon to quantify the "distance decay effect" – the decreasing propensity to attend as one lives further away from a venue. This effect differs by geographic location and is governed by the transport infrastructure as well as the location of competing offers.

For Odeon gravity models are useful in predicting sales or admissions, the likely impact on own or competitor outlets, and market share by small area. It is not only about opening or closing outlets, says Mr Halsall, it is also about performance versus potential, location planning, repositioning or even marketing and media planning. Odeon have applied the use of GIS to help in site openings, campaign analysis at the local, regional or national level, and in customer acquisition and retention. Luke Vetere, Marketing Manager at Odeon Cinemas, says that the GeoBusiness work based on Mapinfo technology plays a "vital role in the company's decision support process".

Market research

The census underpins most mainstream market research conducted in Britain. According to Corinne Moy, Director of Statistics at NOP, it provides the bedrock of information about the dispersion of populations and households, which is essential for planning, controlling and executing all types of consumer research. Some populations – such as ethnic minorities or very affluent people – are almost absent from many areas of the country, and targeting can ensure that survey resources are used to maximum effect. The new questions on religion and caring and the more detailed information on ethnic groups will improve the value of the data.

Market researchers use the census to ensure that they achieve representative samples of particular populations. These may be used to plan interviews of predetermined quotas of people in particular age and sex categories. In other instances, the census is used with the Postcode Address File to draw up sample frames of addresses. In both cases a scientific approach achieves more accurate results at a lower cost.

The market research business also makes use of the Samples of Anonymised Records. These samples – around 2 per cent – of individuals and households allow the investigation of relationships and variables for distinct groups of the population in a flexible way. They were introduced for the first time after the 1991 census and are supported by the Centre for Census and Social Research in Manchester. These would allow, for example, analysis of the family structure of mothers under 25 with certain qualifications.

Lottery terminals – Camelot

One of the largest network optimisation projects ever carried out was for Camelot Group to optimise the location of the National Lottery Network of terminals. In 1999, Camelot commissioned the development of an integrated model and map-based GIS (Geographical Information System) known as "Optimum". The aim of Optimum was to provide a decision support tool to ensure that 35,000 National Lottery Terminals were in the ideal locations to maximise lottery sales.

The project by Business Geographics and GeoBusiness Solutions was described as a "milestone in spatial interaction modelling" in a review carried out by the Oxford Institute of Retail Management.

Camelot used the model results and methodology in their successful bid to retain the National Lottery Franchise. Chris Green, Director, Player and Retailer Services at Camelot said that the system "maps out the detailed geographic performance of the network and provides key decision support on the future location of terminals".

RNLI

The Royal National Lifeboat Institution is a registered charity that saves lives at sea. It provides, on call, the 24-hour service necessary to cover search and rescue requirements to 50 miles out from the coast of the United Kingdom and the Republic of Ireland. The RNLI depends on voluntary contributions for its income and volunteer crew to operate the lifeboats and the census plays a role in determining policy in both these areas.

As Ginette Tessier, research manager at the RNLI, says, "Knowing where to place a lifeboat station is a combination of local knowledge, experience and detailed risk assessment." Once an assessment has been made of the type of rescues likely to be required in an area – and therefore the type of boat that will best perform the job – the RNLI needs to work with the local community to assess the best place for a station.

It is that immediate community that provides the lifeboat crew, so it is vital that it has a good supply of men and women who meet the rigorous fitness levels, are readily available for a call out 24 hours a day, 365 days a year and are likely to volunteer. The improved availability of the small area census data will, say the RNLI, increasingly allow the organisation to monitor population demographics and migration for a particular area, to gauge the likely success in recruiting volunteer crew.

The RNLI raises money in many ways but legacies are a big source of income. The census information on mortality and life expectancy plays a part in income forecasting – it is only by studying the data that a reasonable estimate can be made of when pledged monies will arrive.

Pub redevelopment – matching customers with outlets – Inn Partnership

Following a change of ownership in 1999, the Inn Partnership decided to develop the way it evaluated a site for redevelopment and targeting new opportunities. Previously ideas had been developed through operational teams at the front line in conjunction with the Licensees. Inn Partnership developed this process through their marketing team by analysing the estate and looking at successful pubs by pub type (for example, community local, town bar, rural characters, young venues) and by their consumer profiles, finding areas to replicate the success by either developing existing sites or taking over new ones.

CACI produced reports for each business development manager so that they could further understand the profiles of people in their areas. This allowed the managers to look at data at an individual pub level. The information could be combined with data from other sources to show what sort of products are being drunk and where, and an idea of how Inn Partnership is comparing to the competition. The resulting reports gave the company a clearer view as to the type of customer they are targeting, providing vital facts and figures to support acquisitions, refurbishments and disposals.

Source: Briscoe, S. (2003) Private users: how shops use the information, FT.com, 7 October.

Optimisation models – under a variety of names – are used successfully across very different organisations.

Formulating the problem

The first stage in the solution process is to translate the problem faced into a mathematical formulation. We require this both for the constraints we face and for the objective, profit, we are seeking to maximise.

Constraints

In this problem we face four constraints, or restrictions, in terms of what we can, and cannot, do to resolve the problem. The four constraints relate to:

- availability of Mix A at 20 000 litres;
- availability of Mix B at 15 000 litres;
- availability of containers for product H at 4000;
- availability of containers for product C at 4500.

For each constraint we can express the restriction mathematically. Consider the first constraint, relating to availability of Mix A. We have a maximum of 20 000 litres available. This supply will be used to produce units of H and/or C. Each unit of H produced requires four litres and each unit of C requires two litres. If we denote the number of units of the two products produced as H and C respectively then the amount of Mix A required for any combination of H and C will be given by:

$$4H + 2C$$

For example, if we decided to produce 1000 H and 500 C then the quantity of Mix A required would be:

$$4H + 2C = 4000 + 1000 = 5000 \text{ liters}$$

So, for any given combination of production we can quantify the requirement using this expression. The supply of Mix A is restricted to a maximum of 20 000 litres. If we incorporate this into the expression we then have:

$$4H + 2C \leq 20\,000$$

which indicates that the quantity required (4H + 2C) must always be less than or equal to (≤) that available (20 000). This is the first mathematical constraint for the problem.

Progress Check 11.1

Formulate an equivalent expression for each of the remaining constraints in the problem.

The constraints would be:

$$4H + 2C \leq 20\,000 \quad (\text{Mix } A)$$
$$1H + 3C \leq 15\,000 \quad (\text{Mix } B)$$

The demand for Mix B arising from producing units of H and C cannot exceed the available supply at 15 000.

$$1H \leq 4000 \quad (\text{Containers for } H)$$
$$1C \leq 4500 \quad (\text{Containers for } C)$$

Note that the last two constraints are formulated in terms of only one variable rather than two since the limitation imposed is only on one variable. We can produce no more than 4000 units of H and no more than 4500 units of C.

Other types of constraint

In this problem all the constraints are expressed in terms of a less than or equal to formulation ($\leq$). It is common to encounter other types of constraint which may be formulated in terms of $\geq$ or $=$. The $\geq$ term implies that some *minimum* value must be satisfied. For example, the company may have a contract with a national hotel chain to supply *at least* 2500 units of C each week. This would then give rise to a constraint:

$$1C \geq 2500$$

indicating a minimum value for this variable. Similarly, a constraint involving $=$ implies that the left-hand side (LHS) and right-hand side (RHS) of the constraint must be exactly the same. For example, suppose the company's marketing department has redesigned the label that is used on the front of each bottle. However, the company is keen to use up existing stocks of the old labels before using the new ones. If stock of the old labels is 4000 and the label can be used on either product then a constraint:

$$1H + 1C = 4000$$

would be appropriate, forcing the company to produce appropriate quantities regardless of profitability.

The objective function

Just as we have formulated a mathematical expression for the constraints, so we can do the same for the objective of the problem: profit in this case. The profit achieved from any combination of production would be given by:

$$\text{Profit} = 0.30H + 0.25C$$

where profit would be measured in £s. Each unit of H produced contributes 30p to profit and each unit of C 25p. This expression is known as the *objective function*. Note that, unlike the constraints, the objective function has no numerical value attached to it (like 20 000 for the first constraint). We do not yet know what profit we will make, since we have not yet determined the optimum combination of H and C to produce.

The complete formulation

We can bring these expressions together into a full LP formulation:

Maximise $0.30H + 0.25C$

subject to:

$$4H + 2C \leq 20\,000$$
$$1H + 3C \leq 15\,000$$
$$1H \qquad \leq 4000$$
$$1C \leq 4500$$
$$H, C \geq 0$$

This indicates that we are seeking to maximise the value of the objective function subject to the restrictions imposed by the four constraints. Note that we have added an extra 'constraint', known as the *non-negativity condition*, $H, C \geq 0C \leq 0$. This is an expression which simply indicates that negative values for the two variables are not permitted: they clearly would make no sense in a business context. We should note two further points about the formulation of an LP problem.

- The number, and type, of constraints will be determined by the problem.
- Some problems may require a minimum value for an objective function. For example, we might want to minimise production costs rather than maximise profit. Such an objective function would then be shown as a minimisation rather than maximisation.

Progress Check 11.2

Return to the chemical mix problem in the chapter. The company now decides that instead of maximising profits it wishes to minimise the total costs of producing the two products. The cost per unit of C is £1.10 and of H £0.85. In addition to the existing constraints, the firm has also decided that minimum acceptable production of H is 2000 units and of C is 2500.

Formulate the new problem.

Solution is given on p 581.

Graphical solution to the LP formulation

Having formulated the problem we now seek some general method of solution. In fact the problem as formulated involves expressions which are all linear in format: they would give straight lines on a graph (you may want to revisit the section Graphs in Chapter 2). We can use this feature to develop a graphical solution method which follows a logical sequence of stages as follows.

- Graph the constraints.
- Graph the objective function.

- Determine the solution visually.
- Check the solution algebraically.

Graph the constraints

The first stage in the solution process is to graph all the constraints to the problem. Given that all the expressions are linear, this implies that to draw each one we require two sets of coordinates for the graph. The line representing each expression in the formulation can then be obtained by joining the two coordinate points together. Consider the first constraint:

$$4H + 2C \leq 20\,000$$

The two sets of coordinates are typically obtained by setting each variable in turn to zero and solving for the other. Let us set H to zero. Logically this then implies that all 20 000 litres of Mix A are available to produce C, which requires two litres of Mix A per five-litre bottle. Maximum production of C will then be given by:

$$20\,000/2 = 10\,000$$

One set of coordinates is then:

$$H = 0, C = 10\,000$$

Repeating the logic but this time setting C to zero we have:

$$H = 5000, C = 0$$

These are then the two coordinate sets for this first constraint, which can now be plotted on a graph.

Progress Check 11.3

Obtain similar coordinate sets for the remaining constraints.

We obtain the following coordinate sets:

For constraint 2: $H = 0, C = 5000; H = 15\,000, C = 0$
For constraint 3: $H = 4000$ for any value of C
For constraint 4: $C = 4500$ for any value of H

Note that to solve these equations we consider the equal ($=$) sign. This is to find the coordinates in order to draw the corresponding lines for the equations. Obviously the figure may represent the maximum or the minimum value for that variable, depending on the equation.

Figure 11.1 shows the graph for the first constraint. The two points are marked at $C = 10\,000$ and $H = 5000$ and the line representing this constraint then joins these two points. We need to consider carefully the information implicit in the diagram. The line

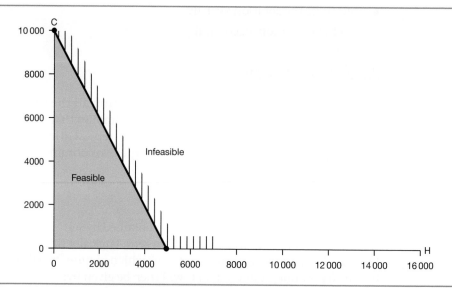

Figure 11.1 Feasible area for first constraint

itself actually represents all combinations of H and C which require *exactly* 20 000 litres of Mix A (in other words where the constraint takes the form =). The area below the line represents all combinations of H and C which require *less than* 20 000 litres (where the constraint takes the form <). Together this area and the line itself represent what is known as the *feasible* area: those combinations of H and C which are feasible for this constraint. It follows that the area above the line represents the *infeasible* area: combinations which cannot be achieved given the restriction of 20 000 litres. Typically the infeasible side of the line is marked as shown on the diagram. What this effectively means is that we have now limited where the optimal solution to this problem must be: it can only be in the feasible area. Clearly this feasible area relates only to the first constraint. As we add further constraints to the graph, however, the feasible area will alter and will show the feasible area for *all* constraints.

Progress Check 11.4

Add the other three constraints to the graph and mark the area which is feasible for all four constraints.

Figure 11.2 shows all four constraints for the problem. Take a few moments to study the diagram. All four constraints are shown and marked (1) to (4). The infeasible side of each constraint line has been marked. The area which is feasible to all four constraints simultaneously is marked. Its boundary is marked by the origin, by 4500 on the C axis, the intersection of constraints (2) and (4), the intersection of constraints (1) and (2), the intersection of constraints (1) and (3), 4000 on the H axis and back to the origin. This area, by definition, must contain the solution to the problem since it shows all possible solutions which are feasible. Clearly, in order to determine which of the many feasible solutions is optimal, we require the objective function.

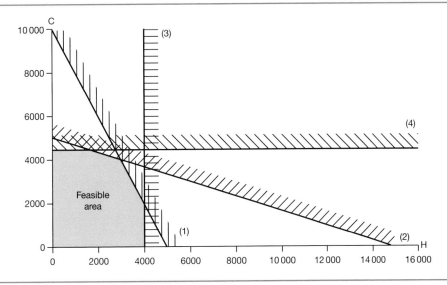

Figure 11.2 Feasible area for all constraints

Graph the objective function

To graph the objective function, we must adopt a slightly different approach to that for the constraints. The reason for this is that we currently have no numerical value for the objective function (indeed that is what we are actually seeking to determine). To graph the objective function line, however, we can give the function some arbitrary numerical value. One convenient arbitrary value can always be found from a multiple of the two coefficients in the function. If we multiply 0.30 and 0.25 we obtain 0.075. If we scale this result upwards to 750 we can use this to ascertain the graphical characteristics of the objective function.

Progress Check 11.5

Using a profit of 750 determine the two sets of coordinates of the objective function for the graph.

Setting profit to £750 we would then obtain coordinates:

$$H = 0, C = 3000$$
$$H = 2500, C = 0$$

However, these coordinates and the corresponding line are associated with a level of profit that was entirely arbitrary. A different profit value would clearly have given different coordinates. Figure 11.3 shows a series of such profit lines from £750 to £1500 (and we could go higher as well but as you will see this won't be needed). It is evident that the different profit lines are all parallel (mathematically they must be because they have the same slope, which is given by the ratio of the two profit coefficients). Equally, the higher the profit value then the further away the line is from the origin.

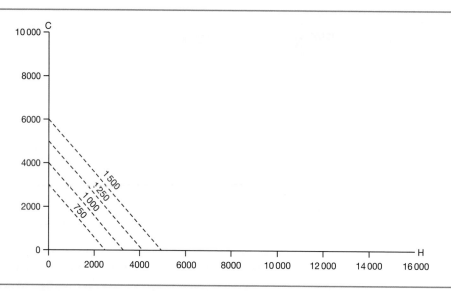

Figure 11.3 Objective function for differing profit values

Progress Check 11.6

From the manager's perspective, which of these four profit lines would you prefer?

Clearly, given the objective of maximisation, we would prefer to be on a profit line which was as far above the origin as possible. £1500 would be preferable to any of the others shown. A related aspect to this is that we would be indifferent as to *where* on a particular profit line we were since all points on the same line generate the same profit. That is, as long as we were on the £1500 profit line it would not matter where on that line we were: i.e. what combination of H and C we were producing as long as it generated this much profit. Returning to the feasible area in Figure 11.2, however, it becomes apparent that some profit lines may well lie outside the feasible area: they represent a value for the objective function which cannot be achieved given the constraints we face.

Determine the solution visually

What we require is to combine the graphical information about the feasible area with that for the objective function to help us determine the optimal solution. The general principles are evident. We seek a profit line as far above the origin as possible yet still within the feasible area. The principles involved are shown in Figure 11.4. To help understand the process involved the diagram shows only the feasible area rather than the full graph of the constraints, and the scale has been enlarged. Also shown on the diagram are two profit lines for £750 and £1500. Let us consider the profit line of £750. All combinations of H and C which generate this particular level of profit fall within the feasible area, hence all of these are solutions to the problem. However, we see that it is possible for the profit line to move further away from the origin and still remain in the feasible area. The profit line for £1500, for example, is preferred to that of £750 (given the maximisation objective). Although some parts of this profit line fall outside

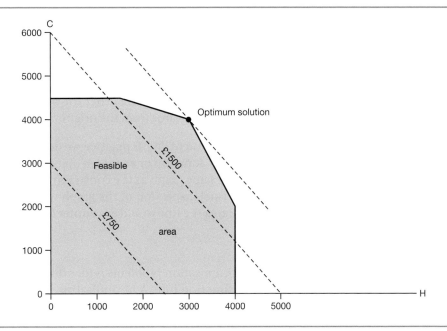

Figure 11.4 Optimum solution

the feasible area (representing infeasible solutions), part of the line is still within the area. Hence we conclude that it is possible to generate a profit of £1500 and still satisfy all four constraints. However, it is clear that there are still further profit lines above £1500 that are feasible.

Consider the principles, however. It is apparent that as the profit line moves away from the origin, less and less of the line remains in the feasible area. Clearly there will come a time when a particular profit line has part of it just within the feasible area and the rest outside: literally one point on the line will be feasible and the rest will not. Consider the next possible – and higher – profit line. Given that the last one had only one point in common with the feasible area then the next higher line will have left the feasible area entirely. None of the solutions on this line will be feasible. So, we are searching for a profit line which just passes through a single point of the feasible area. This point will represent the combination of the two products which represents the optimal solution: this point will generate the highest possible profit that is feasible. Such a point is marked on Figure 11.4 and can be seen to represent H = 3000 and C = 4000. Obviously this profit line – like all others – will be parallel to the two we have already drawn. It is also important to note that the solution to such a problem will invariably occur at one of the corner points of the feasible area. The reason for this is to do with the mathematics underpinning the approach, but we can take advantage of this fact for any LP problem. Effectively what we must do to determine the solution is identify all the corner points for the feasible area and decide, in the context of the objective function line, which of them represents the optimum solution.

So, the solution is:

$$H = 3000$$
$$C = 4000$$
$$\text{Profit} = £1\,900 = (0.3(3000) + 0.25(4000))$$

To summarise the graphical solution process:

- Graph the constraints to the problem.
- Mark the feasible area.
- Graph the objective function by assigning it an arbitrary numerical value.
- Visually locate the point of the feasible area that the objective function line would encounter *last* as it is pushed outwards from the origin.

This last point needs some comment. With practice we do not actually need to draw a separate graph for the objective function or a series of objective function lines. If we simply draw *one* such line on the same graph as the constraints we know that all other lines will be parallel to this. By visual inspection of the graph we can then determine which corner point of the feasible area the line would encounter *last* as it is pushed outwards.

Minimisation problems

The solution process for minimisation problems is identical except for the direction we would push the objective function line. A minimisation line is seeking to get as close as possible to the origin (rather than as far away as possible). Typically, the feasible area will prevent a minimisation line from actually reaching the origin but the point the line intersects last as it approaches the origin will be the minimisation solution.

Binding and non-binding constraints

So the solution to the maximisation problem is to produce 3000 units of H and 4000 units of C. From the objective function we determine that this will generate a weekly profit of 1900. From each constraint we note that:

(1) $4H + 2C \leq 20\,000$

$12\,000 + 8000 = 20\,000$

That is the optimal solution, using all available supply of Mix A;

(2) $1H + 3C \leq 15\,000$

$3000 + 12\,000 = 15\,000$

and all the available supply of Mix B;

(3) $1H \leq 4000$

$3000 < 4000$

but there are 1000 unused containers for product H; and

(4) $1C \leq 4500$

$4000 < 4500$

there are 500 unused containers for product C.

The first two constraints, for Mix A and B, are technically known as *binding* constraints: at the optimal solution they limit (or bind) the objective function from taking an improved value. From Figure 11.2 we note that the optimal combination of H and C actually occurs on the line of both these constraints (and remember that for any point on the constraint line the RHS of the constraint expression equals the LHS). The other two constraints are *non-binding*: at the current optimal solution they do not prevent the objective function from taking an improved value. We could produce more of H and C as far as these two constraints are concerned. From the graph we note that the optimal combination lies below these two constraint lines: there are surplus resources available for these two constraints. In fact we can use the binding constraints to confirm the graphical solution using mathematics.

Check the solution algebraically

The two binding constraints at the optimal solution can be rewritten as:

(1) $4H + 2C = 20\,000$

(2) $1H + 3C = 15\,000$

We also note from the graph that the solution occurs where these two constraint lines intersect: where the equations are equal. Using the method of *simultaneous equations* we then confirm the solution. This is a simple method for finding the values of two variables (here H and C) when we have two equations. From Equation 1 we take the numerical coefficient associated with the first variable: here the coefficient is 4 (associated with H). We then multiply each term in Equation 2 by this coefficient, 4, and subtract the result from Equation 1 to get:

$$
\begin{array}{rl}
(1) \quad 4H + 2C = & 20\,000 \\
\underline{-4H - 12C =} & \underline{-60\,000} \\
-10C = & -40\,000
\end{array}
$$

giving $C = 4000$. Substituting this value for C back into either Equation 1 or 2 we obtain $H = 3000$ to confirm the graphical solution. It is always worthwhile using simultaneous equations in this way to confirm the graphical solution. However, such an approach can also generate useful management information through what is known as sensitivity analysis.

So to summarise, we started with a problem where we were seeking to maximise profit subject to a variety of constraints on what we could, and could not, do. Through the application of LP we now know that we can maximise profit at £1900 by producing 3000 units of H and 4000 units of C. This combination of production will use all the available supply of Mix A and Mix B but leave 1000 unused containers for product H and 500 for product C. And if you're wondering why the technique is called linear programming it's because we're dealing with linear relationships and have found a sequence of steps (or programme) for solving an LP problem.

Sensitivity analysis

Clearly LP is useful as a means of determining the optimal solution to a given problem. Management are likely to be interested in more than this, however. Typical questions are likely to be: what would happen to the solution if we could obtain an extra 5000 litres of Mix A? What would happen if H's profitability per unit increased? What would happen if the supplier of containers decreased their availability? One approach to providing an answer to such what-if questions would be to recalculate the entire problem and determine the solution to the amended formulation. Even for small problems, however, this can be time-consuming and tedious. A different approach is to examine the sensitivity of the current solution to marginal changes in the problem formulation. This allows us to assess readily a change in one part of the problem without the need for an entire recalculation. Typically, such sensitivity can be undertaken on the constraints and on the objective function.

Constraints

Let us return to the optimal solution, where we found that the two binding constraints were the availability of the two chemical mixes. Consider Mix A. We have a weekly supply of some 20 000 litres, all of which is used at the optimum. If we pose the question: would it be worthwhile obtaining extra supplies of Mix A then the answer clearly has to be 'yes'. Additional supplies of this mix will allow additional production and hence more profit, other things being equal.

Progress Check 11.7

Consider the related question. How much would extra supplies of Mix A be worth to the company?

This is more difficult. In principle the answer would relate to profit. Given that extra supplies of Mix A will lead to increased profit via increased production then the 'worth' or value of this extra supply will clearly be linked to extra profit. What we obviously require is some method for calculating this effect. Let us consider the following scenario. The company decides it is possible to obtain one extra litre of Mix A for use in the production process.

Progress Check 11.8

Examine Figure 11.2. What would happen to the constraint line for Mix A? What would then happen to the optimum production of C and H?

Figure 11.5 shows the principles of the situation. We see that constraint line (1) would be pushed outwards by a small amount as one extra litre became available. The feasible area would change marginally also, although it would be impossible to show such a small change on the solution graph. The corner point of the feasible area representing the optimal solution would also change: it would move down the constraint (2) line. This would represent a slight (or marginal) reduction in C and a marginal increase in H. Using simultaneous equations, we can quantify this effect. We now have:

(1) $4H + 2C = 20\,001$

(2) $1H + 3C = 15\,000$

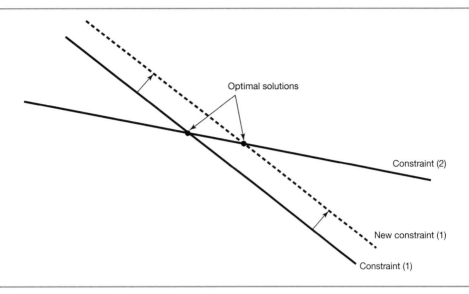

Figure 11.5 Sensitivity analysis: a marginal change in Constraint 1

and we obtain:

$$
\begin{aligned}
(1)\quad 4H + 2C &= 20\,001 \\
-4H - 12C &= -60\,000 \\
\hline
-10C &= -39\,999
\end{aligned}
$$

giving a new solution for C = 3999.9 and therefore H = 3000.3. That is, a reduction of 0.1 units of C and an increase of 0.3 units of H. The new profit will be:

$$0.3(3000.3) + 0.25(3999.9) = £1900.065 \; 0.3(3000) + 0.25(4000) = £1900.65$$

– an increase of £0.065 in profit achieved. What we now have is a means of assigning a monetary value to the extra supply of Mix A. An extra litre of Mix A adds 6.5p to profit and this is its *marginal value*: the value to the company over and above what it would normally pay for a litre of Mix A. This marginal value in LP is often referred to as *opportunity cost* or *shadow price*. It shows the change in the objective function for a marginal, one-unit, change in the right-hand side of a binding constraint.

If one extra litre of Mix A is worth 6.5p, does it then follow that two litres are worth 13p, 3 litres 19.5p and so on? The answer is a qualified 'yes'. Further marginal increases in the supply of Mix A will lead to further marginal increases in profit at a rate of 6.5p per litre of Mix A. However, this cannot continue indefinitely. The only reason that Mix A has a positive opportunity cost is because it is in scarce supply. As we increase the supply of this resource we gradually change the feasible area. There will come a point where some additional constraint becomes binding and the current binding constraint for Mix A becomes non-binding. In fact we can usually identify this from the graph. In Figure 11.2 we see that as constraint line (1) moves outwards as we increase supply of Mix A, it will eventually reach the point where constraint lines (2) and (3) intersect. This will be a new corner point of the feasible area and, given the slope of the profit line, which remains unchanged, will be the new solution. The new solution will now be:

$$H = 4000$$

and from constraint (2) when H = 4000, C = 3666.67. This combination of C and H will require from constraint (1) a total of 23 333.33 litres of Mix A. The maximum worthwhile increase in supply of Mix A is then 3333.33 litres. Increasing the supply of Mix A past this amount will not lead to any further increase in profit, since we will have run out of containers for product H: all 4000 will now be in use. Such a sensitivity analysis, therefore, allows us not only to put a value, or opportunity cost, on scarce resources but also to quantify the maximum worthwhile change in resource availability.

Progress Check 11.9

Undertake a similar sensitivity calculation for constraint (2).

For constraint (2) we would have:

(1) $4H + 2C = 20\,000$

(2) $1H + 3C = 15\,001$

and we obtain:

$$
\begin{array}{r}
(1) \quad 4H + 2C = 20\,000 \\
-4H - 12C = -60\,004 \\
\hline
-10C = -40\,004
\end{array}
$$

giving C = 4000.4 and H = 2999.8 with a profit of £1900.04 – an increase in profitability of 4p per extra litre of Mix B. Using the same approach as before, we note from Figure 11.2 that the new maximum solution point will occur at the intersection of constraints (1) and (4), where by default C = 4500. This gives H = 2750. This combination of C and H would require a total of 16 250 litres of Mix B, which represents the maximum worthwhile amount before constraint (4) becomes binding. An extra 1250 litres would be worthwhile obtaining. Such sensitivity analysis also allows us to prioritise in the context of scarce resources. The opportunity cost of Mix A is 6.5p per litre and that of Mix B 4p per litre. Other things being equal, it will be more profitable to increase supplies of Mix A before those of Mix B.

Progress Check 11.10

Consider increasing the supply of resources in a non-binding constraint. What would be the associated opportunity cost?

It is important to realise that a positive opportunity cost is associated only with constraints that are binding at the current optimal solution. Non-binding constraints, by definition, must have a zero opportunity cost. Since a non-binding constraint already has unused resources then increasing the total supply of this resource will not allow an increase in production and hence in profit. Opportunity cost is often referred to in an LP context as *the dual value* or *shadow price* of a binding constraint.

The objective function

Just as we can undertake sensitivity analysis on constraints, so we can do the same for the objective function. In this case we are considering changes in the coefficients for the two variables in the objective function: in this example the profit contributions made by each product. In principle, a change in either profit contribution will affect the slope of the objective function line. If the slope of the objective function line changes sufficiently then it will move the optimal solution to a new corner point of the feasible area. The mathematics of calculating when this will occur are too complex for our consideration of the topic here but it is worthwhile noting that this information can be produced for a specialist LP computer program.

Computer solutions

In practice, of course, LP problems are solved using an appropriate computer package. This might be available as part of a spreadsheet program, for example SOLVER in Microsoft Excel. It might also be a specialist LP program such as LINDO or XPRESS-MP. The reason for this is that such problems will typically involve more than two variables – and hence cannot be solved on a two-dimensional graph – and a considerable number of constraints. However, the information such solutions typically generate is no different in principle from that we have produced. Table 11.2 shows typical computer output that

Table 11.2 Computer output

basis	value		
H	3000.00	zmax	1900.00
C	4000.000		
S3	1000.000		
S4	500.000		

Sensitivity on constraint

con	opp. cost	constr constant	permitted range of variation* from	to
1	0.06500	20000.0	15000	23333.3
2	0.04000	15000.0	10000	16250
3	0.00000	4000.00	0	+∞
4	0.00000	4500.00	0	+∞

Sensitivity on objective

var	optimal value	obj fun coeft	permitted range of variation* from	to
H	3000.00	0.30000	0.083	0.50
C	4000.00	0.25000	0.15	0.90

*The current basis remains optimal in this range

was obtained for this problem. The optimal solution is shown first with the objective function (shown as zmax) taking a value of 1900 and the values for H and C as calculated. This is then followed by two variables labelled S3 and S4. LP programs typically refer to the *slack* for each constraint at the optimal point: the difference between the LHS of the constraint expression and the RHS. For constraints 3 and 4 these are, respectively, 1000 and 500 and represent the two types of unused container. Slack for constraints 1 and 2 is zero since these are binding. Sensitivity analysis results are then shown for the constraints. The opportunity cost for each binding constraint is shown, together with the range of variation. This shows the range within which the RHS of that constraint can vary and still remain a binding constraint. Although we only calculated one side of this range manually – at 23 333.3 – a reduction in the RHS value can also be calculated. Finally, sensitivity analysis for the objective function is shown. This indicates that for the H variable, for example, the profit coefficient could vary between £0.083 and £0.50 without altering the corner point of the feasible area at which the optimal solution occurred.

Assumptions of the basic model

Like all the quantitative models we introduce, it is important to be aware of the implicit assumptions behind the model. If these are not appropriate to the business problem to which the model is being applied then the output from that model must be suspect.

Linearity

The model assumes that all relationships are linear in form. One of the implicit aspects behind such an assumption is that of proportionality. In this example, this assumes that if we produce twice as much C then we require twice as much of all the resources that C requires. Clearly in the real world this may not always be appropriate. Economies of scale may come into play after some output level is reached, for example, meaning that we may not require twice as much labour for twice the output.

Divisibility

The second assumption is one of divisibility: that all variables are continuous rather than discrete. In our context this implies that we can have fractions of products or resources. Again, for some problems this is not a difficulty, while for others it might be. Clearly if our solution had shown that we had to produce, say, 3000.2 bottles of C, this is a physical impossibility.

Certainty

The third assumption relates to certainty: that we know for certain the numerical values of the linear relationships specified. In practice this can be a major difficulty in applying LP to real problems.

Single objective

The last assumption relates to the fact that we specify a single objective which we seek. Again, in practice a manager may be searching for a solution which satisfies several objectives simultaneously and not just a single one.

Dealing with more than two variables

Extensions to the basic LP model are not difficult to incorporate with ready access to computer solution packages. Additional variables are easily incorporated into programs, as are larger numbers of constraints. Naturally, once additional variables are added to the problem, the graphical method can no longer be used (since the graph has only two axes for two variables). Such larger problems are solved through the use of a suitable computer program, which typically will use what is known as the *simplex* method of solution. Briefly, this is a set of mathematical and arithmetic rules for checking the corner points of the feasible area for the problem to see which represents the optimum solution. To illustrate the solution output we would typically obtain, let us amend our basic problem. Let us assume that the company is now considering a third type of detergent for the export market (X). This would contribute 35p to profit per five-litre bottle and would consist of 3 litres of mix A and 2 litres of mix B. The problem formulation would then be:

$$\text{Maximise } 0.30H + 0.25C + 0.35X$$

subject to:

$$4H + 2C + 3X \leq 20\,000$$
$$1H + 3C + 2X \leq 15\,000$$
$$1H \qquad\qquad \leq 4\,000$$
$$\qquad 1C \qquad \leq 4\,500$$
$$1H, C, X \geq 0$$

Table 11.3 shows the computer output for this problem. The first part of the table, labelled tableau, shows details of the optimal solution. The objective function (labelled zmax) takes a value of 2350. From the last column of the tableau we see that X takes a value of 6000, C a value of 1000, S3 a value of 4000 and S4 a value of 3500. Any variable that does not appear in this column takes a value of zero. The solution, in other words, is to produce:

0 units of H

1000 units of C

6000 units of X

which will generate a profit of £2350. Such a combination of production will use all of chemical Mix A (S1 = 0 by default), all of chemical Mix B (S2 = 0 by default). The slack associated with constraint 3 will be 4000 (since H is zero at the optimal solution) and the slack associated with constraint 4 will be 3500. The optimal solution may seem surprising since, per unit, H is more profitable than C and yet we are producing zero H. The answer, of course, lies not in the unit contribution as such but the contribution in relation to the use of the limited resources available. We see from the solution that it is preferable to produce C instead of H. Sensitivity analysis is shown in the rest of the table: on the constraints first, then on the objective function. For the constraints we see confirmation that constraints 1 and 2 are binding whereas 3 and 4 are not. The opportunity cost for each of the binding constraints is shown as 0.11 (11p) for constraint 1 and 0.01 (1p) for constraint 2. Interpretation is as before. Increasing the available supply of Mix A would allow an increase in profit of 11p per extra litre obtained. This extra profit would occur for increases in the supply up to 22 500 litres (shown in the last column).

Table 11.3   Computer solution

```
Tableau

basis    X1       X2       X3       S1       S2       S3       S4       rel value

zmax    -0.15    0.000    0.000   -0.11    -0.01    0.000    0.000    = 2350.000

X        2.000    0.000    1.000    0.600   -0.40    0.000    0.000    = 6000.000

C       -1.00     1.000    0.000   -0.40     0.600    0.000    0.000    = 1000.000

S3       1.000    0.000    0.000    0.000    0.000    1.000    0.000    = 4000.000

S4       1.000    0.000    0.000    0.400   -0.60     0.000    1.000    = 3500.000


Sensitivity on constraint

                                           permitted range
         opp.             constr           of variation*
con      cost             constant         from             to

1        0.11000          20000.0          11250.0          22500.0

2        0.01000          15000.0          13333.3          20833.3

3        0.00000          4000.00          0.00000          +∞

4        0.00000          4500.00          1000.00          +∞


Sensitivity on objective

                                           permitted range
         optimal          obj fun          of variation*
var      value            coeft            from             to

H        0                0.30000          -∞               0.45000

C        1000.00          0.25000          0.23333          0.40000

X        6000.00          0.35000          0.27500          0.37500
```

*The current basis remains optimal in this range

For the objective function, the sensitivity analysis is particularly revealing given that we are only producing two of the three products in the product range. For C and X, the range of variation can be interpreted as before: for X, for example, the unit profit contribution can vary between 27.5p and 37.5p without affecting the profit-maximising combination of production. Let us examine H, however. This is a product not currently being produced (since it is not profitable to do so given the limited resources). The value of 45p shown actually indicates the minimum profit contribution this product would have to make in order for it to take a non-zero value in the solution. That is, the per-unit profit contribution of H would have to be at least 40p in order for the company to find it worthwhile (in terms of increased profit) to produce this product. Clearly this now provides management with the opportunity of assessing where such a profit contribution could be realised: either by increasing the selling price and/or by reducing the production costs of this product.

QADM IN ACTION

Capgemini – optimising the supply chain

Capgemini's client was a global manufacturer in the consumer packaged goods sector. The client was undertaking a complete review of their operations across Europe. One of the major elements of the review focused on improving the performance of the supply chain. The client was considering several options for the future supply chain infrastructure and they need a technique to explore these options against a number of possible future demand scenarios.

It was decided to adopt an optimisation model approach to the problem. A supply chain model was developed incorporating costs, product demands and supply chain resources. The model was then used to demonstrate how costs could be minimised for each given supply chain configuration that was being considered by management.

The model was designed from the outset as a decision support tool for senior management. This allowed them to assess the impact of potential changes through the modelling environment. An LP model was formulated for a supply chain which consisted of 15 factories; 14 distribution centres; 2500 products; 7500 components; 1000 component suppliers; 25 000 customers.

Data on procurement, manufacturing, warehousing and distribution was collected for the entire European supply chain. Data analysis allowed activity costs to be obtained. A specialist optimisation package, XPRESS-MP, was used together with a Windows graphical user interface to make it easy for senior management to understand and explore the results of the optimisation model.

The figure illustrates the complexity of the supply chain that had to be modelled.

The benefits are as follows:

- As a result of restructuring its supply chain the business achieved savings of around 10 per cent per annum (c. £10m).

- For the first time the client was able to view the complexity in the supply chain and the associated costs.

- For the first time the client was able to develop a European-wide view of the supply chain.

Source: Based on a Capgemini case study, with thanks to Capgemini for permission to use their material.

Extensions to the basic LP model

Because of some of the assumptions underpinning the model, a variety of additional programming models have been developed. *Integer* programming is concerned with those problems where some or all of the variables can take only integer values. *Non-linear* programming has been developed for use in situations where some, or all, relationships are non-linear. *Goal* programming allows the relaxation of the assumption of a single objective. In addition, a number of models have been developed for specialist use in more restricted applications, a common example being the *transportation* model, which is concerned with 'transporting' items from a variety of origins to a variety of destinations. All of these are developments that are worth exploring.

Drillers turn to big data in the hunt for more, cheaper oil

Under pressure from renewables, energy groups are again looking to tech for answers

By Ed Crooks in Menlo Park

Source: huyangshu/Shutterstock

Just a few miles down the road from Facebook's headquarters, Schlumberger's Software Technology Innovation Center in leafy Menlo Park feels like just another Silicon Valley business with dreams of changing the world. ... What Schlumberger is doing, however, is far from typical for Silicon Valley: it is working to increase output and cut costs for an activity at the heart of the old economy, oil and gas production. ... The technology centre that the oilfield services group has created is a sign of the huge changes under way in oil and gas, as the industry begins to adopt the latest innovations in information technology. Techniques such as advanced data analytics, used by Google, Facebook, Amazon and others mainly to disrupt consumer-facing businesses, are now increasingly being applied to the energy industry. Many oil executives believe the results could be similarly dramatic. ... BP's chief executive Bob Dudley said last week that it had worked with a Silicon Valley start-up to develop an optimisation model, and had been able to raise production at the 180 wells in its pilot project by 20 per cent.

Source: Crooks, E. (2018) Drillers turn to big data in the hunt for more, cheaper oil: Under pressure from renewables, energy groups are again looking to tech for answers, *Financial Times*, 12 February. © The Financial Times Limited. All Rights Reserved.

Optimisation models like LP are finding new areas of application across business and industry.

Worked example

A local health board is producing a healthy-living guide for sale primarily to schools, voluntary agencies, hospitals and clinics. The guide provides advice on health education, healthy lifestyles and the like. The board intends to produce the guide in two formats: one will be in the form of a loose-leaf printed binder, the other as a short video. The board is currently trying to decide how many of each type to produce for sale. The video will sell for £5 and the binder for £3. Given the effort that has gone into the guide, the board is keen to maximise the revenue it gets from sales. It has estimated that it is likely to sell no more than 10 000 copies of both items together. However, it thinks that it will be able to sell at least 4000 copies of the video and at least 2000 copies of the binder, although sales of the binder are not expected to exceed 4000 copies. The company manufacturing the video on the board's behalf has also indicated that it takes 24 minutes to make each video and that for the fixed price it has quoted it can allocate only 5000 hours to the video production.

We are seeking to maximise the revenue earned from sales of these two products. Denoting the video as V and the binder as B we can obtain the following problem formulation:

Maximise $5V + 3B$

subject to:

$$1V + 1B \leq 10\,000$$
$$1V \qquad \geq 4\,000$$
$$1B \geq 2\,000$$
$$1B \leq 4\,000$$
$$0.4V \qquad \leq 5\,000$$
$$V, B \geq 0$$

The fifth constraint shows that the time required to make each video (24 minutes or 0.4 hours) multiplied by the number of videos made cannot exceed the time available, 5000 hours. Using a computer package we obtain the information in Table 11.4 regarding the optimal solution. (You may wish to produce your own graphical solution.)

First of all we see that the optimal solution is to produce 8000 videos and 2000 binders and that this will generate a revenue of £46 000. As usual with optimisation problems, the solution is rarely our sole interest and, in this case, we might wish to assess some of the implications surrounding the optimal solution. We see that constraints 2, 4 and 5 are non-binding. Constraint 2 relates to the minimum production of videos, which, at 4000, is being exceeded at the optimal solution by another 4000. Constraint 4 relates to the maximum production of binders and our optimal solution is some 2000 binders below this. Constraint 5 is the constraint imposed by the video manufacturer. We can see that the 5000 hours currently budgeted for will not all be required, with some 1800 hours not needed (and we may wish to go back to the video manufacturer to renegotiate the production contract). We see that by default constraints 1 and 3 are binding. The sensitivity analysis provides information about the extent to which the optimal solution remains stable if we change the right-hand side values of constraints.

We see first of all that only constraints 1 and 3 have non-zero opportunity costs (since they are the two binding constraints). For constraint 1 we see an opportunity cost of 5. This implies that if we were able to find a market for more than 10 000 of these guides

Table 11.4   Computer solution

```
basis      value

V          8000.00                zmax    46000.00
B          2000.00
S2         4000.00
S3         2000.00
S4         1800.00


Sensitivity on constraint

                                        permitted range of
           opp.           constr       variation*
con        cost           constant      from              to

1          5.0            10000.0       6000.0            14500.0
2          0.0            4000.0        0                 8000.0
3          2.0            2000.00       0                 4000.0
4          0.0            4000.00       2000.0            +∞
5          0.0            5000.00       3200.0            +∞


Sensitivity on objective

                                        permitted range of
           optimal        obj fun       variation*
var        value          coeft         from              to

V          8000.00        5             3                 +∞
B          2000.00        3             +∞                5>
```

*The current basis remains optimal in this range

(perhaps by getting health boards in other areas interested in them) the sales revenue would go up by £5 for each extra guide, implying that we would produce extra units of the video. Equally, of course, if this 10 000 figure proved optimistic and we realised we could sell fewer, the sales revenue would decrease by £5 each time. We see that this constraint will remain binding in the range from 6000 to 14 500. The opportunity cost of £2 for constraint 3 needs more thought, since it does not appear to be the revenue either from videos (at £5) or from binders (at £3). This constraint relates to the minimum sales of binders, estimated at 2000. Effectively, if we reduced this constraint by one (to 1999) we would produce one less binder. Given that constraint 1 would still be binding, one less binder means we could produce one more video (since we still have unused video production hours). The net change in sales revenue then would be a loss of £3 and a gain of £5, a net gain of £2. In summary, then, we might suggest to the board that, as well as determining the optimal combination as 8000 videos and 2000 binders, it should:

● attempt to renegotiate the contract with the video manufacturer, since this appears to be based on a need for 5000 production hours, 1800 more than will be needed;

● attempt to find other markets for the guide, since each extra guide sold above the 10 000 limit will generate an extra £2. Up to 4500 additional guides could be produced with the currently unused production time (and of course if we were able to increase sales in this way, we would not want to renegotiate the contract with the video manufacturer);

- reconsider whether a minimum of 2000 binders should be available. Given the anticipated fixed demand for the guide of 10 000, the board should consider producing only video versions (unless it has other information that some purchasers would not buy a video version but only a binder version).

Summary

In this chapter we have introduced and developed the linear programming model as an example of a model applied to constrained optimisation problems. The LP model, in its many different forms, is a widely used technique and has been applied to a considerable variety of problems in both public and private sector organisations. The principles of the model are relatively simple, requiring a problem formulation, a solution, and an evaluation of the solution. Often the first part of this process, the formulation of a business problem into a linear programme, can be particularly difficult and may call for considerable skill on the part of the practitioner. The solution process is typically computer-based, although the graphical method is useful for illustrating general principles in a form a manager can understand.

QADM IN ACTION   Blue Bell Inc.

Blue Bell Inc. is a US-based company that few people outside the USA have heard of. Yet, in the 1980s at the date of this application, the company achieved annual sales of over $1.2 billion, generated an annual net income of almost $50 million and employed almost 30 000 people worldwide. While the company itself may not be well known, its product ranges certainly are. The largest part of its business consists of the Wrangler Group, producing and selling denim jeans and related clothing. In the early 1980s senior management in the company became increasingly concerned about one aspect of the Group's operations: that relating to stock control and the amount of capital tied up in stock. The business itself was classed as one which was very intensive in terms of working capital. The number of product lines, styles of product and markets served had increased markedly. Figure 11.6 illustrates the product complexity for one particular product, jeans. Given that annual output of jeans at the time was around 35 million pairs scattered across 37 production facilities the stock control problem was a severe one. At a time when short-term interest rates were particularly high, the company as a whole found that its interest charges had increased from just over $1 million in 1979 to almost $22 million by 1982, with the obvious consequences on operating costs and corporate performance. A company task force was established with the aims of:

- assessing the opportunity for reducing stock levels
- developing a suitable programme for achieving such stock reduction
- implementing such a programme.

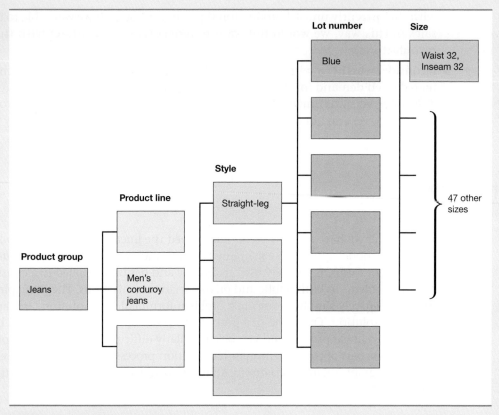

Figure 11.6 The product hierarchy for jeans

Source: Reprinted by permission of J.R. Edwards, H.M. Wagner and W.P. Wood. Taken from 'Blue Bell trims its inventory', Interfaces, 15(1), 1985. Copyright held by the Operations Research Society of America and the Institute of Management Sciences.

The task force investigated this complex problem from a number of different perspectives – forecasting sales, assessing required stock levels, planning the production process – which were all an interrelated part of the overall problem. One aspect in particular that was investigated related to what is known as marker planning and selection. A simplified overview of the production process is that, on a weekly basis, sufficient fabric must be cut to shape to form the components for manufacturing into a pair of jeans. Typically, layers of the appropriate fabric are placed on a cutting table and a marker – a pre-prepared pattern showing the parts to be cut – placed on top of the fabric to be used as a cutting guide. An example of a marker is shown in Figure 11.7.

Figure 11.7 Example of marker

Source: Reprinted by permission of J.R. Edwards, H.M. Wagner and W.P. Wood. Taken from 'Blue Bell trims its inventory', Interfaces, 15(1), 1985. Copyright held by the Operations Research Society of America and the Institute of Management Sciences.

Given the complexity of possible production plans – with the variety of jeans in terms of sizes, designs and fabrics – a library of such markers is available. The design and use of appropriate markers in the cutting process is of critical importance. Fabric may form over 50 per cent of the production cost of an item and any increase in fabric waste will have an obvious consequence for profitability. The design of the marker itself will contribute to fabric waste, which may be anything up to 15 per cent of the fabric used. The problem for the company in this context was to try to minimise fabric waste while at the same time ensuring that the utilisation of cutting room capacity was in line with production requirements. A linear programming model to assist in this part of the task was formulated. The model took into account a number of critical factors:

● the number of different stock parts (which could vary from 75 to 125)

● the production lead time required

● the estimated production requirements over the planning period for each stock part

● the fabric waste on markers

● the frequency of use of the different markers.

The LP formulation was a particularly complex one, given the production set-up in the company, and the model actually used had to be adapted to ensure it was cost-effective to run the model on the required weekly basis. Understandably, given the complexity of the new approaches and the consequences should they fail to work satisfactorily, the new systems were pilot-tested in a single profit centre. The testing consisted of utilising the new approach in parallel with the planning systems currently in use. The first stage was to use the new approach as part of the planning process. Later this was extended to use the new approach for scheduled production, again on a test-site basis first of all. The reported results were impressive. Within a two-year period, stock levels had been reduced by some $115 million without affecting sales volumes or requiring a reduction in the size of the product line. Raw material costs – through reduced fabric waste – were also substantially reduced, with annual cost savings estimated at $1 million.

Source: This application is based on the article: Edwards, J.R., Wagner, H.M. and Wood, W.P. (1985) Blue Bell trims its inventory, *Interfaces*, 15(1), pp 34–52. Copyright is held by the Operations Research Society of America and the Institute of Management Sciences, 290 Westminster Street, Providence, Rhode Island 02093, USA.

Exercises

1   A manufacturer is trying to determine the combination of two products, A and B, that should be produced. Each product passes through a three-stage production process: Stages I, II and III. For product A Stage I takes three hours of labour, Stage II four hours and Stage III one hour. For product B the comparable data are four hours, two hours and two hours. Labour hours currently cost £4.50 per hour. Product A sells for £38 a unit and B for £40. At present 11 people are employed on Stage I, 12 on Stage II and 10 on Stage III, with all employees working 40 hours each week.

(a) Formulate this problem in terms of determining the profit-maximising combination of the two products on a weekly basis.

(b) Solve the problem graphically.

(c) Confirm the solution using simultaneous equations.

(d) Identify the binding and non-binding constraints.

(e) Undertake sensitivity analysis on each of the binding constraints and evaluate the management information that this generates.

(f) What rate of overtime should the firm be willing to pay its employees?

2   For the problem in Exercise 1 assume the firm now wishes to maximise revenue rather than profit.

(a) Formulate this problem in terms of determining the revenue-maximising combination of the two products on a weekly basis.

(b) Solve the problem graphically.

(c) Confirm the solution using simultaneous equations.

(d) Identify the binding and non-binding constraints.

(e) Undertake sensitivity analysis on each of the binding constraints and evaluate the management information that this generates.

(f) What rate of overtime should the firm be willing to pay its employees?

3   A small engineering company makes two products for export, A and B. Both products go through a four-stage process: turning, grinding, polishing, finishing. The two products are produced in batches of 100 items and the time taken, in hours, for each batch to go through each stage is shown in Table 11.5.
   Profit contribution per batch of product A is £4 and for product B is £5.

(a) Formulate this problem in terms of determining the profit-maximising combination of the two products on a weekly basis.

(b) Solve the problem graphically.

(c) Confirm the solution using simultaneous equations.

(d) Identify the binding and non-binding constraints.

(e) Undertake sensitivity analysis on each of the binding constraints and evaluate the management information that this generates.

(f) What is it worth to the company to have extra hours available in turning?

4   A small electrical repair shop finds it has two main types of work. Major and minor repairs. Customers bring items in for repair: TVs, DVD players, etc. require major repair; other repairs are classed as minor. At present the shop has more business than it can handle and is trying to prioritise the work it should do. The firm charges £25 per hour for effecting a major repair and £10 per hour for a minor one. The shop currently has two trained repair engineers, who each work a 40-hour week. The shop will not allow overtime. The manager of the store has the following requirements:

- Repair work must generate at least £800 per week income.
- Major repairs should form at least 60 per cent of the weekly work.
- Minor repairs should form at least 30 per cent of weekly work.

Table 11.5   Time taken for production processes

Stage	Hours per batch		Hours available
	Product A	Product B	
Turning	12	18	240
Grinding	30	45	450
Polishing	20	60	480
Finishing	40	30	480

(a) Formulate this problem in terms of determining the revenue-maximising combination of the two types of work on a weekly basis.

(b) Solve the problem graphically.

(c) Confirm the solution using simultaneous equations.

(d) Identify the binding and non-binding constraints.

(e) Undertake sensitivity analysis on each of the binding constraints and evaluate the management information that this generates.

(f) What is it worth to the company to allow the engineers to work overtime?

Appendix: Solving LP problems with excel

Note the following instructions are based on Excel 2016. Some of the details may vary slightly depending on which version of Excel you are using.

Excel can be used to solve LP problems (although not using the graphical method). Excel has an add-in called Solver. You should be able to see this listed under the Data tab. If not, go to File, Options, Add-Ins, click on Solver in the list, click on Go, then Ok (you only have to do this once). To use Solver we first have to create a spreadsheet with the problem data. We'll illustrate using the two variable chemical mix problems we used in the chapter. Our spreadsheet for the problem is shown in Figure 11.8.

The way we actually set out the spreadsheet doesn't matter as long as it's logical and complete. In the top part of the spreadsheet (rows 4–14) we've shown the data for the problem – the constraints and their parameters and the profit function. The bottom part of the spreadsheet shows the LP model that we want Excel to solve (rows 17–27).

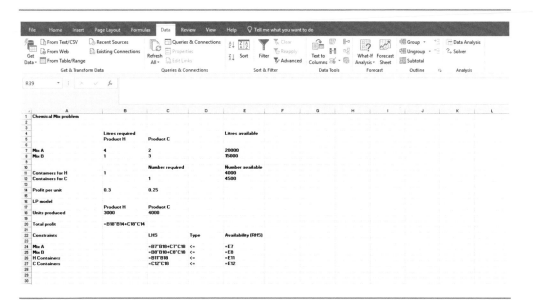

Figure 11.8 Initial spreadsheet

Cells B18 and C18 will show the optimal units to be produced (currently blank). Cell B20 shows the total profit achieved. Note that we have entered an appropriate formula here so Excel can calculate the actual profit achieved. The four constraints are then shown in rows 24–27. We first show the formula for the left-hand side (LHS) of each constraint, then show the type of each constraint (here all <=) and then the value of the right-hand side (RHS) for each constraint. Care must be taken to ensure that all formulas are correct.

We then call up the Solver module in Excel as shown in Figure 11.9.

Solver shows a dialogue box requesting parameters for the problem.

The **Set Objective** is the cell containing the objective function formula: here this would be $B20.

We then can select the **To** option of **Max**(imising), **Min**(imising) or **Value Of** for the objective function. Here we would choose Max.

Then we specify **By Changing Variable Cells**. Here we select B18:C18 as the cells that Excel can alter to find the optimal solution (most probably the Solver has already guessed this and it appears).

Finally we have **Subject to the Constraints:** Constraints can be added in different ways. Click on the **Add** button.

Enter C24 in the **Cell Reference**.

Select <=

Enter E24 in the **Constraint**

Repeat this for each of the other three constraints. We then have a Solver dialogue box as in Figure 11.10.

Under the **Subject to the Constraints** box make sure **Make Unconstrained Variables Non-Negative** is ticked (which means we don't need to specify the non-negativity constraints we had in the chapter). For the **Select a Solving Method** choose **Simplex LP** from the drop box.

Now click on the **Solve** button and the solution is shown on the spreadsheet as in Figure 11.11 (note that from the **Solve** button you also have the option of producing separate sheets (**Reports**) for the **Answer** and for **Sensitivity**).

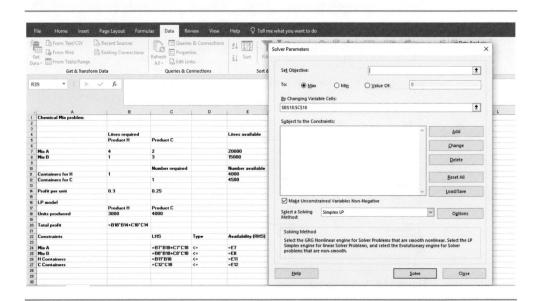

Figure 11.9 Solver dialogue

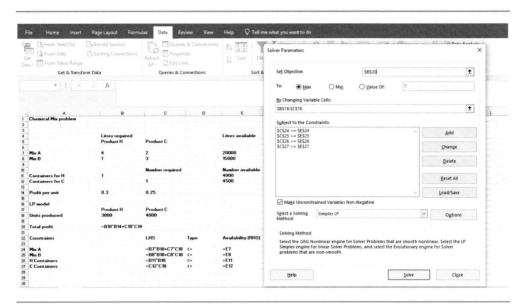

Figure 11.10 Solver dialogue completed

	A	B	C	D	E	F	G
1	**Chemical Mix problem**						
2							
3							
4		**Litres required**			**Litres available**		
5		**Product H**	**Product C**				
6							
7	Mix A	4	2		20000		
8	Mix B	1	3		15000		
9							
10		**Number required**			**Number available**		
11	Containers for H	1			4000		
12	Containers for C		1		4500		
13							
14	Profit per unit	0.3	0.25				
15							
16	**LP model**						
17		**Product H**	**Product C**				
18	Units produced	3000	4000				
19							
20	Total profit	1900					
21							
22	Constraints		**LHS**	**Type**	**Availability (RHS)**		
23							
24	Mix A		20000	<=	20000		
25	Mix B		15000	<=	15000		
26	H Containers		3000	<=	4000		
27	C Containers		4000	<=	4500		
28							
29							
30							
31							
32							

Figure 11.11 Solver solution

12 Stock Control

Learning objectives

By the end of this chapter you should be able to:

- explain the stock-control problem
- identify the major stock costs
- calculate the basic EOQ model
- be aware of the MRP and JIT approaches to stock control

In this chapter we examine a specialised – but important – area of management decision making. Every organisation faces what are known as stock-control problems – the difficulty of maintaining adequate stocks of certain goods to ensure that customers' requirements are met or services can continue to be provided. Consider the following scenarios. A small neighbourhood shop runs out of certain products and the shelves are empty. Customers coming in to buy goods are told that those products are out of stock and they'll have to wait or shop elsewhere. The local hospital runs out of a particular blood type and has to postpone or cancel planned treatments and operations on patients. Mechanics at a major international airport are undertaking routine maintenance on several jumbo jet airliners and find that certain parts needed are out of stock in the warehouse. The airliners are grounded until the spare parts arrive. A major car manufacturer finds that one component needed on the assembly line is out of stock and production grinds to a halt until supplies arrive. Clearly such situations would not be seen as acceptable in any organisation. Shortage of stock – often called inventory – causes problems of lost sales, disruption of activities and service, lost production and customer dissatisfaction. However, the issue of managing stock/inventory so that adequate supplies are available is not as straightforward as it seems. It's tempting for an organisation to play safe and maintain high stock levels to avoid such problems. But high stock levels bring high costs.

So the dilemma for the manager lies in balancing the stock levels needed to meet likely demand, against the costs incurred in keeping stock levels high. In this chapter we shall examine some of the basic problems of stock control and some of the approaches that can be taken to help resolve the problem.

The stock-control problem

Assume that we have been asked to assist the manager of a company with a stock-control problem. The company specialises in the maintenance and repair of business PC systems and much of its market consists of local small- and medium-sized businesses which have taken out an annual contract with the repair company. Under this contract the repair company guarantees to repair a customer's PC within 24 hours or to provide an equivalent replacement until the repair is effected. The company prides itself on customer service, so it is keen to ensure that its 24-hour target is met wherever possible. No other local company offers this type of guarantee and the company sees this as a major part of its competitive advantage in the marketplace. However, in order to meet this target, the company has to have an efficient and effective stock system so that adequate supplies of spare parts are readily available. Clearly if the service engineer finds that a PC requiring repair needs a specific replacement part – say a new graphics card – then the company cannot afford to be in the position of having to order this from the supplier and wait for delivery if it is to meet its guaranteed repair time. In fact, to help us focus on the key features of the stock-control problem, let us examine in detail just one of the key parts the company has to have in stock: a Super VGA graphics card. The company can purchase these from the supplier at £100 each and anticipates that over the coming 12 months 250 cards will be needed. The supplier will supply any quantity we require and, because the supplier is local, delivery of the order is immediate. The company, however, also realises that placing an order incurs certain costs: someone has to find the time to get the order sent off, when the order is received it has to be checked to ensure that what was ordered has been supplied, payment then has to be authorised and so on. The best guess of the company is that all of this 'costs' the company £50 each time an order is sent. The basic problem the company currently faces is: how many of these cards should be ordered now from the supplier?

Progress Check 12.1

Can you advise the company on a suitable decision?

One approach we might take is to say: order the quantity of cards now that we require over the next 12 months. This way we can effectively guarantee we will have the card in stock when required (at least for virtually all of the year). However, the problem with this is that the company will have to spend £25 000 (250 × £100) on the stock now and this capital will be tied up in the stock for most of the year. The company also has the problem of looking after the stock over this period – costs relating to security, insurance, obsolescence, etc. The alternative appears to be that of placing several orders throughout the year. For example, the company might place an order now for 50 cards and then a further order, say, every two months. This has the advantage of keeping the capital invested in stock lower but the total ordering cost per year will be higher than the first approach, where there is only one order throughout the year. The other potential problem with the second approach is that the firm may be increasing the chance of not having a card in stock when needed. In fact this is the classic dilemma of the manager with stock-control responsibility: on the one hand trying to minimise the costs incurred and on the other trying to ensure that a 'stockout' (running out of stock) does not occur. Let us clarify the various costs involved in the problem.

How Sports Direct won a place in the premier league of retail

By Andrew Hill and Andrea Felsted

Source: mubus7/Shutterstock.com

Sports Direct has become one of Britain's fastest-growing retailers by harnessing the experience of a group of long-serving senior executives to the energy of its youthful staff, some of whom benefit from generous incentives and exceptional autonomy. Through its stores – 400 in the UK, 260 in the rest of Europe – its website, and its clever handling of its brands such as Dunlop and Karrimor, Sports Direct has gained enormous influence in a growing market, even with big suppliers such as Nike or Adidas. A more than twentyfold share price increase since 2008 has propelled Sports Direct into the FTSE 100 index of blue-chip UK companies.

In hard hat and steel-toed shoes, Karen Byers, Sports Direct's head of retail, is explaining how the group operates at its new Oxford Street store in central London, while keeping an eye on contractors refurbishing the cavernous former theatre around her. The

pace is unrelenting. The previous night at 10pm, Ms Byers called the project manager's home from the store to insist he demolish a wall to create a new children's section. "I pride myself on my people: we work hard to make sure the staff work hard," says Ms Byers.

That ethos comes from the founder – Mike Ashley. Mr Ashley "works hard and has fun and he expects other people to work hard and have fun", according to one former executive. The former squash coach started with one shop in 1982 when he was 17, backed by his parents. Meetings about store design used to be held in the Ashleys' kitchen. People who know Mr Ashley say he remains indispensable for his insights and obsessive eye for detail, particularly in the back-office retail arts of sourcing, supply chain and inventory management, which he assesses with the help of statistics analysts he refers to as his "stattos".

On a recent visit new store managers – in Sports Direct manager strip of blue and red short-sleeved shirts and tracksuit bottoms – were undergoing a two-week induction course. It is not all classrooms and flip-charts: downstairs, Sports Direct also bloods recruits in practical skills such as how to handle pre-dawn stock deliveries. The group offers a degree of responsibility to teams of young employees at head office unusual in UK retail. As head of buying, Sean Nevitt insists his team members learn about stock control first. Contrary to retail orthodoxy, he does not run separate teams of buyers, merchandisers and allocators of stock. Everyone is responsible for all aspects of a product range

Having staff that understand and can manage stock control effectively is a key part of Sport Direct's success.

Costs involved in stock control

We can distinguish between a variety of key costs:

- order costs;
- purchase costs;
- holding costs;
- stockout costs.

Order costs

Order costs are the costs incurred whenever a stock order is generated. These relate to the costs involved with all the stages from the time an order is placed through to when the order is paid for. These might involve the costs relating to clerical, administrative and managerial activities linked to the order process; costs of transportation; costs of receiving and inspecting orders; costs of finance and accounting support. Order costs are often assumed to be fixed, regardless of the size of the order, in stock-control models. In our problem the order cost is assumed to be £50. In real life this cost may be difficult to quantify and the full cost often remains hidden.

Purchase cost

Purchase cost is the actual cost of purchasing the stock item from the supplier. In the simpler stock-control models this cost is usually assumed to be constant. In more sophisticated models, however, it is possible to build in discount systems, i.e. lower unit purchase cost with larger orders. We have already assumed a fixed cost of £100 per item for our problem.

Holding costs

Holding costs are those associated with the company holding a fixed quantity of stock over a given period of time. Such costs can include the cost of capital tied up in the value of the stock, storage costs (heating, lighting, security), depreciation, insurance and obsolescence. Typically the holding cost is calculated as a cost per unit held in stock per year. We shall assume that for this company the holding cost is £15 per item per year. That is, if the company held one graphics card in stock for one year it would cost £15 (made up of the opportunity cost of the £100 purchase cost, insurance, obsolescence, security costs and the like).

Stockout costs

The final cost we consider is that incurred when stock is not available. This is typically made up of two elements. The first is the cost that may be incurred in obtaining supplies of the item at short notice. It may be possible, for example, for the firm to obtain supplies of the card at short notice by going to another supplier who charges a higher price, or by sending someone to the supplier's premises to collect directly. The second element is more difficult to quantify but represents a 'goodwill' cost: the customer may in future take their business elsewhere or complain to other customers, ultimately leading to a loss of business. Such costs are understandably difficult to quantify and for the purposes of the basic stock-control model we shall ignore shortage costs.

Debenhams' costly problems are bricks, not clicks

By Matthew Vincent

Are Britain's bricks-and-mortar retailers in terminal decline? Two days, two answers. No, suggests clothing to homeware chain Next, where Christmas sales rose 1.5 per cent, pushing its shares up four times that amount. Yes, suggests occasionwear to dishcloth store Debenhams, where festive sales fell 1.3 per cent, and its shares by 11 times as much.

These are, of course, two very different stores. But investors must now decide if they are telling two very different stories.

In some ways, they describe the same challenges. Both are trying to offset falling high street sales with revamped ecommerce offerings – but higher costs mean they are already resigned to lower annual pre-tax profit. It is their short-term and long-term strategies for coping with this that differentiates them. And, here, the differences seem stark.

Debenhams' short-term answer to falling sales has typically been more discounting. This year, it tried it again – but it stopped working: "tactical" promotions to combat rivals' Black Friday promotions lifted sales 1.2 per cent for 6 weeks, only for sales to fall back post-Christmas. Next, by contrast, increased its full-price sales despite taking part in Black Friday for the first time, and its end-of-season sale stock was 6 per cent lower than last year.

Debenhams' other short-term fix – more cost cuts – offers less scope, too. It has found £10m of further savings, but that still means costs will rise 1 per cent. Next said its cost inflation would fall from 2 per cent to zero by the second half. This difference matters. Debenhams' discounts and costs will cut its gross margin by 150 basis points. Analysts reckon just a 50 bps shift can wipe out 20 per cent of pre-tax profit.

Long-term strategies are arguably a fairer way to judge Debenhams turnaround plan, under boss Sergio Bucher. And some of these seem to be working. Tighter stock control means Debenhams will end the half with less inventory. That creates more space to expand its still-growing "destination categories" of food and beauty. Sales in both areas are up, and the aim is to take food from £150m to £300m, and beauty from £750m to £1bn, of total revenue in three to five years. New format stores, and "right-sized" old stores, will focus on these destinations, to entice customers back. Increasing the average number of customer visits per year from three to four could add £1bn to sales, Mr Bucher claims.

 Source: Vincent, M. (2018) Debenhams' costly problems are bricks, not clicks, *Financial Times*, 4 January. © The Financial Times Limited. All Rights Reserved.

Stock control is big business – and for good reason.

QADM IN ACTION — Capgemini – improving stock management

Capgemini's client was a global manufacturer of packaged consumer goods. As part of their review of European operations, the client was reviewing its supply chain (see also the QADM in Action on p 417). Capgemini were called in to examine ways of improving supply chain performance in terms of stock levels currently maintained, raw material and packaging costs and sales forecasting. Inadequate forecasting of sales or inadequate reporting of existing stock levels can both lead to inefficiency and higher cost in terms of stock control. Similarly, better use of the existing supplier base can generate significant cost savings. Equally, given that product sales forecasts drive the entire supply chain, the accuracy of such forecasts is critical to the cost efficiency of the supply chain operations.

Data was collected for around 2500 product lines across the client's European operations on weekly production, sales and forecasts for a 12-month period. Purchase ledgers were used for component and supplier information. The data collected was stored in a central database for detailed analysis.

A comprehensive analysis of the data was undertaken across the areas of stock levels, raw material and packaging costs and sales forecasting. Some of the findings from the analysis include:

- Average stock levels were excessive when compared with weekly demand.
- In principle stock levels could be reduced by 50 per cent together with an improvement in average service levels of 98 per cent.
- Similar components were purchased from numerous different suppliers (with potential for rationalisation of purchasing).
- A large percentage of suppliers provided only one component to the client.
- Sales forecasts on average were 30 per cent above actual sales figures and in some cases 100 per cent higher.
- Further analysis indicated that the forecasting methods used across the various European markets had wide differences in approach.

The graph below is taken from part of the analysis and shows the percentage of stock items against the number of weeks of stock cover.

The analysis:

- provided the client with information and motivation to develop new stock control processes;
- demonstrated the opportunity for restructuring purchasing and procurement and was the first step towards supplier partnering;
- provided the evidence and motivation to develop new approaches to forecasting.

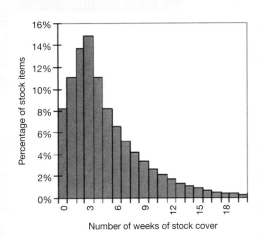

Number of weeks of stock cover

Source: Based on a Capgemini case study, with thanks to Capgemini for permission to use their material.

The stock-control decision

Clearly the major decision the manager must face in terms of the stock-control problem is what quantity of stock to order at any one time. Following from this decision, a subsequent decision needs to be taken on how frequently to order stock. As we have already seen, the manager faces an inherent conflict between the order costs involved and the holding costs involved in the decision, since both of these will vary depending on the quantity ordered each time. To add to the problem, these two costs are affected in different ways by the order-quantity decision. The larger the quantity ordered at any one time then the lower the total order costs over a year (since fewer orders will be made to meet annual demand). Holding costs, however, will increase with the order size, since larger quantities of stock will be held at any one time. It seems sensible, therefore, for the manager to consider trying to minimise the total costs involved – the sum of both the order costs and the holding costs.

Let us consider the effect of different decisions. We first define the notation we shall be using:

D = the annual demand for the item, here 250

C_0 = the cost of placing each order, £50

C_h = the cost of holding an item for one year, £15

Q = the size of the order to be placed (currently unknown)

OC = total order costs

HC = total holding costs

TC = total cost (of ordering and holding the stock items)

Consider setting $Q = 10$: that is the manager decides to place a stock order for 10 items. This will necessitate 25 (250/10) orders through the year at a cost of £50 each order and will lead to total order costs, OC, of £1250. Conversely, if we decide to set $Q = 250$ we will require only one order each year and total order costs will be £50. But what of holding costs for these two options? This is slightly more complicated since we need to consider the average number of items held in stock at any one time and then multiply this by C_h. Consider the manager's position. They know that, in our first scenario, a stock order will consist of 10 items. On some given day, then, 10 items will arrive from the supplier. Gradually over time these will be used up. Ideally, what the manager would like to see is that on the day that the last of these 10 items is used the next order for 10 items arrives from the supplier so that no stockout ever occurs, while at the same time ensuring we are not carrying too many stock items. From this it follows that, at any one time, the average number of items held in stock will be Q/2 (since at the beginning we will have Q items and at the end we will have 0 items). The total holding costs will then be given by:

$$Q/2 \times C_h = 10/2 \times £15 = £75$$

So, with an order size of 10 units, OC will be £1250 and HC £75. But what of our other option – ordering 250 items?

Total holding costs, using the same Q/2 argument, will be calculated as follows:

$$HC = 250/2 \times £15 = £1875$$

and this compares with OC = £50 for this value of Q. We see, numerically, that the two cost elements move in opposite directions as we alter Q, the size of our stock order. Order costs will decrease as Q increases but holding costs will increase. Clearly we require some compromise position between the two. Table 12.1 shows the order costs, holding costs and total costs for a variety of order sizes, Q. It starts with the order size of 10 and then increases to reach the order size of 250.

It can be seen that as we increase the order size, Q, the order costs, OC, decline. At the same time, however, holding costs, HC, increase. Total costs exhibit a different pattern altogether. At first as Q increases TC decreases. After some point, however, TC begins to rise again with Q. Consider Figure 12.1, which shows a graph of the two cost elements,

Table 12.1   Order costs and holding costs

Q	Orders	OC	HC	TC
10	25	1250.00	75.00	1325.00
25	10	500.00	187.50	687.50
50	5	250.00	375.00	625.00
75	3.33	166.67	562.50	729.17
100	2.50	125.00	750.00	875.00
125	2	100.00	937.50	1037.50
150	1.67	83.33	1125.00	1208.33
175	1.43	71.43	1312.50	1383.93
200	1.25	62.50	1500.00	1562.50
225	1.11	55.56	1687.50	1743.06
250	1	50.00	1875.00	1925.00

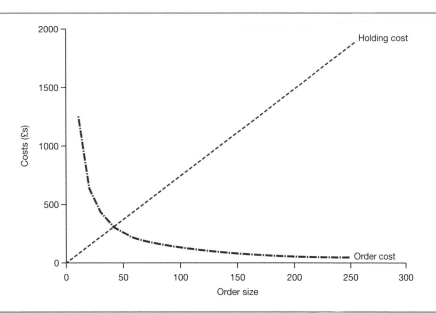

Figure 12.1   Order costs and holding costs

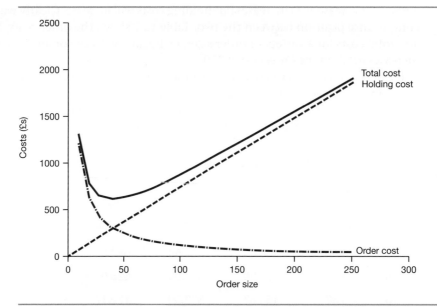

Figure 12.2 Total costs

OC and HC, up to Q = 250. We see that total order costs are especially high when Q takes low values but gradually decrease as Q increases. Total holding costs, on the other hand, steadily increase with Q (in fact you may recognise this as a linear relationship). You can also see from the graph that OC and HC take equal values (they intersect) when Q is around 40 units. Consider the implications of this. The manager is trying to balance the conflicting cost pressures. For Q less than 40, OC will be higher than HC. For Q greater than 40, the position is reversed, with HC greater than OC. At Q = 40 (or thereabouts) the two cost elements are the same. This is reinforced if we consider Figure 12.2, where the total cost (that is OC + HC) is shown on the same diagram. We see clearly that total cost will be minimised where OC = HC. In other words, this value for Q will minimise the total cost involved in stock.

The economic order quantity model

In fact what we have developed here is technically known as the *economic order quantity model*: establishing the value for Q that minimises total cost. This value for Q is referred to as the economic order quantity (EOQ). Clearly, the graphical solution method is a clumsy and tedious one and we require a more direct and accurate method for deriving Q. Using some fairly complex algebra, which we won't show here, we can derive a suitable formula for determining the value of Q where OC = HC. This formula – the EOQ formula – allows us to calculate the optimum quantity of stock to order and is presented as:

$$Q = \sqrt{\frac{2 \, C_0 \, D}{C_h}}$$

Progress Check 12.4

Using the appropriate values for the variables shown, calculate the EOQ for this problem.

The calculation simply requires direct substitutions of our problem values:

$$Q = \sqrt{\frac{2(50)(250)}{15}}$$
$$= 40.82$$

where the EOQ is found to be 40.82 units. This is the order size, Q, that will minimise the total costs involved and balance the conflict between order costs and holding costs. We can readily determine that these two costs will be equal at this value of Q, allowing for rounding errors.

Order cost: $\dfrac{250}{40.82} \times £50 = £306.22$

Holding cost: $\dfrac{40.82}{2} \times £15 = £306.15$

The total cost will be: $306.22 + 306.15 = £612.37$. Again, allowing rounding errors, we can be assured that based on EOQ, this will be the minimum total cost of inventory.

Clearly, in a practical sense, the manager will need to order either 40 or 41 units with each order, rather than 40.82 units. In fact we can calculate that 41 units offers a very marginal cost saving over 40 units, although the manager may prefer keeping the number more straightforward at 40. With the EOQ formula the manager has a ready means of determining the size of the stock order that will keep costs to a minimum.

The reorder cycle

From the EOQ calculation we can also determine what is known as the *reorder cycle* – the frequency or timing of orders through the year. This offers potential advantages to the manager in terms of administration and management involved in the stock process. Warehouse staff can be notified in advance as to the next expected delivery date; the finance department will know the expected delivery dates and hence invoice and payment requirements and so on. Equally, if a larger organisation is considering its policy on several hundred – or thousand – different stock items, it is unlikely to want all of these items to be delivered on the same day of the week. Calculating the cycle is straightforward. In our problem, let us assume the manager has opted for 40 units as the preferred number. The number of orders each 12-month period will then be:

$250/40 = 6.25$ orders

and the number of (calendar) days between each order will be:

$365/6.25 = 58.4$ days

or approximately every two months.

Assumptions of the EOQ model

It will be worthwhile at this point to review the implicit assumptions behind the above EOQ model. Although we have not articulated them, the key assumptions underpinning our calculations have been:

- demand is known for certain;
- demand (the usage of the stock level) is constant over time;
- orders are received as soon as they are made;
- a stock order is made when existing stock levels reach zero (as the result of the above assumption);
- the order quantity remains constant over time;
- all costs are fixed and constant.

Clearly, most if not all of these assumptions are unrealistic for many organisations. It is worth stressing, however, that the basic EOQ model is readily adapted to allow some of these assumptions to be relaxed. Our concern, however, is to illustrate the basic principles rather than the more complex solution methods. However, we will consider one extension to the basic model.

Incorporating lead time

Let us consider a variation on our basic problem. We shall assume that over a year there are 50 working weeks. This implies that with $D = 250$ the company will use five items each week. Let us further assume that the supplier of the items can no longer guarantee immediate delivery but indicates that delivery of a stock order may take up to two working weeks from the time the order is placed.

Progress Check 12.5

Consider how the manager might change the stock policy from the previous problem.

The problem is now slightly different in that one of our key assumptions of the basic EOQ model – that orders are received as soon as they are made – no longer applies. We were assuming before that we could allow stock levels to fall to zero on any given day since the next order would arrive the same day and we would thereby avoid running out of stock. We can no longer afford to do this. If we allow stock to fall to zero before placing our next stock order we may have to wait up to two weeks for delivery. During this time we will have no stock items left to meet demand. Clearly we must now ensure that we place the order at a time which ensures that we have sufficient stock to meet demand while we are waiting for the next delivery. Given that we might have to wait up to two weeks for delivery, we must ensure that when we place an order we still have two weeks' stock left. This implies that we know we will have sufficient items in stock to meet daily demand, even if the order takes the maximum time to arrive. Given that we require five items to meet demand each week, this implies that we need to reorder stock when our stock levels reach 10 items. The two weeks we may have to wait for delivery is known as the *lead time*. We can generalise the required calculation as:

$$R = d \times L$$

where R is the reorder level, d is the demand per time period and L the lead time. In our problem we would have d = 5 and L = 2, giving R = 10. The situation is shown in Figure 12.3. This shows R and the stocks available over time. As stocks are gradually depleted there will come a time when they hit the reorder level, R. An order is placed for Q items and, allowing for the lead time, the order is delivered, replenishing stock levels. The cycle continues.

The management implications of this also need to be considered. We now need some system in the organisation for regularly keeping track of stock levels. Under the simple model we could predict how many weeks would elapse before another order needed to be placed. With more complex, and uncertain, models someone must have the responsibility for monitoring stock levels and ensuring that the next stock order is issued when stock levels fall to R. Much of this is done with the aid of IT systems these days, although obviously system maintenance and management is still essential.

It is also worth noting that many companies maintain a Safety Stock for their most valuable items of inventory. Safety Stock is there to keep the production line going even if some unusual incidents resulted in EOQ not being enough for a cycle period. When Safety Stock is used then its cost needs to be added to our calculations for the inventory control costs.

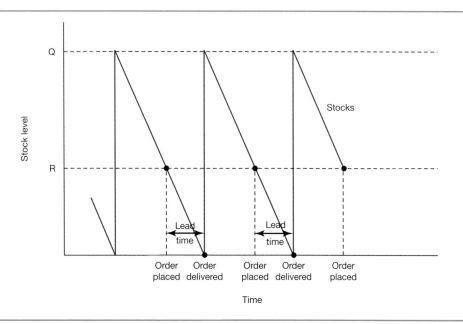

Figure 12.3 Reorder model

Some technical insights

The above inventory control system is called the Continuous Review System. As noted above, the inventory needs to be monitored continuously (by people or IT). EOQ is based on the Continuous Review System.

Due to the assumptions that were held for this problem, both the order quantity and the order cycle remain constant. If we remove the assumption that demand is constant over time then while order quantity remains constant, the order cycle will vary. We order based on the reorder level and the reorder level may emerge at different cycles of time due to the demand not being consistent.

This is where an alternative system may be adopted. This is called Periodic Review System. In a Periodic Review System the order cycle is constant but the order size varies. When the order time arrives we order enough to fill the inventory to a predetermined maximum level. This then means there are no guarantees that the order size will be equal to the Economic Order Quantity for each cycle. This may be seen as a disadvantage of the Periodic Review System but some companies still prefer this system due to its overall low cost of administration compared to the Continuous Review System. Also, many suppliers will prefer receiving orders at equal periods of time rather than different cycle times.

Again, note that when demand (or usage of the inventory in the production line) is constant, and with the other assumptions in place, both order size and cycle time will remain constant and therefore Continuous and Periodic Review Systems will become the same.

Classification of stock items

So far we have assumed that the manager simply has to establish a suitable policy for stock ordering for one single item. Clearly this is unrealistic, since the organisation will use or require a large number of items in its production or service provision. One of the difficulties the manager faces is that of prioritisation: deciding which stock items are worthy of detailed attention in terms of decision making and which are not. It would not be a productive use of the manager's time to try to determine a suitable EOQ policy for the reordering of paper clips used in the office. Such a trivial item – trivial in the sense of both its unit cost and the cost to the organisation of running out of stock – would not warrant serious management attention. Other items, however, clearly will justify management attention.

One approach that has been developed tries to classify stock items into different categories, with the different categories requiring different approaches to stock control. The system is known as the *ABC system* that is based on the *Pareto rule* also known as the *80/20 rule* or *the law of the vital few*. This is a theoretical rule that has implications in many aspects of work and in fact life. It is a very helpful rule when it comes to inventory management. The method is simple in principle. All stock items are categorised into one of three groups – A, B and C – in terms of their relative importance to the organisation. Category A items are the most important and C the least important. Importance may be defined in different ways. It may relate to the financial contribution that each item makes to the organisation's activities, to the costs of the organisation, to the overall business strategy, to frequency of use, to opportunity cost and so on. For example, in a retail organisation, a tin of soup could be categorised as C, whereas a high-price DVD system would be category A since the contribution to the company's sales and profitability will be much larger for the DVD system than for the tin of soup. Similarly, the opportunity cost of a lost sale due to stock not being available will be much higher. The notion of importance will not, however, necessarily relate directly to monetary value. In a production organisation low-cost component parts may have serious knock-on effects in terms of production if they are not available. Running out of stock for car headlight bulbs that cost a few pennies each may well halt the whole production process in a car assembly plant and cost thousands in lost production. Figure 12.4 illustrates a typical stock classification. Category A items are few in number but important in terms of value, while category C items are many in number but low in terms of value. Category B items fall in the middle.

In practice, for most organisations the number of items falling into the A classification will be relatively small – often around 20 per cent of all stock items. But these items have a disproportionate effect in terms of importance, often accounting for around 80 per cent of whatever measure of importance the company is using. Thus 20 per cent of items may contribute 80 per cent to, say, profit. Category B items typically comprise the next 10 to 20 per cent of all items and contribute about 10 to 20 per cent (i.e. a relatively proportionate impact) to importance, while category C items make up the bulk of stock (around 70 per cent) but contribute only 10 per cent to importance. From a management perspective, therefore, it clearly makes sense to focus attention on category A items first, followed by B and C. The implications are that category A items

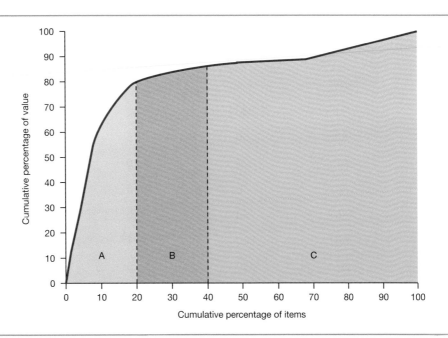

Figure 12.4 ABC analysis

are worthy of a detailed investigation in terms of a suitable stock policy – determining order costs, holding costs, usage patterns, lead times and the like – and variations of the basic EOQ model – or any other suitable model – will be potentially worthwhile developing. Equally, regular management monitoring of the situation should be ensured. For category B items some formal stock process – like the EOQ model – is probably appropriate, with less need for ongoing monitoring. For category C items the effort and cost of applying stock control methods is probably not justified and simpler stock systems are needed – possibly as simple as just ordering another box of paper clips when the last box has been used.

To illustrate, consider the following situation. A company is investigating its stock policy on 10 different items. Table 12.2 shows the 10 items, coded A1 to A10, together with the level of annual demand for each item and the cost per unit of each item. So, for example, item A1 has an annual level of use of 250 units and costs £10 per unit. To categorise these items under the ABC system involves a series of simple calculations. First of all we calculate the total number of items required over the year by the company, 2590, and show each stock item as a percentage of this total. We then calculate the total cost for each stock item (annual level of use × unit cost) and again express this as a percentage of the total costs for the year. The resulting calculations are shown in Table 12.3.

We see, for example, that stock item A1 accounts for 9.7 per cent of all stock items by volume and 6.8 per cent by value. We now take these percentage volume and value figures and rank them in ascending order by volume. That is, we show the lowest volume item first, the second lowest next and so on. For this ranked data we then calculate cumulative percentage volume and value figures as shown in Table 12.4. This indicates that stock item A4 accounts for only 1.5 per cent of stock items by volume but 12.5 per cent by value, whereas at the other extreme stock item A7 accounts for only 11.3 per cent

Table 12.2 ABC classification: use and value

Code	Annual level of use (units)	Cost per unit (£)
A1	250	10
A2	80	75
A3	320	10
A4	40	115
A5	90	95
A6	500	1
A7	830	5
A8	120	30
A9	150	18
A10	210	5

Table 12.3 Percentage use and costs

Code	Annual use	% of total	Cost per unit (£)	Value	% of total
A1	250	9.7	10	2500	6.8
A2	80	3.1	75	6000	16.3
A3	320	12.4	10	3200	8.7
A4	40	1.5	115	4600	12.5
A5	90	3.5	95	8550	23.2
A6	500	19.3	1	500	1.4
A7	830	32.0	5	4150	11.3
A8	120	4.6	30	3600	9.8
A9	150	5.8	18	2700	7.3
A10	210	8.1	5	1050	2.8
Total	2590	100.0		36850	100.0

Table 12.4 Ranked cumulative percentages

Code	% Use	Cumulative % use	% Value	Cumulative % value
A4	1.5	1.5	12.5	12.5
A2	3.1	4.6	16.3	28.8
A5	3.5	8.1	23.2	52.0
A8	4.6	12.7	9.8	61.7
A9	5.8	18.5	7.3	69.1
A10	8.1	26.6	2.8	71.9
A1	9.7	36.3	6.8	78.7
A3	12.4	48.6	8.7	87.4
A6	19.3	68.0	1.4	88.7
A7	32.0	100.0	11.3	100.0

by value but 32 per cent by volume. Figure 12.5 shows the Pareto diagram produced for this example and using this we might identify items A4, A2 and A5 as category A; A8, A9, A10 and A1 as category B; and items A3, A6 and A7 as Category C. It should be noted that the exact classification is somewhat subjective and will depend on what the manager regards as a suitable measure of importance for that stock item.

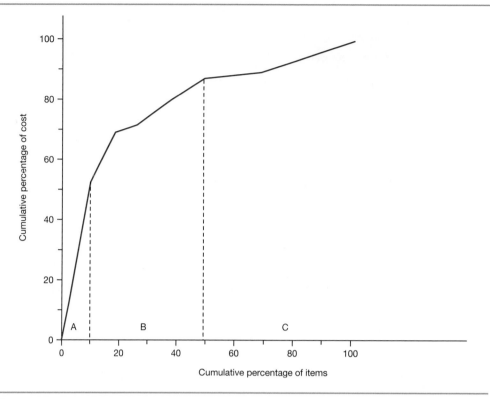

Figure 12.5 Pareto diagram

Analytic programs can learn to make accurate predictions

By Michael Dempsey

Businesses these days are not short of data. However, making sense of the mountain of facts contained in large corporate applications remains a challenge, which is where data analytics comes in. Analytic tools can scan millions of pieces of information and pin down very practical lessons for companies. The rate at which a discount on a particular line in a specific location will make sales climb and then tail off is typical of the questions data analysis has to answer. So-called "machine learning" allows the software to come up with its own set of "rules", directions the software can follow when a similar stocking problem arises. For example, executives can assess and approve the rules so the software can be allowed to follow a particular avenue when stocks of a popular brand are running low during a sales promotion. These are flagged up in plain language for executives to assess and approve. Once activated, the rules can run forecasts on the likely impact of a given sales promotion on stock levels in warehouses and across the shelves

of stores. Jeff Bodenstab, a vice-president at Dutch software house ToolsGroup, says machine learning programs can quickly interpret large volumes of data to measure the accuracy of sales forecasts or logistics plans. Mr Bodenstab says the big breakthrough in recent years has been in producing software that can deal with the incomplete data that inevitably come from busy shop-floors. "With machine learning, we can see through the 'noise', use all the data that don't add up." The ability to translate columns of numbers that would have been previously buried inside spreadsheets into simple visual images boosts the effectiveness of data analysis. These images are presented using colour-coded symbols such as traffic lights to represent the success or failure of a service. We can see through the "noise" [and] use all the data that don't add up. ToolsGroup customer Granarolo, an Italian dairy products company, uses data analysis to help juggle the shelf-life of many of its products. For instance fresh milk lasts for six days while the company's yoghurt has 40 days to sit in the supermarket. Seasonal taste adds to the complexity of shipping products across Europe, with items such as mozzarella cheese selling better in summer. Another factor is that 60 per cent of Granarolo's products are sold via promotions and discounts. The consumer response to each of these deals has to be carefully calculated by the Bologna-based company. Granarolo, applying past experience of how well promotions have worked in different outlets, uses the machine learning program to generate suggested stock levels. These predictions rely on data from 60,000 sites across Europe. Data analysis has replaced spreadsheet-based work and produces accurate forecasts that cover Granarolo's 200 best-selling lines in great detail. Sales of lines such as fresh milk are being forecast with 98 per cent accuracy, meaning stock levels are almost precisely aligned to meet demand.

Visual data and human insight identify where action is needed. Peter Williams, an information analytics manager at Marks and Spencer, the British retailer, uses software from US group Tibco to improve the company's logistics. M&S sells clothing and food and household goods from its 809 UK stores. It needs to know how many units of a given item to ship to stores, so that a line neither runs out nor is overstocked and wasted. Tibco's Spotfire analytics platform takes information from a variety of corporate programs and displays it in a simple visual format. In perishable food

lines, data analysis consists of isolating the sales characteristics of products and deciding an acceptable level of waste. Spotfire studies contrasting sales in large and small stores to determine the right quantity of various foodstuffs for each outlet. The picture is different for clothing, which is subject to changing seasons and fashions. Each line exhibits a trading pattern, a sales curve that rises, then tails off. The company has to determine the angle of that curve and the point at which any line will sell out. The detailed breakdown from Spotfire lets Mr Williams narrow his focus to an individual store. While the machine learning model can dish out lessons based on its own algorithms, M&S does not allow it to have the last word. He explains: "Machine learning is great in itself, but you have to apply human insight to it." The secret sauce of retailing, the sense of what a customer base feels and desires, is still at the heart of the business. Additionally, a supplier dashboard has been developed. This breaks fresh ground in sharing information directly with suppliers, says Mr Williams. He adds: "building this was relatively cheap, but the value is massive". The dashboard covers a set of key indicators, which lets suppliers see just how near they are to the levels of service expected by M&S. Mr Williams says the strength of data analysis is in its clarity. "Visualising data changes people's perceptions of what we can do. We can bypass the spreadsheets and identify where action is needed."

Because stock control is big business it often needs a big investment and careful planning. Use of strong Information technology and computing programs is often essential.

Worked example

A local education authority has responsibility for purchasing supplies for all the schools in its area. One of the items it buys in and then supplies to schools is packs of pens to supply to teachers and support staff. Over the past couple of years annual demand for these packs has been around 75 000 with each pack costing the authority 50p and bought directly from the manufacturer. The supplies manager has estimated that each order that is placed with the manufacturer costs the authority about £5. For financial purposes it is assumed that holding costs for any item are 20 per cent of the purchase cost of that item. The manager currently orders 2750 packs at a time (the EOQ is actually 2738.6 but the manager has rounded this for convenience). However, the supplying manufacturer has recently sent round a letter indicating that it is willing to offer volume discounts on the purchase price: that is, customers who order in quantity will be sold the packs at a lower unit price. The details of the scheme are as shown in Table 12.5.

So, for instance if the manager decides to order between 3000 and 4000 packs each time, a discount of 5 per cent of the pack price of 50p will be offered, effectively bringing

Table 12.5   Purchase price discounts on pens

Order band		Discount (%)	New unit price (pence)
A	up to 3000 packs	0	50
B	3000 < 4000	5	47.5
C	4000 < 5000	10	45
D	5000 < 20000	17.5	41.25
E	20000 or more	18	41

Table 12.6   EOQ calculations

Band	Discount	Unit price (pence)	Ch (pence)	EOQ
A	0	50	10.00	2738.6
B	5	47.5	9.50	2809.8
C	10	45	9.00	2886.8
D	17.5	41.25	8.25	3015.1
E	18	41	8.20	3024.3

the unit price per pack down to 47.5p. Larger orders result in higher discounts. Naturally the supplies manager has expressed interest in this since her annual budget is constantly under pressure and any potential cost savings have to be considered. However, it is clear that the current EOQ of 2750 packs falls short of the minimum of 3000 required to earn a discount. The question for the supplies manager is then how the various costs (purchase, order, holding) will be affected by the discount scheme. The approach she has decided to take is to perform the required calculations on a spreadsheet. Her first step is to calculate the EOQ for each order band. Note that C_h – the holding cost per item – is linked to the purchase cost and since this will change depending on the order size, so might the EOQ. The calculations are shown in Table 12.6.

For each band the holding cost per item per year is shown (at 20 per cent of the unit price) together with the EOQ for that band. The apparent bad news for the manager is that in each order band the calculated EOQ is below that required to trigger the price discount. In band C, for example, the EOQ is calculated as 2887, this is while the minimum order of 4000 is needed to obtain the unit price discount for this band. However, the manager also knows that one of the key assumptions of the EOQ approach is that costs remain constant. This is clearly not the case here, with C_h varying and the unit price varying. She then decides to recalculate all the various costs for each order band assuming that the minimum order size has been placed. That is, for example, calculating the order costs, the holding costs and the purchase costs for band C assuming the minimum order of 4000 packs has been placed. The total costs associated with each order band can then be evaluated. The relevant calculations (with figures rounded to the nearest £) are shown in Table 12.7. As a reminder, note OC = $(D/Q) C_o$; HC = $(Q/2) C_h$.

Table 12.7   Total order costs

Minimum order size	Orders per year	Order costs (£s)	Holding costs (£s)	Purchase costs (£s)	Total costs (£s)
(2750)	28	140	138	37 500	37 778
3 000	25	125	143	35 625	35 893
4 000	19	94	180	33 750	34 024
5 000	15	75	206	30 938	31 219
20 000	4	19	820	30 750	31 589

So, for example, with the EOQ of 2750, 28 orders will need to be placed each year at a cost of £140 (28 × 5). Holding costs will be £138 and purchases costs £37 500 (75 000 × £0.50) giving a total cost of £37 778. If the manager decides to place orders of 20 000, however, to gain the maximum benefit from the price discount, the total cost drops to £31 589 (with purchase cost and order cost both decreasing but holding cost increasing). From the calculations we see that, based on this information, placing orders of 5000 packs each time will lead to the lowest total cost of £31 219. Although the maximum price discount is not earned, the balance between the three costs is maximised. The manager knows that an annual saving of £6559 (37 778−31 219) can be achieved, although clearly additional storage space will need to be found for the extra order size (with the order size effectively doubling from the EOQ level).

Summary

In this chapter we have introduced the basic dilemma facing a manager with stock-control responsibility and considered how the differing cost pressures can be reconciled to try to determine a suitable stock-control policy. We looked at stock control based on a Continuous Review System that can result in Economic Order Quantity (EOQ). Although the model we developed is essentially a simple one based on rigid assumptions, the principles involved are readily transferable to more complex situations. The models we have looked at in this chapter are a key element of effective logistics and supply chain management.

Exercises

1   What are the basic decisions that a manager with stock-control responsibility faces and what are the likely objectives of such a manager in this context?

2   Describe the quantitative techniques that are available to assist a manager with stock-control responsibilities of a continuous review system in an organisation.

3   A company requires a particular item from an outside supplier for its production process. Annual demand for the item is 3000 units. Order costs are estimated at £15 and holding costs at 20 per cent of the purchase price of the item, which is £5.50 per unit.

  (a) Determine the optimum (economic) order quantity.

  (b) What are the critical assumptions behind this calculation?

4   A local authority operates over a large geographical area. The Education Department is responsible for ensuring that stocks of a certain item are kept for distribution to schools through the area on request. In order to try to ensure supplies reach the schools promptly, the department currently operates two store warehouses, which operate independently of each other. The department is trying to assess the pros and cons of merging the two store warehouses and offering a centralised facility. For one item under consideration demand is 250 items per annum via Store A and 100 items per annum via Store B. Order costs are £10 at Store A and £11 at Store B, with holding costs 20 per cent of the purchase price of the item. The item costs £4 per unit.

  (a) Calculate the impact on costs if the two stores merge and place combined orders for this item.

  (b) What other factors would you want to take into account before making a decision as to whether or not to merge the two stores?

5   Following internal reorganisation in a large brewing company, a comprehensive review of stock-control procedures is currently being undertaken. You have been asked to investigate stock control in the context of one of the firm's products: low-alcohol lager. The company operates a sophisticated forecasting and production planning system to forecast demand for this product from its own pubs and from other customers (off-licences, supermarkets, hotels) on a four-weekly cycle. That is, the company tries to forecast four weeks ahead and updates these forecasts each week. Over this four-week period, production of lager takes place and the output is stored until delivery to customers takes place at the end of the four-week cycle. Customers are able to place and receive orders outside this cycle but only at additional cost. Additionally, the company is thinking of installing a new computer network which will link all the company's pubs so that the stock-control manager will be able to monitor stock levels and sales.

  Draft a management report outlining the importance of an efficient and effective stock-control policy for the company. You should include in your report a suggested stock-control policy that you feel is appropriate for the company and this should include reference to:

  ● the links between the forecasting role and stock control;
  ● the choice between continuous versus periodic review system;
  ● the potential benefits of the new computer system;
  ● the data requirements of your suggested stock-control policy;
  ● the problems and difficulties that you think might arise if your policy is implemented.

6   A domestic appliance manufacturer is evaluating its delivery system from the production plant to showrooms around the country. One item used in the transportation of large appliances is a prefabricated polystyrene-foam packing case. These are supplied by an outside contractor and have to be ordered well in advance. Over the last few years, annual output of large appliances at the production plant has been 4000 units a year. The cost of placing an order is estimated at £25. Traditionally, the company has charged 15 per cent of the purchase cost of any item as the stock holding cost. The supplier charges £7.50 for each packing case.

(a) Determine the optimum order quantity and the time between placing orders for the company.

(b) Describe the key assumptions that you have made to determine (a).

(c) Realistically what effect do these assumptions have on the method adopted in (a) to solve this problem?

(d) If the supply of packing cases had a variable lead time how would this affect your suggested solution?

7   A large construction company has recently won the contract for routine inspection and maintenance of the Channel Tunnel linking the UK to France. Obviously, routine maintenance and repair work, unless carefully planned, will have adverse consequences on traffic flows through the tunnel and on operating revenue. You have been asked to investigate policies that might be appropriate for stock control in terms of the building and construction materials that will be required to support these routine maintenance and repair operations. Effectively you have been asked to investigate appropriate policies for such items as cement, steel girders, rail track, electrical wiring and the like.

Draft a management report discussing in detail how the Pareto analysis may help with this situation. Provide a guideline on how the analysis may be carried out.

13 Project Management

Learning objectives

By the end of this chapter you should be able to:

- explain why complex projects require planning and managing
- develop a network diagram for a project
- incorporate time information into a network diagram and identify the critical path for a project
- construct a Gantt chart for a project
- incorporate uncertainty into network models
- be able to use information on crash times and costs

Most managers will, from time to time, be involved in the management of a project. The project might be large – such as the construction of the Channel Tunnel – or it might be small – such as the purchase of some new item of office technology. The manager's involvement might be central to the project – the manager may have full responsibility for managing the project – or it might be as part of a larger team. Given both the frequency with which managers become involved in projects and the degree of importance of such projects for the organisation, it is not surprising that models have been developed to assist the manager in the task of managing some project. In this chapter we shall be developing and using the basic project planning model that is available.

Characteristics of a project

Given the focus of this chapter on project management, we should begin by ensuring we understand what is meant by a project. Although there is no hard-and-fast definition, projects have a number of key characteristics.

Progress Check 13.1

Think of a project that you have personally been involved in. It might be a personal project, such as planning the next holiday, or a work-based project. List the key features that make this a 'project' and that distinguish this from routine day-to-day activities.

Projects are typically self-contained and involve a set of related activities. They usually:

- have clearly defined aims and objectives;
- have a set completion date;
- are often unique, one-off events or at least different from routine activities;
- involve a set of related activities which comprise the project;
- have resources allocated specifically to them, often in the form of a project budget;
- involve a team of people.

A project almost always has a clearly defined set of aims, objectives or goals. Very often these may be 'imposed' on the project manager from above and may often be both varied and in conflict with each other. A construction company, for example, may have to complete a new building for a client to the agreed specification. Such a project will also have some specified completion date, very often with financial penalties for late completion if the project is a major one, and involve a number of related activities, all of which have to be completed to 'finish' the project. Projects typically have some sort of budget allocated. This may be a financial budget or it may be expressed in terms of other key resources: skilled staff, essential equipment, computer time. Large projects almost invariably involve a team of people and can rarely be completed by one individual working in isolation.

Crossrail to demand 'hundreds of millions' in fresh bailout

By Gill Plimmer and Jim Pickard

Crossrail will demand "hundreds of millions" of pounds from the government in its third bailout of the year, according to people familiar with the growing crisis at the London rail project. . . . Ministers were furious in August after Crossrail management admitted that the project's completion would be delayed by a year to the autumn of 2019.

Project delays can be very expensive.

Project management

The manager responsible for the project typically faces a dilemma in project management terms. The project manager is expected to deliver the project:

● on time;

● within budget;

● on target (in terms of key aims, objectives or quality standards).

Although each of these individually presents no major difficulties, the problem is that these requirements will frequently clash with each other during the life of the project. If the project falls behind schedule in terms of the timescale and completion date, this can often be rectified, and the project brought back to schedule, by increasing costs (paying overtime rates to the workforce, for example) or by reducing the targets, perhaps lowering the quality standards specified. Similarly, if the project looks as if it is going over budget or if it looks as if the project will not be to target, we can bring it back under control by altering the other two requirements: putting back the completion date to ensure we are still within budget, for example. Problems with any one of the requirements can usually be resolved by altering the others. However, this is usually unacceptable since the project manager is generally required to meet all three features simultaneously. The project management problem then becomes one of simultaneous achievement of these requirements rather than a trade-off between the three. From the project manager's perspective, therefore, there will be a number of tasks involved in managing the project:

● ensuring that individual activities are completed on time so that later activities – and the project completion – are not delayed;

● being able to identify potential problems before they occur so that appropriate corrective action can be taken to head off a potential problem;

● having an effective monitoring system for the project so that progress can be assessed easily and effectively at any time;

● being able to react quickly to planned or accidental deviations from the project in terms of both identifying the likely knock-on effects and assessing options for re-establishing control;

● being able to plan resource requirements to fit into the project timescale to ensure that critical and scarce resources are in the right place at the right time;

● being able to prioritise between different activities and their resource requirements.

As we shall see, the model we shall be developing in this chapter will meet these requirements and help considerably in the simultaneous achievement of the three features of projects.

Saudi Aramco gets ready for 'no ordinary IPO'

By Anjli Raval

A year ago Mohammed bin Salman, Saudi Arabia's deputy crown prince and the power behind the throne, electrified the global energy industry by revealing plans to float the world's largest oil producer. The ambitious proposal for an initial public offering in state-owned Saudi Aramco is the centrepiece of the hard-charging 31-year-old's vision to overhaul an economy seen as too heavily dependent on natural resources. One year on from Prince Mohammed's statement of intent, many key issues are still to be resolved: notably those pertaining to the precise shape of Saudi Aramco as a public company, its tax rate and dividend policy, and where it will take a stock market listing. . . .

Saudi officials are seeking to transform Saudi Aramco into the world's most valuable publicly traded company, which they say is worth about $2tn. . . .

Staff at Saudi Aramco have spent months untangling the company's finances from those of the government, and separating its core oil operations from projects that reflect its broader role in Saudi society. Saudi Aramco aims to exclude as many of these non-oil projects as possible from the company that floats, by establishing joint ventures and other arrangements to take responsibility for such activities. The company is working with the government to create a project management entity that can handle development of critical infrastructure, says one person with knowledge of the matter.

 Source: Raval, A. (2017) Saudi Aramco gets ready for 'no ordinary IPO', FT.com, 8 January.

Good project management is critical for business success.

What went wrong at Britain's prison of the future?

By Sarah O'Conner and Cynthia O'Murchu

In the hours before the first inmates arrived at Britain's newest and biggest prison, governor Russ Trent said he was feeling proud. Nick Dann, the project's deputy, confessed he had butterflies. . . .

The two men knew that a lot was riding on HMP Berwyn. The rest of the prison system in England and Wales was spiralling into crisis. Prisoner numbers had almost doubled since the 1990s as a result of tougher sentencing, but prison places had not kept pace, leaving the government to stuff about 85,000 people into buildings originally designed to hold about 65,000. . . .

If those were the problems, the government hoped HMP Berwyn would be the blueprint for the solution. The £220m Category C prison (prisons are ranked from A to D, with A the most secure) would hold 2,100 men, making it one of the biggest in Europe. Its size would bring economies of scale, but it wouldn't just be a vast warehouse in which to store criminals cheaply.

Trent, a charismatic former Royal Marine, promised a rehabilitative culture that would turn lives around. Prisoners would be referred to as men, cells as rooms, and wings as communities. Men would have phones, laptops (offering internal services, not the internet) and showers in their rooms. . . .

Two years after it opened, mystery surrounds the government's prison of the future. As inmates continue to be crowded into older, dilapidated prisons, HMP Berwyn remains 40 per cent empty. Without the planned economies of scale, the prison that was forecast to be one of the cheapest Category C jails to run in England and Wales (at £14,000 per year per place) is currently one of the most expensive, at £36,000 per year per place. . . .

The Ministry of Justice declined to let the FT visit the prison and refused a request to interview any managers or officials. But information from prisoners' families, prison officers, contractors and lawyers, together with reports and statistics gathered through Freedom of Information requests and MPs' written questions to ministers, suggest HMP Berwyn remains half empty because key elements of the project have veered off track. When the prison opened, some buildings were either unfinished or unusable. The Interserve workshops, which were meant to provide prison jobs for 520 inmates, are delivering a fraction of what was promised, according to data the FT obtained through an FOI request.

 Source: O'Conner, S. and O'Murchu, C. (2019) What went wrong at Britain's prison of the future?, FT.com, 7 February.

And getting it wrong brings its own problems.

Business example

We shall illustrate the development and use of the model with the following example. As part of its new overall corporate strategy, a local authority is keen to ensure that the services it provides to local citizens match the needs and aspirations of the local community. As part of this matching process it has been decided to undertake a survey of citizens' current attitudes to the services provided. This will enable managers in the local authority to develop a view of customers' perceptions of current services as well as trying to identify needs not currently being met. You have been put in charge of the survey, including analysing the collected data, and are under pressure from both senior managers and elected officials to get this 'project' completed as soon as possible. Naturally, the 'quality' of the information collected must not be compromised and, understandably, the resource costs of this project will need to be carefully monitored and controlled.

Clearly, in this context, we have a typical project that has all the characteristics we discussed earlier. To develop the model to help us in project management we will need to follow a sequence of tasks.

- Identify the key activities that will make up the project.
- Determine the estimated time each individual activity will take to complete.
- Identify the sequencing of activities in terms of their interdependencies.

With this information we will then be able to develop a suitable model which will not only allow us to determine the expected completion date of the project but will also fulfil the other requirements of a project-planning system that we identified earlier. In practice, of course, these three tasks can prove problematic and time-consuming in their own right. For our purposes we will take the relevant information as given but the time and effort to obtain this in practice should not be underestimated. We will assume that the key activities that will make up the project have been identified and are as shown in Table 13.1.

A list of key activities is shown together with a description of what that activity involves. Take a few moments to study the information carefully. It is evident that the list of activities is an abbreviated one (to help us develop a manageable model in the text). In practice the list of activities will typically be much longer. It is easy to see how, for example, Activity K could be broken into its set of individual sub-activities. Each major activity could be treated as a sub-project in its own right, perhaps with another manager having delegated responsibility for it.

However, the requirements of the model now become clear, as do the difficulties faced by the project manager. All these activities have to be managed, and as the project manager you are now being asked how long the project will take. To answer this, of course, we need additional information, which brings us to the second task: estimating the time taken by each activity. For our purposes we will develop a model based on the time information shown in Table 13.2.

For each activity, its duration, shown in days, is given. Activity A, for example, is expected to take three days; Activity B six days and so on. Once again this can in practice be a difficult task. At best such activity durations should be seen as estimates of the time to be taken to complete each activity. We shall see later in this chapter how we can incorporate uncertainty about these times into the model, but for now we will take them as given and assume they are definite and certain.

Table 13.1 Key activities

Activity	Description	Activity	Description
A	*Agree survey objectives* The key objectives of the survey will need to be agreed with senior managers and key elected officials to ensure there is consensus over what the survey is trying to achieve, what information is being collected and why it is being collected.	H	*Print questionnaire* The questionnaire to be used in the main survey will need to be printed and got ready for use.
		I	*Select sample* The sample of local citizens who will be surveyed will need to be chosen according to the agreed methods.
B	*Design questionnaire* It has already been decided that data will be collected through the use of a face-to-face interview conducted with a sample of local citizens. Each interview will follow the structure specified in a specially designed questionnaire.	J	*Conduct survey* The main survey will be conducted and completed.
		K	*Enter data* The results from the completed questionnaires will be entered into the organisation's computer system ready for analysis.
C	*Agree method of sample selection* Since the survey will collect information from only a sample of local citizens, there must be agreement on the method to be used to identify the sample. It is expected that this will require an input from specialist advisers both in and outside the organisation.	L	*Debrief interviewers* A formal debriefing of interviewers will take place to help assess qualitatively the information that has been collected. Interviewers may well be able to provide feedback on whether they felt those being interviewed were providing honest and reliable answers to questions, for example.
D	*Conduct pilot survey* Because of the importance of the survey and its likely use in the strategy-planning process it has been decided that a pilot survey is essential. This pilot will test both the questionnaire design and the sample selection procedure before the full survey is conducted.	M	*Analyse data* The analysis of the data collected can take place. This will be done by the project manager together with a small team of specialist staff.
E	*Amend questionnaire and sample selection* Depending on the results from the pilot survey, it may be necessary to amend the questionnaire design and/or the methods used to select the sample. However, this will be entirely dependent on the results of the pilot survey and cannot be predicted at this stage.	N	*Produce report* The project manager is responsible for producing a final report on the project to include its findings as well as information on completion dates, quality and resource costs. This report will go to senior managers and to elected officials. Because of the committee structure in the local authority, the chair of the appropriate committee that will receive the final report needs to know now when the report will be available so as to ensure it appears in the appropriate agenda. This particular committee meets only once every three months.
F	*Recruit interviewers* Following the pilot survey, those people who will do the interviewing in the main survey will need to be recruited.		
G	*Brief interviewers* Before the main survey actually gets under way it will be necessary to provide a briefing session for all interviewers to ensure they fully appreciate what is expected of them and understand their role in the survey and to ensure consistency between different interviewers.		

Table 13.2   Time required

Activity	Description	Time taken
A	Agree survey objectives	3 days
B	Design questionnaire	6 days
C	Agree method of sample selection	4 days
D	Conduct pilot survey	10 days
E	Amend questionnaire and sample selection	5 days
F	Recruit interviewers	10 days
G	Brief interviewers	1 day
H	Print questionnaire	5 days
I	Select sample	8 days
J	Conduct survey	15 days
K	Enter data	5 days
L	Debrief interviewers	2 days
M	Analyse data	10 days
N	Produce report	2 days

Progress Check 13.2

Using the information in Table 13.2 can you suggest how long, in days, it might take to complete the project?

At first sight, it might appear that the information we have in Table 13.2 is sufficient to allow us to determine the duration of the entire project. It looks as if we can simply add together all the individual activity durations to find the project duration. However, on reflection this will be inaccurate. Such a calculation assumes that all the activities are sequential – that they take place one after the other. Clearly in any project this will not be the case. Some activities will be strictly sequential of course: Activity B cannot take place until Activity A is complete, for example. However, other activities will not be sequential; they can take place simultaneously with other activities. Consider Activities B and C. There appears to be no reason why these two activities cannot take place simultaneously (although both of them would have to wait for Activity A to be completed first). So, before we can answer the question relating to the completion time of the project, we need to consider the third task: determining the dependencies or interrelationships between the various activities. Again, in practice this can be a complex task and frequently requires a teamwork approach: getting those staff with first-hand experience of each activity to evaluate what must be done first before this activity can start. For our purposes we shall assume that the dependencies are as shown in Table 13.3.

Table 13.3 Dependencies

Activity	Description	Dependencies
A	Agree survey objectives	None
B	Design questionnaire	A
C	Agree method of sample selection	A
D	Conduct pilot survey	B, C
E	Amend questionnaire and sample selection	D
F	Recruit interviewers	D
G	Brief interviewers	E, F
H	Print questionnaire	E
I	Select sample	E
J	Conduct survey	G, H, I
K	Enter data	J
L	Debrief interviewers	J
M	Analyse data	K
N	Produce report	L, M

For each activity we show the immediately preceding activities that must be completed first. We see, for example, that Activity A has no dependencies – none of the other activities have to be completed before this one. Activities B and C, however, both have A shown as a dependency. This indicates that, before either of these activities can start, A must have been completed. The interpretation of the rest of the table is similar. Note that some activities have several dependencies shown, indicating that several activities must be completed first. Note also that only the immediately preceding dependencies are shown. For example, Activity E shows only D as a dependency. D in turn, however, is dependent on B and C, and B and C in turn are dependent on A. Activity E, therefore, is implicitly dependent on A, B and C, although this is not explicitly shown. We are now in a position to develop the model we can use to help us manage the project.

Network diagrams

Project-planning models are built around the concept of a network diagram. As we shall see, such diagrams are particularly helpful at providing the information about the project we indicated earlier that a manager would require. Network diagrams will be familiar to most readers – although not necessarily by that name. When looking at a map, for example, you are actually using a road network showing the road connections between various towns or cities. An Underground or subway map is a network diagram to show

how you can travel between various parts of a city. In project management we develop such a diagram along very simple lines but using a standard format. Figure 13.1 shows a typical component of a network diagram that we shall be constructing. The diagram shows two activities – each denoted with circle and known as a node – joined together with an arrow. The arrow itself represents moving from an activity (X) to a subsequent activity (Y).

Figure 13.1 Simple network diagram

The network diagram for a project such as ours is made up of a series of components like that shown in the diagram. Drawing a network diagram is relatively straightforward, although there are one or two aspects which do require practice. Such diagrams follow a series of 'rules' or conventions. Most are obvious, but some take getting used to in terms of their implications.

- All diagrams will have one start node and one end (finish) node.
- Except for the start node, every other node must have at least one preceding node.
- Except for the end node, every other node must have at least one subsequent node.

In addition we should note that it is conventional to label each activity to help identification, and that the completed structure of the diagram will show the logical sequencing of all activities making up the project. Also note that the arrows between the nodes are only used to show dependency between the activities. They do not have any implications in terms of time. The length of these arrows is determined by whatever is appropriate to produce a diagram that accurately describes the relationship and linkages between the activities in the project. It is worth getting into the habit of drawing one or two rough attempts at such a network diagram before producing the final and correct version. In practice, of course, for complex projects, project planning software is readily available.

To illustrate all of this, let us develop a smaller and simpler example before applying these principles to our problem. Table 13.4 shows a small illustrative project consisting of six activities.

Table 13.4   Illustrative project

Activity	Dependency
A	None
B	A
C	A
D	A
E	B, D
F	C

We show the dependencies but not the durations, as we do not require these at present because we wish simply to illustrate the principles of diagram construction. Figure 13.2 shows how these activities are connected to each other using nodes and arrows. Note that we are following the above-mentioned rules, that is, the diagram starts with a Start node and ends with a Finish node and all nodes (except these two) have at least one preceding and one subsequent node.

You will see that the diagram conforms to all the required rules while showing the sequencing and dependencies specified in the project.

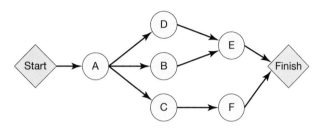

Figure 13.2 Simple network diagram for the illustrative project

You should check the initial network diagram at this stage for any errors. An easy way to do this is to read the diagram from left to right (start to finish) activity by activity, and to check that the dependencies for each activity, as illustrated in the diagram, are correct.

We shall see later how we incorporate duration and other information into the diagram. No matter how complex the project, we can, in principle, construct such a diagram and this diagram is at the heart of the model we wish to develop to assist the project manager.

Progress Check 13.3

For the survey project draw a comparable diagram. This may take you more than one attempt and you should check your completed diagram carefully to ensure it follows the rules yet at the same time shows the dependencies specified in the project.

The completed network diagram for the survey problem is shown in Figure 13.3. Take a few moments to study it and compare it with your own. The diagram may look different from your own version but this is unimportant, as long as it shows the sequencing correctly.

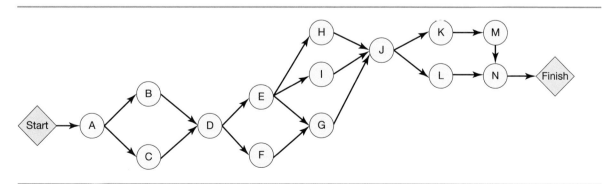

Figure 13.3 Network diagram: survey project

Developing the network diagram

We are now in a position to start to use the network diagram to help us produce information about time that we can use in managing the project. Let us first review what this information consists of. There are six figures related to time for each activity that are recorded in a typical network diagram. These are:

- Duration of the activity
- Earliest start time (EST)
- Earliest finish time (EFT)
- Latest start time (LST)
- Latest finish time (LFT)
- Float (LST – EST or LFT – EFT)

The first item in the above list should be known or assessed before developing the network diagram. The other items are found by carrying out a network diagram analysis.

Not all activities in a project have to start at a definite time in order to meet the project deadline. There are normally many activities that have some flexibility in terms of starting and ending time. These activities therefore have different earliest and latest starting times and also different earliest and latest finish times. The duration of flexibility (that is, time between EST and LST or EFT and LFT) is called *float*. An activity that does not have any float (where the float is zero) is a critical activity. For such an activity EST and LST as well as EFT and LFT are the same. This means, unlike other activities, any slight delay in starting this (critical) activity results in delay in completion of the whole project. On the diagram, the path that connects the critical activities to each other is called the *critical path*. The critical path will actually identify the time taken to complete the entire project.

For recording these pieces of information on the network diagram, there is a well-established format. This is illustrated in Figure 13.4. It can be seen that there are six cells in an activity node to record time-related information. We have EST and EFT of an activity

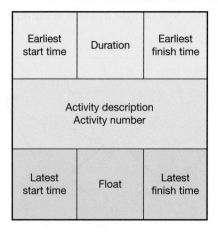

Figure 13.4 Standard format of the activity node

in the first row, with duration recorded in the cell between them. We then have LST and LFT in the third row, with Float recorded in the cell between them. We simply use the same format for our survey project network diagram. Consider Figure 13.5.

Incorporate time information for durations into the network

This is a straightforward task and we simply add the estimated duration of each activity onto the diagram as shown in Figure 13.6. Note the duration for the Start and Finish activities is zero. These are not real activities and we added them just to keep the network tight and to avoid possible errors in calculations.

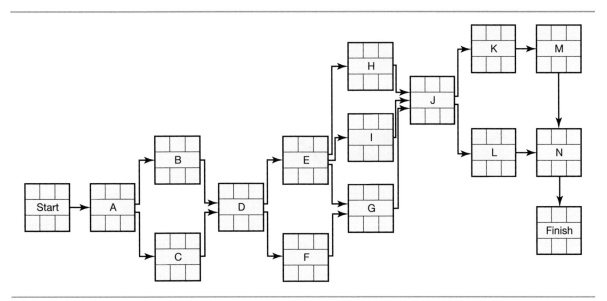

Figure 13.5 Network diagram, survey project

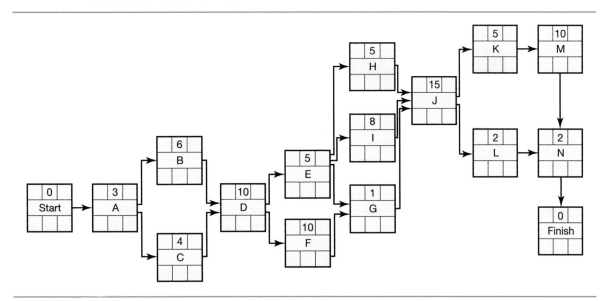

Figure 13.6 Network diagram: survey project with activity durations

Calculate earliest start and finish times for each activity

The next stage is to calculate the earliest start and finish times (EST, EFT) for each activity. To do this, we first put 0 for the EST and EFT of the Start activity (again, note that the duration of the Start activity is 0). We then move towards the Finish activity in the diagram, identifying for each activity in turn the EST and the EFT. In doing so we follow these simple and logical rules:

1 The EST of activity X is equal to the largest EFT of the activities that X depends on.
2 The EFT of activity X is equal to its EST plus its duration.

Let us calculate the ESTs and EFTs of the network diagram for the survey project. While doing this we will also appreciate the logic behind the above rules. As noted above, the EST and EFT for the Start activity will be 0. Activity A depends on the Start activity only. So based on the above rule it can start on Day 0. Activity A has a duration of three days, so we add that to 0 to find 3 as the EFT for Activity A. In other words, the earliest that Activity A can finish is Day 3. Activity B can start as soon as Activity A ends, that is Day 3. Activity B has duration of six days so the EFT for Activity B will be 9. We now look at Activity C. Activity C too can start as soon as Activity A ends. That will be Day 3. With a duration of four days the EFT for Activity C will be Day 7.

Progress Check 13.4

What is the EST for Activity D?

We have now reached Activity D. Based on the first rule, the EST will be the largest EFT for the activities that Activity D depends on. Activity D depends on both Activities B and C. Their EFTs respectively are 9 and 7. Therefore the EST for Activity D will be 9 and its EFT – with a duration of 10 – will be 19. Look at the diagram again to see why this rule applies. Can Activity D start on Day 7 when Activity C is finished? Of course not! We also need to wait for Activity B to finish as Activity D depends on both of these activities. This is the logic behind rule one.

The rest of the calculations too follow the above two simple rules. We need to make sure that when an activity depends on more than one activity we apply rule number 1.

Progress Check 13.5

Complete the rest of the EST and EFT calculations for the network.

Figure 13.7 shows the calculations for the EST and EFT of all activities. Check to see if your answers are the same. Did you notice that Activity J is dependent on three activities, H, I and G? The calculations show that their EFTs respectively are 29, 32, 30. So based on rule one, Activity J can only start on Day 32, and its EFT – with a duration of 15 days – will be 47. Similarly, Activity N depends on Activities L and M with ESTs of respectively 49 and 62. Activity N therefore can only start on Day 62 and its earliest finish time will be Day 64. Therefore, the Finish activity (which, like the Start activity, is not a real activity) will have the EST and EFT of 64.

We now have one critical piece of information: how long the project will take to complete. The answer is given as 64 days – the EFT of the Finish activity. Literally, the earliest we can complete the project is at the end of Day 64, based on the information we currently have. This is obviously useful to the project manager and answers one critical

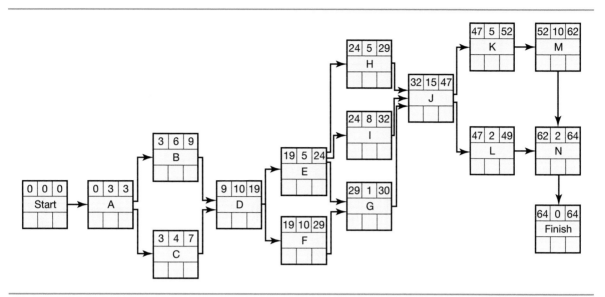

Figure 13.7 Network diagram: survey project with earliest start and finish times

question about the project. However, this was not the sole information requirement of the project manager and it will be worthwhile completing the rest of the calculations we said we required to see what other information we can generate.

Calculate latest finish times and start times for each activity

Just as we have calculated the ESTs and EFTs for each activity, we now require the latest start and finish times (LSTs and LFTs). This is the latest time by which each activity must start and finish if the project is to be completed by the end of Day 64. To obtain these, we work backwards through the diagram from the Finish activity. Before doing the calculations, we will make the LST and LFT figures for Finish activity the same as – respectively – EST and EFT figures (that is 62 and 64). This is because – like the Start activity – the Finish activity has duration of 0 as it is not a real activity.

Similar to the calculations for the ESTs and EFTs, we will now follow the following two rules:

1 The LFT of activity X is equal to the smallest LST of the activities that depend on activity X.

2 The LST of activity X is equal to its LFT minus its duration.

Moving backwards from the Finish activity, Activity N will have the LFT of 64. Deducting the duration time of 2, the LST for Activity N will be 62. The first point in the diagram where rule 1 will become helpful is for Activity J. Activities K and L depend on Activity J and their LST – based on calculations – are respectively 47 and 60. Based on rule 1, the latest time for completing Activity J will be 47. This is of course logical, since if Activity J ends anytime later than day 47 then this will not allow Activity K to start on day 47. Similarly, Activity E is one that the three activities of H, I and G are depending on. Based on rule 1, the LFT for Activity E will be 24 (that is the shortest LST for Activities H, I and G based on calculations).

Progress Check 13.6

Calculate the LSTs and LFTs for the entire network.

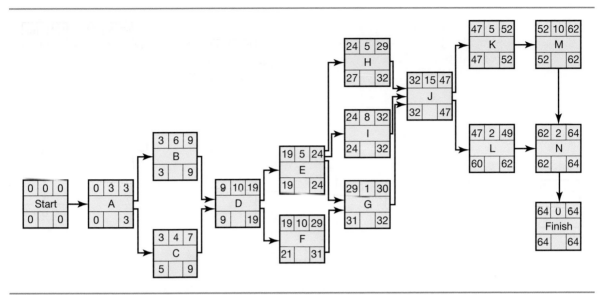

Figure 13.8 Network diagram: survey project with latest start and finish times

Figure 13.8 shows the LST and LFT information. Once again, the only parts we need to be careful about are those where there are multiple routes through the network. In calculating the LSTs and LFTs, we have to reach the figure of 0 for the LST and LFT of the Start activity. If this does not occur, it is an indication of an error somewhere in our diagram.

Identify the critical path through the network

The last part of the analysis requires us to determine what is known as the *critical path* through the network. We can use the EST and EFT (or LST and LFT) information to determine those activities whose completion dates are, literally, critical to the project being completed on time, and those activities which are non-critical. Consider Activity A. This starts on Day 0, takes three days to complete and must be completed on Day 3 (the EST and EFT are the same), otherwise the entire project will be delayed. Activity A is therefore designated a critical activity. Similarly, Activity B is critical. The earliest it can start is Day 3, it takes six days to complete and must be completed by Day 9. However, Activity C is non-critical. Its earliest start time is Day 3 while its latest start time is Day 5. This effectively gives us two spare days (or two days' float time as the terminology of project planning has it). We literally have two days' flexibility with Activity C, which could be used to alter exactly when it starts, when it finishes or how long it takes. If Activity C takes five days rather than the estimated four, it will not affect the completion date of the project. It is evident that, by definition, critical activities have zero float whereas non-critical activities have positive float time. We can then continue to determine the float for the other activities in the network diagram and in this way let the critical path reveal itself. Such a path is continuous and the length of this path (in time) shows the duration of the project.

Progress Check 13.7

For the remaining activities in the project determine whether they are critical or non-critical and, for the non-critical activities, determine the float associated with each.

Figure 13.9 shows the floats – in the middle cell of the bottom row for each activity – and shows the critical path by bold arrows. The critical path in this project is A – B – D – E – I – J – K – M – N. Note that the critical path stretches from the Start activity to the Finish activity. If this was not the case then, again, we should check the calculations, We can now summarise the information associated with each activity, as shown in Table 13.5.

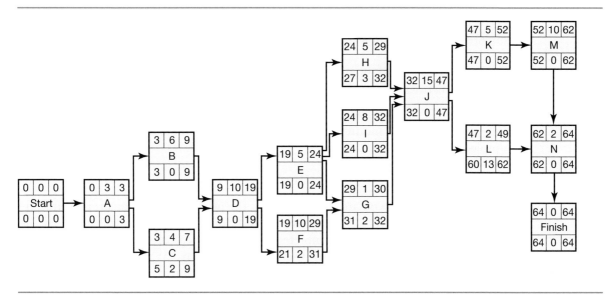

Figure 13.9 Network diagram: survey project showing floats and the critical path

Table 13.5 Critical and non-critical activities

Activity	Duration	EST	EFT	LFT	Float
A	3	0	9	9	0
B	6	3	9	9	0
C	4	3	7	9	2
D	10	9	19	19	0
E	5	19	24	24	0
F	10	19	29	31	2
G	1	29	30	32	2
H	5	24	29	32	3
I	8	24	32	32	0
J	15	32	47	47	0
K	5	47	52	52	0
L	2	47	49	62	13
M	10	52	62	62	0
N	2	62	64	64	0

This shows for each activity its duration, its earliest start time, EST, which is the EFT of the preceding event, its EFT, its LFT and the float time associated with it (the difference between LFT and EFT). Activity L, with 13 floating days, is the most flexible activity.

Using the network diagram

It is by now clear how useful the completed network diagram and the information it contains can be to the project manager. We are now able to:

● determine the project duration;

● prioritise between activities and their relative importance;

● assess the impact on the project duration of any changes in activity duration;

● use the diagram as a monitoring tool to check actual progress against planned as the project develops.

To illustrate we shall consider one or two examples.

● As project manager you are approached by the person responsible for printing the questionnaire: Activity H. This individual indicates that if you are willing to pay the workforce a bonus they can complete this activity ahead of schedule and take only three days to complete this, rather than the estimated five. What would your reaction be? Based on the diagram we know that Activity H is non-critical and we have three days' float associated with it. Completing this activity early will be of no benefit in terms of completing the entire project any earlier. If the activity had been a critical one then we would have considered the option of reducing its duration. If, for example, the same offer had been made regarding data entry, Activity K – a critical activity – then the project manager would need to weigh up the extra costs with the time saved in completing the entire project.

● The IT Department, which will be responsible for data entry, is understaffed and the departmental manager is trying to plan staff requirements over the next few months. You are approached as project manager and asked exactly when you will require the data-entry staff to be available for your project. From the diagram we see that – as long as everything goes according to plan – the data-entry activity, K, is scheduled to start on Day 47 and end on Day 52. This duration is when these staff will be needed. From the IT Department manager's perspective, this indicates that it will serve no purpose having these staff available early: this will not help completion of this project. From a resource management viewpoint, project plans offer considerable potential. Consider that in a wider perspective, the project plan allows the resource management to study how by the use of floats a smoother resource utilisation might be possible. Exercise 2 at the end of this chapter illustrates this.

● Let us assume that most of the activities incur costs as soon as they start. The Finance Department is concerned that by the time the project reaches around 47–50 days there might be some issues with cash flow. She would like to know whether there is any chance to reduce the number of activities during these days. You can now advise her that this is indeed possible since you can delay the start of Activity L from Day 47 to Day 60.

● Part way into the project, you have reached the stage of having just completed Activities A, B, C, D, E and about to start Activity F. However, it is now Day 26 and you should have reached this stage of the project – that is end of Activity E – by Day 24. Once again, the diagram will help you plan through the consequences of this delay. Other things being equal, and unless we take some positive action, such a delay clearly means the entire project will be delayed by two days (note Activity E is a critical activity). It is a straightforward matter to recalculate start and finish times for the activities still to be completed and communicate these as appropriate (for example to the data-entry staff). However, we can also evaluate our options in terms of trying to claw back some of this lost time. Activities I, J, K, M and N are all critical and still have to be undertaken. We would need to review urgently the estimated durations to see if the time taken for any of these activities can be reduced. Such information may well help us determine whether incurring extra costs – by paying the data-entry staff overtime, for example, to complete this activity early – is worthwhile in the context of the overall project objectives and resource allocation.

The network diagram that we have developed offers the project management a valuable tool not only in managing the project to ensure it is completed on time but also as a planning tool to resolve problems that, inevitably, will occur during the life of the project.

Technical point

The network diagram that we developed is technically called an activity on node (AoN) diagram. This is an easy diagram to make with straightforward calculations. Also computer programs for project control calculations often adopt this type of network diagram. However, there is another type of network diagram where the activities are represented by arrows and the nodes are showing the start or end of activities. That kind of network diagram is called an activity on arrow (AoA) diagram. There can be more complications in developing AoA network diagrams (due to use of what is called dummy activities) and it is also more difficult to develop appropriate computing programs. This type of network diagram (AoA) is generally considered outdated and its use is declining.

Gantt charts

A further development we can introduce, based on the diagram and the information we obtained in Table 13.5, is to produce what is known as a *Gantt chart*, which presents the information in the network diagram in a different way. This is particularly useful in meeting one of the requirements we had of the project planning model: that it would serve as a useful tool in the constant monitoring of the project. Such a chart for this project is shown in Figure 13.10. On the horizontal axis we show the duration of the project in days, up to the expected completion date of 64 days, and on the vertical axis we show each activity. A bar is then drawn for each activity, starting at the EST and ending at the EFT. If the activity has float time associated with it then the LFT is also added. Typically, the actual duration is shown as a solid bar with any float time as a dotted bar. It is easy to picture such a chart on the project manager's office wall (indeed many of you may well have seen one of these already on someone's office wall without realising what it was). The chart shows clearly the sequencing of activities and the critical activities, and

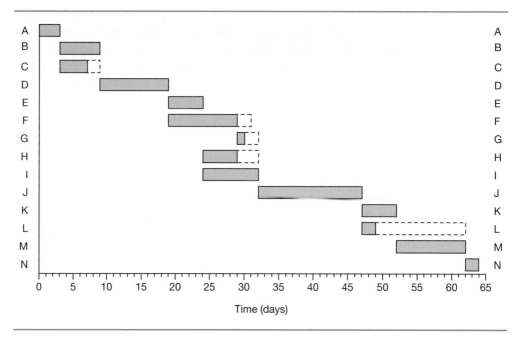

Figure 13.10 Gantt chart

also enables the manager to monitor progress and deviations from the project plan at a glance. For example, it is now very evident that Activity L, debriefing the interviewers, can take place any time between Day 47 and Day 62. Such an activity can be completed at the convenience of those involved. It will also be evident that, although the Gantt chart presents the same information as the network diagram, for many managers it will be seen as much more user-friendly.

QADM IN ACTION

Capgemini – contingency planning in project management

Capgemini's client was a leading mobile phone company. The client had launched a major project to replace their billing and administration system. The timescale for this was particularly aggressive and, given that the system was critical to the business and the possibility of a delay in its delivery, a contingency planning project was commissioned. This project was to run in parallel with the replacement project. In the event of a delay it was proposed to extend the operational life of the existing system although this would then raise issues over its capacity to handle existing levels of business growth.

Much of the client's billing and administrative work took place on an overnight basis. Capgemini

developed a model of the system's overnight batch processes with simulation built into the model to allow for uncertainty.

Three key factors were assumed to influence the amount of work required of the system and its level of utilisation: the size of the customer base, the number of calls being made by customers, and end-user generated activity. Capgemini analysed the relationship between overnight batch job times and these key influences. The performance relationships were built into a spreadsheet model. Because of uncertainty and variability in predicted job times and significant variation in the levels of daily activity, model experimentation was carried out using simulation. This allowed a picture of overnight system

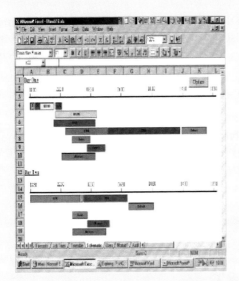

Source: Based on a Capgemini case study, with thanks to Capgemini for permission to use their material.

performance to be built up and the probability of batch failure to be assessed for forecast levels of monthly business activity. Finally, the model was used to evaluate the impact of a number of potential contingency measures on the system life expectancy.

The benefits are as follows:

● An objective assessment of the system's life expectancy.

● Identification of the key influences affecting overnight system performance.

● An assessment of the effect of alternative contingency measures on the system's life expectancy.

Uncertainty

It will be evident that, no matter how useful the model we have developed, its accuracy will only be as reliable as the information which has gone into it: the estimated duration of each activity. No matter how much effort has gone into producing such estimates, it is clear that these must be seen as uncertain to a lesser or greater extent. Although we can use the model to help us assess the effects of such uncertainty on a piecemeal basis (what is the effect of Activity J, for example, taking 17 days rather than 15) this is clearly unsatisfactory. However, under certain assumptions we can incorporate uncertainty over activity durations into the model explicitly. The extension of the basic model in this way is technically a complex one and we shall present only the key parts of the development.

We begin by assuming, realistically, that for any particular activity we could produce not one estimate of its duration but three:

● an *optimistic estimate* (OD), which is the minimum time this activity would take to complete if everything went exactly as expected without any difficulties or problems whatsoever;

● a *most likely estimate* (MD), which is the most likely duration, assuming normal conditions;

● a *pessimistic estimate* (PD), which is the expected duration if major difficulties are encountered.

Although we could produce these three estimates for all the activities making up the project, we shall do so only for three to help keep the principles manageable: E, J and M.

Activity	OD	MD	PD
E	4	5	8
J	12	15	25
M	8	10	15

That is, for Activity E, for example, the OD estimate is four days, the MD estimate five days and the PD estimate eight days. Using the three estimates for each activity we can now calculate an estimated duration for each activity using the formula to give a weighted average:

$$\text{Expected duration} = \frac{OM + 4MD + PD}{6}$$

Notice that the most likely estimate is given a large weight in the calculation and that the pessimistic and optimistic estimates have equal weights. This then gives, for the three activities:

Activity	OD	MD	PD	Expected duration
E	4	5	8	5.33 days
J	12	15	25	16.17 days
M	8	10	15	10.5 days

We could now rework the network diagram incorporating these durations and assessing the impact this will have on the project duration. In some cases, the critical path itself may alter as a result of these calculations: in others (as this one) it does not, although the overall project duration time is now 66 days rather than 64. However, this hardly seems worth the effort, since all it provides is a variant of the original critical path network. We can use such estimates, however, to assess probabilities in the context of the project duration. For example, we may wish an answer to the question: how likely is it that the project will be completed no later than Day 60 – at least six days ahead of schedule? To answer this we return to the Normal distribution. Without going into details to prove it we state that:

- if there are a large number of activities on the critical path and
- if the duration of each activity is independent of other activities

then the overall duration of the project will follow a Normal distribution. Such a distribution has:

- a mean equal to the total of the expected durations of the activities on the critical path
- a variance equal to the sum of the variances of the activities on the critical path.

For our revised problem, the critical path is as before and the estimated duration for each activity is shown in Table 13.6. We note that for those critical activities which have only one duration (as opposed to three) the estimated duration remains the same as in the original problem. The mean of the distribution is then 66 days. We should remember that variance is the square of the standard deviation. The variance of each activity is given by the formula:

$$\text{Variance} = \frac{(PD - OD)^2}{36}$$

Table 13.6 Estimated durations

Activity	Estimated duration	Variance
A	3	0
B	6	0
D	10	0
E	5.33	0.44
I	8	0
J	16.17	4.69
K	5	0
M	10.5	1.36
N	2	0
Total	66	6.49

and is shown in the table. For those activities with only one duration estimate the variance by definition is zero. The total variance for all activities on the critical path is then 6.49. Given that the variance is the square of the standard deviation, this means we have a standard deviation of:

$$SD = \sqrt{6.49} = 2.55 \text{ days}$$

We therefore have a Normal distribution showing the project duration with a mean of 66 days and a standard deviation of 2.55 days. Using the principles of the Normal distribution (see Chapter 5) we can calculate a Z score for this distribution and, using probability tables, determine the relevant probability. We require:

$$Z = \frac{X - \text{Mean}}{SD} = \frac{60 - 66}{2.55} = -2.35$$

which, from the table in Appendix B, gives a probability of 0.0094. That is, there is a probability of only around 1 per cent that this project will be completed at least six days ahead of schedule. Similarly, if we wanted to know the probability of the project being completed no more than three days late we have:

$$Z = \frac{X - \text{Mean}}{SD} = \frac{69 - 66}{2.55} = 1.18$$

giving a probability of 0.1190 or around 12 per cent. However, this is the probability in the area of the tail of the distribution and we require the area up to the tail, since we are asked the probability that the project will be completed no more than three days late. This probability is then (1.0 – 0.119) or 88 per cent. The general principles of this approach are shown in Figure 13.11 and can clearly be used to quantify the uncertainty over the exact durations of activities. In this example we have introduced uncertainty with only three activities; the method is readily extended to all activities where uncertainty might apply.

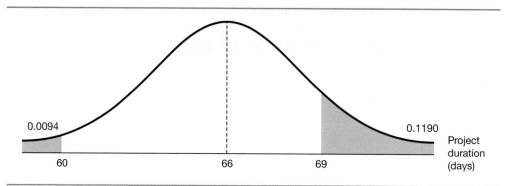

Figure 13.11 Project duration distribution

Project costs and crashing

We have seen that the project-planning model we have developed can be used to help the project manager prioritise, particularly if parts of the project have not gone to plan and delays have occurred. So far, the project manager has been able to identify critical activities and assess subjectively whether reductions in the duration of these might be possible and worthwhile in terms of trying to bring the whole project back on schedule. For some projects it may also be possible to add detailed cost information to the project-planning model and use this to help prioritisation. This is achieved through the introduction of what are known as *crash costs* and *crash times*. Consider Activity K, data entry. We can visualise that this activity has been costed in terms of its resource implications: staff costs, machine time and so on. Let us assume that this cost has been put at £1000. Such a cost is referred to as a normal cost, since it is linked to the estimate of the activity duration of five days, referred to as normal time. Clearly, for this activity, it might be possible to reduce the duration. However, this almost inevitably will incur additional costs: paying the data-entry staff overtime, using computing facilities at peak times, delaying other projects. Let us assume that we could reduce the duration of this activity to three days but at an additional cost of £500. This second duration and cost are known as crash time and crash costs respectively. However, what the project manager now has is information on the cost of reducing overall project duration – since Activity K is critical. On a daily basis we can reduce the project completion date at an extra cost of £250 per day for a maximum of two days. That is, the project could be completed in 62 days rather than the current 64 days. Obviously, management would need to determine whether this extra cost and the reduction in completion date was worthwhile in the context of the overall project.

This principle of crashing, however, can be taken one stage further. It would clearly be possible to establish a crash time and a crash cost for several of the activities. Consider the data shown in Table 13.7.

This shows for several activities the normal times and costs and the crash times and costs. Activity B, for example, could be reduced by one day at an extra cost of £300.

Table 13.7 Crash times and crash costs

Activity	Normal Time (days)	Normal Cost (£s)	Crash Time (days)	Crash Cost (£s)
B	6	1200	5	1500
D	10	3800	7	4500
H	5	750	4	850
J	15	11000	10	20000
K	5	1000	3	1500
M	10	3000	7	3900

Table 13.8 Crash cost per day

Activity	Normal Time (days)	Normal Cost (£s)	Crash Time (days)	Crash Cost (£s)	Crash cost per day (£s)
B	6	1200	5	1500	300
D	10	3800	7	4500	233
H	5	750	4	850	–
J	15	11000	10	20000	1800
K	5	1000	3	1500	250
M	10	3000	7	3900	300

Clearly, the options we face in terms of crashing – and thereby reducing the overall project completion time – are several. The first decision we can make is a simple one: there is no point incurring extra costs to reduce the completion time of a non-critical activity. Activity H is non-critical and therefore should not be crashed. All the other activities are critical, however, and it will be worthwhile calculating the crash cost per day's reduction in duration for each of them. This is shown in Table 13.8. We see, for example, that Activity B has a crash cost per day of £300 and Activity J of £1800, where each cost is calculated by taking the extra costs incurred in crashing this activity and dividing by the reduction in the number of days' duration for that activity. It is clear that we can now use these daily costs to prioritise. Other things being equal, Activity D is the one which should be crashed first as it has the lowest crash cost per day, although the decision to crash at all is still a subjective one.

Worked example

Your company has decided to run a short management training course on project management. You have been asked to project manage the initiative. You have identified the key activities required for the project, shown in Table 13.9.

Table 13.9 Key activities for planning management training course

Activity	Description	Duration (weeks)	Preceding activity
A	Agree course outline and publicity	4	–
B	Identify suitable tutors	2	A
C	Agree detailed course structure	6	B
D	Circulate publicity and application forms	6	A
E	Agree contract with tutors	2	B
F	Select participants	1	C, E
G	Send confirmation to participants	2	D
H	Agree teaching material	2	F, G
I	Prepare teaching material	5	H
J	Prepare venue for event	1	G
K	Run programme	–	I, J

For certain activities there is some uncertainty as to the exact duration and you have provided alternative duration figures:

Activity	Optimistic	Most likely	Pessimistic
A	3	4	6
B	2	2	10

In addition, you have made estimates of the costs of the various activities, as shown in Table 13.10.

To put our project plan together we can start with the relevant network diagram, shown in Figure 13.12. The overall project duration is 20 weeks, with critical activities shown as A, B, C, F, H and I. Other activities are non-critical and float time is shown for each in the relevant precedence box.

We know, however, that for two activities, A and B, uncertainty about the expected durations exists. We can now obtain the expected duration of the project (from the expected duration of all activities on the critical path) as 22.34 weeks. More usefully though, with the project variance at 10.92 and the standard deviation at 3.30, we can determine a range of completion dates and the associated probability:

● a 90 per cent probability that the project will be completed within 26.6 weeks;
● a 95 per cent probability that the project will be completed within 27.8 weeks;
● a 99 per cent probability that the project will be completed within 30 weeks.

Table 13.10 Costs of activities

Activity	Extra cost (£s)	Minimum possible duration
A	1000	2
B	750	1
C	300	3
D	1200	8
E	100	1
G	1500	1
H	200	1

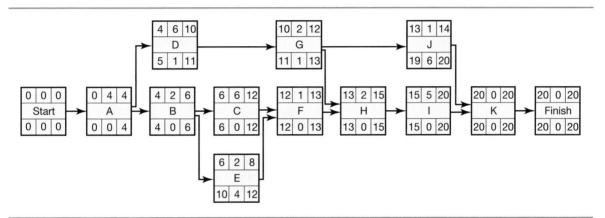

Figure 13.12 Network diagram for training course

We can also apply the crashing information to the problem. From the information given we can calculate the crash cost per week for each activity:

Activity	Crash cost per week	Maximum possible time saved
A	500	2
B	750	1
C	100	3
D	1200	1
E	100	1
G	750	2
H	200	1

Recollect that only critical activities are worth considering for crashing. The current critical activities are A, B, C, F, H and I. It looks tempting to say we can crash C by three weeks at a cost of £300. However, closer inspection of Figure 13.12 reveals that we have limited float time with activities D and G. In fact, for these two activities combined, we have only one week of float time available (since G has an EFT of 12 while F currently finishes in Week 13). So, we can only crash Activity C by one week before D and G also become critical. Visual inspection of the crash costs indicates the next option is to crash Activity H by the one week, available at a cost of £200. Activity A is the next possibility, at a cost per week of £500, but it would probably be sensible to determine what our available budget was for such crashing before completing the rest of the calculations.

Summary

In this chapter we have examined the issues and problems that typically arise for managers who have the responsibility for controlling a project. We have also developed a model – usually referred to as the critical path model (CPM) – which allows us to identify discrete activities which make up the project and use these to represent the project diagrammatically. With additional information about linkages between the different activities and their durations we can use this model to identify the critical path: the key activities which directly affect the overall duration of the project. We have also seen that the basic model can be extended to incorporate uncertainty through what is known as the project evaluation and review technique (PERT). This allows a manager to quantify the likelihood of a given completion date for the project. So, the main difference between CPM and PERT is that CPM is used when the activity duration is predictable while PERT is for the situation where there is uncertainty about at least some of the activity durations.

We cannot finish this chapter, however, without repeating the message that project management involves far more than simply applying these models and using the information they generate. Project management calls upon a whole range of skills on the part of the project manager, many of them 'people' skills relating to teamwork, motivation, control and delegation. These are far more important than the simple quantitative models that we have developed. Such models can, however, provide valuable information to the project manager to assist in this wider management task.

UK Whitehall projects worth £500bn at risk of failure

By Sarah Neville

Successful delivery of about one in five government projects, including new aircraft carriers and the HS2 high-speed rail line, is in doubt and requires urgent action, according to ratings released on Friday by the Major Projects Authority.

A total of 41 out of 199 projects, with a collective value of close to £500bn, have been given a "red" or "amber-red" rating, compared with 31 projects a year ago. Of the eight projects rated "red" in September 2012, only one still held that status a year later, the Queen Elizabeth Class Aircraft Carrier project. The project has been dogged by cost overruns and late last year Philip Hammond, defence secretary, disclosed that the price of building two of the carriers would rise by another £800m to £6.2bn, due in part to the need to build a sophisticated aircraft landing system on the ships.

Universal Credit, the government's flagship welfare reform, which last year fell into the "amber-red" category, has not even been assigned a rating, on the grounds that it was "reset" last year – an omission that is likely to fuel doubts over the progress of the troubled project. The Department for Work and Pensions insisted: "Universal Credit is on track. The reset is not new but refers to the shift in the delivery plan and change in management back in early 2013."

Margaret Hodge, who chairs the Commons public accounts committee, welcomed the transparency inherent in publication of project ratings but said the failure to rate Universal Credit suggested a "veiled compromise" within government, designed to avoid revealing the "chaos" surrounding the project. Meanwhile, the amber-red rating for HS2, unchanged since last year, showed that "the focused attention that is being applied to addressing the remaining issues must continue", said the MPA, while stressing that many projects in their early stages still had problems to overcome.

The decision to publish assessments of progress by the MPA, established three years ago to oversee big ticket spending, is part of a Cabinet Office attempt to drive up performance through greater transparency and improving civil servants' skills. Francis Maude, Cabinet Office minister, said that before the last general election there had been "no central assurance of projects, a lack of the right skills and problems were not systematically highlighted before they spiralled out of control". Improving project management had helped to save £1.2bn in 2012–2013 alone, Mr Maude said.

Of the 31 projects rated either red or amber-red last year, more than half did better this year and only one had got worse, said the MPA. However, of the 122 projects that were assessed both this year and last, 32 had got worse while only 27 had improved.

Poor project management can be very costly, but good project management doesn't happen by accident.

Exercises

1   Consider the situation of waking up in the morning and going to the kitchen to make yourself a cup of tea or coffee. Identify the various activities you would need to complete for this project and determine the dependencies between each activity. Use this information to construct a network diagram. When you have your result, try following the sequencing you have identified to make yourself a cup of tea or coffee and see if it works.

2   A business organisation is trying to improve staff morale and motivation and has decided to replace the existing staff canteen with a modern cafeteria. The works department has drawn up a detailed list of the various activities that will need to be completed, together with an estimate of how long each activity will take and the sequencing of activities. This information is shown in Table 13.11.

(a) Using this information construct a network diagram for the project.

(b) Identify the critical path.

(c) Determine float times for all activities.

(d) To try to keep the project within budget it has been decided that ideally no more than five personnel should be involved in the project at any one time. Is this feasible?

3   A large banking organisation is installing a network of automated teller machines (ATMs) for use by its customers in a large town. A number of major activities that have to be completed have been identified, along with estimates of the duration of

Table 13.11   Cafeteria project

	Activity	Duration	Preceding activities	Personnel required
A	Purchase construction materials	12 weeks	–	3
B	Purchase catering equipment needed for new cafeteria	3 weeks	–	2
C	Appoint supervisory architect	2 weeks	–	1
D	Clear site	3 weeks	–	3
E	Produce final building details	8 weeks	C, D	1
F	Prepare site for construction	3 weeks	E	2
G	Construct cafeteria	12 weeks	A, F	5
H	Install utility services	4 weeks	G	2
I	Install catering equipment	4 weeks	B, H	2
J	Decorate internally	2 weeks	B, H	2
K	Stock cafeteria	4 weeks	I, J	1
L	Hire catering staff	8 weeks	–	2
M	Train staff on site	2 weeks	I, L	3

Table 13.12   ATM project

Activity	Preceding activities	Normal duration (weeks)	Normal cost (£s)	Crash duration (weeks)	Crash cost (£s)
A	–	9	900	3	6 300
B	–	7	2800	5	4 000
C	A	12	8400	6	13 800
D	A	10	7000	6	16 600
E	B	12	7200	4	12 800
F	C, E	6	3000	4	4 600
G	C, E	7	4900	6	6 800
H	F	14	4200	10	6 200
I	G, D	8	3200	3	6 700
J	H, I	3	1500	–	–

each activity and the normal cost of each activity. Crash times and costs have also been estimated. The relevant information is shown in Table 13.12.

(a) Construct a network diagram using this information.

(b) Determine the critical path.

(c) Determine the expected normal completion time for the project.

(d) The bank has decided that in terms of increased customer satisfaction and new accounts it is worth up to £1000 a week to reduce the completion time of the project. Determine by how many weeks it would be cost-effective to reduce the completion date.

4   In the project detailed in Table 13.13, activity labels indicate the major activities to be completed in a project. The duration and cost of each activity have been identified, on both a normal basis and a crash basis.

(a) Construct a network diagram for this project.

(b) Identify the critical path, the normal completion time and the normal cost of the project.

(c) By successively crashing activities, find the shortest possible time for the project as a whole and calculate the associated cost.

Table 13.13 Project

Activity	Preceding activities	Normal duration (weeks)	Normal cost (£s)	Crash duration (weeks)	Crash cost (£s)
A	–	10	2000	4	2600
B	–	2	500	–	
C	A, B	3	1500	1	2000
D	A	12	3000	4	4600
E	C, D	5	900	3	1200
F	E	3	700	–	
G	E	5	1110	3	1340
H	C, D	9	2500	4	4000
I	F, G	16	4200	6	5200
J	H, I	2	400	–	–

5   You have been appointed secretary of a student group which has an annual programme of invited speakers from the business world. The group has suffered from a membership decline over the last few years and you are keen to reverse this trend by planning a more ambitious programme of guest speakers. Table 13.14 shows the individual activities you have determined to make up the project and the estimated duration.

(a) Estimate the overall completion time for the project.

(b) Construct a Gantt chart for the project.

6   A project comprises the activities shown in Table 13.15, which also shows the duration of each activity.

(a) Construct a network diagram for this project and determine the expected completion time together with the critical path.

(b) Determine the probability that the project will take longer than 50 weeks.

(c) Determine the probability that the project will take less than 42 weeks.

Table 13.14 Programme project

	Activity	Preceding activities	Duration (days)
A	Book individual dates for programme	–	2
B	Contact key speakers to agree availability	A	20
C	Arrange sponsorship to help with costs	–	15
D	Send out membership renewal details	–	5
E	Membership renewals returned	D	15
F	Send reminder notice to those who have not renewed membership together with list of key speakers	B, E	5
G	Membership renewals returned	F	15
H	Compile membership list	G	5
I	Print detailed programme	B, C	5
J	Mail final programme to members	I, G	5

Table 13.15 Activities and duration of project

Activity	Preceding activity	Duration in weeks		
		Optimistic	Most likely	Pessimistic
A	–	2	3	3
B	–	10	12	15
C	A	4	5	8
D	B	2	2	2
E	A, D	3	3	3
F	B	3	4	5
G	C, E, F	8	10	20
H	G	2	3	5
I	G	2	2	2
J	H	4	5	10
K	I, J	2	4	6

7 A firm is making minor alterations to its automated stock-handling system in one of its warehouses. The relevant information relating to this project is shown in Table 13.16.

Table 13.16 Activities relating to stock-handling system

Activity	Expected time (weeks)	Preceding activities	Extra crash costs (£s)	Crash time (weeks)
A	3	–	6 000	2
B	2	A	–	–
C	8	–	16 000	5
D	1	C	–	–
E	6	B, D	18 000	4
F	4	C	20 000	2
G	5	E, F	15 000	4
H	1	E, F	–	–
I	1	G	–	–
J	5	G	5 000	3
K	6	H, I	12 000	3

The table shows the activities that must be completed, their expected duration times in weeks, and the activities that must precede each activity shown. Also detailed in the table are potential time savings for some activities and the extra costs that would be associated with such time savings.

(a) Construct a suitable diagram to determine the completion time of this project. The diagram should clearly show the critical path and all appropriate times.

(b) The warehouse manager has expressed concern about the disruption caused during the project and has indicated that an extra £25 000 of funding for the project would be available if the overall completion time could be reduced. Using the principles of crashing, determine by how much it would be feasible to reduce the overall completion time and which activities would be affected.

8   For a particular project, the information in Table 13.17 has been obtained.

(a) Construct a network diagram for this project showing ESTs, EFTs, LSTs, LFTs, floats and the critical path.

(b) The company concerned has indicated that it would like the project completed in no more than 16 days. Determine the additional cost of achieving this.

(c) What is the minimum possible time for completing the project?

Table 13.17 Project information

Activity	Preceding activities	Normal time (days)	Crash time (days)	Normal cost (£s)	Total crash cost (£s)
A	–	3	1	900	1700
B	–	6	3	2000	4000
C	A	2	1	500	1000
D	B, C	5	3	1800	2400
E	D	4	3	1500	1850
F	E	3	1	3000	3900
G	B, C	9	4	8000	9800
H	F, G	3	2	1000	2000

14 Simulation

Learning objectives

By the end of this chapter you should be able to:

- describe the features of a simulation approach in business
- construct a simulation flowchart
- complete a manual simulation
- interpret information generated from a computer simulation

We have developed and used a number of quantitative models through the text. These models have had one key feature in common: they are primarily *deterministic*. That is, they are concerned with determining or finding the specific solution to the problem as formulated, very often with this solution being seen as the 'best' or optimal solution. There are very many situations in business decision making, however, where it may be unrealistic to expect there to be an optimum solution. One group of models – simulation models – are concerned with this type of situation and differ from most other quantitative models in that they are primarily descriptive rather than deterministic: they are concerned with describing in modelling terms the business problem we are investigating rather than finding the solution to such a problem. Simulation models typically generate additional information about the situation – frequently information that is difficult if not impossible to produce with other models – and this information must then be assessed and utilised by the user to reach an informed decision.

The principles of simulation

Consider the following scenario. The manager of a small supermarket is reviewing policy in terms of the number of checkouts that are available at any one time for serving customers. The manager has recently received a number of complaints from customers who have to wait for an unacceptably long time at the checkout before being served by the checkout operator. That is, they have to wait in a queue of customers before receiving service and the time they have to wait is unacceptable, or to put it in technical terms, is beyond their tolerance time. Naturally this is a potentially serious situation for the manager.

Progress Check 14.1

As supermarket manager what action would you consider taking?

It is evident that one option that would be seriously considered would be the possibility of increasing the number of checkouts that were in use at any one time. Consider the logic of the situation which the manager faces. A number of customers will be in the supermarket at any one time and will be wandering around completing their shopping. When they are finished they will make their way to the checkout to pay for their goods and will leave the store. The number of customers who can be served in a given period of time will, then, be largely determined by the number of checkouts in use at any one time. In principle, the more checkouts in use then the shorter the time a customer is likely to have to wait before service. Naturally having more checkouts in use will not guarantee that every customer will receive faster service – we are in the realms of 'on average' once again.

Progress Check 14.2

If the solution to the problem is this simple and obvious then why, as customers, do we always seem to face long queues in supermarkets?

Clearly, although in principle the manager has a simple solution to the problem, a number of other factors will have to be considered. Foremost of these is likely to be the issue of the extra cost incurred by opening additional checkouts – in particular, the manager will want to know how cost-effective the decision will be. The difficulty is clear. Opening an extra checkout will cost money: in terms of the equipment that has to be made available, the staff who have to be employed and the training that has to be provided. These costs have to be weighed against the impact such a decision will have on the size of the queues in the store and the length of time that customers have to wait. What is clearly required is some sort of analytical approach to assist the manager in reaching a decision about whether to bring additional checkouts into use and if so how many. Even so, the decision as to how many checkouts to have open will to some extent still remain a subjective one.

It is not difficult to see that, in reality, the problem would be much more complex than the one we have described. Patterns of customer behaviour are likely to complicate matters: the fact that the store will be busier at some times of the day than at others, will be busier on some days than on others, that the number of customers will not only vary during the day/between days but also be uncertain and so on. We face a technically complex situation. It may also have occurred to you that even if we can develop a suitable quantitative model for such a situation the model is unlikely to be able to produce an optimal solution, simply because, from the manager's perspective, there will be no ideal solution to the problem. From the customers' viewpoint, of course, the ideal solution is to ensure there are sufficient checkouts in use so that a customer never has to wait for service. In practice, however, this would be too costly for the store. We can readily envisage that under such a situation many of the checkouts would be unused for large parts of the day: although customers would not have to wait for service, it is likely that checkouts would need to wait for customers! The manager, then, faces a trade-off situation: trying to reach some compromise between the amount of time customers spend in the queue and the 'waste' of resources tied up in underutilised checkouts. Even in this simple situation it is easy to see that the manager is trying to reconcile two conflicting objectives:

- minimising the time customers spend queuing;
- minimising the resources the store requires.

The manager's difficulty is the absence of any hard, quantitative information about alternative trade-off positions. That is, what would happen to the length of time spent in the queue if an extra checkout were in use, or two extra checkouts, or three and so on.

This example typifies the problem that many managers in many different organisations face, a problem that is generically referred to as the *queuing problem*. In such a problem some operations are in place to provide a service either to the external customer (like the checkout service in our example) or to provide service to an internal customer (like a service that takes place on a production line, or a service that occurs in a stock-control system). The rate at which such a service can be provided is typically subject to variability. At the other end of the queuing system we typically have arrivals: of customers, production items, stock items, vehicles, aircraft, computer jobs and so on. Once again, the rate of arrivals will be subject to variability. The manager involved then has the task of trying to balance the service rate and the arrival rate. Clearly, if the service rate is lower than the arrival rate then a queue will form: of customers at a checkout, of items on a production line, of stock items at the delivery depot. Too high a service rate and the queue disappears but the manager will be left with the resources committed to providing the service being underutilised: waiting for arrivals to serve at certain times.

What if the arrival and the service rate are equal? Do you think there will be a queue? Remember 'on average' when you think about this!

Returning to the supermarket problem, there are of course quantitative modelling techniques like queuing models that can help with the analysis. However, for a rather complex problem like these, such models are often too narrow-minded and limited. Any attempts to add new analytical dimensions to these types of models can make the model too difficult to make and work with. So what other solutions we have?

In principle, of course, returning to the supermarket problem, the manager could experiment. For one week the manager could add an extra checkout to those in use and measure the effect this has on customers' queuing time, on costs, on profits and so on. A second week's experiment would have a different number of checkouts again. In principle, over time, we could then begin to see the impact different numbers of checkouts had on the key parameters of the problem. This would then help the manager assess an acceptable trade-off position between the two different objectives. It is evident, however, that for a variety of reasons such experimentation is simply not possible in the real business world. The practicalities of such experimentation would be prohibitive. Furthermore, such experimentation may reveal the result of the changes (what), but hardly reveal the dynamics that led to the result (why).

It is in situations like this that *simulation models* come into their own. Using principles primarily of logic and observation – and supported by computer technology – we can develop a simple descriptive model of such a situation that will, literally, simulate the situation we are keen on investigating. Effectively such a model allows us to experiment and observe the results in terms of key parameters without actually having to do such experimentation for real. Such a model also allows us to investigate both the 'what' and the 'why' questions about the operational situation.

You may agree or disagree with some of the author's opinions in the following article, but the article provides a very good example on how simulation can help to better understand a complex problem and reach some informed decisions.

Lesson I learnt tackling financial crisis that never was

Sometimes the biggest potential risks are staring you in the face, writes Ed Balls

One of the stranger experiences you can have as a Treasury minister is engaging in a tense discussion with the governor of the Bank of England about a problem that does not exist.

My contretemps with the governor came during a three-hour meeting in early 2007, as we decided what action to take to tackle a purely theoretical banking crisis at the end of a 10-day simulation exercise. As the UK's financial services minister, I had decided that we should conduct that exercise to test our systems. Little did we know that the real thing was just around the corner.

If Bank of England officials are holding similar drills today — and I hope they are — they will not struggle for plausible scenarios. In the past year, fears of tighter US monetary policy have triggered enough jitters in the equity and commodity markets to warrant the simulation of a full-blown transatlantic stock market correction.

Set aside the crisis engulfing Greece. Officials could wrestle with the impact of a sharp slowdown in China or Brazil, or a further escalation of hostilities in eastern Europe or the Middle East. If they wanted to look at a narrower market that is worryingly overheated, they would be spoilt for choice — from London housing to subprime US car loans. If they wanted to try out a scenario similar to the 2007 crisis, they might look beyond the formal banking sector, where rules are now much tougher, and focus on the frothier end of asset management and shadow banking.

In retrospect, the current economic situation — apparently healthy growth but with plenty of downside risks — contains some disconcerting echoes of the situation in 2006, a year before the global financial crisis began. Back then, with inflation and interest rates historically low, the consensus was that economies were still recovering from the oil and dotcom shocks of the early 2000s.

Economists debated whether continued loose monetary policy was necessary to maintain that recovery, or whether it was simply serving to fuel the next, bigger crisis. But in both the US and UK, central banks were inclined to believe the "great moderation" was delivering a more benign cycle, with lower household savings the result.

In retrospect, the current economic situation — apparently healthy growth but with plenty of downside risks — contains some disconcerting echoes of the situation in 2006

While at the time, I remember spending hours in the European Council listening to the German finance minister lecturing Britain about "irresponsible" hedge funds, even while German banks were falling over themselves to buy US subprime mortgages and Greek debt. It was in that uncertain environment that I decided to initiate our simulation.

It envisaged a lender collapsing after an unexpected legal ruling, and a large UK clearing bank being exposed to huge liabilities as a result, turning a local difficulty into a systemic event. The simulation ended with my tough meeting with the governor of the Bank of England and the chairman of the Financial Services Authority. We debated the risk that stepping in might send the wrong message and encourage recklessness by signalling that institutions could expect rescue if they ended up on the rocks. But we decided that the failure of a clearing bank would cause immense damage. So we opted to arrange a takeover.

When the real crisis struck later in the year, it did help that officials had been through that simulation — although I know many of the same arguments resurfaced. Here are three longterm lessons, relevant today, that I learnt from that exercise.

First, if weaknesses are exposed, they must be fixed quickly. Our simulation at the start of 2007 revealed that our deposit insurance system was old and creaking, and that EU state aid rules could obstruct decisive action to find an acquiring bank. The Treasury agreed a plan with the BoE to sort out those problems. But only on an 18-month timetable — too slow to help when Northern Rock foundered eight months later.

Fortunately, the structural reforms recommended by the international Financial Stability Board are happening much more urgently, particularly in the UK.

Second, procedures really matter. Even in a simulation exercise, our three-hour meeting was arduous. It helped greatly that there were three institutions in the room, able to debate the issues and hammer out an agreement.

Of course, the tripartite system did not spot the real crisis coming. Almost nobody did. But I am concerned that, under the new arrangements which replaced that system, the equivalent discussion would now take place exclusively within the Bank of England, with just one principal at the top.

In my view, the head of the Prudential Regulation Authority must also have a direct line to the chancellor, underpinned by proper structures for crisis decision-making which currently do not exist.

My third lesson is that sometimes the biggest potential crises are staring you in the face. In our simulation, the lending institution that collapsed was, in fact, a northern building society. And when a buyer was needed for the large clearing bank, who did the FSA propose? ABN Amro. Just a few months later, we were still taken by surprise when Northern Rock collapsed for real; while the misplaced confidence in ABN Amro's stability was doubtless one of the reasons Royal Bank of Scotland was allowed to go ahead with its disastrous takeover.

Policymakers need to be alive to all the distant threats to stability, from emerging market slowdowns to new financial activities beyond their regulatory reach, as they make the difficult and delicate judgment about whether and when to tighten monetary policy.

But, while continuing to scan the horizon, they must always keep one careful eye on what is going on at the end of their nose.

The writer is a senior fellow at Harvard Kennedy School and a former shadow chancellor and cabinet minister

Simulation is seen by some organisations as a key competitive edge.

Business example

To illustrate the principles and to help us develop a specific model we shall consider the following problem in detail. The manager of a local hospital is under pressure from patients, medical staff and politicians to extend the range of medical services offered to the local population. The problem, as ever, is one of limited and scarce resources and these must be prioritised. One particular medical service is currently under serious evaluation. The typical situation encountered by the hospital is as follows. An individual may visit their family doctor or general practitioner (GP). After an initial examination the GP may decide to refer the patient to the hospital, where they can be examined by an appropriate specialist and where use can be made, as necessary, of specialist equipment. Typically, the patient will be referred to the hospital by the GP and will stay in the hospital a few days until the necessary examinations and tests have been completed. On completion of the examinations, the patient will typically be discharged as not at risk or will be moved to another part of the hospital to await specialist treatment.

The hospital manager is currently trying to assess how many beds to make available for this particular unit. Naturally, this will be only one of many related decisions about resource allocation but it will enable us to focus easily on the principles of the simulation model. Some limited information has been obtained on the number of patients per day likely to be referred to the unit. This information is shown in Table 14.1.

This indicates that, on any given day, the unit could expect up to four new patients to be admitted. Also shown are the percentage frequencies associated with each number of patients. So, for example, there is a probability of 30 per cent that on any given day no new patients will be admitted and a probability of 10 per cent that four new patients will

Table 14.1   Patient referrals per day

No. of patients	Percentage frequency
0	30
1	25
2	20
3	15
4	10

Table 14.2   Patients' length of stay

Length of stay (days)	Percentage frequency
1	10
2	10
3	30
4	30
5	10
6	10

be admitted. Naturally, from the manager's perspective, this variable is beyond control. The decision to refer a patient is taken by the GP, not by the manager (you will realise that this is the same situation the supermarket manager faces in terms of how many customers will use the store at any one time, although in the supermarket context some marketing tools may be used in an attempt to influence the demand). Similar information is available on the length of time patients stay in the unit before discharge (either back home or to another part of the hospital for treatment). This is shown in Table 14.2.

We see that length of stay could be anywhere between one and six days. Once again, this variable is beyond the control of the manager – it will be a medical decision made by the specialist.

We now see clearly the problem facing the manager regarding the decision over how many beds to put into the unit. On the one hand, if too many beds are made available then it is likely that some of these will remain unused for long periods – a waste of scarce resources. On the other hand, too few beds and the unit will run the risk of having all beds in use when another patient is referred and not being able to cope with that patient. In fact this situation is typical of many to which simulation is applied. The problem is clearly compounded by the uncertainty over the number of patients that could be expected on any one day and over the length of time they will need to stay in the unit. It is also evident that there will not be any ideal solution to the manager's dilemma as to how many beds to make available, only compromise and subjective preference. What the manager is lacking is information on the likely consequences of alternative decisions.

Progress Check 14.3

From the two tables calculate the mean number of arrivals per day and the mean length of stay. How could this information be used to decide how many beds to have in the unit? What problems would using this approach have?

Developing the simulation model

Clearly, we could use basic statistical information to try to help us with this problem. The mean number of arrivals per day is calculated at 1.5 and the mean length of stay at 3.5 days. We might be tempted simply to multiply the two together – to get 5.25 – and say that five or six beds would be adequate on average. The problem with this of course relates to the consequences of the arrival rate or the service rate not being average. All we would need in such a situation is to have three or four days when we have an above-average number of arrivals or three or four days when we have a below-average rate of service and we would have problems. We might also think about trying to use the variability information – perhaps through a standard deviation – although again it is not clear how this could be done. Here is where a simulation approach comes to rescue, where the aim is to develop a descriptive model which will mimic the behaviour of the unit.

In order to develop the model for use we need to describe accurately the key elements of the process for this problem – remember that a simulation model is descriptive in essence. For this unit we might describe the situation in a number of stages. Before doing so it will usually be necessary to decide on a set of 'rules' that govern key parts of the process. In practice these will already be in place for the particular problem under examination. In our case we will impose the following rules:

● any patient due for normal discharge from the unit is discharged at the start of the day;

● new patients seeking admission to the unit do so at the start of the day;

● if a new patient seeks admission and the unit is full then an existing patient is moved to an adjacent unit. The patient who will be moved in this way will be the patient who is scheduled for the earliest discharge.

These 'rules' are to some extent arbitrary and we could develop a different simulation model if we allowed different rules to operate. They will suffice for our purpose, however, as they allow us to describe the operation of the unit in the following sequence of events.

1 The unit 'opens' at the start of the day.
2 Patients due for discharge leave the unit.
3 Any new patients are admitted to the unit.
4 If empty beds are available new patients are allocated to them.
5 If empty beds are not available, existing patients are discharged early to an adjacent non-specialist ward. These beds are then used for new patients.
6 The unit 'closes' at the end of the day.

What we have is a simple verbal description of the operation of the unit. The purpose of this verbal description is to provide a detailed – and hopefully realistic – description of the sequence of events in this situation. Clearly, in this example we have a simple process to describe. The more complex the situation under investigation, the more complex and detailed the description will need to be. The key point is that the description should represent accurately the stages of the service process.

A simulation flowchart

It may also be desirable – and for larger simulation models essential – to show this process in diagrammatic form through a simulation flowchart. Such a flowchart is shown in Figure 14.1. The diagram will need careful consideration but it shows the sequencing of key events and activities and the decisions that need to be taken at various stages of the process. The flowchart represents the process of the management of the unit for one day. The flowchart starts at the beginning of the day. Note that conventionally the oval shape is used to denote the start and end events. We then assess whether any existing patient is scheduled for normal discharge today (remember the rules we imposed earlier). If the answer is 'yes', then we need to empty these beds and keep track of how many empty beds we now have. If the answer is 'no', then clearly these actions are not required. Note again that conventionally we use a diamond-shaped box whenever a 'decision' takes

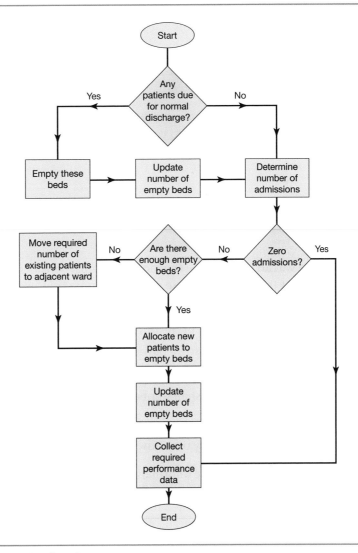

Figure 14.1 Simulation flowchart

place (or a question has to be answered) and a square box to denote some action being taken. We then move to determine the number of admissions today. If we have zero admissions then effectively the simulation for that day is at an end. If we do have some number of admissions, however, we first need to check if we have sufficient empty beds for these admissions. If the answer is 'yes', we allocate patients to empty beds and update the information we have about beds still vacant (for use at the start of the next day's simulation). If the answer is 'no' then we must effect the policy of moving existing patients to an adjacent ward to free up sufficient beds for the new admissions. Finally, no matter which route we took through the flowchart we need to collect data on the performance of the unit during today before ending today's simulation. Clearly we can then repeat this process for the next day and the next and so on.

The amount of detail we show in the flowchart is to some extent subjective, as long as it serves to describe accurately the process in the model. Like the network diagrams we introduced in Chapter 13, simulation flowcharts can take some getting used to but they are an excellent way of both describing a situation and indeed checking that we have got the description right (since if we find ourselves going down part of the flowchart we did not expect, it signifies the flowchart does not model the situation accurately). We can now begin to use the sequencing, detailed in the flowchart, to use the model and to start to generate management information.

Progress Check 14.4

Consider the last action in the flowchart of collecting performance data. What measures of performance would you want data collected for?

Using the model

Before we can begin to use the model, we must consider what information the manager will want from it. In this case we shall assume that two key performance measures are required:

- the level of utilisation of the resources, beds, over the period of the simulation;
- the rate at which existing patients were discharged early from the unit because of shortage of beds.

and that in addition we shall want data on:

- the number of admissions over time;
- patients' length of stay over time.

In practice, of course, the information required might be far more detailed than this. We shall also assume that the manager has already decided that somewhere between five and ten beds will be allocated to the unit. We therefore require the model to simulate these alternatives and generate information on the likely consequences – in terms of our performance measures – from each simulation. Let us see how we can use the model to simulate the unit's performance with five beds.

It is evident that there are two main determining characteristics in this simulation model:

● the rate of daily admissions to the unit;
● the rate of daily discharges.

As far as the manager is concerned, both of these events are variable and – within the limits set – are unpredictable. Consider the manager's position in terms of admissions. At the start of any given day the manager has literally no idea how many patients will seek admission (apart from knowing that it must be between zero and four). However, in the long run, the manager does expect the distribution of admissions to follow that shown in Table 14.1. The same logic applies to the length of stay of patients. It seems that somehow we should be able to use the probability information to help simulate this situation, although at this point it may not be clear how. The next section can help to make this clear.

The use of random numbers

In fact we simulate the variability in key variables through the use of what are known as *random numbers*. Consider the approach we could take for determining the number of admissions on a particular day. We could take 100 slips of paper and on each write one number from 1 to 100. If we put these slips into a bag we could then choose entirely at random one slip of paper from all those available. If the slip of paper had a number in the range 1 to 30 (since there is a probability of 0.3 from Table 14.1 that there are no admissions on a particular day) we could assume that zero patients were admitted that day; if it had 31 to 55, that one patient was admitted, and so on for the rest of the distribution. Clearly, in the long run, we would expect the number of slips of paper we drew from the bag which fell into each category to follow the probability pattern (assuming that we replaced the slip of paper in the bag after use). We could also undertake a similar process for determining the length of stay of patients once admitted.

Although this approach is logical, it is somewhat tedious and time-consuming. We can replicate this process, however, in one of two ways. We can use pre-calculated tables of random numbers or we can obtain random numbers (or pseudo-random numbers) directly from a computer system. Effectively what both these methods do is mimic the process of us choosing a slip of paper at random. Such a set of computer-generated random numbers is shown in Table 14.3.

Table 14.3 Random numbers

90	5	62	24	73	50	13	27	86	6
7	78	18	44	51	70	99	82	77	36
67	87	7	25	47	61	15	72	68	69
77	21	29	91	20	38	78	60	27	13
6	36	25	48	91	80	11	38	33	20
46	78	70	13	92	6	91	40	55	80
20	9	87	48	56	20	11	87	62	2
65	6	0	62	57	53	86	10	78	30
2	5	16	39	36	27	10	59	13	89
13	90	20	24	48	22	73	53	59	64

By definition the sequence of numbers in the table is entirely random and shows no pattern. There are a few points we need to make about the use of such tables before proceeding.

- We can start to use the table from any point. We do not have to start with the top-left corner but could start from anywhere in the table.
- When using such tables, in order to ensure complete randomness, we must use the numbers in strict sequence. That is, if we started at the top-left corner (although we could decide to start anywhere in the table) with 90, we must move in sequence either by row or by column. We cannot jump about the table for the next random number needed.
- We should use a separate, and different, table for each variable in the problem we want to simulate. However, to keep things simple for our purposes we shall use just the one table for both admissions and length of stay. We shall start admissions at the top-left corner with 90 and move down the column. For length of stay we shall start at the bottom-right corner with 64 and move up the column.
- To keep the random numbers to two digits (rather than three) the first possible random number is zero. This means we can expect numbers to occur between 0 and 99, thus 100 numbers in total to represent all the possible percentages. The corresponding tables for admissions and length of stay will then be as shown in Tables 14.4 and 14.5 respectively.

Beginning the simulation

We are now in a position to begin the simulation, following the structure of the flowchart. Remember that we are assessing the performance of the unit with five beds. At the start of the simulation, therefore, all five beds will be empty and we will have no patients for discharge that day. We now need to simulate the number of patients being admitted on Day 1, and to do this we must use the random numbers shown in the table. From the

Table 14.4   Admissions and random number range

No. of patients	Percentage frequency	Random number range
0	30	00–29
1	25	30–54
2	20	55–74
3	15	75–89
4	10	90–99

Table 14.5   Length of stay and random number range

Length of stay (days)	Percentage frequency	Random number range
1	10	00–09
2	10	10–19
3	30	20–49
4	30	50–79
5	10	80–89
6	10	90–99

selected starting point of the table for admissions we have a random number of 90. From Table 14.4 we see that this corresponds to four patients admitted on that day. Since we have five empty beds we can allocate each of these four patients to one empty bed. This leaves us with one empty bed and brings us to the end of Day 1. To summarise, we then have at the end of Day 1:

> Bed 1 Occupied
>
> Bed 2 Occupied
>
> Bed 3 Occupied
>
> Bed 4 Occupied
>
> Bed 5 Empty
>
> 4 patients admitted
>
> 0 patients discharged early

We will now simulate the length of stay required for each patient at the time of their admission. Clearly this is not what would happen in practice but it will make the simulation more manageable and it will not actually affect any results. We require four random numbers for the four patients and these will be 64, 89, 30 and 2. Using these in turn for the four patients we then have:

Day 1		
	Length of stay	Due for discharge beginning of day
Bed 1 Occupied	4 days	5
Bed 2 Occupied	5 days	6
Bed 3 Occupied	3 days	4
Bed 4 Occupied	1 day	2
Bed 5 Empty		
4 patients admitted		
0 patients discharged early		

We can now move on to simulate Day 2. We start this by checking whether any existing patients are scheduled for discharge (remember the decision rule that discharges would take place at the start of the day). The patient in Bed 4 is due for discharge (admitted on Day 1 for one day). So, we know that on Day 2 we will have two beds available for any new patients. To simulate arrivals, we take the next random number in sequence, 7, which equates to zero admissions on Day 2. The position at the end of Day 2 is then:

Day 2		
	Length of stay	Due for discharge beginning of day
Bed 1 Occupied	4 days	5
Bed 2 Occupied	5 days	6
Bed 3 Occupied	3 days	4
Bed 4 Empty		
Bed 5 Empty		
4 patients admitted		
0 patients discharged early		

The position for Day 3 follows the same logic. There are no discharges due today and the next random number, 67, indicates two admissions and that they will stay for five and three days respectively (using the random numbers 80 and 20). We then have:

Day 3		
	Length of stay	Due for discharge beginning of day
Bed 1 Occupied	4 days	5
Bed 2 Occupied	5 days	6
Bed 3 Occupied	3 days	4
Bed 4 Occupied	5 days	8
Bed 5 Occupied	3 days	6
9 patients admitted		
0 patients discharged early		

At the end of Day 3 the unit is full, although one patient is scheduled for discharge at the start of Day 4. On Day 4 we encounter a capacity problem for the first time. Three patients require admission today (random number 77) but we have only one free bed, Bed 3. Accordingly we must implement the specified policy of moving two existing patients to other wards; freeing Beds 1 and 2, which are the beds with patients due for the earliest discharge. The three new patients have a scheduled length of stay of two, four and three days respectively. At the end of Day 4 we then have:

Day 4		
	Length of stay	Due for discharge beginning of day
Bed 1 Occupied	2 days	6
Bed 2 Occupied	4 days	8
Bed 3 Occupied	3 days	7
Bed 4 Occupied	5 days	8
Bed 5 Occupied	3 days	6
9 patients admitted		
2 patients discharged early		

The principles of the simulation approach are also becoming evident. As we progress on a day-by-day basis we simulate arrivals and discharges as they might happen in real life. This allows us to assess the impact of a particular decision – having five beds – on the performance criteria.

Progress Check 14.5

Complete the simulation for Days 5 to 10. When using the random number table for arrivals, jump to the top of the next column to continue, and for discharges jump to the bottom of the next column.

By the end of Day 10 we have the following situation:

Day 10		
	Length of stay	Due for discharge beginning of day
Bed 1 Occupied	4 days	12
Bed 2 Empty		
Bed 3 Empty		
Bed 4 Empty		
Bed 5 Empty		
12 patients admitted		
2 patients discharged early		

It is also evident that as we progress through the simulation we can determine the use of beds on a day-by-day basis. Any day a bed remains unoccupied is effectively a waste of that resource. Similarly, we can monitor our other key measure of performance: the rate at which patients were discharged early because there were no empty beds for new admissions. Although the manual simulation process is not difficult, it is tedious, and it is clear that we would require the simulation to cover several hundred, perhaps thousand, days before we regard the results as a reliable indicator of what might happen in the real world. (In fact the comparison between simulation and taking a sample of observations in statistical inference is a valid one.) Clearly, in practice, simulation has to be undertaken by using one of the specialist simulation packages that are available or building an appropriate model in a spreadsheet. Table 14.6 shows the results of such a simulation on this problem.

The computer simulation was run for 1000 days with five beds available. The information provided shows the following:

- The total number of patients admitted over this period. This would provide the manager with an indication of demand and would also indicate the trend of demand in the context of the information in Table 14.1.
- The average number of patients admitted. Although this is simply 1401/1000 it also serves as a check on the randomness of the simulation process. Remember from Table 14.1 the probability distribution in terms of patient arrivals. This has a mean number of patients per day of 1.5, which we would expect the simulation to approach. In this instance we see that the mean number of patients in the simulation is slightly below the 'population' mean. It can be expected that a higher number of simulation days (i.e. more than 1000 days) will bring the mean number of patients in the model closer to the statistically calculated 'population' mean.
- The total number of patient days required. This is the total length of stay for all patients and could provide the manager with information on staffing levels required in the unit.
- Mean length of stay in the simulation is 3.48 days. Again, from Table 14.2 we would expect this to approach 3.5 in the long run.
- Mean percentage bed occupancy at 79 per cent. This is an indication of the level of utilisation of the key resource under investigation.

Table 14.6   Computer simulation results

End of this simulation with five beds available for 1000 days	
Total number of patients admitted	1401
Mean number of patients admitted per day	1.40
Total number of patient days required	4869
Mean length of stay (days)	3.48
Mean bed occupancy	79%
Number of early discharges	584
As percentage of total admissions	42%

● Early discharges were 584 patients. Although bed occupancy at 79 per cent gives the impression of spare capacity, it is now clear that there were frequent occurrences when the unit was full and existing patients had to be moved to adjacent wards.

● As a percentage of total admissions we see that early discharges were 42 per cent.

It is evident from this example that simulation is an extremely useful source of information – information that may not be available from any other source. To reinforce the use of simulation, however, it is also clear that the model does not suggest a solution to the manager's problem of how many beds to allocate to the unit. The manager must decide whether the trade-off between bed occupancy and early discharges – at 79 per cent and 42 per cent respectively – is acceptable. What is also clear is that the manager would wish to see comparable results for the other available options: six beds through to ten beds. Once again, such information is readily generated from the simulation model. The only amendment we require is to increase bed capacity from five to six, then to seven and so on.

Progress Check 14.6

In the context of the two key performance criteria – percentage bed occupancy and percentage of early discharges – what would you expect to happen to these two values if we increase the number of beds to six?

Table 14.7 shows the summary results for all the bed options obtained from the computer simulation. It is evident that as we increase the number of beds available we see an improvement in the percentage of patients discharged early: this falls from 42 per cent for five beds to 2 per cent for ten beds. However, we see a marked – and simultaneous – deterioration in the other measure of performance. Percentage bed occupancy falls from 79 per cent to 51 per cent. Once again we must stress that simulation is basically a what-if model. It does not indicate which of the bed options is 'optimal' but simply quantifies the likely outcomes of alternative decisions. However, it is also clear that the manager is now in a far better position to rationalise the decision that must be taken.

Although such simulated outcomes are not guaranteed, we know the likely results of the alternative decisions for this situation, and the manager can assess qualitatively (and

Table 14.7 Computer simulation results

	5 beds	6 beds	7 beds	8 beds	9 beds	10 beds
Total number of patients admitted	1401	1483	1455	1516	1434	1478
Mean number of patients admitted per day	1.40	1.48	1.46	1.52	1.43	1.48
Total number of patient days required	4869	5217	5085	5287	4955	5174
Mean length of stay (days)	3.48	3.52	3.49	3.49	3.46	3.50
Mean bed occupancy	79%	76%	68%	63%	54%	51%
Number of early discharges	584	471	253	162	47	23
As percentage of total admissions	42%	32%	17%	11%	3%	2%

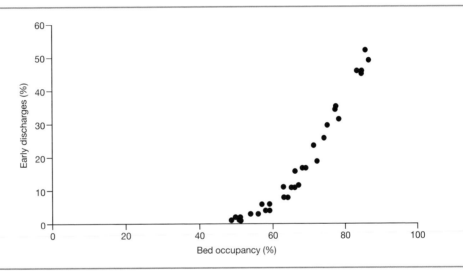

Figure 14.2 Scatter diagram for different bed options

based on policies and strategic objectives as well as the wisdom obtained from past experience) the trade-off that will be acceptable. It can also be instructive to show the results of such simulations graphically when they have been repeated many times. Clearly, if we repeated the simulation for each scenario (number of beds), we would expect similar but not identical results due to the use of random numbers (just as would happen in real life). Figure 14.2 shows the results of repeating the simulation of each bed option five times and plotting the results for the two performance criteria in a scatter diagram. The (non-linear) relationship between the two parameters is clearly shown and it is evident that the manager could use this to assist decision making, as it enables us to quantify the expected trade-off between the two objectives. For example, we see from the diagram that a bed occupancy performance of 80 per cent is linked to an early discharge performance of around 40 per cent. If the manager is under pressure to reduce the early discharges, say to 20 per cent, it is evident that, other things being equal, this will require additional resources (more beds) and that the consequence of this will be a reduction in bed occupancy to around 70 per cent.

QADM IN ACTION	Capgemini – simulating airport management

Capgemini is a multinational professional services and consulting corporation. One of Capgemini's clients was an airport operator. The client had initiated a major programme to investigate the use of IT throughout the business. Part of the project involved examining and improving the passenger 'experience'. As we all know from our own experiences as passengers, at an airport passengers have to move through several different stages or processes: parking the car, checking in, passport control, etc. Some of these processes are the responsibility of the client, and some are the responsibility of other businesses such as the airlines using the airport. The client was interested in simulating the passenger flow through the airport to allow it to investigate the effect that changes to the various processes might have.

A simulation model of the airport processes from the passengers' perspective was developed using specialist simulation software.

Capgemini developed a simulation model for the key processes. The model was designed from the outset as a management support tool and the visual aspects of the model were important in this respect. The model allowed for various process inputs to be set, such as passenger arrival rates, availability of key resources and process or throughput times, so that the effect of resourcing decisions could be investigated. The model allows managers to visualise (and quantify) the impact of decisions such as opening or closing additional check-in facilities

or passport control desks. In addition, the model allows managers to identity those parts of the airport system where delays occur because of a mismatch between passenger flows and resource availability.

The figure shows a screen shot from the simulation model. The screen shows the arrival of passengers at the check-in area, where two airlines are processing passengers.

The benefits are as follows:

- A management tool to test 'what-if' scenarios for airport resource management.
- The ability to assess the effect of changes in key variables such as passenger growth and technology improvement on passenger flow.
- Demonstrating the importance of seeing the business as a complete set of interrelated processes.

Source: Based on a Capgemini case study, with thanks to Capgemini for permission to use their material.

Worked example

A popular coffee shop on the outskirts of Edinburgh is reviewing its customer service strategy. The shop is located on a prime commuter route into the city and during the morning rush hour attracts considerable business of commuters driving into work who stop off to pick up coffee and cakes. Some preliminary market research has indicated that some customers would prefer to use a drive-in facility to save time. The shop is

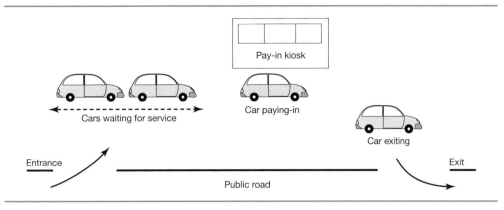

Figure 14.3 Pay-in facility layout

considering how many of these drive-in facilities to open during the morning rush hour, which lasts around two hours.

The provisional design of the pay-in facility will provide an off-street area where cars can queue while waiting for service at the kiosk, and the kiosk itself. The intended system and its layout are shown in Figure 14.3. Cars will enter from the public road, form a queue waiting for service (if necessary), take their turn at paying their bill and then exit back onto the public road.

One of the key variables in this type of situation is the inter-arrival time. This is the time between the arrival of two successive customers (note in the example of the local hospital we simplified this by assuming that patients were admitted or discharged at the start of the day, an assumption that may not be very realistic). The shop has collected some data and the inter-arrival times seem to be uniformly distributed between 0 and 2 minutes. In such a situation we state that the inter-arrival time for the next customer is given by 2r, where r is a random number between 0 and 1. Suppose we generated a random number of 0.62. The inter-arrival time for the next customer would then be 2(0.62) or 1.24 minutes – that is, the next customer will arrive 1.24 minutes after the current customer.

The shop has also estimated the time taken to serve a customer at the drive-in facility. This information is shown below. So 81 per cent of customers would take 1 minute to serve, 14 per cent would take 2 minutes and so on.

Time taken to serve a customer/car (minutes)	Probability
1	0.81
2	0.14
3	0.04
4	0.01

We can associate random numbers between 00 and 99 with the above percentages as follows:

Probability	Random Numbers
0.81	00–80
0.14	81–94
0.04	95–98
0.01	99

Another area of concern relates to the amount of space this facility will physically take up. The amount of space available for vehicles queuing while waiting for service is limited, and the local manager has indicated that they do not want to be faced with a problem of cars queuing back onto the public road. Not only will this cause annoyance to other passing motorists (with subsequent adverse perceptions of the company), it might also get the company into trouble with the local police. We have been asked to advise on the initiative.

Given the uncertainties that exist over arrivals, service times and possible queue lengths, it appears that simulation would offer a useful management approach to the situation. Not only would this allow us to simulate the existing initiative in terms of its overall performance, we could do some what-if analysis on the two data distributions (arrivals and service times) and we could also simulate the performance of different designs – for example that of a two-kiosk operation. Clearly, any sensible simulation will need to be computer-based, but we might wish to explain the principles, so that management are aware of the approach, using a few iterations of a manual approach.

Let's illustrate with some of the random numbers from Table 14.3, say row 5 for arrivals and column 2 for service times.

Row 5:	6	36	25	48	91	80	11	38	33	20
Column 2:	5	78	87	21	36	78	9	6	5	90

The first inter-arrival time is 2(0.06) or 0.12 minutes. So the first customer arrives at 0.12 and can be served straight away given no one else is waiting. The service time for this customer is determined by random number 5, which is associated with 0.14 probability for 2 minutes. The service therefore ends at 2.12 minutes. The second customer arrives 0.72 minutes, 2(0.36), after the first at time 0.84. The first customer is still being served at that point so the second customer needs to wait till 2.12 when the service for the first customer is completed. Service time for the second customer is determined by random number 78, which is associated with 0.81 probability for 1 minute. So the service for customer two will be completed at time 3.12. We can carry on in this way with the first 10 customers (you may want to do this yourself at this stage) with the results in Table 14.8. The inter-arrival times are shown and the actual arrival time of each customer together with the service time. The table then shows the time that service starts

Table 14.8 Simulation of the first 10 customers

Customer	Inter-arrival time	Arrival time	Service time	Service starts	Service ends	Waiting in the queue	Total time
1	0.12	0.12	1	0.12	1.12	0	1
2	0.72	0.84	1	1.12	2.12	0.28	1.28
3	0.5	1.34	2	2.12	4.12	0.78	2.78
4	0.96	2.3	1	4.12	5.12	1.82	2.82
5	1.82	4.12	1	5.12	6.12	1	2
6	1.6	5.72	1	6.12	7.12	0.4	1.4
7	0.22	5.94	1	7.12	8.12	1.18	2.18
8	0.76	6.7	1	8.12	9.12	1.42	2.42
9	0.66	7.36	1	9.12	10.12	1.76	2.76
10	0.4	7.76	2	10.12	12.12	2.36	4.36

for each customer, together with the time service is completed. Also shown is the time, if any, that the customer had to wait for service (the difference between arrival time of the current customer and the time that service ended for the previous customer) plus the total time that the customer is in the service area.

A quick look at Table 14.8 reveals a disturbing trend of waiting time increasing as time passes and more customers arrive. Based on the random number series used the 10th customer will spend over four minutes in the system, the majority of which is just waiting in the queue. The figures reveal that the total time in the system and the waiting time are increasing as time passes and more customers arrive. If you continue this manually you will see that the 40th customer arrives around half an hour after the start of the drive-in service and will have to wait around 22 minutes in the queue (obviously the number may vary depending on which random number series you use). This is hardly in line with the whole idea of saving customer's time through a drive-in service. Not only this is not efficient but it is also not feasible (would you wait for 22 minutes in the queue in the morning just to get coffee?!). It is not difficult to appreciate that as time passes an even longer queue will be formed in this situation and that even the traffic in the area can be easily affected by this. Seeing the results of the simulation models, the manager can immediately conclude that this set-up is not at all acceptable. An obvious solution will be to have two service points in the drive-in. In the next section we use computing simulation software to see how helpful this solution can be.

Naturally, all we are trying to do with this data is ensure the principles of the simulation approach are understood by the relevant managers, so that they are then in a position to understand, and evaluate, the output we get from a computer-based simulation. As we've emphasised, simulation modelling does not provide a solution to the manager – it provides additional information and insight, which may help the decision maker.

Note that in simulation we are interested in covering all the significant variations. This is an important point that can explain why in the hospital example we wanted to simulate more than one day (we simulated 1000 days), however, in this coffee shop example we only need to simulate one (typical) day. What is the difference between the two scenarios?

In the hospital the item (patients) can stay overnight, therefore at the start of the day there are already patients (work in progress) from previous days in the hospital. This is not the case for a coffee shop where customers leave the service area at the end of the day (or at the end of the service time). In a coffee shop every day starts afresh. Therefore, unless there are specific days (like weekends or holidays) where inter-arrival times are different, there won't be any point in running the simulation for more than one day.

However, in both cases (i.e. 1000 days of the local hospital and one day or two hours for the coffee shop) we need to run the simulation more than once (with different series of random numbers) to get a representative idea of likely performance.

In the Appendix we will develop a spreadsheet model to simulate the coffee shop scenario.

Using simulation software

In the above two examples we used manual calculations to simulate the operations. As noted, we can also use spreadsheet software like Excel for the purpose. However the best tool for simulation is dedicated simulation software. There are many good simulation packages available. Here we first explain some of the common features of a typical simulation package and will then illustrate this with a simulation software called Simul8.

The real benefit of simulation can only be appreciated when we use a dedicated computing program in the form of a simulation package. This is mainly due to a number of powerful features of a typical simulation package:

A simulation package requires input information. These are typically 'inter-arrival times', 'service times' and process flow. It is normally possible to choose from a variety of probability distributions for both inter-arrival and service times. The software normally allows you to define different inter-arrival times and service times based on the time of day or the type of service required. This is a very useful feature that allows for a more realistic simulation. Typical simulation software also allows you to define different types of customers, each with a different service requirement. It is also normally possible to introduce shifts in the model so that the user can try different combinations of staffing during the day.

Almost all (discrete event) simulation packages today are on the basis of visual simulation, meaning, instead of working with formulas (as in Excel) you are working with icons on the screen that represent working stations, material, customers, storage areas and flows. You simply put these icons together like a LEGO to build your model and play with them to see the results of different decisions. This is why they are referred to as 'Visual Interactive Simulation'.

A simulation package also has an inbuilt clock that makes a simulation model time-based. It is normally very easy to go forward or backward in time within the simulation model. The programme generates random numbers or pseudo-random numbers for each run of simulation and you can normally run a reasonably complex simulation model hundreds of times within a few minutes.

A simulation model normally provides you with numerous output measures, including time in the system, waiting times, number of items or customers in the queue, utilisation of resources, idle times, etc. These normally come with statistical features like means, standard variations and confidence intervals.

The above features along with many other technical elements of a typical simulation package provide a very rich and strong tool for analysing a complex decision-making problem (where simulation is a suitable tool to use). It will be very easy to trace back the effect of different operational decisions on the model and to explore how the operational outputs are affected by the inputs. It will be very difficult or nearly impossible to do the same level of analysis using formulas and calculations in a spreadsheet or a mathematical model.

Figure 14.4 shows the simulation model of the coffee shop drive-in using the Simul8 software.

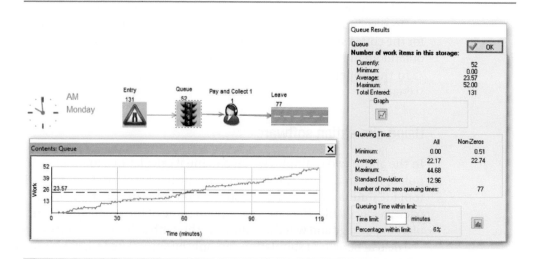

Figure 14.4 Simulation model for the coffee shop with one server, using Simul8

You can see that two hours of the drive-in system is simulated (8:00–10:00 a.m.). As we expected from the short manual calculations in the last section the situation is far from acceptable, let alone ideal. At the end of the two hours there are 52 cars still in the queue and out of 131 cars only 77 are served. The queue graph shows how the queue builds up. The average time in the queue is 22.17 minutes with on average around 24 cars in the queue. The simulation has recorded that the maximum number of cars in the queue has reached 52. If we assume that people are happy to stay in the queue for no more than two minutes, then the bad news is that only 6 per cent of the customers (cars) have a queuing time within the two minutes tolerance.

Let us now examine an obvious solution, that is, adding a second service point. Figure 14.5 shows the simulation of two servers in the system.

As you can see from the graph the queue does build up but only occasionally; at no point are there more than three cars in the queue, and there are plenty of times with no or very little queue. The average queue time is only 0.13. According to the results, all customers (cars) stay in the queue within the 2 minutes tolerance time. This is of course an excellent situation from the customers' point of view. However this is only one side of the story. From the operational side, the situation is still far from acceptable. The utilisation of the servers (as indicated in the model) is only slightly above 50 per cent. This means the two operators are idle almost half of the time, which is clearly a waste of resource.

For easy comparison, the results from the two simulation models are put next to each other in Table 14.9.

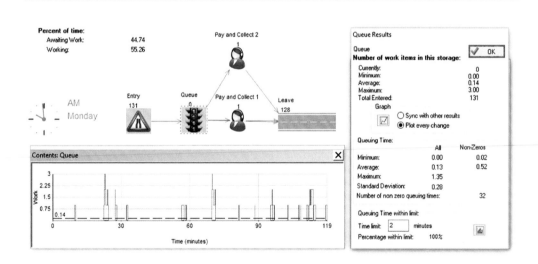

Figure 14.5 Simulation model for the coffee shop with two servers, using Simul8

Table 14.9 Comparison of simulation models for two hours

	Single kiosk	Two kiosks
Average number of cars in the queue	23.57	0.14
Maximum number of cars in the queue	52	3
Average time in the queue	22.17	0.13
Maximum time in the queue	44.68	1.35
Queuing time within two minutes	6%	100%
Awaiting customer	0.86%	44.74%

The striking difference between the outcome of the two models is clear from Table 14.8. We are looking at full utilisation at the cost of long customer waiting times (in the case of one kiosk) versus very short customer waiting times at the cost of very low utilisation (in the case of two kiosks). It is now up to the manager to consider all practical points and to decide what is next. The simulation model can keep exploring options.

What other options do you think may be available here?

Hedge funds eye glamour of movie land

By Matthew Garrahan

Aside from the size of their respective bank balances and a shared fondness for extravagant cars, Hollywood film executives and hedge fund managers would seem to have little in common. After all, hedge funds like to invest in volatile quoted vehicles whereas Hollywood studios put their money into film franchises that can be exploited by their quoted parents. But after a spate of deals that have seen private equity and hedge funds pour money into film production "slates", the two industries are increasingly finding common ground.

The latest example of Hollywood courting the world of high-margin investment came this week when the Paramount studio, a subsidiary of Viacom, struck a $300m financing deal with Dresdner Kleinwort, the investment bank. Under the agreement, Dresdner arranged the funding, which mostly came from hedge-fund and private equity investors. The deal followed similar slate arrangements between rival studios and financial partners, with Warner Brothers, Fox and Universal among those to have bought in outside backers.

Co-financing is not a new phenomenon. High net worth individuals keen on a slice of Hollywood glamour have long associated themselves with the industry by funding film productions. But the interest shown by hedge funds and private equity firms is relatively new, and has been driven on by the need for those investors to find new homes for excess cash. "Private equity and hedge funds are awash with capital and are looking to invest in different asset classes," says Laura Fazio, managing director and head of media, global banking, at Dresdner Kleinwort.

Hollywood has never been an easy place to make money. Over-paid stars, poor accounting practices and box-office flops have historically been enough to deter seasoned financial investors. However, investing in a slate of films helps investors offset the risk of backing a box-office dud. "[Hedge funds and private equity] look at a slate as a portfolio investment, similar to investing in a basket of stocks," says Bill Block, chief executive of QED, which sells and distributes film projects in the US and in international markets.

When the average cost of a film was $40m, says Ms Fazio, co-financing "wasn't as high a priority. But with average budgets having grown to $75m, studios have been more motivated to bring in outside financing partners. Most of the studios are releasing 8–16 films a year which represents a sizeable capital investment."

Like other deals, though, returns will be determined by the success of the films on the slate. Relativity Media, a broker, has enjoyed success with its two Gun Hill Road funds. The first fund raised $600m for investment in 18 projects being developed by Sony Pictures Entertainment and Universal Pictures. An additional $700m was raised for Gun Hill Road II.

The marriages between hedge funds and Hollywood have not always worked, however. Warner Bros' recent $530m six-picture deal with Virtual Studios, a hedge fund backed vehicle, produced *Poseidon*, the year's biggest box-office flop. Equity holders in the movie are believed to have had the value of their investments written down to zero. Other deals have also struggled. Legendary Pictures, founded by Thomas Tull, whose background is in private equity, invested in Warners' *Superman Returns*, *The Lady in the Water* and *The Ant Bully*. All three films produced below-par box-office returns.

But such setbacks have not deterred risk-loving hedge funds. Using a computer model known as a Monte Carlo simulation, fund managers can analyse data from historical slates to estimate returns from unmade films.

Source: Garrahan, M. (2006) Hedge funds eye glamour of movie land, FT.com, 9 October.

Even Hollywood makes use of business simulation!

Practical tips in simulation

Being a descriptive model, it takes some experience to develop and use a suitable simulation model to help with decision making. Here are some practical points to consider when working on a simulation project:

- Always start by determining what performance measures you want to study.
- Simulation is not designed for mimicking every detail of the operations. Keep it simple and use it as a tool to understand how the key performance measures may be affected by different operational scenarios. A very complicated and detailed simulation model is not necessarily a useful one.
- Often an initial analysis of the problem in hand is needed in order to understand what to simulate and what the main elements of the simulation model are.
- Before studying alternative scenarios, make sure that the simulation is representative. Your model should generate figures that are reasonably close to what is happening in reality.
- Keep documenting the simulation elements and check and double check for errors and mistakes.
- Where possible compare the results of a simulation model with the results obtained from a different type of model (e.g. spreadsheet).
- You may find that some parts of the system can easily be studied by simple calculations and that adding these to the simulation model will make the model unnecessarily complicated.
- Simulate only the length of time that contains variations. There is no point in simulating identical situations (as in the coffee shop example where simulating one day was enough).
- Carry out enough runs for your simulation model so that it provides you with representative findings. This is normally done by the use of confidence intervals for the output of the numerous runs of a simulation model (trials).
- There is no standard ending for developing and running a simulation model. In reality and in practice you keep running the model with different scenarios and may change and develop the model as you experiment with it. You continue to do so till you feel you are ready to make an informed decision (or your client/manager is ready to do so).
- Do not get over-excited by the magic of simulation! Only use simulation when it fits the problem in hand. Many problems can be approached much more easily by using simple calculations, spreadsheets, mathematical models or other already established solutions.

Summary

In this chapter we have introduced the principles of simulation modelling as an aid to decision making. We have seen that simulation models are descriptive and frequently based on logic rather than mathematics. They can produce information on the likely outcomes from alternative decisions. As such they can be particularly useful to management when multiple objectives, or qualitative objectives, are being sought. Because the models are built primarily on logic and a description of the key elements of the problem, they can prove attractive to management and decision makers who are unfamiliar with formal quantitative models.

Simulation is a very flexible model and has been developed and applied across a variety of business problems. It is evident from the simple examples used in this chapter that the model could readily be developed to become more complex, and hence realistic. We could add staffing levels to the model, budget allocations, equipment and the like. Equally we could use such a simulation model to assess the impact of changes in the arrival and service rates brought about by some separate management initiative. For example, we might be able to introduce some sort of appointments system for certain patients which might affect the arrivals distribution. The simulation model would allow us to quantify the effects of this on our performance parameters. Equally, medical specialists may be considering altering their diagnosis and treatment methods, which will have a knock-on effect on the service rate (the length of stay).

In one sense, the usefulness of simulation is limited only by the extent to which our imagination and knowledge limit our ability to develop a realistic descriptive model of some situation. Considerable progress has been made in the area of simulation programmes to the extent that for much simulation software you no longer need a working knowledge of computer programming. Visual interactive simulation in particular has made the process of making a simulation model and using it for analysis reasonably easy and fast. There are many Discrete Event Simulation programs available in the market and most of them are good enough for carrying out simple analysis of business operations scenarios. Some programs are more popular than the others and each provides different sets of design capabilities and analytical tools. INFORMS, a global institute of operations management and analytics, has been carrying out a detailed Discrete Event Simulation software comparison survey every two years since 1991, the results of which are published in *OR/MS Today Journal*. This is a well-respected survey supported by the simulation programme vendors themselves. The most recent survey can be found on the INFORMS website.

As a last point, note that in this chapter we are specifically discussing Discrete Event Simulation (DES) and for ease of reference we call it Simulation. In contrast, there is a different type of simulation called Continuous Simulation. DES and Continuous Simulation are both very helpful and widely used. However, in business scenarios where we are looking at the operations level DES is more applicable. Also in general a DES model can run much faster than a Continuous Simulation model. Many of the principles that are discussed here are also true for a Continuous Simulation model.

(For more on the difference between Discrete Event Simulation and Continuous Simulation refer to Michael Pidd (2004) *Computer Simulation in Management Science*, 5th Edition, Wiley.)

QADM IN ACTION Planning theatre time to achieve 18-week elective targets

Summary

Simulation modelling was used to forecast waiting time for elective orthopaedic procedures using different theatre schedules and different rules for allocating patients to surgeons. Spare theatre time is required to absorb fluctuations in demand; waiting time in the model increased rapidly above 85% theatre utilisation. Waiting time could be reduced by using pooled waiting lists, where a patient could be placed on the waiting list of the surgeon with the shortest waiting time. Nearly all the benefits of pooling could be achieved if ~40% of patients were suitable for joining the pooled list. A balance may therefore be struck where most patients can be allocated to a specific specialist surgeon but with others allocated to any surgeon.

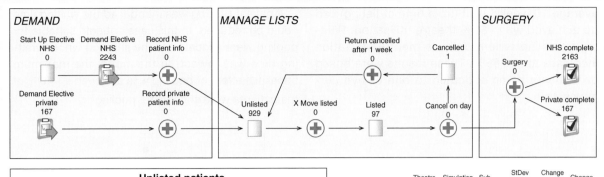

DEMAND

Start Up Elective NHS	Demand Elective NHS	Record NHS patient info
0	2243	0

Demand Elective private	Record private patient info
167	0

MANAGE LISTS

	Return cancelled after 1 week	Cancelled
	0	1

Unlisted	X Move listed	Listed	Cancel on day
929	0	97	0

SURGERY

Surgery	NHS complete
0	2163

	Private complete
	167

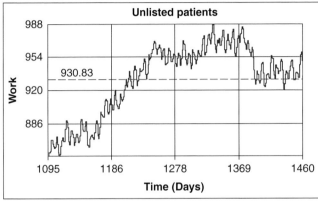

Unlisted patients

Work vs Time (Days)

930.83

| Time values: | 1095 | 1186 | 1278 | 1369 | 1460 |

| Work values: | 886 | 920 | 954 | 988 |

NHS waiting time [weeks]	18.8
NHS % complete in 12 weeks	55

Code	Procedures	Theatre time	Simulation proc ID	Sub specialist	StDev Theatre time	Change over mean	Change over SD
A031	1	176	1	1	56	37	21
A608	1	57	2	1	18	37	21
A611	3	63	3	0	6	16	12
A648	1	165	4	0	53	16	12
A651	159	29	5	0	22	16	12
A661	1	125	6	0	40	16	12
A678	1	69	7	1	22	37	21
A683	11	78	8	0	5	16	12
A688	1	278	9	1	89	37	21
A692	2	30	10	0	1	16	12
A733	19	65	11	0	19	16	12
C866	1	90	13	1	29	37	21
G451	1	123	15	1	39	37	21
L911	1	55	20	1	18	37	21
M421	1	26	24	1	8	37	21
NULL	4	68	25	0	50	16	12
O088	1	172	26	1	55	37	21
O251	1	106	27	1	34	37	21
O278	2	134	28	0	48	37	21
O278	1	149	29	0	48	16	12
O291	160	71	30	0	3	16	12

Session ID	Specialty	Sub Specialty	Weekday	Session length	Theate #	Weekend catch-up
1	14	0	1	210	1	0
2	14	0	2	210	1	0
3	14	0	2	210	1	0
4	14	0	3	210	1	0
5	14	0	3	210	1	0
6	14	1	8	210	1	0
7	14	1	9	210	1	0
8	14	1	9	210	1	0
9	14	1	10	210	1	0
10	14	1	10	210	1	0
11	14	2	2	210	2	0
12	14	2	3	210	2	0
13	14	2	5	210	2	0
14	14	0	8	210	2	0
15	14	0	9	210	2	0

Context

Yeovil District Hospital were planning theatre schedules for new commissioned contracts. They had various possible scenarios and wished to check whether the planned scenarios could cope with the new contracted workloads, whilst achieving 18-week referral to treatment targets.

Method

A simulation was built where patients are referred in proportion to the predicted frequency of required procedures. They were allocated to surgeons' waiting lists with any specialist need (e.g. requirement for specialist theatre). Theatre lists were constructed according to priority of patient and time on waiting list. Cancelled procedures rejoin the waiting list with a higher priority.

Outputs

As the number of scheduled theatre hours increases waiting times reduce but unused theatre time also increases. It is predicted that an average 10 weeks' wait (from time of listing) can be achieved with ~85% theatre utilisation. Waiting times increase rapidly as theatre utilisation increases above 85%. These results were based on patients being allocated to one of five surgeons' lists.

If patient pooling was introduced the waiting time could be reduced. In this case patients suitable for pooling were allocated to the surgeon whose waiting time was lowest. In the model the maximum beneficial effect of pooling was achieved if ~40% of the patients were suitable for pooling

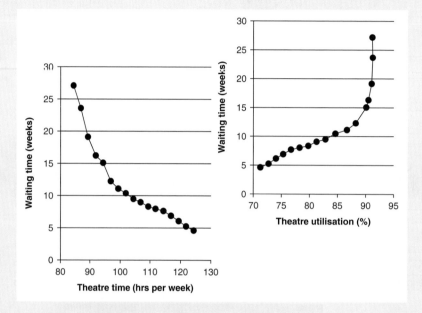

Discussion

There is frequently a pressure to maximise theatre utilisation, as it is one of the most costly resources in a hospital. Complete utilisation can only be achieved when there is a guarantee that all lists can be filled with suitable patients and there is a good range of procedures such that theatre times can be filled (e.g. after a long procedure there may only be time for one short procedure in order to fill theatre time). These conditions can only be met when there is a large pool of patients to draw from, which will necessarily be associated with long waiting time. A compromise therefore must exist between waiting time and theatre utilisation targets. Our modelling suggested this was likely to be at about 85% theatre utilisation.

Waiting times in the model reduced when patients could be pooled between surgeons. Importantly this benefit did not require an 'any patient may be seen by any orthopaedic surgeon' model. Even a small amount of pooling improved waiting times and

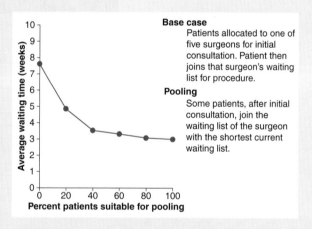

near-maximum benefit was achieved with 40% of patients being suitable for pooling.

Implementation

Yeovil are currently implementing a new theatre schedule backed, in part, by this simulation modelling.

Source: A research report published by PenCLAHRC, NIHR.

Exercises

1   An investigation is being carried out into a local authority's housing policy. The local authority has a limited supply of housing which it owns and rents out. It receives requests for housing from a number of individuals and families throughout the year. Some of these applications come from those who have moved into the area, others from single-parent families, married couples who have separated and so on. With the limited housing stock at its disposal, the authority is unable to allocate every applicant a house or apartment immediately, and inevitably a waiting list has been developed. Elected officials are expressing concern over the size of this waiting list and have told the housing manager to review the existing situation and to class all such applications into one of two categories: urgent and non-urgent.

Urgent cases include those who are homeless at the time of the application and other needy applicants such as those who are victims of domestic violence, those facing eviction from their existing accommodation, and those in substandard housing. Non-urgent cases are subdivided into general applications and those from disabled individuals who have special accommodation requirements.

Once classified as urgent, an application goes to the top of the housing waiting list (or straight into accommodation phase if available) provided no other urgent case is already on the list. If this is the case, then the latest urgent case goes to the end of the list of all other earlier urgent cases. Non-urgent cases are allocated housing points by the housing manager. These points depend on the circumstances of the applicants, with points allocated depending on the number of children in the family, the gender of the applicant, age, income level and whether the applicant is disabled. Housing points allocated to an applicant can vary from zero (the lowest) to 100 (the highest). After all available accommodation has been allocated to urgent cases, remaining vacant housing is allocated to those applicants with the highest number of points.

Applications for housing can be anything up to five per day. Only limited information is available and this is shown in Table 14.10.

Elected officials are pressing for the disabled to be automatically classed as urgent cases. You have decided to carry out a simulation of the existing system to be followed by a simulation of the policy of classifying all disabled applications as urgent.

(a) Draft a short report to elected officials indicating why you think simulation would be suitable for this investigation.

(b) In addition to the information currently available, what other information would you require to enable you to undertake the simulation?

(c) Assuming that such information is available, construct a flowchart for the current policy and the suggested new policy.

Table 14.10   No. of applications for housing

Case type	% of applicants	Number of working days to obtain housing
Urgent	5	3
Non-urgent		
General	80	18
Disabled	15	27

2   You are currently employed by a loan company and have been asked to investigate the company's policy in one particular area of its operations: small amount loans to individual customers. The loans in question are usually short term and for a maximum amount of £2000. The manager responsible for these loans has been asked by head office to recommend a suitable maximum amount that should be available each week. The manager has asked you for advice in this matter and you are considering the use of simulation to assess alternatives.

The information you currently have is limited, but from past records you have noted that the number of customers requesting a loan could be up to five on any one day. Table 14.11 shows the historical distribution of customer requests. You have also determined that, within the maximum allowed loan of £2000, the amount customers wish to borrow could vary, with the full distribution as shown in Table 14.12. When requesting such a loan a customer is given a risk rating on the basis of their past borrowing history, their income level and credit status, with this rating varying between one and three (one indicating the lowest-risk customer). This information is given in Table 14.13. As long as sufficient funds are available on a weekly basis, loans are allocated on a first-come, first-served basis.

Table 14.11   Customer distribution

No. of customers per day	Probability
0	0.10
1	0.20
2	0.30
3	0.15
4	0.15
5	0.10

Table 14.12   Loan requested

Amount borrowed	Proportion of customers (%)
up to £750	5
from £751 up to £1000	15
from £1001 up to £1500	20
from £1501 up to £2000	60

Table 14.13   Priority rankings

Priority rankings	Proportion of customers last year (%)
1	25
2	70
3	5

However, if the demand for loans exceeds the supply of funds, the company has a policy of allocating the following week's funds on a risk-priority basis. So, for example, if a priority 1 customer is unable to get a loan this week because all funds have been allocated, that customer will have priority over any risk 2 or 3 category customers the following week. At present the company makes £20 000 per week available for these loans but is keen to assess whether this sum should be altered.

(a) Develop a suitable simulation flowchart for modelling this situation.

(b) For the current policy of allocating £20 000 of funds each week, simulate the company's operations for 10 days (the company has a five-day week). Use the random number table shown in Table 14.14.

(c) Explain how you would use your model to assist management decision making.

(d) Comment on any assumptions you have had to make to develop the simulation model and the effect these might have on the model's validity.

3   A utility company is currently reviewing its manpower requirements in the domestic-appliance servicing department. One feature of the servicing work relates to domestic central-heating systems. For an annual fee, a trained engineer will undertake a safety check on a customer's domestic central-heating system. As part of the check the engineer will inform the customer of any repair work that needs to be completed, although this work is not done at the time. The majority of such safety checks take place in the autumn of each year. Last year, in one geographical area served by an engineering team, the demand for such servicing was as shown in Table 14.15.

Table 14.14   Random numbers

79	9	44	11	1	50	70	41	6	80
10	47	52	40	59	89	29	95	72	63
77	92	48	85	56	27	5	42	10	55
18	30	52	55	58	85	96	64	92	84
39	28	97	93	78	82	15	59	48	19
35	41	6	1	53	68	32	61	14	29
69	23	19	38	99	59	31	42	79	29
43	72	10	19	16	49	99	82	68	92
60	17	99	24	55	38	54	19	95	87
91	23	97	93	39	64	60	73	29	81

Table 14.15   Gas simulation: service demands

No. of safety checks per day	No. of days
up to 100	10
from 101 up to 125	25
from 126 up to150	30
from 151 up to 175	20
from 176 up to 200	15

Table 14.16 Gas simulation: servicing time

Small-bore system		Large-bore system	
Time required	Probability	Time required	Probability
up to 45 minutes	0.50	up to 35 minutes	0.40
from 46 up to 50 minutes	0.25	from 36 up to 40 minutes	0.40
from 51 up to 55 minutes	0.15	from 41 up to 45 minutes	0.10
from 56 up to 60 minutes	0.10	from 46 up to 50 minutes	0.10

Typically, gas domestic central-heating systems fall into two types: small-bore and large-bore systems. Approximately 25 per cent of engineer visits are to small-bore systems, although this percentage is increasing slowly over time. Depending on the type of system to be checked, some variability occurs in how long each service check takes. Information from last year is shown in Table 14.16.

Naturally, the engineer does not know in advance how long a particular service check will take. The times shown in this table include the engineer's travel time, rest breaks and so on. Engineers typically work an eight-hour shift and are allowed to travel home after completing their last job that day. If, as sometimes happens, an engineer has to work beyond the eight-hour total to complete a job then an overtime payment of £15 per hour or part hour is paid. Normal pay rate for engineers is £10 per hour. The company is trying to review the number of engineers who should be in the team covering this area.

(a) Produce a simulation flowchart for this situation.

(b) Using the random numbers in Table 14.14 simulate this situation for 10 days for a given number of engineers in the team.

(c) Draft a report to management explaining why you think funding should be made available to develop a computer-based simulation model for this problem.

4 You have been asked to help a factory in scheduling production of two products. Product A requires 5 days working on the process I and 22 days working on the process II. Product B requires 3 days working on the process I and 3 days working on the process II. The production manager is interested to know what schedule of production will result in the lowest average completion time for products A and B.

The production manager has heard about simulation and has asked you to use simulation modelling to help with his inquiry.

Explain why and how you should convince the production manager that this is not a simulation problem case and that it is easier to use other methods to reach the desired solution.

Appendix: Simulation with excel

Clearly manual simulation is time-consuming and tedious. In practice simulation problems are developed and solved using specialist simulation software. However, less complex problems can be solved with Excel, or other spreadsheets. We'll illustrate with the simulation we used in the Worked example in the chapter looking at the one kiosk option.

We need to set up a spreadsheet that is effectively in two parts: one part sets out the basic model and the other part shows the simulation results. To model a simulation in Excel we need to use a number of in-built functions. Figure 14.6 shows the basic set-up. We have the service time information in the top left and information about the inter-arrival times in the top middle. The basic performance information we require is shown top right.

In the bottom part of the spreadsheet we show the information that will be calculated for each customer in turn.

We now need to input the formula that will be used for each customer simulation.

Cell B12 = 2*RAND()   Calculate the inter-arrival time for Customer 1

RAND() is an in-built function in Excel that generates a random number greater than or equal to 0 and less than 1.

Cell C12 will show the cumulative arrival time of customers. For Customer 1 this will be the inter-arrival time (= B12) For Customer 2 (and onwards) this would be the cumulative time:

Cell D12 = C12+B13   Calculate the service time for that customer

To do this for our probability distribution we use an Excel function VLOOKUP. This generates a random number using RAND(). Then, using specified cells, Excel looks up the value (= service) associated with that random number. The formula is:

$$= VLOOKUP(RAND(),\$A\$4:\$C\$7,3)$$

	A	B	C	D	E	F	G	H	I	J	K	L
1												
2	Service Time											
3	Lower random	Upper random number	Service time			Inter-arrival time minutes						
4	0	0.8	1			minimum		0		Mean service time		
5	0.81	0.94	2			Maximum		2		Mean waiting time		
6	0.95	0.98	3							Maximum waiting time		
7	0.99	0.99	4							Number waiting		
8												
9												
10	Customer	Inter-arrival time	Arrival time	Service time		Service starts	Service ends	Waiting time				
11												
12	1											
13	2											
14	3											
15	4											
16	5											
17	6											
18												

Figure 14.6 Worksheet, the basic set-up

The specified cells are shown as $A$4:$C$7 and we indicate the values to be used are in column 3.

Cell F12   Calculate the service start time for that customer

For Customer 1 this will be the same as the arrival time

For subsequent customers, this will depend if the previous customer has been served or not. We can use the IF function in Excel.

$$= IF(C13 > G12,C13,G12)$$

(Alternatively we can use Max function: $= MAX(C13,G12)$)
Here, if the arrival time for Customer 2 is greater than the service ends time for Customer 1 then the cell takes the value in C13 otherwise it takes the value in G12.

Cell G12   Calculate the service end time (= Service start time + Service time)
Cell H12   Calculate the time this customer had to wait (if any)

This is the difference between the arrival time and the service start time
Finally we require the performance statistics.
Mean service time: the mean for Column D for Customer 1 to n (use Average function)
Mean waiting time: the mean for Column H for Customer 1 to n (use Average function)
Maximum waiting time: the maximum time in Column F for Customer 1 to n (use MAX function)
The number waiting: a count of the number of customers whose waiting time was greater than 0 (use COUNTIF function)

Obviously the formulas in the spreadsheet need to be copied in the rows till we reach the arrival time of around 120 minutes (given the randomness of the times). This (two hours) will be the end of the service for the drive-in.

Figure 14.7 is a snapshot of the full results for one simulation run. You can see from the summary results that the findings are quite close to the findings of the simulation programme (Figure 14.4).

	A	B	C	D	E	F	G	H	I	J	K	L	M	N
1														
2	Service Time					Inter-arrival								
3	Lower rando	Upper random number	Service time			time	minutes							
4	0	0.8	1			minimum		0			Mean service tim	1.2672		
5	0.81	0.94	2			Maximum		2			Mean waiting tim	20.233		
6	0.95	0.98	3								Maximum waiting	41.303		
7	0.99	0.99	4								Number waiting	112		
8														
9														
10	Custom	Inter-arrival time	Arrival time	Service time		Service starts	Service ends	Waiting time						
11														
12	1	0.573689818	0.573689818	1		0.573689818	1.573689818	0						
13	2	0.717364755	1.291054573	1		1.573689818	2.573689818	0.2826						
14	3	1.943116868	3.234171442	1		3.234171442	4.234171442	0						
15	4	0.877470849	4.11164229	1		4.234171442	5.234171442	0.1225						
16	5	1.357631449	5.469273739	1		5.469273739	6.469273739	0						
17	6	1.621557761	7.0908315	2		7.0908315	9.0908315	0						
18	7	1.291365825	8.382197325	1		9.0908315	10.0908315	0.7086						
19	8	0.723599167	9.105796492	2		10.0908315	12.0908315	0.985						
20	9	0.680660272	9.786456764	1		12.0908315	13.0908315	2.3044						
21	10	1.718052316	11.50450908	3		13.0908315	16.0908315	1.5863						
22	11	1.969339958	13.47384904	1		16.0908315	17.0908315	2.617						
23	12	0.852876942	14.32672598	1		17.0908315	18.0908315	2.7641						
24	13	1.088331835	15.41505781	1		18.0908315	19.0908315	2.6758						
25	14	0.210413895	15.62547171	1		19.0908315	20.0908315	3.4654						
26	15	0.034002859	15.65947457	3		20.0908315	23.0908315	4.4314						
27	16	0.487879029	16.1473536	1		23.0908315	24.0908315	6.9435						
28	17	1.808415128	17.95576873	1		24.0908315	25.0908315	6.1351						
29	18	0.114595061	18.07036379	1		25.0908315	26.0908315	7.0205						
30	19	0.811174154	18.88153794	1		26.0908315	27.0908315	7.2093						
31	20	0.859783801	19.74132174	1		27.0908315	28.0908315	7.3495						
32	21	1.989587942	21.73090968	1		28.0908315	29.0908315	6.3599						
33	22	0.985753875	22.71666356	1		29.0908315	30.0908315	6.3742						
34	23	1.557902432	24.27456599	2		30.0908315	32.0908315	5.8163						

Figure 14.7 Snapshot of the worksheet for the full results

15 Financial Decision Making

Learning objectives

By the end of this chapter you should be able to:

- explain the principles of interest rate calculations
- explain the difference between nominal and effective interest rates
- calculate the net present value
- evaluate investment alternatives using different methods
- calculate and explain the internal rate of return
- evaluate alternative replacement decisions

Many of the models we have developed in earlier chapters have used financial information as part of the decision-making process, although frequently this has simply been one source of information used. In this chapter, we focus specifically on the use of financial information and we shall introduce a number of techniques applied specifically to the evaluation of such information. At the heart of most of these is the principle of interest and interest rate calculations. This leads into an examination of the principles involved in assessing the value of money over time and seeing how this information can be used to evaluate alternative financial decisions. A word of caution is necessary before we start, however. The financial decision area is a veritable minefield in the real world, hedged as it is with tax implications, depreciation allowances, investment and capital allowances and the like. This is one area in particular where the financial expert is needed. Nevertheless, the principles of such financial decision making are established through the concepts of interest and present value – two concepts which we detail in this chapter.

Shareholders need better boards, not more regulation

By Professor Theo Vermaelen

Sir, Prof Eric De Keuleneer blames the "dramatic lowering of ethical standards in the financial sector" for all types of evils, such as the fact that acquirers on average lose money in acquisitions (*Letters*, January 8).

Why do many bidders lose money in acquisitions? While bankers can advise companies, it is ultimately the chief executive who makes the decision. So, one explanation could be that some chief executives do not care too much about shareholder value and benefit personally from becoming bigger (through higher salaries, acquisition bonuses, prestige).

Alternatively, it could be that many chief executives simply do not want to learn finance and rely on their advisers for the valuation of acquisition targets. Whatever the reason, I do not think that the problem can be cured by regulation of the financial sector.

What we need is better governance; that is, board members who defend shareholder interests and understand finance, in particular the subtleties of discounted cash flow valuation techniques.

Theo Vermaelen,
Professor of Finance,
Insead, 77305 Fontainebleau,
France

 Source: Vermaelen, T. (2008) Shareholders need better boards, not more regulation, *Financial Times*, 11 January. © Professor Theo Vermaelen.

A plea for those at the top to better understand financial statistics.

Interest

Most of the principles of financial decision making are based on a simple concept: that of *time preference*. Other things being equal, we would prefer to receive a sum of money now rather than that same sum at some time in the future. Offered a simple choice between receiving £500 now or £500 in one year's time the choice is clear: we would take the money now. The reasons for this are several.

● The future is uncertain, the present less so.
● Inflation will erode the purchasing power of a future sum of money.
● Our personal cash flow might be such that we need the money now.
● There is an opportunity cost involved in waiting to receive the sum of money, since if we took the money now we could invest it or we could use it to purchase goods and services from which we derive satisfaction now.

This last point is particularly relevant for financial decision making, since it leads directly into the issue of interest. Consider your local bank. It approaches you, the customer, with the offer that if you deposit your savings of £500 with the bank for a year, at the end of that time the bank will return £500 to you. Clearly such an offer is totally unattractive, given the 'sacrifice' you have to make over the next 12 months: going without the £500 for one year. The bank has to offer you some inducement to part with your cash. Such an inducement is the interest it is willing to pay. In effect, the bank will offer to pay you not £500 in a year's time but £500 plus a financial reward.

Interest rate calculations are straightforward but they lead us into some important areas, so we shall take some time to explore their principles. Let us consider the sum of money you have available, £500, and denote this as the principal, P. The bank offers to pay you interest on the amount you give it at a rate of 8 per cent per year (per annum, or p.a.). At the end of the year your savings with the bank would be worth:

$$£500 + 8\%(£500) = £500 + £40 = £540$$

If we show the rate of interest as a decimal, we can generalise this as:

$$500 + 0.08(500) = 500(1 + 0.08)$$

or denoting the rate of interest as r:

$$P(1 + r)$$

If you left your savings in the bank for a second year you would have:

$$540(1 + 0.08)$$

but since:

$$540 = 500(1 + 0.08)$$

this gives:

$$500(1 + 0.08)(1 + 0.08) = 500(1 + 0.08)^2$$

It is easy to see the pattern and what the calculation for Year 3 would be:

$$540(1 + 0.08)^3$$

or in general:

$$P(1 + r)^t$$

where t is the number of periods for which we wish to calculate the interest payment. In fact this formula can be used in a variety of ways. If we denote V as the value of a sum of money in the future, we have:

$$V = P(1 + r)^t$$

but we can rearrange this as:

$$P = \frac{V}{(1 + r)^t}$$

to show the sum we must invest now, P, in order for this to increase to V in t periods of time at a rate of interest, r. Similarly, we can obtain:

$$r = \sqrt[t]{\frac{V}{P}} - 1$$

to determine the rate of interest which will increase a given principal to a known future sum after t periods. To illustrate, consider the following example. A small company knows that in five years a piece of equipment will need replacing. The best estimate is that at that time the equivalent equipment will cost £30 000. The company has the option of investing a sum of money now at a rate of interest of 6 per cent per annum to fund the equipment purchase.

Progress Check 15.1

How much does the company need to invest now in order to be able to purchase the equipment in five years?

Using the second formula we have:

$$P = \frac{V}{(1 + r)^t}$$

with V = 30000, r = 0.06 and t = 5 giving:

$$P = \frac{30000}{(1.06)^5} = \frac{30000}{1.3382} = £22418$$

as the sum that must be invested now. This sum, £22 418, will have increased to £30 000 in five years at a rate of interest of 6 per cent. Consider a variant on this problem. The company has decided that its current cash flow will not allow such an investment to be made at present. The maximum amount the company can afford at the moment is £20 000.

Progress Check 15.2

What rate of interest is required if the company's investment is to grow sufficiently to purchase the equipment in the future?

Using the third formula we have:

$$P = 20000$$

$$V = 30000$$

$$t = 5$$

$$r = \sqrt[t]{\frac{V}{P}} - 1$$

$$r = \sqrt[5]{\frac{30000}{20000}} - 1$$

$$= 1.084 - 1 = 0.084$$

Or a required rate of interest of 8.4 per cent. Clearly, if the company cannot find such an investment opportunity, it will have to budget for a shortfall in the money it has available for purchasing the replacement equipment in the future.

Nominal and effective interest

The formulae we have developed have been shown for periods of a year or more. In practice they can be used for any calendar period: quarters, months, days. For example, consider a credit card company charging interest on the amount of outstanding debt that you owe. Such an interest charge will typically be calculated monthly. The formulae can be used, as long as we divide the annual rate of interest by 12 and multiply the number of time periods by 12. However, it is more instructive to consider the difference between what is known as the *nominal* rate of interest and the *effective* rate of interest. Consider a situation where you invest £500 in a savings account which adds interest at the end of every month, and that the current annual rate is 9 per cent. After five years the money in the account will be:

$$V = 500(1 + 0.09/12)^{60} = 500(1.0075)^{60} = £782.84$$

You will be able to see that if the interest had been calculated annually the sum would have been £769.31. The rate of interest quoted – 9 per cent per annum – is generally referred to as the *nominal* rate of interest. The rate actually earned, which is more than 9 per cent per annum, is known as the *effective* rate or the *annual percentage rate* (APR) frequently seen quoted in financial advertisements. The APR can be calculated using the formula:

$$APR = \left(1 + \frac{r}{t}\right)^{t} - 1$$

where r is the nominal rate and t the number of periods during the year when interest is calculated. Here this would give:

$$\begin{aligned} APR &= \left(1 + \frac{0.09}{12}\right)^{12} - 1 \\ &= 1.094 - 1 \\ &= 0.094 \end{aligned}$$

or 9.4 per cent as the APR. The APR is a quick and easy method of comparing different options when the frequency of interest calculations might vary. For example, you are thinking of investing a sum of money for a 10-year period. One investment firm is offering a rate of interest of 6.4 per cent with interest added quarterly. A second is offering 6.2 per cent added monthly. Which is preferable? By calculating and comparing the APRs we see that option 1 has an APR of 6.56 per cent and option 2 has an APR of 6.38 per cent. Option 1 is therefore to be preferred.

I am confused about the meaning of different quoted interest rates – e.g. APR, AGR, AER. Please explain?

By Sarah Ross

You are not alone in your confusion, particularly because banks and credit card companies have different ways of calculating and applying rates. Things should improve a bit in the future since, from March, banks have to include an "honesty box" in all credit card marketing which gives consumers clear information on what annual percentage rates and other charges they will pay. All companies will have to use one method of calculating annual rates on cards rather than the two used up until now.

APR (Annual Percentage Rate) is the term used on a fixed repayment schedule – for example a fixed rate loan involving fixed repayment amounts. It means the customer will know the number of repayments, the repayment amount and the time period for the repayments.

AER or EAR (Equivalent Annual Rate) is quoted for overdrafts so that (in theory) customers can compare rates across institutions. The calculation does not include fees, which are quoted separately.

Barclaycard says the main difference between APR and AER (or EAR as it prefers to call it) is that EARs are a "cut-down" version of an APR applicable to overdrafts (because an overdraft does not have key features needed to do a full-blown APR calculation). They also say they have never heard of AGR although they guess it may be a reference to an annual gross rate on a savings product. That would be the rate, gross of tax, on a product which paid interest annually.

In the savings world, the term AER (Annual Equivalent Rate) is used and is the same as EAR, that is, the annualised gross rate to show the effect of compounding interest (even though in fact interest may be paid monthly or quarterly).

 Source: Ross, S. (2004) Is money in my account mine?, FT.com, 7 April.

Confused by rates? You're not the only one.

Present value

We can also use these basic principles to introduce a particularly important concept in financial decision making: that of *present value*. Using the formula we have developed, we are able to calculate what a sum of money now would be worth at some time in the future. For example, £1000 now would grow to £1050 in one year at a rate of interest of 5 per cent, to £1102.50 in two years and so on. Consider this information from a slightly different perspective. If you were offered £1000 now or £1050 in one year, which would you prefer? If we make a number of heroic assumptions, the answer will be that you are indifferent between the two; you have no preference. The logic behind this is that if you took the £1000 now it would be worth the same as the £1050 in one year's time anyway. Effectively what we have done is to calculate the value *now* of a future sum of money. The £1000 is denoted as the *present value* of £1050 in one year's time. Of course it is also the present value of £1102.50 in two years' time. As we indicated, such indifference is based on a number of assumptions. In particular that:

● we ignore the effects of inflation;
● there is no risk involved in waiting;
● interest rates will remain stable.

In more complex applications it is possible to incorporate the relaxation of such assumptions into the calculations, but for our purposes we shall ignore them as they do not alter the fundamental principles involved. In general the present value of a future sum is given by:

$$PV = \frac{V}{(1 + r)^t} \text{ or } V \times \frac{1}{(1 + r)^t}$$

with r generally referred to as the *discount rate* and the term $1/(1 + r)^t$ as the *discount factor*.

This is basically the same formula that we had before, but here instead of P (Principal) we are using PV (present value).

Pre-calculated tables of discount factors are available and are also easily calculated in a spreadsheet. Present value is particularly important in the area of investment appraisal, which we shall turn to shortly. For the present we shall illustrate its use with a simple example. Some years ago you invested a sum of money into a scheme which guaranteed a return of £5000 at a specified future date. That date is six years from today. However, you really would like to get your hands on the money now if at all possible because you want to buy a car. A friend has indicated that he is willing to give you £3500 now in return for your savings scheme. That is, he will give you £3500 and you sign over your rights to the £5000 return in six years' time. Should you take his offer? To help make a decision we can apply the present-value principles. Let us assume that current interest rates are 7 per cent per annum and you believe they will remain at that level for the next six years.

Progress Check 15.3

Calculate the present value of the £5000 and decide whether you would take up your friend's offer.

The present value of the £5000 is then:

$$PV = \frac{5000}{(1.07)^6} = £3332$$

That is, £5000 in six years' time has an equivalent value of £3332 today. If offered £3332 today or £5000 in six years' time you would not be bothered which you received (other things being equal). However, your friend is actual offering you £3500 not £3332. In this case you are being offered more than the present value of your investment. Other things being equal, you should take your friend's offer. Of course, the catch lies in the term 'other things being equal'. We would clearly want to consider all other factors in the situation as we usually do with all our models. In particular we might wish to consider the assumption about the rate of interest remaining at 7 per cent and the effect this has on our decision.

Progress Check 15.4

Recalculate the PV if the interest rate is 5 per cent.

Logically at a different rate of interest the PV of the future sum will alter. In general, if the rate of interest is higher, the PV falls and vice versa. In this case, with an interest rate of 5 per cent, the PV increases to £3731. Your friend's offer is now less than the PV based on a discount rate of 5 per cent and should not be accepted. This may well explain of course why your friend is making such an offer. He may well have a different view from yourself about future interest rates. If he believes interest rates will fall – and they do – he will stand to gain from the transaction.

Inflation

As we indicated, one critical assumption in the calculations relates to that of zero inflation. In practice, if we have a view about future levels of inflation we can take this into account by using, as the discount factor, not the actual rate of interest but the real rate of interest, where:

$$\text{Real rate of interest} = \text{Actual rate} - \text{Rate of inflation}$$

So, if the actual rate of interest is 7 per cent and we anticipate a rate of inflation of 2 per cent, the real rate of interest is 5 per cent. Again, different perceptions of the future rate of inflation can explain differences in behaviour and choice.

Investment appraisal

Present value is particularly useful when it comes to evaluating alternative projects in financial terms. To illustrate this, and introduce related methods, we shall develop an example. A printing firm is reviewing its current production facilities. Some of its printing equipment has reached the end of its useful working life and the firm is considering replacing this with the latest computer-based equipment. Such equipment will be costly but the firm expects to be able to reduce its staffing levels to compensate. Two options are currently under review.

Option A   Under Option A the firm will purchase a standard piece of equipment at a cost of £12 000 payable now. Over the next five years, however, the firm expects to be able to reduce its staffing costs by £4000 per year in the first three years and then by £3500 in Year 4 and £3000 in Year 5. At the end of the five years the equipment would have reached the end of its life and would need replacing.

Option B   Under Option B the firm would purchase a slightly more sophisticated piece of equipment for an initial cost of £15 000. In the first two years staff cost savings are estimated to be £4500 and £5000 respectively. In Year 3, however, the equipment would need major refurbishment at an additional cost of £5000. Staff cost savings in Years 3, 4 and 5 would be £5500, £6000 and £6500. At the end of the five years the equipment would have reached the end of its life and would need replacing.

The firm is seeking advice, in financial terms, as to its recommended decision. Clearly the firm faces two alternative decisions (actually three, since it could decide to buy neither machine) with different financial consequences. It will help if we summarise the financial information we have in tabular form. Table 15.1 shows the cash flow of the two options. For each option we show cash outflows (expenditure) and the cash inflows (income or cost savings), with the cumulative net cash flow being the difference between the two as every year passes. We see that Option A generates a positive net cash flow at the end of the five years of £6500 and Option B of £7500. On the face of it, Option B looks preferable since it generates a higher positive cash flow. However, there are a number of different approaches we could take in terms of identifying a preference for either option. The approaches we will be looking at here are payback method, rate of return and net present value. We will also look at the internal rate of return approach that relates to net present value.

Table 15.1 Cash flow projections

Period	Option A			Option B		
	Cash outflow	Cash inflow	Cumulative net cash flow	Cash outflow	Cash inflow	Cumulative net cash flow
0 (now)	12 000		−12 000	15 000		−15 000
1		4 000	−8 000		4 500	−10 500
2		4 000	−4 000		5 000	−5 500
3		4 000	0	5 000	5 500	−5 000
4		3 500	+3 500		6 000	+1 000
5		3 000	+6 500		6 500	+7 500
Total	12 000	18 500	6 500	20 000	27 500	7 500

QADM IN ACTION

Capgemini – cost–benefit analysis

Capgemini's client was a group of companies in the heavy buildings material business. The client had recognised the need for an IT system that would allow it to streamline business process across the group's companies. A joint client/Capgemini team was required to undertake a scoping exercise to assess whether a bespoke system should be developed or whether a specific off-the-shelf system would meet the client's needs. To enable the comparison to be made, cost and benefit information for the two options for each of the companies was pulled together into a summary model. This model then provided the basis for the client's capital expenditure proposal allowing the different IT options to be assessed.

Working closely with the company financial directors and other members of the joint team, one of the consultants developed a spreadsheet-based cost/benefit model.

The spreadsheet-based model used the incremental costs and benefits of the different IT options.

The model manipulated the cost/benefit streams over time into a format that was suitable for input into the client's own capital expenditure appraisal model. A common template was used across the companies to ensure that a consistent approach was used to collect the necessary data. A workshop was also organised to ensure that the quantification of expected benefits was also consistent.

The benefits are as follows:

- The development of a management tool to identify and quantify the expected benefits from the IT options.

- Generating summary financial information in the format required by the client's own capital expenditure appraisal model.

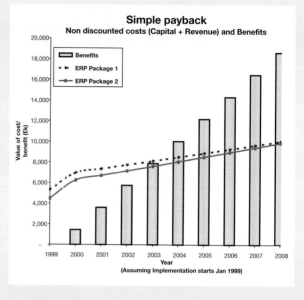

Source: Based on a Capgemini case study, with thanks to Capgemini for permission to use their material.

Payback method

This approach is particularly simple and measures the number of time periods, years and months in this case, it would take to recover the cost of the investment. Effectively the payback method determines when the net cash flow turns positive. In the case of Option A this occurs at the end of Year 3, so this option would have a payback period of three years. In the case of Option B the net cash flow turns positive before the end of Year 4. If we assume a constant stream of cash flow in Year 4 the exact payback period would be 3 years 10 months. On this basis, Option A would be preferred since it has a shorter payback period, meaning it will pay back the original investment in a shorter time.

Although crude and simple, the method does have the advantage of weighting early positive cash flows at the expense of later ones. Given that, in principle, cash flows at later periods are more uncertain and hence riskier, the payback method adopts a relatively 'safe' approach. However, it does have obvious disadvantages. It ignores the total profitability of projects and it ignores cash flows after the end of the payback period.

Rate of return

The second method calculates a rate of return on projects, showing annual profit as a percentage of capital investment. In the case of Option A the total profit is £6500 and over a five-year period this gives an annual profit of £1300, which as a percentage of the total investment, £12 000, gives 10.8 per cent as a rate of return on the investment. For Option B we would obtain a return of 7.5 per cent on investment (note the total investment for Option B is 15 000 + 5000), and Option A would be preferred as it gives the higher return. Although the calculation relates profit to the size of the investment, it clearly does not take the timing of the returns into account, simply preferring those projects which have a higher overall return regardless of when in time this return occurs.

Table 15.2 Net present value: Option A

Period	Cash outflow	Cash inflow	Net cash flow	Discount factor	Present value
0	12 000		−12 000	1.0000	−12 000
1		4 000	4 000	0.9259	3 703.60
2		4 000	4 000	0.8573	3 429.20
3		4 000	4 000	0.7938	3 175.20
4		3 500	3 500	0.7350	2 572.50
5		3 000	3 000	0.6806	2 041.80
Total	12 000	18 500	6 500		2 922.30

Net present value

The final method brings us back to the concept of present value. Clearly, given the timings of the cash flows of the two projects, we ought to assess the present values of the two alternatives to help us choose between them, something neither of the other two methods considered. To apply this method we need to establish a discount rate, which we will set at 8 per cent ($r = 0.08$). This might, for example, represent the real cost of capital for the company. Table 15.2 shows the calculation for Option A.

In addition to the cash flows the calculated discount factor ($1/(1 + r)^t$) is shown, together with the net cash flow for each period multiplied by this factor (the present value of each of these cash flows). The column total that we obtain, £2922.30, is the net present value for this option. That is, assuming a discount rate of 8 per cent, the sum of £2922.30 now and the stream of cash flows as shown for Option A over the next five years are seen as being identical. Such a calculation weights individual cash flows using the present-value principle. We could repeat the calculation for Option B to help choose between them. Other things being equal, a higher net present value (NPV) is the preferred option.

Progress Check 15.5

Calculate the NPV for Option B at a discount rate of 8 per cent. Which option would you recommend?

The NPV for Option B is calculated at £2683.85. On this basis, Option A would be recommended since it generates the higher NPV. The reason for this is clear. Although Option B generates a higher net cash flow, much of this occurs some years in the future. By definition, the opportunity cost of such future sums is high and the NPV takes the timings of the cash flows into account, giving more priority to those early on in the life of the project.

In practice, the NPV method is the one to be favoured in project appraisal, although the first two methods do have their uses. However, the one problem with the NPV method is that it assumes a particular, constant discount rate. We have seen earlier how a different rate may well affect the decision we take. Higher rates, other things being equal, lead to a lower NPV and vice versa. To avoid this problem, a method which relates to NPV is often used.

Internal rate of return

This method calculates what is known as the internal rate of return (IRR). Effectively this is the discount rate for a given project which will give an NPV of zero, and each project will have a different IRR. It may seem odd that we would want to calculate such a result, but logic will help us see why. Consider Option A. At a rate of 8 per cent it has a positive NPV. If this rate increases, the NPV will fall. We repeat this process until we find the rate – the IRR – which gives a zero NPV. We now have a yardstick with which to assess the project. As long as the actual discount rate is lower than the IRR then we know the project will have a positive NPV. In other words, the IRR method removes the need to justify a specific discount rate and simply requires us to assess whether we think it will ever exceed the IRR during the life of the project.

There are a number of ways of determining the IRR for a project. One method uses a formula. To use this requires us to calculate the NPV for a project at two different discount rates, preferably one with a positive NPV and one with a negative. For example, for Option A we already have:

$$NPV_1 = £2922$$
$$r_1 = 8\%$$

Terra Firma sued over 'modelling flaw'

By Megan Murphy in London

The pressure-cooker working environment of Guy Hands' Terra Firma may have driven two executives to conceal a critical error in the cash flow projections for the collapsed television rentals business Boxclever, a court was told on Monday. Natixis, the French bank, is suing the private equity firm for allegedly producing a flawed financial model for Boxclever during a £750m ($1.5bn) refinancing in 2002. The company defaulted on the debt less than a year after the deal closed.

Joe Smouha QC, Natixis's lawyer, compared the alleged modelling blunders to the rogue trader scandal at Société Générale, suggesting that high-earning bankers paralysed by "fear of failure" might have dug themselves deeper into a hole. "What this case is about is what life is really like in the City, where enormous amounts of pressure are put on individuals," Mr Smouha told the High Court.

The high-profile dispute, originally scheduled to start last month, poses a threat to more than Terra Firma's reputation. Natixis, which once held £200m worth of Boxclever notes, has already settled a related lawsuit against two other financial institutions that worked on the securitisation: Germany's WestLB and the Canadian lender CIBC. Terra Firma, as the only remaining defendant, faces a pay-out of tens of millions of pounds if it loses the case.

Natixis's case now centres on whether two Terra Firma executives, Paul Spinks and Quentin Stewart, knew the financial model for the Boxclever deal was flawed but failed to raise the alarm. Like most securitisations, the financing was based on a complex model of future cash flows, such as rental income from customers. Natixis claims Mr Spinks introduced a crucial error into those projections, leading to an overstated calculation of Boxclever's "net present value".

While Natixis bought £200m worth of Boxclever debt based on an estimated net present value of £943m, the real NPV was as much as 44 per cent lower, the French lender said. Mr Smouha claimed the Terra Firma team working on the securitisation was under constant pressure to close the transaction. With the private equity firm in the midst of launching its first fund, a failure to complete the Boxclever deal would have been "disastrous", Mr Smouha said.

Terra Firma denies wrongdoing and says Mr Spinks and Mr Stewart had no motive for concealing an obvious modelling flaw that would have destroyed their careers and the firm's reputation.

The case continues.

NPV calculations can be very contentious.

If we were to repeat the calculation for, say, r = 20% we would obtain an NPV of −£681. If we denote:

$$NPV_2 = -£681$$
$$r_2 = 20\%$$

then the formula for estimating the IRR is given as:

$$IRR = r_1 + (r_2 - r_1)\frac{|NPV_1|}{|NPV_1| + |NPV_2|}$$

where $|NPV|$ is the absolute value of the NPV figure. We would then have:

$$IRR = 8 + (20 - 8)\frac{|2922|}{|2922| + |681|} = 17.73\%$$

That is, a discount rate of 17.7 per cent would give Option A an NPV of zero. Logically, as long as the discount rate in the real world is below the IRR, we know that Option A will have a positive NPV. If management are convinced that over the life of this project the discount rate will not rise above 17.7 per cent, they know the project will continue to have a positive NPV.

Progress Check 15.6

Calculate the IRR for Option B.

Using a second rate of 20 per cent we calculate the IRR for Option B at 14.9 per cent. The IRR is another method for choosing between projects. We made our earlier decisions, based on the NPVs, assuming a discount rate of 8 per cent. It is unlikely that this would remain constant over the life of the project. However, we know that as long as the discount rate does not exceed 17.7 per cent then Option A will generate a positive NPV. For Option B, however, the IRR is lower, so a smaller rise in the discount rate would turn the current positive NPV into a negative. Option B is more 'at risk' from an increasing discount rate than is Option A.

We should note that the formula we have used provides an estimate of the IRR. The reason for this is somewhat technical but basically relates to the fact that the formula allows us to calculate a linear approximation to the IRR when, in practice, the relationship is a non-linear one. Generally, the loss in accuracy is small and irrelevant for the use to which the IRR is put. A more accurate estimation can usually be provided by developing a small spreadsheet program which allows for iterative calculations. If we were to do this we would find the IRR for Option A to be 17.29 per cent and for Option B to be 14.16 per cent.

Deal offers distant benefits for consumers and security for EDF

By Sylvia Pfeifer, Elizabeth Rigby and Jim Pickard

Why is the government's deal with EDF to build a new nuclear plant in Somerset so important?

The two new reactors at Hinkley Point will provide 7 per cent of the UK's electricity and are a key building block in the government's attempts to attract £110bn of investment into low-carbon energy infrastructure. Around 60 per cent of the country's current generation capacity – ageing nuclear power stations and polluting coal-fired plants – is due to close in coming years. Ministers say Hinkley Point is crucial to help Britain keep the lights on and meet carbon reduction targets.

The government has agreed a "strike price" of £92.50 per megawatt hour (MWh), linked to inflation, to be paid for 35 years to EDF and its partners. In essence, it is guaranteeing them a price for their electricity. The aim is to help reduce the investment risk of the project which has high upfront capital costs and is expected to cost £16bn.

EDF says it expects an internal rate of return (IRR) of around 10 per cent. According to Tony Ward, head of power and utilities at EY, the consultants, this is "quite a tight IRR" given the scale and size of the project and the fact that EDF and its partners are taking on the construction risk. Investors in gas-fired power plants would typically expect an IRR above 10 per cent, while those in wind generation would expect an IRR of 10–13 per cent during the construction phase, he says, although this typically drops to 7–8 per cent once the plants are operational.

 Source: Pfeifer, S., Rigby, E. and Pickard, J. (2013) Deal offers distant benefits for consumers and security for EDF, FT.com, 21 October. © The Financial Times Limited. All Rights Reserved.

IRR calculations can be critical in assessing the viability of large projects.

Replacing equipment

Every business organisation is periodically faced with decisions about the replacement of equipment. On a production line the decision relates to a robot-controlled machine tool, in an office to the photocopier, in many organisations to the company car, in a hospital to a specialised brain scanner. The decision for the manager relates to staying with the existing equipment – and probably incurring additional costs in terms of maintenance and repair – or buying a replacement, which requires a hefty initial investment.

Obviously, there will come a point with any piece of equipment where it will be cheaper to buy new equipment than to keep incurring the expense of repairing the old. Naturally, any such decision will not be made purely on a comparison of these costs. Other factors will need to be taken into account: whether the company's cash flow will finance a replacement this year, whether the capital budget has sufficient funds for the new equipment, whether the general manager will sanction such an investment, whether quality is adversely affected to the point where the decision has to be made. One approach that can be developed is to assess the financial information available in terms of keeping the existing equipment and determining when these costs are at a minimum in terms of the replacement decision. Consider the following example. An organisation has bought a piece of equipment for £50 000. The value of the machine – in terms of its potential resale value – decreases over time as the equipment gets older, but the organisation's accountant has estimated that the resale values will be as shown in Table 15.3.

That is, after one year the equipment will have dropped in value to £20 000 and to £1000 by the end of Year 7. (If you have ever bought a new car you will know the feeling of such 'depreciation'.) Clearly, this loss in value over time represents a 'cost' to the organisation: at the end of every year it has 'lost' a sum of money that it could have had by selling the machine one year earlier.

The other obvious cost that the organisation will incur by keeping the machine will be the running costs: operating costs, energy costs, maintenance and repair. For this piece of equipment the estimated running costs over the next seven years are shown in Table 15.4.

Table 15.3   Resale value

	Value (£s)
Now	50 000
End Year 1	20 000
End Year 2	15 000
End Year 3	12 000
End Year 4	10 000
End Year 5	9 000
End Year 6	5 000
End Year 7	1 000

Table 15.4   Resale value and running costs (£s)

Year	Resale value	Running costs
1	20 000	7 000
2	15 000	7 700
3	12 000	8 500
4	10 000	9 500
5	9 000	10 500
6	5 000	13 000
7	1 000	18 000

As we might expect, the running costs associated with the equipment increase over time as the equipment ages. It seems logical to try to assess when the equipment should be replaced by seeking to determine when these costs are at a minimum (remember the approach in Chapter 12 on stock control). The approach we can develop is to calculate the total costs incurred by keeping the equipment a certain length of time and comparing the average annual cost of the various replacement options. For example, at the end of Year 1 the costs we have incurred (as a result of deciding not to replace the equipment) are:

Loss of resale value: £30 000 (50 000 − 20 000)

Running costs: £7000

giving total costs of £37 000. This is the total cost of deciding not to replace before the end of Year 1. Since the machine has had a useful life of one year, the average total cost will be £37 000/1 or £37 000. For Year 2 a similar approach can be taken. Since the equipment had an initial value of £50 000, the loss in resale value of not replacing in either Year 1 or Year 2 is:

Loss of resale value: 50 000 − 15 000 = 35 000

Running costs: 7 000 + 7700 = 14 700

giving a total cost over the first two years of £49 700 and an average cost per year of £24 850 (49 700/2). Clearly, we can repeat these calculations for each further year we keep the equipment.

Progress Check 15.7

For Years 3 to 7 calculate the average total cost incurred by not replacing the equipment.

Table 15.5 shows the detailed calculations.

The column headed Value cost indicates the cost incurred by keeping the equipment to that time in terms of the resale value, and is calculated as £50 000 less that year's resale value. The next column – Cumulative running costs – shows the total running costs incurred up to that point. The Cumulative total cost is the sum of the previous two columns. The last column – Average cost – is the Cumulative total cost divided by the number of years the equipment has been in use. We see that these average costs are at their lowest at the end of Year 5. This is when, other things being equal, this equipment should be replaced.

Present value

This decision, however, does not take the time value of money into account. It is evident that we could use the discounting principles introduced earlier to examine the average cost expressed in present-value terms rather than money terms. Let us first consider the resale value. By the end of Year 1 the resale value is £20 000. However, because this is in the future its present value will be lower. Assume the organisation's cost of capital is 5 per cent per annum calculated on a monthly basis. The discount factor will then be:

$$\frac{1}{(1.00417)^{12}} = 0.9513$$

and the present value will then be £20 000 × 0.9513 = £19 026. The corresponding value cost will be:

$$£50\,000 - £19\,026 = £30\,974$$

Table 15.5　Average cost (£s)

Year	Value	Running costs	Value cost	Cumulative running costs	Cumulative total cost	Average cost
1	20 000	7 000	30 000	7 000	37 000	37 000
2	15 000	7 700	35 000	14 700	49 700	24 850
3	12 000	8 500	38 000	23 200	61 200	20 400
4	10 000	9 500	40 000	32 700	72 700	18 175
5	9 000	10 500	41 000	43 200	84 200	16 840
6	5 000	13 000	45 000	56 200	101 200	16 867
7	1 000	18 000	49 000	74 200	123 200	17 600

Progress Check 15.8

Calculate the discount factors for the remaining years and the value cost each year in present-value terms.

Table 15.6 Value cost in present-value terms (£s)

Year	Value	Discount factor	Present value	Value cost at present value
1	20 000	0.9513	19 026	30 973
2	15 000	0.9050	13 575	36 425
3	12 000	0.8609	10 330	39 668
4	10 000	0.8189	8 189	41 809
5	9 000	0.7791	7 011	42 987
6	5 000	0.7411	3 706	46 294
7	1 000	0.7052	705	49 295

Table 15.6 shows the value cost each year in present-value terms.

Clearly, discounting has the effect of increasing the value cost. The same calculation can be undertaken on running costs. However, it is more realistic here to assume that running costs are incurred through the year rather than at the end of the year. The discount factor for the first year will then be calculated as:

$$\frac{1}{(1.00417)^6} = 0.9513$$

We use a discount factor for six months to allow for the fact that running costs will average at half their end-of-year amount. This will give a present value for the annual running costs of £6827. The calculation for Year 2 will be the same but using 6 + 12 as the exponent for the discount factor.

Progress Check 15.9

Calculate the present value for running costs for Years 2 to 7.

Table 15.7 shows the running costs expressed in present-value terms together with the cumulative running costs.

The same logic can now be applied as before. We can calculate the total costs each year (value cost plus cumulative running costs) but with this expressed in present-value terms. This total cost can then be averaged over the life of the equipment to assess what time period represents the least-cost replacement. Table 15.8 shows the summary results.

This indicates that the optimal replacement occurs at the end of Year 6. Clearly, as with any present-value calculation, the result is based on the assumption that the cost of

Table 15.7 Running costs in present-value terms (£s)

Year	Running costs	Discount factor	Present value	Cumulative present value
1	7 000	0.9753	6 827	6 827
2	7 700	0.9278	7 144	13 971
3	8 500	0.8826	7 502	21 473
4	9 500	0.8396	7 977	29 450
5	10 500	0.7987	8 387	37 837
6	13 000	0.7598	9 878	47 715
7	18 000	0.7228	13 011	60 726

Table 15.8 Total costs in present-value terms (£s)

Year	Value cost at present value	Cumulative running costs at present value	Total cost	Average cost
1	30 973	6 827	37 800	37 800
2	36 425	13 971	50 396	25 198
3	39 668	21 473	61 141	20 381
4	41 809	29 450	71 259	17 815
5	42 987	37 837	80 824	16 165
6	46 294	47 715	94 009	15 668
7	49 295	60 726	110 021	15 717

capital at 5 per cent will remain constant. It is evident, however, that this basic model is easily updated to allow management to perform 'what-if' analysis in terms of changes to the key parameters.

Worked example

A company, WWE, has decided to install a new networked computer system. Initial discussions with the preferred supplier have indicated that WWE faces two basic options.

Option 1   WWE can purchase the system outright for an initial sum of £45 000. The sum includes a maintenance contract from the supplier for the first 12 months. At the end of the first year (and at the end of each subsequent year) WWE can purchase an annual maintenance contract for £2500. At the end of five years the system will be obsolete and will have a scrap value of £1000.

Option 2 Alternatively, WWE can lease the system from the computer supplier. WWE will pay £12 000 now and a further £12 000 per annum at the end of each subsequent year. So, the second lease payment will be due at the end of the first year (to pay for the system through Year 2) and so on. At the end of five years the system will be scrapped, but its scrap value will go to the supplier not to WWE. The leasing fee also includes maintenance.

Assume again, the group's current cost of capital is 10 per cent.
Quite simply, which of the two alternatives should WWE choose?

It is usually essential to draw up a table of the timings of any cash flows in this sort of problem. As we have seen with NPV calculations, the timings are at the heart of the calculations. The cash flows for the options are shown in Table 15.9.

Note that in this case the 'year' refers to the end of the year shown. In this case, both projects generate negative cash flows, since we are not relating the project to any income generation or cost savings. At face value, the leasing option looks more expensive, generating a larger negative cash flow than purchasing outright. However, these totals ignore the timings of these flows and it is apparent that we must determine the relevant NPVs. The appropriate calculations are shown in Table 15.10.

Table 15.9 Cash flow of Options 1 and 2

	Option 1: Purchase	Option 2: Lease
Now	−45 000	−12 000
end of Year 1	−2 500	−12 000
end of Year 2	−2 500	−12 000
end of Year 3	−2 500	-12 000
end of Year 4	−2 500	−12 000
end of Year 5	+1 000	
Total cost	−54 000	−60 000

Table 15.10 NPVs for both options

Year	Discount factor	Purchase		Leasing	
		Net cash flows	Present value	Net cash flows	Present value
0	1.0000	−45 000	−45 000	−12 000	−12 000
1	0.9091	−2 500	−2 272.75	−12 000	−10 909.20
2	0.8264	−2 500	−2 066.00	−12 000	−9 916.80
3	0.7513	−2 500	−1 878.25	−12 000	−9 015.60
4	0.6830	−2 500	−1 707.50	−12 000	−8 196.00
5	0.6209	+1 000	+620.90		
Total		−54 000	−52 303.60	−60 000	−50 037.60

In Table 15.10 the two series of net cash flows have been discounted at 10 per cent. For the purchase option the NPV is –£52 304. Similarly, the figure for the leasing option is –£50 038. Comparison of the two NPVs reveals that the leasing option has the lower negative value. This indicates that, other things being equal, the leasing option is to be preferred. The present value of the cash outflows is smaller than that of the alternative – purchase.

Naturally, in practice, we would not recommend that the decision be taken simply on the basis of the NPV calculations. We would need to assess other factors in reaching the decision: tax allowances, the likely rate of inflation and so on, as well as a view as to whether the rate of interest used to calculate the NPVs will remain constant at 10 per cent. This last point is critical for NPV calculations. Should the rate of interest/cost of capital change over this period then the present values will also change and possibly the recommendation we would make. We might wish to undertake some sensitivity analysis on the two options to see how sensitive the decision is to interest rate changes. Such analysis reveals that we would prefer to lease, based on this information, for any interest rate of 6.85 per cent or higher. If the rate fell below this figure, the NPV of the buy option would fall below that of the lease option. Management could be asked to indicate their expectations of future interest rate changes to help them evaluate their decision.

Summary

Although financial decision making in the real world is an area where financial experts must be involved because of the complexity of the tax and legal systems that surround these decisions, in principle the decisions revolve around the calculations of interest and present value in their many forms. At the heart of these calculations is the fundamental principle of the time value of money. The concept of interest is a critical one both to individuals and to business organisations. We have shown in this chapter, based on a variety of approaches, how interest payments can be calculated and evaluated. Equally, the ability to evaluate projects in financial terms is clearly important to any organisation. Because most project investments will have financial consequences over a period of time, it is necessary to allow for time preference in this financial evaluation. This can be achieved through the calculation of present values.

QADM IN ACTION　Tomco Oil Inc.

As was discussed in the QADM in Action in Chapter 6, the oil industry is one characterised by high levels of uncertainty and, linked to such uncertainty, high financial returns/high financial losses. Although one tends to think of the oil industry in terms of the large multinationals – Shell, BP, Exxon/Esso – the industry also contains many smaller, independent operators. Among these are the so-called wildcat operators – typically companies involved in exploration, drilling and production on a smaller scale and who have no pipeline or distribution systems of their own. For such companies the wrong decision about a particular operation can have fatal consequences for the organisation's survival.

One such operator is Tomco Oil, which was faced with a choice of two sites in Kansas, USA. It was seen in Chapter 6 that the sequential decision problem a company faces in such circumstances is typified by inadequate and uncertain information. Yet, based on this information, the organisation has to reach a decision about the likely financial consequences in terms of future cash flows. Figure 15.1 shows the various elements of the decision model and their interrelationship in this context. Tomco was faced with choosing between two sites: Blair East and Blair West. The available information on Blair East was less than that of the alternative site and this is reflected in the added complexity of the relevant part of the decision tree for Blair East, shown in Figure 15.2. While there were only five possible outcomes from the decision to develop Blair West, there were over 70 for Blair East.

To help assess the options, a financial evaluation was added to the model. For each outcome a financial contribution was calculated, consisting of the net cash inflows after deducting operating costs. Given that any given well is expected to have an economic life lasting a number of years, it is clearly appropriate to evaluate the options in terms of discounted cash flows rather than simple totals. This in itself required a detailed assessment of the future in terms of:

● future oil prices;

● estimates of oil reserves on the sites. These varied between 10 000 barrels and 40 000 barrels;

● annual oil production from each site;

● annual operating costs and taxes.

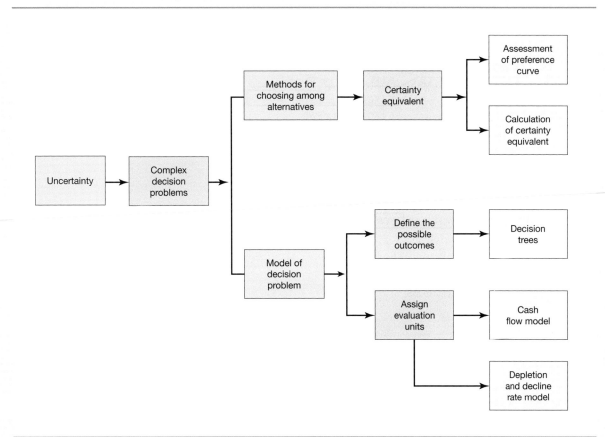

Figure 15.1 The structure of an integrated model of decision making under uncertainty

Reprinted by permission of J. Hosseini. Taken from 'Decision analysis and its application in the choice between two wildcat adventures', J. Hosseini, *Interfaces*, 16(2), 1986. Copyright held by the Operations Research Society of America and the Institute of Management Sciences.

Table 15.11 shows the calculations for some of the options considered at a discount rate of 14 per cent.

The recommendation was made, at the end of the modelling process, to drill at Blair West. The president of Tomco later commented:

'Before we actually utilised decision-tree analysis to aid in our selection of drilling-sites, we were skeptical as to the applicability . . . in oil exploration. [Such] analysis provided us with . . . a clearer insight into the numerous and varied financial outcomes that are possible.'

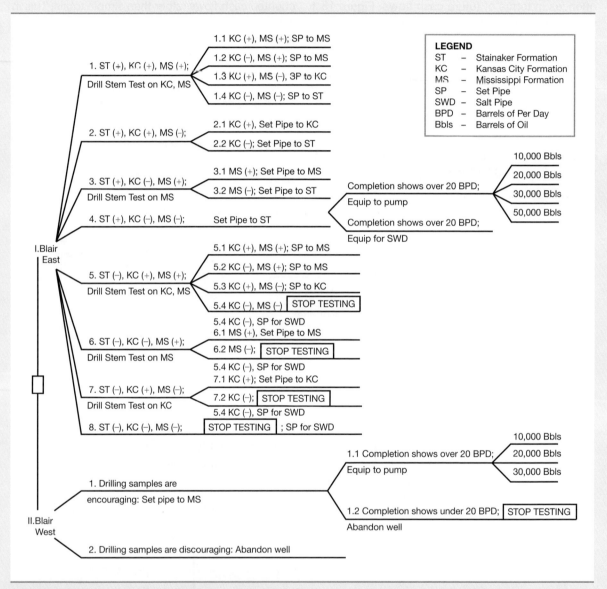

Figure 15.2 The decision-tree model used to help oil producers decide between the two site locations, Blair East and Blair West. A plus (+) indicates a promising sample. A minus (–) indicates a negative sample

Table 15.11   Calculation of net present value for a reserve of 10 000 barrels of capacity, pumped off at a 20 per cent depletion rate and discounted at 14 per cent

Year	Price ($)	Bbls.	Total ($)	Operating expenses ($)	Net cash flow ($)	NPV factor	Net present value ($)
1	29.00	2 000	58 000	11 630	46 370	0.877	40 666.50
2	29.00	1 600	46 400	11 630	34 770	0.769	26 738.13
3	30.74	1 280	39 347	12 238	27 019	0.675	18 237.83
4	32.58	1 024	33 362	13 852	19 510	0.592	11 549.92
5	34.53	819	28 246	14 683	13 563	0.519	7 039.20
6	36.60	655	23 973	15 564	8 409	0.456	3 834.50
7	38.80	524	10 331	16 497	3 834	0.400	1 533.60

Total net present value of cash flows $109 589.68

Exercises

1   You have the choice of investing a sum of money in four alternative schemes:

(a) one which will pay 10 per cent per annum interest compounded daily;

(b) one which will pay 10.25 per cent per annum interest compounded monthly;

(c) one which will pay 10.5 per cent per annum interest compounded quarterly;

(d) one which will pay 10.75 per cent per annum interest compounded annually.

Which would you choose and why?

2   The company you work for is considering acquiring several of the latest generation desktop computers for use in an office. The company expects the equipment to have a useful life of three years. The finance director has asked you to recommend whether the equipment should be purchased outright or whether it should be leased from the supplier. If the equipment is purchased outright the total cost will be £4200. At the end of the three years it is estimated that the equipment will have a scrap value of £500. If the machine is leased then the rental charge will be £1660 per annum payable at the start of each year. The company's cost of capital is currently 10.5 per cent per annum.

Draft a report advising the company whether it should purchase or lease the equipment and comment on any other factors the company may want to consider before making a decision.

3   A production company is considering purchasing a new piece of equipment for the production process for one of its products. The product itself is due to be withdrawn from the market in five years' time. The equipment will cost £600 000 and have a scrap value of £5000. Included in this price is a one-year service guarantee from the supplier of the equipment. Each additional year the equipment is in use the company will take out another service contract with the supplier at a cost of £7500.

  Calculate the net present value for this project assuming a cost of capital of 15 per cent. Explain how this calculation might help the company in its decision making.

4   A hospital has decided to replace an important piece of medical equipment at a cost of £30 000. The expected life of the equipment is five years and it will have a resale value of £4000 at this time. The hospital is trying to decide how to finance the purchase. One option is to buy the equipment outright. A second option is to obtain the equipment under a credit agreement with a finance company. Under this agreement the hospital will pay £10 000 now and £5500 at the beginning of each subsequent year. A third option is to enter into a leasing agreement. Under this agreement the hospital will pay an initial amount of £9000 at the start of the first year. At the start of each subsequent year another payment will be needed which will be the previous year's payment less 12 per cent. The current cost of capital for the hospital is 9 per cent.

  Which of the three options would you recommend?

5   A local authority is under severe financial pressure and is considering selling some of the land it owns to a building company. The building company is offering to pay £150 000 for the land now or a payment of £40 000 a year for the next five years.

  (a) If the current interest rate is 8 per cent, which option would you advise the local authority to take?

  (b) How would your recommendation be affected by changes in the interest rate?

  (c) What other factors should the local authority take into account?

6   A large organisation is considering replacing part of its vehicle fleet with the latest equipment. Although such a decision is expensive, it is felt that the investment will be worthwhile in terms of generating future cost savings in repairs, maintenance and running costs and will also help improve the quality of service provided. The company's current cost of borrowing is 12 per cent per annum. Two suppliers have been asked to tender for the project. The relevant costs of the project and the corresponding savings (in terms of reduced costs, increased efficiency, etc.) are shown in Table 15.12.

  (a) Which supplier would you recommend?

  (b) Calculate the IRR for each supplier and explain how this could be used.

Table 15.12   Project costs and savings (£s)

Year	Supplier A Cost	Supplier A Savings	Supplier B Cost	Supplier B Savings
Now	120 000	0	85 000	0
1	0	25 000	35 000	0
2	0	30 000	0	60 000
3	0	40 000	0	45 000
4	0	50 000	0	35 000
5	0	25 000	0	35 000

7   An organisation has recently purchased a company car for one of its senior managers at a cost of £25 000 and is trying to determine the most suitable time for replacement. It is estimated that the car will depreciate by £5000 in the first year, £2000 in each of the next two years and £3000 in each of the next two years. Running costs in the first year are estimated at £5000 and are estimated to increase by 15 per cent per annum thereafter.

(a) Determine a suitable time for replacing the car.

(b) The company has a capital cost for such projects of 5 per cent per annum and expects inflation to average 2 per cent per annum over the foreseeable future. Using present-value techniques determine a suitable replacement time for the vehicle.

Postscript: A quick look at recent developments in QADM

The main quantitative analysis tools that you need to know for helping with decision making have already been covered. The aim of this postscript is to briefly highlight some of the recent and important trends in quantitative analysis for decision making. Most of the analytical tools and techniques that we've looked at are not new – they've been around for a while. It is however the extensive and developing application of these tools and techniques that is the subject of this section.

We're not introducing any new techniques in this section; rather we would like you to sit back and learn about the exciting developments that are presented here – they will affect your own management career. There are no progress checks and no exercises at the end. Instead there are brief reading lists at the end of each section in case you are keen to read more. The topics that are covered in this section are:

- Big Data and data analytics
- Artificial Intelligence
- Multi-criteria decision analysis and data mining
- Agent based simulation
- Data visualisation

We encourage you to think about how these topics link together. We will revisit this at the end of this section.

Big Data and data/business analytics

Remember the first worked example in this book? That was in Chapter 2 on UK credit and debit card purchases. Have another look at Table 2.1. The data that you see is quite limited, it simply gives you the total number and the total value of transactions for debit credit cards in the UK between certain years. Ask yourself, is this all the information that is available to the financial institutions involved? You do not need to be a financial expert to appreciate that this amount of data is only the tip of the iceberg. Every individual transaction that is completed will be recorded somewhere – who used the card, when they used it, what they bought, how much they spent, who they bought it from, where they bought it. Table 2.1 is simply a summary of some of these transactions. The mass of real raw data is out there. Imagine you have this huge amount of data on every card transaction for every (anonymised) individual in the UK. Is that scary? It might be. Is it exciting? It definitely is from the data analysis point of view.

Don't make the mistake of assuming that we're talking about a few megabytes of data, we are not even talking about a few gigabytes of data. We are dealing with terabytes and zettabytes here! Even the name of the measurement unit is new! This is a really big amount of data. The *volume* is huge. Think about the specific challenges that you would have if you were to access and analyse this gigantic volume of data. To start with, how do you want to capture it? In an Excel sheet? Really?! And how do you want to make some sense of it? Looking at averages? Column charts? And what analytical techniques do you want to apply to this data and more importantly, how?

Now consider this: card users produce other data that may not be in the form of simple transaction data. They write reviews for some of the products that they have purchased and satisfaction ratings for some of the financial services providers that they use. They may tweet about them. They may post photos of these products publicly or amongst their friends. Imagine all this data was also anonymised and added to the huge amount of transaction data. You now not only have data on card transactions but also data on product use, reviews and even photos. Now what?! Well, as if volume was not enough challenge we now also have *variety*. We have data in the form of financial figures, texts, including often not very formally written tweets, and we also have images.

Let us add another complexity to this already very complex amount and type of data. Don't forget that this is data that is produced every fraction of second – 24/7/365. Literally at every second you can update the data. This is in fact a never-ending flow of data. We had volume, we had variety, we now also have *velocity*. Given that this volume and variety of data are coming at you constantly, how often would you want to analyse and act on the results as a decision maker?

Put the three features of volume, variety and velocity together and you are facing what is commonly known as Big Data. What makes Big Data different from normal data is not just its features of volume, variety and velocity, but the type of analysis that could fit with these features.

Think about Big Data as a mysterious ocean of data that needs to be explored by a variety of analytical techniques. This exploration of data is often referred to as *data* (or *business*) *analytics*. Analytics is interested in discovering patterns in data and to analyse them to help with decision making. The more traditional ways of analysis that we've introduced in this book are a key part of such analytics. However, they may not be adequate by themselves. More advanced analytical techniques may also be needed, involving advanced statistics, data mining, multi-criteria decision analysis (MCDA), textual analysis and many other techniques.

This is why in differentiating between analysis and analytics we can consider analysis to be about 'What' and mostly related to the past, while we associate analytics more with 'Why' and mostly related to the future. One useful way of looking at analysis and analytics is to use the following categorisation:

Descriptive analytics: focusing on the question – what happened?

Descriptive analytics does exactly what it suggests – we use analytical techniques to describe, or summarise, available historic data. Such analysis describes the past in numerical terms and typically involves many of the techniques we've looked in this text: data presentation, management statistics, hypothesis testing, trend analysis, correlation, regression.

Predictive analytics: focusing on the question – what might happen in the future?

Predictive analytical techniques look to the future and use historical data and analytical models try to forecast or predict trends, outcomes and behaviour. Again, some of the topics we've covered in the text fall into this category: probability, decision making under uncertainty, market research, forecasting techniques, stock control, project management, simulation.

Common areas of application of predictive analytics include: clinical decision support systems, cross selling, customer relationship management, direct marketing, fraud detection, project risk analysis, risk analysis on vulnerable people, and more

Prescriptive analytics: focusing on the question – what could/should we do?

Prescriptive analytics builds on predictive analytics by not only anticipating what will happen but also why it will happen. Prescriptive analytics also highlights decision options available to the organisation and the potential implications/of each decision option. Prescriptive analytics updates data to re-predict and re-prescribe improving prediction accuracy and providing better decision options. Prescriptive analytics typically combines numerical data with more varied data analysis such as video, images, sounds, texts. A number of the topics we've covered form the basis for prescriptive analytics: decision analysis, linear programming, simulation, financial decision making.

Common areas of application include: credit scoring, crime pattern analysis, healthcare risk management, logistics management, managing telecoms networks, prisoner reoffending, production optimisation, crew and staff scheduling, stock control management, supply chain optimisation, vehicle routing, waste and recycling management, and more.

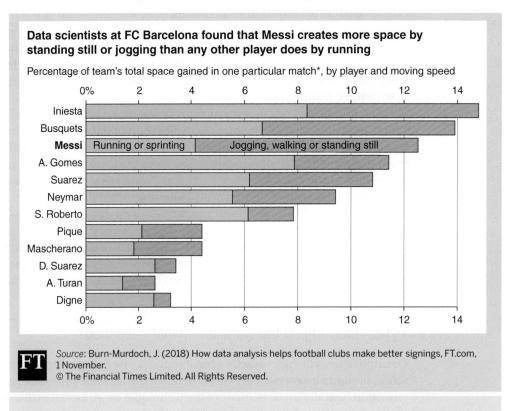

Data scientists at FC Barcelona found that Messi creates more space by standing still or jogging than any other player does by running

Percentage of team's total space gained in one particular match*, by player and moving speed

Big Data analytics can be found in unusual applications, such as this one from the world of football.

Big Data analytics is increasingly being utilised to provide important insights in to a variety of businesses and disciplines, including marketing, human behaviour, media, health care, internet, etc. The Commonwealth Bank of Australia has used Big Data analytics to gain a better understanding and assessment of risk when working with customers. US Express – a provider of transportation solutions – collects a variety of data on different aspects of transportation, including use of fuel, condition of tyres and information from GPS systems to run smooth and efficient operations across the country. The powerful search ability of Google, and its fast progress in recent times, is to a large extent due to the use of Big Data derived from users. Uber is utilising passenger Big Data to provide the UberPool service, where passengers share the cost of the journey by riding common routes together whilst saving fuel and reducing their carbon footprint. LinkedIn uses Big Data, thanks to its members, to provide appropriate and relevant offerings for its members. Singapore Health Care has used Big Data to provide individual targeted treatment for the patients based on their individual requirements and circumstances. Walmart uses Big Data including text analysis to better understand online shoppers, leading to a significant increase in the rate of completed online purchases.

Opinion on Wall Street

Illuminating Big Data will leave governments in the dark

Private firms such as hedge funds are benefiting most from mining 'alternative' stats

By Robin Wigglesworth

Source: Rawpixel.com/Shutterstock

The amount of digital data around the world is already unimaginably vast

Imagine a world where interminable waits for backward-looking, frequently-revised economic data seem as archaically quaint as floppy disks, beepers and a civil internet. This fantasy realm may be closer than you think.

The Bureau of Economic Analysis will soon publish its preliminary estimate for US economic growth in the first three months of the year, finally catching up on its regular schedule after a government shutdown paralysed the agency. But other data are still delayed, and the final official result for US gross domestic product won't be available until July. Along the way there are likely to be many tweaks. Collecting timely and accurate data are a Herculean task, especially for an

economy as vast and varied as the US's. But last week's World Bank–International Monetary Fund's annual spring meetings offered some clues on a brighter, more digital future for economic data. The IMF hosted a series of seminars and discussions exploring how the hot new world of Big Data could be harnessed to produce more timely economic figures – and improve economic forecasts.

Jiaxiong Yao, an IMF official in its African department, explained how it could use satellites to measure the intensity of night-time lights, and derive a real-time gauge of economic health. "If a country gets brighter over time, it is growing. If it is getting darker then it probably needs an IMF programme," he noted. Further sessions explored how the IMF could use machine learning – a popular field of artificial intelligence – to improve its influential but often faulty economic forecasts; and real-time shipping data to map global trade flows. . . .

The amount of digital data around the world is already unimaginably vast. As more of our social and economic activity migrates online, the quantity and quality is going to increase exponentially. The potential is mind-boggling. Setting aside the obvious and thorny privacy issues, it is likely to lead to a revolution in the world of economic statistics. Consumer price movements can be measured instantaneously through scraping retailers' websites, data from Swift – the interbank payment network – maps global capital flows, and spending patterns can be gauged through credit card data. The Federal Reserve now gets the latter with a mere three-day lag . . .

Most of all, mobile phones are evolving into tiny data beacons, beaming incomprehensible amounts of information about us to the wider world. Ultimately they could form nodes in a vast, granular and instantaneous measure of global economic activity. This is still some way off, and may prove a practical impossibility, but data scientists say it is far from science fiction.

But there are obviously weaknesses in all these funky alternative data sets. For example, the intensity of night-time lights is highly correlated to growth in poorer countries, and works pretty well in middle-income ones, but it has a negligible relationship with economic health in wealthy countries, Mr Yao admitted. Trade volumes are estimated from the depth of a ship's draft, but if the goods are moved both off and on at a port it complicates the calculations from real-time shipping data.

Yet the biggest issues are not the weaknesses of these new data sets – all statistics have inherent flaws – but their nature and location. Firstly, it depends on the lax regulatory and personal attitudes towards personal data continuing, and there are signs of a (healthy) backlash brewing. Secondly, almost all of this alternative data is being generated and stored in the private sector, not by government bodies such as the Bureau of Economic Analysis, Eurostat or the UK's Office for National Statistics. Public bodies are generally too poorly funded to buy or clean all this data themselves, meaning hedge funds will benefit from better economic data than the broader public. We might, in fact, need legislation mandating that statistical agencies receive free access to any aggregated private sector data sets that might be useful to their work.

That would ensure that our economic officials and policymakers don't fly blind in an increasingly illuminated world.

 Source: Wigglesworth, R. (2019) Illuminating Big Data will leave governments in the dark: private firms such as hedge funds are benefiting most from mining 'alternative' stats, Opinion on Wall Street, *Financial Times*, 19 April. © The Financial Times Limited. All Rights Reserved.

Big Data and analytics offer opportunities to the public as well as the private sector – but brings its own challenges.

Some helpful further reading on Big Data and Analytics

Beyond the hype: big data concepts, methods, and analytics (2015). Authors: Amir Gandomi and Murtaza Haider, in *International Journal of Information Management*, vol. 35, no. 2.

Big Data in Practice: How 45 Successful Companies Used Big Data Analytics to Deliver Extraordinary Results (2016). Author: Bernard Marr, published by: John Wiley & Sons.

Big Data: Using Smart Big Data, Analytics and Metrics to Make Better Decisions and Improve Performance (2015). Author: Bernard Marr, published by John Wiley & Sons.

Business Intelligence, Analytics, and Data Science: A Managerial Perspective (2016). Authors: Ramesh Sharda and Dursun Delen, Efraim Turban, published by: Pearson.

How 'big data' can make big impact: findings from a systematic review and a longitudinal case study (2015). Authors: Samuel Fosso Wamba, Shahriar Akter, Andrew Edwards, Geoffrey Chopin and Denis Gnanzou, *International Journal of Production Economics*, no. 165.

Traffic Flow Prediction with Big Data: A Deep Learning Approach (2015). Authors: Lv Yisheng, Duan Yanjie, Kang Wenwen, Li Zhengxi and Wang Fei-Yue, in *IEEE Transactions on Intelligent Transportation*, vol. 16, no. 2.

What can big data and text analytics tell us about hotel guest experience and satisfaction? (2015). Authors: Zheng Xiang, Zvi Schwartz, John H. Gerdes Jr and Muzaffer Uysal, *International Journal of Hospitality Management*, no. 44.

In addition, useful and user-friendly case studies regularly appear on the websites of: the UK Operational Research Society: www.theorsociety.com and INFORMS: www.informs.org

Artificial Intelligence

If you review the methods that we covered in this book so far you will see that they all have one common feature: they rely on the human brain – on people. Someone has to decide what data to collect. Someone has to decide what analytical techniques to use. Someone has to decide what action to take based on the analysis undertaken. You don't need to be a fan of science fiction movies to appreciate that we are in an era where machines are used to do much of the thinking – and decision making – that only people have done in the past. What makes people useful when it comes to decision making is our 'intelligence' and today this intelligence – or some of it at least – can be captured, copied and cloned and artificially utilised. It's commonly referred to as Artificial Intelligence (AI).

It is important to understand what exactly we are referring to when talking about AI. The fact is, any use of a computer-based machine to do part of the thinking for the human being can technically be referred to as AI. This is why in general AI is categorised into the following types:

- **Assisted Intelligence** is nothing more than the use of machines to undertake a basic task or provide basic help (think of a warning system in a car telling you you're exceeding the speed limit).

- **Augmented Intelligence** takes a further step by providing a platform for the exchange of data and information with the user (human being). Here the user provides data to the machine and in return, the machine provides the user with more insights by analysing the data. A GPS system in a car is an example of this where the GPS needs to know your destination before computing a route.

- Then we **have Autonomous Intelligence** – here the human being is not actually involved. The machine collects and analyses the data, makes decisions and acts accordingly (an example is self-driving cars).

The level of AI referred to in this section is between Augmented Intelligence and Autonomous Intelligence. In most of the cases where AI is helping businesses with decision making, the degree of independence of the machine in gathering and analysing data is much more than a typical Augmented Intelligence. However, in most of these cases people are still in place to approve the decisions and to authorise acting on them.

The thought of machines thinking for us might be scary, but the fact is that AI, while having its own risks, is already helping in many areas of decision making in our lives, private and not-for-profit sectors alike. In the United States, AI is used in some states to assist with decision making about prisoner parole. The New South Wales government in Australia uses AI in order to identify cyber threats on time. Netherlands police use AI to process a huge amount of investigation requests, making sure that crucial pieces of information are not lost in the mass of information flow. While the use of AI in some of the public sectors may be controversial, in businesses and business decision-making situations AI is becoming increasingly popular. AI is used in particular for analysing markets, customer relationship management, personalisation of services and products, data trends, forecasting, quantifying uncertainty and identifying complex algorithms.

If you are a regular customer of online shopping then most probably you have seen AI yourself (even if you didn't know it as such). Have you noticed that increasingly when you do online shopping, you tend to receive relevant advertisements in your email or as pop-up messages? Have you noticed that the virtual assistant on the webpages of some businesses are not as useless as they used to be in the past and in fact in many cases do provide helpful assistance? Have you also fallen into the trap of chatting with a sales representative online only to find out later that you were chatting with a machine? Coca - Cola uses AI to understand customer reactions to different beverages and to develop new products accordingly. EDF energy is using AI to provide real-time advice to power station operators to help with efficiency and reduce waste. BP uses AI to help with efficiency and better performance levels. Netflix uses AI to recommend movies and documentaries based on the past viewings of the customers and their ratings of them. Walmart, one of the largest retailers in the world, uses face recognition system to study customers' reactions to some of the products.

Big Data is closely linked to AI. Multi-level and complex analytics of Big Data can be done more readily by AI. PwC a multinational professional service holds data of more than 300 million financial decisions by US consumers. AI is used to analyse this data on a live regular basis to evaluate a company's financial decisions in real time.

McDonald's to buy AI company Dynamic Yield

Acquisition will help burger group customise its menu displays based on differing variables

By Alistair Gray in New York

Source: Paul Thomas/Bloomberg via Getty Images

McDonald's serves about 68m customers each day from almost 38,000 outlets

McDonald's is spending about $300m to buy an artificial intelligence company in the fast-food chain's latest technology investment. In a rare move for the burger group, which has for years avoided acquisitions, McDonald's announced a deal on Monday to buy Dynamic Yield, a machine learning specialist founded seven years ago. The technology will allow McDonald's to customise its menu displays based on variables such as the weather and the time of day – McFlurry ice creams in the heat or Sausage McMuffins at breakfast, for instance – as well as previous customer choices. It will also assess restaurant footfall to suggest food that

is faster to prepare when the kitchen is busy, or more elaborate items in quieter stretches.

McDonald's, which serves about 68m customers each day from almost 38,000 outlets, plans to roll out the technology at its drive-through locations in the US this year before expanding it overseas. The Chicago-based company also plans to introduce it inside restaurants and on mobile phones. Steve Easterbrook, McDonald's chief executive, said: "This technology has the capability and the flexibility to work on all of our digital platforms." Deal terms were not disclosed but people familiar with the matter said the consideration was about $300m. Dynamic Yield, based in Tel Aviv and New York, employs 200 people. Clients include furniture retail group Ikea, football club Tottenham Hotspur and online supermarket Ocado.

Following the acquisition it will continue to be run as a standalone business by Liad Agmon, co-founder. "We're thrilled to be joining an iconic global brand," he said. While small in the context of McDonald's, which has a market capitalisation of about $142bn, the purchase is its biggest in 20 years. It is also strategically significant as the company turns to big data to gain an edge over rivals in the highly competitive fast food

business. Self-order kiosks, mobile order and payment, and delivery via UberEats are among the tech initiatives introduced by Mr Easterbrook, a Briton who took charge in 2015. The company has also been smartening up its outlets, rolling out new decor, kiosks, free-to-use tablets and phone chargers.

McDonald's said it would be Dyanmic Yield's sole owner and would "continue to invest" in the business following the deal. It would continue to serve its other clients, which also include beauty chain group Sephora, retail company Urban Outfitters and betting and gambling group Ladbrokes.

 Source: Gray, A. (2019) McDonald's to buy AI company Dynamic Yield: acquisition will help burger group customise its menu displays based on differing variables, FT.com, 25 March.

AI, Big Data and Big Macs do go together!

One of the most important issues that AI raises, however, is the question of ethics. How far and to what extent should businesses be allowed to use AI to study the market, customers, employees, social media, etc.? At what point is this no longer business analysis and starts to become breaching of privacy? Some of the material shown below discusses this important issue.

Some helpful further reading on the use of AI in decision making

Artificial Intelligence and Machine Learning for Business: A No-Nonsense Guide to Data Driven Technologies (2018). Author: Steven Finlay, published by: Relativistic.

Artificial intelligence arrives in the library (2018). Author: Bruce Massis, in *Information and Learning Science*, vol. 119, no. 7/8.

Artificial Intelligence: A Modern Approach (2016). Authors: Stuart Russell and Peter Norvig, published by: Pearson.

Artificial Intelligence Brings Out the Worst and the Best in Us (2019). Author: Lisa Burrell, in *MIT Sloan Management Review*, 60:2.

Incorporating ethics into artificial intelligence (2017). Authors: Amitai Etzioni and Oren Etzioni, in *The Journal of Ethics*, vol. 21, no. 4.

Multi-criteria decision analysis and data mining

Multi-criteria decision analysis (MCDA) and data mining are not new but in the past few years applications of these analysis tools have developed rapidly both as standalone techniques and as an integrated bundle. In this section we look at some of their most recent applications. In Chapter 14 we looked at the example of a takeaway coffee shop. We used at two criteria to study this business situation using simulation modelling. One was customer waiting time, the other was staff idle time. The simulation model generated results for two scenarios of having one kiosk and two kiosks for service. Remember this sentence at the end of the analysis: '*It is now up to the manager to consider all practical points and to decide what is next*'?

In a more realistic situation the number of criteria for making a decision about the situation may be more than just two. What about avoiding wasting the available space? What about maintaining staff satisfaction with different scenarios? What about minimising the cost of the inventory? What about avoiding extra staff costs? Clearly the 'what about' questions can continue, implying that in a decision-making situation we are often faced with a number of criteria for making decisions where, very often, these criteria conflict with each other. In this example, having more service kiosks is likely to improve customer satisfaction but will not help with avoiding extra staff cost. In every decision-making situation we face multiple criteria for making decisions and there is always *trade-off* between these criteria. In smaller and simpler situations we may manage to find a decision that would reasonably satisfy every criteria. However in more complex decision-making situations the criteria may be so many and their relationship with each other may be so complicated that straightforward analysis using basic tools would fail to provide a satisfactory solution. This is where multi-criteria decision analysis can help (also referred to as multi- or multiple-criteria decision making, MCDM). MCDA is decision-making tool where there are a number of decision-making criteria with trade-offs between them, aiming to provide the best decision based on the perceived importance of each criterion.

In its simplest form what MCDA does is that it lists the criteria and assigns relative weights to each; then it studies the available options (decisions) to see to what extent each option satisfies each of the criteria. This is recorded by giving scores (values) against each option in terms of each criterion. The chosen option will be the one that gains the highest weighted sum of the scores. The table below gives a simple example.

Sample MCDA calculations

	Criterion 1 (10%)	Criterion 2 (30%)	Criterion 3 (20%)	Criterion 4 (25%)	Criterion 5 (15%)	Weighted sum
Option A	3	5	4	8	2	4.95
Option B	1	6	6	9	3	5.8
Option C	8	5	5	2	1	3.95

Here we have five criteria that have to be satisfied and for each we have noted relative weighting to show importance as seen by the decision maker. Criterion 2 is seen as most important with a weight of 30 per cent and Criterion 1 least important with a weight of 10 per cent. The decision maker has three alternative options (A, B, C). How well each option meets each individual criterion is then shown with a score (here out of 10). Option A, for example, does best in meeting Criterion 4 (a score of 8/10) and worst at meeting Criterion 5 (2/10). Weighted scores are then calculated for each option. Here Option B has the highest weighted score indicating that it does 'best' at meeting the criteria specified.

It seems a very simple approach but in practice it's very powerful. MCDA has been used successfully in many areas of decision making and in a variety of situations, including health care, logistics, environmental planning including water regulation policies, point systems for immigration purposes, student admissions for sensitive and popular degrees such as medical schools, supplier selection, public housing allocation, evaluation of e-government systems and much more. MCDA, of course, goes well beyond this simple illustration. There are processes in place to assure the assigned criteria and assigned scores are appropriate. This often involves group decision making among the people who are closely involved with the problem in hand. Sensitivity analysis takes place and different outcomes based on different views on weightings and scores are studied. Problem structuring, behavioural aspects of making decisions and optimisation are among the most common components of a typical MCDA project.

One particular technique that has recently been used with MCDA to provide a more powerful analytical tool is data mining. Data mining is used extensively in Big Data analytics generally. The idea is to recognise patterns in data by the use of techniques like classification, clustering and regression analysis. These patterns are normally not identifiable by simple statistical approaches. This also includes detecting anomalies (deviations from a routine pattern). In other words, data mining explores hidden links between events and recognises patterns accordingly, and consequently it also recognises situations where events are not happening in the expected pattern. As a result data mining produces information about entities that we do not have direct information about. This may be a description of what is happening or a prediction of what is going to happen with a very high likelihood. Service providers use data mining to predict when it is likely that a customer starts thinking about switching to another provider. They use data available to them including records of interactions with the customer, billing information and possibly website visits. They send offers and incentives to customers who according to the analysis are most likely to be thinking about leaving.

In health care data mining can be used to foresee potential health risks in individuals and to give early warning. The story of Target, a large retailer in the US, went viral when it sent coupons for baby products to a female customer when no one knew she was pregnant. Target was simply following the outcome of their data mining analysis done by machines! Insurance agencies can use data mining on claims to recognise anomalies, signalling fraud cases that need further investigation. In education, data mining can be used to study the factors that may lead to behaviour in students that is detrimental to their education.

How Facebook could target ads in age of encryption

Zuckerberg promises privacy, but experts warn metadata can be mined to build behavioural profiles.

By Hannah Murphy in San Francisco

Source: Reuters/Alamy Stock Photo

Mark Zuckerberg believes the future of social networking lies in private messaging.

His convictions are so strong that he plans to merge the messaging services of Facebook, WhatsApp and Instagram into one encrypted system, meaning only the people who send and receive messages can view them. But the Facebook founder has yet to say how the world's biggest social media network, which generated $16.9bn in revenues in the fourth quarter of last year – largely from advertising on its news feed – will make money from such a radical overhaul.

Experts say there is one obvious solution: metadata, the vast amount of context surrounding a message that can be viewed even when the content is encrypted. Even though Mr Zuckerberg has cast the shake-up as a pivot towards privacy, Facebook could still mine and analyse users' messaging metadata to help build detailed profiles for targeted advertising, in a move that could irk privacy activists and even regulators.

"By abstracting out and looking at who's talking to who, for how long, and when . . . you can build up a very statistical picture of people very quickly," said Alan Woodward, encryption expert and professor at the University of Surrey."

"In many ways, it is the context of what you say in those messages that is more important than the messages themselves," he added.

Facebook has faced mounting pressure to give users more clarity and control over how their information is handled in the wake of the Cambridge Analytica scandal, as well as reports that it allowed device makers to access users' personal data through special deals. Earlier this month, Mr Zuckerberg responded to those concerns by announcing dramatic plans to integrate the three messaging services and introduce end-to-end encryption. At present, only WhatsApp encrypts users' messages.

But the chief executive did not outline the group's policy around metadata, which was first thrust into the spotlight in 2013 after it emerged in the Edward Snowden leaks that the National Security Agency collected phone call metadata of US citizens on a mass scale. Facebook has declined to provide precise details of the messaging metadata it currently collects, but said it was largely used to rank people by how often they use Messenger, as well as monitor for abuse and spam. The company also said it was too early to comment on how much or how little metadata it will gather when its three apps are integrated, although Mr Zuckerberg has suggested limiting how long metadata is stored for. Facebook hopes to launch the combined platform next year.

Still, experts argue there are reams of this "data about data" that Facebook could potentially collect if user habits shift more towards walled-off messaging. According to Jon Callas, a senior technology fellow with the American Civil Liberties Union and a former encryption expert at Apple, the information could include the host website of links that are shared, and picture or file names if they are shared between users. Metadata could also help to classify what was in a photo – for example, a dog or a house – without a third party viewing the photo itself, he said. "There could be a lot of intrusive scanning going on while only having metadata," he added.

Research suggests that by analysing these patterns of communication, it is possible to make relatively accurate predictions about people's personal lives, such as their age, gender, sexual preferences or personality traits. Sophisticated machine learning technology, where algorithms learn from large data sets and improve over time, can provide further

insights. One 2018 study by University College London researchers analysed the metadata alone of 10,000 Twitter users and found that it could match this information to their identity with approximately 96.7 per cent accuracy.

In the case of Facebook, the platform could also combine messaging metadata with the other personal information that it holds on users, such as what they like and share in its news feed, in order to build a behavioural profile of an individual and their friends.

"Applying statistical analysis to the metadata from messages with other data harvested by Facebook can lead to all kinds of inferences about what you are interested in, and predict what you might be interested in if exposed to it," said Mr Woodward.

A Facebook spokesperson said the company does not currently use machine learning on metadata for targeted advertising.

One method is known as pattern-of-life analysis, where data including location is used to understand a user's habits over time. Using this, a platform such as Facebook might easily be able deduce where a user's home and work is. Taken to its logical conclusion, that platform could establish that a user typically walks from a train station to their office every day at a certain time – allowing them to serve that user with adverts for a particular coffee shop within a certain radius of that journey during that timeframe, for example. Another method, known as link analysis, assesses a person's network of connections to map out who is influencing who and what they might have in common. "If you speak to someone regularly, it can assume that a lot of the behavioural indicators that it has for them, probably apply to you," said Kalev Leetaru, senior fellow at Auburn University.

Critics warn metadata could become the next battleground for privacy, particularly in the case of Facebook. "When it comes to large-scale, very rich data sets and the privacy of those data sets, we need to think beyond whether a particular piece of information is sensitive or not, and take into account what this data could reveal about the person now or in the future when using a machine learning algorithm," said Yves-Alexandre de Montjoye, assistant professor at Imperial College London's department of computing.

Mr Callas said: "I want Mr Zuckerberg to say in very specific terms what they are going to do. [Otherwise] I worry they are going to be like the genie in the story that grants your wish but not in the way that you like."

Facebook is not alone in having huge data sets that can be mined for commercially useful information but there's lots of controversy around this.

MCDA and data mining have recently been integrated as one strong analytical tool for decision making. One of the challenges that analysts face in MCDA is to get the managers or clients to come up with a reasonable understanding of relevant criteria and their relative weightings as well as valid scores for each option per criteria. As noted earlier, group decision-making tools are used for this purpose but other analytical tools may also help. Data mining has come to the rescue here by revealing what seems to be leading to what, therefore providing some input when it comes to defining criteria, their relative weightings and the scores for the available options. In France the technique was used for improving road safety. The associations between different variables in road accident records were explored and used to utilise MCDA in order to make decisions for improving road safety. It was concluded that more investment was needed to change the behaviour of road users including both drivers and pedestrians. In Iran, data mining was used to explore the probability of flood and landslide in the Gorganrood Basin. This was then fed into an MCDA analysis to identify the safest and the most at-risk cities in the region. Articles related to these two case studies are included in the following reading list for this section. There have also been developments in integrating MCDA with data mining where the output of the former is fed to the latter, resulting in improving and empowering the data mining techniques.

Some helpful further reading on multi-criteria decision making and data mining

An integrated data-mining and multi-criteria decision-making approach for hazard-based object ranking with a focus on landslides and floods (2018). Authors: Ghasem Mirzaei, Adel Soltani, Milad Soltani and Morad Darabi, in *Environmental Earth Sciences*. vol. 77, no. 16.

CLUS-MCDA: A novel framework based on cluster analysis and multiple criteria decision theory in a supplier selection problem (2018). Authors: Abteen Ijadi Maghsoodi, Azad Kavian, Mohammad Khalilzadeh and Willem K. M. Brauers, in *Computers & Industrial Engineering*, vol. 118.

Data mining combined to the multicriteria decision analysis for the improvement of road safety: case of France (2019). Authors: Fatima Zahra El Mazouri, Mohammed Chaouki Abounaima and Khalid Zenkouar, in *Journal of Big Data*, vol. 6, no. 5.

Data Science for Business: What You Need to Know about Data Mining and Data-Analytic Thinking (2013). Authors: Foster Provost and Tom Fawcett, published by: O'Reilly Media.

Multi-Criteria Decision Analysis: Methods and Software (2013). Authors: Alessio Ishizaka and Philippe Nemery, published by: John Wiley & Sons.

Preferential data mining in the context of MCDA (July 2013). Authors: Alexandru Liviu Olteanu and Raymond Bisdorff, in *Proceedings of the European Conference of Data Analysis*, Luxembourg.

Agent-based simulation

In Chapter 14 we looked at simulation modelling and its use in studying time-based operations. Since its flourishing use in the late 1990s, simulation has made vast improvements in both technology and application and we shall look at one important development, that of agent-based simulation (ABS). Consider the patients referral example in Chapter 14. This was about deciding how many beds to make available in a hospital unit. We used simulation to help with this. Now imagine a rather stressful situation. The hospital has been informed that a patient with a dangerous contagious disease has discharged themselves from hospital (think Ebola virus). What processes need to be improved to stop such incidents will be an important subject to look at later, but for now, the important problem is to understand how quickly the disease may spread in the city and which city zones are in most danger. This analysis is needed to help the police and medical teams understand how best to control the spread of the disease and which areas may need to be quarantined.

Many variables need to be taken into consideration. The point of entry of the patient from the hospital exit to the street. The routes and places that they visited. The routes and places that those who first came into contact then took. It will clearly be impossible to seek information directly from infected people as they won't yet know they've been infected. Obviously we're in a very difficult situation from a modelling and analytical perspective. Can simulation help? Yes. Is it the same type of simulation approach that we discussed in Chapter 14? Definitely not. It is agent-based simulation that can help here. Unlike typical discrete event simulation, ABS does not follow work items (e.g. customers, material) through processes. Rather it follows agents (individuals, groups, organisations) to study their interaction with each other and the way that this affects the whole system. In this example, the agents are the public, the effect that we are looking at is how fast the disease may spread and the system is the city population. Areas of application include: the process and speed of decision making in organisations, issues related to organisational behaviour, bidding systems, biological scenarios (like the above example), combat modelling, team working, consumer behaviour and word of mouth, road traffic, economic studies and pedestrian flow in cities. Examples of successful use of ABS are: Southwest Airlines in the USA studying the effect of decisions on freight traffic; Procter and Gamble studying the dynamics in markets; and Hewlett-Packard studying the effect of hiring strategies on their organisational culture. ABS is also used for training in a variety of decision-making areas like controlling fire, community outreach and controlling crowds. The application of ABS models is becoming increasingly varied and extensive. A survey of 181 articles published between 2000 to 2016 reveals that within the scope of organisation management, operations and logistics, marketing and organisational behaviour, in turn, have been the most popular areas for application of ABS. The result of the study is presented in the figure.

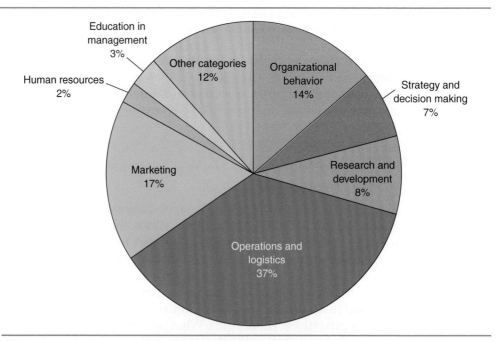

Application of agent-based simulation in organisation management

Source: Nelson Alfonso Gómez-Cruz, Isabella Loaiza Saa, Francisco Fernando Ortega Hurtado (2017) Agent-based simulation in management and organizational studies: a survey, *European Journal of Management and Business Economics*, 26 (3), pp 313–328.

Some helpful further reading on agent-based simulation

Agent based modelling and simulation tools: a review of the state-of-art software (2017). Authors: Sameera Abar, Georgios K.Theodoropoulos, Pierre Lemarinier and Gregory M.P. O'Hare, in *Computer Science Review*, vol. 24.

Agent-based modeling: an introduction and primer (2016). Authors: Christopher W. Weimer, J.O. Miller and Raymond R. Hill, in *Proceedings of the 2016 Winter Simulation Conference*.

An introduction to agent-based modeling for undergraduates (2014). Authors: Angela B. Shiflet and George W. Shiflet, in *Procedia Computer Science*, vol. 29.

Introductory tutorial: Agent-based modeling and simulation (2014). Authors: Charles Macal and Michael North, in *Proceedings of the Winter Simulation Conference 2014*.

Data visualisation

In Chapter 3 we discussed some popular tools for visualising data like bar charts, graphs and scatter diagrams. There is no doubt that basic visualising tools like these are still the most common and helpful tools of the trade when it comes to data presentations and analysis. Yet the increasing variety of data and its massive volume sometimes require more creativity when it comes to visualisation. Consider some of the examples that we discussed earlier in this chapter (card transactions, passenger routes, movie streaming). How easy is it to study this kind and size of data only by bar charts and scatter diagrams? The huge amount of data, its variety and its never-ending flow require new features to be added in data visualisation. Interactive visualisation and animation are among these new features. The latter is particularly helpful when data is visualised in platforms like social media where the elements of attracting attention and speed of delivering the message are required.

Another required feature for many cases of data visualisation is the ability to present the data in a concise and limited space. Guess where there's one use for such a feature. Look at your mobile phone and you'll find the answer! An analyst will always need plenty of time and space to study the data. However when it comes to visualising it for the attention of a manager who is very busy and does many things only by IT or mobile phone, then it will be important to use tools to make it mobile screen friendly. From here come mobile visualisation tools and apps.

The effect of the internet and the ease of producing and receiving data also means visualising links and connections between different types of data. New advancements in technology, like the internet of things, and complex systems, like network theory, require analysts to look beyond simple visualisation tools. One of the other limitations of classical visualisation tools is the two-dimensional aspect of these tools. Even your 3D column chart in Excel is still in two dimensions. Here is where virtual reality can help. With the use of advanced technology you literally walk through data in a virtual world and observe visualisation of data in more than two dimensions and in various formats. Data visualisation is also going beyond just a static image. It can now be presented in an interactive mode where the analyst or user can visually 'discover' the data by interacting with the system in many ways. This includes zooming in and out, looking at the visualisation from different viewpoints and choosing between different levels of data presentation. All the above factors and advancements have made data visualisation more than just an analytical skill. Both technology and art are now essential components of data visualisation when we need to move beyond simple visualisation tools. The title of this section is 'Data visualisation'. The following case study suggests that the title could have been 'Data visualisation and sonification'!

Sonification: turning the yield curve into music

By Alan Smith

. . . It always pays to be aware of a chart's limitations, even useful ones. Take the iconic yield curve, a chart that shows the yields of government bonds of varying maturities. Analysts use the shape of the curve to gauge market expectations. It might even help predict recessions.

But with yields changing on a daily basis, showing how the curve evolves over time is not easy. That is

time running from left to right. On the yield curve, that axis is occupied by each bond's maturity date. Instead, analysts often chart the "spread" – the percentage point difference between two bonds (typically 2-year and 10-year). This produces a useful summary of the cyclical peaks and troughs of market expectations and how they might relate to recessions, but it also throws away a lot of information from the underlying yield curve.

How to read a yield curve

The curve shows the yields of different government bonds, ordered by their date of maturity

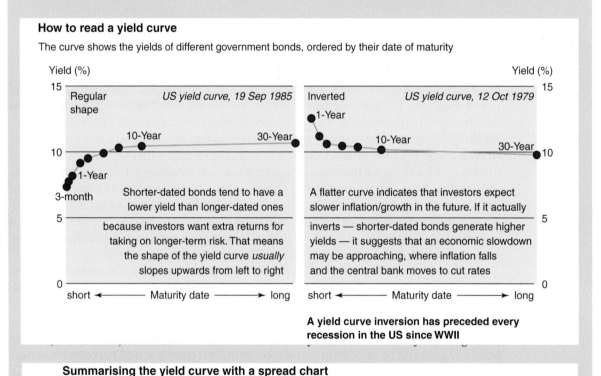

A yield curve inversion has preceded every recession in the US since WWII

Summarising the yield curve with a spread chart

Spread between 10- and 2-year Treasuries (% point)

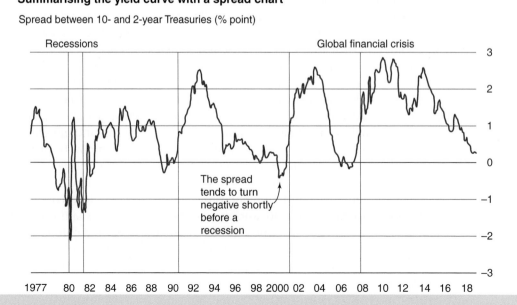

is always the risk that the particular spread chosen might not be representative of the shape of the entire curve. And how much does the curve change on a daily basis anyway? . . .

Animation is another approach worth investigating – after all, using time itself to represent time seems logical. A rapid daily animation of the yield curve shows a month's worth of data in half a second, a year in around six seconds. Tiny daily oscillations in the curve are now visible alongside more significant monthly and annual movement. . . . One problem with animation is that, with data changing so fast, it becomes difficult to remember key moments in the yield curve's progression. Adding "memory lines" with text annotations of the curve's "peak inversions" allows us to directly compare the yield curve at different points in time. Extending the animation, to show how the yield curve has changed on a daily basis since 1979 to the present day, results in a video just over three minutes long. It is compelling, but over such a duration, almost eerily silent. . . .

Of course, we could choose to add a Hans Rosling-style commentary – but could we use the data itself to produce a soundtrack? The process of turning spreadsheets into sound is known as data sonification. And it might just be the next big thing in data presentation. With our animation, the first challenge is to map the bond yields (the y-axis of the chart) to musical pitches.

While it might be tempting to think in terms of orthodox musical scales ("recession in C minor", "the great bear run in F# major"), our "music" ideally needs to preserve equal spacing between pitch in the same way as tick marks preserve distance on the chart's y-axis. The more unusual whole tone scale – beloved of Debussy – ensures that our data will be proportionally spaced in pitch. The scale was also used last year by Berliner Morgenpost to sonify SDP party polling data.

Sonification has tremendous potential to not only support and reinforce visuals, but to take data to new audiences. Chancey Fleet is assistive technology co-ordinator at New York's Andrew Heiskell Braille and Talking Book Library. She has a particular interest in accessible technology and how it can bring data into the everyday life of those who, like herself, cannot directly see data visualisations.

Watching Ms Fleet listen to the yield curve and sketch its shape on her tactile drawing tablet provides a tantalising glimpse of what sonification might be able to do for blind or visually impaired users. She immediately suggests an improvement: a "sonic legend" to provide a primer on interpreting the data. And while sensible audio defaults are a good starting point, sonification is something users should be able to personalise. But, overall, she considers the experimental yield-curve music to be a promising approach that allows her to parse information from a complex time series of over 100,000 data points. I sonified the yield curve by writing code and using specialist music software. But for this technique to truly take off into the everyday, it needs to be publicly accessible.

A new open source tool funded by Google's Digital News Initiative promises to do just that. To coincide with New York Open Data 2019 week, NYC-based Datavized has released TwoTone, an interactive tool for making music with data. The company has already explored virtual and augmented reality, but according to co founder Hugh McGrory, the first mass adoption of immersive data storytelling will be in audio "because the barrier to entry is zero – everybody already has a pair of headphones".

According to Mr McGrory, pre-release testing of TwoTone saw everything from "millennials chair dancing to music made from spreadsheets", to intense interest from cyber security outfits keen to listen to data in real time. Some might be inclined to dismiss sonification as a novelty, but a new generation of screenless devices with voice interfaces, such as Amazon's Alexa, marks the end of silent interaction with computers. It is perhaps naive to think that data will continue to just be seen and not heard. . . .

Some helpful further reading on data visualisation

Communicating Your Research with Social Media: A Practical Guide to Using Blogs, Podcasts, Data Visualisations and Video (2017). Authors: Amy Mollett, Cheryl Brumley, Chris Gilson and Sierra Williams, published by SAGE Publications.

Data Visualisation: A Handbook for Data Driven Design (2019). Author: Andy Kirk, published by: SAGE Publications

Data Visualization: A Practical Introduction (2019). Author: Kieran Healy, published by: Princeton University Press

Information is Beautiful (2012). Author: David McCandless, Published by: Collins

Quick and Dirty Guide to Data Visualisation in R: For Business People (2018). Authors: Marvilano Mochtar, Morenvino Mochtar and Michaelino Mervisiano, published by: Create Space Independent Publishing Platform.

Storytelling with Data: A Data Visualization Guide for Business Professionals (2015). Author: Cole Nussbaumer Knaflic, published by: John Wiley & Sons

Summary

We've briefly reviewed some of the most recent trends impacting on QADM. The message is clear. As the world becomes more complex, so does decision making. Analysts may never fully understand all that is happening but they never fail to develop more advanced tools in order to develop as much an understanding as possible. As a result of facing a huge amount of data in many decision-making situations, the concepts of Big Data and business analytics have developed. Artificial Intelligence emerged to make up for the limitations of the human mind when facing scenarios that involve hugely complex data and the need for fast decisions. Many analytical tools that once were used in isolation as standalone tools are now integrated and work together, like MCDA and data mining, to provide wider and more reliable results. Agent-based simulation that once had very limited use now is widely used in a variety of decision-making platforms. Data visualisation joins hands with arts and technology to bring out the best possible illustrative tools for data.

We encouraged you at the start of this section to think about how these tools are related. We presented MCDA and data mining under one title to emphasise the recent trends in integrating them as one mega-tool. The fact is, we could have presented all these topics under one title. Artificial Intelligence is one of the most useful tools when it comes to Big Data analytics, and data visualisation needs to be at its most artistic and technologically modern to be able to present the data for such complex analysis. Agent-based modelling can easily be part of a wider data analytics project and it is totally possible to link it with tools like data mining or MCDA.

As analytical tools become more advanced and find ever more applications in decision making, their links and dependency on each other also become clearer and stronger. This link itself has been one of the most important trends in the past decade and we expect it to continue at an increasing rate. It is however important to note that the analytical tools and techniques that we introduced in the text have remained and will continue to remain the main tools and techniques of the trade when it comes to decision analysis. Despite advances in organisations and businesses, most of the decision-making situations that managers face can be tackled and helped by using these tools and techniques. And as we said at the beginning of this text, our aim is not to turn you into a business analyst or statistician but rather to help you understand the quantitative analysis tools and techniques that can help you become a better manager and decision maker. Your own decision-making journey begins here.

Appendix A
Binomial Distribution

	p =	0.01	0.02	0.03	0.04	0.05	0.06	0.07	0.08	0.09
n = 2	r ≥ 0	1.0000	1.0000	1.0000	1.0000	1.0000	1.0000	1.0000	1.0000	1.0000
	1	.0199	.0396	.0591	.0784	.0975	.1164	.1351	.1536	.1719
	2	.0001	.0004	.0009	.0016	.0025	.0036	.0049	.0064	.0081
n = 5	r ≥ 0	1.0000	1.0000	1.0000	1.0000	1.0000	1.0000	1.0000	1.0000	1.0000
	1	.0490	.0961	.1413	.1846	.2262	.2661	.3043	.3409	.3760
	2	.0010	.0038	.0085	.0148	.0226	.0319	.0425	.0544	.0674
	3		.0001	.0003	.0006	.0012	.0020	.0031	.0045	.0063
	4						.0001	.0001	.0002	.0003
n = 10	r ≥ 0	1.0000	1.0000	1.0000	1.0000	1.0000	1.0000	1.0000	1.0000	1.0000
	1	.0956	.1829	.2626	.3352	.4013	.4614	.5160	.5656	.6106
	2	.0043	.0162	.0345	.0582	.0861	.1176	.1517	.1879	.2254
	3	.0001	.0009	.0028	.0062	.0115	.0188	.0283	.0401	.0540
	4			.0001	.0004	.0010	.0020	.0036	.0058	.0088
	5					.0001	.0002	.0003	.0006	.0010
	6									.0001
n = 20	r ≥ 0	1.0000	1.0000	1.0000	1.0000	1.0000	1.0000	1.0000	1.0000	1.0000
	1	.1821	.3324	.4562	.5580	.6415	.7099	.7658	.8113	.8484
	2	.0169	.0599	.1198	.1897	.2642	.3395	.4131	.4831	.5484
	3	.0010	.0071	.0210	.0439	.0755	.1150	.1610	.2121	.2666
	4		.0006	.0027	.0074	.0159	.0290	.0471	.0706	.0993
	5			.0003	.0010	.0026	.0056	.0107	.0183	.0290
	6				.0001	.0003	.0009	.0019	.0038	.0068
	7						.0001	.0003	.0006	.0013
	8								.0001	.0002
n = 50	r ≥ 0	1.0000	1.0000	1.0000	1.0000	1.0000	1.0000	1.0000	1.0000	1.0000
	1	.3950	.6358	.7819	.8701	.9231	.9547	.9734	.9845	.9910
	2	.0894	.2642	.4447	.5995	.7206	.8100	.8735	.9173	.9468
	3	.0138	.0784	.1892	.3233	.4595	.5838	.6892	.7740	.8395
	4	.0016	.0178	.0628	.1391	.2396	.3527	.4673	.5747	.6697
	5	.0001	.0032	.0168	.0490	.1036	.1794	.2710	.3710	.4723
	6		.0005	.0037	.0144	.0378	.0776	.1350	.2081	.2928
	7		.0001	.0007	.0036	.0118	.0289	.0583	.1019	.1596
	8			.0001	.0008	.0032	.0094	.0220	.0438	.0768
	9				.0001	.0008	.0027	.0073	.0167	.0328

	p =	0.01	0.02	0.03	0.04	0.05	0.06	0.07	0.08	0.09
	10					.0002	.0007	.0022	.0056	.0125
	11						.0002	.0006	.0017	.0043
	12							.0001	.0005	.0013
	13								.0001	.0004
	14									.0001

	p =	0.01	0.02	0.03	0.04	0.05	0.06	0.07	0.08	0.09
n − 100	r ≥ 0	1.0000	1.0000	1.0000	1.0000	1.0000	1.0000	1.0000	1.0000	1.0000
	1	.6340	.8674	.9524	.9831	.9941	.9979	.9993	.9998	.9999
	2	.2642	.5967	.8054	.9128	.9629	.9848	.9940	.9977	.9991
	3	.0794	.3233	.5802	.7679	.8817	.9434	.9742	.9887	.9952
	4	.0184	.1410	.3528	.5705	.7422	.8570	.9256	.9633	.9827
	5	.0034	.0508	.1821	.3711	.5640	.7232	.8368	.9097	.9526
	6	.0005	.0155	.0808	.2116	.3840	.5593	.7086	.8201	.8955
	7	.0001	.0041	.0312	.1064	.2340	.3936	.5557	.6968	.8060
	8		.0009	.0106	.0475	.1280	.2517	.4012	.5529	.6872
	9		.0002	.0032	.0190	.0631	.1463	.2660	.4074	.5506
	10			.0009	.0068	.0282	.0775	.1620	.2780	.4125
	11			.0002	.0022	.0115	.0376	.0908	.1757	.2882
	12				.0007	.0043	.0168	.0469	.1028	.1876
	13				.0002	.0015	.0069	.0224	.0559	.1138
	14					.0005	.0026	.0099	.0282	.0645
	15					.0001	.0009	.0041	.0133	.0341
	16						.0003	.0016	.0058	.0169
	17						.0001	.0006	.0024	.0078
	18							.0002	.0009	.0034
	19							.0001	.0003	.0014
	20								.0001	.0005
	21									.0002
	22									.0001

	p =	0.10	0.15	0.20	0.25	0.30	0.35	0.40	0.45	0.50
n = 2	r ≥ 0	1.0000	1.0000	1.0000	1.0000	1.0000	1.0000	1.0000	1.0000	1.0000
	1	.1900	.2775	.3600	.4375	.5100	.5775	.6400	.6975	.7500
	2	.0100	.0225	.0400	.0625	.0900	.1225	.1600	.2025	.2500
n = 5	r ≥ 0	1.0000	1.0000	1.0000	1.0000	1.0000	1.0000	1.0000	1.0000	1.0000
	1	.4095	.5563	.6723	.7627	.8319	.8840	.9222	.9497	.9688
	2	.0815	.1648	.2627	.3672	.4718	.5716	.6630	.7438	.8125
	3	.0086	.0266	.0579	.1035	.1631	.2352	.3174	.4069	.5000
	4	.0005	.0022	.0067	.0156	.0308	.0540	.0870	.1312	.1875
	5		.0001	.0003	.0010	.0024	.0053	.0102	.0185	.0313
n = 10	r ≥ 0	1.0000	1.0000	1.0000	1.0000	1.0000	1.0000	1.0000	1.0000	1.0000
	1	.6513	.8031	.8926	.9437	.9718	.9865	.9940	.9975	.9990
	2	.2639	.4557	.6242	.7560	.8507	.9140	.9536	.9767	.9893
	3	.0702	.1798	.3222	.4744	.6172	.7384	.8327	.9004	.9453
	4	.0128	.0500	.1209	.2241	.3504	.4862	.6177	.7430	.8281
	5	.0016	.0099	.0328	.0781	.1503	.2485	.3669	.4956	.6230

	p =	0.10	0.15	0.20	0.25	0.30	0.35	0.40	0.45	0.50
	6	.0001	.0014	.0064	.0197	.0473	.0949	.1662	.2616	.3770
	7		.0001	.0009	.0035	.0106	.0260	.0548	.1020	.1719
	8			.0001	.0004	.0016	.0048	.0123	.0274	.0547
	9					.0001	.0005	.0017	.0045	.0107
	10							.0001	.0003	.0010
n = 20	r ≥ 0	1.0000	1.0000	1.0000	1.0000	1.0000	1.0000	1.0000	1.0000	1.0000
	1	.8784	.9612	.9885	.9968	.9992	.9998	1.0000	1.0000	1.0000
	2	.6083	.8244	.9308	.9757	.9924	.9979	.9995	.9999	1.0000
	3	.3231	.5951	.7939	.9087	.9645	.9879	.9964	.9991	.9998
	4	.1330	.3523	.5886	.7748	.8929	.9556	.9840	.9951	.9987
	5	.0432	.1702	.3704	.5852	.7625	.8818	.9490	.9811	.9941
	6	.0113	.0673	.1958	.3828	.5836	.7546	.8744	.9447	.9793
	7	.0024	.0219	.0867	.2142	.3920	.5834	.7500	.8701	.9423
	8	.0004	.0059	.0321	.1018	.2277	.3990	.5841	.7480	.8684
	9	.0001	.0013	.0100	.0409	.1133	.2376	.4044	.5857	.7483
	10		.0002	.0026	.0139	.0480	.1218	.2447	.4086	.5881
	11			.0006	.0039	.0171	.0532	.1275	.2493	.4119
	12			.0001	.0009	.0051	.0196	.0565	.1308	.2517
	13				.0002	.0013	.0060	.0210	.0580	.1316
	14					.0003	.0015	.0065	.0214	.0577
	15						.0003	.0016	.0064	.0207
	16							.0003	.0015	.0059
	17								.0003	.0013
	18									.0002
n = 50	r ≥ 0	1.0000	1.0000	1.0000	1.0000	1.0000	1.0000	1.0000	1.0000	1.0000
	1	.9948	.9997	1.0000	1.0000	1.0000	1.0000	1.0000	1.0000	1.0000
	2	.9662	.9971	.9998	1.0000	1.0000	1.0000	1.0000	1.0000	1.0000
	3	.8883	.9858	.9987	.9999	1.0000	1.0000	1.0000	1.0000	1.0000
	4	.7497	.9540	.9943	.9995	1.0000	1.0000	1.0000	1.0000	1.0000
	5	.5688	.8879	.9815	.9979	.9998	1.0000	1.0000	1.0000	1.0000
	6	.3839	.7806	.9520	.9930	.9993	.9999	1.0000	1.0000	1.0000
	7	.2298	.6387	.8966	.9806	.9975	.9998	1.0000	1.0000	1.0000
	8	.1221	.4812	.8096	.9547	.9927	.9992	.9999	1.0000	1.0000
	9	.0579	.3319	.6927	.9084	.9817	.9975	.9998	1.0000	1.0000
	10	.0245	.2089	.5563	.8363	.9598	.9933	.9992	.9999	1.0000
	11	.0094	.1199	.4164	.7378	.9211	.9840	.9978	.9998	1.0000
	12	.0032	.0628	.2893	.6184	.8610	.9658	.9943	.9994	1.0000
	13	.0010	.0301	.1861	.4890	.7771	.9339	.9867	.9982	.9998
	14	.0003	.0132	.1106	.3630	.6721	.8837	.9720	.9955	.9995
	15	.0001	.0053	.0607	.2519	.5532	.8122	.9460	.9896	.9987
	16		.0019	.0308	.1631	.4308	.7199	.9045	.9780	.9967
	17		.0007	.0144	.0983	.3161	.6111	.8439	.9573	.9923
	18		.0002	.0063	.0551	.2178	.4940	.7631	.9235	.9836
	19		.0001	.0025	.0287	.1406	.3784	.6644	.8727	.9675
	20			.0009	.0139	.0848	.2736	.5535	.8026	.9405
	21			.0003	.0063	.0478	.1861	.4390	.7138	.8987
	22			.0001	.0026	.0251	.1187	.3299	.6100	.8389
	23				.0010	.0123	.0710	.2340	.4981	.7601

p =	0.10	0.15	0.20	0.25	0.30	0.35	0.40	0.45	0.50
24				.0004	.0056	.0396	.1562	.3866	.6641
25				.0001	.0024	.0207	.0978	.2840	.5561
26					.0009	.0100	.0573	.1966	.4439
27					.0003	.0045	.0314	.1279	.3359
28					.0001	.0019	.0160	.0780	.2399
29						.0007	.0076	.0444	.1611
30						.0003	.0034	.0235	.1013
31						.0001	.0014	.0116	.0595
32							.0005	.0053	.0325
33							.0002	.0022	.0164
34							.0001	.0009	.0077
35								.0003	.0033
36								.0001	.0013
37									.0005
38									.0002

	p =	0.10	0.15	0.20	0.25	0.30	0.35	0.40	0.45	0.50
n = 100	r ≥ 0	1.0000	1.0000	1.0000	1.0000	1.0000	1.0000	1.0000	1.0000	1.0000
	1	1.0000	1.0000	1.0000	1.0000	1.0000	1.0000	1.0000	1.0000	1.0000
	2	.9997	1.0000	1.0000	1.0000	1.0000	1.0000	1.0000	1.0000	1.0000
	3	.9981	1.0000	1.0000	1.0000	1.0000	1.0000	1.0000	1.0000	1.0000
	4	.9992	.9999	1.0000	1.0000	1.0000	1.0000	1.0000	1.0000	1.0000
	5	.9763	.9996	1.0000	1.0000	1.0000	1.0000	1.0000	1.0000	1.0000
	6	.9424	.9984	1.0000	1.0000	1.0000	1.0000	1.0000	1.0000	1.0000
	7	.8828	.9953	.9999	1.0000	1.0000	1.0000	1.0000	1.0000	1.0000
	8	.7939	.9878	.9997	1.0000	1.0000	1.0000	1.0000	1.0000	1.0000
	9	.6791	.9725	.9991	1.0000	1.0000	1.0000	1.0000	1.0000	1.0000
	10	.5487	.9449	.9977	1.0000	1.0000	1.0000	1.0000	1.0000	1.0000
	11	.4168	.9006	.9943	.9999	1.0000	1.0000	1.0000	1.0000	1.0000
	12	.2970	.8365	.9874	.9996	1.0000	1.0000	1.0000	1.0000	1.0000
	13	.1982	.7527	.9747	.9990	1.0000	1.0000	1.0000	1.0000	1.0000
	14	.1239	.6526	.9531	.9975	.9999	1.0000	1.0000	1.0000	1.0000
	15	.0726	.5428	.9196	.9946	.9998	1.0000	1.0000	1.0000	1.0000
	16	.0399	.4317	.8715	.9889	.9996	1.0000	1.0000	1.0000	1.0000
	17	.0206	.3275	.8077	.9789	.9990	1.0000	1.0000	1.0000	1.0000
	18	.0100	.2367	.7288	.9624	.9978	.9999	1.0000	1.0000	1.0000
	19	.0046	.1628	.6379	.9370	.9955	.9999	1.0000	1.0000	1.0000
	20	.0020	.1065	.5398	.9005	.9911	.9997	1.0000	1.0000	1.0000
	21	.0008	.0663	.4405	.8512	.9835	.9992	1.0000	1.0000	1.0000
	22	.0003	.0393	.3460	.7886	.9712	.9983	1.0000	1.0000	1.0000
	23	.0001	.0221	.2611	.7136	.9521	.9966	.9999	1.0000	1.0000
	24		.0119	.1891	.6289	.9245	.9934	.9997	1.0000	1.0000
	25		.0061	.1314	.5383	.8864	.9879	.9994	1.0000	1.0000
	26		.0030	.0875	.4465	.8369	.9789	.9988	1.0000	1.0000
	27		.0014	.0558	.3583	.7756	.9649	.9976	.9999	1.0000
	28		.0006	.0342	.2776	.7036	.9442	.9954	.9998	1.0000
	29		.0003	.0200	.2075	.6232	.9152	.9916	.9996	1.0000

p =	0.10	0.15	0.20	0.25	0.30	0.35	0.40	0.45	0.50
30		.0001	.0112	.1495	.5377	.8764	.9852	.9992	1.0000
31			.0061	.1038	.4509	.8270	.9752	.9985	1.0000
32			.0031	.0693	.3669	.7669	.9602	.9970	.9999
33			.0016	.0446	.2893	.6971	.9385	.9945	.9998
34			.0007	.0276	.2207	.6197	.9087	.9902	.9996
35			.0003	.0164	.1629	.5376	.8697	.9834	.9991
36			.0001	.0094	.1161	.4542	.8205	.9728	.9982
37			.0001	.0052	.0799	.3731	.7614	.9571	.9967
38				.0027	.0530	.2976	.6932	.9349	.9940
39				.0014	.0340	.2301	.6178	.9049	.9895
40				.0007	.0210	.1724	.5379	.8657	.9824
41				.0003	.0125	.1250	.4567	.8169	.9716
42				.0001	.0072	.0877	.3775	.7585	.9557
43				.0001	.0040	.0594	.3033	.6913	.9334
44					.0021	.0389	.2365	.6172	.9033
45					.0011	.0246	.1789	.5387	.8644
46					.0005	.0150	.1311	.4587	.8159
47					.0003	.0088	.0930	.3804	.7579
48					.0001	.0050	.0638	.3069	.6914
49					.0001	.0027	.0423	.2404	.6178
50						.0015	.0271	.1827	.5398
51						.0007	.0168	.1346	.4602
52						.0004	.0100	.0960	.3822
53						.0002	.0058	.0662	.3086
54						.0001	.0032	.0441	.2421
55							.0017	.0284	.1841
56							.0009	.0176	.1356
57							.0004	.0106	.0967
58							.0002	.0061	.0666
59							.0001	.0034	.0443
60								.0018	.0284
61								.0009	.0176
62								.0005	.0105
63								.0002	.0060
64								.0001	.0033
65									.0018
66									.0009
67									.0004
68									.0002
69									.0001

Appendix B
Areas in the Tail of the
Normal Distribution

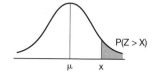

Z	.00	.01	.02	.03	.04	.05	.06	.07	.08	.09
0.0	.5000	.4960	.4920	.4880	.4840	.4801	.4761	.4721	.4681	.4641
0.1	.4602	.4562	.4522	.4483	.4443	.4404	.4364	.4325	.4286	.4247
0.2	.4207	.4168	.4129	.4090	.4052	.4013	.3974	.3936	.3897	.3859
0.3	.3821	.3783	.3745	.3707	.3669	.3632	.3594	.3557	.3520	.3483
0.4	.3446	.3409	.3372	.3336	.3300	.3264	.3228	.3192	.3156	.3121
0.5	.3085	.3050	.3015	.2981	.2946	.2912	.2877	.2843	.2810	.2776
0.6	.2743	.2709	.2676	.2643	.2611	.2578	.2546	.2514	.2483	.2451
0.7	.2420	.2389	.2358	.2327	.2296	.2266	.2236	.2206	.2177	.2148
0.8	.2119	.2090	.2061	.2033	.2005	.1977	.1949	.1922	.1894	.1867
0.9	.1841	.1814	.1788	.1762	.1736	.1711	.1685	.1660	.1635	.1611
1.0	.1587	.1562	.1539	.1515	.1492	.1469	.1446	.1423	.1401	.1379
1.1	.1357	.1335	.1314	.1292	.1271	.1251	.1230	.1210	.1190	.1170
1.2	.1151	.1131	.1112	.1093	.1075	.1056	.1038	.1020	.1003	.0985
1.3	.0968	.0951	.0934	.0918	.0901	.0885	.0869	.0853	.0838	.0823
1.4	.0808	.0793	.0778	.0764	.0749	.0735	.0721	.0708	.0694	.0681
1.5	.0668	.0655	.0643	.0630	.0618	.0606	.0594	.0582	.0571	.0559
1.6	.0548	.0537	.0526	.0516	.0505	.0495	.0485	.0475	.0465	.0455
1.7	.0446	.0436	.0427	.0418	.0409	.0401	.0392	.0384	.0375	.0367
1.8	.0359	.0351	.0344	.0336	.0329	.0322	.0314	.0307	.0301	.0294
1.9	.0287	.0281	.0274	.0268	.0262	.0256	.0250	.0244	.0239	.0233
2.0	.0228	.0222	.0217	.0212	.0207	.0202	.0197	.0192	.0188	.0183
2.1	.0179	.0174	.0170	.0166	.0162	.0158	.0154	.0150	.0146	.0143
2.2	.0139	.0136	.0132	.0129	.0125	.0122	.0119	.0116	.0133	.0110
2.3	.0107	.0104	.0102	.0099	.0096	.0094	.0091	.0089	.0087	.0084
2.4	.0082	.0080	.0078	.0075	.0073	.0071	.0069	.0068	.0066	.0064
2.5	.0062	.0060	.0059	.0057	.0055	.0054	.0052	.0051	.0049	.0048
2.6	.0047	.0045	.0044	.0043	.0041	.0040	.0039	.0038	.0037	.0036
2.7	.0035	.0034	.0033	.0032	.0031	.0030	.0029	.0028	.0027	.0026
2.8	.0026	.0025	.0024	.0023	.0023	.0022	.0021	.0021	.0020	.0019
2.9	.0019	.0018	.0018	.0017	.0016	.0016	.0015	.0015	.0014	.0014
3.0	.0014	.0013	.0013	.0012	.0012	.0011	.0011	.0011	.0010	.0010

Appendix C
Areas in the Tail of the t Distribution

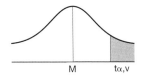

			α		
ν	0.10	0.05	0.025	0.01	0.005
1	3.078	6.314	12.706	31.821	63.657
2	1.886	2.920	4.303	6.965	9.925
3	1.638	2.353	3.182	4.541	5.841
4	1.533	2.132	2.776	3.747	4.604
5	1.476	2.015	2.571	3.365	4.032
6	1.440	1.943	2.447	3.143	3.707
7	1.415	1.895	2.365	2.998	3.499
8	1.397	1.860	2.306	2.896	3.355
9	1.383	1.833	2.262	2.821	3.250
10	1.372	1.812	2.228	2.764	3.169
11	1.363	1.796	2.201	2.718	3.106
12	1.356	1.782	2.179	2.681	3.055
13	1.350	1.771	2.160	2.650	3.012
14	1.345	1.761	2.145	2.624	2.977
15	1.341	1.753	2.131	2.602	2.947
16	1.337	1.746	2.120	2.583	2.921
17	1.333	1.740	2.110	2.567	2.898
18	1.330	1.734	2.101	2.552	2.878
19	1.328	1.729	2.093	2.539	2.861
20	1.325	1.725	2.086	2.528	2.845
25	1.316	1.708	2.060	2.485	2.787
30	1.310	1.697	2.042	2.457	2.750
40	1.303	1.684	2.021	2.423	2.704
50	1.299	1.676	2.009	2.403	2.678
∞	1.282	1.645	1.960	2.326	2.576

Appendix D
Areas in the Tail of the χ^2 Distribution

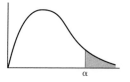

Degrees of freedom	Level of significance α		Degrees of freedom	Level of significance α	
	0.05	0.01		0.05	0.01
1	3.84	6.63	20	31.41	37.57
2	5.99	9.21	21	32.67	38.93
3	7.81	11.34	22	33.92	40.29
4	9.49	13.28	23	35.17	41.64
5	11.07	15.09	24	36.42	42.98
6	12.59	16.81	25	37.65	44.31
7	14.07	18.48	26	38.89	45.64
8	15.51	20.09	27	40.11	46.96
9	16.92	21.67	28	41.34	48.28
10	18.31	23.21	29	42.56	49.59
11	19.68	24.72	30	43.77	50.89
12	21.03	26.22	40	55.76	63.69
13	22.36	27.69	50	67.50	76.15
14	23.68	29.14	60	79.08	88.38
15	25.00	30.58	70	90.53	100.43
16	26.30	32.00	80	101.88	112.33
17	27.59	33.41	90	113.15	124.12
18	28.87	34.81	100	124.34	135.81
19	30.14	36.19			

Appendix E
Areas in the Tail of the F Distribution, 0.05 Level

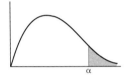

ν_2 \ ν_1	1	2	3	4	5	6	7	8	9
1	161.45	199.50	215.71	224.58	230.16	233.99	236.77	238.88	240.54
2	18.513	19.000	19.164	19.247	19.296	19.330	19.353	19.371	19.385
3	10.128	9.5521	9.2766	9.1172	9.0135	8.9406	8.8867	8.8452	8.8323
4	7.7086	6.9443	6.5914	6.3882	6.2561	6.1631	6.0942	6.0410	5.9938
5	6.6079	5.7861	5.4095	5.1922	5.0503	4.9503	4.8759	4.8183	4.7725
6	5.9874	5.1433	4.7571	4.5337	4.3874	4.2839	4.2067	4.1468	4.0990
7	5.5914	4.7374	4.3468	4.1203	3.9715	3.8660	3.7870	3.7257	3.6767
8	5.3177	4.4590	4.0662	3.8379	3.6875	3.5806	3.5005	3.4381	3.3881
9	5.1174	4.2565	3.8625	3.6331	3.4817	3.3738	3.2927	3.2296	3.1789
10	4.9646	4.1028	3.7083	3.4780	3.3258	3.2172	3.1355	3.0717	3.0204
11	4.8443	3.9823	3.5874	3.3567	3.2039	3.0946	3.0123	2.9480	2.8962
12	4.7472	3.8853	3.4903	3.2592	3.1059	2.9961	2.9134	2.8486	2.7964
13	4.6672	3.8056	3.4105	3.1791	3.0254	2.9153	2.8321	2.7669	2.7444
14	4.6001	3.7389	3.3439	3.1122	2.9582	2.8477	2.7642	2.6987	2.6458
15	4.5431	3.6823	3.2874	3.0556	2.9013	2.7905	2.7066	2.6408	2.5876
16	4.4940	3.6337	3.2389	3.0069	2.8524	2.7413	2.6572	2.5911	2.5377
17	4.4513	3.5915	3.1968	2.9647	2.8100	2.6987	2.6143	2.5480	2.4443
18	4.4139	3.5546	3.1599	2.9277	2.7729	2.6613	2.5767	2.5102	2.4563
19	4.3807	3.5219	3.1274	2.8951	2.7401	2.6283	2.5435	2.4768	2.4227
20	4.3512	3.4928	3.0984	2.8661	2.7109	2.5990	2.5140	2.4471	2.3928
21	4.3248	3.4668	3.0725	2.8401	2.6848	2.5727	2.4876	2.4205	2.3660
22	4.3009	3.4434	3.0491	2.8167	2.6613	2.5491	2.4638	2.3965	2.3219
23	4.2793	3.4221	3.0280	2.7955	2.6400	2.5277	2.4422	2.3748	2.3201
24	4.2597	3.4028	3.0088	2.7763	2.6207	2.5082	2.4226	2.3551	2.3002
25	4.2417	3.3852	2.9912	2.7587	2.6030	2.4904	2.4047	2.3371	2.2821
26	4.2252	3.3690	2.9752	2.7426	2.5868	2.4741	2.3883	2.3205	2.2655
27	4.2100	3.3541	2.9604	2.7278	2.5719	2.4591	2.3732	2.3053	2.2501
28	4.1960	3.3404	2.9467	2.7141	2.5581	2.4453	2.3593	2.2913	2.2360
29	4.1830	3.3277	2.9340	2.7014	2.5454	2.4324	2.3463	2.2783	2.2329
30	4.1709	3.3158	2.9223	2.6896	2.5336	2.4205	2.3343	2.2662	2.2507
40	4.0847	3.2317	2.8387	2.6060	2.4495	2.3359	2.2490	2.1802	2.1240
60	4.0012	3.1504	2.7581	2.5252	2.3683	2.2541	2.1665	2.0970	2.0401
120	3.9201	3.0718	2.6802	2.4472	2.2899	2.1750	2.0868	2.0164	1.9688
∞	3.8415	2.9957	2.6049	2.3719	2.2141	2.0986	2.0096	1.9384	1.8799

ν_2 \ ν_1	10	12	15	20	24	30	40	60	120	∞
1	241.88	243.91	245.95	248.01	249.05	250.10	251.14	252.20	253.25	254.31
2	19.396	19.413	19.429	19.446	19.454	19.462	19.471	19.479	19.487	19.496
3	8.7855	8.7446	8.7029	8.6602	8.6385	8.6166	8.5944	8.5720	8.5594	8.5264
4	5.9644	5.9117	5.8578	5.8025	5.7744	5.7459	5.7170	5.6877	5.6381	5.6281
5	4.7351	4.6777	4.6188	4.5581	4.5272	4.4957	4.4638	4.4314	4.3085	4.3650
6	4.0600	3.9999	3.9381	3.8742	3.8415	3.8082	3.7743	3.7398	3.7047	3.6689
7	3.6365	3.5747	3.5107	3.4445	3.4105	3.3758	3.3404	3.3043	3.2674	3.2298
8	3.3472	3.2839	3.2184	3.1503	3.1152	3.0794	3.0428	3.0053	2.9669	2.9276
9	3.1373	3.0729	3.0061	2.9365	2.9005	2.8637	2.8259	2.7872	2.7475	2.7067
10	2.9782	2.9130	2.8450	2.7740	2.7372	2.6996	2.6609	2.6211	2.5801	2.5379
11	2.8536	2.7876	2.7186	2.6464	2.6090	2.5705	2.5309	2.4901	2.4480	2.4045
12	2.7534	2.6866	2.6169	2.5436	2.5055	2.4663	2.4259	2.3842	2.3410	2.2962
13	2.6710	2.6037	2.5331	2.4589	2.4202	2.3803	2.3392	2.2966	2.2524	2.2064
14	2.6022	2.5342	2.4630	2.3879	2.3487	2.3082	2.2664	2.2229	2.1778	2.1307
15	2.5437	2.4753	2.4034	2.3275	2.2878	2.2468	2.2043	2.1601	2.1141	2.0658
16	2.4935	2.4247	2.3522	2.2756	2.2354	2.1938	2.1507	2.1058	2.0589	2.0096
17	2.4499	2.3807	2.3077	2.2304	2.1898	2.1477	2.1040	2.0584	2.0107	1.9604
18	2.4117	2.3421	2.2686	2.1906	2.1497	2.1071	2.0629	2.0166	1.9681	1.9168
19	2.3779	2.3080	2.2341	2.1555	2.1141	2.0712	2.0264	1.9795	1.9302	1.8780
20	2.3479	2.2776	2.2033	2.1242	2.0825	2.0391	1.9938	1.9464	1.8963	1.8432
21	2.3210	2.2504	2.1757	2.0960	2.0540	2.0102	1.9645	1.9165	1.8657	1.8117
22	2.2967	2.2258	2.1508	2.0707	2.0283	1.9842	1.9380	1.8894	1.8380	1.7831
23	2.2747	2.2036	2.1282	2.0476	2.0050	1.9605	1.9139	1.8648	1.8128	1.7570
24	2.2547	2.1834	2.1077	2.0267	1.9838	1.9390	1.8920	1.8424	1.7896	1.7330
25	2.2365	2.1649	2.0889	2.0075	1.9643	1.9192	1.8718	1.8217	1.7684	1.7110
26	2.2197	2.1479	2.0716	1.9898	1.9464	1.9010	1.8533	1.8027	1.7488	1.6906
27	2.2043	2.1323	2.0558	1.9736	1.9299	1.8842	1.8361	1.7851	1.7306	1.6717
28	2.1900	2.1179	2.0411	1.9586	1.9147	1.8687	1.8203	1.7689	1.7138	1.6541
29	2.1768	2.1045	2.0275	1.9446	1.9005	1.8543	1.8055	1.7537	1.6981	1.6376
30	2.1646	2.0921	2.0148	1.9317	1.8874	1.8409	1.7918	1.7396	1.6835	1.6223
40	2.0772	2.0035	1.9245	1.8389	1.7929	1.7444	1.6928	1.6373	1.5766	1.5089
60	1.9926	1.9174	1.8364	1.7480	1.7001	1.6491	1.5943	1.5343	1.4673	1.3893
120	1.9105	1.8337	1.7505	1.6587	1.6084	1.5543	1.4952	1.4290	1.3519	1.2539
∞	1.8307	1.7522	1.6664	1.5705	1.5173	1.4591	1.3940	1.3180	1.0214	1.0000

Appendix F
Solutions to Chapter
Progress Check Questions

Note: if a particular activity does not have a solution shown here, the solution has been given in the chapter text following that activity.

Progress Check 2.1

(a) the number of private houses built last year
This will be discrete as only a whole number of houses can be built.
(b) the average price of a house
This is more problematic. The price will be measured in terms of a given number of £s. Financial data is technically discrete as it can take only fixed, numerical values. However, it is often treated as a continuous variable and we shall do so in this text.
(c) the number of people employed in the construction industry
Nominally, this will be discrete as we would normally think of counting the (whole) number of people employed. Even if we had fractions of people (perhaps representing those employed on a part-time basis) this would still be discrete (taking fixed, numerical values).
(d) the number of tonnes of concrete used in house construction
Technically continuous, as our measurement could, in theory, be to any required degree of accuracy.
(e) the different types of houses constructed
This would be an attribute variable.

Progress Check 2.2

25% can be expressed as 0.25 as a decimal or 1/4 as a fraction (i.e. we want to find 1/4 of the two original numbers). Using a pocket calculator it is easiest to use 0.25:

We require $0.25 \times 12\,098$ which gives 3024.5
and for 0.25×139.5 we get 34.875.

It is always a good idea when you are doing this sort of arithmetic (even on a spreadsheet) to have some mental idea as to the size of the number you should get as an answer. This will help you do a quick visual check as to whether the answer looks about right. Here we want 1/4 of each number. The first number is about 12 000 and mentally we can figure out that a quarter of this will be about 3000. Our calculated answer of 3024.5 is obviously in the right ballpark. Similarly a quarter of our second number, which is about 140, will be about 35. Get into the habit of doing this every time.

For the other calculations it is again best to convert them into decimals:

0.33
0.90
0.05 (take care over this one for 5%)
0.33
0.125
0.375

and using these in turn with each of the two original numbers:

0.33 gives 3992.34 and 46.035
0.90 gives 10888.2 and 125.55
0.05 gives 604.9 and 6.975
0.33 gives 3992.34 and 46.035
0.125 gives 1512.25 and 17.4375
0.375 gives 4536.75 and 52.3125.

Progress Check 2.3

(a) £1 078 245.7
(b) £1 078 250
(c) £1 078 000
(d) £1 100 000

Progress Check 2.4

(a) 100.2(34 − 7)/13
The arithmetic order is to do the arithmetic inside the bracket first, then the multiplication, then the division. This gives:

$$100.2(27)/13$$

$$= 208.108$$

$$= 208.1 \text{ (rounded)}$$

(b) $0.5 - 0.8 \times 13 + 3$
Here, the arithmetic order is multiplication, addition, subtraction:

$$0.5 - 10.4 + 3$$
$$= 0.5 - 7.4 \text{ (taking care that } -10.4 + 3 \text{ is done correctly)}$$
$$= -6.9$$

Note also that it would have been better to write (b) as:

$$0.5 - (0.8 \times 13) + 3$$

(c) $(100 \times 2) - (5/2) \times 10$
Here we have two sets of brackets, so we need to do each of these first (it doesn't matter in what order), then the multiplication, then the subtraction:

$$(200) - (2.5) \times 10$$

$$= 200 - 25$$

$$= 175$$

Progress Check 2.5

(a) We wish to multiply two numbers so we must take their logs and add these together, then find the antilog.

$$\log 1098.2 = 3.0406814$$
$$\log 34 = 1.5314789$$
$$(\log 1098.2) + (\log 34) = 3.0406814 + 1.5314789 = 4.5721603$$
$$\text{antilog}(4.5721603) = 37\,338.8$$

(b) We have:

$$\log 345.6 = 2.5385737$$
$$\log 23.7 = 1.3747483$$
$$\log 109.3 = 2.0386202$$

giving

$$2.5385737 - 1.3747483 + 2.0386202 = 3.20244$$
$$\text{antilog}(3.20244) = 1593.84$$

(c) We take the log of 12.569, multiply by 5 and find the antilog:

$$\log 12.569 = 1.0993007$$
$$\text{multiply by } 5 = 5.4965035$$
$$\text{antilog}(5.4965035) = 313\,692.04$$

(d) We take the log of 156, divide by 8 and find the antilog:

$$\log 156 = 2.1931246$$
$$\text{divide by } 8 = 0.274140575$$
$$\text{antilog}(0.274140575) = 1.88$$

Progress Check 2.6

(a) We require the sum of all the X values:

$$\Sigma X = 2 + 3 + 7 + 9 = 21$$

(b) Similarly, we require the sum of the Y values:

$$\Sigma Y = 10 + 12 + 14 + 18 = 54$$

(c) Here we require the sum of the X^2 values – that is, we square each X value and then add these resulting numbers together:

$$\Sigma X^2 = 2^2 + 3^2 + 7^2 + 9^2 = 4 + 9 + 49 + 81 = 143$$

(d) Here we find the total of the X values and square this total:

$$(\Sigma X)^2 = (21)^2 = 441$$

(e) This is the same as ΣY^2:

$$\Sigma Y^2 = 10^2 + 12^2 + 14^2 + 18^2 = 764$$

(f) We multiply each pair of Y and X values and then total:

$$\Sigma YX = (10 \times 2) + (12 \times 3) + (14 \times 7) + (18 \times 9) = 316$$

(g) $10! = 3\,628\,800$

(h) $3! = 6$

(i) $10! - 3! = 3\,628\,800 - 6 = 3\,628\,794$

Progress Check 2.8

We recognise this as a linear equation and following the steps set out we have the following:

Step 1
The price variable, P, corresponds to the X, horizontal, axis. It seems logical to set the minimum value for P at 0 (after all the firm cannot charge a negative price). The maximum value for P can logically be set at 20, since some mental arithmetic indicates that with $P = 20$ Q will equal zero and again negative values for Q have no business meaning. Accordingly, we have an X scale from 0 to 20.

Step 2
The Y (or Q) scale will go from 0 to 100, following on from the logic used in Step 1. Our two points will be:

$$P = 0, Q = 100$$
$$P = 20, Q = 0$$

Step 3
We need to ensure labels, scales, etc. are appropriately drawn.

Step 4
The two points, and the line joining them, are shown in Figure A.1.

From the graph we can determine Q when $P = 7$ as 65 (000). We can also determine that when $Q = 40$ (000) then P must be 12. Both results can also be confirmed directly from the equation.

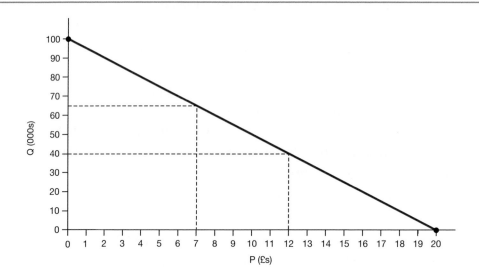

Figure A.1 $Q = 100 - 5P$

Progress Check 2.9

We calculate:

$$26\,000 \times \frac{100}{115} = £22\,609 \text{ (rounded)}$$

That is, the £26 000 is worth the same as £22 609 in 2015. After allowing for inflation over this period, we would be £2609 better off in real terms.

Progress Check 3.1

A retail organisation would probably be interested in reviewing such data as part of its overall strategic review. Changes in expenditure patterns and growth/decline in spending behaviour are clearly of critical importance to a retail organisation. From Table 3.1 itself a number of key points can be made:

● Overall, total expenditure has increased over this period by about 100 000 (£million).
● Over the expenditure categories shown, consumers' expenditure has changed in different ways.

However, it is also clear that without performing additional calculations it is difficult to assess relative changes over this period.

Progress Check 3.2

We'd probably go for Figures 3.4 and 3.7 as these highlight the key patterns and changes.

Progress Check 3.4

The histogram is shown in Figure A.7.

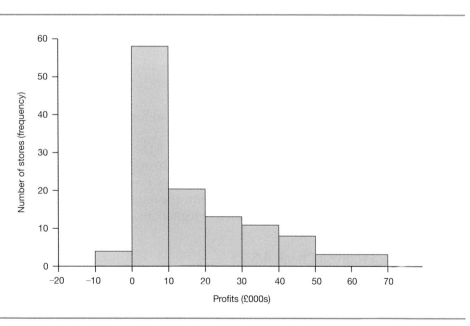

Figure A.7 Histogram of store profits for Region B

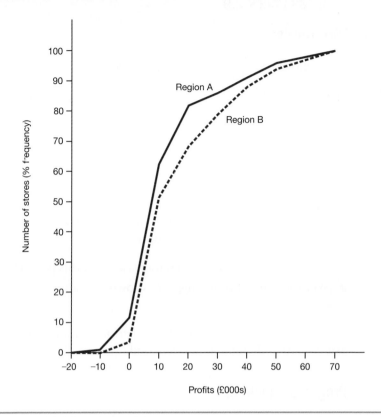

Figure A.8 Ogives for Region A and Region B

As with the histogram for Region A (Figure 3.9), we need to adjust the frequencies for the last interval. As before, these are divided by two and a frequency of 3.5 should be plotted for the last interval. Comparing the histograms of the two regions we note that they give a very similar profile across the X axis, with both having a 'peak' in the 0–10 interval and then showing a tailing off effect as we move into higher profit intervals.

Progress Check 3.5

Figure A.8 shows the two ogives. That for Region A, of course, is identical to that in Figure 3.12. We note that the two ogives are different and the implications of this need to be considered. We see that for Region B the ogive is below that for Region A. This implies that for any given profit level – say £30 000 – there is a smaller percentage of Region B's stores below this figure than Region A's. Conversely, there must be a higher percentage of Region B's stores above this profit. The implications of Region B's ogive being lower then is that, typically, its stores have higher profits than Region A's.

Progress Check 4.3

If one of the data items increases from 38 to 48, then the mean will increase (by 10/11 since we are adding 10 to the total, Σx, and there are still 11 numbers in the data set, n). However, the median for Month 1 will remain unchanged since in our ordered array we start at the smallest value and count along until we get to the sixth value, which is the median value. In other words, the mean will be slightly higher as a result, but the median will remain unchanged. This is a feature that will be helpful later.

Progress Check 4.6

The standard deviation for Month 2 works out at 3.3 days (the sum of the squared deviations is 122).

Progress Check 4.8

The various statistics are shown below:

	Before media campaign	After media campaign
Mean	234.2	277.5
SD	39.7	45.0
Min	173	204
Max	317	381
Range	144	177
Q1	205	241
Median	228	279.5
Q3	262	311
IQR	57	70
CofV	0.17	0.16
CofSk	0.47	−0.13

Note that figures have been calculated in an Excel spreadsheet and rounded.

All figures are in £s except for the Coefficient of Variation (CofV) and the Coefficient of Skewness (CofSk).

Let us examine the Before situation first. We see that there is a mean number of users of 234, although there is considerable variation around this, as shown by the standard deviation (calculated using the sample formula) of 40 and by the range of 144. The coefficient of variation indicates relative variability of 17 per cent around the mean. The median value is 228, slightly lower than the mean, implying a small number of high values in the data set. We see from the median that half the time the centre has less than 228 customers. The quartiles indicate that 25 per cent of the time there are less than 205 users and 25 per cent of the time there are more than 262. Half of the time, therefore, the centre has between 205 and 262 users.

After the campaign there are some interesting differences. The mean number of users per day has increased by over 40 (and we could use this to estimate the increase in revenue as a result). The median has increased by over 50, though, pushing it above the mean (as confirmed by the skewness coefficient, which is now negative at −0.13). This tends to imply that there are still some days where the number of users is quite low, although in general the campaign has pushed most days higher in terms of user numbers. This is confirmed by the minimum and maximum, with the former increasing by 20 and the latter by 60. Similarly, the upper quartile has increased more than the lower. In general, then, user numbers have typically increased after the campaign by about 40 per day, although we must be cautious about inferring cause and effect: we have no direct evidence that the media campaign has caused the increase in user numbers.

Progress Check 4.9

Region B m	f	fm	m²	fm²
−15 000	0	0	225 000 000	0
−5 000	4	−20 000	25 000 000	100 000 000
5 000	58	290 000	25 000 000	1 450 000 000
15 000	21	315 000	225 000 000	4 725 000 000
25 000	13	325 000	625 000 000	8 125 000 000
35 000	11	385 000	1 225 000 000	13 475 000 000
45 000	7	315 000	2 025 000 000	14 175 000 000
60 000	7	420 000	3 600 000 000	25 200 000 000
Totals	121	2 030 000	7 975 000 000	67 250 000 000

The mean for Region B is calculated as £16 776.86 (with Σ fm at 2 030 000). Again note the difference between the mean calculated from the aggregated data and that for the raw data.

Progress Check 4.10

For Region B we have:
Substituting into the formula:

$$\sqrt{\frac{\Sigma fm^2}{\Sigma f} - \left(\frac{\Sigma fm}{\Sigma f}\right)^2}$$

$$= \sqrt{\frac{67\,250\,000\,000}{121} - \left(\frac{2\,030\,000}{121}\right)^2}$$

$$= \sqrt{555\,785\,123.967 - 281\,463\,014.821}$$

$$= 16\,562.67$$

Note again the difference between the standard deviation based on the raw data and that for the aggregated data.

Progress Check 4.11

From Table 3.4 we have:

MI = 61
LCL = 0
CF = 4
CW = 10 000
F = 58

$$\text{Median} = 0 + (61 - 4)\frac{10\,000}{58} = £9828$$

It is always worthwhile looking at your solution to see whether it looks 'sensible' in the context of the problem (it is not unknown in exams, for example, to see a negative standard deviation given by a student as an answer – think about it). Here the median item is item number 61, which must be close to the upper limit of the median interval (0 < 10 000), so the answer of 9828 at least appears to be in the right numerical area.

Progress Check 4.12

For Q1 we have:

> Quartile item = 28.25
> LCL = 0
> CF = 14
> CW = 10 000
> F = 56

So that:

$$Q1 = 0 + (28.25 - 14)\frac{10\,000}{56} = £2545$$

and for Q3:

> Quartile item = 84.75
> LCL = 10 000
> CF = 70
> CW = 10 000
> F = 22

giving:

$$Q3 = 10\,000 + (84.75 - 70)\frac{10\,000}{22} = £16\,705$$

Progress Check 5.1

'Common sense' would tell us that there is a one in six chance of throwing the die and showing a six. This would be a theoretical probability since we know that there are six possible outcomes (the numbers 1 to 6) but only one of them can occur, and that each of them has the same chance of occurring (1/6).

However, consider the scenario that we have been throwing the die and noting which numbers are shown. We have done this 100 times and, as yet, have never thrown a six. We pick up the die one more time to throw. What would you say the probability is of throwing a six next time (assuming the die has not been tampered with in any way)?

The answer will depend on which of the three approaches to probability you adopt. On a strictly theoretical basis the answer must still be 1/6. On an empirical basis you might say the answer is 0 since a six has never appeared. On a subjective basis you might say the answer is 1 (or close to it) – that is, you're certain a six will appear because it hasn't been thrown for such a long time and has to appear sooner or later.

Progress Check 5.11

The mean and standard deviation are easily calculated:

> Mean = np = 50 000(0.12) = 6000
> Standard deviation = $\sqrt{npq}$ = $\sqrt{(50\,000)(0.12)(0.88)}$ = 72.7

Potentially, these results and the principles of the Binomial could be used in a number of ways. First, by estimating the likely number of returns we can determine what these returns will cost us in postage, handling, etc. We also know that this cost has to be recouped from somewhere, so we can build this likely cost into the calculations for the profit margins we need to realise on the sales we achieve (estimated at 44 000). Equally, we can use this information for production and ordering. If we anticipate sales of 44 000 from orders of 50 000, there is clearly no point producing 50 000 items, as we will at some time have 6000 unsold items on our hands. We could also do some 'what-if' analysis around the problem. Clearly, the orders of 50 000 and the return rate of 12 per cent are not guaranteed outcomes – they are based on empirical observations. We could readily use the Binomial to determine the consequences of the number of orders differing from 50 000, and equally for the return rate to differ from 12 per cent to assess the consequences on our production decision and our profit.

Progress Check 5.13

Using the Z score formula we have:

Machine 1

$$X = 475, \ Z = -2.5$$
$$X = 505, \ Z = 0.5$$
$$X = 518, \ Z = 1.8$$

Machine 2

$$X = 745, \ Z = -0.33$$
$$X = 725, \ Z = -1.67$$
$$X = 759, \ Z = 0.60$$

Progress Check 7.17

We can treat the age distribution from government statistics as our expected (E) distribution. If our sample were representative then we should have a distribution by age group like the one in the government statistics. The sample we have obtained is clearly the observed (O) distribution. As with all these types of test, the null hypothesis is that O = E (that is, that our sample distribution is representative, based on the government statistics). Presumably, it is important for the market research company to know whether or not the sample is representative so let us choose $\alpha = 0.01$. The calculations are then:

Observed	Expected	$(O - E)$	$(O - E)^2$	$(O - E)^2/E$
54	65	−11	121	1.86
63	60	3	9	0.15
167	190	−23	529	2.78
85	75	10	100	1.33
131	110	21	441	4.01
500	500	–	–	10.14

Notice that the expected frequencies total to 500 (the sample size). We have obtained a calculated χ^2 of 10.14. We have 4 degrees of freedom and from Appendix D we obtain a critical statistic of 13.28. Given the calculated statistic is less than the critical we have no reason to reject the null hypothesis. Remember that this is that O = E, so we cannot reject the hypothesis that the sample is representative compared with the government statistics.

Progress Check 8.3

The relevant information for the construction of a control chart is that we anticipate an average of 12 customer complaints per day averaged over 14 days (the sample period of two weeks). This would give warning limits of:

$$12 \pm 1.96\,(5/\sqrt{14}) = 12 \pm 2.62$$

and action limits of:

$$12 \pm 3.09\,(5/\sqrt{14}) = 12 \pm 4.13$$

One of the implications of these calculations, amongst others, is that a reduction in the mean number of customer complaints is not necessarily an indication that the number of complaints is falling. A reduction in one two-week period, for example, to 11 complaints would still be within the warning limits and could not be taken to indicate that the mean number of complaints had actually fallen (we would explain the reduction through the concept of sampling variation). The relevant control chart, with the first seven sets of results also plotted, is shown in Figure A.9. Our commentary on these results might be as follows.

We observe that in period 3 the result of 14.8 exceeds the upper warning limit. We would take this as evidence that the process might be out of control and we should obtain another sample as soon as is practical. We also observe that from period 3 onwards a clear downward trend is evident and although this is, by period 7, still within the warning limit we might anticipate period 8 being below the lower warning limit. In one sense this is not a problem for the supermarket since it implies a declining mean number of complaints. However, the store manager would still be advised to try to assess why this trend was occurring. Is it linked to some management initiative intended to improve customer satisfaction? Is it linked to a customer care training programme introduced by the store? Is it linked to a change in the way customers are encouraged to complain (perhaps deliberately or accidentally the store has made it more difficult for customers to make complaints)?

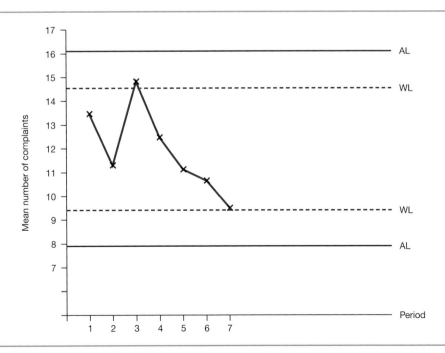

Figure A.9 Complaints control chart

Progress Check 10.2

Graphical solutions to Activity 10.2 are shown in Figure A.10.

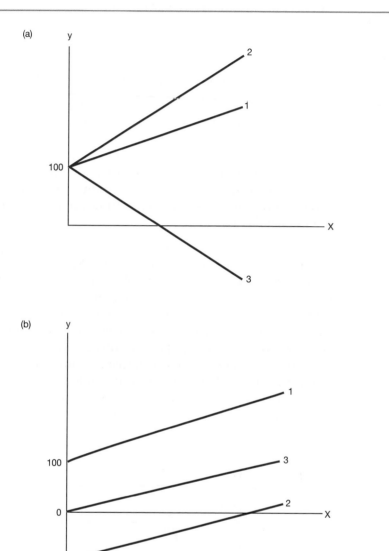

Figure A.10 Graphical solutions to Activity 10.2

```
SUMMARY OUTPUT          Scenario B
                   Regression Statistics
Multiple R                          0.864570639
R Square                            0.74748239
Adjusted R
Square                              0.732628413
Standard
Error                               349.057928
Observations                        19
```

```
ANOVA
                  df          SS              MS              F          Significance F
Regression        1       6131309.352     6131309.352    50.32203738     1.80125E-06
Residual          17      2071304.431     121841.4371
Total             18      8202613.783
```

	Coeffi-cients	Standard Error	t Stat	P-value	Lower 95%	Upper 95%	Lower 95.0%	Upper 95.0%
Intercept	28199.09307	166.6985241	169.162224	7.17652E-29	27847.38993	28550.79621	27847.38993	28550.79621
X Variable 1	-103.7144304	14.62042774	-7.093802745	1.80125E-06	-134.5608363	-72.86802449	-134.5608363	-72.86802449

This confirms a forecast for the trend in 2018 IV (T = 24) of 23.76. We also see that R^2 at 0.75 is lower than that for the model for Scenario A, implying a worse fit of the regression line to the data. This would also be confirmed by comparing the two prediction intervals for Scenarios A and B. The trend forecast for Scenario A is statistically 'better', although whether it provides a better forecast in a business context is another matter, since both forecasts imply that the respective trend will remain unchanged.

Progress Check 11.2

We have a formulation:

Minimise $0.85H + 1.1C$

such that $4H + 2C \leq 20\,000$

$1H + 3C \leq 15\,000$

$1H \leq 4000$

$1C \leq 4500$

$1H \geq 2000$

$1C \geq 2500$

$H, C \geq 0$

Solutions and feedback on Progress Checks for Chapters 12–15 are contained in the chapter text.

Index